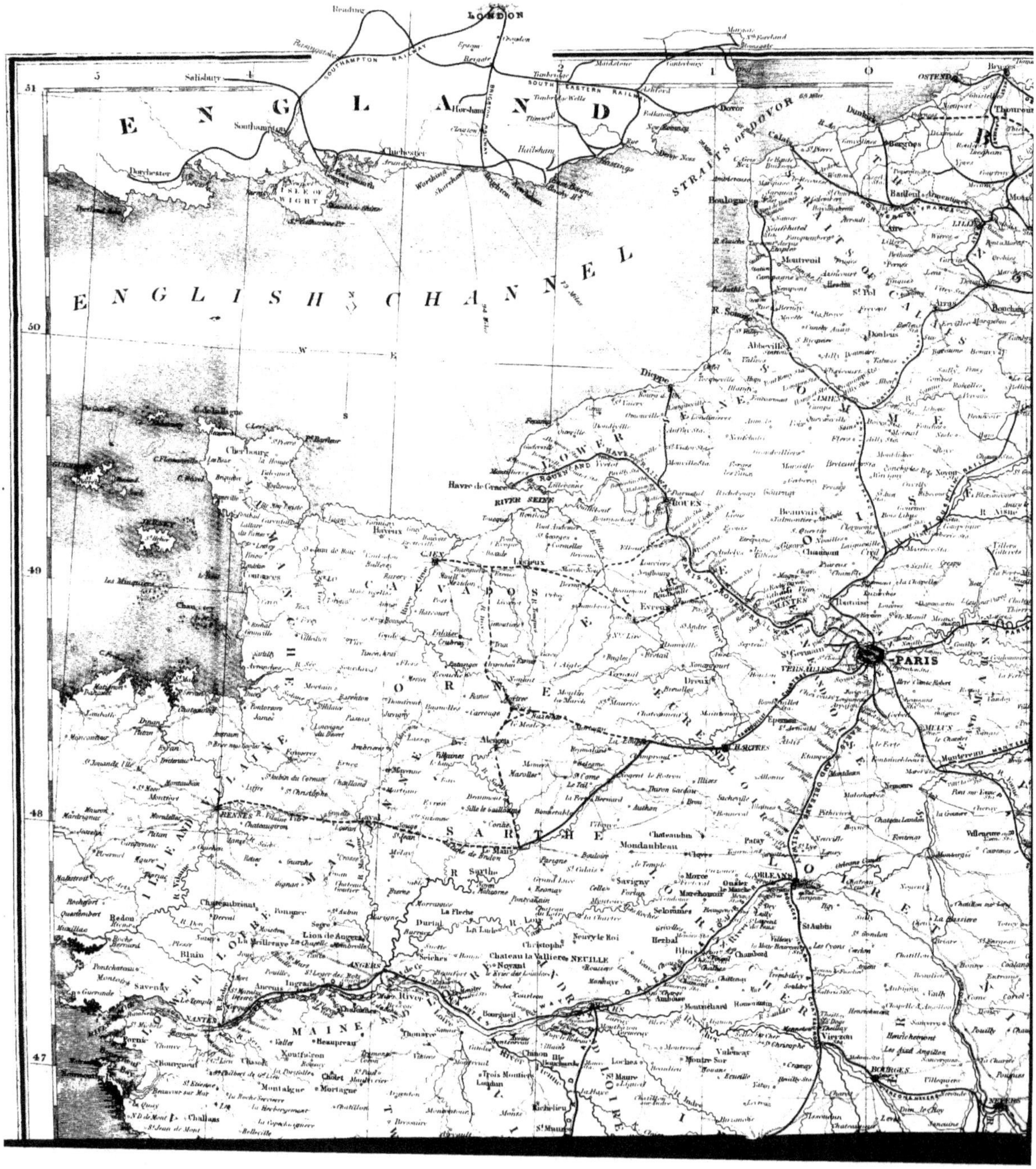

LONDON
ENGLAND
ENGLISH CHANNEL
STRAITS OF DOVOR
SOUTHAMPTON RAILWAY
SOUTH EASTERN RAILWAY
Salisbury
Southampton
Chichester
Dorchester
Brighton
Hastings
Tunbridge
Maidstone
Canterbury
Folkstone
Dover
Ashford
Horsham
Hailsham
Worthing
Shoreham
Reigate
Epsom
Reading
ISLE OF WIGHT
OSTEND
Bruges
Dunkirk
Calais
Boulogne
Bergues
Lille
St Omer
Arras
Amiens
Abbeville
Dieppe
Beauvais
Havre de Grace
ROUEN
RIVER SEINE
CAEN
Lisieux
Evreux
Mantes
PARIS
Versailles
St Germain
Pontoise
Chartres
Rambouillet
Etampes
Melun
Fontainebleau
Nemours
Montargis
Pithiviers
ORLEANS
Blois
Amboise
Chambord
Vierzon
Bourges
Nevers
Tours
Saumur
ANGERS
NANTES
RENNES
Laval
Le Mans
Alençon
La Fleche
Chateau la Valliere
Cherbourg
Coutances
Avranches
St Malo
Dinan
Redon
Savenay
Guerande
Ancenis
Cholet
Mortagne
Chinon
Loches
Valençay
Mondaubleau
Bonneval
Chateaudun
Nogent le Rotrou
Mortagne
Dreux
CALVADOS
ORNE
SARTHE
EURE
MAINE AND LOIRE
LOIRE
RIVER SEINE
51
50
49
48
47
5
4
3
2
1
0

MAP OF THE RAILWAYS IN
FRANCE,
BELGIUM,
AND
SWITZERLAND.
BY C. BRADSHAW. ASSOC. INST. C.E.

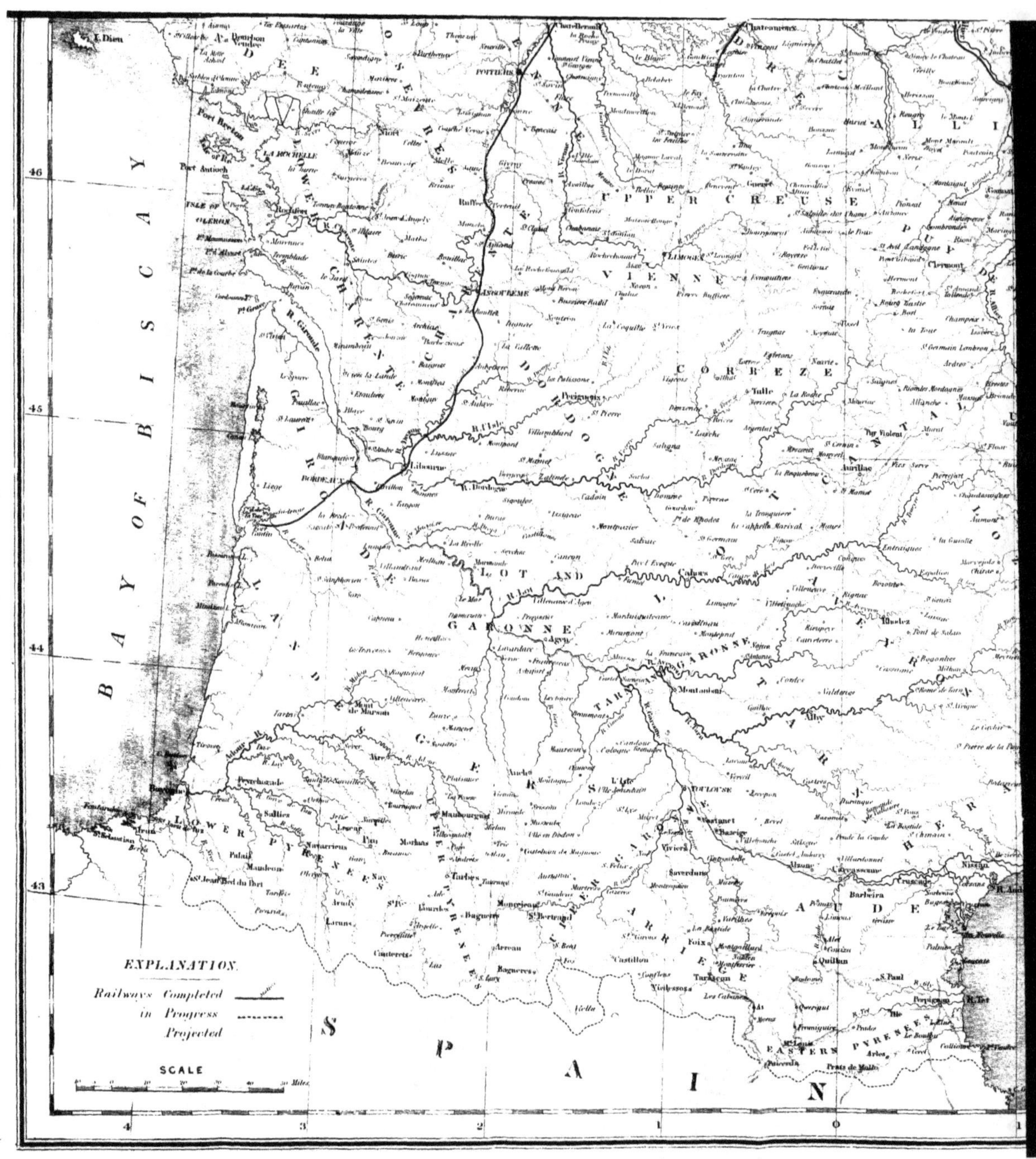

BAY OF BISCAY
EXPLANATION.
Railways Completed
in Progress
Projected
SCALE
Miles
SPAIN
UPPER CREUSE
VIENNE
CORREZE
DORDOGNE
LOT AND GARONNE
GARONNE
LOWER PYRENEES
EASTERN PYRENEES
AUDE
LA ROCHELLE
POITIERS
ANGOULEME
BORDEAUX
Libourne
Perigueux
Cahors
Agen
Montauban
TOULOUSE
Tarbes
Carcassonne
Perpignan
LIMOGES
Tulle
Aurillac
Clermont
Niort
Rochefort
Saintes
Mont de Marsan
Auch
Pau
Foix
Alby
46
45
44
43
4
3
2
1
0
1

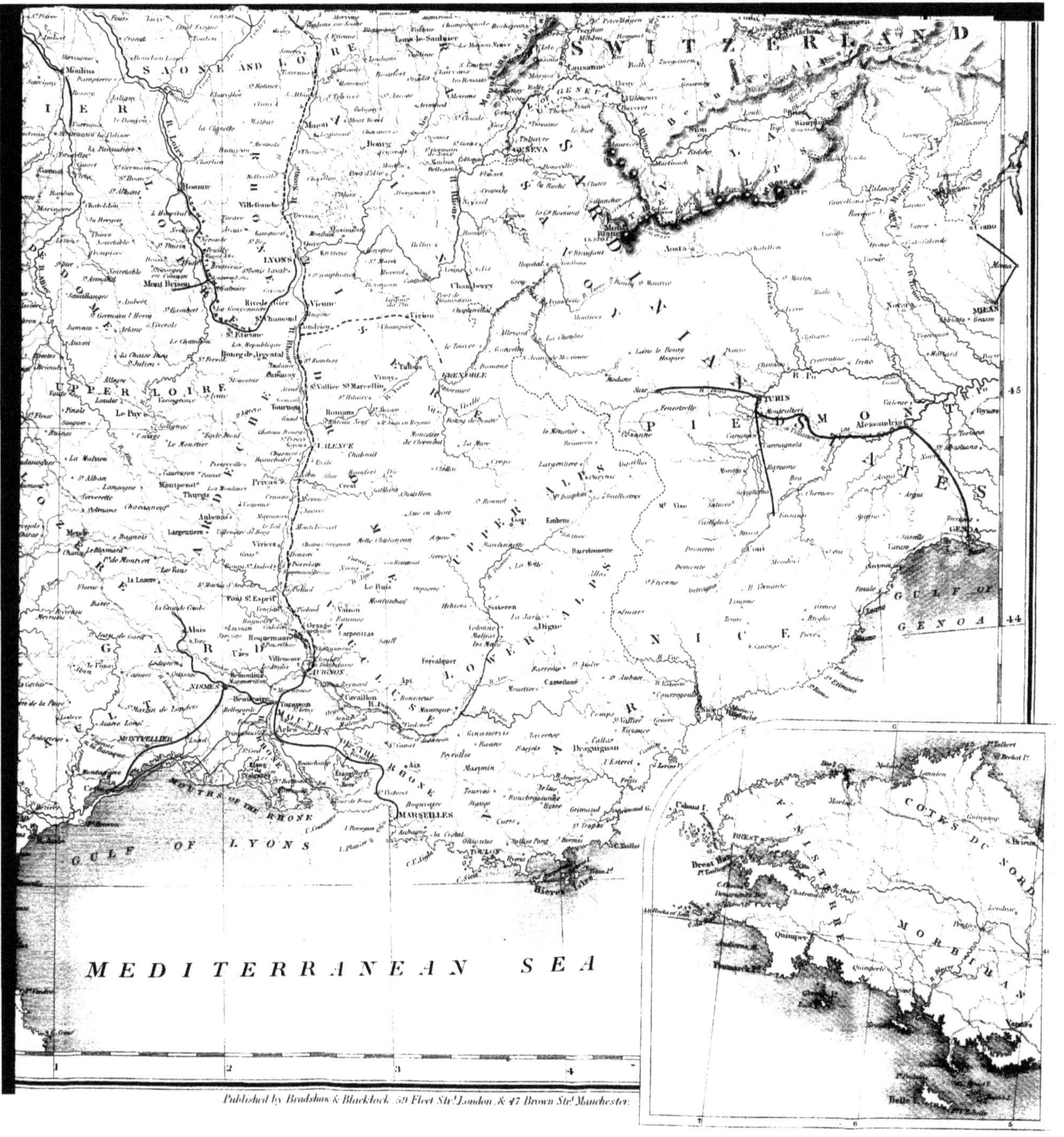

Published by Bradshaw & Blacklock, 59 Fleet Str.t London, & 47 Brown Str.t Manchester.

SOUTH EASTERN RAILWAY,

THE DIRECT MAIL ROUTE TO ALL PARTS OF THE CONTINENT, WITH THE SHORTEST SEA PASSAGE.

DAILY COMMUNICATION BETWEEN LONDON AND PARIS IN TWELVE HOURS;

London and Brussels in Fourteen Hours; London and Cologne in Twenty Hours; Sea Passage only Two Hours.

SUMMER SERVICES, 1854.

LONDON TO PARIS BY TIDAL TRAINS,

VIA FOLKESTONE AND BOULOGNE.

THIS is the quickest and most comfortable means of communication between London and Paris; it is performed every day, the time of departure varying in accordance with the tide. (Time Table published daily in front page of "The *Times*.") The Passengers are conveyed by Express Train to Folkestone, where they find a powerful Steamer waiting in the harbour to receive them; they walk on board, and two hours afterwards are landed at Boulogne, where another Train is in readiness to convey them immediately to Paris. The whole journey is thus accomplished without interruption, in the shortest possible time, no small boats for embarking and disembarking being required.

By these trains, luggage can be registered for Paris direct, relieving the Passenger from all trouble about it until the arrival in Paris, and avoiding the Customs examination at Boulogne.

The same correspondence of trains and Steamers is arranged for the journey from Paris to London.

FIXED CONTINENTAL SERVICES VIA DOVER AND CALAIS.

FROM LONDON.

London	departure	8 10 a.m.	*11 30 a.m.	*8 30 p.m.
Dover	„	11 0 „	2 30 p.m.	11 15 „
Calais	„	2 30 p.m.	6 30 „	3 0 a.m.
Paris	arrival	9 40 „	5 5 a.m.	10 0 „
Brussels	„	10 10 „	5 0 „	10 50 „
Cologne	„	5 0 a.m.	1 30 p.m.	4 45 p.m.

TO LONDON.

Cologne	departure	11 30 p.m.	6 15 a.m.	*9 30 a.m.
Brussels	„	7 0 a.m.	2 0 p.m.	3 0 p.m.
Paris	„	7 0 „	11 45 „	7 30 „
Calais	„	3 0 p.m.	10 0 „	2 30 a.m.
Dover	„	7 30 „	2 0 a.m.	5 20 „
London	arrival	10 15 „	4 50 „	7 45 „

*** These Trains are not direct on Sundays.**

For further details see Bradshaw's British and Continental Guides.

Offices for through Tickets, Time Bills, &c.:—

IN LONDON—40, Regent Circus, Piccadilly;
IN PARIS—4, Boulevard des Italiens;
IN BRUSSELS—74, Montagne de la Cour.

G. S. HERBERT, *Secretary*

London Bridge Terminus, May, 1854.

THE LOWER SEINE.

REGULAR SERVICE FOR THE SUMMER OF 1854.

BETWEEN HAVRE AND ROUEN,

By the Steamers **Meustrie** and **Courier,** calling at HONFLEUR, QUILLEBŒUF, VILLEQUIER, CAUDEBEC, LA MAILLERAYE, and DUCLAIR, in connection at Rouen with the Paris Steam Packet Company between Rouen and Paris.

DEPARTURES FOR THE MONTHS OF

JULY.				AUGUST.				SEPTEMBER.				OCTOBER.			
		From Havre.	From Rouen.			From Havre.	From Rouen.			From Havre.	From Rouen			From Havre.	From Rouen.
1	S	1030 mrn	6 30 mrn	1	T	1115 mrn	7 45 mrn	1	F	1 0 aft	8 45 mrn	1	S	2 30 aft	10 0 mrn
2	S	11 0 „	7 45 „	2	W	1230 aft	8 15 „	2	S	2 15 „	1045 „	2	M	3 15 „	1215 aft
3	M	1215 aft	8 15 „	3	T	1 15 „	9 45 „	3	S	4 30 mrn	1115 „	3	T	5 0 mrn	1 45 „
4	T	1 0 „	9 50 „	4	F	2 45 „	1030 „	4	M	5 0 „	1 15 aft	4	W	5 30 „	2 0 „
5	W	2 30 „	10 0 „	5	S	3 15 „	1215 aft	5	T	5 30 „	2 0 „	5	T	6 15 „	2 30 „
6	T	3 0 „	1145 „	6	S	5 0 mrn	1245 „	6	W	5 45 „	3 0 „				
7	F	5 0 mrn	1215 aft	7	M	5 30 „	2 30 „	7	T	7 15 „	4 30 mrn				
8	S	5 15 „	1 30 „	8	T	6 30 „	3 0 „	8	F	7 45 „	5 0 „				
9	S	5 45 „	2 0 „	9	W	7 0 „	5 0 mrn	9	S	8 30 „	5 0 „				
10	M	6 15 „	4 15 mrn	10	T	8 15 „	5 0 „	10	S	9 0 „	5 30 „				
11	T	7 30 „	4 45 „	11	F	8 45 „	5 15 „	11	M	9 30 „	5 30 „				
12	W	8 0 „	5 0 „	12	S	9 30 „	5 30 „	12	T	10 0 „	6 30 „				
13	T	9 15 „	5 30 „	13	S	10 0 „	6 30 „	13	W	11 0 „	7 0 „				
14	F	9 30 „	6 15 „	14	M	11 0 „	7 0 „	14	T	1145 „	8 0 „				
15	S	1045 „	6 45 „	15	T	1130 „	8 0 „	15	F	1 0 aft	9 0 „				
16	S	1115 „	8 0 „	16	W	1245 aft	9 45 „	16	S	2 30 „	11 0 „				
17	M	1245 aft	8 15 „	17	T	1 30 „	1015 „	17	S	4 30 mrn	1130 „				
18	T	1 30 „	10 0 „	18	F	4 30 mrn	11 0 „	18	M	5 0 „	1 15 aft				
19	W	2 45 „	1030 „	19	S	4 30 „	1245 aft	19	T	5 30 „	1 45 „				
20	T	3 15 „	1215 aft	20	S	5 0 „	1 15 „	20	W	6 0 „	2 30 „				
21	F	5 0 mrn	1 0 „	21	M	5 45 „	2 30 „	21	T	6 30 „	2 45 „				
22	S	5 15 „	2 0 „	22	T	6 30 „	2 45 „	22	F	7 0 „	4 30 mrn				
23	S	6 0 „	2 30 „	23	W	7 0 „	4 30 mrn	23	S	7 30 „	4 30 „				
24	M	6 15 „	4 15 mrn	24	T	7 30 „	4 30 „	24	S	7 45 „	5 0 „				
25	T	7 15 „	4 30 „	25	F	7 45 „	5 0 „	25	M	8 30 „	5 0 „				
26	W	7 30 „	5 0 „	26	S	8 30 „	5 0 „	26	T	8 45 „	5 30 „				
27	T	8 15 „	5 0 „	27	S	8 45 „	5 15 „	27	W	9 45 „	6 0 „				
28	F	8 30 „	5 15 „	28	M	9 30 „	5 30 „	28	T	1015 „	6 45 „				
29	S	9 30 „	5 30 „	29	T	1045 „	6 30 „	29	F	1115 „	7 15 „				
30	S	10 0 „	6 15 „	30	W	11 0 „	7 0 „	30	S	12 0 „	9 0 „				
31	M	1045 „	6 45 „	31	T	1130 „	8 0 „								

AGENTS.

Havre: Messrs. E. Deschamps & Co., 13, Grand Quai; Messrs. Louis Bertin & Co., 7, Rue Bernardin de St. Pierre.

Rouen: M. Louis Bertin, 55, Quai Napoleon.

Honfleur: M. Elie, Hotel du Cheval Blanc.

Paris: At the Paris Steam Packet Office, 17, Quai Molaquais; at the Office de Publicité, 12, Place de la Bourse, and on board the Steamers.

MANUFACTURER OF REGISTERED PORTMANTEAUS.

JOHN HILL, TRAVELLING EQUIPAGE MANUFACTURER TO THE ARMY AND NAVY.

97, REGENT STREET, QUADRANT, AND 212, PICCADILLY, *Six Doors West of Regent Circus,* LONDON.

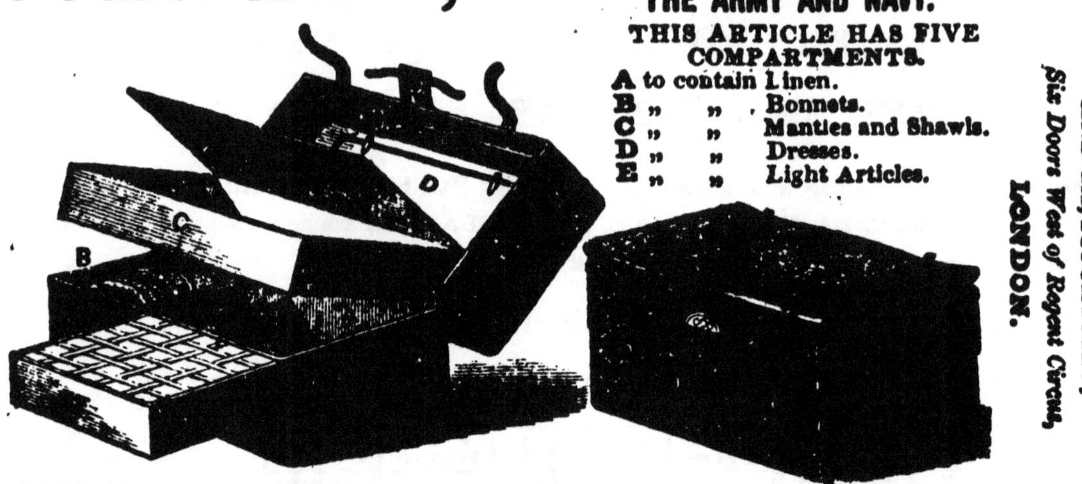

THIS ARTICLE HAS FIVE COMPARTMENTS.

A to contain Linen.
B " " Bonnets.
C " " Manties and Shawls.
D " " Dresses.
E " " Light Articles.

JOHN HILL respectfully solicits the attention of the Nobility, Gentry, and all persons travelling to any part of the Globe, to his newly-invented LADY'S EXPANDING PORTMANTEAU, which for strength, portability, and capacity for containing, excels all others ever invented; is strongly recommended for continental, railway, and general travelling. To be had only of the inventor, where all other articles connected with the business are of first-rate quality. Leather and carpet bags; various descriptions of hat cases, boxes, and trunks; writing, dressing, and brush cases of every description; air tight tin boxes for India; wood cases made and lined with tin, zinc, or copper; paper boxes. Patentee of the Choretikopas.

HILL'S NEW REGISTERED SOLID LEATHER FIVE COMPARTMENT PORTMANTEAUS, constructed so that the five compartments are accessible at once, and entirely distinct from each other, rendering it unnecessary for luggage being disturbed or moved in passing through the customs.

Hill's Improved Metallic Revited Hinged Bottom Bag, with wide opening, superseding all others for convenience.

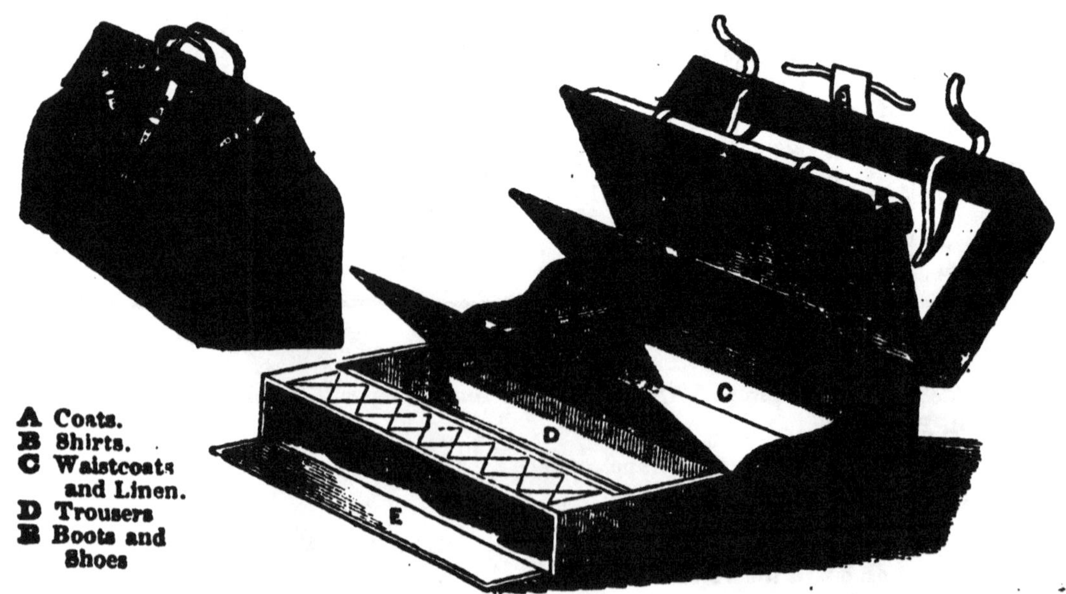

A Coats.
B Shirts.
C Waistcoats and Linen.
D Trousers
E Boots and Shoes

212, Piccadilly, and 97, Regent Street, London.

BRADSHAW'S

HAND BOOK FOR TRAVELLERS

IN FRANCE.

BRADSHAW'S
ILLUSTRATED
TRAVELLERS' HAND BOOK IN FRANCE.

ADAPTED TO ALL THE RAILWAY ROUTES;

WITH

A SHORT ITINERARY OF CORSICA,

AND

A GUIDE TO PARIS.

WITH MAPS, TOWN PLANS, AND ILLUSTRATIONS.

"The scene
Is now transported, gentles, to Southampton;
And thence to France shall we convey you safe,
And bring you back, charming the narrow seas
To give you gentle pass."—*Shakspere.*

LONDON:
W. J. ADAMS, BRADSHAW'S GUIDE OFFICE, 59, FLEET STREET.
MANCHESTER: BRADSHAW AND BLACKLOCK, 47, BROWN STREET.
LIVERPOOL: T. FAIRBROTHER, 2, OLD HALL STREET.
EDINBURGH: W. CORNS AND CO., 26, WATERLOO PLACE.
GLASGOW: JAMES REID, 138, ARGYLE STREET.
DUBLIN: ROBERT CHADDERTON, 62, GRAFTON STREET.
PARIS: J. DAWES, 3, PLACE VENDOME, (THREE DOORS FROM RUE ST. HONORE).
CONTINENTAL MANAGER: W. MIDDLETON, BRUSSELS.

1854.

ADDRESS.

The present work is offered to the public as one of a series of cheap and portable Hand Books, which are in preparation for the use of travellers at home and abroad,—adapted to the requirements of the day, and to the great alterations produced by the extension of the railway system. In writing it, the Editor has endeavoured to steer midway between tedious descriptions and a meagre list of names. But while he has chosen such a plain business-like style and selection of matter as may recommend it to the tastes of the majority of travellers, whose object is to see as much as possible with the least expenditure of time and money, he believes that the resident in France will here find as much information collected as will serve for the full examination of any particular locality.

Besides the authorities referred to in the text, the Editor has been under great obligations for many details in the compilation of this Guide to an excellent and interesting work, entitled *France Pittoresque*, by A. Hugo, the brother of Victor Hugo. It is a complete summary of France, by departments, with engravings, &c.; and the traveller could hardly bring back with him a more instructive and useful remembrance of his visit to that country. Another general authority has been F. Didot's *Guide Pittoresque du Voyageur en France.*

It is scarcely necessary to add that the production of a good guide is a work of time, and the result of much patient thought, and gradual digestion of matter. Those, therefore, into whose hands this little book may fall, are earnestly invited to lend their assistance in perfecting it, by transmitting such corrections or additional information as may be derived from personal experience or good authority. Notices of alterations in conveyances, hotels, and other useful heads, will be received with thanks.

June, 1854.

NOTICE.

The Editor of the Travellers' Hand-Book in France is extremely solicitous that travellers and friends, who make use of this book, should favour the Publishers with corrections of any omission or mistakes that may come under their observation. Tourists, &c., kind enough so to favour them, will please direct their communications to their London Office, 59, Fleet Street. In all cases the name of the writer, in confinence, as a guarantee of the genuineness of the information, will be required.

To Innkeepers and others.—The Editor of Bradshaw's Hand-Book wishes to intimate, that no person or persons are authorised to procure or receive money from Hotel Keepers, Artists, or Tradespeople abroad, under pretence of procuring the insertion of favourable notices of their establishments, &c., in the Hand-Books; recommendations in these books are not to be purchased; they are the result of personal experience. or well-founded and *disinterested* information. Nor will self-laudatory letters from Innkeepers in praise of their own houses be received.

The sole *Continental Manager* is William Middleton, 94. Montagne de la Cour, Brussels, through whom all communications concerning Hotels, &c, must be sent.

LIST OF MAPS AND ILLUSTRATIONS.

CONTENTS.

INTRODUCTION.

SECTION I.

SECTION II.

SECTION III.

SECTION IV.

SECTION V.

SECTION VI.

SECTION VII.

INDEX.

*** Chief Towns and Sous-Préfectures are distinguished by the *department* being placed after them in a parenthesis.

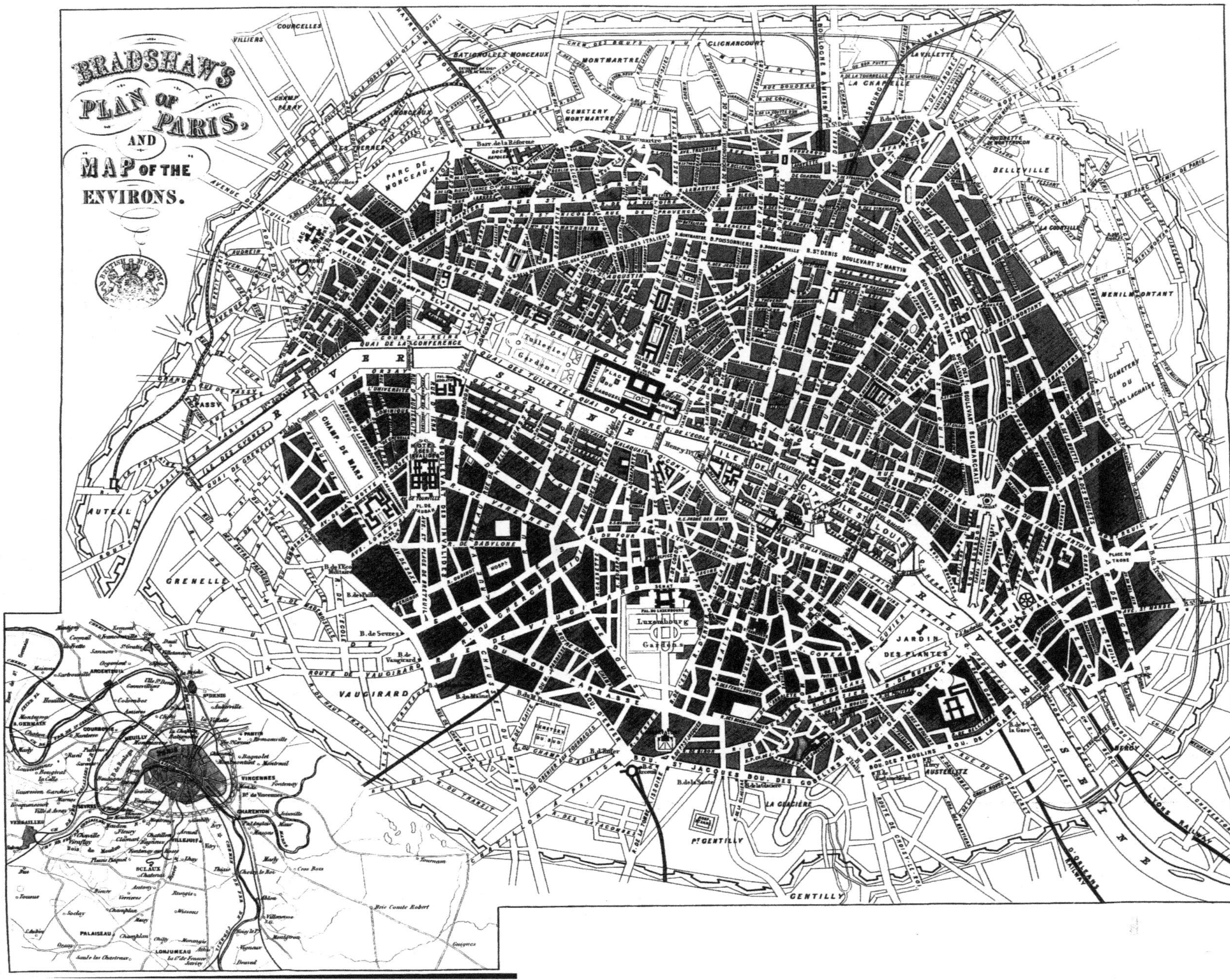

BRADSHAW'S
PLAN OF PARIS,
AND
MAP OF THE
ENVIRONS.
COURCELLES
VILLIERS
BATIGNOLLES MONCEAUX
MONTMARTRE
CLIGNANCOURT
LA CHAPELLE
LA VILLETTE
CEMETERY MONTMARTRE
PARC DE MONCEAUX
BELLEVILLE
MENILMONTANT
Tuileries Gardens
CHAMP. DE MARS
PASSY
AUTEIL
GRENELLE
VAUGIRARD
Luxembourg Gardens
JARDIN DES PLANTES
LA GLACIÈRE
P.t GENTILLY
GENTILLY
BERCY
VERSAILLES
PARIS

INTRODUCTION.

We believe there was much truth in the remark we once noticed in an article of the Atheneum, "that every copy sold of a Continental Hand-Book becomes a missionary in the work of civilization, and in the promotion of good fellowship among nations. With an annual issue of many thousands of these *Souvenirs*, suggesting and recalling the wonderful, the magnificent, and the beautiful, existing throughout Europe,—who shall say that the cause of peace is not materially promoted? Each hand-book is a standing memento of its blessings and advantages.

The compilation, however, of a good guide-book is not the easiest of tasks, if anything more is attempted than a mere monotonous parrot-like repetition of what is known, and has been said in a hundred ways.

How to hit a fortunate medium between not being over garrulous, and yet sufficiently suggestive,—how, in fact, to lead every one to explore for himself, indicating sufficiently what is worthy to be explored,—how to discriminate between the valuable and the valueless,—are aims of a good guide-book.

But after all the help which hand-books can afford, the pleasure of foreign travel are in a great measure dependent on the intelligence and information which the traveller carries with him. Every thing, both in nature and in art, as well at home as abroad, is pretty much a prize or a blank as we draw it ourselves.

The briefest directory is an ample guide for eyes and ears that *can* see and hear, whilst the most diffuse instructions may be too brief for the blind and the deaf.

There are two points whence countries may be viewed—their high-ways and their bye-ways. Along the former flow the great concourse of travellers, and the main volume of observation. It would be difficult to find a continental high road, or line of ordinary route not thoroughly developed, and of which each object is not amply discussed in guide-book, tour, or journal. Not so with the bye-ways, which are as it were the veins of a country, wherein life moves, and the character of its real constitution can be best tested. There is much, very much, to be seen, especially of scenery and sights on the high road, but though the scenery may, the society, manners, morals, habits, and character of a country do not, lie on the highways. Unfortunately we are prone to build general opinions on our railway train views and table d'hôte experiences.

The tourist, who excursionizes for a few weeks in a foreign country, feels it almost essential to the character and dignity of a traveller, to import a settled code of opinions on the manners, morals, minds, politics, and arts, sciences and literature, manufactures and commerce of the people and empire, whose high roads and hotels have been honoured by his observation.

And yet of all travellers the Englishman, who comes abroad for the first time, is the least likely to give anything more than snperficial opinions on what he sees, hears, or learns, in a flying visit from one end of Europe to the other.

Too often the grand business of a majority of the English out of England is eating; there is no doubt they carry a mighty stomach with them everywhere. If the climate is hot, it exhausts them and they must recruit; if cold, they get hungry with astonishing celerity, the air is so keen and bracing—change of air, change of scene, change of diet, the excitement of moving from place to place, the clatter of a new language—every thing contributes to this one end; as if the sole aim and business of travelling was to get an appetite.

Another remarkable trait in their character, is their dissatisfaction with almost every thing abroad, and their freezing hauteur and unsociable bearing even towards their fellow countrymen.

The Englishman on his first visit to the Continent is quite out of his element. He misses the unmistakeable cookery, the rugs and carpets, the order, decorum, the wealth and its material sturdiness. He comes out of his fogs and sulphurous atmosphere of his sea-coal fires, into a *laughing climate.*

His ears are stunned with songs and music from morning till night; every face he meets is lighted up with enjoyment. This lightness of the heart, joined to the lightness of the atmosphere, produces that open-air festivity and community of enjoyment which makes the taciturn heavy hypocondriacal man stare. *He* is used to think of taxes—but the people of the Continent are not bowed down by an old man at their backs in the shape of a glorious National Debt.

The fundamental error of the travelling English consists in bringing their English feelings, and grievances, and modes, with them abroad, instead of leaving them behind, to be taken care of with their pictures and furniture.

You can detect an Englishman abroad by that repulsion of manner which covers him over like a frost-work, and within the range of which nobody can enter without being bitten with cold. His sense of superiority freezes the very air about him; you would think he was a statue of ice, or a block dropped from a glacier of the loftiest Alps. It would be as easy for the sun to thaw the eternal peak of the snowy *Jung-frau*, as for any ordinary warmth of society to melt that wintry man into any of the cordial courtesies of intercourse.

The same thing that happens upon a great scale in political affairs is illustrated in a minor way in the intercourse of travellers. Our *social tariff amounts almost to a prohibition.* We are as reluctant to open our mouths or our ears, as we were to open our ports, and have as profound a horror of foreign vivacity and communicativeness, as we had of foreign corn before the potatoe famine.

We have a similar difficulty in relaxing our manners. The bulk of our continental travellers enter an hotel with as much severity and suspicion in their looks, as if they wished to produce the very thing mentioned by the author of Zig-Zag travels.

"Inn keepers, he says, are in some degree what travellers make them. You arrive, haughty, exacting, surly, placing between you and your host the immense distance which separates the rich gentleman from the miserable official. The nature of the contract between you is thus established by yourself; service, alacrity, and respect, appear in due course in the bill, which you think extravagant, and which you pay with anger.

"You arrive, good-natured, considerate, without noise or bustle; you treat your host like a man whose attention and whose good graces are personally agreeable to you; whose respectful manner is to be acknowledged but not paid for; he gives all these but does not sell them; your bill stripped of all false charges is found reasonable, and you pay it with pleasure. People are occasionally met with who speak ill of all inns; these are individuals, whom with more justice, all inns could speak ill of."

When a Frenchman, or an Italian, comes to England, he brings his sunshine with him, when an Englishman goes to France or Italy, it is said he cannot leave his fogs behind him. He is apt to think everything wrong which does not happen to harmonize with his usages, without making allowances for the difference of habits and modes of life. But it ought to be remembered that some national traits may jar with our customs, and yet harmonise perfectly with the general characteristics and necessities of others—and that many of the very traits we desiderate in them would be totally irreconcilable with the whole plan of their society—perhaps even with their climate, which frequently exercises an influence that cannot be averted over society itself.

It is surprising, however, how a little knocking about in steam-boats, and railways shakes a man out of his sluggish thonghts and opaque humors. It is the best of all constitutional remedies for mind and body, although it acts but slowly on the whip-cord nerves of the English; it is good for the brains and the stomach; it invigorates the imagination, loosens the blood, and makes it leap through the veins with redoubled and healthy action.

There is nothing in this leveling world of ours, which so effectually annihilates conventional respectability, as the modern mode of travelling—in which speed and safety are rightly judged to be valuable compensations for state and seclusion. The Frenchman avails himself of this advantage, to observe the habits and manners of the nations he visits—but our countrymen are generally too shy and too exclusive—too fearful of unwittingly compromising themselves, by contact with persons not quite up to their standard of gentility, to encourage conversation, or court the society of foreigners.

If they can only overcome this restraint no man abandons himself so utterly to the charms of this mode of travelling as an Englishman, once he allows himself to give way to it. Observe with what curiosity he peers into shop windows and bazaars; with what vivacity he hunts through royal parks and palaces, to collect gossip for the table d'hôte; how he climbs lofty steeples and boasts of his lungs; what a dinner he makes amidst a bewildering chaos of provocatives; showing very plainly that the previous restraint was contrary to his real character, and he is much more happy when he throws it off—proving that there is nothing like a plunge into new worlds of human faces for the recovery of youth, with all its giddy joys and airy fallacies. The only difficulty is to get him to make this plunge. Instead of running wild and joyous amongst the people of the Continent, and giving free vent to his pleasure-seeking feelings, he generally takes umbrage at everything.

He goes to an Hotel and orders a private dinner in a room apart—his sense of exclusiveness being offended at the indiscriminate crush of the salle à manger.

But when he has overcome this repugnance, and reconciled himself to this universal custom on the Continent, no man enjoys it better than he does; and it is amusing to hear him direct your attention to "its magnificence," "the regal splendour with which it is set out and appointed;" "how brilliantly it is lighted up, gilt, and draperied with oriental pomp;" "the dinner served and laid out with exquisite taste;" "the manner in which the company glide in, noiselessly, and gracefully take their places;" "persons of every class—from the Marquis to the negociant; nobleman and commoner, with their families; military and civilians of all professions. All observing the strictest propriety and manners of the best tone of the highest society."

This is quite correct. Moreover, from this usage, which we deprecate so much because it infringes upon our dignity and sullenness, a manifest advantage is gained, in the practical education of men for any intercourse with general society to which they may be called. Nor is it of less value in conferring upon them that ease and self-possession and versatile command of topics, for which the people of the Continent are so much more distinguished thau our own countrymen.

Few English (Lady Blessington observes) shine in conversation with the French. There is a lightness and brilliancy, a sort of touch and go, if I may say so, in the latter, seldom, if ever, to be acquired by Englishmen. Never dwelling long on any subject, and rarely entering profoundly into it, they sparkle on the surface with great dexterity, bringing wit, gaiety, and tact into play.

Conversation is, with the French, the aim and object of society. All enter it prepared to take a part.

Nevertheless (the same writer adds) there is a repose in the society of clever and refined Englishmen to be met with in no other—the absence of all attempts to shine; the mildness of manners, the low voices, the freedom from any flattery, &c., are peculiarities which Lady Blessington naively observes, "have a great charm for me."

The tone of society at Paris is very agreeable. A strict observance of deferential respect from the men towards the women, and the entire freedom from those marked attentions engrossing conversations, and from that familiarity of manner often permitted in England, gives to Parisian society in the high circles an air of greater dignity and decorum.

A French woman talks well on every subject. Her talent in this art is daily exercised, and consequently becomes perfected; while an English woman, with more various and solid attainments, rarely, if ever, arrives at the ease and self-possession—or confidence—which would enable her to bring the treasures with which her mind is stored into play. An English woman, more concentrated in her feelings as well as in her pursuits, seldom devotes the time given by French women, to the superficial acquirements of a versatility of knowledge, which, though it enables them to converse fluently on various subjects, they would dread entering on unless well versed. This does not, however, detract from a talent, or art (for art it may be called), that renders society in France not only so brilliant but agreeable, and which is attended with the salutary effect of banishing the ill-natured observations and personal remarks, which too often supply the place of more harmless topics with us.

From this descriptive contrast observable in the higher circles of society in England and in France, a comparison between the characteristic peculiarities of the two capitals will be natural and interesting.

The improvements which are being carried out in the French capital are on a scale so vast, and of a character so remarkable, both in an architectural and political point of view, that the following brief sketch will form an appropriate preface to our description of Paris.

These improvements and works were undertaken to find employment for the workmen of the metropolis and its environs.

At the present rapid rate of construction three or four years only will be required for their completion; and by that time the present government hopes to have so far consolidated its power, as to be able to dispense with these means of preserving peace in the capital.

It is not in Paris alone that this course is being pursued. In most of the great municipal towns of France, cathedrals, churches, or public buildings are being restored, or new churches or municipal buildings erected.

Not a small proportion of all this immense outlay is being devoted to the church. Large sums are being expended throughout France in restoring the ecclesiastical edifices.

By this means, what the municipalities are obliged to pay is made to serve the double purpose—first, of buying the favour of the clergy; and secondly, of buying the support of the *Ouvriers*. Most of these works are as admirable as they are splendid and costly: for instance, a railway is being carried, at an immense expense entirely round Paris, and so constructed that it will unite all the metropolitan lines of railway together, so that in a few months a passenger will be able to take his seat in the train at Boulogne, or Calais, and proceed to Bordeaux or Strasburg without changing the carriage at all.

Two magnificent streets are being made through some of the most populous parts of Paris. One, which is already open for traffic, extends from the gardens of the Tuileries for a mile in a strait line along the Tuilleries and the Louvre, to the front of the Hotel de Ville.

The houses on each side, are palaces of six and seven stories in height, and built of a beautiful white stone. The ground floors will form magnificent shops, the upper stories some of the noblest houses in Paris. When this street is completed it will form one line of palaces, of about a mile and a half in length, from the Place de la Concorde to the front of the Hotel de Ville.

The other street will also be very handsome—beginning at the Hotel de Ville it crosses the Boulevards to the Strasburg railway station; this street will be planted with trees.

All the houses which formerly incumbered the Place de Carousel and shut out the view of the Louvre from the Tuilleries have been pulled down, and the original plan of the two palaces is being at length carried out in all its splendour. The wing of the Tuilleries facing the river has been entirely restored, while the outer wing, which forms one side of a great part of the Rue de Rivoli, is being built in the most magnificent and solid manner, with massive stone walls, and in many parts with stone arched roofs. In two years, or before the Great Exhibition of 1855 is opened, if nothing happen to interrupt the works, the Louvre and the Tuilleries will form one splendid palace, and will enclose the grandest square in Europe.

The interior of the Louvre has been restored and most gorgeously decorated. All its treasures have been re-arranged, and although the classification is not yet so complete as in the Berlin Gallery—a great step has been made in the last four years, to present a history of arts, by arranging the school in a somewhat more chronological sequence.

The quays are being completely finished and put in order, so as to make them worthy of the palaces which stand upon them; and several of the oldest of the stone bridges are being completely rebuilt.

The Cathedral of Notre Dame, the exquisite chapelle called La Sainte Chapelle, and other churches have been, or are being carefully restored within and without; the Pantheon has been newly decorated, and converted into a splendid church; the Dome of the Invalides is to be re-gilt; and the interior of the church (which corresponds to our Chelsea Hospital) has been lavishly decorated, to make it worthy to be the shrine of Napoleon's tomb; and beneath the dome the tomb itself is nearly completed: what that will be under the finishing touch of his nephew, Napoleon III., may be imagined!

In addition to these national works there is one which promises to be not less magnificent or costly, and which to Englishmen ought to be the most pleasing, as it is certainly the most flattering of all, namely, the vast palace erecting for the *Exhibition* of 1855.

This remarkable building, which is intended to remain as one of the grandest palaces of Paris, is being built entirely of stone in the most solid and substantial manner, and, considering the materials, of extraordinary dimensions. It is between 800 and 900 feet long, by about 400 feet broad. The walls are a long series of massive arches rising above one another, each arch being intended to form one great window of glass.

Each long side is broken by a great building, which projects some distance, and contains one of the principal arched entrances, and the offices and apartments for the superintendents and officers of the Exhibition. The building promises to be a noble palace. It is admirably situated on the left side of the great avenue leading to the Arc de Triomphe, about half way between the Triumphal Arch and the Tuilleries.

These extensive improvements and embellishments will render Paris the most splendid city in the world; science and art, and apparently inexhaustible resources of money, accomplishing artificially what nature has done for some of the beautiful cities in Italy and along the shores of the Mediterranean.

And thus the Anglo-Saxon of the other hemisphere may still be expected to expatiate in the highest eulogistic terms of the capital of France, to the disparagement of London.

Even our own provincial countrymen re-echo the reproach against their own metropolis—alleging, however, that it cannot be otherwise, while our Minister of Public Works knows nothing about architecture, and that nearly all our national works are merciless less.

The Author of the Classical tour through Italy accounts for this in a more generous spirit.

I feel some regret, he observes, in being obliged to acknowledge that the metropolis of the British Empire, though the first city of Europe for neatness, convenience, and cleanliness, is yet inferior to most capitals in architectural embellishments. This defect is owing in a great degree to the nature of the materials of which it is formed, as brick is ill calculated to receive the graceful forms of an *Ionic Volute*, or a *Corinthian Acanthus;* while the dampness of the climate seems to preclude the possibility of applying stucco to the external parts with permanent advantage. Besides, some blame may justly be attributed to architects, who either know not, or neglect the rules of proportion and the models of antiquity; and in edifices, where no expense has been spared, often display splendid instances of wasteless contrivance and of grotesque ingenuity. But it is to be hoped that the industry and the taste of the British nation will ere long triumph over this double obstacle,—inspire artists with genius, teach even bricks to emulate marble, and give a becoming beauty and magnificence to the seat of government and the capital of so mighty an empire. Augustus found Rome of brick and in his last moments boasted that he left it of marble. May not London hope at length to see its Augustus.

But if our "Minister of Public Works" cannot accomplish this by decrees—we can refer with satisfaction to the modern works of national importance constructed in all parts of the United Kingdom, by private capital and skill, and what this as already done in "Public Works" on the Continent. We are reconciled by these drawbacks by other considerations. Much as we admire the genius of Stevenson, of a Barry, a Paxton, Watt, and justly proud as we may be of the people's palace at Sydenham, we are prouder of the "great facts" enumerated by the Author of Paris re-visited.

If England, he remarks, was not among the earliest to distinguish herself in the Fine-Arts, we must derive some consolation under the reproach of this, from the circumstance that religion was reformed of its most absurd superstitions, and political tyranny was chequed and controlled among us for some hundreds of years before any of our neighbours stirred in these public undertakings which are surely not insignificant. Literature, being essential to the deliverance of the human mind and the elevation of human feelings, was always sedulously attended to in England; and in regard to it she has no reason to blush either for her want of taste or want of power.

Painting and Sculpture certainly lagged behind, and it would be easy enough to account for their lateness, in a way that would rather prove it to reflect credit than dishonour on the minds of the people; but it is not necessary to say anything invidious of two elegant arts. When the accomplishment of great public duties, involving gallant enterprises, had afforded a fair opportunity for relaxation,—when the process of thoughtful enquiry, and the fiery trials of conflict and disputation, had issued in the settlement of a substantial fabric of public strength, freedom, and opulence,—when the useful having been pretty generally attained, the merely-agreeable might be safely cultivated, England evinced neither a want of taste or talent for elegant imitation. Reynolds, Hogarth, and Wilson, are names which suggest high degrees (some of them the highest) of almost all the variety of excellence belonging to painting.

London is certainly deficient in elegancies of architecture, though less so than common report declares, in consequence of the little parade that is made there of anything we have. Our palaces are very mean and clumsy; and as they are the first objects to which a foreigner looks, he seldom looks beyond them, being satisfied that they would be elegant if any of our buildings were so. But he ill-understands England, he must turn to what has been done by private wealth or popular spirit, by commercial prosperity or public charity, for her most magnificent displays;—her sovereigns have seldom had it in their power to build even a cottage but subject to the severest questioning. The point to be settled is, which is most honourable to a country's taste, to say nothing of its general character, the enjoyment of public liberty, exercising a control over the authorities of the state, or the erection of such beautiful palaces, as those which the Bourbons gave to their favourites.

In conclusion, we would express the hope, that while England emulates France in all that appertains to the Fine Arts, and the sciences, and her Educational Institutions, for all classes of her people, France may be able to emulate Old England in her glorious institutions of civil and religious government, so that in course of time, moving onwards side by side in the march of civilization, rival competitors in the Arts of Peace, the similarity in their institutions, shall exercise such an influence over the minds of both people, that it shall be impossible to disturb their friendly and commercial relationship, to "exhume" old animosities, and much less to revive a warlike disposition between two nations, who now, for almost the first time in their histories, appreciate the advantages of a sincere "Eutente Cordiale," and that under the reign of a Napoleon, whose conduct in this respect is alike honourable to his feelings and to his character.

PRACTICAL INSTRUCTIONS TO THE TRAVELLER.

In drawing up the following instructions, it has been presumed that the traveller will have provided himself with *Bradshaw's Continental Railway Guide*, as indispensable to railway travelling on the Continent; and reference is, therefore, made frequently to that book, in order to avoid unnecessary repetition here. As extensions of the railway system cause alterations in the number of the pages of that book, from time to time, where a reference is made to a particular page, if the information required is not found there, it will probably be on one of the adjoining pages.

1. What should be done in London—Passports—Money—Luggage.—The first thing the traveller must see about is his passport, for which ample instructions are found at pp. 19-22 of *Bradshaw's Continental Guide*. Mr. W. J. Adams, our London agent, will answer any inquiries on this head, or take the necessary steps to procure a passport for those who desire it.

2. Money.—See pp. 23-5 of *Bradshaw's Continental Guide*, and the table below. Bank-notes are negociable in some of the principal towns, and sovereigns are received; but the best plan is to change your English money into French napoleons at a respectable money-changer's at London or in France *(changeur)*. English gold, however, will pass anywhere (silver is useless), so will the louis d'or or napoleon, and the five-franc piece. As to expenses, 10s. to 20s. per head per day may be allowed. The latter sum will cover all charges of living in the best hotels, and travelling by first class railway and the best places in the coach. In the country inns board and lodging may be had for 6 francs to 10 francs a-day. Living is so cheap in Brittany, that 'Nimrod' says a man may live there like a prince on £6 to £100 a-year; but, course, at a sacrifice of many English *comforts*.

3. Luggage and Dress.—The less luggage you take the better. A carpet-bag is enough, with half-a-dozen shirts, two pairs of socks, and as few other things as possible. The socks should be woollen or worsted, which may be bought as you go, throwing the worn-out ones away. Brown, grey, or dark dresses are fitted for men or ladies; and as to the style, let it be simple. A light overcoat, and an umbrella for a stick are essential. Soap is not common, and being charged in the bills abroad, you should provide yourself with a stock before taking up your quarters. The pedestrian should, of course, put on a stout pair of double-soled shoes, and wear gaiters, especially as the roads are more dusty than ours. Where shoes chafe in walking, take a sheet of writing paper, grease it over, and wrap it round the foot next the skin. Good knapsacks may be got abroad.

4. Letters.—The traveller will find it convenient to have his letters addressed to him to the "Poste Restante," in the various towns at which he expects to be. They will be delivered on the passport being shewn, or, in some cases—as Paris, for instance —the name-card only is required. There are now two posts daily (one in the morning and the other in the evening) leaving London for France. All letters for France go through the London post-office, and for the morning mail must be in the London office before 7 45 a.m., and the evening mail before six p.m. The time required for conveying them to any part of France can be ascertained by reference to *Bradshaw's Continental Railway Guide*, and in very little more than this time the traveller may expect them at their appointed place.

5. Way to get to France, and Landing there.—See pp. 140-1 of *Bradshaw's Continental Guide*, from which the following is extracted:—

a. Calais Route.—London to Paris direct, *viâ* Dover and Calais, 346 miles, in 12¼ hours, viz.:—Departure from London for Dover (1st class only) at 8 30 *p.m.;* arrival at Dover 11 15 *p.m.;* departure from Dover 11 30 *p.m.;* arrival at Calais 2 *a.m.;* arrival at Paris 10 *a.m.* *(See page 30, Route 10, of Hand Book; and read the descriptions in an inverted order back to page 21).* Through tickets, 61s. There are 26 miles only of sea by this route, which in the old coach days took 58 to 60 hours between London and Paris. By the direct train the luggage is examined only on arrival at Paris. Another direct train (1st and 2nd class) starts at 8 10 *a.m.*, reaching Dover at 11 *a.m.*, Calais at 3 *p.m.*, and Paris at 11 5 *p.m;* through tickets, 61s. and 43s. 9d. Travellers for Marseilles, on landing at Boulogne or Calais, should have their passports *visé* for that place direct, to save delay at Paris; they will receive a provisional passport for 2 francs. The station, refreshment room, and douane at Calais are close to the quay. Two departures from Calais for Dover daily. Calais may be also reached by the General Steam Navigation Company's steamers, direct from London Bridge Wharf, twice a-week, in 9 to 10 hours. Fares 12s. and 8s.

b. Boulogne Route.—London to Paris direct in about 12 hours, by South Eastern Railway and Packets from Folkestone, according to tide. *(See pp. 35-6, Route 12; and read back).* Through tickets, 51s. 6d. and 37s. Or by General Steam Navigation Company's boats four times a-week, and Commercial Steam Company's boats twice a-week, direct from London Bridge Wharf, in 10 hours. Fares 12s. & 8s.; or through 31s. and 22s.

c. Dieppe Route.—Direct, in 12 to 15 hours, by Brighton Railway, steamer from Newhaven to Dieppe, according to tide, and railway to Rouen and Paris. *(See pp.*

12-13, *Route* 2; *and read back*). About 72 miles of sea passage. Through fares, 28s. and 20s.

d. Havre Route.—By South Western Railway to Southampton, steam to Havre, and railway to Rouen and Paris. *(See pp.* 10-12, *Route* 1; *and read back*). Through fares 28s. and 20s. N.B.—Steamer only three times a-week; sea passage, 102 miles.

e. Dunkirk Route.—By steamer direct from Irongate Wharf, two or three times a week, in about twelve hours. Fares 10s. and 7s. *(See pp.* 38-9, *Route* 14).

In addition to what is here stated, you may take the route to Jersey from Southampton or Newhaven; thence to Avranches, Granville, St. Malo; and through Brittany to Nantes, &c. Before you land at a French port, make up your mind as to the hotel you choose, as, by so doing, you secure to yourself the services of the porter of that hotel directly you land, and are saved annoyance from the touters who crowd at the landing. No baggage, except it may be a small parcel, or a carpet bag, (if at night) is allowed to be taken ashore by the passengers, but is detained at the Douane (custom-house), where you may clear it yourself or pay a porter (*commissionnaires*, as they are called) to clear it.

Your passport is taken from you at the Douane, and a provisional passport given you instead, which will take you on to Paris. Or if you make a stay of a day or two at the port, you apply for the provisional pass on leaving it. This you may do through the commissionnaire, who will also clear your baggage. It is much better in either case to make use of such an agent, who will for a franc or two take all the trouble off your hands, and save much bother and loss of time. The regular charge when you clear it, is, per package, 7 sous (3½d.) if under 10lb., 14 sous from 10 to 56lb., 1 franc above that weight; every package being charged, so that the fewer you have the better. For carriage to the hotel you pay a porter 50 cents (5d.) for the first package, and 25 cents for each of the others. When leaving a French port for England, a *permis d'embarquement* may be had at the Douane one hour before the steamer starts, or between one and three *p.m.* when she leaves at night. Once on board you cannot go ashore again without special permission. You may bring back, free of duty, a pint of spirits, and half-pint of eau-de-Cologne. By a new arrangement, luggage direct to London, by some of the trains on the South Eastern Railway, is not examined at Dover or Folkestone, but at the London Bridge station. Luggage, also, in Steamers from abroad, may be examined, if desired, by the officer on board, between Gravesend and London.

6. Living in France.—When you go to an inn choose your bed at once, *au premier*, *au second*, *au troisième*, &c., on the 1st, 2nd, or 3rd story; the higher stories being the cheapest. In your bed room, if you desire it, there is no objection to your taking tea and seeing your friends, if you have not a private sitting room. It is not indispensable that you take your meals in the hotel, though it may be advisable to do so as often as convenience will permit. At other times you may find a *café* or *restaurant* desirable for eating or drinking, and there is often one of these attached to good hotels in Paris and other large cities in France. To make the most of your time for sight-seeing, two meals a-day may suffice, a good breakfast to start with, and a dinner at the end of it. Frenchmen seldom make more than two regular meals. If you come back to the *table d'hôte* (ordinary), kept at every hotel at a fixed hour, and at a charge of from 3 to 5 francs), you may safely trust yourself to the landlord who presides. The courses

are something in this order, soup *(potage)*; *bouilli*, or the meat from which the soup is made; veal or some made dish; fish *(poisson)*; poultry *(volaille)*; cutlets; vegetables, separately; roast meat; pastry *(pâtisserie)*; then fruit, biscuits and cheese. Coffee and liqueurs are a separate charge. The drink is *vin ordinaire* (common wine), a bottle of which is *usually* included in the charge for dinner. Few dishes in France require a knife. Servants are paid in the bill, 1 to 1½ franc a day for each person.

If you order a dinner at an hôtel or restaurant, order a 'diner à la français,' or at so much a-head; as a 'diner à deux francs et demi 2½ francs),' 'diner à trois or quatre francs (3 or 4 francs),' &c.; or call for the bill of fare *(carte)* and choose for yourself, out of a list of 100 or 200 dishes, filling a respectable volume. Coffee houses &c., where you may smoke in the large towns are called *estaminets*; common wine and *eau de vie* (brandy) are sold at the cabarets. Where you make a stay at any place, the cheapest plan of living, is to take a furnished room at a private house or hôtel *(hôtel garni*, or *maison meublée* You may get them at all prices; the furniture is much more simple than in Englan Have a written agreement, signed by both parties, with an inventory of every article, however trifling, and if advisable, a stipulation that the landlord pays the furniture tax (levied in November).

Servants are engaged by the month; but it is most economical to hire one to come a little while every day to your lodgings, and to bring meals from the nearest *traiteur* (cook-shop), who will regularly send you his bill of fare to choose from, and supply hot dishes at any hour you please. This convenient arrangement is very common in France. If you want to examine any town &c. in a hurry, the best thing is to hire a *laquais de place*, at 5 or 6 francs a day (finding himself), to act as a guide and servant.

When travelling, "a pair of leather sheets may be placed beneath the seat cushions, as a precaution against damp beds, which however, are seldom met with in France or Italy. Essence of ginger is an useful stimulant; and a tea-spoonful in a cup of tea, on arriving after a day's journey, is very refreshing. Those who are in weak health, and travellers in general, should eat very sparingly of animal food on a journey, as it tends to produce heat and flushing. Black tea is one of the most useful articles travellers can be provided with, as it is seldom good in small towns or at inns on the road." (Edwin Lee, *Companion to the Continent*; a most useful Hand Book for the invalid).

As to personal demeanour, it is scarcely necessary to add, that civility and kindness will procure a welcome anywhere. 'One touch of nature makes the whole world kin,' says the poet. Always carry your passport about with you; 'Je suis Anglais' (I am an Englishman), and the production of this document, will gain you admission to almost every public exhibition. Where the authorities (gendarmes, &c.) ask for explanation, be ready to give it with temper and openness. The smallest official abroad participates in the cares of government, and assumes in consequence a very dignified air when dealing with a stranger; but do not mind this, touch your hat (this goes a great way indeed with every native you speak to) and answer him as politely as if he were the Préfet de Police. Above all things do not trouble your head about French politics.

In returning to England it will be necessary to get back the passport which was exchanged for the *passe provisoire* at the port you touched at, and thence sent on to Paris. Apply for it again when you reach Paris, or if you return by another way, write for it from some large town, to which end all the préfectures and sous-préfectures are carefully noted in this Hand Book.

7. RAILWAYS, DILIGENCES, &c. A full list of Railways is given in *Bradshaw's Continental Guide*, and they are so clearly marked by the *black line down the page* in this Hand Book that it is useless to say much about them here. The map shews that daily all the important localities in France are brought into communication with Paris and with each other. A system is projected for uniting Bordeaux, Toulouse, Perigueux, Clermont, Marseilles, and Lyons, in the south and most hilly part of the kingdom.

About 2,320 miles are laid down, while England and Wales have about 6,000 miles. The earliest railways were those from Paris to St. Germains, and from Lyons to St. Etienne; both constructed in 1837. The longest direct line from the capital is that to Bordeaux (opened throughout June, 1853), a distance of 360 miles; but from Calais down to Bordeaux, there is now a direct line of 596 miles; that from Nantes to Strasbourg is a little less, 582 miles. (Plymouth to Aberdeen is 664 miles; Bordeaux to Vienna, 1,900 miles).

The traffic is carefully parcelled out to each line, so that vehicles to places off it run from certain stations, and from those only. One line, the Paris and Lyons, is under the management of government officials. In France, before a line is opened, not only the rail, but the carriages, engines, stations, and all other details are looked into by the authorities, with a paternal eye to the safety of the public, who on this side of the water are considered able to take care of themselves. Nevertheless, French railways are cheaper and more comfortable than English; both 1st and 2nd class seats are stuffed; they are heated in winter with metal cases of hot water, covered with sheep skins, and first class fare is 1½d. per mile, on the average; while in England it is 3d. Children, however, pay full fare above six or eight years; in England not till ten or eleven years. Trains do not run so often or so fast, but still they run much faster than in Belgium or Germany.

Full lists of coaches (omnibuses and diligences) running from the stations on the railways and the towns along the roads are given in this work; as well as of the steam boats *(bateaux-à-vapeur)* from the ports. Nearly all the the *malles-postes* (mail coaches) have been superseded by railways; diligences (stage coaches) run six to ten miles an hour, at an average rate of 1½d. per mile.

COMMON FRENCH WORDS AND PHRASES.

A few of the commonest phrases, however ill chosen or arranged they may be, are better than nothing to the inexperienced traveller; and we therefore add a short list for his benefit.

Des Repas.	**Of Meals.**
Le Déjeuner	Breakfast
Le goûter, le second déjeuner	Luncheon
Le diner	Dinner
Le thé	Tea
Le Souper	Supper

Le Manger.	**Of Eating.**
Un pain, du pain	A loaf, bread
Un petit pain	A roll
Du pain blanc	White bread
Du pain de ménage	Household bread
Du pain bis	Brown bread
Du pain frais	New bread
Du pain rassis	Stale bread

La Carte.	**The Bill of Fare.**
Du bouillon	Broth
Un consommé	Gravy soup
De la Soupe	Soup
Soup à la vermicelle	Vermicelli soup
Soupe au riz	Rice soup
Soupe à la purée	Pease soup
De la viande	Meat
Des côtelettes demouton	Mutton chops
Un gigot	A leg of mutton
Des rognons	Kidneys
De vagneau	Lamb
Du lard	Bacon
Du jambon	Ham
Du gibier	Game
Un pâté	A pie
De la volaille	Poultry
Un poulet	A fowl
Un dinden	Turkey
Du poisson	Fish
Des soles	Soles
Des huitres	Oysters
Des legumes.	Vegetables
Uu chou	A cabbage
Un choufleur	A cauliflower
Des pommes de terre	Potatoes
Des œufs	Eggs
Un œuf	An egg
Des œufs frais	New laid eggs
Des œufs à la coque	Soft boiled
Une omelette	An omelet
Une salade	A salad
Du Sel	Salt
Du poivre	Pepper
De la moutard	Mustard
Des biscuits	Biscuits
Des gateaux	Cakes
Du fruit	Fruit
Du fromage	Cheese
Du beurre frais	Butter
Du sucre	Sugar
Du thé	Tea
Du café	Coffee

De la Boisson.	**Of Drink**
De l'eau	Water
De l'eau rougie	Wine and water
Du vin	Wine
Du vin blanc	White wine
Du vin rouge	Red wine
Vin ordinaire, ou vin de Bordeaux	Claret
Du vin de champagne	Champagne
Du vin de Bourgoyne	Burgundy
Du vin d'Oporto	Port wine
Du vin de Xeres	Sherry
De la bierre	Beer
De l'eau de vie, de cognac	Brandy—cognac

Un couteau	A knife
Une fourchette	A fork
Une cuiller	A spoon
Une apiette	A plate

LES PLATS QU'ON TROUVE GENERALEMENT CHES LES RESTAURATEURS EN FRANCE.	THE DISHES GENERALLY FOUND AT THE FRENCH RESTAURATEURS.
LA CARTE.	**THE BILL OF FARE.**
Pottages.	**Soups.**
Au macaroni	Macaroni soup
Au riz	Rice soup
Au vermicelle	Vermicelli soup

A la julienne	Soup, with chopped carrots and herbs
A la purée	Peas Soup
Consomme	Gravy soup

Bœuf.	**Beef.**
Bœuf au naturel	Boiled beef
Bœuf à la sauce tomate	Beef with love-apple sauce
Bœuf à la sauce piquante	Beef with savoury sauce
Bœuf aux choux	Beef with cabbage
Entrecôte	Ribs of beef
Filet santé	Fillet of beef with gravy
Rosbif aux pommes de terre	Roast beef with potatoes
Aloyau de bœuf	Sirloin of beef
Langue de bœuf	Neats' tongue
Palais de bœuf	Palate of beef
Bifteck à l'Anglaise	Beefsteak in the English manner
Bifteck aux pommes de terre	Beefsteak with potatoes
Bœuf à la mode	Beef larded

Veau.	**Veal.**
Fricandeau au jus	Larded veal in gravy
Friandeau au epinards	Larded veal with spinage
Fricandeau à l'oseille	Larded veal with sorrel
Fricandeau à la chicoreé	Larded veal with boiled endive
Côtelette de veau au naturel	Veal chops fried or boiled
Côtelette en papillote	Veal chops broiled in papers with sweet herbs
Cotelette au jambon	Veal chops with ham
Cervelle appreteé de différentes manière.	Calf's brains cooked in different ways
Tête de veau a la vinaigrette	Calf's head with oil and Vinegar
Tête de veau d'autres manières	Calf's head in different ways
Langue à la sauce piquante	Calf's tongue with savoury sauce
Pieds de veau de vinaigrette	Calf's feet with oil and vinegar
Blanquette de veau	Fricaseed veal with white sauce.
Ris de veau	Calf's sweet bread
Fraise de veau	Calf's fry

Mouton et Agneau	**Mutton and Lamb**
Côtelettes panées	Chops fried in bread crumbs
Côtelettes en papillottes	Chops broiled in papers with fine herbs
Côtelettes au naturel	Chops fried or broiled
Gigot au jus aux haricots	Leg with gravy or French beans
Royons au vin de champagne	Kidneys done in champagne
Pieds de mouton à la vinaigrett	Trotters with oil and vinegar
Rognons à la brochette	Kidneys broiled
Rognons aux truffes	Kidneys with truffles

Volaille.	**Poultry.**
Chapon au gros sel	Capon (boiled)
Chapon au riz, etc	Capon with rice
Poulet sauté	Chicken in gravy
Poulet à la tartarre	Chicken devilled
Cuisse de poulet en papillote	Leg of a chicken in paper with sweet herbs.
Dinde truffée	Turkey with truffles
Dindonneau	Young turkey
Poulet aux champignons	Chicken with champignon sauce
Capilotade de poulet	Chicken hashed
Salade de volaille	Cold chicken in slices and vinegar
Galantine de volaille	Brawned fowl
Poulet au truffée	Chicken, with truffles
Filets de poulet	Slices of chicken (breast)
Canard aux navets	Duck and turnips
Canard aux poids	Duck and green peas.
Caneton	Duckling
Pigeon à la crapandine	Broiled pigeon
Fricasseé de poulet	Fricasseed chicken

Gibier.	**Game.**
Côtelette de chevreuil	Venison chops
Filet de chevreuil	Fillet of venison
Perdrex apprêteés de differentes manières	Partridges dressed in different ways
Perdreaux en salmis	Young partridges jugged
Maurrettes differentes manières	Larks, variously dressed
Gibelotte de lapin	Rabbit smothered
Laperau sauté aux champignons	Young rabbit with champignon sauce
Becasse	Woodcock dressed in different ways
Becassine	Snipes
Canard Sauvage	Wild duck
Caille	Quails
Faisau	Pheasant
Ortolans	Ortolans
Grives	Thrushes
Canard sauvage en salmis	Wild duck jugged
Sarcelle en salmis	Teal jugged

Poissons.	**Fish.**
Saumon	Salmon
Turbot	Turbot
Raie	Skate
Morue	Cod
Truite	Trout
Soles	Soles
Merlans	Whiting
Maquereau	Mackerel
Eperlans	Smelts
Alose	Shad
Carrelet	Flounder
Homard	Lobster
Ecrevisse	Cray-fish
Heutres	Oyster
Brocket	Pike
Anguilles	Eels

Legumes.	**Vegitables.**
Asperges	Asparagus
Pointes d'asperges	Heads of asparagus
Choux de Bruxelles	Brussels sprouts
Chou-fleur	Cauliflower
Haricots blanc	French beans (shelled)
Haricots verts	French beans (green)
Chicorée	Endive
Pommes de terre à la maître d'hôtel	Potatoes sliced with parsley and butter
Petits pois	Green peas
Epinardo	Spinage
Artichauts	Artichokes
Céleri	Celery

Hors D'oeuvre.	**Extras.**
Omelette aux fines herbes	Omelet with sweet herbs
Omelette au sucre	Omelet with sugar
Omelette au jambon	Omelet fried with ham
Œufs pochés	Poached eggs
Œufs sur le plat	Fried eggs
Beignets de pommes, etc	Apple fritters
Gâteau de riz	Rice pudding or cake
Charlotte russe	Syllabub in light paste
Tourte aux fruits	Tarts of various fruits
Plum pouding	Plum pudding
Fromage (différentes sortes)	Cheese (different sorts)
Beurre frais, salé	Butter, fresh, salt
Petits pâtés	Savoury patties
Truffes au vin de champagne	Truffles done in champagne
Gelée de groseilles ou de framboises	Jellies (currant or rasberry)

Dessert.	**Dessert.**
Melon	Melon
Raisin de Fontainebleau	White grapes of Fontainbleau
Pêches	Peaches
Fraises au sucre	Strawberries with Sugar
Ananas	Pines
Figues	Figs
Pruneau cuits au sucre	Prunes cooked with sugar
Quatre mendicants	Raisins, almonds, nuts and figs (four beggars)
Cerises à l'eau de vie	Cherries preserved in brandy
Prunes de Monsieur	Orleans plums
Prunes de reine, Claude	Green gages
Pommes et poires	Apples and pears
Amandes vertes	Green almonds
Compotedes differents fruits	Stewed fruits
Geleé des groseilles, etc.	Currant jelly and others
Meringues	Trifle
Abricots á l'eau de vie	Apricots with brandy
Biscuits de Rheims	Sponge cakes
Macarons	Macaroons

Vins et Liqueurs.	**Wines & Liquors.**
Bordeau ou Mâcon ordinaire ou vieux	Claret, of Bordeaux, or Burgundy, ordinary or old
Bourgogne, ordinaire ou vieux	Burgundy, ordinary or old
Château Margot	Claret, Chateau Margot
Chablis	Chablis
Grave	Grave
Sauterne	Sauterne
Saint Peray	Saint Peray
Du Rhin	Rhenish
Champagne	Champagne
Volnay	Volnay

Habillements d'Hommes, etc.	**Of Men's Clothes, &c.**
Une chemise(d'hommes)	A shirt
Un calecon	Drawers
Une camisole	An under-waistcoat
Une robe de chambre	A morning-gown
Un pantolon	Trowsers
Une cravatte	A neck cloth
Un col	A stock
Un gilet	A waistcoat
Des bas	Stockings
Un cure dents	A tooth pick

Un tire botte	A boot jack
Se raser	To shave
Un necessaire	A dressing case
Des chaussons	Socks
Des pantoufles	Slippers
Des souliers	Shoes
Des bottes	Boots
Un chause pied	A shoe horn

Habillement des Femmes.	Of Women's Clothes.
Une chemise	A chemise
Un jupon	A petticoat
Un corset	Stays
Un lacet	Stay lace
Une pelerine	A tippet
Une robe	A gown or dress
Des volants	Flounces
Des manches	Sleeves
Un fichu	A neck handkerchief
Un mouchoir de poche	A pocket handkerchief
Des gants	Gloves
Un châle	A shawl
Une echarpe	A scarf
Un chapeau	A bonnet
Un voile	A veil
Un neglegé	A morning gown
La coiffure	Head dress
Une robe d'enfant	A frock
Des papellotes	Curl papers

Miscellanea.	Miscellaneous.
Du Savon	Soap
Une Eponge	A sponge
Une serviette, essuie-main	A towel
Des épingles	Pins
De la soi	Silk
Du satin	Satin
Du velour	Velvet
De la dentelle	Lace
Chambre a coucher	Bed room
Une petit salon	Sitting room
Un cabinet de toilette	A dressing closet
Le salon	The drawing room
La salle à manger	The dining room
Un rez de chaussée	A ground floor
Les appartments	The apartments
Un poële	A stove
Un miroir, une glace	A looking glass
Un lit	The bed
Le bois de lit	The bedstead
Un lit de plume	A feather bed
Un matelas	A mattress
Un oreiller	A pillow
Les draps	The sheets
Une couverture de laine	A blanket
Une courtepointe	A counterpane
Une bassinoire	A warming pan
Une table de nuit	A night table
Une chandelle	A candle
Une bougie	A wax candle
Une lampe	A lamp
Une veilleuse	A night lamp
Les mouchettes	The snuffers
Un augnoir	An extinguisher
Un bain (chaud)	A bath (warm)
Des allumettes	Matches
Du charbon	Coals
Du bois	Wood
Un acquit	A receipt
Un billet de banque	A bank note
La cherté—cher	Dearness—dear
Bon marché	Cheap
La douane	The custom hous
Le bureau de la poste	The post office
La grande poste	The general post office
Le facteur	The postman
Le post des lettres	Postage
Un banquier	A banker
Un changeur	A money changer
Un joallier—un orfevre	A jeweller or goldsmith
Un marchand de soieries	A silk mercer
Un marchand des nouveautés	A linen draper
Un medicin	A doctor
Un pharmacien	An apothecary
Un dentiste	A dentist
Une marchande de mode	A milliner
Une couturière	A dress maker
Un coiffeur	A hair dresser
Un gantier	A glover
Un patissier	A pastry cook
Chemin de fer	Railway
Voyageur	Traveller
Billet ou coupon	Ticket
Bagage	Luggage
Franchise de port	Luggage allowed
Voiture	Carriage
La gare	Station
Salle d'attente	Waiting room
Facteurs	Porters

Train, *or* convoi	Train
Station, *or* embarcadère	Terminus
Chevaux	Horses
Chien	Dog
Moitié prix	Half-price
Matin (m.)	Morning
Soir (s.)	Evening
1re. cl. (première classe)	1st class
2e. cl. (seconde id)	2nd do.
3e. cl. (troisième id)	3rd do.
De grande vitesse, *or* exp.	Fast train
Duret du trajet	Time taken
Prolongement	Extension
Service d'hiver	Winter service
Service d'été	Summer do.
Par tête	So much a head
Administration	Office
Billets d'aller et de retour	Return tickets
Voyage simple	A run one way
Trains ixtes	Mixed trains
Trains irects	1st and 2nd class

Buffet	Refreshment room
Trains express	1st class only
Articles de messagerie	Goods, &c, for luggage van
Conducteur, or mécanicien	Engineman, or driver
Chauffeur	Fireman, or stoker

Bateau à vapeur	Steam-boat
Bateau à vapeur à hélice	Screw steamer
Bateau de post	Post-office packet
Paquebots	Packet boats
Deux fois par jour	Twice a day
Deux departs par semaine	Twice a week
1re. Chambre	Chief cabin
2e. do.	Fore cabin
Navigation à vapeur	Steam navigation
Pavillon (*in Rhine steamer*)	1st cabin(one half more than saloon)
Salon (do.)	2nd cabin
Chambre de devant(do)	3rd. do. (half of Saloon)
Nourriture	Living, or provisions
Une malle	A trunk
Un porteur	A porter
Telegrahe sous-marin	Submarine telegraph
Bains de mer	Sea baths
Uu commis de la douane	Custom-house officer

Ville	Large town, or city
Bourg	Walled town
Boulevards	Site of old walls, or *bulwarks*
Faubourg	Suburb
Rue	Street
Chausée	Causeway
Chemin	Road
Pont	Bridge
Bac	Ferry
Porte	Gate
Hôtel de ville, or mairie	Town-house
Place	Square
Eglise	Church
Poste aux lettres	Post-office
Bibliothèque	Public-library
Musée	Museum
Jardin des plantes	Botanic garden
Salle de spectacle	Theatre, &c.
Hôpital, *or* Hôtel Dieu	Infirmary
Hospice	Asylum
Fonderie	Iron work
Verrerie	Glass work

Dimanche	Sunday
Lundi	Monday
Mardi	Tuesday
Mercredi	Wednesday
Jeudi	Thursday
Vendredi	Friday
Samedi	Saturday

Le printemps	Spring
Les semailles	Seed-time
L'eté	Summer
L'automne	Autumn
La recolte	The harvest
Les vendanges	The vintage
L'hiver	Winter

Janvier	January
Fevrier	February
Mars	March
Avril	April
Mai	May
Juin	June
Juillet	July
Aout	August
Septembre	September
Novembre	November
Decembre	December

Une demi-douzaine.	Half a dozen.
Qu' est-ce que cela, Monsieur?	What is that, Sir;
Que dites-vous?	What do you say?
Monsieur, je ne vous ai pas entendu, *or*. Je ne vous entend pas, monsieur ('Nong tong paw' of the old song).	I do not understand you.
Où allez-vous?	Where are you going?
Que voulez-vous?	What do yon want?
Quel est le chemin de Paris? *or* Ayez la bonté de me montrer le chemin, &c.?	Which is the way to Paris? or, Have the goodness to tell me the way, &c?
Allez tout droit.	Go straight on.
Tournez à gauche (*or*, à droite).	Turn to the left (or, to the right).
Merci, *or*, bien obligé.	Thank you.
Il fait beau.	It is fine weather.
Le temps est convert; il va pleuvoir; prenez un parapluie.	Ii is cloudy weather, and going to rain; take an umbrella.
Il fait mauvais temps; nous aurons de l'orage.	It is bad weather; we shall have a storm.
Le soleil luit; il fait bien chaud.	The sun shines; it is very hot.
Le soleil est couché	The sun is set.
Il fait clair de lune.	It is moonlight.
Il fait un brouillard épais.	There is a thick fog.
Le vent est changé.	The wind is changed.
Il fait beaucoup de poussière.	It is very dusty.
Quelle heure est-il, Monsieur?	What o'clock is it, sir?
Il est environ deux heures; *or*, Deux heures vont sonner.	About two o'clock-
Il est deux heures et quatre.	Quarter-past two.
Il est deux heures et demie.	Half-past two.
Il est deux heures moins un quatre.	Quarter to two.
Il est deux heures moins cinq miuutes.	Five minutes to two.
Il est midi.	It is twelve (uoon).
Aujourd'hui.	To-day,
Ce matin; ce soir.	This morning; this evening.
Demain matin; après demain.	To-morrow morning; day after.
Hier; avant hier.	Yesterday; day before.
Il y a deux jours.	Two days ago.
Dans huit jours; *or*, D'aujourd'hui en huit.	In a week.
Tous les jours.	Every day.
J'ai faim.	I am hungry.
Que-voulez-vous manger?	What will you eat;
Donnez-moi à boire.	Give me something to drink.
Donnez-moi un verre d'eau de vie.	Give me a glass of brandy.
Apportez le diner.	Bring the dinner.
Donnez-moi des œufs.	Give me some eggs.
Voulez-vous une tasse de café, (du vin, de la viande, du jambon, du thé, de l'eau de vie!	Will you take a cup of coffee, (some wine, meat, ham, tea, brandy)?
Comment vous portez-vous?	How do you do?
Fort bien; *or*, Très bien, je vous remercie.	Very well, 1 thank you.

Je suis Anglais.	I am English.
Parlez-vous Anglais!	Do you speak English.
Soyez le bien-venu, Monsieur.	Sir, you are welcome.
Où demeure Monsieur A?	Where does Mr. A. live?
Il demeure Rue B.	He lives in B. street.
Appelez-moi un fiacre (*or* cabriolet)	Call a coach (or cab).
Vous pouvez aller par la diligence, ou prendre une chaise de poste.	You may go by the stage coach, or take a post chaise.
A quelle heure la diligence part-elle d'ici?	When does the coach start?
Combien prend-on par place? *or*, Combien prenez-vous?	What is the fare? or, what do you charge?
Combien de jours serons nous en route.	How many days will it take?
Quell reute prenez-vous?	Which way do you go?
Quel est le meilleur chemin?	Which is the best road?
La route qui passe par B. est la plus courte.	The road through B. is the shortest.
Combien de ——— à ———?	How far from ——— to ———?
A qui est ce château?	Whose seat is this?
Quel est le nom de cet endroit?	What is the name of this place?
Y-a-t-il des cabinets de tableaux?	Are there any pictures to be seen?
Quel magnifique paysage!	What a beautiful country?
Comment appelle-t-on cette ville?	What town is this?
Où nous arrètrons-nous?	Where shall we stop?
Quand partirez-vous?	When do yon sail?
Au point du jour, *or*, à la marée.	At day break, or, high water.
Nous allons partir.	We are going directly.
Quand nous embarquons-nous?	When do we go on board?
Combien de temps serons-nous en mer?	How long shall we be at sea?
Je me sens mal, je puis à peine me tenir sur mes jambes; la tête me tourne.	I am very sick; I can hardly stand on my legs; my head turns round.
Je loge à l'hôtel de C.	I am staying at the hotel de C
Quel est le meilleur hôtel; *or*, la meilleure auberge?	Which is the best inn?
Un diner à table d'hôte.	A dinner at the ordinary.
Un diner seul.	Dinner alone.
A quelle heure voulez-vous diner?	At what time do you wish to dine?
On a servi.	Dinner is on the table.
Voulez-vous un pen de soupe; *or*, de potage?	Will you take soup?
Non, je vous remercie, je commencerai par du poisson.	No, I thank you, I will take some fish.
Permettez que je vous presente du bœuf.	Allow me to offer you some beef.
De quel vin voulez-vous.	What wine will you take?
Garçon, donnez-nous une bouteille de vin de Bourgogne.	Waiter, bring us a bottle of Burgundy.
Vous enverrai-je une tranche de ce gigot?	Shall I send you a slice of mutton?
Vous servirai-je des légumes?	Will you take some vegetables?
Vous servirai-je des pommes de terre?	Will you take some potatoes?
Pas davantage.	Not any more.
Garçon, changez cette assiette.	Waiter, change this plate.
Uue cuiller, s'il vous plait.	Give me a spoon.

Je vous remercie, c'est assez.	Thank you, that's enough.
Mettez les verres sur la table.	Put the glasses on the table,
Apportez-moi un verre d'eau.	Bring me a glass of water.
Garçon, une bouteille de vin ordinaire.	Waiter, a bottle of ordinary claret wine.
Donnez-nous le dessert.	Let us have the dessert.
Voulez-vous avoir la bonté de sonner?	Be so good as to ring the bell.
Le thé est servi.	Tea is ready.
Combien vous devons-nous?	What have we to pay?
Je désire avoir mon compte.	I wish to have my bill.
Voici la note Monsieur.	Here is the bill, Sir.
Voici votre argent.	Here is your money.
Pouvons-nous coucher içi?	Can we sleep here.
J'aimerais mieux une chambre au premier (*or*, au second, au troisième).	I should like a room on the first floor (or, second floor, third floor).
Il me faut du savon.	I want a piece of soap.
Les lits sont-ils bien bassinés?	Are the beds well warmed?
Les draps sont-ils bien secs?	Are the sheets quite dry.
Apportez-moi encore un oreiller.	Bring me another pillow.
Emportez la chandelle.	Take away the candle.
A quelle heure voulez-vous que je vous appelle?	When shall I call you?
Monsieur, je vous souhaite une bonne nuit.	I wish you good night, Sir.
Bon jour, Monsieur (*or* Madame, *or* Mademoiselle).	Good morning, sir.
Apportez-moi de l'eau chaude.	Bring me some hot water.
Apportez-moi mes bottes.	Bring me my boots.
Le déjeûner est il prêt?	Is breakfast ready?
Je prendrai du café, si vous voulez bien.	I will take coffee, if you please.
Il nous faut encore des tartines.	We want more bread and butter.
Une tasse de thé.	A cup of tea.
Déjeûner à la fourchette.	A meat breakfast.
Voilà de la viande; voici des saucisses, du jambon, une volaille.	Here is cold meat; here are sausages, ham, fowl.
Avez-vous des chambres à louer	Have you apartments to let?
Meublées ou non meublées?	Furnished or unfurnished?
Quel est le prix du loyer?	What are the terms.
Voudriez-vous me donner de la monnaie de France pour ces souverains?	Will you be so good as to give me French money for these sovereigns?
Banquier.	A banker.
Négociant.	A merchant.
Où est le bureau de poste?	Where is the post office?
Je voudrais acheter un chapeau.	I want to buy a hat.
Je voudrais acheter des souliers.	I want to buy a pair of shoes.
Je voudrais acheter une robe.	I want to buy a dress (ladies').
Voulez-vous me raser.	Will you shave me.
Voulez-vous me couper les cheveux (chevaux *means* horses).	Will you cut my hair.
J'ai du linge à laver; lavez le avec soin.	I have some linen to wash; wash it carefully.
Quand me le rapporterez-vous?	When will you bring it home?
Il faudra que vous rapportiez la note.	Bring the bill with you.

Voulez-vous que nous allions faire un tour de promenade ?	Shall we take a walk.
De bien bon cœur, *or*, très volontiers.	With great pleasure.
Peut-on passer à travers ce champ.	Is there a way across the fields ?
Quel est ce joli hameau ?	What pretty place is that ?
Où peut-on lire les journaux ?	Where can we see the newspapers ?
On lit les ouvrages périodiques et les journaux aux cabinets de lecture au Palais Royal.	You may see the periodicals and papers, &c., at the reading rooms of the Palais Royal.
Donnez-moi un verre de limonade.	Give me a glass of lemonade.
Je vous suis bien obligé.	I am obliged to you.
J'aime mieux une tasse de café et un verre de liqueur.	I prefer a cup of coffee and a glass of liquor.
Je suis à vos ordres ; allons nous en, *or*, partons.	I am ready ; let us go.
J'ai besoin d'un cheval de selle.	I want a horse to ride.
Donnez-lui une mesure d'avoine.	Give him a feed of oats.
Il me faut une belle voiture à quatre roues (*or* voiture de voyage).	I want a good four-wheeled carriage (or travelling carriage).
Combien demandez-vous ?	What is the price ? If the reply is not understood, as English figures are used, it will be clear if written ; therefore say ecrivez le, si vous plait.
C'est trop cher.	It is too dear.
Bon jour.	Good day.

CARDINAL NUMBERS.

Un, une	1	Neuf	9	Seize	16	Cinquante	50
Deux	2	Dix	10	Dix sept	17	Soixante	60
Trois	3	Onze	11	Dix huit	18	Soixante dix	70
Quatre	4	Douze	12	Dix neuf	19	Quatre-vingt	80
Cinq	5	Trieze	13	Vingt	20	Quatre-vingt dix	90
Six	6	Quatorze	14	Trente	30	Cent	100
Sept	7	Quinze	15	Quarante	40	Mille	1000
Huit	8						

ORDINAL NUMBERS.

Le premier / L'unième	the First	Le dixième	the Tenth
Le second / Le deuxième	the Second	L'onzième	the Eleventh
Le troisième	the Third	Le douzième	the Twelfth
Le quatrième	the Fourth	Le treizième	the Thirteenth
Le cinquième	the Fifth	Le quatorzième	the Fourteenth
Le sixième	the Sixth	Le quinzième	the Fifteenth
Le septième	the Seventh	Le seizième	the Sixteenth
Le huitième	the Eighth	Le dix septième	the Seventeenth
Le neuvième	the Ninth	Le dix huitième	the Eighteenth
		Le dix neuvième	the Nineteenth
		Le vingtième	the Twentieth

MONEY.

Money accounts in France are kept in francs and centimes, or hundredths; the décimes or tenths, which come between, being seldom mentioned.

1 (silver) franc = 10 décimes = 100 (copper) centimes = 20 sous or sols = 10d. English.
(1 sous therefore = 5 centimes = ½d.)
24 francs = 1 Louis d'or (gold) = 19s.
20 francs = 1 napoleon (gold) = 15s. 10d.
100 francs = £4
The franc exceeds the old livre by 1¼ per cent. (1¼ centimes).

£1 = 25¼ or 25½ francs,
According to the rate of Exchange.
1s. = 1¼ franc or 25 sous.
1d. = 10½ centimes or 2 sous.
The modern French *gold* coins are pieces of 10 fr., 20 fr., and 40 fr. The *silver* coins are pieces of 20 centimes, 50 cents. or ½ franc, 1 franc, 2 franc, and 5 franc pieces.

The above equalities of French and English moneys will vary a little with the rate of exchange; but the prevailing rate has been adopted.

WEIGHTS AND MEASURES.

Weights and measures are reckoned by the metrical system, so called from the *mètre*, the unit for long and square measure. Other units are—the *litre* for measures of capacity (cubic measure), the *stère* for wood, the *are* for land, and the *gramme* for weights. These are divided according to the numeration system; but to express tens, hundreds, &c., the French use the Greek prefixes of increase, *deca*, *hecto*, *kilo*, *myria*, *i.e.* tenfold, hundredfold, &c.; while for tenths, hundredths, thousandths, they use the Latin prefixes of decrease, *deci*, *centi*, *milli* (all ending in i), *i.e.* tenth part, hundredth part, thousandth part. Thus they answer to decimals, altering their name and value according to the place of the decimal point.

	ENGLISH FEET.
So that a *mètre* being	3.281
a decimètre is	.3281
and a centimètre is	.03281
but a decamètre is	32.81
a hectomètre is	328.1

	CUBIC INCHES.
In the same way a *litre* being	61.028
a decilitre is	6.1028
but a decalitre is	610.28

	GRAINS (TROY).
Again, a *gramme* being	15.432
a decigramme is	1.5432
but a decagramme is	154.32

This system is simple and convenient, in spite of the fine names with which it is encumbered, nly one or two of which need be used at a time.

For example, all measures of *length* may be reckoned in *mètres* and *parts*; thus,

1 mile	= 1609.315 mètres, *i.e.* 1609 mèt. 315 millimètres.
1 furlong	= 201.164 mètres, or 201 mèt., 164 millimètres.
1 yard	= .914 mètres, or 914 millimètres.
1 foot	= 304 mètres, or 304 millimètres.

Measures of *capacity* in *litres* and *parts*; thus,

1 gallon (imperial)	= 4.54 litres, or 4 lit. 54 centil.
1 quart	= 1.13 litres, or 1 lit. 15 centil.

Measures of *weight* in *grammes* and *parts*; thus,

1 pound (avoirdupois)	= 453.59 grammes, or 453 gr. 59 centig.
1 ounce	= 28.35 grammes, or 28 gr. 35 centig.
1 pound (troy)	= 373.24 grammes, &c.
1 ounce	= 31.10 grammes, &c.

FRENCH INTO ENGLISH.

1 French foot (old) = 1.066 English foot.
1 Ditto (new) 1-3rd of the mètres = 1.094 feet.
1 aune or ell = 4 feet nearly.
10 French feet = 10⅔ English feet.
100 French feet = 106½ English feet.
(being about 6 per cent., or 1 in 16 longer).

1 *mètre* = 1.094 English yard = 3.281 English feet = 39.37 inches (or about 1 1-10th yard or 3¼ feet nearly, or 10 per cent. longer).

To turn mètres into yards nearly, add 1-10*th.*

100 mètres = 328 English feet.
1000 mètres (or 1 *kilomètre* = 3281 English feet. or 5 furlongs nearly (4 furlongs 213 yards 2 feet exactly).

N.B. Distances on the French roads and railways are now measured in *kilomètres* and *parts.*

As a kilomètre is 3281 feet, and a mile 5280 feet it will be useful to remember, in comparing them, that

1 kilomètre = 5-8ths mile nearly.
or 6 miles = 10 kilomètres „
or 10 miles = 16 kilomètres „

10,000 mètres (or 10 kilomètres or 1 myriamètre) = 6.214 English miles, or = 6¼ miles nearly.
1 lieue de poste (or 4 kilomètres, or 2,000 toises) = 2 4-9ths English miles.
10 „ = 24 3-7ths „
1 toise = 6.396 feet = 6 feet 4½ inches.
10 „ = 64 feet, or 10⅓ fathoms nearly.
1 *kilogramme* = 2 lbs. 3 oz. (avoirdupois).
10 „ = 22 lbs. 1 oz.
51 „ = 112 lbs. or 1 cwt. nearly.
1 hectare = 2.471 acres, or 2½ acres nearly.
10 „ = 24⅘ acres.

ENGLISH INTO FRENCH.

1 foot = 3.084 décimètres.
1 yard = .9144 mètres, or 9-10th mètre nearly.
(To turn yards into mètres nearly, take off 1-10th)
1 fathom = 1.829 metres. 1 pole = 5.029 mètres.
1 mil = 1609.315 mètres = 1.609315 kilomètres; or 6 miles = 10 kilomètres, or 10 miles = 16 kilomètres nearly, as in the opposite column.
100 miles = 22 marine leagues = 41.3 legal leagues (lieues de postes, now abolished).
1 square yard = 0.836 metre square.
1 acre = 4.000 square mètres nearly,
1 square rood = 10.117 ares.
1 gallon = 4.543 litres.
1 bushel = 36.348 litres.
1 quarter = 290.78 litres, or 2.9078 hec.

Short Table of miles and kilomètres for long distances.

1 m. =	1·60931 kil.	1 kil. =	·621 m.
2 „ =	3·21862 „	2 „ =	1·242 „
3 „ =	4·82793 „	3 „ =	1·863 „
4 „ =	6·43724 „	4 „ =	2·484 „
5 „ =	8·04655 „	5 „ =	3·105 „
10 „ =	16·0931 „	10 „ =	6·210 „
100 „ =	160·931 „	100 „ =	62·1 „

Remember that 2 miles (for instance) being 3·21862 kilomètres, 20 miles will be 32·1862 kilomètres, and so on; therefore, if you want to turn 127 miles into kilomètres, say

	MILES.	KIL.
	100 =	160·9
	20 =	32·2
(4 and 3 together, or)	7 =	11·3
	127 =	204·4

To compare *thermometers*, remember that

	FAHR.	CENTIGRADE.	REAUM.
Boiling point	= 212°	= 100°	= 80°
Freezing point	= 32°	= 0°	= 0°
therefore	180°	= 100°	= 80°
or	9°	= 5°	= 4°

That is, 1° Reaum. = 2¼° Fahr.
and 1° Centig. = 1° 4-5ths Fahr.

For the *barometer*, 704 and 779 millimètres Fr., correspond to 27·7 and 30·7 inches.

Reaumur's thermometer is generally used on the Continent. To convert degrees of Reaumur into Fahrenheit multiply by 9, divide by 4, and to the quotient add 32° Thus, to convert 20° R. into F. 20 + 9 = 180 ÷ 4 = 45, to which add 32 = 77° Fahrenheit.

PARIS.

We have hitherto avoided encumbering modern travellers with diffuse histories of the Continental Cities they visit under our guidance; and we think it advisable to adhere to this rule, even with respect to the French Capital.

It would be a waste of time to give the early history of the old city, from the period it became the Metropolis of France down to the Revolution, 1789, and we spare our readers the details of the tragical events of which it has been the theatre since then, and wish we could

"Erase them from the Book of Time."

If any of our readers have a peculiar interest in the reminiscences connected with the names and incidents of civil wars, there are inumerable works replete with these details, by means of which he may people almost every house in Paris with some celebrity of other times. Leaving, therefore, every traveller, inquisitive, or sentimental, to indulge his own predilections, we revert to our external description of Paris.

Continental towns are generally of great antiquity, having a remote origin in forts and castles, and becoming gradually enlarged. They are consequently built without method, piled up of all orders and ages, paved all over with sharp stones, fantastic and irregular façades—all sorts of roofs and angles. The old town of Paris, built on La Cité, one of the islands in the Seine, has all these characteristics to the present day, and bears no resemblance whatever to the other parts of the great capital.

The extreme beauty of which, as seen in fine weather—its projections of massy buildings and single towers, standing in the clear blue atmosphere, is very striking.

This Paris of to-day is the Paris of yesterday, and the Paris of to-morrow is one unchanging attribute. It has always been, is still, and will no doubt continue to be, the cynosure which all travellers desire to behold — in illustration of the French adage "See Paris and die" as if the sight of that city were the supremest enjoyment in which man could participate.

"Other towns, compared with her, appear
Like shrubs, when lofty Cypresses are near."

And now that a net work of railway communication is gradually connecting it with all the principal cities of the Continent, making it as it were the heart of Europe, from which the iron arteries extend and connect it with the sea ports on the Mediterranean, with the capitals of Belgium and Holland, with the cities of Prussia, the shores of the Baltic, and the banks of the Rhine; with the cities of Austria and the shores of the Adriatic, with the cities of Poland, and ere long with the banks of the Neva; with Switzerland, Italy, and Spain, Paris will become the Babylon of modern Europe.

The English visitor, on leaving London to visit the French capital, no longer considers he his going among foreigners; he goes to Paris as a provincial comes up from the south or north to pass a few days in London, without thinking of the difference between the people of the two countries, and would scarcely be reminded of it in his sojourn among the Parisians, except by his visits to the marvellous attractions of the beautiful city they are so justly proud of.

The journey between the two capitals is now performed with so little fatigue, with such remarkable facilities, and smoothened with all those small courtesies of life, by which the English and French now so happily reciprocate an "Entente cordiale," that there is a constant stream of travellers passing to or from the two capitals of France and England throughout the year.

Formerly the English visited Paris principally during the summer months, whereas they now appear all the year; but the mode of their visiting the numerous objects of attraction in Paris and its environs must necessarily depend in a great measure on the season. If it be in the spring and the weather will admit of walking, this is the most agreeable mode, as there is something worthy of being seen and admired at almost every step. Leaving the hotel, after partaking of a substantial breakfast, the traveller should proceed to the Rue de Rivoli; thence to the Place du Carousel, and passing through the Court of the Tuilleries, obtain admission to the Palace.

The Tuilleries dates from the time of Catherine de Medecis, and consists of five parts, *i.e.*, a lofty pavilion in the centre, two long low buildings at each side, and again a lofty pavilion at each end—the whole forming a magnificent pile of buildings. On its southern side it is united to the Louvre by the long picture gallery bordering the Seine; and it is intended to complete the union with the palace of the Louvre, by continuing the northern side to form an immense quadrangle.

The interior is no less grand and regal. It was much injured in 1848 by the mob, which had possession of it for several weeks, during which they committed every act of vandalism they could think of, destroying most of the beautiful works of art belonging to Louis Phillipe and his family.

It is now restored to its former sumptuous splendour, but the numerous priceless gems alluded to cannot be replaced, they are irrevocably gone.

The first splendid Saloon is the hall of the Marshalls of France, on the first floor, which contains full-length portraits of the Marshalls of the French Army.

The Saloon of Peace is a magnificent room, the ceiling of which is exquisitely painted; representing the course of time: Spring succeeded by Plenty, and Fame announcing the happy intelligence to the world.

The suite of apartments succeeding these are embellished with most beautiful paintings, tapestry, vases, sculpture, &c., which must elicit many a lingering look of longing admiration from the amateur or connoiseur.

On leaving the palace, the traveller should proceed to the garden in front, called the Tuilleries Gardens, and if the morning be fine and genial, a walk in these delightful grounds, will be most agreeable. The walks and avenues—the magnificent and fine old elm or chestnut trees, in their deep green and rich luxuriant foliage; the beautiful variety of flowers, orange and laurel trees, the elegant and admirable statuary, the front view of the Tuilleries; and above all a clear and cloudless sky, produce a charming scene that will make a delightful impression on the traveller. At a later hour of the day it is the resort of the fashionable beau-monde of Paris.

Walking down the central avenue, and then ascending the steps leading to the terraces fronting the Place de la Concorde, the view thus obtained is one of the finest it is possible to conceive.

Proceeding thence to the side of the Egyptian Obelisk, between the fountains in the centre of the square, there will appear trees of majestic size, gardens, and architectural magnificence, mingling in one view of surpassing beauty. Including the palace and garden of the Tuilleries, the Madeleine church, the bridge de la Concorde, the chamber of the Legislative Body, the splendid avenue of trees called the Champs Elyseés or Elisian Fields, at the end of which, towering in grand architectural magnificence, appears the Triumphal Arch, crowning as it were the coup d'œil, of certainly and unquestionably the finest sight in Europe.

The traveller should linger long enough to retain a vivid recollection of this beautiful view, and should not omit to notice the eight pavillions around the square, surmounted by allegorical figures representing the great towns of France.

Time and inclination must determine whether the traveller will proceed at once up the Champs Elyseés to examine the Triumphal Arch, or direct his steps in a different direction. It is considered preferable to ride up this delightful promenade in the afternoon or evening, when it is thronged with splendid equipages, equestrians and pedestrians in their exquisite "Parisian toiletts" of the latest fashion. At this time of day, when the rays of the setting sun are thrown up from the horizon upon the Triumphal Arch, bringing out each feature and form of the basso-relievo groups, representing the most remarkable scenes and incidents of the French armies, this splendid piece of architecture is seen to great advantage, and looks indeed a triumphant work of art.

If the traveller will ascend to the top of the Arch and take a panoramic view of Paris, bathed in the glowing effulgence of a deep orange sun-set, we are persuaded it will elicit feelings of glowing admiration.

Returning at this hour, and on foot, *down* the Champs Elyseés will be found a most charming promenade.

Assuming, however, that this visit be deferred agreeably to the above suggestion, the traveller should then cross over the bridge de la Concorde, and pay a visit to the Hotel des Invalides, containing the Tomb of Napoleon, immediately under the dome of the church, and which, from what can be seen of it, will be every thing the genius of a great architect, the late Mr. Visconti, the co-operation of the greatest celebrities in the arts and sciences of France, the wealth of a great nation, and the affection of the Nephew can accomplish, in deference to the wish so often expressed by Napoleon himself:

> "That his ashes might repose on the banks of the Seine,
> Amidst the people he had loved with a fatherly affection."

And the traveller will not fail to observe how wonderfully Providence has permitted the fulfilment of this wish—to the very letter.

Beyond this, on the same side of the river, is the celebrated Champ de Mars, which is unworthy a visit, except to witness a grand military review.

On leaving the Hôpital des Invalides, and returning towards the Tuilleries, the traveller will pass in front of the Chamber of the Legislative Body, or Palais Bourbon, the beautiful front of which is much admired—the twelve Corinthian pillars supporting the pediment—the bas-reliefs, representing Law, Strength and Justice, Peace and Commerce, are considered very fine. The figures at the foot of the staircase are those of Sully and Hôpital on the left; Aquessean and Colbert on the right—Minerva and Themis.

Further on is the Palace of the Legion of Honor, and beyond this the Palace d'Orsay, one of the finest buildings in Paris, and the noble proportions of which are seen to so much advantage on the quay which borders this part of the Seine. The Tuilleries on the opposite side of the river has also a truly regal appearance from this view.

Proceeding on to the third bridge, the Pont Neuf, the traveller will enjoy one of the most striking sights to be seen in all Paris. The Palace of the Louvre and the great gallery which joins it with the Tuilleries expand before the view along the right-hand bank of the Seine, and give the two palaces the appearance of one magnificent range of buildings. Crossing this bridge, and approaching the Louvre, the traveller will perceive a small church on the right, St. Germain L'Uxerrois, the portal of which is considered remarkably fine. The great object of attraction, however, is the celebrated Façade or Colonade of the Louvre, admired and esteemed as the most precious specimen of architecture in the French capital, and which the French deem their chef d'œuvre. It consists of a central compartment and two wings, united by a beautiful double colonade of fluted Corinthian columns, and bas-reliefs on the pediment—of the Muses bearing the attributes of the arts and sciences.

Each side of the Louvre has a splendid entrance, and the traveller, passing through the one under the colonade, will find himself in the grand court of the palace, and on reaching this celebrated spot, he will no doubt be impatient to see the wonders in the interior. To connoisseurs and persons of taste it offers a very great treat; and to visitors in general this Museum will afford unfeigned pleasure, so true it is that art is not destined for artists alone, but for the world, to refine and elevate the human mind, and many of our fair readers evince as much discernment of the beautiful paintings in this collection as they do in the merits of *Lace* and *Cachemeres*. The Museum is divided into several branches or collections—the Museum of Antiquities on the ground floor—the Egyptian Museum, the Naval Museum, and the Picture Gallery at the top of the grand staircase, which gallery is divided into three schools, the French, the Flemish and Dutch, the Italian and the Spanish.

Our space will not admit of a description of the first museums, but we cannot omit a short notice of the "Gallery of Paintings." The coup d'œuil on entering this is very striking, and the array of works of art most imposing, extending the whole length of the superb gallery—"the length of which lends enchantment to the view," and on beholding which we are always reminded of the memorable and honorable homage paid by Frederick the Great to a similar collection at Dresden. After taking this city, instead of abusing his right of conquest to obtain possession of its works of art, he merely evinced an impatient desire to see its paintings; and on being conducted to the Gallery, expressed himself "Proud of the honor of being allowed to admire so beautiful a collection." And our readers will probably give expression to the same sentiment on visiting the Gallery of the Louvre.

It is usual on a first visit to run through the rooms, to take a rapid view of the collection, and then to examine them again and again at leisure. This is Indispensable, as the dazzling splendour of the saloons, the carved, painted, and gilt ceilings, the marble pillars, mirrors, statuary, polished oak floors, &c., so divert the attention from an examination of the pictures, that the first visit only leaves a confused impression of this wonderful display of art and opulence in unrivalled magnificence.

Though the Gallery of the Louvre "has been shorn of many of its brightest beams," has lost a large number of those matchless works taken in the conquests of the First Napoleon, from the finest collections in Europe, which were restored to them in 1815, it still possesses so many master pieces of all the great schools, as to afford one of the most comprehensive views of the works of art to be seen.

Commencing with the productions of Raphael, the prince of painters—there are several of his very best paintings, all distinguished by that exquisite, calm, and ethereal expression which give that inexpressible loveliness, beatitude, and dignity to his Madonnas. That which has always excited the greatest admiration is where the Madonna is lifting the veil to show the infant Jesus. The deep beauty of expression in the face of the mother is most exquisite. The Cartoons of Hampton Court are esteemed the most valuable of his works, containing in perfection those displays of character, action, and expression in which Raphael's excellence peculiarly consists. There are four copies of the great Frescoes in the Vatican, in another department,

Several other specimens of the Italian school are objects of general attraction: "*The Bacchus and Ariadne*"; "*The Feast at Cana*"; "The two Magdalens"; "The Salutation"; "Paris and Helen"; the glowing and magnificent Sun-set of Claude; the Landscapes of *Poussin*; "Truth in an Allegory"; the "Shepherds in Arcadia"; "Summer and Paradise"; "Winter and the Flood."

The great works of the Flemish school, the paintings of Rubens, next claim attention; and though they have not the purity of design or the delicacy of tints of the Italian school, yet they are masterly productions. His females are plump rosy burgomasters' wives, and daughters, and produced in admirable variety; but no one can behold his series of paintings in this Gallery allegorically representing the history of Marie de Medecis, in 21 pictures, each of which is a work of imposing merit, without being struck with the genius of the great Antwerp painter, his matchless art in the grouping of figures, his variety of models, and warmth of colouring, and the display of highly poetical powers of imagery in these series, which are known as Ruben's Poem.

The portraits and madonnas of Van Dyck combine the Flemish with the Italian school; having studied in Italy he retains the Flemish forms, but gives them the attitudes and expression of the best Italian masters.

There are several valuable and rare gems of the Dutch painters—by Rembrandt, Gerhard Dow, Cuyps, Holbein, and Wovermans, &c. whose beautiful productions are so much admired in England.

The Spanish gallery is one of the most interesting in the whole collection, although from the number of monks who figure in most of the Spanish paintings, it would seem as if the painters lived in a world of monks. The "Nativity," and two of the "Saviour crowned," by Murillo, are superb; and two others on the same subject by Morales are, in point of expression, still more exquisite.

In this very cursory reference to the works of the great masters whose works adorn the Louvre, we have purposely avoided lengthened details, our intention being merely to awaken the curiosity and attention of the traveller to the compositions of transcendent beauty, and to the splendour and riches of this celebrated gallery. There are innumerable other pictures of great merit, and these will display their beauties gradually in proportion to the frequency of the visits paid to them, and the minuteness of inspection.

On leaving the Louvre the traveller can return to his hotel in time for the Table d'Hôte dinner, and then spend the evening in the manner most agreeable to himself at whichever place of amusement offers the greatest attraction.

On the following morning, the traveller should visit the object he most desires to see, or if time and opportunity permit, we would recommend him to visit the Palace of the Luxembourg, which is considered the next in importance for a stranger to visit, and because, in proceeding to this place, he can see several other remarkable objects in going and returning. For instance, in starting from the Rue de Rivoli and turning to the left, the traveller can visit the Palais Royal and Hotel de Ville, thence across the Arcole Bridge or Pont d' Arcole, and the Rue d' Arcole, he will see the celebrated Cathedral of Notre Dame lifting its majestic form far above the Churches and Palaces of Paris. This is reputed to be one of the finest monuments in Europe, and excites general interest from its antiquity—the historical events with which its name is connected—as well as by the grandeur of its architecture. This noble relic of the Middle Ages will remind the traveller of the piety and munificence of

"Christian Zeal and Papal piety"

of our ancestors when

"Those tow'rs a Monarch built to God—and grace'd
"With golden pomp the vast circumference."

Continuing in a straight line from the façade of the Cathedral to the third Bridge, the traveller crosses the river and ascends the Rue de la Harpe, at the top of which is the Luxembourg Palace, with its beautiful garden, its walks and flowers, its historical associations, the death of Marshall Ney, the bravest of the brave, and to whom a statue has recently been erected on the spot where he was shot!

This palace, though much smaller than the Louvre or Tuilieries, is very handsome. The grand staircase on the right wing, ornamented with bas-reliefs and statuary, is much admired. The saloon, appropriated to the Senators for their legislative labours, is a splendid hall in the form of a Greek Amphitheatre. This was formerly the chamber of Peers, and where they also judged political prisoners.

The gallery of paintings contains the most remarkable of French pictures by modern painters, among the number, E. Delacroix' "Dante and Virgil in the boat with the souls, the damned around them trying to enter"; the "School of Raphael"; the "Slaughter of the Mamelukes" and "Judeth," by Horace Vernet, claim the most attention. The First Secret (le Premier Secret, by Jouffroy), is considered very beautiful —a girl in the bloom of youth is raising herself on tip-toe to a level with the head of a Venus and whispering her secret into the ear of the goddess; this picture is exquisitely painted, and is a general favorite.

If the traveller can spare the time, there are many other pictures of considerable merit, which he can criticise or praise as he thinks due. On leaving the Luxembourg, the traveller should proceed down the Rue des Grecs, and in a few moments will find himself in front of the celebrated Pantheon, originally built for a church, but subsequently appropriated to the reception of the remains of the great men of the French nation. It is now restored to its original purpose, and is known as the church St. Genevieve. The beautiful fresco painting of the Cupola, under the dome, is well worth seeing.

Returning by the Rue des Grecs, the Rue des Princes, Mazarin, &c., the traveller will soon reach the Pont des Arts, Facing the Louvre, from whence he can easily reach his hotel.

On the third day his visits may be more discursive, but he should not omit going to see the Palais des Beaux Arts, and the celebrated fresco painting by Delaroch. The subject is a congress of the greatest men of genius who have contributed to the glory of the fine arts. The painter has drawn an assemblage of the dead "who graced their age with new invented arts" from every age and clime, and clad in every fashion. The painting may be described in a few words: a long portico of graceful proportion, coming off from a clear blue sky, occupies a large portion of the back ground. On a raised seat of marble, in the front of this portico, sit the three principal judges of the supposed assembly for the reward of the successful competitors in the annual distribution of prizes. The one is Appelles, the second Phidias, and the third Ictinis. At their feet are the two muses of antique art. Nearer the spectator are two other female figures; the one with fair long hair is the ancient genius and spirit of painting, whose classic and stern attributes were purity of design, creative genius, chaste yet brilliant colouring, the secret of light and shade, and all the wondrous powers in the art, by means of which she produced her matchless votaries of the middle ages.

The other figure is the genius of modern art, with a caress and a coquetry for every school and every mode. These two figures are the means by which the eye is carried from the central group to the extremities. On the right side are the Architects, and on the left are Sculptors; on this side the great masters of outline, on that, the great apostles of colour. In the centre, and in front of the principal group, is a lovely girl lifting a wreath from the ground to cast out of the painting. This splendid composition is considered very beautiful; the easy and diginified attitudes, and the expressive but serene countenances of the different men of genius here represented, fills the spectator with admiration; they seem to look down on a crowd of votaries, and once more to challenge the homage of mankind. After having seen these emporiums of the works of art, the traveller can revisit each as he thinks proper; and if time will admit he should see "Pere la Chaise" cemetry, the "Gobelin's Manufactory of Tapestry," and a few other remarkable places enumerated in the list at page lv., &c.

All these places can be seen at leisure, and if the weather be favorable, the environs of Paris are very beautiful, particularly the Bois de Boulogne, Neuilly,

St. Cloud, Versailles, St. Germain, all of which can be reached in a very short time.

During the winter months, instead of excursions to the above places, there are diversions sufficiently attractive in Paris, rendering it the most charming and exciting city in the world.

The Theatres, Operas, Concerts, Bals Masqués, &c., &c., ad-infinitum, so that Paris life may be said to resemble a railway panoramic view—at one moment we may enjoy a delightful scene, and the next it has disappeared, with this difference, that the train pursues its steady course through all the fascinating scenes, and conveys the traveller to his destination; whereas the youthful traveller may sometimes linger in spots whence prudence would warn him to depart. The pastimes of a luxurious capital like Paris should be indulged in with circumspection, as the object of travelling of the peripatetic philosopher is to "see a good deal of men and manners—to admit the good and reject the bad of all nations—to learn mutual toleration—as mutual toleration teaches us mutual love."

GUIDE TO PARIS.

Paris, the capital of, and perhaps the finest city in Europe, is on the Seine, 143 miles from Havre, 236 from Calais, and about 360 from London, from which it may be reached in eleven or twelve hours. It lies in an oval, 15 miles round, on both sides of the river; that on the north side being the largest; whilst the oldest part is on the two Iles de la Cité and St. Louis between, or in their neighbourhood. Within the barrières it contains 1,200,000 souls, 50,000 houses, 1,350 streets, 200 covered avenues, 30 boulevards, 12 parishes or arrondisements, 40 churches, 27 theatres, 50 caserners or barracks, and 90 public establishments. Thirty-seven communes beyond the barrières compose the Banlieue, or environs, including Neuilly, Belleville, Batignolles, and other well-known spots. Both banks of the Seine (a mere canal in comparison with the Thames) are lined with 33 broad Quays, and large buildings, and joined by 28 bridges. The houses are so numbered, that you can tell how near you are to the river (which runs nearly east and west), and whether you are going from or towards it; the streets parallel to the river being painted in black letters, with the numbers *down* the stream (or west,) and those perpendicular to it in white letters, with the numbers *from* the stream: the odd numbers are on one side of the street, and the even on the other.

The principal places are the Champs Elyseés, Tuilleries, Palaise Royal, Hôtel de Ville, Portes St. Denis and St. Martin, July Column, and Père la Chaise, on the north side; the Hôtel des Invalides, Luxembourg, Panthéon, and Jardin des Plantes, on the south side; the Pont-Neuf and Notre Dame, in the centre. Among the most lively streets are, Rues St. Honoré, Vivienne, Richelieu, Neuve-des-Petits-Champs, the Boulevards (which thread the outskirts or faubourgs), the Quays, &c. The unrivalled Passages, or Arcades, are also very gay, as Passages des Panoramas, de l'Opera, du Saumon, Jouffroy,

Vivienne, Colbert, Choiseul, Vero-Dodat, Delorme, &c.; here all the knick-knacks, or *articles de Paris*, are sold. A circle of fortresses, 26 miles round, commands every point near the city.

On passing the barrière, the passport is asked for (to be immediately returned), and the baggage examined. Porters, called commissionaires, ply at every railway station or coach office, who will convey the traveller to any of the hôtels for 6d., or 1 franc, with luggage.

HOTELS.—There are a great many hotels in Paris, some magnificent in appearance, but dear and uncomfortable; others cheap, but questionable. The following are carefully selected as deserving our recommendation:—

Hôtel de Lille et Albion, 323, Rue St. Honoré, a well-conducted, good house.

Hôtel Bedford, 11, Place de l'Arcade, near the Madeleine, excellent in every respect.

Hôtel Wagram, good, very clean, and well conducted.

Hôtel Victoria, very good, comfortable, and reasonable.

Grand Hôtel de Lyon, 12, Rue des Filles St. Thomas, with a large frontage in the Rue Richelieu, very comfortable and charges moderate.

Hôtel Folkestone, 9, Rue Castellane, very comfortable, and charges moderate.

Hôtel des Etrangers, 3, Rue Vivienne, very comfortable and reasonable.

Hôtel de York, Rue St. Anne, is a new house, well furnished; everything very clean and comfortable.

Grand Hotel d'Oxford et Cambridge, exceedingly good in every respect.

Hôtel de Normandie, 240, Rue St. Honoré, good and moderate.

The *Hotels des Princes*, *Meurices*, *du Rhin*, are good but dear.

RESTAURANT—*British Tavern* (Taverne Britannique), Rue Richelieu, 104, near the Boulevard. This restaurant commands a greater assemblage of persons of distinction of all nations than is to be found in any other restaurant in Paris. The elegance of the establishment, its excellent cellar of wines, and its English cookery, constitute its chief recommendation.—For English Directory to Paris, see page lxxi.

We recommend to such of our readers as may be desirous of attaining that desideratum, a pure French pronunciation, Mr. Emile, of No. 320, Rue St. Honoré. His assistance will be found especially valuable to medical men who purpose walking the Paris hospitals, and to military candidates preparing for the Sandhurst examination. He speaks English well.

British Embassy and Consulate, 39, Rue du Faubourg St. Honoré. Hours for passports, eleven to two.

In the short description which follows, the subjects run alphabetically, as most convenient for reference. Streets will be found under the proper name, as 'Rivoli (Rue de)' for 'Rue de Rivoli,' or Rivoli Street. When the stranger comes upon a large building, church, &c., he has only to look down this list for the street it is in, and he will find it described there, or else described under its own head. Places in the immediate neighbourhood of Paris, must be looked for in the general index to the Hand Book. For further details, see Galignani's Guide to Paris *(French or English), and Chaix's* Nouveau Guide à Paris.

*N.B.—Those most worthy of notice are marked *. Though special days for visiting are sometimes mentioned, yet nearly all are accessible to strangers upon the production of the passport.*

* *Arc de Triomphe de l'Etoile*, at the end of Avenue de Neuilly, and so called because seven or eight roads spread from it like a star, is an enormous triumphal arch, begun 1806, and finished 1836. It is 152 feet high, 137 broad, and 68 thick; the centre arch, 90 feet high, by 45 wide; and is covered with groups and bas-reliefs of the events of the revolution and the empire, from 1792 to the peace of 1815. By this arch, the Grande Armée entered Paris after the peace of Tilsit; and Louis Napoleon on his return from the provinces, 1852. A fine view from the top. Outside of it, on the Neuilly road, is the beautiful *chapel* of St. Ferdinand, built 1842-3, on the spot where the Duc d'Orleans was killed by his horses taking fright. One fine marble group is by his sister, Marie of Würtemburg, who sculptured the well-known Joan of Arc. Open by passport, from one to four, except Wednesday. The Château de Neuilly, ruined by the mob 1848, was sold 1853.

Bac (Rue de), contains the Musée d'Artillerie, and (No. 120) St. François Xavier church. Near it is St. Thomas d'Aquin.

Banque de France, Rue de la Vrillére, a large but plain building, built, 1720, by Mansard, for a private hôtel.

Bernard (Rue St.) contains Ste. Marguerite's church.

Bibliothèque de l'Arsenal, Rue Sully, where cannons were cast till the time of Louis XIV., is now a library of 200,000 vols.; open daily, 10 to 3.

Bibliothèque St. Geneviève, near that church, in the old abbey buildings (fourteenth to sixteenth centuries), contains 200,000 vols. and 3,000 MSS., with portraits of sovereigns from Philippe le Hardi to Louis XV.

* *Bibliothèque Impériale*, or Imperial Library, Rue Richelieu, No. 58, was once Cardinal Mazarin's hôtel, and is now a large pile, 540 feet by 130. It contains 1,400,000 printed vols.; 125,000 MS. genealogies (30,000 being French); 150,000 medals; gems; 9,600 vols. of engravings, from the fifteenth century; 90,000 portraits; 300,000 maps; 150 vols. of French history; 500 vols. of plans, views, &c.; besides several marbles. In the ground floor are Voltaire's bust, a silver missal, the first psalter printed with a date (1459), models, &c. Readers bring their own pens as well as paper. Among the MSS. are those of Galileo, St. Louis' prayer-book, Fenelon's Telemachus, and autograph letters from Henry IV. downwards. Some of the missals are as old as the fifth and sixth centuries. Cardinal Mazarin's painted gallery is 140 feet long. Visitors, Tuesday and Friday, 10 to 3.

Boulevard du Temple. Opposite Jardin Turc, is No. 50, whence Fieschi discharged his infernal machine, 1835, against Louis Philippe, which killed Marshal Mortier, &c.

Bicêtre—See page 181 of the Hand Book.

* *Bourse*, or Exchange, Rue Vivienne, was built by Brongniart and Labarre, 1808-26, is 212 feet by 126, with 66 corinthian pillars round it, and a metal roof. The large

doric hall is 116 feet by 76, and has a painted ceiling and a marble pavement, at the east end of which is the *parquet*, a space railed off for stock brokers. Galignani's library and news-room is at No. 18, near this.

BRIDGES.—*See Ponts.*

Catacombs, in the gypsum under the south side of Paris, long ago excavated for houses, and, after 1786, used as a receptacle for bones from the crowded graveyards, but now stopped up. They extend over about 200 acres, and are reckoned to contain 3,000,000 skeletons, piled in order along the galleries. One entrance is in a garden, near Barrière d'Enfer, but it is not opened without a special order. Some *made* logan stones are seen below, with a collection of remarkable skulls, and the well-chosen inscription '*Memento, quia pulvis es*' (Remember, for thou too art dust!) The smell is close and disagreeable. A part of the quarries under Rue du Marché aux Chevaux is turned into cellars for Dumesnil's brewery.

* *Cemetery of Père la Chaise*, a pleasant spot, outside the Barrière d'Aunay, so called from the confessor of Louis XIV., Father Lachaise, the superior of the Jesuits, who had a seat here. It was turned into a burial ground, 1804; covers 100 acres, and is prettily laid out, with groups of trees, cypresses, &c. The most remarkable monuments are in this cemetery, which is the largest and most celebrated. A guide will point out the best. There are about 15,000 tombs, among which are those of Abélard and Heloise (gothic); C. Perier, the minister; Labedoyère, who led the revolt from the Bourbons, in the Hundred Days; Volney; Abbé Sicard; Beaumarchais; Marshals Davoust, Lefèbre, Ney ('*Sta viator, heroem calcas*'), Junot, Massêna, Suchet; General Foy, with sculptures by David; B. Constant; Molière; Lafontaine; Madame de Genlis; Laplace; Aguado, the banker; Talma; Prince Demidoff, &c. The doric chapel is 56 feet by 28, and commands a fine view over Paris and the neighbouring country. Here the Russians bivouacked, 1814.

Chaise (Rue de la) has the Hospice des Ménages.

Champ de Mars (Field of Mars), a vast space between Ecole Militaire, and Pont de Jéna, 2,700 feet by 1,320, planted with trees, and bordered by sloping banks and ditches, now used for reviews, races, &c. The slopes were made in eight days by the voluntary labour of all ranks of the people in 1790, when Louis XVI. swore at the Autel de la Patrie (erected here 14th July) to maintain the new constitution. Other signal events have marked it since that disastrous period. A splendid stone building for a permanent Industrial Exhibition, will be opened in 1855; it is on arches 800 feet long by 400 feet wide.

Champs Elysées are rows of stunted trees, planted 1616 by Marie de Medicis, and replanted 1764. The Allies encamped here 1814-15, and here the fêtes are held. It includes the French Crystal Palace; the Chapel Marboeuf (Protestant); and a Circus or Cirque (1 to 2 francs). In its neighbourhood are the Panorama, Géorama (a globe like Wyld's, 35 feet diameter), Swimming School, Jardin d'Hiver (Winter Garden), Jardin Mabille, and other dancing places. A wide planted walk, called the Avenue de Neuilly, leads down it, past the Rond Point Fountain in the middle, to the Barrière and Arc de l'Etoile, on to Neuilly and St. Cloud.

**Church of St. Etienne du Mont*, is chiefly in the renaissance style of the sixteenth century, with a tower as old as 1222, and is one of the most striking churches in Paris, containing many parts worth notice and good pictures. It has lately been restored. Pascal, Racine, Rollin, &c. were interred here.

**Church of St. Eustache*, Rue Coquillière, the largest after Notre Dame, is cross-shaped, 318 feet by 132, and 90 high, the style being a mixture of gothic and grecian. It was built 1532-1617. The north door and high altar are good. Colbert the minister was buried in it. It has been lately restored.

Church of St. François d'Assise, Rue d' Orleans.

**Church of St. Germain l'Auxerrois*, near Rue St. Denis is on the site of Childebert's church, which the Normans destroyed 886. It was the court church, (being near the Louvre) and highly decorated, and is now restored. Its bells gave the signal for the St. Bartholomew massacre. It is cross-shaped, and includes a door (1649), a west front of the thirteenth century with five portals in it, and a porch built 1431-7, with frescoes by Mottez.

**Church of St. Germain des Prés*, near Rue Ste. Marguerite, one of the oldest in Paris, is on the site of one built by Childebert 550-7 called the Golden Basilica, and destroyed by the Normans. It was part of a benedictine abbey, fortified like a castle, and belonging to the learned Congregation of St. Maur. In front was the promenade called the Pré aux Clercs (Clerks' field). The church, as restored, is 200 feet by 65, and 60 high, and includes parts of two east towers as old as 990, an ancient west front (spoilt by a doric porch) and tower, norman arches in the nave, effigies of a Duke of Douglas (1645) and of Casimir of Poland (who died about 1672), and a fine marble front. Some pieces of Notre Dame chapel (thirteenth century), and the abbot's brick house, remain. The Abbaye prison is near.

Church of St. Gervais, of the sixteenth century (though dated 1420), has a tower 130 feet high, and a west grecian front; but the remainder is gothic, especially the beautiful lady chapel with its stained glass and paintings.

Church of St. Jacques du Haut Pas, Rue St. Jacques, No. 252, was built 1650-84 in the grecian style.

Church of St. Laurent, Rue du Faubourg St. Martin, begun 1429, is chiefly gothic with a doric porch (1622) in which you see the saint's gridiron. The north aisle of the choir is the most ancient. Some good tracery is observed over the north door and tower; and pendants hang in the nave.

Church of St. Leu and St. Gilles, Rue St. Martin, was mostly rebuilt 1611; and has a tower dated 1236, (but really much later), with a gable front. Many genuine relics are shown here to the faithful.

Church of St. Louis en l'Ile (in the Island), built 1664, has a tall open-work spire erected 1765, with stained windows and frescoes.

Church of Ste. Marguerite, Rue St. Bernard, built 1625-1712 in the shape of a cross, the nave being the oldest part. Besides many good pictures, it contains, they say, the grave of the Dauphin, Louis XVII. The poor boy died through the ill-treatment he received from his master, one Simon a cobbler, to whom he was apprenticed by the bloodhounds of the Revolution, after the execution of his unfortunate father.

Church of St. Médard, Rue Mouffetard, is gothic of the fifteenth century, with a norman porch, square tower, stained windows, &c., but spoilt by modern additions. An old painting on wood in one of the chapels. Nicole and Abbé Paris were buried here. At the latter's tomb the Convultionists began their antics 1730.

Church of St. Merri, Rue St. Martin, No. 2, as rebuilt 1560-1612, includes a beautiful florid gothic west front, niched figures, porches, rose windows, stained glass, &c., and an old wood painting of the fourteenth century near the altar.

**Church of Notre Dame de Lorette*, Rue St. Lazare, begun 1823 by Le Bas; 224 feet by 96, with a square campanile tower and corinthian portico. Its interior is highly decorated, with eight frescoes of the Virgin, &c.

**Church of St. Roch*, Rue St. Honoré, so celebrated in all the revolutions, was built 1653-1740; and is cross-shaped, 159 feet long, with a wide flight of steps leading to a grecian portal, 84 feet by 91 high. Paintings and bas-reliefs are seen. P. Corneille and Abbé de l'Epée were buried here.

**Church of St. Sulpice*, near the Luxembourg, begun 1655, and not finished till 1797, is cross-shaped, 432 feet by 174, and 99 high. The fine double portico consists of doric pillars 40 feet high, supporting another range of ionic columns 38 feet high, by Servandoni 1745. The north tower 210 feet high, is made up of four stories of columns; both it and the south tower carry telegraphs. The holy water basins (benetières) are two large shells given to Francis I. by the Venetian states. A good pulpit rests on two flights of steps. The organ is highly carved, with seventeen various figures playing music. On the pavement a meridian line is traced. There is an image of the Virgin and Child on a globe, with the light falling on it from an opening, producing a very striking effect. Pictures and frescoes in the twenty-one chapels around. It was called the Temple de la Victoire in the Revolution. A herb market and seminary in front.

**College de la Sorbonne*, near Rue St. Jacques, on the site of the famous theological school or university founded 1253 by Robert Sorbon. It is a quadrangle, begun 1629 by Richelieu; including a grecian church, built 1635-59 by Lemercier, in which there is a good dome, painted by Philippe de Champagne, and Girardon's famous statue of the Cardinal, supported by religion, &c. The library of 50,000 volumes, open daily, 10 to 2.

**Conservatoire des Arts et Métiers* (Museum of Practical Arts and Trades), Rue St. Martin, No. 208, on the site of St. Martin's abbey (of which a round tower is left at the fontaine), was formed 1798, as a repository of models, patents, machines, &c., of all classes and countries. Some are placed in the old gothic chapel of the thirteenth century, and the beautiful eight-sided refectory. Strangers on Tuesday, Wednesday and Saturday, from 11 to 3, by passport. Lectures on Science and Art, gratis.

CONVEYANCES.—*Omnibuses* called Béarnaises, Citadines, Constantines, Dames-Réunies, Diligentes, Excellentes, Favorites, Gazelles, Parisiennes, Tricycles, &c., run through all the principal lines, at one fare of 6 sous (3d.) They correspond with each other, so that you may go from any part of Paris to any other part, by showing your ticket or *cachet* when you change at certain points. But their slow travelling will be sure to try the patience of an Englishman.—*Cabs* and hackney coaches run by time or by the course, whichever you choose, the *course* being a single run, long or short (within Paris), without stopping, for which the fare is 1 fr. 10 c. for a cab, 1½ fr. for a hackney.—*Glass Coaches* or voitures de remise, of a better sort, may be hired for 20 to 30 fr. a day, or 400 to 500 fr. (£16 to £20) a month.

COACH FARES IN THE INTERIOR OF PARIS.

Kind of Vehicle.	From 6 a.m. till 12 night.						From 12 night till 6 a.m.			
	The Journey.		First Hour.		2nd hour and following		The Journey.		The Hour.	
	f.	c.	f.	c.	f.	c.	f.	c.	f.	c.
Hackney coaches, two horses	1	50	2	25	1	75	2	0	3	0
Small hackney coaches. Four places. Glass coaches (one or two horses).	1	25	1	75	1	50	1	65	2	50
Cabs (two or four wheels)	1	00	1	50	1	25	1	65	2	50

Cabs at Livery Stables, 1 fr. 50 c. the journey. The hour, 2 fr.

READY RECKONER FOR COACHES TAKEN BY THE HOUR.

Hours.	Hackney Coaches. 2 Horses.		Glass Coaches and small Hackney Coaches.		Cabs.		Livery Stables, Cabs.	
	f.	c.	f.	c.	f.	c.	f.	c.
1 hour 0 minutes.	2	25	1	75	1	50	2	0
1 " 5 "	2	40	1	90	1	60	2	20
1 " 10 "	2	55	2	0	1	70	2	35
1 " 15 "	2	70	2	15	1	80	2	50
1 " 20 "	2	85	2	25	1	90	2	70
1 " 25 "	3	0	2	40	2	0	2	85
1 " 30 "	3	10	2	50	2	15	3	0
1 " 35 "	3	25	2	65	2	25	3	20
1 " 40 "	3	40	2	75	2	35	3	35
1 " 45 "	3	55	2	90	2	45	3	50
1 " 50 "	3	70	3	0	2	55	3	70
1 " 55 "	3	85	3	15	2	65	3	85
2 " 0 "	4	0	3	25	2	75	4	0
2 " 5 "	4	15	3	40	2	85	4	20
2 " 10 "	4	30	3	50	2	95	4	35
2 " 20 "	4	60	3	75	3	15	4	70
2 " 30 "	4	85	4	0	3	40	5	0
2 " 40 "	5	15	4	25	3	60	5	35
2 " 50 "	5	45	4	50	3	80	5	70

Coquillière (Rue) contains the church of St. Eustache.

Culture Ste. Catherine (Rue), No. 23, is the Hôtel de Carnavalet, a fine house of the sixteenth century, once the seat of Madame de Sevigné and her daughter, to whom her letters were written. It was built 1544 by Bullant; carvings by J. Goujon.

Denis (Rue St.) has the Entrepôt des Glaces, and (near the bottom) the church of St. Germain l'Auxerrois.

Depôt des Fourrages (Forage Stores), for the garrison, is near Barriére de la Rapée and Pont d'Ivry, and is 300 feet long.

Depôt de la Guerre, Rue St. Dominique, Nos. 82 and 86, is a large building, and contains the state papers of the time of Louis XIII., the letters of Louis XIV. to his grandson, Philip of Spain, Napoleon's letters, the survey of France, plans of battles, &c. The War Minister's head quarters are fixed here.

**Elysée Bourbon Palace*, opposite the Champs Elysées, 59, Rue St. Honoré, was built 1718; belonged to Madame de Pompadour, the Duchess de Bourbon, &c., and was the residence of Murat, Napoleon, Alexander of Russia, Duke of Wellington, Duc de Berri (when assassinated, 1820), &c. In one room is Napoleon's bed, with other memorials.

**Ste. Geneviève* or Panthéon, not far from the Luxembourg, is the St. Paul's of Paris, and takes name from its patron saint, to whom Clovis built a church, in which she was buried 512, and which Louis XV. began to rebuild 1764, in the grecian style, from Soufflot's designs. It makes a cross 602 feet by 255 (the nave being 105 long), with a dome 268 feet high and 66 diameter, painted by Baron Gros. In the front, which is 129 feet broad in the whole, is a range of eleven steps, leading up to a fine portico of six corinthian pillars, sixty feet high, besides sixteen others behind them. The pediment is filled up by David's fine bas-relief of France (a figure fifteen feet high) distributing honours to her great men, represented by Fenelon, Malesherbes, Mirabeau, Voltaire, Rousseau, Lafayette, Carnot, Monge, Manuel, David the painter, Napoleon, &c.; below them is this inscription in gilt letters,—'*Aux Grands Hommes la Patrie reconnaissante*,' a concise idiom difficult to translate, but meaning—Thus the country rewards her famous children. Altogether the portico is so good, that the architect has been said to 'mis à la porte toute son architecture,' turned his building out of doors. There are 258 pillars about this church, of which 130 are inside. The carved vault is eighty feet from the marble pavement, under which are the crypts on doric pillars, wherein are the remains of Voltaire ('poete, historien, philosophe,') and Rousseau, Lagrange, Bougainville, Admiral de Winter, Marshals Lannes and Bugeaud. A fine prospect from the top, one of the highest points in Paris.

**Halle au Blé*, or Corn Exchange, Rue des Deux Ecus, a vast circular pile on the site of a royal seat, built 1763-7 by Le Camus, 126 feet diameter; the shape and size of the Pantheon at Rome. It is entirely of stone and iron, with an iron domed roof and skylight (built 1811). It has an arcade round it, and large granaries. Outside the south part is Catherine de Medicis' doric pillar (1572) and sun-dial 100 feet high, built by her astrologer.

**Halle aux Vins* (Wine Stores), Quai St. Bernard, was rebuilt after 1813, on the site of St. Victor's abbey, and makes seven great piles, divided by streets, called Rue de Champagne, Rue de Bordeaux, &c., after the wines bonded here. The river front is 800 feet; the whole covers 6½ acres, and will hold 450,000 casks. The spirit (eau-de-vie) stores behind are built of hollow bricks, without wood or iron. Open, 6 to 6.

**Hôtel Cluni*, Rue des Mathurins, No. 16, a fine old building, begun 1480, by an abbot of Cluny, and finished 1505. After many changes it came to M. de Sommerard, who formed a large mediæval collection, which the government, having bought, turned into a museum of antiquities, such as carvings, furniture, stained glass, tapestry, arms, MSS., pictures. The old chapel rests on a single pillar in the middle. Across the court is the *Palais des Thermes*, a solid pile, about 90 feet long, supposed to be the old seat of the roman governors, whence a roman way struck along Rue St. Jacques, and an aqueduct went to Arcueil. Its thick walls are made of stones and bricks with stucco; and roman remains are kept in it. Open Wednesday and Friday, by passport, 10 to 4.

**Hôtel Dieu* close to Notre Dame, the oldest hospital in Paris, was founded in the seventh century, rebuilt by Philippe Auguste, and enlarged by St. Louis, and forms a vast solid pile, with eight hundred and fifty beds; but all that is left of the old building is a chapel of the thirteenth century. There are several statues, portraits, &c., of benefactors and eminent medical men.

**Hôtel des Invalides*, the French 'Chelsea Hospital,' opposite the Champs Elysées, is known by its conspicuous gilt dome, and stands on an esplanade, 1,440 feet by 780 feet, which reaches to the Seine, and is ornamented with trees, Marochetti's statue of Napoleon, and cannons, some of them from Algiers. The buildings, begun by Louis XIV., include fifteen courts, and cover sixteen acres; and about three thousand soldiers and one hundred and seventy officers, under a governor (the senior Marshal, now Jerome Bonaparte), lieutenant governor, &c., are sheltered here. The river front is 612 feet long, and has ionic pilasters, with *lucarne* windows (formed of military trophies, cut in stone) and a bas-relief of Louis XIV. on horseback. The cour royale is 315 feet by 192. Portraits of great soldiers in the council chamber. There is a gallery of plans and fortresses. Dining rooms 150 feet long. One dormitory is called after the famous republican soldier, Latour d'Auvergne, who refused promotion on principle, preferring to be called the premier grenadier of France. The large kitchens are worth seeing. In the old church, 210 feet long, are many tablets to governors; 1,400 flags here, taken from the enemy, were burnt by Marshal Serrurier, 1815, to save them from the Allies At its south end is the great dome, 323 feet high, under which the ashes of Napoleon (brought from St. Helena, 1840), are placed, with his sword, hat, crown and star, covered by a most splendid tomb. Twelve medallions of kings here were transformed into greek and roman philosophers, at the revolution, two being Voltaire and Rousseau! There are paintings of apostles. On the ceiling of the cupola, 51 feet diameter, is Delafosse's St. Louis entering Heaven. Strangers, by passport, Tuesday, Thursday and Saturday, 10 to 4.

**Hôtel de la Legion d'Honneur*, Rue de Lille, was built 1786, for the Prince de Salms, (who was beheaded, 1793), and was sold by lottery to a hair-dresser; in 1803 it came to the government, and is the seat of the Grand Chancellor of the Legion, whose head quarters are here.

**Hôtel des Monnaies* (Mint), on Quai Conti, built 1768-75, is 360 feet long, with eight courts, ornamented by pillars and busts. Many of the scales used here and at the branch mints were made from cannon taken at Austerlitz. It has a museum of medals and coins from Childebert's time (511), including English from 1621 (Henry VI.), Spanish from 560, and other countries, of which there is a catalogue. Strangers, by passport, Monday and Thursday, 1 to 3.

**Hôtel-de-Ville* (Guildhall), opposite the Place-de-Grève (the scene of many a bloody deed), near the Pont d'Arcole, was begun 1533–1628, on the site of the Maison de la Grève, in the renaissance style; to this other large piles were added, 1838–41, so as to make a large quadrangle, with pillars between the windows, and about sixty statues, of which twenty-eight are in the west, or principal front, besides a bas-relief of Henry IV. In one of the three courts is a statue of Louis XIV. Two very rich staircases lead to the great room, called Salle de Danse; another leads to the Grande Salle, the largest and most ancient of all, ornamented with great marble fire-places, paintings, busts, escutcheons, &c. They shew the room were Robespierre held his councils. From the middle window, looking into the square, Louis XVI. spoke to the people, with the 'bonnet rouge' on his head; and Lafayette presented Louis Philippe to them, 1830. There are above one hundred and sixty public rooms here; among which are the public library of sixty thousand volumes, open daily, 10 to 3; the Salle du Conseil; the Prèfect's apartments; the Salle d'Introduction, in which is Bozio's statue of Henry IV.; Salle de Jeu, containing a model of the artesian well of Grenelle; the Salle de Bal, 70 feet by 40, with portraits, &c.

Imprimerie Impériale, Rue Vieille du Temple, belonged to Cardinal de Rohan, of the time of Louis XVI., but is used as a government printing office, since 1809, about seven hundred and fifty hands being employed. When Pope Pius VII. visited it, the Lord's Prayer was printed for him in one hundred and fifty languages. Seen on Thursday, by application, in writing, beforehand, to the director.

Institution Impériale des Jeunes Aveugles (Youthful Blind) Rue de Sèvres, was founded 1784, by Valentine Haüy, a blind man. It is a fine large building, with gardens, on a space four thousand feet square, built 1843, by Philippon for three hundred, and includes a grecian chapel, &c. The teachers are blind; weaving, brush and basket making, printing, music, mathematics, &c., are taught. Strangers, on Wednesdays, 1 to 5, by passport. A public examination on the last Saturday in every month, which foreigners may attend.

**Institution Impériale des Sourds-Muets* (Deaf and Dumb), Rue St. Jacques, in St. Magliore's seminary, was founded by Abbé de l'Epée, 1775(?), and has about one hundred and sixty cases. The good Abbé's portrait, by Camus is here; one of his pupils, A. Dubois, died in it lately, upwards of ninety years old. A work by a deaf and dumb artist adorns the chapel.

**Jardin des Plantes* (Botanic Garden), opposite Pont d'Austerlitz, near the Halle aux Vins, was founded by Louis XIII., in 1635, and increased by the care of Tournefort, Vaillant, Jussieu, Buffon, Fourcroy, Cuvier, Brongniart, and other learned men. In this vast collection there are, a botanic garden of twelve thousand plants and trees; a botanic gallery, with fifty thousand specimens; a mineral gallery, 540 feet long, with sixty thousand specimens; zoological gallery of 390 feet, in six rooms, with two hundred thousand specimens, of which two thousand are mammalia, ten thousand are birds, five thousand are fishes, two thousand are reptiles; comparative anatomy gallery in twelve rooms, with fifteen thousand specimens, chiefly arranged by Cuvier, whose bust, by David, is here; menagerie; lecture-rooms for one thousand two hundred, which the public attend gratis; and a library of forty-five thousand volumes, besides ninety splendid volumes of plants, &c. (coloured, on vellum), open every day, except Thursday, 11 to 3. There is in the grounds a cedar, given by Collinson, the english naturalist, near the pavilion and dial, on a height commanding a good view, and not far from the grave of Daubenton. Strangers to the galleries, by passport, Monday and Thursday, 11 to 3 (comparative anatomy); Monday, Thursday, and Saturday (zoology).

**Louvre* (Rue de Rivoli), begun 1528, by Francis I., on the site of Dagobert's castle, was enlarged by Louis XIV. (who finished the long gallery to the Tuilleries) after

Perrault's designs, and improved by Napoleon. The west side or Old Louvre, was built by Henry II., and has sculptures by Goujon. Charles IX. was here on the infamous Bartholomew day: they pretend even to shew the window he fired from. Henrietta Maria, widow of Charles I., also resided here. The best part (and best seen from Pont Neuf) is the east front, which has C. Perrault's colonnade of 28 pillars, 38 feet high: it is 525 feet long and 85 high, and includes Napoleon's bronze gates. In the south front (towards the river) are 40 pilasters. The decorated court inside is 408 feet square, and held Marochetti's bronze statue of the Duke of Orleans (1842). The Louvre is now used as a vast *Museum* of paintings and works of art; including about 2,000 specimens of every school of painting (1,400 being French, Flemish, German, Italian,—and 450 Spanish), with drawings, models, busts, marbles, Egyptian antiquities, bijous, &c. Admission by passport, 10 to 4, every day (except Monday). Catalogues are sold at the door. The whole has been rearranged and decorated anew.

Lune (Rue de la), contains the church of Notre Dame de Bonne Nouvelle.

Luxembourg.—See *Palais du Luxembourg*.

**Madeleine Church*, Rue Royale, at the upper end near the Boulevards, was begun 1764 (being the fifth church on that site), and lately finished. Vignon was the principa architect. It stands on a platform 328 feet by 138, and — high, with flights of 28 steps at each end; is in the style of a grecian temple, and has 52 pillars round three sides, each 64 feet high, with 32 statues of saints between. In the south pediment is a fine alto-relief, by Lemaire, 126 feet long, of Christ and the Magdalene; the bronze door beneath is 32 feet by 16½, covered with bas-reliefs from Scripture. Inside are six chapels, adorned with paintings of the Magdalene; over the altar (by Marochetti) is Ziegler's picture of the Progress of Christianity.

**Manufacture Impèriale des Gobelins*, Rue Mouffetard, No. 280, on the Bièvre (where tanners, dyers, &c. have settled for ages) takes its name from Jean Gobelin, a tapestry worker about 1450, and was turned, 1662, into a government factory by Louis XIV., who employed Lebrun to paint the designs. Large, elaborate pictures are here copied, with all the effect and smoothness of an oil painting—not for sale, but as presents. A carpet factory is attached to it, called La Savonnerie, from a soap work in which Marie de Medicis placed it, 1615. Some carpets take ten years to make, and cost 180,000 francs. Strangers, on Wednesday and Saturday, 2 to 4. A catalogue may be had.

**Marchè des Innocens*, Rue St. Denis, so called from a church of that name, pulled down 1788, is used for fruit and vegetables, and has in the midst, an old fountain in the renaissance style, 42 feet high, built 1551, by Lescot and Goujon.

Morgue, a plain doric building, near Notre Dame, where persons, found drowned or accidentally dead, are brought, to be recognised by their friends. If not claimed, the bodies are given up for dissection.

**Musée d'Artillerie* out of Rue du Bac, in an old Jacobin convent, is a collection (something like the Woolwich Repository) of guns of all kinds, models, suits of armour, portraits of Generals, &c. Strangers on Thursdays, 12 to 4, by passport.

Musée Dupuytren, Rue de l'Ecole de Medicine, No. 15, in the Old Cordeliers convent, was founded by the great surgeon whose name it bears. Dissecting-rooms are attached to it.—At No. 18, Murat was stabbed in his bath by Charlotte Corday.

**Notre Dame Cathedral*, on Ile de la Cité, on the site of a roman temple, and of an early Christian church. Bishop Maurice began the present building about 1180; another bishop Maurice built the west front, 1223, and the south or Stephen's porch 1251; Philippe le Bel the north transept and the Virgins' porch 1312; and Jean Sans-Peur the beautiful porte rouge (in the choir) 1407. The west doors were made by Biscornette 1570-80. It is cruciform on the plan, with an eight-sided apse at the east end, 390 feet by 144, and 102 high to the chesnut roof; and the style, early gothic, of the thirteenth and fourteenth centuries. One stained circular window is 36 feet diameter; west front is 128 feet wide, with a triple portal deeply recessed, and set off with figures of saints, &c., and carved Scripture subjects. The towers, square and massive, are 204 feet high; in one is an old clock, and the Bourdon bell in the other (south). Flying buttresses and pinnacles are seen all around. The pillars in the aisle are plain and clustered alternately; double-pointed windows light the clerestory. The organ contains 3884 pipes. In the choir are the carved stalls and pictures, with 24 alto-reliefs coloured. In one (St. Charles) of its 30 chapels is Dessine's statue of Cardinal Belloy. At the sacristy the coronation robes are kept. The space in front of the cathedral is called the Parvis, and was formerly many feet higher than the inside. To the south stood the archbishop's palace, destroyed 1830. A gothic fountain, 60 feet high, built 1845, is behind.

Orléans (Rue d'), has the church of St. François d'Assise.

**Palais* and *Ecole des Beaux Arts*, Rue des Petits Augustins, is a school of painting, sculpture, and architecture, in the remains of an old convent, to which a modern pile was added 240 feet by 60. In one of the courts stands the beautiful renaissance front of Cardinal d'Amboise's château, brought from Gaillon, in Normandy; also the portal of the Château d'Amet (where Diane de Poitiers lived), forming the entrance to a chapel now used as a magazine. Among casts in it is a model of the great elephant, which was to adorn Place de la Bastille. Several specimens of old buildings from different quarters of France are here. There are also galleries of ancient and mediæval sculpture, and Delaroche's great picture of celebrated artists, with 75 figures in it, presided over by Zeuxis, Phidias and Apelles; besides portraits, models, &c. Strangers, 10 to 4, by passports.

**Palais Bourbon*, opposite the Pont de la Concorde, was built 1722 by the Prince de Condé, of the Bourbon family; used by the Council of Five Hundred at the first Revolution, latterly by the Chambre des Deputés, now by the Legislative Corps. The north front (towards the river) was built 1802, and is 100 feet broad, with twelve grecian pillars, flights of steps, with figures and busts. Inside are marble statues and frescoes, leading to the semicircular chamber, with its raised seats, president's chair, tribune for the speakers, bas-reliefs, public gallery, and memorials of a constitutional order of things, since swept away by anarchy and despotism. Here the Duke of Orleans took the oath as King of the French, 9th August, 1830. A temporary building, erected near this for the late national assembly, was pulled down by Louis Napoleon.

Palais de l'Institut, on Quai Conti, near the Hôtel des Monnaies, was the Collège Mazarin, or College of the Four Nations, built 1662, now granted to the Institute of France. The dark front, known by its Lion fountains at each end, is crescent-shaped, with a chapel in the middle, at present used as a hall of sittings and adorned with busts,

&c. The *Mazarin Library*, of 1,500,000 vols., with 3,700 MSS., is open to the public daily, 10 to 3; but the Institute library, of 100,000 vols., rich in works of science, &c., can be seen only by a member's ticket. It has Pigalle's famous *statue* of Voltaire. The *French Institute* is divided into five sections, viz., the Académie Française, Académie des Inscriptions et Belles Lettres, Académie des Sciences, Académie des Beaux Arts, Académie des Sciences Morales et Politiques.

**Palais de Justice* or Law Courts, on Ile de la Cité, was the seat of the French kings till the fourteenth century. A dome stands over the front. In one corner of the square (in which the pillory stands) the guillotine carts received their victims to carry them to the scaffold. The Salle des Pas Perdus, as rebuilt 1622, by Desbrosses (another part in 1766,) is 216 feet by 84, and contains a monument by Dumont (1822) to Malesherbes, the courageous counsel of Louis XVI. The Cour de Cassation (the highest court of appeal), formerly called 'Grande Chambre de Louis,' has statues of d'Aguesseau and l'Hôpital, two great lawyers. Other courts, &c., are, the Chambre des Requêtes; Court of Première Instance; Gallery of portraits of Lawyers; the Conciergerie or prison, with towers, &c. in the feudal style; Chapel and dungeon where Marie Antoinette and the Princess Elizabeth were confined; the Parloir, whence Lavalette escaped by his wife's help; and the Sourcière or St. Louis' kitchen, now a prison, with a labyrinth of winding corridors, staircases, &c. About 240 prisoners were massacred in cold blood here, 2nd and 3rd September, 1792., Close to it is the *Hôtel de la Prefecture de Police*, where passports are got. Also the *Sainte Chapelle*, a beautiful specimen of florid gothic (1245-8), 110 feet by 34, in two stories, now restored; it has a fine rose window, a spire of 180 feet, and stained windows. Boileau satirizes the chapter of this foundation in his 'Lutrin.'

**Palais du Luxembourg*, Rue de Vaugirard, on the site of the Duc d'Epernay-Luxembourg's house, was built after 1612 by Desbrosses, for Marie de Medicis, on the plan of the Pitti Palace (Florence), and came to the Orleans and other families. The Directory sat here, 1795; also the Consuls, 1799; and the Peers, after 1814, till the Revolution of 1848. It is now occupied by the new imperial senate. It is a solid, well-proportioned square pile, with pilasters in front, and a court 360 feet by 300. Paintings in the Salle des Messagers, and a large one on wax in the Salle des Conferences. The Salle des Séances (or sittings) is a splendid semi-circle, 92 feet diameter, with a painted vault, and statues of French statesmen. The Salle du Trone is ornamented with tapestry, and the First Consul's state chair. Other rooms are, the painted library, with 15,000 vols.; Marie de Medicis' Chapel and bed-chamber; also another chapel, with Pujol's great fresco. A gallery of modern artists is shewn here, with vases, &c.; open daily (except Monday), 10 to 4, by passport. The large gardens behind are in the style of the Tuilleries, with parterres and statuary, and a pepinière, or nursery, through which a broad avenue (near the spot where Ney was shot, December, 1815) runs up to the observatory. At the Petit Luxembourg, close to the principal building, the ministers of Charles X. were confined, till tried, after the events of 1830.

**Palais Royal*, Rue St. Honoré, was first built as Palais Cardinal, by Richelieu, and given, 1642, to Louis XIII. Louis XIV. granted it to his nephew, Philip of Orleans. The Regent Orleans here collected his gems and medals, as well as his 'Orleans Gallery' of pictures, which was dispersed at the Revolution. Philippe Egalité re-built the front, 1763, after a fire, and let most of it out as shops after 1780. The Jacobin and other clubs met here at the first Revolution; in that of 1848, the royal apartments were completely gutted, but are now occupied by Jerome Bonaparte and his son. Here are many restaurants, cafés (Véry's, &c.) in the noble-looking court, which is 700 feet by 300, planted with trees, and adorned with a fine jet d'eau. People come here to read the papers (lent out at six sous each), and it presents a very gay scene of a summer's evening. Close to the statue of Eurydice a cannon is fired daily, at noon, by means of the sun, when he comes to the meridian. Blind musicians regularly play at the Café des Aveugles.

Panthéon. See *Ste. Geneviève.*

Ste. Pelagie, Rue de la Clef, once a nunnery, is a place where 550 political prisoners may be kept.

Père la Chaise. See *Cemetery.*

Pères (Rue des Saints), has, at No. 24, the Ecole Impériale des Ponts et Chaussées.

Petits Augustins (Rue des) contains the Palais des Beaux Arts.

**Place de la Bastille*, Rue St. Antoine, where the Bastille stood, till captured by the mob, 14th July, 1789, and pulled down 1790. It was a castle-shaped pile, where state prisoners were kept at the mere command of the king or his ministers, called *lettres de cachet.* An elephant, 72 feet high, was to be placed on the spot, with water pouring from his trunk; but this is superseded by the *Column of July*, to the memory of 504 'Citoyens Français,' who fell in the Revolution of 1830 (27th, 28th, and 29th July). It was designed by Alavoine, is 163 feet high, 12 diameter, and contains 67 tons of bronze metal. Being unsupported by masonry inside, it shakes sensibly with the wind. There is a good view from the top.

**Place du Carrousel*, Rue de Rivoli, between the Tuilleries and Louvre, so called from a tournament, 1662. On one side is Napoleon's fine *Triumphal Arch*, 47 feet high, 64 wide, pierced by three arches, built 1806. It is covered with bas-reliefs of the events of 1805 (Austerlitz, Ulm, &c.); and the horses of St. Mark were placed on it, till carried back to Venice, 1814; but this loss is made up by a bronze copy by Bosio. The band plays here at the daily guard-mounting. Henri IV. and Louis XIV. built the long gallery towards the river, joining the Tuilleries and Louvre; that to the north (near Rue de Rivoli), about half done, is being completed by Louis Napoleon, after Visconti's designs.

Place du Châtelet, on the site of an old château-prison, has Bralle's palm-tree fountain, with a column 58 feet high.

**Place de la Concorde*, or *Place Louis Quinze*, Rue de Rivoli, opposite the Tuilleries, was laid out in the time of Louis XV., whose statue was pulled down at the Revolution. The horses on the west side were set up by Coustou, 1763-72; those on the east, by Coysevox. It is surrounded by a dry moat (now planted), and allegorical pavilions to eight large cities. In the midst between two fountains, 50 feet diameter, is the famous Luxor *obelisk*, erected at Thebes, 1550 B.C., brought by ship from Egypt, 1831-3, to Cherbourg, and set up here, 1836. It is a single block of reddish granite, 72¼ feet, 7½ feet broad at the base, and covered with 1,600 hieroglyphical characters. The pedestal is of Brittany granite, 27 feet high. Louis XVI. and Marie Antoinette were executed here, 1793, as well as Charlotte Corday and Philippe Egalité; Danton, Robespierre, St. Just, &c., in 1794. In two years 2,800 victims suffered on this spot by the guillotine,—*la petite* *fenêtre nationale*, or little national window, as the republicans called it (from the hole which received the neck),—the very instrument which, in 1815, belonged to a carpenter in Rue Pont-aux-Choux, near the Marais, and perhaps may be there now. The centre of the Place is one of the finest points of view in Paris.

Place Royale, Rue St. Louis, on the site of the Palais des Tournelles (so called from its little towers), in which Henry II. was killed 1559, when tilting with Montgommerie; on which account his widow, Catherine de Medicis, pulled it down a few years after. A statue of Louis XIII. here.

**Place Vendôme*, Rue St. Honorê, was built by Mansard on the site of the Duc de Vendome's Hôtel. The centre is marked by *Napoleon's Column*, built 1806-10; a copy of Trajan's (but one-twelfth larger), 135 feet high, 12 diameter, with the statue of Napoleon at top, 11 feet high. On the pedestal and shaft are a series of bronze bas-reliefs of the victories of 1805—from the departure of the troops to the battle of Austerlitz, where the cannon which furnished the metal were taken. They run in a spiral, 840 feet long, and include as many as 3,000 figures, 3 feet high. A staircase inside leads to the top, which is open from 10 to 6 for a small fee to the old soldier who keeps it.

Place des Victoires is circular, and has a bronze statue of Louis XIV., by Bosio.

PLACES OF WORSHIP—(*Protestant*).—Church service at the Embassy Chapel, in Rue d' Aguesseau, Faubourg St. Honoré, at 11½ and 4; Episcopal Chapel, Avenue Marbœuf, on the Champs Elysées, at 11 and 3; Wesleyan Chapel, No. 21, Rue Royal St. Honorê, in French and English, at 12 and 7; British and American Church, Rue Chauchat, Boulevard des Italiens, at 4; Friends' Meeting Room and Library, at R. Develay's Boarding House, 19, Rue Neuve des Mathurins, near the Madeleine; Jews' Synagogue, 14, Rue Neuve St. Laurent, in Rue du Temple, at 11½ and 3.—*French Protestant Churches* (called Temples) of the Reformed Communion: Temple de l'Oratoire, 157, Rue St. Honorê, at 11½; Temple de St. Marie, 216, Rue St. Antoine, at 11½; Temple de Pentamont, 108, Rue de Grenelle St. Germain, at 11½; Temple de Batignolles-Monceaux, 38, between the Barrières de Clichy and Monceaux, at 12½. The pastors are Rev. MM. Juillerat, Coquerel (Unitarian), Martin-Paschoud, Vermeil, Monod, &c.—Of the Augsbourg Confession: Church, 16, Rue des Billettes, at 12, in French, at 2, in German; Eglise de la Redemption, Rue Chauchat, at 11, in French. Rev. MM. Cuvier, Verny, Meyer, Vallette.—Sunday schools (held at 9½ *a.m.*) are attached to nearly all.

Police Office. See *Palais de Justice*, page xxxvi.

Pont d'Arcole, a suspension bridge, near the Hôtel de Ville, was *not* named after Napoleon's feat at Arcole, as might be supposed, but was suggested by a similar act of daring by a young man who led the Parisians against the troops, 1830, and whose name curiously enough was Arcole.

Pont des Arts, between the Louvre and Palais des Beaux Arts, was the first built of iron (1804), and is 546 feet long.

Pont d'Austerlitz (424 feet long), on five iron arches, was built 1801-6, by Beauprê.

Pont au Change, where the money changers lived, at the end of Rue St. Denis, 369 feet long.

Pont de la Concorde, opposite that Place, was built 1787-90, by Peyronnet, on five oval arches, 461 feet long, 61 broad. Some of the stones used were taken from the Bastille. The twelve statues which adorned it are now at Versailles. It is also called Pont Louis Seize.

Pont des Invalides, opposite the Hotel des Invalides, is a suspension bridge 350 ft. long.

Pont d'Jéna, opposite the Champ de Mars, a simple but elegant five-arch bridge on a level, 460 feet long, and so called after the great battle of 1806. Blucher would have blown it up, 1814, but for the interference of the Duke of Wellington.

Pont Louis Philippe, a double suspension bridge from Ile de la Cité, across the end of Ile St. Louis.

**Pont Neuf* (New Bridge), joining Rues Dauphine and de la Monnaie, across Ile de la Cité, was begun 1578 by Henry III., and finished 1604 by Henry IV. It is the 'London Bridge' of Paris, and is on twelve arches, and 1,020 feet long by 78 broad. A little a-one-side of the middle, at the end of the Island, is Limot's bronze equestrian statue of *Henri Quatre*, the favourite hero of France. It was set up, 1818, by Louis XVIII., in place of one erected by Henri's widow; and is fourteen feet high, weighing 30,000lbs. In one of the bas-reliefs on the marble pedestal, the generous king *(qui fut de ses sujets le vainqueur et le père)* feeds the poor people of his rebellious capital which he was then besieging; and in the other he sends a message of peace to them. The shops on this bridge have recently been removed.

Pont Notre Dame, near the Hôtel de Ville, is the oldest bridge in Paris, rebuilt 149 -1507, and is 362 feet long.

Petit Pont, near Hôtel Dieu, is 104 feet long.

Pont Royal, leads from the Tuilleries to the Quai d'Orsay, and to the *Palais* of that name in Rue de Lille, occupied by the Conseil d'Etat.

Popincourt (Rue), contains St. Ambroise church and the Abattoir of Ménilmontat.

**Porte St. Denis*, Rue du Faubourg St. Denis, is a triumphal arch to Louis XIV., built 1672 by Blondel, 72 feet high, the mid arch being 43 high and 25 wide. The carvings refer to the passage of the Rhine, taking of Maestrecht (Trajectum ad Mosam), &c. Much fighting took place here 1830.

Porte St. Martin, in Boulevard St. Martin, built 1674 by Blondel's pupil Bullet, is another arch, raised in honour of Louis XIV., after the taking of Besançon (Vesontio) and Limbourg. It is 54 feet by 54, the centre arch being 15 wide and 30 high. Louis appears as Hercules with a wig; his emblem is the Grand Soleil or Sun. Near it is Girard's château d'eau or reservoir, 1811.

Post Office. General Office (Hôtel des Postes) in Rues Jean-Jacques-Rousseau and Coq-Hêron; there are 16 branch offices called *Bureaux d'Arrondisement*, and 268 smaller, called *Boites aux Lettres.* For Paris, a ¼ oz. letter is charged three sous (1½d.); for the rest of France, an uniform charge of 25 centimes (2½d.) whether unpaid or prepaid, by postage stamps. Letters for the departments, and foreign countries, are in time at the boites till half-past three; at the bureaux till four; at the general office till five, or till three on Sundays and holidays when the Exchange is shut. Letters may be directed to a traveller, 'Poste Restante' *i. e.* to be called for, at Paris, or any other town, and will be delivered upon shewing the passport, between eight and seven (or eight and five on Sunday).—Daily Express Office, for despatch of small parcels, samples, law papers, &c., in Rue Montmatre, No. 121.

The Park of St. Cloud

Paris

Clermont

THEATRES, ETC. *French Opera House*, Rue Lepeletier, near the Boulevard des Italiens, has a front 64 feet high, with a double arcade, and an interior 66 feet wide; the stage 42 feet by 82; a fine saloon, 186 feet long. Places for 2,000. Prices, 2½ to 9 fr. In French Theatres, *loges* are the boxes, *baignoires* boxes near the pit, *parterre* is the pit (used only by men.) Most of them open at six.

Italian Opera, Rue Marsollier, is 154 feet by 110, with a double arcaded front. Prices, 4 to 10 fr.

Opéra Comique, Place des Italiens, has a six column portico. Prices, 1 to 7½ fr.

**Théâtre Français*, Rue Richelieu, corner of Palais Royal, was built, 1787, by Philippe Egalité, and has a doric front 110 feet high. Places for 1500. In the hall and saloon are Houdon's statue of Voltaire, busts, and memorials of Molière, &c. Mesdemoiselles Mars and Rachel have acted here. Prices 1 fr. 10 c. to 6 fr. 60 c.—At the north-west corner is the small Théâtre du Palais Royal, built 1831.

Théâtre du Gymnase Dramatique, Boulevard Bonne Nouvelle, has a six-column front; Scribe's plays were brought out here.

Théâtre Syrique, Boulevard du Temple, was built by Alexander Dumas (1847), and is decorated with sculptures and frescoes. The body is 66 feet wide, 52 deep, and very favourable for seeing. Prices, ¾ to 6 fr.

Théâtre de la Porte St. Martin, Boulevard St. Martin, a large wood and plaster pile, re-built in seven weeks after a fire.

Théâtre des Variétés, Boulevard Montmatre, built 1807 by Collerier, and has a double row of columns in front, with places for 1,240. Prices, ½ to 6 fr.

Théâtre du Vaudeville, Place de la Bourse, built 1827.

Ambigu Comique, Boulevard de Bondy, was re-built 1828, with shops on the ground floor, and has places for 1,900.

Gaîté, Boulevard du Temple, has 1,800 places, at prices from 40 c. to 5 fr.

Ten or eleven other Theatres are in the Boulevards, &c., besides about six outside the Barrières. The Guinguettes are places of amusement like the Eagle, Cremorne Gardens, &c. The *Conservatoire de Musique* is at 2, Rue Bergère; the *Diorama* in Boulevard Bonne-Nouvelle.

**Odéon*, rebuilt 1820 after a fire, has a portico of eight pillars, and stands 161 feet by 112, and 64 high, with places for 1,600.

Cirque National is in Champs Elyseés. The *Hippodrome*, outside the Barrière de l'Etoile, is of wood, in the moorish style, 380 feet diameter, with room for 10,000.

Thevenot (Rue) is a wretched spot, in which is the famous Cour des Miracles described by V. Hugo, a place for thieves and their cant tongue called '*Argot.*'

**Tuilleries Palace*, Rue de Rivoli, so called from the *tile* works here till 1518. Begun 1564 by Catherine de Medicis, enlarged by Henry IV. and Louis XIV., and joined by a gallery behind to the Louvre. It is 336 yards long, in the renaissance style, with a dome and high-pitched roof, and looks grand from its size. The centre part is called the Pavillon de l'Horloge; and at the extremities are the pavillons Marsan and de Flore. It contains many beautiful rooms, adorned with paintings and works of art. The mob broke into it, 20th June, 1792, young Napoleon Bonaparte being a witness to it; the Swiss guards were massacred, 10th August, in the same year; and it suffered in the disastrous revolution of 1848, when it was the residence of Louis Philippe. Napoleon also lived in it. The famous gardens in front, laid out by Lenôtre, are 2,256 feet by 900, and, in summer, crowded with people enjoying the sunshine, and wandering among the statues, parterres, basins, chesnuts and elms. Behind the Venus Pudica, one Henry hid away when he fired at Louis Philippe 1846. The view stretches through Place de la Concorde, down the Champs Elyseés to the Arc de l' Etoile. Behind the palace is the court made by Napoleon (who used to hold his reviews here), with the triumphal arch in Place du Carrousel. Here the troops mount guard daily at 10, and the band plays. The assassin Alibaud stood near the gate towards the river when he attempted Louis Philippe's life, 1836.

Vaugirard (Rue de) contains the Luxembourg, and (at No. 70), the Carmelite convent, where the massacre of the priests began, 1792.

Victoire (Rue de la), No. 52, is the house where Bonaparte and Josephine lived when he started for Italy, 1796, and for Egypt. It received its name on account of his Italian victories; here he planned the revolution of 18 Brumaire which made him Consul, 1799.

Victor (Rue St.) No. 68, now a municipal barrack, was once the Seminary of St. Firmin, where Calvin lived, and 91 unfortunate priests were massacred in 1793.

Vieille du Temple (Rue) has the Imprimerie Impériale.

Vivienne (Rue) contains the Bourse.

Vrillère (Rue de la) has the Banque de France.

ENGLISH DIRECTORY OF PARIS.

Apartment, House, and Commission Agent.—A. Webb, 36, Rue di Rivoli. Persons intending to reside in Paris, or wishing to forward goods to England, will find Mr. Webb's services of great advantage.

Chemist and Druggist.—T. P. Hogg, English Chemist to the Embassy, 2, Rue Castiglione (three doors from Rue Rivoli), highly deserving our best recommendation.

Dancing and Waltzing.—Mademoiselle Victorine and the veteran Coulon, of the Paris opera, give lessons at 320, Rue St. Honoré; just opposite the Hotel de Lille et d'Albion.

Dentist.—Mr. W. Rogers, 270, Rue St. Honoré, author of several important medical and surgical works on Dentistry. Mr. Rogers also enjoys a first reputation as a practical dentist.

Jewellery—Goldsmiths and Jewellers.—Paris being so distinguished in the fine arts, it requires some judgment and care to select the best establishments connected therewith. Deponchel and Co., orfèvre, bijoutier, joaillier, 47, Rue Neuve St. Augustin, are recommended as having an unrivalled stock of jewellery, and as being highly respectable.

Lace.—A visit to the 'French and Belgian Manufactory,' 57, Rue Neuve Vivienne, 15, Boulevard Montmartre, will convince our fair readers that we have selected a house deserving our best recommendation.

Money Changers and Foreign Bankers.—Messrs. Meyer, Spielmann, and Co., of 26, Rue Neuve Vivienne, are well known, and deserving our best recommendation. English and all foreign moneys can be exchanged at this establishment to the best advantage. They grant drafts on London and the principal cities of Europe and America.

Nouveautés.—We have exercised our usual care in choosing the best firm in Paris for these 'articles,' and in recommending the first-rate establishment, the Trois Quartiers, of Messrs. Gallois, Gignoux, and Co., 21 and 23, Boulevard de Madeleine, and 26, Rue Duphot, near the Madeleine; we are confident our selection will be approved.

English Pharmacy.—381, Rue St. Honoré, near the Madeleine. Mr. J. Dalpiaz, agent of Messrs. Savory and Moore of London.

Watch and Clock Maker.—Mr. Raby, 17, Boulevard des Italiens, first floor, opposite *Tortonis.*

Mr. Scott, Surgeon Dentist, Rue Royale St. Honoré, may be consulted from 10 to 4.

Mr. Seymour, Surgeon Dentist, 10, Rue Castiglione, may be consulted from 9 to 5.

Mr. George, Surgeon Dentist, 36, Rue de Rivoli, receives from 10 till 4; Author of 'Un mot sur le Nouveau Systeme de prothese dentaire.'

Furnished Apartments, combining English comfort with economy, may be had at 19, Boulevard Montmartre. We can recommend this as being a highly respectable house, and well situated.

"With respect to climate, the chief advantage which Paris has over London, consists in the greater purity and dryness of the atmosphere, its freedom from smoke and fog, and in the weather being less variable from day to day. The summers are hotter and the winters equally cold, if not colder. The average quantity of rain which falls throughout the year is about as great in the one as in the other capital. It would not, therefore, be advisable to select Paris as a winter residence for delicate invalids, or those whose cases require attention to climate. It agrees, however, with many dyspeptics, to whom the light cookery of the French *cuisine* is better suited than the more substantial fare usually met with in Britain, which requires greater powers of digestion,—provided always that this class of invalids abstain from ragouts, rich sauces, indigestible vegetables, as truffles, and from partaking of a variety of wines." (Lee, *Companion to the Continent*).

SKETCH OF FRANCE.

France is between latitude 42° 20' and 51° 6' north, and longitude 8° 15' east, and 4° 40' west. The greatest length, north and south (Dunkirk to Perpignan), is 787 kil.; the greatest width, east and west (Strasbourg to Brest), 802 kil.; the least width being (Rochelle to Pont-de-Beauvoisin) 735 kil. Area, about 54,452,600 hectares, or 136,131,500 acres, or 212,700 square miles (British Islands are 120,560 square miles). The back-bone of the country, or line of 'water-shed,' is along the Jura and Vosges mountains, then to the west by Monts Faucilles, then south by the plateau de Langres, the Côte d'Or, and the Cevennes, whence it strikes west to the Pyrenees. Its greatest off-shoot, the Dauphiné Alps, rise 14,108 feet at Mont Pelvoux, the highest peak in France; Mont Perdu, in the Pyrenees, is 10,994 feet; Mont Dore, in Auvergne, 6,198 feet; Reculet, in the Juras, 5,683 feet.

Six principal rivers water the surface: the Rhine, Meuse, Seine, Loire, Garonne, Rhône; the smaller ones are the Escaut, Aa, Canche, Authie, Somme, Touques, Orne, Vire, Selune, Rance, Aulne, Blavet, Vilaine, Lay, Sèvre-Niortaise, Charente, Leyre, Adour, Tet, Agly, Aude, Orb, Hérault, and Var. Besides these and ninety-four streams of the second class, there are about 3,664 kil. of canals, making a total of 2,900 leagues of inland navigation.

The roads are in three classes; 1st,—routes impériales (or 'king's highway'), kept up by the state; 2nd,—routes départementales, kept up by the departments; and 3rd,—routes vicinales or cross roads, which are left to the communes. Some of the best are thirteen to twenty mètres broad, paved, and lined with trees; but the cross roads are dreadful. In the 37,187 communes of France, there are about 2,240,000 kil. of public ways.

Its eighty-six departments, made 1789, by the division of the thirty-three provinces, take name from their position with respect to some river, mountain, &c., and with their chief towns, are as follows:—

DEPARTMENT.	CHIEF TOWN.	PROVINCE.	DEPARTMENT.	CHIEF TOWN	PROVINCE.
Ain	Bourg	Bresse	Loiret	Orléans	Orléannais
Aisne	Laon	Ile de France	Lot	Cahors	Guienne
Allier	Moulins	Bourbonnais	Lot-et-Garonne	Agen	Guienne
Alpes (Basses)	Digne	Provence	Lozère	Mende	Gévaudan
Alpes (Hautes)	Gap	Dauphiné	Maine-et-Loire	Angers	Anjou
Ardèche	Privas	Vivarais	Manche	St. Lo	Normandie
Ardennes	Mézières	Champagne	Marne	Châlons	Champagne
Ariège	Foix	Comté de Foix	Marne (Haute)	Chaumont	Champagne
Aube	Troyes	Champagne	Mayenne	Laval	Maine
Aude	Carcasonne	Languedoc	Meurthe	Nancy	Lorraine
Aveyron	Rodez	Guienne	Meuse	Bar-le-Duc	Lorraine
Bouches-du-Rhône	Marseille	Provence	Morbihan	Vannes	Bretagne
Calvados	Caen	Normandie	Moselle	Metz	Lorraine
Cantal	Aurillac	Auvergne	Nièvre	Nevers	Nivernais
Charente	Angoulême	Angoumois	Nord	Lille	Flandre
Charente Inférieure	La Rochelle	Saintonge and Aunis	Oise	Beauvais	Ile de France
Cher	Bourges	Berri	Orne	Alençon	Normandie
Corrèze	Tulle	Limousin	Pas-de-Calais	Arras	Artois
Corse	Ajaccio	Corsica	Puy-de-Dôme	Clermnt-Ferrand	Auvergne
Côte d'Or	Dijon	Bourgogne	Pyrenées	Pau	Bearn & Navarre
Côtes du Nord	St. Brieuc	Bretagne	Pyr. (Hautes)	Tarbes	Bigorre (Gascogne)
Creuse	Gueret	Marche	Pyr.-Orientales	Perpignan	Roussillon
Dordogne	Périgueux	Périgord	Rhin (Bas)	Strasbourg	Alsace
Doubs	Besançon	Franche-Comté	Rhin (Haut)	Colmar	Alsace
Drôme	Valence	Dauphiné	Rhône	Lyon	Lyonnais and Beaujolais
Eure	Evreux	Normandie	Saône (Haute)	Vesoul	Franche-Comté
Eure-et-Loir	Chartres	Beauce	Saône-et-Loire	Macon	Bourgogne
Finisterre	Quimper	Bretagne	Sarthe	Le Mans	Maine
Gard	Nismes	Languedoc	Seine	Paris	Ile de France
Garonne (Haute)	Toulouse	Languedoc	Seine-et-Marne	Melun	Ile de France
Gers	Auch	Armagnac (Gascogne)	Seine-et-Oise	Versailles	Ile de France
Gironde	Bordeaux	Guienne	Seine-Inférieure	Rouen	Normandie
Hérault	Montpellier	Languedoc	Sèvres (Deux)	Niort	Poitou
Ille-et-Vilaine	Rennes	Bretagne	Somme	Amiens	Picardie
Indre	Châteauroux	Berri	Tarn	Albi	Languedoc
Indre-et-Loire	Tours	Touraine	Tarn-et-Garonne	Montauban	Guienne
Isère	Grenoble	Dauphiné	Var	Draguignan	Provence
Jura	Lons-le-Saulnier	Franche-Comté	Vaucluse	Avignon	Venaissin
Landes	Mont-de-Marsan	Gascogne	Vendée	Napoleon Vendée	Poitou
Loir-et-Cher	Blois	Orléannais	Vienne	Poitiers	Poitou
Loire	Montbrison	Forez	Vienne (Haute)	Limoges	Limousin
Loire (Haute)	Le Puy	Velay	Vosges	Epinal	Lorraine
Loire (Inférieure)	Nantes	Bretagne	Yonne	Auxerre	Bourgogne

Each department is under a préfect (appointed by the state), and is divided into three to six arrondisemênts or sous-préfectures; these are parted (seven on the average) into cantons (2,834 in all) under juges de paix, and these again (six to fifteen each) into communes, each having a maire, a parish priest or curé, and his subordinate or vicaire. There are 40,430 priests in the 37,013 communes, besides 565 monasteries (for monks) and 3,400 nunneries. Before the revolution of 1848, each arrondisement had an electoral college comprising all persons paying 200 francs direct taxes, which returned deputies to the Chambre; under the present system, the Legislative corps are elected by direct universal suffrage. Each arrondisement has a tribunal de premiére instance (or quarter sessions court); and the departments are joined so as to make twenty-seven cours impériales (or assize courts), twenty-one military governments and eighty-one diocesses (fourteen being under archbishops).

About 47,000 primary schools are established in the communes, superior schools or colleges in the towns, normal schools and university faculties in the chief cities. Chambers of commerce exist at the ports and manufacturing towns; public libraries in most large places. There are 183 fortified places of war, in four classes.

Some of the best cathedrals are, Chartres, Bourges, Strasbourg, Rheims, Troyes, Amiens, Abbeville, Beauvais, Metz, Rouen, Bayeaux, Coutances. The romanesque style corresponds to the round-arched norman in England; flamboyant to the florid gothic (with wavy, *flame-like* tracery); and renaissance to the tudor and later styles.

The soil is very fruitful, and best cultivated on the borders of Belgium, thence to the south it gets worse. Fields are unenclosed; farmers live near the villages away from their farms. Most of these are mortgaged, and grow smaller and smaller by the law of equal shares. Corn is not drilled in, so that a fine crop of weeds spring up. Women reap, and the produce is threshed in the open air. Manures used, but no more cattle kept than actually wanted. The best pasture is in Normandy and the west, where good breeds of cattle and sheep are seen.

About three acres in seven are arable, and half as much waste; there may be twenty-million acres of forest, and five of vineyards. Wheat, rye, oats, potatoes, are the chief crops, the return being one-third less than in England; beet root is grown for sugar, the annual production of which is 46,000 tons; french beans and other vegetables in profusion; maize for food; flax, hemp, tobacco, and a few hops; rape and cole seed.

Cider, perry, and a little poor wine are made in the north down to a line running east-north-east and west-south-west through Paris. Vineyards are common, south of this; and at another line through Rochelle and Dijon the maize or Indian corn begins. From a third line, east and west through Lyons, the olive and mulberry flourish; and the orange, lemon, &c., are pretty common on parts of the south coast.

The Vine (grown in seventy-six departments,) yields nine-hundred and twenty-four million gallons of wine, of which one-sixth is for brandy (eau-de-vie) from the Charente, &c., and one-tenth is exported. Champagne, Burgundy, Bordeaux (claret), Roussillon, Dauphiné, Lyonnais, &c , are the best sorts; stoney soils are the most suitable. Bercy is the central market for wine, and Béziers for brandy.

The forests are not too great for the vast consumption of charcoal for fuel. Elm is the most common timber; others are the oak, lime, maple, and various ornamental woods, pine (in the Landes, Vosges, &c.), cork tree (Pyrenees); the chesnut for food, walnut for oil, mulberry for the silk worm (in the Drôme, Ardèche, &c.).

Coal is found more or less in thirty-three departments, but worked only round Valenciennes, St. Etienne, Angers, &c., so that of the small annual consumption (4,150,000 tons?), part is imported. Iron is plentiful, and forged at 4,400 furnaces. Copper worked near Lyons; brick and porcelain clay, chalk, gypsum, limestone (in most of the mountains), marble, granite (in Brittany, &c.), manganese, antimony, lead and silver, rock salt, and slate, are abundant.

Of eight hundred mineral springs counted, there are eighty principal (under medical inspectors), such as Bagnères, Bagnères de Luchon, Cauterets, Bourbonne, Bourbon-Lancy, Mont Dore, Vichy, Rennes, &c., annually used by 50,000 persons, one-half being strangers.

Linen, lace, cotton (at Rouen, Mulhouse, &c.), broad cloths, woollens, carpets, &c., are made in the north; silk in the south. Beavers and flamingoes still breed in the Rhone; the bear, wolf, wild boar, chamois, &c., otter, with the ortolan, becafico, gecko, salamander, are also seen in the south of France, where the musquito *bites*. Sardines or pilchards caught in Brittany; tunny and anchovy, in the Mediterranean.

Perhaps the most striking parts of France, are Normandy, the Seine, the Lower Loire, Brittany, the Upper Garonne and Pyrenees, Auvergne and its volcanoes in the Upper Loire, the Cevennes Mountains, the Rhône below Lyons, Dauphiny, the Vosges mountains.

We may add a few notices of its past history. In Cæsar's time it was Gallia or Gaul, including the Belgae to the north and north-east; Celts in the west, middle, and south; the Aquitani in the south-west; with some Greek colonies round Marseilles. (Fine roman remains still exist at Nismes, Orange, &c., in the south, and even as far north as Lillebonne). It was afterwards divided into four, and then seventeen, provinces by the emperors. Later still, it was occupied by the roving nations from central Europe, as the Visigoths and Ostrogoths, in the south; the Burgundians, on the Rhine; and the Franks (fourth century), on the Lower Rhine, who were descended from Meroveus, and under Clovis (481-511) the *Merovingian* obtained so much ascendancy as to give it their name.

Upon his death his four sons shared his power and dominions, which were again united under the survivor, Clotaire. After several kings, and many divisions, during which parts of it took the names of Austrasia (east and north-east); Neustria (north-west, where many Armorican Britons, &c., driven out of England, had settled); Aquitan (south and west); Bourgogne (east and south-east); it was re-united and extended under the vigorous sway of Charlemagne (768-814), son of Pepin, and head of the *Carlovingian* race, which expired with Louis V. (prior to which the Northmen, under Rollo, settled in Normandy).

His successor was Hugues *Capet*, 987, from whom the descent is tolerably regular, though the kingly power was but weak for several reigns. A succession of fourteen kings of this house (including Philippe Auguste and Louis IX., or St. Louis), ended in the direct line with Charles IV., who was succeeded, 1328, by Philippe VI. of *Valois*. Six kings of this branch (among whom are Charles V., called le Sage, who however, lost Crecy and Poitiers; Charles VII., in whose time the English lost nearly

all they had gained in France; and the crafty Louis XI.) ended with Charles VIII. Louis XII. of *Valois-Orléans* comes next, 1498. After him, Francis I. (1515) of *Valois-Augoulême*, and four princes of the same stock, including Charles IX., the author of the Bartholomew massacre. Henry IV., or Henri Quatre of *Valois-Bourbon*, ascended the throne, 1589, and was succeeded by Louis XIII. and other Bourbons, down to the Revolution, and execution of Louis XVI. (1793).

***Napoleon* became emperor 1806. Louis XVIII. was restored 1814 (the child of his murdered brother had the nominal title of Louis XVII.), and, except the 'Hundred Days,' reigned till 1825. His brother, Charles X., was driven from the throne, 1830, when Louis Philippe of *Orléans* succeeded, and reigned till 1848, when the Third Revolution and Second Republic was effected, which terminated, 1851, with the restoration of the Empire, under Napoleon III. (son of Napoleon's second brother Louis). The direct survivor of Louis Philippe is his grandson, the Count de Paris; and of the Bourbons, Charles X.th's grandson, the Count de Chambord, or Henry V. as his partisans style him.**

Population of France (1851), 35,781,628; regular army, 454,000; fleet, 330 vessels (90 being steamers), with 8,000 guns; revenue, about 1,375,000,000 francs (£55,000,000); public debt, £230,000,000.

The same items for the British Islands are,—population (1851), 27,452,000; army, 129,000; fleet, 678 vessels, with 18,000 guns; revenue, £52,250,000; debt, £765,000,000.

GUIDE TO FRANCE.

*** A *Black Line* down the page in any part of the book serves to shew that the RAILWAY runs in that quarter; and a short line projecting from the *centre* line signifies that the Railway terminates at that point. For examples, see pages 50 and 57.

Ten kilomètres = *six* English miles, nearly.

SECTION I.

ROADS TO THE NORTH-WEST;

IN CONNEXION WITH THE PARIS AND ROUEN-HAVRE-DIEPPE RAILWAYS, SUPPLYING EVREUX, ROUEN, DIEPPE, HAVRE, CAEN, BAYEUX, ST. LO, CHERBOURG, ETC., IN THE OLD PROVINCE OF NORMANDY. ROUTES ONE TO SEVEN.

ROUTE 1.

Paris to Rouen and Havre,

BY railway, opened 1843, 84 miles, or 137 kil.; five trains a-day, in 2½ to 4½ hours; fares, 16, 13, and 10 fr. (or through to London, *viâ* Havre and South Western Railway; and *viâ* Dieppe and Brighton Railway; same fare for each, 30, 25, and 17 fr.) or by steam-boat direct to London.

Embarcadère, No, 15, Rue d' Amsterdam, behind the Madeleine; the station is large and handsome. To each passenger 15 kilogrammes (or 33 lbs.) of luggage are allowed; beyond that a charge is made according to weight and distance, besides 10 cents for booking. Other booking offices in Paris; Rue St. Martin, No. 247; Rue de la Jussienne, 25; Cour des Messageries Nationales; Place St. Sulpice.

The stations going down the Seine are :—

	kil.		kil.		kil.
Asnières	4	Meulan	16	St. Pierre	14
Colombes	3	Epône	8	Pont-de-l'Arche	12
Bezons Bdge.	3	Mantes	8		
Maisons	7	Rosny	6	Tourville	5
Confians	5	Bonnières	6	Oissel	2
Poissy	5	Vernon	11	Rouen (S.)	11
Triel	8	Gaillon	13	Rouen (N.)	14

LES BATIGNOLLES (dept. of the Seine), near the Railway Engine Shops, is the first place outside the barrière, and gives name to one of the short tunnels, by which you pass (the longest is 1322 feet) under the plain of Monceaux. Clichy-la-Garenne, a little further, near the Seine, with its square town, was a country seat of le bon roi Dagobert, who was married here. Neuilly lies above it, on the Seine, and St. Denis below, with the hills of Montmorency behind. A five-arch bridge leads over to

ASNIERES (2½ miles), where the Rive droite (right, or north bank of the Seine) line to Versailles (*see* Route 3) turns off, up the river, among several country houses. Coach to Gennevilliers.

At COLOMBES, the branch line to St. Germain turns off to the left (*see* Route 3*a*). Rollin wrote his Ancient History in this pleasant neighbourhood. (Coach to Houilles.) A short branch, leads 3 kil. north-west to Argenteuil, (population 4,600) on the Seine, having parts of its old walls, a hospital, founded by Vincent de Paul, and Marais château. It was to the Bernardine convent here (founded 656), that Heloise retreated after leaving Abélard. Coaches to Sannois, Franconville, St. Leu-Taverny, and Eaubonne.

At BEZONS (in department Seine-et-Oise),

the rail crosses the Seine (which winds three or four times hereabouts), on a wooden viaduct of nine arches, each 98½ feet span. The early French kings had a mint here. Anoth.. wooden bridge over the river brings you to

Maisons (10 mls.), or Maisons-Lafitte, so called after the banker, whose widow lives in a château, built 1658, by Mansard, and which came to Comte d' Artois (Charles X.) and Marshal Lannes, Duke of Montebello. Voltaire was here when he caught the small-pox. Herblay château lies 5 miles north-north-east, across the river.

L'Etoile-de-Conflans (3¾ miles), in the middle of the forest of St. Germain, (that town is to the south) leaves *Conflans* 4 kil. north, across the Seine, near the Oise's mouth, and having a church of the eleventh and twelfth centuries, where St. Honorius was buried, besides a picturesque château.

Poissy (½ mile), at the old bridge, on the river, was a country seat of the early kings, from Charles the Bold (860), and has a high-roofed gothic church, with buttresses and two slender spires, containing the font which Louis IX., or Louis de Poissy, (a native) was baptized in, and the tomb of Philippe his brother. Another church, founded by his son, Philippe le Hardi, 1314, (and destroyed 1793) belonged to the Ursuline abbey, where the famous conference was held, 1561, between the Catholics and Protestants, Beza and Peter Martyr attending, on the part of the latter; but it led to no result except the massacre of St. Bartholomew. There are also an old hospital, and a central house of detention. A great cattle market for Paris, on Thursday. *Hotels*—De Rouen, de la Marine. Population 4300.

The rail follows the south side of the river, hence, almost all the way to Rouen; the limestone banks begin to rise, and the scenery improves. Opposite Verneuillet (north side) where Talleyrand's brother lived, is

Triel (7½ miles), and its old-fashioned church, with a centre tower, built by Francis I.; it has some stained windows, and Poussin's Adoration of the Magi, which the Pope gave to Christiana of Sweden. The Princess of Condé had a seat here before the revolution. Population 2000. At Mureaux, is a skew bridge over the Ruplat; and a road turns off to

Meulan (3¾ miles), north of the rail, beyond the Seine, which an old bridge, resting on Ile Belle, here crosses. It was a fortified town, which the Duc de Mayenne unsuccessfully besieged in the civil wars. One of its two churches, (it had also a priory and convent) is now a corn-market. Chateaubriand had a seat here. Population 2000. *Hotel*—Royal.

[At 7 miles north is Vigny château, which belonged to Cardinal d'Amboise, minister of Louis XII., and a munificent patron of the arts. Ingen, further on, was a country house of the bishops of Chartres; and near Epône, is a Dolmen or druid pile.]

Mantes (10¼ miles), opposite Limay, at the bridge of 3 arches (each 127 feet span, resting on Ile Champion), is called *la jolie*, or pretty, because of its situation, and is a sous-préfecture with 4600 souls. William the Conqueror burnt it, in 1096, to revenge himself on Louis, and received the hurt of which he died a little after; it was taken from the English by Du Guesclin, and again by Charles VII. Notre Dame church, with its triple portal, tall square towers of different ages, lofty nave, 105 feet high (supported by buttresses), delicate choir, pillars, etc., was founded by Jeanne of France. Of another church, St. Maclou, only a beautiful slender tower (1340-4) is left. The old château in which Philippe Auguste died, was pulled down, 1721. The public library contains 4000 vols. and there are several fountains. with some parts of the old walls. *Hotels*—Le Grand Cerf (Stag), la Chasse Royale.

Limay has a hermitage, to which pilgrimages are made. Trade, in wine, corn, leather, and timber. (Coach to La Roche Guyon, 20 kil.) A new bridge leads out of the town.

[At 26 kil. south-west is Anet, near the Eure, with a wing, chapel, and other remains of the beautiful château, built by Delorme, for Henry the Second's mistress, Diana de Poictiers (buried here), and pulled to pieces at the revolution. Dreux is 16 kil. further. (*see* Route 91.)

At 27 kil. south south-west, is Houdan, on the Vègres (where the Opton meets it) and the Brest road, once a fortified place, and having an old tower, with an excellent gothic church, as ancient as Robert the Pious. Population 2000.

At 21 kil. north, is Magny, a little village, on the Aubette, in a fertile corn country, with a good church, and manufactures of woollen, paper, &c.]

Rosny (3½ miles), close to that forest, has the old high-roofed brick château, in which Rosny, Duc de Sully, the faithful friend and minister of Henry IV. was born, 1539. It belonged to the late Duchess de Berry.

[At 22 kil. south-west, is *Ivry-la-Bataille*, under a hill, on the Eure, celebrated for the victory of Henry IV., and his Protestant subjects, 1590, over the Leaguers, under their Captain General, the Duke of Mayenne, assisted by the "hireling chivalry of Gueldres and Almayne." The field contains a pyramid 56 feet high. Macaulay's noble lines on this victory are marked by one of those generous traits which have endeared Henry IV. to his countrymen.

"And then we thought on vengeance, and all along our van,
'Remember Saint Bartholomew,' was passed from man to man.
But out spake gentle Henry, 'No Frenchman is my foe.
Down, down with every foreigner, but let your brethren go.'"]

The pretty village, of Rolleboise (which has part of the castle taken from the English, by Du Guesclin), on the slope of the river, a little further, is close to a tunnel 8,682 feet long through the chalk, which cost twenty months, and nearly half a million pounds of powder to make.

Bonnieres (3½ miles), where conveyances to Evreux, Caen, &c., are taken; and the road to Caen and Cherbourg turns off. (*see* Route 4.)

[At 7 kil. north, on the bend made by the Seine, here crossed by a suspension bridge, is La Roche Guyon, with the Norman tower and chapel of an old castle, taken by the English, 1418; below which is the more modern seat of the Rochefoucaulds, where they shew the bed, portrait, and furniture of Henry IV. Here Francis de Bourbon was killed, by a box being thrown on his head, 1545.]

Soon after Port-Villez (opposite the Epte's mouth, and near the Camp-de-Cæsar) you enter department Eure, and the province of Normandy.

Vernon (7 miles), belonged to the Norman ancestor of the Vernons, of Kinderton, in England. It stands in a fine hollow, at the 22 arched bridge to Vernonnet; as a frontier town it was fortified by Henry II., and frequently suffered in the wars with France. An old tower, built by Henry II., remains; also a good gothic church (Nôtre Dame) having a carved black marble tomb; and St. Just's hospital, or Hôtel Dieu, founded by St. Louis, and rebuilt 1776, by the Duc de Penthièvre. It has besides an artillery depôt, and a small salle-de-spectacle. To the west is the charming Park, and Château de Bisy, which belonged to the Orleans family. A tower at Vernonnet, is called Julius Cæsar's; the Château de la Madeleine was the seat of Casimir Delavigne, the poet. Population 6,300. *Hotels*—Du Lion d'Or, (Golden Lion); Grand Cerf, (Stag).

[At 36 kil. north-east, is Gisors, a pleasant old town, on the Epte, having the keep and other remains of a feudal castle, begun by William the Conqueror and Henry I. (who received Pope Calixtus here, 1120,) and finished by Henry II. (who met Philippe Auguste here, 1188, about a new crusade). Philippe Auguste fled hither some time after, on his defeat by Richard I., at Courcelles, and was nearly drowned by the falling of the bridge. The town walls and moats are now turned into promenades; a gothic church of the 13th century, has a well carved renaissance portal, a jubé and marble figure by Goujon, and stained windows. St. Paer's tower, of the 13th century, is outside. Population 3,700. *Hotels*—Du Bras d'Or (Golden Arm); de l'Ecu, (Crown-piece).

Further down, across the river, in the forest of Vernon, are Pressagny, called l'Orgueilleux, (the Proud), though it has little to be proud of,—and Port-Mort, where Louis VIII. married Blanche de Castile. The Seine is crowded with pretty islands here.]

Gaillon (8 miles), 2 kil. west of the railway, in a fine spot, has a House of Correction on the site of the château of the Rouen archbishops, built about 1262, burnt by the English, and restored in the renaissance style of the 16th century, by Cardinal d'Amboise, but ruined at the revolution. Its gate is at the Palais des Beaux Arts, in Paris, and a picture of it at the primate's palace at Rouen. Part of the beautiful park remains. It was a favourite retreat of Francis I. This is the most northerly place in France for wine,—a poor sort, of a small black grape. Near this is the Château de Navarre, built by Jeanne of Navarre, 1532, and rebuilt 1686, by Mansard for the Ducs de Bouillon, and for a time the seat of the Empress Josephine. Grisolle and Rotoirs are also near, and Abloville, where Marmontel died.

[Courcelles is across the river. At 10 kil. north of it, at the suspension bridge, on a bend of the Seine is *Les Andelys*, a sous-préfecture of 5,000 souls, near Château Gaillard, a fine picturesque ruin, on a peak, built 1197, by Richard Cœur de Lion, at Petit Andely, to command the river, and dismantled by Henry IV. The vicious Margaret de Bourgogne was strangled here, 1315, by order of Louis X.; and Cardinal Balue shut up his victim Charles de Mellieu in it. At the hospital founded by the Duc de Penthièvre, is a plaster figure of St. Main, which mothers rub their children against to cure them of colic. Grand Andely, on the Gambon, further inland, and older, grew out of a monastery founded by Clothilde, and burnt 1170, by the English. Near the curious old chapel, called after her, (now a vinegar work), is her fountain, into which sick persons and new born infants are plunged. The half gothic church has a good portal, stained windows, and Lesueur's "Jesus in the Temple." At the Hôtel de Ville is Poussin's "Coriolanus." Blanchard the æronaut was a native; Henry IV.'s father, Antoine died here, 1552, of a wound at the siege of Rouen; T. Corneille had a house here in which he died. Cloth is made, and pèche d'ablettes, for false pearls, are caught. *Hotels*—Du Grand Cerf (Stag); des Trois Rois (Three Kings).]

At VILLERS, where N. Poussin, the painter was born, 1594, is a tunnel 5,643 feet long, cut through in seventeen months; another at Venables, 1,410 feet long. The river makes several islands here.

ST. PIERRE-DU-VAUVRAY ($8\frac{3}{4}$ miles), near Praslin Park.—Coaches to Louviers, Beaumont-le-Roger, Neubourg, Bernay (*see* Route 4). Evreux is 22 kil. beyond Louviers, (*see* Route 4.)

[*Louviers* (4 kil. south west), a sous-préfecture of 10,300 persons, chiefly weavers of fine cloth, is a flourishing and ancient town, in the rich plain of the Eure, where Richard I. and Philippe Auguste made a treaty, 1196. It was taken by Edward III., and again by Henry V. who dismantled it, except a small part of the walls. An old church of the twelfth century, partly norman in its style; a Knight Templar's house of the twelfth century, and timber houses (in the old town) are seen; besides several factories, dye-works, a bibliothèque, salle-de-spectacle, three bridges, &c. *Hotels*—Du Rouen, du Grand Cerf (Stag), du Mouton d'Argent, (Silver Sheep or "Golden Fleece").]

At MANOIR, on the north side of the Seine opposite the Eure's mouth, the railway crosses by a viaduct of 6 arches, each 98 feet span. At 8 kil. north-east, is Romilly, and its large copper founderies, on the Andelle, which employ 1100 or 1200 hands. Here Cardinal d'Amboise's great cathedral clock was brought from Rouen and melted down for cannon, at the revolution. Fleury, 6 kil. further up, has good views of the valley of the river. About 10 kil. beyond this is Lyons-la-Foret, on the Lieur, near the remains of the abbey church of Mortemer, founded by Henry II. of England; and on a hill roman remains have been found.

PONT-DE-L'ARCHE, ($7\frac{1}{2}$ miles) to the south, across the Seine, here spanned by a long 22-arch bridge, to which it owes its name, is a pretty place, in Ouche district, in Upper Normandy, and was built and fortified 854, by Charles the Bold, who held two councils there. Its high roofed church, has a spire and buttresses, with stained glass of the fourteenth century. A house stands in the middle of the bridge, near an island on which it rests, once covered by a fort. Behind stretches a large forest. (Coach to Louviers, 12 kil.)

[At 10 kil. west, at the suspension bridge across a bend of the river, is *Elbœuf*, a thriving cloth town, of 16,500 people, among factories, in a valley bordered by a chain of hills, which crop out at the chalk cliffs of Orival in the river. It has two churches, St. Etienne being the older and smaller, and both ornamented with stained glass, and it is watered by artesian wells. Steamers to Rouen daily. *Hotels*—Le Bœuf d'Or (Golden Bull); Lion d'Or.]

The tunnel at Tourville, 1,440 feet long, leads over the Seine again, by a narrow viaduct of 6 arches, of the same span as the previous ones, to

Oissel (4½ miles,) which has a church with a tall tower and spire. The railway passes by St. Etienne de Rouvray, and the forest where William the Conqueror was hunting when he heard of the death of the Confessor, to Rouen 5 miles further, the debarcadère or terminus being in the Cours de Reine, on the south side of the river and the town. The train through to Havre and Dieppe, turns off before this at Sotteville, (after waiting 15 minutes), through St. Catherine's hill to the north side of the town, where there is an embarcadère (de la rive droite). The total fall of the railway from Paris is 91 feet.

Rouen—55½ miles from Havre, 37¾ from Dieppe.

Hotels.—D'Albion, kept by Mrs. Smith, deserves our best recommendation; d'Angleterre, by Mr. Delafosse, is a very excellent house. *Cafés.*—Thillard and Fontaine, Rue des Charrettes; de France, Place des Carmes. *Restaurants.*—Hiesse and Jacquinot, Cours Boieldieu; Busmont, in Vieux Marché.

Omnibuses from the stations to all parts of the town, 40c.,—or 1fr., with 132 lbs. of baggage; but the baggage may be left at the station.

English vice-consul, M. Dacaen, 42, Rue de la Vicomté. English physician, Dr. Walton, 1, Rue Nationale. Post Offices, Quai du Havre (near the Custom House) and Place des Carmes. Money changers, M. Barette, 46, Rue Vicomté; M. Henault, 46, Basse-Vieille Tour. Rev. MM. Paumier and Allègre are French Protestant pastors here.

Population 91,500. This fine old city and port, as remarkable for its past history as for its present commercial eminence, is the chief town of department Seine-Inférieure (Lower Seine), seat of a military division, an archbishoprick, cour impériale, college, school of navigation, &c., and of the French cotton trade, and stands in a very agreeable spot, on the Seine, at the bottom of a circuit of low hills, open to the south. By the bending river it is 75 or 80 miles from the sea at Havre; the direct distance being only 45 miles. Green islands, such as Petit Gay, Lacroix, Brouilly, &c., occupy the middle of the stream, which is only about 500 to 650 feet wide, and lined with tall modern houses and broad bustling quais, deep enough for small craft of 200 tons to come up to. High water at full and change, 1 hour 15 min. Mont Gargan, or St. Catherine's Hill, to the south, commands a full prospect of the city, styled by V. Hugo—

> * * * * La Ville aux vieilles rues,
> Aux vieilles tours, debris des races disparues,
> La Ville aux cents clochers carillonnant dans l'air,
> Le Rouen des chateaux, * * * *

with its noble cathedral, its steeples, towers, factories, crooked streets, planted boulevards, and spreading suburbs. Darnetal Hill, further off, where Carville church stands, is another good point of view. It is the *Rothomagus* of Ptolemy, which under Clovis became the capital of Neustria. Wrolf, or Rollo, the Northmen leader (912) made it the head of his province of Normandie, which Charles the Simple gave him with his daughter, and which King John, upon the murder of his nephew Arthur, in Basse Vieille tower, forfeited to his suzerain Philippe Auguste, 1204. Henry V. took it 1418, before the battle of Agincourt, which laid France at his feet. "Joan of Arc here expiated the crime of having saved her country,"* being burnt for a witch by the English, 1431. The French retook it, 1449, and it was given up to Henry IV. 1543, after a siege, in which his father, Antoine de Navarre was mortally wounded. The works he threw up are still seen on St. Catherine's Hill, but the old towers and walls (extended for the fifth time from Rollo, by Louis IX.), are replaced by open boulevards, planted 1770-83. This line includes the old town and the buildings worth notice; outside are the faubourgs of Martainville and Hilaire (east), Beauvoisine and Bourreuil (north), Cauchoise (west), and the large suburb of St. Sever, on the south bank, where most of the factories lie; but many small works—between 200 and 300, for tanning, dyeing, &c.,—are placed on the little rivers Aubette, Robec, and Rouelle, which creep through to the Seine. Three streets, running north and south, namely, Rues Grand Pont, des Carmes, and

* J. Janin's *Voyage de Paris a la Mer*,—a beautifully illustrated book.

Beauvoisine, make the principal thoroughfares past the cathedral, &c., and are in line with each other, and with Rue de Ernemont to the north, and with the suspension bridge and Rues St. Sever and d'Elbœuf to the south,—a line about two miles long. The new suspension bridge, 646 feet long, opened 1st September, 1836, hangs on a cast-iron arched tower in the middle, with a pont-levis or drawbridge for shipping to pass. Two piles a little above it mark where the old pont-à-bateaux, or bridge of 15 boats crossed, as built, 1626, by Friar Nicholas. Further up is the Pont d'Orleans, between Quais de Paris and Grand Cours, built 1811-31, by Lunasson, of six stone arches, (the 2nd and 5th each 102 feet span), resting in the middle on the west corner of Ile Lacroix, where a David's theatrical bronze of P. Corneille was placed 1834. Beyond this is the railway bridge across Ile Brouilly, on ten arches. Quai de Havre, below the suspension bridge, where the steamers and shipping lie, is the most lively; the barges up the river lie at Quai de Paris, &c. Grand Cours, or Cours la Reine, on the St. Sever side, near the rail, is a promenade 4,300 feet long, planted in the seventeenth century, on the site of Grammont priory, founded by Henry II. of England; other walks are at Cours Dauphin, Avenue du Mont Riboudet on the Dieppe road, and the hills of St. Hilaire, Bons Guillaume, and St. Aignan, where you look down on the town. The climate is changeable and cold, but healthy in the upper parts.

Highly carved mediæval timber and stone houses meet the stranger at every turn, mostly as old as the fifteenth century; but the first object of attraction is the *Cathedral* of Nôtre Dame, in Rue Grand Pont, begun about 1,200, (on the site of that wherein Rollo was baptized), by King John, and finished 1509-30, by Cardinal d'Amboise. Length of cathedral, 434 feet; breadth, 105 feet; length and breath of transept, 175 feet by 25; height of nave, 90 feet. The cardinal built the richly carved front, between the towers, 180 feet broad, consisting of three deep portals, with six large windows, a rose window, and two spires above, besides the central porch. Two unlike towers, of an older date, flank it, 253 feet high; one, St. Romain's with a low pyramid at the top, has the oldest part of the cathedral at the base, and was finished 1477; the other, with a beautiful eight-sided crown, is called Tour de Beurre, because built 1485-1505, with the money of those who bought leave to eat butter in Lent, and is also called after d'Amboise, on account of his famous brass clock, which was melted down 1793, for cannon and for medals, and bore the republican rhyme:—

> "Monument of Vanity,
> Destroyed for Utility,
> Year II. of Equality"!

The great wooden spire, or lantern, 420 feet high, burnt by lightning in 1822, is re-placed by one of cast-iron open work, by M. Alavoine, 460 feet high, made of 2,540 pieces of metal, weighing 517 tons. The Portal de la Calendre, in the north transept, is full of sculptures of the Life of Christ; that in the south transept or Portal des Libraires, near the chapter-house, is decorated with subjects of the Last Judgment. In the inside are three rose windows, and 130 others, mostly stained, and of the thirteenth century; and 25 chapels the sides, including the Virgin chapel, in which are Philippe de Champagne's "Adoration of the Shepherds," effigies of Richard I., and the beautiful renaissance marble tombs of Louis de Brézé (husband to Diana of Poictiers) by J. Goujon, and Cardinal d'Amboise. The latter is a most elaborate profusion of carved pilasters, figures, and arabesque ornaments, and has the two kneeling statues of the Cardinal and his nephew, both archbishops. Several of the early dukes, three kings, and fifteen prelates are buried here. The palace behind was begun 1461, and finished by Cardinal d'Amboise, though altered since; in the gallery of the States are four large views by Robert.

St. Ouen's Abbey Church, near the Hôtel de Ville, is a chef-d'œuvre of gothic art, and one of the most beautiful structures existing. It was begun in 1318 by Abbé Marcdargent, and makes a cross, 443 feet by 83, and 107 feet high to the vault, with flying buttress, pinnacles, 125 windows, in three rows (stained with the miracles of St. Romain, &c.,) and an extremely elegant tower of the 15th century, 260 feet high to the crown, which rests on a square pinnacled base, and is full of traceried windows and open work. The unfinished west front and rose windows, stand between small towers 43 and 54 feet high. Rose windows are also seen in the transept; that over the south door (which has a host of figures and carvings) being the work of Berneval, (buried in St. Agnes' chapel) the master sculptor, who they say, stabbed his apprentice because he was outdone in the opposite window. Eleven chapels surround the oval choir, (finished 1340) and its clustered pillars. What remains of the abbey, (one of the oldest in Normandy, where Henry IV. and other kings used to stay,) is enclosed in the Hôtel de Ville, which has a simple corinthian façade, built 1818, and grand staircase, with busts of Louis XV., and the Corneilles. It contains the Musée, founded 1809, with a gallery of French and other pictures, (open from 10 till 2,) and Caffieri's statue of P. Corneille; and the Bibliothèque, (open on Thursdays,) of 36,000 volumes, besides 1,200 MSS. from the 11th century, including D. d'Aubonne's graduel or missal, with 200 paintings, &c. in it, (which took thirty years to fill, is 2¾ feet long, and weighs 79 pounds!) and Bishop Jacques de Lieur's Livre des Fontaines (given 1525) full of arabesques, &c.

Of other churches, (14 left out of 37,) there are —St. Maclou, in Rue Malpalu, ranking next to St. Ouen's, and built 1472; it has a finely-carved triple portal, a dome 154 feet high, much stained glass, a good staircase to the organ, &c. St. Patrice, near Boulevard Bouvreuil, built in 1535, in the renaissance style, cross-shaped, with good stained windows. St. Vincent, in Rue de la Vicomte, in the same style, with a good porch, &c. St. Amand, another renaissance church, in Rue St. Nicholas, belonged to an abbey founded 1030, of which a small part is left, covered with wood carvings of abbesses, &c., among whom is Anne de Souvré (died 1654), whose body was found in 1800, undecayed. St. Romain, near the railway station (rive droite,) built 1679, has the granite tomb of its patron saint, whose life is pictured in the dome, &c., besides stained windows saved at the revolution, from the churches of St. Maur, St. Etienne, and St. Martin, all now turned into magazines, &c. St. Godard, in Rue de l'Ecole, of the 16th century, has the genealogy of Christ in one of its stained windows, and a painting by Letellier, Poussin's nephew. At St. Eloi's, near the poultry market and Theatre Français, and used by the protestants since 1803, there was a well in the choir, with an iron chain to it, which gave rise to a proverb, "It is as old as the well-rope of St. Eloi." In Rue Chasselièvre, in the north-west outskirts, is St. Gervais' Church, with a very ancient crypt, and once attached to the abbey which William the Conqueror died in. Near St. Lo's, behind the Palais de Justice, traces of the Roman wall were found in the eighteenth century. St. Nicaise, built 1388, and St. Vivien, are not far behind St. Ouen's. St. Hilaire, near the Rue de Darmetal. St. Paul's stands on the Cour de Pais, near the river side, including a fragment of the old one in the sacristy. St. Sever's, in the midst of that faubourg, is in Rue d'Elboeuf. In this part also are St. Yon's Asile des Aliénés, (Lunatic Asylum) on a large scale. The new Jardin des Plantes, open daily. The Gas Works. A large well regulated abattoir or slaughter house, in the Rue de Sotteville, built in 1835. The Circus. A Caserne or Barrack for cavalry, on the site of Bonnenouvelle priory, founded by the Conqueror's queen, and burnt and rebuilt in 1665; and a foot barrack in Place St. Sever, near the bridge, in what was an immense salt store. A third barrack is that of Martinville, built in 1776, in front of the Champ de Mars.

The *Prefect's Hôtel*, is in Rue de Fontenelle, so called after the philosopher, whose birthplace, (marked "Fontenelle est né dans cette maison, le 11 Fevrier, 1657,") is a little distance off, in the Rue des Bons Enfans, while that of his uncle, the dramatist, is close by the Prefecture, in the Rue de la Pie, (marked "Ici est né, le 9 Juin, 1606, Pierre Corneille.") On the Quai du Havre are, the Douanes or Custom House; the Bourse (Exchange,) and Tribunal de Commerce, in a building called the Consuls, (opposite Boieldieu's statue,) in which is a hall with a Christ, by Vandyke, and two pictures by Lemonnier, a native; and the Théâtre des Arts, near the bridge, having an ionic front, with a medallion of the "Grand Corneille." The Théâtre Français, built in 1793, is in the Vieux Marché (or Old Market place), the oldest in the city, where the scaffold is erected.

A short turn leads into the Place de la Pucelle, so called after the unfortunate Maid of Orleans, who was burnt at the stake on a spot marked by a fountain and a ridiculous bronze of her, by Bonet. Opposite it is an excellent subject for the artist and antiquary, an old house, called Hôtel du Bourg-Theroude, in the mixed gothic and italian style of the 15th century, with a turret hanging over the front, and, in the court, various carvings and bas-reliefs of the Field of the Cloth of Gold, (see Ardres) and other subjects; Elizabeth's ambassador, Shrewsbéry, (the French call him "Scherosbèry,") was lodged here, in Henry the Fourth's time. The Rue de la Grosse Horloge, is so called from the gothic clock tower, dated 1389-98, (the great clock, which sounds the couvre-feu or curfew, is a century later,) to which 200 steps lead; it is joined to part of the old Hôtel de Ville, built 1527, and has on the fountain, bas-reliefs of Arethusa and Alpheus, which the people take for "Le Bon Homme Rouen," the founder of the town. A little further in Rue des Carmes, near the cathedral, are, the half gothic Bureau des Finances, built 1509, decorated with arabesques, and the écu de France, supported by porcupines; and the old Chambres des comptes, built 1525, by Francis I. In the Rue aux Juifs (Jew street,) is one of the most beautiful things in Rouen, the

Palais de Justice, opposite the Neuf Marché (New Market), a low-pitched gothic structure, built 1493-9 by Louis XIIth's minister, Cardinal d'Amboise, for the ancient Echiquier or provincial states, and lately restored; the front towards the court is 212 feet long, with pinnacled windows in the roof, and an octagon tower in the middle; a staircase, built 1607, leads to the Salle des Procureurs, 181 feet by 53, which has a woodwork ceiling compared to the frame of a ship.

In Rue du Grand Maulevrier is the *College*, first built for the Jesuits, by Cardinal de Joyeuse, whose tomb is in the chapel which Catherine de Medicis added, 1614. Behind is the seminary for priests. Between Rues Caquerel and Cavilles is the Bicêtre, or House of Correction; and nearer the Boulevard Martinville, the General Hospice, or asylum, an extensive pile, where 2,000 orphans and poor people are kept. At the opposite side of the town, in Rue de Lecat, is the great hospital for the sick, the *Hôtel Dieu*, or Madeleine, built 1749-56, and having 600 beds, and a chapel, built 1781, with a dome and corinthian portico, and two pictures by Vincent.

At or close to the site of Basse Vieille Tour (near the Quai de Paris), where they say John murdered his nephew Arthur, are the three *Halles*, or market halls (328 feet long) for corn, linen, cotton tissues, and checks, called Rouenneries, &c, which have a very lively appearance on Wednesdays, between six and twelve. To the west is the old Fontaine de Lisieux, built 1518; another, the Fontaine-de-la-Crosse, at the top of Rue des Carmes, has many arabesque ornaments about it; the Fontaine de Croix-de-Pierre, in Rue St. Hilaire; altogether there are 38 fountains, fed by four different sources. Of eight open places for markets, that for butter is at Rougemar (in Rue Bourglabbé), where Duke Richard, in 949, beat the French and Germans; the Boulingrin (bowling-green), in Beauvoisine Boulevard, is used for the sale of horses. The road here leads up to the churches of Longpaon and Carville, and Leveillé's spinning works, at Darnetal. Near the Champs de Foire (Fair field), the site of the old palace built by Henry V., is the tower of Mal-s'y-frotte (which means "He meddled for the worst,") lying on this side of the field where Will. Long-sword, son of Rollo, routed the people of Cotentin.

Two towers, called Donjon and Gascon, in Rue de la Glacière, are left of Philippe Auguste's château, built 1205, and made an Ursuline convent. Many local, middle-age and other antiquities, including Cœur de Lion's heart in a box, are preserved in the departmental museum at the old convent of St. Marie, Rue de Poussin, not far from this, besides a collection of natural history; open Tuesday and Thursday, from twelve to three. Old carved houses may be noticed in Grand Rue (Nos. 115, 120, &c.), Rue du Change, Rue Eloupée (No. 4), the house of Jouvenet, the painter, and many more. On Sapins hill is the Cimetiére Monumental; there are six others, one being for Protestants. Ecoles de Natation, or swimming schools, on Iles Lacroix and Petit Gay.

Besides the Corneilles and Fontenelle, Rouen claims as *natives*, Benserade the poet, Pradon, the Jesuits Brumoy and Daniel, Paul Lucas the traveller, Adam the chemist, Madlle. Champmeslé the tragedian, Jouvenet, Restoul and Géricault the painters, Boieldieu the composer, Count Mollier, Napoleon's minister of finance, Armand Carrel, and Louis Brune, who saved the lives of more than 60 persons; on his house you see "A Louis Brune, la Ville de Rouen."

The *Manufactures* are the cotton rouenneries already mentioned, callicoes, prints, linen, thread, flannels, cloth, soap, chemicals, steam-engines, leather, refined sugar, confitures of great fame, &c.; and it is an entrepôt for wine and spirits, grain, salt fish, spices, dyewoods, cotton, wool, hemp, slate, iron, tar, &c. The shipping and foreign trade are about one-third that of Havre.

Conveyances—By rail, to Paris, Dieppe, Havre, &c.; by coach, to Alençon, Amiens, Argentan, Avranches, Beauvais, Caen, Falaise, Forges-des-Eaux, Gisors, Gournay, Pont-Audemer, Lisieux, Le Mans, Laigle, Pont-l'Evèque, Neufchâtel, Seez and Vire; by steamer, to Elbœuf and Bouille. Steamers to Havre have ceased running since 1847.

ROUTE 1, *continued.*

Rouen to Havre.

By railway (92 kil., or 59½ miles, 5 trains, 2 to 3½ hours), from the branch station at Sotteville (rive gauche). Made 1842-3, at a cost of forty-five million francs; and passes through five or six tunnels, and over eight or ten heavy viaducts.

The stations (all on the north side of the Seine) are—

	kil.		kil.		kil.
Maromme ...	6	Motteville ...	11	Beuzeville..	6
Malaunay ...	3	Yvetot	8	St. Romain.	8
Barentin ...	8	Alvimare ...	11	Harfleur ...	11
Pavilly	2	Nointot	8	Havre	7

From Sotteville, where the railway engine works of MM. Alcard and Buddicom are established, you cross the ten-arched wooden railway bridge over Ile Brouilly, each 131 feet span—Bon Secours new church being to the right, and Rouen on the left—to St Catherine's tunnel, 3 445 feet long; thence past Leveillé's and other large spinning and dyeing mills at Darnetal, on the Robec, which command a fine prospect of the city—(from the detached gothic tower of Longpaon church, the latter being joined to another of modern date)—through two more tunnels (the second 4828 feet), under boulevards St. Hilaire and Beauvoisine, to the rive droite station, in Rue Verte. A fourth and fifth tunnel (3118 feet, and 1167 feet), in the chalk under Cauchoise faubourg, &c., bring you, at length, with the Seine in view, to Bapeaume, Deville, and Maromme—the last having a population of 3300, and manufactures of cotton, paper, powder, &c., on the Cailly.

[About 5 kil. south is Cantelou, in the forest of Roumar, on a height, near the river, with a château of the time of Louis XIV.; and 2 kil. west of this, is the church of the abbey of St. George des Boscherville, founded 1144, by William de Tancarville; it is a good norman specimen, cross-shaped, with round towers and windows (except in the pointed ones of the west spires), an east apse, pilasters, &c., and a transition chapter-house.]

MALAUNAY (5½ miles from Rouen), has paper and cotton mills, on the Cailly, crossed by a viaduct of eight arches, 82 feet high. The railway to Dieppe (*see* Route 2) turns off to the north-east a little beyond, up the valley of the stream, near which you come to Notre Dame-des-Champs tunnel (7218 feet long), under Poville hill.

BARENTIN (5 miles) on the Austreberte (which falls into the Seine at Ducler cliffs, 11 kil. south-south-west in the forest of Trait) has cotton works, and a great viaduct on twenty-seven arches, 108 feet high, 1640 feet long, as rebuilt by the contractors, after a fall in 1846.

PAVILLY, further up the stream, in a pretty spot, has an old château of the thirteenth century (now a cotton work), and a church, in which the first wife of Diana de Poictier's husband is buried.

[At 15 kil. south-south-east are the fine Norman ruins of the abbey church of *Jumièges*, founded 661, by St. Philbert, and rebuilt in the eleventh century. It has two conspicuous towers over the west front, and parts of the central towers, &c. To this abbey the Confessor sent Harold to renew his promise of the kingdom to William. Charles VII. was here when his mistress, Agnes Sorel, died at Mesnil château (3 miles south-east) now a farm house, near the river, opposite Mauny forest.]

MOTTEVILLE (8½ miles) in the wide and fertile plain of the Pays de Caux, near the last tunnel on the line (Flamanville) 541 feet long. Coaches go to Yerville, St. Laurent, Luneray (35 kil.), on one road; and to Dondeville and St. Valery (38 kil.) on another.

YVETOT (5 miles) to the left, in a fertile spot, a sous-préfecture of 8600 souls, with a brick church, old wooden houses, and manufactures of ribbons, cotton velvets, &c., is celebrated for its roi d' Yvetot, a burlesque title, first conferred in an edict of 1392, on its seigneur (like the king of Kippen, in Perthshire), and taken up in Beranger's well-known song. At Allonville, 6 kil. south-west, is an oak 36 feet round, and eight centuries old. Coaches to Cany, Ourville, Valmont, and Caudebec (11 kil. south.)

[Caudebec is a pretty fishing village of 2500 souls, in a gap of the cliffs on the Seine, where the sands begin to be troublesome. It belonged to St. Wandrille's abbey. Henry V., of England, Charles VII., and Henry IV., took it. The last event was in 1592. The old walls are gone, but it retains many wooden houses, and a beautiful gothic church, built 1416-48, having a richly carved triple-portal (the old arms, "three pearls,on a blue field," are seen), a side tower, with a tiara-shaped spire, and a Virgin chapel, with its great pendant hanging from the roof. Biscuits, beer, &c., are made; at one time it was noted for gloves and hats, called caudebecs. The ruined churches of St. Gertrude and Nôtre Dame-de-Barre-y-va, are near—the latter being of the thirteenth century, and a votive chapel for the bargemen, &c. Opposite it was an island, which sunk in 1641, with a monastery on it.

At 4 miles east are the gothic remains of a church, on the site of the abbey founded 684, by St. Wandrille, kinsman of Clovis, and called Fontenelle, but burnt in 1230. Theodoric, son of the last Merovingian king died here. The buildings round it are used for a cotton factory. St. Saturnin's little norman chapel is near; and there was another, Caillouville, so full of statues that it was called the "gathering of Paradise." Across the river (4 kil. south), in Brotonne forest, is the old château of Meilleraye, or Meslerèe, seat of Madame de Mortemarte.

At 4 kil. south-west of Caudebec, is the pretty village of Villequier, and its spire church in a gap of the river.]

Nointot (11¾ miles), to the south of which (3 kil.) is Bolbec, a thriving town of 9800 people, where four valleys meet, on a stream which runs down to the Seine. Cotton and linen goods, leather, &c., are made. *Hotels*—De Rouen; de l'Europe.

[At 8 kil. south of this, is *Lillebonne*, in a hollow on the Bolbec, once the Roman *Julia Bona*, so called after Cæsar's daughter. It remained a place of some note under the Norman dukes, and has been revived by the cloth manufactures. Population 5200. A semi-circular theatre, about 200 feet across, cut of the hill side, was traced 1826; and baths, coins, pieces of statuary, &c., have been discovered. There is a good spire church. Above it are the tower and ruined walls of the Harcourts' old castle.]

Further on you come to Mirville aqueduct, 1640 feet long, on forty-eight arches, some 108 feet high.

Beuzeville (3¾ miles) whence there is a coach to Goderville (7 kil.), and to Fécamp (19 kil. north, Route 2*a*). Further on and 2 kil. south, is

St. Romain-de-Colbose, in a pleasant country, with 2000 population, and manufactures of stockings and prints.

[At 8 kil. east-south-east, on the high cliffs opposite Quillebœuf, are the fine remains of *Tancarville* castle, including the gate and its massy round towers, chapel &c. It belonged to the Conqueror's chamberlain (ancestor of the English Tankervilles), the Harcourts, Dunois the soldier, Law the financier, and now to the Montmorencies, but is not inhabited.]

The railway winds round the hills at the back of

Harfleur (12 miles) a decayed village on the Lezarde, now 3½ kil. from the Seine's mouth (here seen to advantage), but once the chief port of Normandy. Henry V. took it after seven weeks' seige, 1415, and sent the population (8000) to Calais and elsewhere—which was the ruin of it. The church has a slender tower, and good portal, but the beautiful crocketed spire is gone. Coach to Montvilliers (5 kil. north) up the river (*see* Route 2*a*).

A little east is Orcher château, seat of Madame Mortemarte, once belonging to Law.

At 4½ miles beyond this (leaving Graville and its old abbey church to the north) is Havre terminus, in Cours Napoleon.

Havre, or le Havre de Grace. *Hotels*—Wheeler's Hotel, a comfortable and highly respectable house, strongly recommended to travellers; de France; de la Amirauté (Admiralty), on Grand Quai; de l'Europe, in Rue de Paris; de Richelieu, in Place Richelieu; d'Angleterre; d'Albion; de Lilbonne; de New York; de Brazil; de la Paix. *Cafés*—Etats Unit; Frascati. Dinner, 2½ to 3 fr.; bed, 1½ to 3 fr.; wine, 1½ to 2 fr.

English consul: G. Featherstonehaugh; English chapel, in Rue d'Orleans; American chapel, in Rue de la Paix; Rev. MM. Poulain and Amphoun are French Protestant pastors here. Post-office, in Place Louis Seize. Large sea baths, besides those at the Frascati Hôtel. On landing here you give up your English passport for a provincial one; and when you embark, you must ask for a permit. Travellers through to Marseilles should declare to that effect, to save delay about the passport at Paris. Omnibuses run to Ingouville.

Population about 32,000, including English, &c. Havre is a thriving fortified port, sous-préfecture, packet station, &c., in department of Seine-Inferieure, in the old province of Normandy. It ranks as the second port in France, by which the Paris foreign trade is carried on; and its harbour is perhaps the best in the Channel, on the French side. It stands in a flat damp spot, on the north side of the Seine's mouth (where it is 5 miles wide), 143 miles from Paris, 100 from Southampton, and 80 from Newhaven. Francis I. walled it round, Richelieu added a citadel, &c., and others have improved it; but before the fifteenth century it was an insignificant fishing place, near which Henry V. of England landed on his way to Agincourt, and whence Henry VII. embarked as Earl of Richmond. Warwick held it for Elizabeth, 1562, but gave it up after a long siege; and Rodney bombarded it, 1759.

The Rue de Paris is the most bustling street, as it leads to the docks and quais; but the newest houses are up Ingouville Hill, where most of the English live, and which has the best views. Four basins or docks, les Bassins du Roi, du Commerce, and de la Barre, opening into the Port Neuf (opened 1843), and Avant Port, will hold about 700 shipping; there is also a new steam dock: they are cleared by sluices. The tide rises 20 to 27 feet, so that large ships may come in three hours before and after high water. In the Roads—one of which is 8 kil. off—there is anchorage, with plenty of water, but the current often runs with dangerous swiftness. Few of the buildings are of any note. The Hôtel de Ville, built in 1753, stands in Place Francis I., whose crest (the Salamander) is over the door, whence there is a fine view. The Custom-house, or Douane, is on Quai Notre Dame, so called after that church, built in the sixteenth century, cross-shaped, in the renaissance style; the front was restored 1829. St. François Church was built between 1553 and 1681. Exchange, or Bourse, was built 1785; Salle de Spectacle (theatre), began 1817, and rebuilt, 1845, by Charpentier; at the Circle de Commerce the merchants meet. The old prétoire, in the Market Place, is the Palais de Justice; a public library, of 16,000 volumes, is at the new Museum, on the site of the ancient Hôtel de Ville, with statues of Saint Pierre and Delavigne in front. A telegraph, on Francis I.'s old tower (69 feet high, 85 round), communicates with La Hêve Lights. There are military barracks, an arsenal, &c., and the government tobacco factory. A museum of natural history at Ingouville. A marble slab marks the house in Rue de la Corderie (No. 47), where Saint Pierre, the author of Paul and Virginia, was born. Mad. de Scuderi, Mad. de la Fayette, C. Delavigne, &c., were also natives. The low space to the north-west is lined with windmills, and leads to Cape la Hêve, where the chalk cliffs begin, on which stand the fixed lights, 446 feet above sea. The Seine runs with such power past the pier-heads of the harbour, as to prevent the water inside from falling sensibly for even three hours after high water; so that 120 sail have been known to leave in one tide, with the wind against them. Both sides of the river above Havre are well lighted, to guide small craft past the shifting sands. It was off this port that Sir S. Smith was captured, 1796, and sent to the Temple.

Ship-building and kindred trades are carried on. Many ships are engaged in the Newfoundland cod, the herring, and other fisheries. Among the articles manufactured are tobacco, soap, pottery, iron, cordage, starch, vitriol, paper, beer, refined sugar, lace, &c. The imports are sugar, coffee, spices, cotton, &c., to the value of £10,000,000, of which cotton is one-fourth; and the exports include silks, cloths, gloves, perfumes, trinkets, wine, brandy, &c.

Conveyances—by rail, to Rouen, Dieppe, Paris, &c.; by coach to Fécamp, Dieppe, Monbrilliers, &c. By steam to Honfleur, daily, 1 hour; Caen, daily, 4 hours; Cherbourg, twice a week, 10 hours; Dunkirk, weekly, 20 hours; Trouville, daily, 2 hours; St. Malo, three times a month, 20 hours; Morlaix, three times a month, 20 hours; Rotterdam, weekly, 24 hours; Hamburg, weekly, 60 hours; Copenhagen and St. Petersburg, twice a month, 4 and 8 days; Southampton, daily, 12 hours; Brighton, 10 hours; London, weekly, 20 hours; Liverpool, monthly, 60 hours; San Sebastian, Corunna, Cadiz, and Malaga, every 20th day, in 8 days; New York, twice a month, 15 days. There are also lines of sailing packets, &c. See *Bradshaw's Continental Railway Guide.*

From Havre, across the Seine (6½ miles), you come to Honfleur (*see* Route 5).

ROUTE 2.

Rouen to Dieppe.

By rail, 37¾ miles, or 61 kil.; four trains, 1½ to 3 hours. The line turns off at Malaunay (as in Route 1); after which the stations are—

	kil.		kil.		kil.
Monville......	6	Auffay	4	Dieppe	16
Saint-Victor	16	Longueville.	10		

MONVILLE (3¾ miles), up the Cailly (from which a coach goes to Cleres, 7 kil.), was dreadfully ravaged by a storm of wind and lightning, April, 1845.

SAINT-VICTOR (9¾ miles). Coaches to Tôtes, 5 kil.; St. Jaens, 14 kil.; and to Neufchâtel.

[*Neufchâtel*, (28 kil. east-north-east), is a sous-préfecture of 3,430 persons, on a wooded hill-side, by the Bethune, and noted for its excellent cheese, of three sorts,—viz., that from pure cream, the second sort called Hearts of Bray (the district around), and the large round cheese. It was called Driencourt, when Henry I. of England built his new castle (Neufchâtel) here, which suffered in the wars of the League. At Nesnière château they shew his room. There is a church, with painted glass; also manufactures of wool, pottery, cotton, glass, and a trade in cheese, beer, cider, &c. *Hotels*—Du Grand Cerf (Stag); du Lion d'Or (Golden Lion). Coaches to Rouen, Paris, and Abbeville.

At 23 kil. south-south-east is Forges-les-Eaux, so called because of its mineral waters, in a valley near the Forest of Bray, which are drunk from July to September; are clear and sparkling, with a temperature of 43°, and have a tonic quality. Anne of Austria took them before the birth of Louis XIV.; and after her, Louis XIII., and Richelieu, they are named la Reinette, la Royale, and la Cardinale. *Hotel*—Du Mouton d'Or (Golden Sheep, or Fleece).]

AUFFAY (3 miles), in the industrious valley of the Scie, which the railway crosses above twenty times. Coach to Bacqueville, 15 kil.

LONGUEVILLE (6 miles), on a stream which runs to the sea, near Dieppe. Not far from the latter, on the east, is the ruined castle of Arques, on a hill top, below which Henry IV. gained a great victory over the Leaguers and the Duke of Mayenne, 1589. It was built in the eleventh century, with corner towers, &c., and is noted in the history of Condé's sister, the Duchesse de Longueville. The church is worth notice.

At 9¾ miles further is Dieppe, which you reach by a long tunnel of 5,389 feet.

Dieppe. *Hotels*—Gossel's Hôtel de l'Europe, a first-rate old established house; des Bains (Bath), near the Custom House; Royale, facing the sea; de Londres, on Quai Henri IV.; du Commerce; d'Angleterre; d'Albion. *Cafés*—Suisse, in Grande Rue; Robert, Halle au Blé. Dinner, 2 to 3 fr; breakfast, 1½ fr.; bed, 1½ fr. Of all the routes from London to Paris, this is the shortest in actual distance (240 miles), but the sea-passage is 72 miles. Passports are *viséd* on landing; and a permit must be obtained to embark. The Douane is at the railway station, close to the pier; baggage of travellers, direct to Paris, not examined till they get there.

Protestant worship at the Old Carmelite Chapel; Rev. M. Reville is French Protestant pastor here. English physicians, Drs. Moriarty, Davison, Burnett, Sleigh. Bankers, Dufaur and Co., D. Destandes, V. Sanchou.

Population, 16,600. A fishing port, sous-préfecture (dept. of the Seine-Inférieure), and bathing place, the nearest to Paris, and within eight hours of Brighton. It stands under the cliffs of the channel, where the Arques, Bethune, and Aulne fall into the sea. June to September is the bathing season; there are bathing machines, hot and cold baths assembly rooms, with a theatre, &c. The harbour at the north end is made by two piers, one of which carries a light; it will hold about 200 craft, up to 500 tons burden; but the mouth is narrow and sandy. A large street, Grande Rue, leads from the quay towards the Castle at the other end, which has a good prospect. Houses of brick chiefly, with high-pitched roofs and balconies, and mostly built since the English bombarded it in 1694. The old walls are left; there are six places or squares, the principal having a statue of Duquesne (a native); and as many as 68 fountains, supplied by an aqueduct 3 miles long. The fishermen live in Faubourg Pollet; they catch herrings, mackarel, cod, and oysters; and remain a distinct race. Among the buildings are, St. Remi's gothic Church, near the Castle, rebuilt 1500-43; St. Jacques, on the site of an abbey, a gothic church, with buttresses, some good carvings, and a tower, whence you get a fine prospect; Hôtel de Ville, library of 3,000 vols., with a Naval Museum, College, Navigation School, Theatre, &c.

This place was of more consequence formerly, when its seamen discovered Canada, and it sent the first settlers to Senegal. Henry IV. was here before the battle of Arques Castle (6 miles off), in 1589, when he defeated the Leaguers under the Duke of Mayenne. Francis I. visited it in 1532, and was entertained by the merchant Ango, whose seat or manoir still remains at Varengeville (8 kil.), not far from which is Cape l'Ailly light, 304 feet high. Lace, pipes, and ivory trinkets (at St. Nicholas) are made. High water at the moon's full and change, 10h. 30m.

Conveyances, by rail, to Rouen, Havre, Paris, &c.; by steamer, to Newhaven, daily. See *Bradshaw's Continental Railway Guide.*

Château d'Eu (*see* Route 12) is about 30 kil. on the road to Abbeville and St. Valery-sur-Somme. About 4 kil. on this road you pass a large ancient camp called Cité de Limes.

ROUTE 2*a*.

Dieppe to Havre.

From Dieppe, on the road to Havre, you pass (not far from the coast),

Bourg-Dun (18 kil.), with a church of the 15th century.

St. Valery-en-Caux (13 kil.), a fishing port, in a pretty spot. Population, 5,400.

Cany-Barville (12 kil.) has some good seats about it, on the Durdent.

Fecamp (19 kil.), a fishing port, in a healthy spot in a gap of the hills, having the church (all that is left) of the abbey of Nôtre Dame, built between the 11th and 16th centuries, partly norman, but mostly early gothic, with some good carving, effigies of abbots, and a tower, 231 feet high. The lighthouse on Montagne-de-la-Vierge cliff (near a chapel) is 427 feet high, and can be seen 21 miles.

It has a Chamber of Commerce, Navigation School, Theatre, Library, &c.; cotton and saw-mills. Herrings, mackarel, &c., are caught. Population, 10,100. *Hotels.*—De la Porte, du Commerce, du Grand Cerf (Stag).

About 9 miles south-west is Cape de Caux, or d'Antifer, past chalk cliffs all the way, from 150 to 700 feet high.

Goderville (12 kil.) and Epouville (14 kil.) in a fertile country.

About 16 kil. further is Havre. (*see* Route 1.)

ROUTE 3.

Paris to St. Cloud and Versailles.

By rail to Versailles (rive droite, or north bank, opened 1839) and St. Germain (opened 1839); trains hourly, from the Rouen terminus. Omnibuses meet all the trains. Distance to Versailles, 23 kil. or 14 miles; to St. Germain, 18½ kil. or 11 miles.

The stations to Versailles are—

Asnières,	Puteaux,	St. Cloud,
Courbevoie,	Suresnes,	Sèvres.

Asnieres, as in Route 1.

Courbevoie (at the bridge to Villiers), has a large barrack and a church, rebuilt 1789. A little further on, over the river (here crossed by Peronnet's beautiful stone bridge, built 1772, 750 feet long, of five arches, each 120 feet span), is *Neuilly*, the favourite seat of Louis Philippe, but much injured by the mob in 1848. It was built 1755, by Comte d'Argenson, in the italian style; and for a while inhabited by Talleyrand and Prince Murat. The house and grounds were beautifully laid out by the king, to whom the crown was here offered 1830. A pillar marks where he was shot at, just before. Nearer Paris, outside the great triumphal arch over the Avenue de Neuilly, is a chapel on the spot where his son, the Duke of Orleans, was killed, when going to the château, 13th July, 1842.

Puteaux is the next station; then

Suresnes, near the citadel and church, on Mont Calvaire or Valerian, 590 feet above the sea. A suspension bridge crosses the Seine to Longchamps.

St. Cloud, on a hill-side by the Seine (by

which steamers come up), in a charming spot, is so called after Clovis's grandson, St. Clodoald, who was murdered here. It was burnt by the English, 1358; Henry III. was assassinated, 1389; and Henrietta Maria (wife of Charles I.) died here, 1670. The palace, built, 1572, by Gondy, a banker, having been bought by Louis XIV., was given to his brother, the Duke of Orleans, and rebuilt by Mansard, &c. It makes three sides of a square, with a principal front of 170 feet long, and has many painted and gilt saloons full of pictures, statuary, Sèvres china, tapestry, &c. Louis XVI. gave it to his queen; Bonaparte, when consul, carried out the revolution of 18 Brumaire (10th November, 1799,) here; the capitulation of Paris was here signed, 1815; and hence Charles X. issued the ordonnances against the press, 1830. The private grounds and grand park were laid out by Le Nôtre, and are open to the public. In the latter are the water-works and cascades, with a jet d'eau, rising 140 feet, and Napoleon's Lantern of Diogenes, whence there is a fine prospect. A three-weeks' fête is held in September. The unfinished church has two paintings. A fourteen-arch bridge leads over to Boulogne, in the Bois or wood in which the English encamped, 1815; it is noted for its duels, races, and the Longchamps promenade. A tunnel under the park opens out with

Sevres on the left, near the bridge, towards Passy. It was founded 560, and has a population of 4,600, with a church full of new stained windows, and the government factory of porcelain, or Sèvres china, established 1755. The show rooms are open daily; there is also a fine museum of china, pottery, &c., of all ages and countries, to be seen by order.

The line here runs close to the rive gauche, or south bank, past Ville d'Avray, Chaville, Grand Montreuil (where Gen. Hoche was born), to the terminus in Rue Duplessis, at

Versailles. (*see* Route 90.)

ROUTE 3*a*.

Paris to St. Germain.

By railway; the stations to St. Germain are—

Asnières,	Nanterre,	Chatou,
Colombes,	Rueil,	Le Pecq.

Asnieres; as in Route 1. The small branch to Argenteuil turns off before

Colombes, where this branch turns off from the Rouen line. Coaches to Bezons, Houilles.

Nanterre was the birthplace of St. Geneviève the patron saint of Paris, and is noted for its sausages and cakes. The rest of the line to St. Germain is on the atmospheric plan, worked by two fixed engines here, and at Chatou, and St. Germain.

Rueil, to the left, has a large barrack and a church partly as old as the thirteenth century, in which are monuments of Josephine and her daughter Hortense, the latter placed here by her son, the present Emperor. *Malmaison*, the favourite seat of Napoleon and Josephine (who died in it, 1814), belongs now to Queen Christina; it is a plain building, and includes Napoleon's library and cabinet (near the lodge), in which he was nearly captured, 1815, by Blucher's cavalry, but escaped by his guards breaking down the wooden bridge of Chatou, and fled to Rochefort. Coach to Bougival (5 kil. south) near La Jouchère château, once the seat of Louis Bonaparte and Count Bertrand. At La Celle-St. Cloud is the château given by Louis XV. to Madame de Pompadour, and that of Beauregard, in a fine spot, on a hill.

Chatou, in Vesinet wood, where the railway crosses the Seine, resting on Ile Chiard, is to the right. To the left are Croissy and Les Gabillons. Coaches to Le Pecq and Neauphile-le-château.

[Beyond (across the river) are seen Port Marly waterworks and aqueduct of 36 arches, 2165 feet long, 70 feet high, for supplying Versailles; it strikes towards Louveciennes on the hill-side, and Maisons pavilion, which belonged to Madame du Barri. Louis XIV.'s seat at Marly was pulled down at the revolution.]

A short branch turns off to

Le Pecq bridge, opposite St. Germain, but the main line goes round by another bridge to the old palace.

St. Germain-en-Laye, or St. Germains 18 kil. west of Paris, in a healthy spot on a hill-side, is known for its royal château, begun by Louis-le-Jeune, 1143, but rebuilt and enlarged by Francis I. and Louis XIV., who was born here, as were Henry II. and Charles IX. It was the residence of Mary Stuart (in her youth), Henry IV., and James II. of England, who died here, 1701, and was buried in the Italian church, which has a monument to him by George IV. It is a large heavy pile, and after being used as a barrack and military school, is now a military penitentiary. A noble shaded terrace, begun by Henry IV, is above 100 feet broad, and 7870 feet long, and commands a fine prospect. The forest to the north was called *Laia* when the monastery of St. Germain was founded in the eleventh century; it covers 8,000 acres, and two fairs are held in it—one near the Château des Loges. La Muette pavilion is used for a racing stud, under Prince of Newmarket. Population, 13,500. Many English live here. Rev. N. Peyrat is the French Protestant pastor. *Hotels*—d'Angleterre; de Toulouse.

Coaches to Marly, Maule, Meulan, Poissy. At Cambourcy (2 kil.), near Marly forest, are some fine chesnuts, and the domain of Ketz, called the Desert.

ROUTE 4.

Paris to Evreux, Caen, and Cherbourg.

By Paris and Rouen rail to

BONNIERES (69 kil.) as in Route 1; thence by road to Cherbourg, 186 kil. or 115 miles.

PACY-SUR-EURE (15 kil. from Bonnières), a decayed town on the Eure, once fortified, and given up by Richard I. with other places to Philippe Auguste, 1196. About 20 kil. south, higher up the river, is the battle field of Ivry (*see* page 3).

At 18 kil. further is

Evreux. *Hotels*—du Grand Cerf (Stag); du Dauphin; de France; de Rouen; de la Belle Epine (Thorn).

Population, 11,850. Capital of department Eure, seat of a diocess, &c., and once the head of a county, which in norman times gave name to the D'Evreux, or Devereux family, (now Lord Hereford in England). It stands in a hollow, among orchards and gardens, on an island made by the Iton. The old roman town of *Aulerci Eburovices* (of which name the present is a corruption) was Vieil Evreux (9 miles off), where pieces of an aqueduct, baths, &c., have been found. The present town was burnt or harassed many times between 1119 and 1441, when it was finally taken by the French. It has good walks, broad streets, and several old-fashioned houses of wood and plaster.

The *Cathedral* is cross-shaped, and in various styles from norman downwards, to the sixteenth century, the oldest part being that built by Henry I. of England. It has a tower of about 260 feet, a good north portal, and Lady chapel, rose and other windows beautifully stained, besides some good carving in the choir.

St. Taurin's Church (which was part of an abbey founded in the seventh century, and now a priests' seminary,) has a very ancient specimen of the byzantine style (like the norman) in the south transept, and the saint's curious chasse, or ornamented shrine, as old as the thirteenth century. St. Gilles old church is now used as a stable. The Tour de l'Horloge, or belfry, was built 1472-97. Other buildings are the préfecture (over the hospital), the bishop's palace of the fifteenth century, the new hospital, the college or high school, library of 10,000 volumes, with a museum of antiquities, geology, &c. There is also a good botanic garden; and, not far off, there stood till lately, the château de Navarre, rebuilt, 1686, by the Duc de Bouillon on the site of one founded by Jeanne de Navarre, and given by Napoleon to Josephine, who lived in it for a time.

Manufactures of coarse cottons (coutil or ticking, &c.), stockings, linen, leather, and paper. Formerly it made flutes, and ivory and box-wood combs.

Conveyances to Paris, Rouen, Lisieux, Breteuil, Chartres, Dreux, &c.

From Evreux, on the road to Caen, you pass LA COMMANDERIE (18 kil.), where the Knights Templar had a seat.

[A little to the right is Neubourg, with a great hall and other parts of a castle, where Henry of England, son of Henry II. married Louis VII.'s daughter. Dupont de l'Eure, member of the late chamber of deputies, was born here.]

LA RIVIERE-THIBERVILLE (17 kil.), on the Rille, which falls into the Seine opposite Havre.

[A little further on to the left (13 kil.), is *Bernay*, a sous-préfecture in department Eure, on the Charentonne, with 7,000 people, who manufacture linens, flannels, cotton, &c. Besides some old houses and two churches, it has at the corn-hall part of a benedictine abbey, founded 1018, in the norman style. A cattle fair in March is attended by great numbers. *Hotels*—Le Cheval Blanc (White Horse); le Lion d'Or (Golden Lion).

About 10 kil. to the south-west of Bernay, is Broglie with its old church and seat of the Duc de Broglie.

About 6 kil. on the right of La Rivière is Brionne, in a pretty spot on the Rille, with good fishing. A council was held here, 1050.—A little below it is *Bec*, with the church tower (150 feet high), arches, and other remains of an abbey, founded 1034, by Hellouin (or Harlowyn), and used by the Benedictines of St. Maur, before the revolution. It produced archbishops Lanfranc, Anselm, Theobald, and Hubert, besides many bishops, appointed by the norman kings in England.]

L'Hotellerie (24 kil.), in the fertile Pays de Lieuvin, and department Calvados.

Lisieux (13 kil.), a sous-prèfecture in department Calvados, on the Touques where the Orbee joins it in a rich valley. It was the roman *Lexovii*. Henry II. of England married Eleanor here, 1152, and here his rebellious subject, Becket, came when exiled, 1169. Grand Rue is the best built street; the others are narrow and winding, with many curious timbered houses. There are eight Places, four halls, eleven fountains, three churches, an old bishop's palace (with good gardens), public library and museum, communal college, salle de spectacle, hospital, a public garden, &c.; and manufactures of coarse woollens, flannels, cotton, and other goods. St. Peter's cathedral church is mostly early gothic (with some norman portions as old as 1022), and has a good west front with two towers, and a lady chapel built in fifteenth century, by Bishop Cauchon to atone for the share he took in condemning Joan of Arc. Population, 12,000. *Hotels*—de France, de l'Espagne, de la Rose, &c.

[About 18 kil. to the right is Pont l'Evêque (*see* Route 5). At 18 kil. to the left is Livarot, noted for its cheese; and 10 kil. beyond it, Vimoutiers, where large manufactures of coarse linens, employ 20,000 people in and around it.]

Estrees (17 kil.) At 30 kil. further is

Caen. *Hotels.*—De la Place Royale, du Commerce, d'Angleterre, d'Espagne, de France. Dinners, 2 to 3 fr.; beds, 1 to 2 fr.

English Vice-Consul, P. Barrow. Post Office in Rue Hôtel de Ville. Service in English at the French Protestant Church, in Rue de la Geôle: Rev. C. Olive and E. Mellon are resident pastors.

Population, 44,000. A fine old town, where many English settle, capital of department Calvados, head of a military division, &c., in a fertile corn country on the Orne, where the Odon joins it, three leagues from the channel. It was called *Cathein* about the time (1066) that the Conqueror founded St. Etienne's Abbey, in which he was buried, his wife Matilda having founded a nunnery at the same time. The English, under Edward III., plundered it 1346 and again 1417, from which year they held it till 1450. Only the remains of its walls and 21 towers are left. It looks to great advantage as you approach it. The streets are wide, and the houses of stone—the Caen stone—which was used formerly in England; several old wooden gable fronted ones, with carvings, are seen. The best promenades are at Grand Cours, Place St. Sauveur, Place Royale (which has a statue of Louis XIV.), and the Quais, to which vessels of 150 tons come up. Of its 10 or 12 churches the most remarkable are—

St. Etienne's (Stephen's), or the Abbaye Aux Hommes, in the norman style, built 1066-77, and 370 ft. long, with three towers and two turrets, a fine west front, and a marble slab before the altar, marking where the bones of the Conqueror once rested. The building in the early pointed style near it belong to the High School or college.

Holy Trinity, or Abbaye Aux Dames, is also a large and excellent norman specimen, cross-shaped, with low towers, a monument of Queen Matilda the foundress, and having close to it the Hôtel Dieu or general Hospital (built 1726).

St. Pierre (Peter) has a beautiful light spire (built 1308), 240 ft. high, and a good vaulted roof.

St. Etienne-le-Vieil, a pointed church in decay, and serving as a corn market, has a soi-disant figure of the Conqueror. That of St. Nicholas, which he built 1066, in the norman style, is a cavalry stable. At the old castle, now used as a barrack, is another norman chapel. St. Jean's has two unequal towers, and St. Michel is a mixture of norman and other styles. The Château de Calix, or aux Gens d'armes, has some curious carving about it. Hotel de Valois, now the Bourse or exchange, is also ornamented with statues, &c.

Other buildings are the Hôtel de la Prefecture; the Palais de Justice, with a colonnade round it; large Public Library of 48,000 volumes, besides MSS.; Museum, having several good pictures and cabinet of natural history, which includes fossils of the oolite rocks, as the ichthyosaurus, &c.; Botanic Gardens, Deaf and Dumb School, Le Bon Sauveur Lunatic Asylum, &c. There are also an Academie or University, founded as far back as 1431, by the Regent Bedford, Schools of Medicine, Architecture, Navigation, &c., with Antiquarian and other Societies. They shew the house where Malherbe the poet was born; Bishop Huet was also a native, and wrote an account of the town. The unfortunate Beau Brummel died here in a madhouse.

Manufactures of millinery, hose, yarn, oil, paper, sugar, linen, &c., but especially lace, which the people in and around the town make all day long. Trade in oil, grain, cider, eaux-de-vie, fish, horses, &c.

Coaches to Cherbourg, Evreux and Paris, St. Malo, Granville, Nantes, Havre, Alençon, Tours, &c.; by steam, daily, to Havre in 3 or 4 hours. Several good village churches are seen in the neighbourhood; and within a distance of 6 or 8 miles are Ardenne old abbey, Nôtre Dame de la Delivrance (near Douvres, a norman chapel, visited by Louis XI. in 1571), on the road to the bathing place of Courseulles on the coast, and the castles of Creuilly and Fontaine Henri. Falaise is 39 kil. to the S.E. (*see* Route 92.)

From Caen, on the road to Cherbourg, you pass Maladrerie (1½ kil.) or Beaulieu, a house of detention, on the site of a lepers' hospital founded by Henry II. of England.

Bretteville (10 kil.), with a good church spire, is near that of Norrey, in the pure early-pointed style.

Bayeux (16 kil.), an old looking place, the ancient *Civitas Bajocassium*, sous-préfecture, and seat of a bishopric, with 9,800 people, on the Aure, in a fertile spot, is noted for its *Tapestry* or piece of worsted work on coarse linen, about 230 feet long and 20 inches wide, worked by Queen Matilda, to represent the Conquest of England by her husband. It is shewn at the public library (7,000 vols.), and a copy of it at the Antiquarian Society of London.

The *Cathedral*, on the site of that built 1077, by the Conqueror's brother, Bishop Odo, is of the 12th century, and has three carved porches, two towers, 246 ft. high, with good oak stalls, and a crypt under the choir; it is 334 ft. long.

At the *Bishop's Palace* is a series of portraits; the Hôtel Dieu was a chapel, built 1206; the Hôtel de Ville is ancient. There are two other churches, a museum, public baths, a new corn market, college, &c., and a house in Rue St. Malo where A. Chartier, the poet, and his brothers were born in the 15th century. Trade, in cattle, sheep, butter, cider, &c. *Hotels*—Du Luxembourg, Lion d'Or (Golden Lion), Grand Hôtel.

The road to St. Lo and Awranches turns off here, (*see* Route 7.) The country called the Bocage, or woodland, between this and Isigny, is very fine.

Formigny (16 kil.), where the English were beaten in 1405, and obliged, finally, to give up Normandy.

Isigny (16 kil.) a pretty little port in the bay, at the mouth of the Vire and Aure, on the Channel. It is noted for its fresh and salt butter, in which it carries on a large trade, and cider.

Carentan (13 kil.), a fortified town in a marshy spot, at the top of a creek, which runs up from the east side of the Cotentin peninsula. It has a good church, and a ruined château fort.

[About 20 kil. west is the Abbey of Blancheland, founded in the 12th century. On the coast, 10 kil. west-south-west, is the fine Abbey Church of Lessay, in the norman style. Jersey is in the distance.]

St. Mere Eglise (13 kil.) has a good church, and a trade in grain, butter, and cattle. About 10 kil. north-east of it is the Grande Cheminée of Quineville on the coast, a rock 27 ft. high.

[About 17 kil. to the west, at St. Sauveur, on the Douve, is a ruined abbey, founded by the Harcourts, with an old castle, which Edward III. gave to John Chandos.]

Valognes (17 kil.), a sous-préfecture of 6,400 people, on the Murderet, near the site of the roman *Alauna* or *Lonia*. It has a college of some pretensions, and a library of 15,000 vols. Traces of a roman temple, aqueduct, &c., were seen till lately, and it had a castle of William the Conqueror's.

[About 12 kil. west-south-west is Briquebec castle, with a keep 100 ft. high. Near this are the Grosses Roches (druid stones), and a Trappist convent. At 16 kils. north-east is St. Waast-la-Hogue.]

At 20 kil. further, at the end of the peninsula of Cotentin, is

Cherbourg. *Hotels*—D'Angleterre, (on the Quai), du Commerce, de France, du Louvre.

Protestant Chapel, in Rue du Vieux Quai, opened 1835; Rev. M. Robineau, is the resident French Protestant pastor. Post-office, on the Quai.

Population, 27,000. A strong naval station and fortress of the first class, seat of a maritime préfect, &c., in the cliffs, at the mouth of the Divette, which spreads into a wide road or bay, with the great breakwater called the Digue in front. It is about 60 miles due south of the Needles. The town is a collection of narrow streets, and houses of stone and slate. A quay lines the commercial dock (Port du Commerce) at the gap of the river. The Hôtel de Ville has Vauban's original plan of the arsenal, a gallery of pictures, &c., chiefly French and Flemish, bequeathed by a native, T. Henry, whose bust is here; with a library of 2,400 volumes, a museum, &c.; in front is a pillar to the Duc de Berri. St. Trinité Church, near the sea, and an old tower, was built 1450, except the spire, added 1825; it is 151 feet long. The chapel of Nôtre Dame du Vœu (*i.e.* of the Vow) in Chantier de Chantereine, and only 49 feet long, replaces one built by Queen Maude, who landed here in a storm. Another church, in the gothic style, was built in 1831. There are a college, theatre, navigation school, baths, fountains, &c. The naval *Dock* and *Arsenal* to the west was begun by Napoleon, in 1803, and is still unfinished. Two docks (out of three) are opened, each about 950 feet long, and nearly as broad; they have been excavated out of the slaty cliffs by gunpowder. About 2,000 men are still employed upon them; it is calculated they will take ten years yet to complete; but when finished, they will be 60 to 70ft. deep, and large enough to hold all the French navy. Around are six building slips (cales de construction) on granite piers; dry dock (forme de radoub), blacksmiths' shops (ateliers des forges); timber shed (hangar aux bois), 960 feet long; machine shops (ateliers des machines), magazines, park of artillery, museum (salle des modèles), large barracks for seamen and soldiers, telegraph office, &c. The *Digue*, or Dyke, off the town, is a breakwater 3,760 metres, or 4,711 yards long (2½ times longer than the Plymouth), and 31 broad at top. It was begun 1782, carried on by Napoleon and Louis Philippe, and completed 1851; the stones being supplied in making the docks, and sunk in great cones. It was upon one of these that Captain Brenton grounded in the Minerve, 1803, and was taken after a struggle of 36 hours to escape. It is strengthened by Fort du Hommet, near the middle, which carries a light; other lights are at the fort on Ile Pelée, near the east corner, where the way in is 1½ miles broad, and on Point Querqueville (near that fort) on the main land, to the west, where the fair way is ¾ of a mile broad. There are from 6 to 7 fathoms at low water, inside, and room for 100 sail or more. High water at moon's full and change, 7 hours 45 min. Forts on the heights around command any part of the road. The English held this town 1418-50, and again in 1758, when General Bligh burnt the old dockyard, &c. James II. was here at the battle of La Hogue; Charles X. embarked here, 1830; and Don Pedro landed here 1831. A little lace and coarse cloth are made; fish are caught, and eggs, &c. sent to England. A French Mail Company, with 20 or 30 steamers, from here to the United States and West Indies, is talked of.

Conveyances, by coach, to Barfleur, Granville, St. Malo, &c.; by steam, to Havre, twice a-week, in 10 hours,—10 and 12 fr. In summer a steamer to Guernsey and Weymouth. Tourlaville castle, now a farm, or glass factory, lies to the south-east.

(*a*) From Cherbourg, to the east, you pass Maupertuis (10 kil.); St. Pierre, (13 kil.) near Chateau de Tocqueville; and then at about 22 kil. you come to

Barfleur, a decayed port, which Edward III. plundered, 1346, but which, in norman times, was the starting point for England. Upon the rocks, near this, Henry the First's son William was lost in the Blanche Nef,—a loss which struck such a blow to the king's heart that they say he never smiled afterwards. To the north of it is Cape Barfleur, or Cape de Gatteville, which has a granite lighthouse 236 feet high, with an intermittent flash, seen seven leagues off. About 8 miles south of it is Waast La Hogue, which gives name to the naval action of 1692, when Rooke burnt the French fleet, under Tourville.

(*b*) From Cherbourg, to the west, you come to Beaumont (14 kil.), and then to

CAPE LA HAGUE (21 kil.), which is sometimes mistaken for Waast la Hogue, has several reefs round it, and on the Gros de Ray rock, a fixed light, 157 high, seen six leagues round. The Race of Alderney, where the tide runs six and seven miles an hour, divides it from Alderney and the other Channel Islands in the distance.

ROUTE 5.

Rouen to Caen and Cherbourg.

Distance, 133 kil., or 83 miles. A rail is projected in this direction.

ROUEN, as in Route 1.

PETIT QUEVILLY (3 kil.), on the south side of the Seine, so called they say after the fence (cheville) made by the Norman dukes round their hunting-grounds, and having St. Julien's norman chapel (a barn), built by Henry II. of England. A little further is Grand Quevilly, which had an immense Protestant church in Henry IV.'s time, pulled down in 1686. The Princesse de Montmorency's chateau is near.

MOULINEAUX (8 kil.), in a fine spot, opposite the little spire church of Sahur, has on a hill the picturesque remains of the castle of a fierce soldier called Robert le Diable (of Pepin's time), the hero of Meyerbeer's opera. It was destroyed by King John, who some say killed his nephew here.

BOUILLE (4 kil.), to which steamers from Rouen come, stands under the cliffs, and is a favourite trip of the citizens. Le Londe forest, Caumont quarries, and Jacqueline grotto, are near.

BOURZARCHARD (7 kil).

PONT-AUDEMER (23 kil.), a sous-préfecture, of 6,860 population, in the fertile valley of the Rille, called after Odomar, who founded it in the fifth century. It suffered in the English and civil wars. It has three or four churches. Trade in leather (for which it is noted), corn, cider, wool, &c. *Hotels*—De l'Image de St. Pierre, de Lion d'Or (Golden Lion).

[At 12 kil. is Quillebœuf, a pilot station, on a point of the Seine, which the Norman dukes gave to Jumièges Abbey, and whose walls were reduced by Louis XIV. Population, 1,350. The Seine is full of shifting sands here, and the tide frequently rushes in with a bore six feet high, doing harm to the shipping.]

HONFLEUR (23 kil.), a port of 10,000 souls (department Calvados), with three basins, and building slips, whence frigates have been launched. It has several old streets and houses. St. Catherine's Church, which at first was built in the 5th century of wood, has two pictures by Rubens' pupils, Jordaens and Quellin. St. Leonard's is as old as the 12th century. From the little fishermen's chapel of Nôtre Dame de Grace, on the hill outside the town, there is a fine sea view; and an excellent prospect may be got from La Roque, up the river. Various manufactures thrive here; eggs, fruit, butter, &c., are sent to England, and there is a trade in honey, cider, and fish, &c. High water at Moon's change, about 10h. *Hotels*—Le Cheval Blanc (White Horse), la Poste, d'Angleterre, &c.

PONT L'EVEQUE (16 kil.), a small sous-préfecture of 2,200 souls, in the valley of the Touques, where they make lace and good cheese. At the mouth of the river, 11 kil. lower, is the little bathing place and fishing village of Trouville-sur-Mer, which is frequented from June to September, when steamers run to Havre.

DOZULLE (18 kil.), near on the Dive, which is navigable to this point, and remarkable as the river where the Conqueror collected part of his fleet for invading England, in 1066.

At 26 kil. further is Caen; thence to Cherbourg, as in Route 4.

ROUTE 6.

Evreux to Alencon.

Distance, 119 kil., or 74 miles.

EVREUX, as in Route 4.

CONCHES (18 kil.), a village where nails are made. Neuve Lyre is the next place; then Rugles, (population 2,100) on the Rille, with manufactures of nails, pins, and needles; then L'Aigle, (36 kil. from Conches) with a population of 5,600, who make pins, needles, lacets (a kind of lace,) &c. It has two churches, one (St. Barthèlemi), as old as 1115, and chiefly norman; and a brick château.

NONANT (32 kil.); then Seez (12 kil.), as in Route 92. Alençon is 21 kil. further.

ROUTE 7.

Bayaux to Avranches

BY ST. LO.

Distance, 90 kil., or 56 miles.

BAYEUX, as in Route 4.

VAUBADON (13 kil.), on the Dromme.

LITTEAU (12 kil.)

At 9 kil. further is

St. Lo. *Hotels*—Du Soleil Levant (Rising Sun); du Cheval Blanc (White Horse.)

Population 8,300. An ancient town, and capital of department Manche, once the seat of a bishopric, founded by St. Laudus, 549. It stands in a pretty spot on a rock by the Vire. The Normans destroyed it in 890, but afterwards restored it, though it was almost ruined again, in 1346, by Edward IV., who took it by storm.

Notre Dame Cathedral Church is on the hill, near Petit Place; it is chiefly gothic, of the 12th century, with two good tall spires in its west front, which is of later date. A stone pulpit stands outside. Another church, St. Croix, in the early norman style, replaces one attached to the abbey founded by Charlemagne, about 810, when the town was walled round and improved. There is a salle de spectacle, also public baths, a museum of antiquities, a library of 4,500 volumes, &c. A Roman stone, called the Marbre de Torigni, is now at Caen.

Lace, ribbons, and cloth are made, and the trade is in grain, cattle, poultry, butter, cider, fruit, &c., and cavalry horses, which are bred at the haras, near St. Croix. Conveyances to Caen, Cherbourg, Coutances, Granville, &c.

[*Coutances*, 27 kil. west-south-west, a sous-préfecture and bishopric, on a hill 7 kil. from the sea, to which the Soule river or canal runs, is noted for its beautiful early english *Cathedral*, with its two west spires, the clustered pillars in the nave, (which is 100 feet high), and the octagon lantern, which commands a view of the sea and Channel Islands. Other buildings are the churches of St. Nicholas and St. Peter, the library of 4,500 volumes, the theatre, the Hôtel Dieu, &c. Near the Palais de Justice is a bronze figure of Prince Lebrun, arch-treasurer under Napoleon. There are remains of the fortifications, and part of an aqueduct called Les Piliers, from the columns which it rests on. Parchment, cloth, &c., are made. *Hotels*—De France, d'Angleterre.

In the neighbourhood are the Pont-de-la Roque, St. Gerbold's hermitage, the castles of Régneville, Lithenaire, Mauny, Gavray, the abbeys of Blanchelande and Hambye—the latter founded by the Paganels, who settled in Engand at the Conquest.]

VILLEBAUDON (19 kil.), at the head of the Soule.

PERCY (6 kil.), was the seat of William de Percy, who went over to England with the Conqueror, and being surnamed Alsgernon (or whiskered), Algernon has always been a favourite name with that noble family.

VILLEDIEU-LES-POELES (9 kil.), where the roads to Vire (*see* Route 93) and Granville part off, has been noted for its manufactures of copper goods from a very ancient date.

[At 28 kil. west, is *Granville*, on the cliffs, in sight of the Channel Islands, with a good sized but shallow harbour, inside a fine mole, and well fortified. The Vendeans tried to take it in 1793. An old gothic church has carvings in granite, and a spire 312 feet above the sea. The people (7,350) are pilots, fishermen, boat-builders, and carry on a trade in grain, cider, salt, &c. There is a light on Cape Lihou 154 feet from the sea. J. Turnbull is the English consul. High water at full and change, 6h. 30m., the tide setting in with dangerous swiftness. A steamer comes from Jersey, every Monday morning (on the arrival of that from Southampton), and returns on Tuesday, in turn with that to St. Malo. It passes the Chausée, Minquières, and other shoals which abound here.]

AVRANCHES, (22 kil.) near St. Michael's Bay on the coast, a sous-préfecture of 7,269 inhabitants, many of whom are English, who settle here for economy and the pleasantness of its situation among the hills. The Romans called it *Abrincæ Ingenæ*, and it was fortified by St. Louis. St. André cathedral church, built about 1120, by Henry 11. of England, was pulled down at the revolution. A statue of Valhubert, a native, who fell at Austerlitz, stands in the bishop's garden. The public Library of 15,000 vols., has also 200 MSS., (including one of Abelard's which M. Cousin published 1836,) and a Museum. A fine view from the Jardin des Plantes. *Hotels* — de France, de Bretagne, d'Angleterre. Trade in grain, cider, hops, &c. Conveyances—Daily, to Caen, Cherbourg, Rennes, Granville, Mortain, St. Malo.

[The famous *Mont St. Michel* (16 kil., south-west), in name, appearance and history is very like St. Michael's Mount, in Cornwall. It is a heap of rugged granite, very steep on the north side but sloping on the east and south, where the people (300) with their little gardens scraped from the rocks live round the old abbey, now a convict prison. The beach below it is a shelly sand completely covered at high water, but a causeway leads to it when the tide is low, from Ardevon where guides may be got. The Druids had a station here, which the early Christians used as a hermitage, and afterwards turned into a monastery, of which the remains are still picturesque. The great door is flanked by two solid towers; on the north side is a part called la Merveille, or the Wonder, including the large Montgomery rooms, the refectory (90 feet long, a good specimen of gothic), the hall of the Chevaliers (nearly as long), the cloister, the well preserved choir of the church, and the crypt below resting on great pillars of granite.]

SECTION II.

ROADS TO THE NORTH;

IN CONNEXION WITH THE CHEMIN-DE-FER DU NORD (NORTHERN RAILWAY); SUPPLYING ST. DENIS, BEAUVAIS, ST. QUENTIN, AMIENS, BOULOGNE, CALAIS, ARRAS, LILLE, DUNKIRK, BRUSSELS, COLOGNE, (AND THENCE TO BERLIN, VIENNA, ETC.), IN THE OLD PROVINCES OF PICARDY, ARTOIS, FLANDERS.—ROUTES TEN TO FOURTEEN.

ROUTE 10.

Paris to Calais.

Embarcadère, or terminus, Clos St. Lazare, 24, Place Roubaix, near the barrière St. Denis, opened 1846; distance to Boulogne 272 kil. or 170 miles; to Calais, 378 kil. or 236 miles; four trains a day; 6½ to 12½ hours to Calais; 5½ to 9 hours to Boulogne, (changing at Longeau and Amiens). Fares 38½, 29, 21½ fr. to Calais; 28, 21, 15¾ fr. to Boulogne, (or *through* to London, 50½, 37, 27½ shillings). Luggage allowed, 60 lb. Buffets for refreshment at Creil, Amiens, Douai, Lille.

Omnibuses to all the trains. About thirteen trains start for shorter distances; those to Enghein almost hourly. Paris time, which is 15 minutes before London time, is kept.

The stations to Calais, are—

	kil.		kil.		kil.
St. Denis ...	¾	Ile Adam ...	6	Clermont...	8½
Enghein ...	¾	Beaumont...	6½	St. Just ...	12
Ermont	13	Boran.........	7	Breteuil ...	15½
Franconville	3	Brecy	4½	Ailly	16½
Herblay	3	St. Leu	3½	Boves	10½
Pontoise......	8½	Creil	6½	Amiens ...	8½
Auvers	5	Liancourt ...	7	Corbie	5½

	kil.		kil.		kil.
Albert	16	Carvin	6	Hazebrouck	6½
Achiet	18½	Seclin	8	Eblinghem	9½
Boileux ...	9	Lille	12	St. Omer ...	11
Arras	8½	Perenchies	8	Watten......	9
Rœux	9½	Armentières	7	Audruicq ...	11½
Vitry.........	6½	Steenweeck	7½	Ardres	8
Douai	10	Bailleul......	4	StPierre-Cal.	11
Leforest	7	Strazeele ...	8	Calais	2½

The railway passes by Chapelle St Denis, just outside the Barrière, which divides the city from the old province of Ile deFrance now department Seine; then Montmartre, 300 feet above the Seine, with a church, citadel, and reservoir on top, whence there is a fine view of Paris. It is noted for its quarries (plaster of Paris), windmills, and guinguettes. Clignancourt (on the left) and Aubervilliers (right), are next passed; then St. Ouen on the Seine, (6 kil. from Paris) to the left, with a château where Louis XVIII. promised a charter to the nation, 1814. It has, in the caves, large granaries and ice-houses.

St. Denis, (3¾ miles), a sous-prèfecture of department Seine, with 12,500 population, on two little branches of the Seine, and on the canal joining the river to Canal de l'Ourcq, is noted for the burial place of the French kings, in the church of the Benedictine Abbey, founded 613, by Dagobert. Length, 390 feet; breadth, 100; and 80 feet high to the vault. It was rebuilt, 1144–1281; the oldest part being Abbe Segur's front and towers, one of which was till lately, 360 feet high; and has been restored by Napoleon and his successors, with great splendour. The new windows are stained with historical subjects, and the chapels, &c., are full of paintings and frescoes. Among the monuments, &c., are those of Dagobert, (not older than St. Louis's time;) Louis XII. and Queen; Henry II. and Queen; Francis I. and Queen; Duguesclin the soldier; Henry III. and IV.; Francis I. (Mary Stuart's husband), and the twelve apostles in the Chœur d'Hivre; the oriflamme, or banner of France used to be kept here; there is a fine organ. In the crypt below are statues and cenotaphs of all the sovereigns, some as old as the eleventh century. The abbey house as rebuilt by Cotte is used as an asylum for orphans of the Legion of Honour, founded 1809. Omnibuses run to Paris. Many corn-mills, breweries, and tanneries; a large sheep fair in June. A bridge across Ile St. Denis in the Seine, leads to Gennevilliers. *Hotels*—Du Grand Cerf, (Stag), de France; excellent fish and cheese cakes. Coaches to the following places:—

[Epinay (4 kil. east) on the Seine, has many country houses, with that of Brêche, which Gabrielle d'Estrées, Henry IV.'s mistress, lived in. Fourcroy, Lacepède, Marquis Somariva, &c., resided here; Mad. Houdetot at Ormesson. Arnouville to the north-east, on the Crould, has an old unfinished château, of the last century, built by garde-des-sceaux (lord keeper) Machault. A little further on is Gonesse, the birth-place of Philippe Auguste, 1166, and for a long time famous for its bread. At 9 kil. north is Ecouen château on a hill, built in the renaissance style, with high roof, pilasters, &c. Latterly it belonged to the prince of Condé.]

ENGHIEN-LES-BAINS (3½ miles), on lake St. Gratien, is known for its sulphur waters, used between June and September, and a large bathing-house, ball-room, &c. The springs were discovered in 1766, and have about 60° temp.; the neighbourhood is very pleasant. Coaches to Groslay, and

[*Montmorency* (3 kil. north), a pretty place on a hill, founded 1008, by Burchard the Bearded. It gave name to a noble house, the premier Christian Barons, as they used to be called; and came to the family of Condé with the title of Duke, which Louis XIV. changed to that of Enghein, after the above place. The large gothic church of the fourteenth century, has good stained glass. One walk through the chesnut forest leads to Ecouen, past the hermitage where the pernicious sentimentalist Rousseau, wrote his Emile, &c.; it has his bust and furniture; Gretry the composer died in it.]

At Sannois, a little further, a road turns off south to Argenteuil on the Seine.

ERMONT (2 miles), from which coaches go to Margency; to Andilly (a fine spot in Montmorency forest); St. Brix; and Eaubonne, in a pretty valley of the forest, near an oak planted by Franklin, who lived here, as did St. Lambert, Rousseau, &c.

FRANCONVILLE (1¾ miles). Coach to St. Leu-Taverney, (3 kil. north), where Mad. de Genlis had a seat, which the last Duke of Bourbon hung himself in, 1830. The gothic church of the thirteenth and fourteenth century, is worth notice for its interior carving.

HERBLAY (¾ mile), lies to the left, by the Seine.

PONTOISE (5½ miles), a sous-préfecture of 4,300 persons, in department Seine-et-Oise, on a rock, over the Oise, (where the Viosne, joins,) here crossed by a bridge or pont, which gave it its present and its ancient name (Briva-Isaræ). It was held by the Normans, and by Talbot, 1419-41. St. Maclou church is ancient, and has an alarm bell, with an inscription on it. There also a large Hospital, a library of 3000 vols., remains of its old walls and castle. Trade in grain, calves, &c. General Leclerc was a native. *Hotels*—Des Messageries, du Pot d'Etain (Pewter Pot). Coaches to Magny and Gisors (*see* Route 1.) and to Marines, Moyneville, and

[Chaumont-Oise, (30 kil. north-west), on a hill, topped by the gothic church, where there is a wide prospect. The houses are of good brick. Blonde lace, leather, &c., are made; and there are large fairs for cattle and horses.]

The railway here turns north-east up the Oise.

AUVERS (2½ miles), on the Oise.

ILE-ADAM (4½ miles), so called from an island in the river, on which stood a château built 1200, by the seigneurs, one of whom was the famous Grand Master of the Knights of St. John, Philippe de-l'Ile-Adam, who held out so long at the siege of Rhodes, 1522, against 200,000 Turks.

BEAUMONT-SUR-OISE, (4½ miles), on a rock at the bridge over the river, has a tower of its old feudal castle, which commanded the pass here. The promenade overlooks a rich prospect. Coaches to Viarmes, (near Royaumont old abbey, in Chantilly forest); Noailles, (near Pierre-aux-Fées, druid stones); Jouey, Presle, &c.

[At 12 kil. east is Luzarches, on a hill side, with remains of a château on the site of a palace which Charlemagne gave to St. Denis' Abbey. The Collegiate Church, of the thirteeth century, was built over the relics of St. Côme, the patron of surgeons.]

BORAN (4½ miles).

PRECY (2½ miles).

Mortefontaine (18 kil. south-east), has a château, built 1770, which belonged to Joseph Bonaparte when the French treaty with America was signed here, 1800. The preliminaries of the peace of Amiens were adjusted in the Valhère pavilion, in the park, (on the site of a castle of the eleventh century,) where they used to shew the boat in which Sir Sidney Smith was captured, 1796. It is a picturesque mixture of woods, hills, rocks, lakes, canals, falls, &c., and thought to be more English than any other place in France. Traces of a Roman camp are at Butte-Mahet.]

ST. LEU-D'ESSERENT, (2½ miles), in department Oise, on a hill side, with a conspicuous church in the transition style. It has important lime quarries, and lace is made. Coaches to the following:—

[*Chantilly* (4 kil. east), which belonged to the Counts of Senlis, has remains of a seat of the Montmorencies and the great Condé, who was visited by Louis XIV., when Vatel, his cook, killed himself because the fish had not come, and which, as enlarged by his family, was pulled down at the revolution. What remains, including a hunting château on the lake, a chapel, splendid stables, for 180 horses, (built 1719-35.), the English garden and grounds, were sold, 1852, by the Duke d' Aumale, along with the forest of 20,000 acres, and Hez forest of 43,000 acres, to Majoribanks and Antrobus, the bankers, for 11,000,000 fr. Twelve roads meet at the centre of this, called the Round Table, where the 'Derby' and 'St. Leger' are run for, at the annual races of the French Jockey Club. On lake Commelle, is the lodge, built, they say, by St. Louis's mother, Blanche of Castile, and lately restored. Blonde lace, pottery, articles in wood, thread, linen, &c. are made. Population 2,400. *Hotels*—De Bourbon, Condé, d'Angleterre.

Senlis (7 kil. further), a sous-préfecture, 5,800 population, in department Oise, on a hill-side among the forests of Halatte, Chantilly, &c, where the Aunette and Nonette join, was the capital of the *Silvanectes*, in Cæsar's time, and has traces of roman-built walls, with several old gates, as the Porte de Maux, Porte de Bellon, Porte de Compiègne, &c., besides St. Louis' ruined castle. Philippe Auguste was married here, 1180, to Elizabeth of Hainault; and it stood seven or eight fierce assaults of the Leaguers, 1588. The old cathedral church, rebuilt by Louis XII., on the site of Charlemagne's, has a plain front, with a corner spire on a pinnacled tower, 225 feet high; also two good north and south porches, by Francis I. There are besides a theatre in St. Aignan's old church, an hospice, now the Hôtel de Ville, a public library of 8,000 vols. At 2 kil. from it is the old abbey of St. Victoire, a favourite of Louis XI. The cross-bow men of this place were noted in the sixteenth century. Trade in wool, cotton, lace, grain, wine, chicory, stone, &c. *Hotels*—Du Grand Cerf (Stag), de Paris.]

CREIL (4½ miles), where the branch line to St. Quentin, &c. turns off (*see* Route 11) is among hills, on the Oise, and has an old bridge, a church with a good spire, manufactories of pottery and pipes, with traces of the old château, (on an island) where Charles VI. was placed when lunatic, and of St. Evremond's Abbey. Coach to Senlis.

LIANCOURT (4¼ miles), on the Bresche, in a pretty spot, has part of the château (of the time of Louis XIII.) of the late Duc de la Rochefoucald-Liancourt, who after the revolution, established an English farm here, with a school of industry, &c., besides introducing vaccination He is buried in the park, under a plain tomb.

CLERMONT-OISE (5½ miles), a sous-préfecture, of 3,200 souls, was burnt by the English, 1359, and has a famous prospect, on the hill over the Bresche, from the Chatellier promenade, close to the old castle, now a Central House of Detention for women. There are also a museum of agriculture and geology, with a library of 6,000 vols., and manufactures of cotton, linen, leather. At St. Felix, in the neighbourhood, excellent fossil shells are found. *Hotel*—L'Epée (Sword).

Coaches to Beauvais, Mony, Crevecœur, Grandvilliers.

[**Beauvais**, 26 kil. west-north-west of Clermont. *Hotels*—D'Angleterre, des Trois Piliers (Three Pillars, which are seen at a house, near the cathedral), du Cygne (Swan), de l' Ecu (Crown Piece.)

Population, 12,867. Chief town of department Oise, and a bishopric, with a tribunal de première instance, college, societies of agriculture, and arts, and manufactures, &c. standing in a fertile valley, on the rivers Thérain and Avalon, on the old road to Calais. This very ancient town, was the Roman *Cæsaromagus* or *Bellovaci* which joined the league against Cæsar, without success. It gave name to the insurrection of the 'Jacquerie,' in king John's time, after one Jacques, a man of Beauvais, who headed the mob against their feudal oppressors. The English besieged it, 1472, but were repulsed by Jean Lignière. It was again attempted, by Charles the Bold, with 80,000 men, in 1472, when it was so well defended, by the valour of Jeanne Laine, or Jeanne la Hachette, and the women of the town, that they have taken precedence of the men, in an annual procession, in October, ever since. This heroine's picture and banner are in the Hôtel de Ville. In La Cité, the oldest part, some round towers of solid construction may be seen, as ancient as the third or fourth century. The ramparts of the twelfth century are laid out as promenades. You will notice a great number of timbered houses, curiously carved, with their gables turned to the narrow streets.

St. Pierre Cathedral, in Rue St. Pierre, with its buttresses and pinnacles, is the great object of attraction. It was begun, 1225, and is incomplete, having no nave or steeple. The latter was overturned in a storm, 1574. A fine rose window stands over the entrance, in the south porch, which is full of niches and other ornaments. The magnificent choir, is 51 feet broad, but 145 feet high! so that in this respect it exceeds even that at Amiens, by 13 feet, and Westminster, by about 57 feet. It is the highest choir, or perhaps roof, in the world. The transepts were built, 1500-55. The long narrow windows are richly stained. In the chapel is the kneeling effigy of Cardinal Forbin de Janson, by Coustou, and a piece of tapestry, the "Healing of the Paralytic." A part called the Basse Œuvre, on the west side is of the ninth century.

St. Etienne's (St. Stephen's) is a transition Church, older than the cathedral, with good stained windows of the sixteenth century. Formerly this town had three abbeys, seven convents, six collegiate, and thirteen parish churches, a commandery of St. John, &c.

The *Bishop's Palace*, now the Préfecture, is in the castle style, with towers, &c. The Hôtel de Ville, in the grand place, is a fine, regular building, with an ionic front, built 1754. There are also, the college, the bibliothèque, or public library of 7,000 vols., the Hôtel Dieu, a salle de spectacle, or theatre, the government tapestry factory, founded by Colbert, cavalry barracks, &c. L'Ile Adam, grand master at the siege of Rhodes, was a native. Small canals and branches of the Thérain run through the town. Manufactures of woollens, flannels, good carpets, tapestry, shawls, linens (demi-Hollandes), felt for hats, cotton thread, black lace; and commerce in grain, wine, woollen, and other goods. Conveyances, to the railway, to Rouen, Dieppe, &c.

Crèvecœur (20 kil. north), has the fine old brick château, of its seigneurs; and in the church are good fragments of the tomb of Admiral Bonnivet, the favourite of Francis I.

Grandvilliers (11 kil. north-west of this), in a wide plain, was founded, 1213, by a bishop of Beauvais, and has near it the castle of Damerancourt, a curious seven-storied building, with battlements and corner towers, 106 feet high—and the pretty château of Sarcus, built 1522, for one of the mistresses of Francis I.

From Beauvais, on the road to Dieppe, you pass Gournay (31 kil.) a small place on the Epte, near the mineral water of Jouvence. Dieppe is 74 kil. further. (*see* Route 2.)]

St. Just (8½ miles), at the head of the Arre. Coaches to Roye, Ansauvilliers, Cavilly, Montdidier, Rosières.

Breteuil (9¾ miles), 6 kil. from the railway, is at the Noye's head, and takes its name from the roman *Brantuspansium* (1 kil. south-east), where coins, &c., have been discovered, and which was destroyed by the barbarians in the fifth century. It came into notice after St. Marie's abbey was founded, 1049; was fortified, and taken by the English; and belonged to the Montmorencies, and others. The church is as old as 1226. Coaches to the town, and to Beauvais, Crevecœur, Aumale, Montdidier, Roye.

[At 13 kil. west is *Montdidier*, a sous-préfecture of 3,800 souls, in department Somme, on a hill by the Dom, was a seat of the Merovingian kings, and has remains of its walls, with many old houses and buildings in its narrow streets. St. Pierre's Church, though large and ugly, has a carved porch and curious effigies of one of its early counts, Raoul II. In the porch of St. Sepulchre's stands the tomb of another Raoul, as old as 1074; and its pulpit deserves notice. At the Hôtel de Ville, in the belfry is a niched figure, called Jean Duquesne, to strike the hours. The ancient bailliage is turned into the law court, or tribunal, where several pieces of tapestry are to be seen. A cabinet of natural history is placed in the College, a large building; as is the hospital, or Hôtel Dieu. It was an Aubry de Montdidier who was overcome in single combat, and murdered in the forest of Bondy, by Macaire, and the murder discovered by the victim's dog—the dog of Montargis. Trade in grain, cattle, leather, stockings, &c.; excellent pork pies are made. *Hotels*—De Condé; de Grenadier.]

Ailly-sur-Noye (10¼ miles), on the Noye. Coaches to Conty, Hangest, and Moreuil.

[Moreuil (8 kil. east) on the Ayre, or Avre, has paper and stocking factories, and the château of Margaret de Rougé. Near it, on a high hill, is the Folleville Tower, sometimes called Beauvoir, for the fine view it commands. It has a very striking appearance, and stands above 100 feet high. The chapel remains, having the marble effigies of Raoul de Launay (and his wife), viceroy of Naples, with a chain round it, similar to one given him by Louis XI. at the taking of Quesnoy.]

Boves (6¾ miles), on the Noye, where the Ayre joins it. At 5¼ miles further is

Amiens. *Hotels*—De France et d'Angleterre, first-rate, and highly recommended; du Rhin, Place St. Denis, close to the railway, highly recommended; de Londres et du Nord, opposite the railway station, and very good.

Population, 47,117. A large, fortified, and very old town, the capital of department Somme (formerly of Picardy), seat of a cour impèriale (assize court), tribunal, university, college and bishopric, on the river Somme, which divides itself in its course here into eleven or twelve canals, and contributes to its manufacturing prosperity. It was the Roman *Ambiani*. The Spaniards took it by stratagem, 1597, but it was almost immediately recovered. In 1802, the "Peace of Amiens" was signed here as being a sort of half way place between London and Paris—a *petite paix*, at which the English rejoiced so much, that it made Nelson say he was "ashamed of his country," and which lasted about a twelvemonth. They still shew the room where the plenipotentiaries met. The streets and houses are regular; the largest place or square is the Marché aux Herbes (herb market), which extends about 145 yards by 48. Good walks are laid out on the old fortifications; but the best is the Hautoye promenade, which is regularly planted, and has a large piece of water.

Virgin Mary Cathedral, one of the finest in France, was built between 1220 and 1288, Bishop de Fouillay having laid the first stone. Length, about 440 feet, height of spire, an elegant one, 425;

the nave, which is 45 feet broad, is of the surprising height of 141 feet! But the front, flanked by two towers, and pierced at the base by three deep portals, is the finest part. It has a circular window above; and the whole is a wonderful profusion of tracery, bas-reliefs, niched figures, including the 'Last Judgment,' 'Virtues and Vices,' the 'Months and Seasons,' the 'Massacre of the Innocents,' &c. The nave is supported by above 120 delicate pillars, some of which sounds like a bell when struck. Notice also the circular gallery, the fine windows (not stained), the tombs of the founders Godefrey d'Eu and Cardinal Hemart, the carved stalls and pulpit, and the monument of the enfant pleureur (weeping child). It is in course of repair.

Hôtel de Ville, built by Henry IV., stands on arcades, and has some pictures.

The *Public Library* (bibliothèque) is a large building in the ionic style, with a good collection of 45,000 volumes, including 400 volumes of MSS.

Other buildings are the préfecture, the lycée or college, the museum, corn market, citadel, jardin des plantes (botanic garden), cemetery of la Madeleine, hospital of St. Charles, the cavalry barracks, la Barge cloister of the 14th century, the 'King's House,' in the passage of that name (Logis du Roi).

Peter the Hermit, Ducange the scholar, the poet Gresset, Delambre, the astronomer, were born here.

Manufactures of velvet, camlet, plush, ribands, and cotton goods. Good pâtés are made; and savon du nord (soap).

Conveyances, by railway to Abbeville, Boulogne, Calais, Paris; and to Arras, Douai, Valenciennes, Dunkerque, Mons, Brussels, &c. Public carriages to Doullens, Aumale. The old châteaux of Baves and d'Hœilly, may be visited from this point. The railway to Abbeville and Boulogne is described in Route 12.

[Villers-Bretonneux (16 kil. east), on the Peronne road, has a thriving stocking manufacture.

Aumale (43 kil. west-south-west) on the Rouen road, pleasantly seated on the Bresle, gives title to the Duc d'Aumale, and has two columns near the bridge where Henry IV., was wounded on his way from Rouen. The old fort stood about a dozen sieges. On the north side are some useful mineral waters; and the ruins of Auchy abbey are not far off.

Neufchâtel (*see* Route 2) is 25 kil. further; thence to Dieppe 47 kil., or to Rouen 46 kil.]

Corbie (9¾ miles) has the curious portal, &c., of a benedictine abbey, founded 664 by St. Bathilde. Coaches to Harlonnières and Rosières.

Albert (10 miles), on a branch of the river Ancre, which makes a fine cascade here. It has a quarry, in which various fossils are found; and at the church is an image of "our Lady of Breberie," to whom the shepherds and shepherdesses of this part make an annual offering of cakes. Coach to

[*Peronne* (22 kil. east-south-east), a sous-préfecture and fortress, with 4,300 inhabitants, in the marshes of the Somme, was the old capital of Santerre. It has a castle, enclosing a very old tower, called Tour Hébert, where Charles the Simple (placed here by Heribert, Count of Vermandois) died a prisoner, 929, and where, too, the old fox Louis XI. was trapped by his vassal, Charles the Bold, as related in Scott's "Quentin Durward." Having been unsuccessfully besieged by the Spaniards, and by Henry of Nassau, 1536, it styled itself la Pucelle (the maid), but it was taken, 1815. It has an old gothic church, and Hôtel de Ville, with a belfry. At Château d'Applincourt, the famous League against the Protestants was signed by Henry III. and the Guises. *Hotel*—D'Angleterre.]

Achiet (11½ miles.) Coach to Bapaume, a place as old as the eleventh century, fortified by Charles V. against France, but given up 1659. An artesian well was sunk here, 1723, by Feullon. It has a ruined castle.

Boileux (5½ miles). At 5¾ miles further is

Arras. *Hotels*—De l'Europe (good); Petit St. Paul.

A strongly fortified town, chief place of department Pas-de-Calais (formerly of Artois province, which gave title of Comte d'Artois to Charles X.), a third-class military station, seat of a Bishopric, Tribunal, College, Chamber of Manufactures, &c., in a fertile plain on the Scarpe. It was the *Atrebates* of Cæsar, and in St. Jerome's time (fifth century) was noted for its trade.

The city, or old town, on the highest point, was built round the hermitage of St. Waest (founded in the 6th century), which afterwards became a large abbey, and has left some remains in the public Library (36,000 vols). The ville, or lower town, divided from the other by the brook Crinchen, has good houses and streets of hewn stone, and adjoins the citadel, built by Vauban. Near the Hôtel de Ville, a good gothic building, are the great and little squares (place), surrounded with old flemish houses and arcades.

Notre Dame Cathedral was rebuilt, 1832, in the grecian style, on the site of the old gothic one, destroyed by the partisans of the infamous Robespierre, who was born here. Other buildings worth notice are the Préfecture, Museum with remains of antiquity found here, the clock tower, deaf and dumb school, large barracks, riding and military schools, theatre. The ramparts are strong and high, and the country may be soon laid under water. Damiens, who was broken on the wheel for trying to assassinate Louis XV., was also a native. At one time it was held by the Spaniards, who put up this rhyme on the gates—

Quand les Français prendront Arras,
Les souris mangeront les chats ;

which, when it came into French hands some one proposed to retain, merely suppressing the *p*.

Manufactures of cotton, woollen, lace, soap, salt, beet-root sugar, linseed oil, pottery, leather; besides a trade in grain, wine, and spirits—some of the latter being kept in the chalk cellars in the city part. "Arras" tapestry made here.

Near this, at Plancy, is the society of St. Victor, founded 1841, by M. Collin, author of the Dictionnaire Infernal.

At Mont St. Eloy (6 kil.) is a ruined abbey; and two stones at Acq, mark where Charles the Bold was defeated by Baldwin, 863. Coaches to Cambrai (*see* Route 11), Bethune, and St. Pol.

[Lens (14 kil. north-north-east), an old place on the Eleux, where the Prince of Condé, in 1648, gained a victory over the Spaniards. Soap, spirits, leather, linseed oil, &c., are made.

St. Pol (34 kil. north-west), on the old road to Montreuil, a sous-préfecture (population, 3,504), pleasantly seated on the Ternoise, in a healthy spot, where four great roads meet, and having traces of the old castle of the Counts of St. Pol.

Bethune (30 kil. north-north-west), another sous-préfecture on the old road to Calais, and a strong military place of the second class, on the river Brette and two canals, which meet here. The grand place (square) has, near the Hôtel de Ville, a curious and lofty spire tower or belfry. Much of the water is supplied by artesian wells, which were first tried here. It has a good trade. Population, 6,889. *Hotels*—De France; d'Angleterre; du Lion d'Or (Golden Lion).

The wood of Dames Chartreuses offers a fine panorama.]

From Arras, along the rail to Lille, you pass Rœux (5¾ miles); Vitry (4¼ miles), on to

Douai (5¾ miles), a strong town, and sous-préfecture, having a cour impèriale, tribunal, college, and school for artillery and engineers, to which the Duke of Wellington was sent when a boy. It was once a seat of the *Caluaci*, in Belgic Gaul, and stands on the river Scarpe, which is joined to the Escaut, or Schelde, by a canal. Marlborough took it in the wars of Anne's time. The old walls are strengthened with several towers, and there are good walks on the ramparts. It has a large place (square), a gothic Hôtel de Ville, with a belfry tower over it, an arsenal (where the English prisoners were kept in the war), cannon foundry, public library of 30,000 vols., botanic garden, picture gallery, museum, theatre; and every other year an exhibition of works of industry takes place. At the English College for priests, founded by Cardinal Allen, the Douai version of the Old Testament was first published, 1609. Population, 18,793. Tapestry, sewing-thread, bone lace, &c., are made. *Hotels*—Du Commerce; du Noveau Monde (New World); de l'Europe; du Nord, &c. Coach to Cambrai (*see* Route 11).

At Douai, the line to Valenciennes and Brussels parts off, as in Route 13.

From this, the rail proceeds by

Leforest (5 miles),

Carvin (3¾ miles), with its population of 5,000 starch-makers, &c.; and

Seclin (6½ miles); 6 miles further is

Lille. *Hotels*—De l'Europe, Rue Basse, the first in the town, and highly recommended; de Gand; de la Cour Royale; de Flandre; du Nouveau Monde (New World); du Brabant; du Commerce (near the theatre); du France; du Lion d'Argent

(Golden Lion), &c. *Cafés*, on Grande Place. Dinner, 2½ fr.; bed, 1½ fr.

Population 75,433. A large manufacturing town, capital of department du Nord (formerly of French Flanders), a strongly fortified post on the Belgian frontier, head quarters of the 16th military division, &c., standing in a fertile and populous plain, covered with windmills and factories, 15 leagues from the sea, on the Deule and the canal from the Scarpe to the Lys. It grew out of an abbey, founded about 840; was improved by Baldwin V., in 1047, and after many events, including the taking of it from the Spaniards, by Louis XIV., in 1667, and from the French, by Marlboro', in 1708, it was finally given up to France, 1713. In shape it is an oval, about 2,620 yards by 1,300 yards, entirely closed in by ramparts and ditches, strengthened by 15 bastions, by Fort St. Maurice, on the south east side, and a citadel of great extent on the west. The latter, one of Vauban's best, is five-sided, and considered almost impregnable. The Austrians tried to take it, 1792, but without success, a fact commemorated by a bronze figure, in the Grande Place, near the exchange, &c.

Porte St. André is the oldest of its seven gates, having been built in 1670; the Porte de Paris has a triumphal arch, by Volans, built 1682, in honour of Louis XIV., whose bust is here, with figures of Hercules and Mars. The best streets are Rue Royal, Rue de Paris, Rue d' Esquermois, Rue St. Saveur, and Rue St. André. Most of the houses are modern and regular, and generally two stories high; many work people live in cellars. A bread esplanade, near the citadel is planted with trees, and watered by the Deule. The largest open part, next to the Grande Place, is the cattle and wood market, near the Douane (custom-house); some of the oldest houses are in this neighbourhood, with the public baths. Pont Neuf here, is a small bridge of 6 arches, built 1701, on the Grand Rivage, a branch of the Deule, where goods are landed. Pont Royal is ascended by steps and covered over. In this quarter, also, are the general hospital, founded 1783; the government tobacco factory, magazines, barracks, the artillery depôt, &c.

The six parish churches are those of St. André, the best, restored since the revolution; St. Catherine, which has an altar piece by Rubens, and a high tower; St. Etienne, having a good portal; St. Madeleine, a cupola and pictures; St. Saveur, which had a gothic spire battered down, 1792; and the ancient gothic church of St. Maurice (begun 1022), with its side chapels, and Duc de Berri's mausoleum. Part of St. Peter's old tower is all that remains of that church.

Near the Citadel, in Rue de la Barre, stands the *Hôtel de Ville*, called the Palais de Rihoult, when it belonged to the Dukes of Burgundy who began it in the thirteenth century; it is a gothic pile of various dates; and includes the tribunal of commerce (where are two pictures, by Wamps), and various official bureaus; also an old chapel, and a modern belfry. Charles V. and Henry VIII. visited it together, 1542. The Hôtel de la Préfecture is near the Place du Concert.

Not far from Place St. Martin are the following. The Museum, in the old church of the Friars Minors, having several pictures including some by Vandyke, Rubens, &c, portraits of the Dukes, and valuable drawings by Raphael, Giotto, and others, given by Wicar, a native of Lille, who died at Rome, 1834. Next it is the old men's hospital, or Hôpital Comtesse, founded in the thirteenth century, by Countess Jeanne, daughter of the emperor, Baldwin IX., and having a slender spire like a minaret. The Hôtel de Monnaie (or mint) adjoins the cirque, which they say marks the site of the Château de Buc, built by Lyderic, founder of the town. At the college is the public library, of 24,000 volumes, besides MSS.

The *Bourse* stands in Grande Place; it was built 1652, with a square court inside. Behind it is the theatre, begun 1785, but since enlarged, and having a portico of six columns.

A large *Military Hospital* is seen near the Porte Bethune, built 1765. The hospital St. Saveur is near that church, and the Hôtel Dieu.

At the *Administration des Hospices*, are a picture by Vandyke, and the halbert of the famous Jeanne Maillote, leader of the towns-people against the insurgent Flemish, who attacked the place, 1582.

There are several *Casernes*, or barracks, and magazines; abattoirs, or slaughter-houses, schools of medicine, painting, &c.; and a botanic garden. Here died, 1852, an old veteran, aged 88, called Coulombon l'Immortel. Among other escapes, when taken in the Vendéan war and shot for not giving the pass-word, he fell pierced with ten balls and four stabs of the bayonet, and yet survived sixty years after. Revs. MM. Marzian and Deboeck are protestant pastors here.

Chief *Manufactures* are cottons and linen, Lille thread, lace, soap, chemicals, beet-root sugar, linseed oil, eaux-de-vie, and various other articles.

Conveyances, by railway to Calais, Dunkirk, Brussels, Mons, Paris, &c.; by coach, to Bethune, Cambrai, &c.; also by a baraque to these and other places, on the canals. Cysoing, to the south-east, has part of an old abbey, and a pyramid in honour of Louis XV., who was here after the battle of Fontenoy.

[From Lille, on the rail to Ghent or Gand, you pass

Roubaix (5¾ miles), a large town of 31,000 people and seat of the cotton manufactures. *Hotels*—De France; du Commerce.

Tourcoing (1¾ miles), noted for its linge-de-table, or table linen. Population 26,900. *Hotel*—Du Cynge.

Mouscron (3¼ miles), where carriages are changed for

Belgium. Travellers are advised not to have cigars, tobacco, lace, &c., about them, without declaring it at the douane, as the regulations are very strict.]

From Lille, on the rail to Calais, you pass

Perenchies (5 miles).

Armentieres (3¾ miles), on the Lys, and noted for its grain, linen, &c. Population 8,000.

Steenwerck (5½ miles).

Bailleul (2¾ miles), an ancient looking place, with old carved houses, St. Waast's old church, and a Jesuits' college. Population 10,140.

Strazeele (5 miles).

Hazebrouck (4 miles) where the line to Dunkirk turns off, is a sous-préfecture of 7,400 souls, in a fertile spot on a branch of the Lys. It has a large church, built 1490-1520, with a tower of 276 feet; a new Hôtel de Ville, fronted by a portico of twelve pillars; a tobacco factory at the old augustine convent; a library of 4000 volumes. Linen, soap, &c. are made. *Hotel*—Des Trois Chevaux (three horses). Coaches to Lillers and Aire.

[Lillers (14 kil. south-south-west), in department Pas-de-Calais, on the fertile banks of the Nave, where one of the first artesian wells was bored in France. The fountains rise up in jets. Population 5,200. Pottery, linseed oil, leather are made, and bleaching and printing carried on.

Aire (13 kil. west-south-west) a third class fortress, where the Lys and Laquette meet the St. Omer and Bassée canals. It has a belfry of the last century; large barracks; and St. Paul's gothic church, in which is a ridiculous picture of Herodias with the Baptist's head. Mallebranche was a native. Population 8,300. Woollens, hats, soap, starch, oil, paper, spirits, &c., are made. *Hotels*—D'Angleterre; de France.]

Eblinghem (6¼ miles).

St. Omer (6¾ miles), a fortified town of the third class, and sous-préfecture in department Pas-de-Calais, in a marshy spot on the Aa, where six great roads meet. It is surrounded by the canals and gardens of a Flemish-speaking population. St. Audomar founded a church here, and gave his name to the town. Louis XIV. took it from Flanders, 1677. The old cathedral church of Notre Dame was begun in the 14th century, on the site of St. Audomar's, whose tomb it contains, besides good carved work, a picture by Rubens, &c.; it is 321 feet long, and worth examination; the clock shews the moon's changes, the months, the signs of the zodiac, &c. Opposite it stands a tower only of St. Bertin's abbey, where Childeric III. died; it was one of the finest in this part. The Jesuits' college, built 1615-36, for English Roman Catholics, is now occupied by a commercial school; its church is worth notice. The Hôtel de Ville is modern; the museum has some antiquities; and there are 18,000 volumes in the public library. An arsenal was built 1781. Linens, flannels, paper, &c., are made, and a good trade carried on. *Hotels*—De la Poste; du Commerce.

In the neighbourhood are Clairmarais abbey (5 kil.), and the old castle of Arques (2 kil) near the Sept Ecluses, or seven locks of the Aa, which falls 40 feet here, in its descent to Gravelines.

The next station is Watten (5 miles), the old *Itium prom.* to which the sea came up in Cæsar's time. It has an old watch tower on the hill.

Audruicq (7¼ miles). Coach to Bourbourg.

Ardres (5¼ miles), a small fortified town, near the Field of the Cloth of Gold, where Henry VIII. and Francis I. met; so called from the splendid equipages displayed, of which there is a curious picture at Hampton Court. All this part is now covered with willows and flax fields, round the village of Les Saules (population, 900), which grows as much at £80,000 worth yearly. The écoucheurs, or scutchers, prepare steeped flax for the spinners, working in little clay-built huts, or boutiques. Coach to Guines, once a fortress, with 4,760 souls, and a trade in cattle and poultry.

St. Pierre (6¾ miles), the birth-place of the famous Eustache St. Pierre. At 1½ mls. beyond is

Calais. *Hotels*—Hôtel Dessin, one of the oldest and most respectable establishments on the continent; it is highly and deservedly recommended. Hôtel Quillacq; de Paris, opposite the railway station and English steam-packet wharf, quiet, reasonable, and comfortable. *Cafés*—Marine, Legrant, Eudes, Bellevue. Dinners, 2 to 3 fr.; bed, 1 to 1½ fr. Good private lodgings, 20 to 50 fr. a month. The railway station, douane, and passport office are on the pier; passports are *visé* without delay, and they may be procured of the consul for 4s. 6d. Passengers landing here direct to Marseilles, Brussels, &c., should say so, as they need not give up their passports; and luggage, if merely going across France to Belgium and Germany, may be *plombé* (sealed), to save examination till the end of the journey. Luggage, direct to Paris, is not examined till arrival there. On embarking here for London a *permis* must be asked for. Luggage direct to London by rail is not examined at Dover or Folkestone, but at the London Bridge Station.

English consul, E. Bonham; also consuls for Belgium, Holland, &c. English chapel in Rue des Prêtres; banker, M. Guilbert, Grande Place. There are several reading rooms and collections of natural history, antiquities, &c. High water at moon's full and change, 11h. 45m.

Population, 10,700. A well-known half-English port and fortified town of the first class, in a flat corn and flax country on the Pas-de-Calais (which Englishmen call the Straits of Dover), about 25 miles (or two hours' steam passage) from Dover, to which it is joined by the electric telegraph. It was taken, after 11 months' siege (when Eustace St. Pierre defended it, 1347), by the English, who kept it till the Duke of Guise captured it in Queen Mary's time (1588). The Spaniards held it for two years, 1596-8. It makes a long square, surrounded by ramparts (which have a view of the English coast), and ditches, and defended by several forts, as Forts Rouge and Vert (red and white), on the piers; another on the quay; Fort Nieulay on the south-west; while Cardinal Richelieu's strong citadel, to the west, commands the whole. The shallow harbour is the mouth of the river de Hames, between the piers, one of which is three-quarters of a mile long, with a pillar on the spot where Louis XVIII. set his foot in 1814. It was deepened in 1842, but passengers sometimes land in boats still. A gate by Richelieu (the Porte du Havre, which figures in Hogarth's picture of the 'Roast beef of England,') leads from the pier. It was built in 1685. The streets are narrow, the houses chiefly of brick, and common looking. In the Grand Place, or Place d'Armes, are the Lighthouse and the Hôtel de Ville, with busts of St. Pierre, the Duc de Guise, and Richelieu in front; inside is the library of 6,000 volumes. The church, built by the English, is a cross-shaped, gothic structure, with a tower, and contains 11 chapels, a fine marble altar, and a painting by Vandyke. St. Pierre is in Basse-Ville or Lower Town, in the south-east, where many hands (English and others) are employed in the tulle and lace factories.

At the *Museum* (open three days a-week, from 10 to 5) are Blanchard, the æronaut, and car, and some pictures, including Correggio's 'Vierge au Bandeau,' given to the town by the Princess of Canino (Lucien Bonaparte's wife), who was born here in 1788. In Cour de Guise is the old hotel, which belonged to the merchants of the wool staple, and where Henry VIII. lodged. There are a large barracks, a salle de spectacle, or theatre, an old clock-tower, a navigation school, &c., and good baths, to which reading, dancing, and other rooms are attached. A stone outside the Boulogne gate marks where the unfortunate Lady Hamilton was buried. La Place, the astronomer, and Mollier, the traveller, were natives. They shew Sterne's room at Dessin's. A canal is cut to the river Aa, which goes to St. Omer, on the road to which, between Guines and Ardres, was the famous field of the Cloth of Gold, where Henry VIII. and Francis I. met in 1520. The fishermen live in the suburb of Courgaine.

Trade in lace, fish, eggs, spirits, salt, and steam-engines for pressing linseed oil.

Conveyances by rail to Lille, Paris, Brussels, &c. (See *Bradshaw's Continental Guide*); by coach to Gravelines, Dunkirk, and Boulogne (*see* Route 12). By steamer to Dover, 2 hours, or (with rail) 6 hours to London; to Ramsgate, 3½ hours; to London, 10 hours. The electric telegraph is laid down to Boulogne, as well as along the rail to Paris.

(*a*) From Calais, on the road to Dunkerque, or Dunkirk, you pass

GRAVELINES (22 kil.), on a flat, dreary coast, a port of 5,200 people, at the Aa's mouth, where Henry VIII. embarked in 1520. It has an arsenal, and a monument by Girardon, at the church. Flax, hemp, corn, colza, &c., are abundant in this country of dykes and willows. *Hotel*—Lesur.

At 20 kil. further is Dunkirk (*see* Route 14).

ROUTE 11.

Creil to St. Quentin, Cambrai, &c.

By rail to St. Quentin, 102½ kils., or 63⅝ miles; four trains a-day, in about 3 hours.

CREIL, as in Route 9, on the Northern railway. The stations beyond are—

	kil.		kil.
Pont-Ste-Maxence,	11½	Noyon	6½
Verberie	9½	Appilly	8
Compiègne	12	Chauny	8
Thourotte	8½	Tergnier-La-Fère,	7½
Ribécourt	4½	Montescourt	10
Ourscamps	4½	St. Quentin	12

PONT-STE-MAXENCE (6½ miles), in a pleasant part of the Oise, under a wooded hill, has, near the remains of an old one, a good three-arched bridge (pont), by Péronnet, on a level, resting on groups of open pillars, not solid piles. Some old houses are left, though it suffered much in past times. Much grain is sold. Moncel Abbey ruins are turned into a wine depôt. Coaches to Gournay-sur-Aronde and Senlis (*see* Route 10.)

[The former (20 kil. north-east,) was the birthplace of Montaigne's adopted daughter, Mademoiselle de Gournay.]

Before the next station, you pass Sarron, on the Oise, near the château of Plessis-Villette, which belonged to Voltaire's niece, Madame de Villette; they shew here his statue on a pedestal containing his heart, his desk and sofa, &c.

VERBERIE (6½ miles), on a hillside, now much decayed (population 1,800), had once three bridges over the Oise, and a palace, in which Charles Martel died, 741. His son (Pepin) called a council here, and his grandson (Charlemagne) built a chapel. Charles the Bold held the synod of Soissons here, and gave his daughter to Ethelwolf of England. It was burnt by the Normans, and restored by Charles V.; but few traces are left. In the time of Louis XIV., the walls were strengthened, and the town called Villeneuve (new town).

[At 10 kils. south-east is Crépy, on the Grand Morin, founded in the tenth century, along with St. Arnould's Abbey. It was the capital of the Valois country, and a strong place, having a palace called Bouville. Only one (St. Denis, with a good choir,) of its five churches remains, and ruins of another. There are also a tower and part of the château fort. The English took it in 1431, and the leaguers in 1588; but it is best known for the treaty of 1544 between Francis I. and the Emperor Charles V.]

COMPIEGNE (10⅝ miles), a sous-préfecture of 9,800 souls, on a slant of the Oise, where the Aisne joins. It is a quiet place, with narrow ill-built streets. Near its great forest was the roman *Compendium*, and a small hunting seat of the time of Clovis and Charles the Bold, who built an abbey and château. Louis le Begue and Louis V. were buried here; and it was held for Charles VII. by Jeanne d'Arc, when she was taken prisoner (1430), in a sally from Vieux Pont gate, by the Burgundians, who sold her to the English. The château, as rebuilt by Louis XV., and finished by Napoleon (who met Marie Louise here), was the residence of Charles of Spain in 1808. The noble front towards the forest is 624 ft. wide. In the grand gallery, of 100 ft., are Napoleon's victories, painted by Girodet.

St. Corneille, or the Abbey Church, contains some old royal tombs, and had the organ (the first brought into Europe) which Constantine Copronymous, the Greek emperor gave to Pepin, 755. St. André and St. Antoine are gothic; St. Jacques partly in the renaissance style. At the Carmelites is the tomb of the Count of Toulouse, by Lemoine. One of the best buildings is the picturesque gothic *Hôtel de Ville*, with its delicate carvings, high roof, carved spire turrets, and the fine spire belfry in the middle. The three-arched Pont Neuf has a pyramid 33 feet high in the middle of it. There a public library of 28,000 volumes, and a museum of antiquities. Formerly muslins and linens were made. The walks around are pleasant; an avenue of nearly a mile leads from the château to the forest, which covers 29,600 acres (46 square miles), and is pierced with 275 leagues of road; one, called Brunehaut, was a Roman way. *Hotels*—De la Cloche (Clock), du Lion d'Argent (Golden Lion). Coaches to Soissons, Pierrefonds.

[*Soissons* (35 kil. east), a sous-préfecture of 10,200 souls, (department Aisne,) a fortified town, and seat of a diocess, in a fertile valley on the Aisne; was the chief hold of the *Suessones* when Cæsar took it. Clovis made it the capital of the Franks (486), after routing its Roman governor Syagrius. Pepin deposed Childeric here, 752, and Charles the Simple was beaten, 922, by his competitor Robert. In 1315, it suffered from the Burgundians and Armagnacs; the Huguenots ravaged it 1567; and it was taken and retaken twice over 1814. It is well-built, and defended by ramparts. The gothic cathedral of the twelfth century, on the site of that which Pepin was crowned in, by St. Boniface, has a tower 160 feet high, and Rubens' "Adoration of the Shepherds," given they say by him to the Cordeliers here, in gratitude for their care of him when sick. St. Pierre is in the Lombard style, small and round, with buttresses and a dome; St. Leger, in that of the renaissance; only the fine gothic portal and spire are left of St. Jean-des-Vignes Abbey, on a hill, founded in the eleventh century. The old château, on the site of the palace, is flanked by heavy round towers. Other buildings are, the Intendance, the college, Hôtel Dieu, house of correction, museum and library of 19,000 volumes, two barracks, theatre, &c. A bridge leads over to St. Vaast. In the neighbourhood are some remains of St. Medard's Abbey, founded 545, with the dungeon where Louis-le-Debonnaire was for a time confined by his rebellious sons. Clotaire, son of Clovis, king of Soissons (which took in all the north-east of France) was buried in it. Childeric I., Clotaire II., the Duke of Mayenne (the chief of the league against Henry IV.), and Collot d'Herbois, the infamous terrorist, were natives. Linen and pottery are made; trade in grain, vegetables, cattle, &c. *Hotels*—Du Lion Rouge (Red Lion), de la Croix d'Or (Golden Cross). Coaches to Laon (33 kil. further—Route 17*a*), Rheims, Château-Thierry, &c.

At 12 kil. south-east of Compiègne, near one end of its forest, are the picturesque walls and towers of *Pierrefonds Castle*, a vast ruin on a hill. It was so strong that a determined soldier, Rieux, in 1592, held out against three or four of Henry the Fourth's commanders, and was at last only bought over with gold. In 1617, 15,000 men invested it and took it after six day's continual firing, when it was dismantled. It is one of the finest remains of antiquity in France.]

THOURETTE (2¾ miles).

OURSCAMPS (5½ miles).

NOYON (4 miles), the roman *Noviodunum*, became the seat of a bishop, 511, and was the place where Hugh Capet was elected king, 987. It stands on a hill side, among gardens, in the valley of Chaunay, on the Vorse, near the Oise; and is well built, having four gates, and the house in which John Cauvin, or *Calvin*, was born, 1609, his father being diocesan secretary, &c. He went to the school of the Capettes here, and by favour of the bishop, received a benefice when he was only twelve; two years after, to escape the plague, he was sent to Paris. The cathedral church is chiefly romanesque, of the thirteenth century (an earlier one was begun by Pepin), 351 feet long, and 217 high at the west towers. Trade in grain, leather, linen, cottons, coal, &c. Population, 6,300. *Hotel*—Du Nord. Coaches to Roye, Nesles, Guiscard, Ham.

[Roye (15 kil. north-west), a small old place on the Avre, in department Somme (part of Picardy), is said to be the ancient *Rodium*, and has suffered from eleven sieges and three plagues. It has a church with excellent stained windows, a carved timber house on the Place, public baths, mineral springs, and manufactures of stockings, &c. Population, 4,000. A sect of Guerinets, so called after their leader, Guerin, the curé here, were extirpated 1626.

Nesle (10 kil. north-east of this), gave name

to one of the oldest marquisates in France, and has an old church in which nearly all its inhabitants were butchered by Charles the Bold, 1472.

Ham (18 kil. north-north-east of Noyon), on the Somme, is as old as 875, and known for its moated château or state prison, built 1470, by the Count St. Pôl. On the gate is his motto in gothic letters, "Mon Mieux" (my best); the great round keep stands 108 feet high, 108 diameter, and 36 feet thick. The ministers of Charles X., Louis Napoleon (now emperor), and Cabrera, the Carlist, were confined here. The church has a good choir, and carvings of scriptural subjects. General Foy was a native.]

APPILLY (5 miles), in department Aisne.

CHAUNY (4¾ miles), a decayed fortified town, on the Oise, where the St. Quentin canal joins, in a fertile plain. Linens are made. Population, 4,290. The canal opens a way between the Oise and Somme.

TERGNIER-LA-FERE (5 miles). Coaches to La Fère, Laon, Marle, Vervins, Moncornet.

[LA Fère, a little east, on the Oise, where the Serre joins, is an old fortress, where the Spaniards, in 1592, met the Leaguers about putting a Spanish prince upon the throne instead of Henry IV. The Allies took it 1815, after six month's siege. It has the oldest artillery school in France (1719), with a large arsenal and barracks.]

MONTESCOURT, 6¼ miles.

St. Quentin (7½ miles), on a hill between the Somme and St. Quentin Canal, is a sous-préfecture (in department Aisne) of 24,000 souls, who carry on here, as the centre of a wide district, thriving manufactures of cotton, thread, table linens, silk, tulle, muslin, shawls, steam-engines, oil, soap, &c. It was the Roman *Augusta-Vivamanduorum*, but called St. Quentin from 884, after the martyr. It suffered from the Vandals, 401; Attila and his Huns, 451; the Normans, in the eighth and ninth centuries; and was made the head of the Vermandois country by Louis I. for his nephew Pepin. Louis XI. and his rival, Charles of Burgundy, frequently contested it. In 1557, it was defended by Coligny against 50,000 Spaniards under Philip II (King of England) and Emanuel of Savoy, but taken, after a long siege, and a battle lost close to it by Montmorency—a success which led Philip, in fulfilment of a vow he had made, to build the Escurial. The houses are modern; three faubourgs stretch beyond the site of its old ramparts. Overlooking the town, on the hill-top, is the fine *Church*, a large and imposing gothic specimen, about 420 feet long from the large Fulrad porch to the Virgin chapel, and 127 feet high in the nave (which is 212 feet long); it has 110 windows, some stained, and 42½ feet high, with 23 side chapels, and 78 pillars; a tall spire used to rise above the square tower; it was a cathedral till the bishop removed to Noyon.

The *Hôtel de Ville*, in Grande Place, built 1509, in the gothic style, is worth notice for its quaint carvings and lantern tower, in which is a good chime of bells. There are also a college, palais de justice, library of 17,000 vols., new theatre, gas-works, besides a conseil-de-prud' hommes (who arrange prices, &c., between masters and workmen), schools of design, botanic garden, hospitals, &c. The canal, which is part of the system called Canal de Picardie, unites the Oise and Somme to the Schelde, near Cambrai; one of its tunnels, near Bellicourt, is 5,677 metres long (3½ miles). Charlevoix, the Jesuit historian, was a native. Traces of three Roman ways are seen; the old town kept its Latin name for a long time in the form of *Aoste*. *Hotels*—D'Angleterre, de l'Ange (Angel), du Cygne (Swan). Coaches to Cambrai, Le Câteau, Avesnes, Guise.

(*a*) GUISE (26 kil. east-north-east) a small third-class fortress, in a pretty spot on the Oise, is as old as 1050, and was given, 1520, to Claude de Lorraine, first Duke of Guise. Mary, Queen of Scots was his grand-daughter; and Francis, a grandson, surnamed the Balafré, was he who took Calais from the English. The old chateau, 164 feet above the town, now used as a barrack, has a round keep left; Henry IV., against whom the Guises headed the League, burnt it, 1594. Jean de Luxembourg, who sold the Maid of Orleans to the English, and Count Desmoulins, were natives.

(*b*) CAMBRAI (38 kil. north of St. Quentin), on the road to Mezières, a sous-préfecture in department Nord, an ancient and strongly-fortified town of the second class, in the old province of Flanders, and seat of a bishopric, but of an archdiocess when held by the excellent Fénélon, whose monument, by David, is in the present cathedral; the old one which held his grave was rased at the revolution. It was the roman *Cameracum*, and the head of a district called Cambrésis, held by the bishop as a fief of the German empire. It stands in a fertile pasture land, near the source of the Escaut or Shelde, which runs through it. The fortifications are defended by a citadel on a hill. Notre Dame bridge leads out on one side. The Hôtel de Ville fronts the large place d'Armes (exercise ground). The Esplanade is also of great extent. It has a military hospital, a college, a public library of 30,000 vols., mont de piété (loan fund), theatre, and several gable-fronted houses and public buildings. Monstrelet, the historian-antiquary, and General Dumouriez, were natives. Fine linen, cambrics, lace, thread, &c. are made. Population, 17,646. *Hotels*—De l'Europe; des Diligences; de Hollande; du Mouton Noir (Black Sheep). Valenciennes (*see* Route 13) is 50 kil. further.

(c) Cateau Cambresis (24 kil. east-south-east of Cambrai), on the Selle, a place of 5,946 inhabitants, is best known for the treaty of peace, made 1559, between Philip of Spain and Henry II. of France. Marshal Mortier was born here. It had a castle or château built by Bishop Hallais. ——*Avesnes* (30 kil. further), the roman *Avesnae*, a sous-préfecture and fortified town, on the Sambre, near the Belgian frontier, taken by the Prussians, 1815. It has a church with a tower about 320 feet high, Hôtel de Ville, clock-tower, &c., and is noted for prepared boars' heads. Population, 3,600. *Hotels*—du Nord, de la Cloche (Clock).

ROUTE 12.

Amiens to Boulogne and Calais.

By railway to Boulogne, 124 kil., or 77 miles, (170 miles from Paris); four trains a-day, 2½ to 4 hours. The stations are—

	kil.		kil.		kil.
Picquigny ...	15	Noyelle	14	Neufchâtel	14
Hangest......	7	Rue............	10	Pont - de - Brique ...	8
Longpré......	7	Montreuil - Vertin ...	16	Boulogne ...	6
Pont-Rémy	8	Etaples	11		
Abbeville ...	8				

Amiens (as in Route 10), 93 miles from Paris. Then, going down the Somme, you pass Ailly (6 miles); Picquigny (3 miles) and its old castle, Hangest (4 miles); Longpré, (4½ miles); Pont-Rémy (4½ miles), on to

Abbeville. *Hotels*—D'Angleterre; la Tête du Bœuf (Bull's Head); de l'Europe (a fine building). A sous-préfecture and large fortified town, of 17,522 inhabitants, on the river Somme, in department Somme and the old province of Picardy, about 18 miles from the sea. Some of the streets are pretty good, but the greater part are old-fashioned, narrow, and ill-paved. The houses, chiefly brick, with a few stone buildings, and several ancient looking ones of wood. Trees are planted on the ramparts, but the view is not very enticing. It has a communal college, theatre foundling hospital, &c., and a public library of 25,000 vols. At the latter are busts of natives (Sanson the geographer, Millevoye the poet, Lesueur the composer, &c.), and a copy of the Gospels, in gold letters, on purple vellum, which Charlemagne gave to St. Riquier's Abbey.

But the gothic *Cathedral* of St. Wulfran is the most remarkable object. It has a tower 171 feet high, and a noble west front, built by Cardinal d'Amboise, in the sixteenth century, decorated with niched figures of saints; the triple portal has carvings of the apostles, annunciation of the Virgin, &c. The arches of the nave are also good, but the rest is inferior. Manufactures of fine linen (at the Champ de Foire, or Fair Field), first established by Colbert, serges, muslins, cordage, leather; and a brisk trade in grain, wine, cider linen and woollen goods, &c.

Conveyances, Daily to St. Valery-sur-Somme, (by boat), a small bathing-place, whence the Conqueror sailed to England, 1066; by rail to Paris, Amiens, Boulogne, &c.

[From Abbeville, along the road to Dieppe, you pass *Eu* (34 kil. west-south-west), and its château castle, the noble seat of the Dukes of Guise, and of Louis Philippe, who, on his visit to England, embarked at Treport (a little below Eu), which has some fine old mills and a curious church. The château d'Eu, standing in a vast park, contains a large collection of portraits made by the king, 70 principal apartments, 250 inferior ones, with stables, &c. for 180 horses and 60 carriages. At 30 kil. further is Dieppe, (*see* Route 2.)

From Abbeville, along the road to Arras, you pass

Rouen
Nantes
Abbeville
Tours

St. Riquier (10 kil. east-north-east) and the remains of its abbey, founded by Dagobert, in the seventh century; enlarged by Charlemagne, and called Centule, from its hundred towers; and now a college. The church, partly restored, is worth notice for its beautiful front, full of niches and carvings; as well as for its carved stalls, iron gates, and curious frescos (of the sixteenth century) in the treasury, including the dance of the Three Dead and Three Living. An old belfry and remains of the great town walls are seen. At 21 kil beyond this, is the sous-préfecture of

Doullens, which has a good church, and one of Vauban's best constructed fortresses. Population, 4,100. *Hotels*—du Grand Turc, de l'Europe. Arras is 35 kil. further (*see* Route 10.)

From Abbeville, along the road to St. Omer, you pass near the field of *Crescy*, or Crécy, (16 kil. north-east), where the Black Prince, 1346, defeated the French, 30,000 being slain. The walls of the windmill in which they say Edward III. stood to watch the battle, as related by Froissart, are crowded with names of Englishmen who have visited this memorable spot.

Hesdin (35 kil. from Abbeville, further on), in department Pas-de-Calais, was founded 1554, by the Dukes of Savoy, in the midst of a beautiful country, flat, but well wooded and cultivated. The air is healthy, and there is a good Hôtel de Ville. Abbe Prévost was a native. Population, 3,425. Trade in cotton, thread, oil, pottery, salt refining, leather, &c.

Agincourt or Azincourt, 12 kil. beyond, in the old province of Picardy, a small village, with traces of a castle, 16 miles from Crescy, and equally memorable for the great victory gained by Henry V., 25th of October, 1415, with 9,000 men, against a French force of about 55,000, chiefly by means of his archers, with their cloth yard shafts, stationed in a wood still here. Shakspere's King Henry V. speaks of 8,400 "knights, esquires, and gallant gentlemen," who fell, besides others. Fluellen in that play, is the David Gam, or squinting David, of Welsh history, who told the king on this occasion, after counting the enemy, that 'there was enough to kill, enough to make prisoners, and enough to run away.'

Fruges, 5 kil. from this, under a slope, has a mineral water. At 31 kil. beyond is St. Omer, (*see* Route 10.)]

From Abbeville, along the rail, you pass

NOYELLE (7½ m.);

RUE (7 miles), which has St. Esprit's church front richly sculptured, besides its carved pillars, roof, &c. It is still a place of pilgrimage, and stands on a little stream which runs up to the field of Crécy, and Monties forest, where the favourite son of Francis I., Charles, died of the plague, 1545. A coach to Le Crotoy down the Somme.

MONTREUIL-VERTIN (10 miles.)

[*Montreuil-sur-Mer* (8 kil. east), a sous-préfecture of 3,800, and fortified town of the second class, on a hill by the Canche, where Cæsar built a fort called Vinacum, was rebuilt 878, by Heltgaut or Hergot, along with the abbey church, and castle, and called Monastoriolum, whence the modern name. It was besieged by the Normans, 918, held by the English, taken by the Spaniards, 1544, and given up to France, 1665. The houses, divided into Upper and Lower Town, are of brick. A large citadel, with a view of the river and flat sea coast, replaces the castle, of which the gate towers are left; and St. Saulve's abbey is now the Hôtel de Ville. Its church has a fine tall buttressed doorway. *Hotels*—De l'Europe, de France. Trade in soap, leather, spirits, wine, &c.]

ETAPLES (7mls), a decayed fishing port, on a sandy plain at the Canche's mouth, which the Romans used, having some good old houses and remains of a château, built 1160. Coach to Montreuil.

NEUFCHATEL (8½ mls.); Pont de Brique (4½ m.)

At 4 miles further is Boulogne terminus, near Place Belle Vue.

Boulogne. *Hotels*—De l'Europe, close to the railway and steam packet stations, excellent; d'Angleterre; this old-established and first-rate house is highly recommended; Bedford, well situated and good; Brighton, very comfortable for residents. Boarding House, Mr. Roberts, 92, Rue de Boston, is very comfortable and respectable. Besides these there are several French Hotels.—The 'Nord,' 'Londres,'

'Bains,' &c., more remarkable for size than comfort. *Café*—De Paris, Rue St. Croix.

Post Office, No. 8, Rue des Vieillards; open from 7 a.m. to 8 p.m.

English consul, W. Hamilton, at the top of Rue des Vieillards, near the sous-préfecture, open from 10 to 2 and 7 to 8 for certificates to obtain permits to embark. The permit office is at the Douane, on the packet boat quay; they are given gratis,on the presentation of the passport (at present, permits are not required, if the passport is *en règle*). It is here also that the latter is *visé* on first landing from London; between which and Paris this route is 70 miles shorter than by way of Calais (with 29 miles of sea); the company's boats being as regular as those of the government, and the conveniences for landing, &c., equally good. Luggage, ½ fr. each large package; the porters are civil and quick. Omnibuses to the railway station. Passengers by *through* trains (in 10 hours) are not now examined till their arrival at the London or Paris terminus. Those going on to Marseilles should declare to that effect, to save delay at Paris about the passport. Paris time, ¼ hour before London. (See *Bradshaw's Continental Railway Guide*).

English Episcopal Chapel—Upper Town, Rev. George Brooks; Lower Town, Rev. W. K. Groves; Rue Royale, Rev. J. Bewsher, Rue de la Lampe, Rev. J. C. Furlong. Wesleyan Chapel—Rev. Mr. Chapman. Scotch Chapel—Rev. Mr. Stewart. There is a French protestant chapel.

Population, 29,145.

A sous-préfecture, (department Pas-de-Calais), port, military post of the 2nd class, and packet station, on the Channel, 29 miles from Folkestone, 112 from London. In spite of 5,000 of his countrymen who live here, an Englishman feels himself at once in a foreign country on landing, and his first walk up Rue de l'Ecu, is like a scene in a play. The entrance to the harbour is rather imposing, between wooden piers or jetties, made by the mouth of the Liane, 2,200 feet and 1,640 feet long. It was called *Gesoriacum* or *Bononia* by the Romans, who made it a fort, and built a lighthouse here (the Tour d'Ordre), carried away by the sea, 1644, except some traces near the baths. Attila attacked it; as did the Northmen, in the ninth century; and Henry VIII. took it 1544; one of his knights (buried at Hardres, in Kent,) carrying off its gates. Hence the old signs of Bull and Gate (Boulogne Gate) and Bull and Mouth, in London. His son gave it up six years later. Napoleon intended to invade England from here, and collected 200,000 men under Soult, for that purpose, but never ventured out of port.* It is divided into Upper and Lower town, the former, on the hills, being the oldest. Here are Vauban's citadel, and the old walls, now turned into a pleasant promenade, where you may catch a glimpse of Dover. The best and newest houses are at Tintelleries, on the north. Of the gates, only three are left, the principal one being Porte des Dunes (after the dunes or sand hills which line the shore towards Calais.) Place d'Armes is in Upper town. Water is supplied by 17 fountains and a reservoir; the lamps are lit with gas. Among the objects of notice are, Notre Dame church, a grecian pile, built 1827, on the site of the cathedral, which Louis XI. visited; the bishop's palace, now a school; the old hotel of the dukes d'Aumont, and the house which Napoleon stopped at; all in Upper town. In this part also is the Hôtel de Ville, with an old beffroi or belfry tower near it, 140 feet high. The museum, in Grand Rue, has a collection of arms, coins, Roman, and other antiquities, natural objects, &c., and is open three days a-week. The public library (bibliothèque,) has 22,000 vols. and 300 MSS., some being illuminated. There are also a Palais de Justice, hospitals, barracks, many French and English schools, three convents, a house replacing one which Le Sage (who wrote Gil Blas,) died in, a theatre in Rue Monsigny, on the site of the Cordeliers' convent. The splendid new baths have dancing, music, billiard, and reading rooms attached.

The *Napoleon Column*, one mile out of the town, was begun 1804 by the Grande Armée, and finished by Louis XVIII.; a statue of Napoleon was put up 1841. It is in the composite style, 180 feet high, 13 diameter, with a staircase within, and commands a great prospect. Beyond this is a chapel containing the *ex voto* offerings

* It is curious that the British army, when they took Paris, 1814, encamped in the Bois de *Boulogne*, near the city.

of the fishermen, who form a distinct class here as elsewhere.

In the neighbourhood are Mont Lambert, Mont Outreau, Mont St. Etienne, and other points of view, and remains of a roman road; the gardens at Denaire, and the châteaux of the Cregni, Colombert, and de la Cocherie; the botanic gardens of Mont Pelé; the quarries of Marquise and Ferques. A good mineral spring on the Wimille road.

Conveyances to Calais, St. Omer, &c.

(*a*) From Boulogne, on the road to Calais, (to which the telegraph is laid down), you pass (through a flat, sandy, and marshy soil), on to

WIMILLE (4 kil.), where the two unfortunate æronauts, Rosier and St. Romain, are buried. In trying to cross the Channel they fell from a height of 5,000 feet. Lower down the stream is the small port of Wimereau.

MARQUISE (9 kil.), on the Slack, which has a fine linden tree and marble quarries, is near Ambleteuse, where James II. landed, 1688, in his flight from England. Population, 2,550. Near it are the quarries of Ferques and Landretun, with some remains of Beaulieu abbey (founded 1150), and druid stones near the former.

LE HAUT BUISSON (9 kil.)

At 13 kil. further is Calais (*see* Route 10.)

ROUTE 13.

Douai to Valenciennes, Mons, &c.

DOUAI, as in Route 10.

You then pass Montigny (5½ miles), Somain (4½ m.), Wallers (5½ m.), Raismes (3½ m.), to

VALENCIENNES (4½ miles,) a sous-préfecture, in department Nord, a large strongly-fortified town, and second-class military station on the frontier, formerly the capital of Hainault, in the midst of a coal-field and thriving manufactures. It is well built, and divided into two parts by the Escaut, or Schelde, and has one of Vauban's citadels. Population, 18,953. Among the best buildings are, St. Gery's church, founded 1225, by Jeanne, daughter of Baldwin, emperor, of Constantinople, 171 feet long, with two of Rubens' pictures; the half-gothic Hôtel de Ville, built 1612, with three pictures by the same master; and a tall clock tower, 180 feet high, built 1237; public library of 18,000 vols. and MSS.; museum, containing minerals, armour, pictures, &c. An academy of painting, sculpture, and architecture, was founded 1782, by Baron Pujol; at the hospital, founded 1751, is a good chapel; the salle de spectacle (theatre), is by Pujol; and there is a mont de piété. It has several good promenades, and commands a fine view from the tower of the citadel. Froissart, or Froissard, the historian, Watteau, the painter, and d'Argenson, the statesman, were born here. Among the manufactures are muslins, gauzes, excellent lace, linens, wine, saltpetre, linseed oil, chicory, pottery, pipes, soap, leather, toys; it has several sugar and salt refineries, printworks, distilleries of eaux-de-vie, and there is a large trade in these articles, besides coal (the mines at Anzin employ 4,000 hands,) timber, &c. Travellers from Belgium are examined by the douaniers at the station. *Hotels*—Du Canard (Duck); de la Biche (Hind;) du Grand Cygne (Swan;) du Commerce, &c.

At Denain, a pillar stands on the spot where Marshal Villars routed the Allies, 1712.

Coaches to Bavay, Maubeuge, Berlaimont, Avesnes (40 kil. south-east; *see* Route 11), St. Amand-les-Eaux, Landrecies, Quesnoy, Condé, Bonsecours, Solesmes, Le Câteau. Mons, across the *Belgian* border, past Blanc-Misseron, &c., is 19½ miles further.

[Bavay, or Baval (22 kil. south-east), the roman *Bayacum*, has, in the Place, a seven-sided pillar, marking on its faces as many roman ways, and said to replace a roman milliary stone which stood here within the last two centuries.—Maubeuge, 12 kil. further, a small frontier fortress on the Sambre, with a population of 7,400, and manufactures of fire-arms, nails, iron, &c. Coal and marble are got near. The Austrians were defeated here, 1793.

St. Amand-les-Eaux (10 kil. north-north-west) on the Scarpe, with a population of 9,500, who make lace, soap, pottery, &c., is known for its waters, its artesian wells, and its clock tower, 318 feet high, which was the spire (built 1635-6,) to the church of St. Amand's abbey, founded 634. The mineral springs, near Croisette (2 kil.) are three, Fontaine-de-Bouillon, Source de Pavilion, Fontaine de Verité; temperature 77°; they are useful in rheumatism, paralysis, ulcers,

&c. Season, from June to August. There are bathing-houses and an assembly room, &c. Bon-Secours hermitage is near.

Le Quesnoy (15 kil. south-south-east), a fourth class fortress, on a hill, in a wide plain, near Mormal forest, with an arsenal, a curious church, a nail-factory, &c. It was taken by Eugene, 1712, taken and retaken, 1793, and occupied by the Allies, 1815-18.

Condé (11 kil. north-east) on the Schelde, close to the Belgian frontier, is a fourth-class fortress (by Vauban), with a large arsenal and good Hôtel de Ville. It gave title of prince to the Bourbons, to whom it came in the fifteenth century. The Spaniards at one time held it, and the Allies took it, 1793. Population, 5,000. Nails, starch, tiles, &c. are made. Mademoiselle Clairon the actress was a native. Near it is Ermitage, seat of Duc de Croi.

Solesmes (19 kil. south) on the Selle, has the cloister, &c., of an abbey of old date, with a modern church, having a spire 213 feet high. Population, 5,000. Linens, muslins, &c. are made, besides soap and leather. At 8 kil. further is Câteau-Cambrésis (*see* Route 11.)]

ROUTE 14.

Hazebrouck to Dunkirk.

Distance, 41 kil., or 25½ miles.

Hazebrouck, as in Route 10.

Cassel (6½ miles), an old town, once fortified, having a parish church of the thirteenth century, part of a Jesuits' convent, a Flemish mairie, two (out of six) gates, &c., but most remarkable for the prospect it commands from the hill it stands on (800 feet high), over the flat and populous country around. An anchor found here, 1815, about 12 feet down, and other signs, shew that this flat was once covered by the sea. The view takes in part of the North Sea (even to Dover in clear weather), 32 fortified towns, and about 100 villages, including Dunkirk, Nieuport, Ostend, Bruges, Ypres, Courtray, Lille, Bethune, St. Omer, Calais, Hazebrouck, Gravelines, &c. It extends above 30 miles every way. General Vandamme, who fought at Waterloo, was born here; and his house and gardens are shewn.

Arneke (4½ miles).

Esquelbecq (4½ miles).

Bergues (5½ miles), a small frontier post, on the Colme, and a canal which brings vessels of 300 tons up from the sea. It stands among marshes, and has often suffered from war, having been taken or pillaged about sixteen times. It has an Hôtel de Ville, built 1664; a pretty belfry, 164 feet high, two towers of St. Winnoc's abbey, which serve for sea marks, a good public library of 5,000 volumes, and a museum of pictures. The trade is in butter, cheese, grain (for which there is a large market), cattle, linen, lace, eaux-de-vie, &c. Population, 6,000.

At 5 miles further is

Dunkirk, or Dunkerque. *Hotels*—De Flandre, an old established house, where travellers are sure to be comfortable; de la Poste; du Chapeau Rouge (Red Cap); du Sauvage.

English protestant chapel in Rue-des-Sœurs Blanches, Rev. Mr. Thompson. The British vice-consul will visé passports before embarking as well as the Maire. Passengers for Belgium, &c., should have their luggage *plombé* (sealed) to save examination in crossing France.

High water at moon's full and change, 11h. 18m.

Population, 24,600. A sous-préfecture in department Nord, a bustling port, military post of the second class, on the Belgian frontier, grew out of a church founded in the seventh century, by St. Eloi, called the "Church of the Dunes," from the dunes, downs, or sand-hillocks, which line this terribly flat coast. It is about 40 miles due east of Dover, the anchorage lying at some distance in the road; and is as noted for smugglers in peace, as for its exploits in war time,—especially when it sent out Jean Bart, a bold privateer's man, who was a native, and whose statue is in Place Royale. Canal runs inland to Bergues, Ostend, Bruges, &c. White brick houses of two stories make up the neat broad streets, but there is a want of good water. Many of the people, workmen and others, live in cellars. It is defended by ramparts, the citadel, fort Risbau, &c., and has two basins, one of which was restored 1794, and frigates launched in it. There is a jetty at the quay, besides a long pier over the flats, and a light-tower, 194 feet high. The Hôtel de Ville, built 1644, is an old-fashioned pile, with a low spire; a solid square clock tower, of brick, 154 feet high, called Tour de l'Eglise, because once part of the church, is now cut off from it by the road. This church (St. Eloi's) is gothic, with a handsome grecian portico of ten pillars, added by Luis, and some paintings. The Jesuit's church is replaced by the college; the public library contains 7,000 volumes; large barracks are also seen, a salle de spectacle, school of navigation, &c.; and there are sea and other baths. Its position has made it the scene of many contests. A castle was built by the Counts of Flanders, which the English burnt, 1388; they took the town, 1538, but gave it up to Spain the next year. The French (under Condé) took it, 1558, but restored it immediately; again, in 1658, it was taken by Turenne at the "Battle of the Dunes," given up to Cromwell, but sold, in 1662, by Charles II. to Louis XIV., who fortified it. This happened when Clarendon was building his great house in Piccadilly, which the mob nicknamed Dunkirk House. The fortifications were razed, 1715, but afterwards restored. The Duke of York tried to take it, 1793, but without success. Admiral Roussin was born here.

Manufactures of ropes, sugar, candles, &c., and a good trade in eaux-de-vie, gin, coal, soap, leather, salt, tebacco, butter, fish, salmon, cheese, beer, grain, iron, pottery, &c.

Conveyances, by rail, to Lille, Brussels, Paris, &c.; by steamer to Havre, on Saturday (10 and 20 francs, in 20 hours), to Rotterdam (10 and 20 francs, in 12 hours), Hamburg, Copenhagen; by canal-boat to Bourbourg (6 hours), Ostend, &c.; by sailing-packet to Ramsgate and London, Hull, Dundee, &c. (See *Bradshaw's Continental Railway Guide).*

(*a*) From Dunkirk, along the coast, you pass LAFRENOUCK (3 miles); then Laytcoote, near the *Belgian* border (6 miles from Dunkirk), across which the first place is Furnes and its two churches.

SECTION III.

ROADS TO THE EAST;

IN CONNEXION WITH THE PARIS AND STRASBURG RAILWAY (CHEMIN-DE-FER DE PARIS A STRASBOURG); SUPPLYING RHEIMS, CHALONS-SUR-MARNE, BAR-LE-DUC, CHAUMONT, NANCY, METZ (BADEN AND FRANKFORT), EPINAL, STRASBOURG, COLMAR, MULHOUSE, BASLE (THE RHINE AND SWITZERLAND.) ROUTES SIXTEEN TO TWENTY-TWO.

ROUTE 16.

Paris to Strasbourg.

Embarcadère, or terminus, Rue Neuve Chabrol, in Rue de Faubourg St. Martin near the Northern railway. Opened throughout, 1852. Distance to Strasbourg, 501 kil., or 312½ miles; (to Nancy, 220 miles); four trains a day, in 12 to 15 hours; 51½, 39, and 29 fr.; baggage allowed, 30 kil., or 66 lbs.

The stations are—

	kil.		kil.		kil.
Noisy-le-Sec..	9	Meaux	8	Nogent-l'Artand	10
Bondy	2	Trilport	6	Château-Thierry	11
Villemonble .	3	Changis	7	Mezy............	11
Chelles	5	LaFerté-sous-Jouarre ...	8	Varennes......	2
Lagny	9	Nanteuil	8		
Esbly	9				

	kil.		kil.		kil
Dormans	11	Nançois-le-Petit	11	Blainville-la-Grande......	6
Port-à-Binson	9	Loxeville	11	Lunéville	9
Damery	9	Lèrouville ...	13	Marainviller .	8
Epernay	7	Commercy ...	5	Emberménil .	8
Oiry	6	Sorcy	8	Avricourt ...	8
Jalons	9	Pagny-s-Mse.	6	Hèming	14
Chalons	13	Foug............	5	Sarrebourg ...	8
Vitry-la-Villecais	16	Toul	6	Lützelbourg..	17
Loisy............	11	Fontenoy-sur-Moselle	9	Saverne	10
Vitry-le-Fran.	6	Liverdun	9	Steinbourg ...	4
Blesmes	12	Frouard	7	Dettwiller ...	4
Pargny.........	8	Nancy	8	Hochfelden...	8
Sermaize	16	Varangeville.	13	Mommenheim	5
Revigny	7	Rosières-aux-Salines	5	Brumath	5
Bar-le-Duc ...	16			Vendenheim .	8
				Strasbourg ...	9

Outside the barrière is La Vilette, near the basin of the Canal de l'Ourcq, from which the canal of St. Martin runs down to the Seine, and which feeds many of the Paris fountains. It was made 1806-9, and is 2620 feet long. Thence the rail follows the Canal-de-l'Ourcq to Meaux, (passing Vitry, Blancmenil, Aunay, Rosny, Pantin, Baubigny, &c., on the right and left).—Belleville, near to La Villette, has a fine view over Paris from its country seats, and an aqueduct, or reservoir, built by Philippe Auguste, and restored 1602. It was here the pupils of the Ecole Polytechnique distinguished themselves, 1814.—Romainville, a little further, also commands a view of the city, and is covered with wood and ginguettes for pleasure folks; a detached fort and reservoir stand on it. The latter is joined to another at Pré St. Gervais.

Noisy-le-Sec (5½ miles).

Bondy (1½ miles), is an old village of 1,950 souls, near a forest where Childeric II. was killed, and Aubry de Montdidier was murdered by Macaire, (who fought with his victim's dog—the dog of Montargis—before Charles V., at Notre Dame.) Raincy château belonged to Louis Philippe, who laid out the grounds in the English style. For a time it was held by Napoleon.

Coaches to Livry, Sevran, Villepinte, Tremblay, Vaujours, Villeparisis, Mitry.

[Livry, 6 kil. east-north-east, in the forest, near Raincy château, has an Augustine abbey, not far from which dwelt the pious hermit of Livry, "whose name," as D'Aubigny relates, "though written in heaven, history has not transmitted to us," but who, for preaching the gospel, peacefully died at the stake in front of Notre Dame.]

Villemonble-Gagny (2 miles), in department Seine-et-Marne. Coaches to Rosny, Montfermeil, Coubron, Neuilly-sur-Marne, and to Juilly, which has an academy or college founded 1688, by the Fathers of the Oratory.

Chelles (3 miles). Coaches to Torcy, Gournay-sur-Marne, and to Claye, on the canal de l'Ourcq, with bleach-works, &c.

Lagny, 5¾ miles, is across the bridge on the Marne, on its south bank. Coaches to Annet Fresnes, Ferrières, Provins (*see* Route 26), Rosoy Jouy-le-Châtel, Fontenay, &c.

[*Ermenonville* (24 kil., north-north-east), has a country seat, with a lake and fine grounds, built by the Girardins, its Vicomtes (on the site of an older), in which Rousseau died, 1799 (in what is now the lodge). His tomb is among poplars on an island in the lake, but his body lies in the Pantheon. A little circular temple to the Advancement of Philosophy (purposely left unfinished), stands on six pillars, to Newton, Descartes, Voltaire, Montesquieu, Penn, Rousseau; the whole being dedicated to Montaigne. The Emperor Joseph, Gustavus of Sweden, and others, have visited this spot.]

The rail crosses a bend of the Marne twice before Meaux.

Esbly (5½ miles). Coaches to Crécy, Coulommiers, Beton-Bazoche.

[*Coulommiers* (23 kil. south-east), a sous-préfecture in department Seine-et-Marne, of 4,000 souls, in a pleasant part of the Grand Morin, on which is an island with remains of a château built by the Duchesse de Longueville. It grew out of St. Denis' church, founded by the Counts of Champagne, and has a good chapel to the convent established by the duchess. General Beaurepaire, who shot himself rather than give up Verdun, 1792, was a native. Many mills for grain, tan, &c., and a trade in Brie cheese, melons, wool, cattle, &c. *Hotels*—De l'Ours (Bear), la Croix Blanche (White Cross).]

Meaux (5 miles), a well-built town, sous-préfecture (9,400 population), and bishopric, in a pleasant spot on the canal de l'Ourcq and the Marne, which divides it in two; that part to the south being called the Marché, and joined to the other by a wooden bridge overhung with mills, turned by the rapid current. It was the capital of the *Meldi* in Roman times; and, later, of Brie Champenoise; was ravaged by the Normans (eighth century), and the Jacquerie rioters (fourteenth century); taken by the English, 1420, and by Henry IV., 1594. The best building is St. Etienne's *cathedral*, a massive gothic structure, begun 1212, and left unfinished in the sixteenth century; it is 332 feet by 138, and 213 feet high at the north tower, which stands on one side of the west front, and commands a view nearly to Paris. Inside are 32 clustered pillars and a rich choir, with a tomb to the eloquent Bossuet, who died bishop. His statue, by Rutehiel, is at the palace, where they shew his library, &c. There are two other churches, a large hospital or Hôtel Dieu, halle or market, theatre, college, library of 14,000 vols., cavalry barracks, &c., and a Grand Place. Trade in grain, cattle, fromage de Brie (Brie cheese), poultry, and wool, a few muslins are made. *Hotels*—De la Sirène, du Cheval Rouge (Red Horse).

Coaches to Coulommiers (*see* above), Dammartin, Juilly, Nanteuil-le-Hardouin, Villers-Cotterets, La Ferté-Milon, May, Crouy, Lizy.

[Dammartin (19 kil. north-west), on a hill, where there is a fine circle of view. Lace is made.—May-en-Muleien (11 kil. north-east), on the canal de l'Ourcq, has an ancient church, ranking next to Meaux, in this diocess.

La Ferté Milon (12 kil. further), in department Aisne, on a hill by the Ourcq, was fortified as far back as 845, and has a castle dismantled by Henry IV. In front of the Hôtel de Ville is David's statue of Racine (born here 1639), whose bust, by Stabinsky, is in the bibliothèque of 17,000 volumes. Population, 4,800. *Hotel*—Du Soleil d'Or (Golden Sun).

Villers-Cotteret, (10 kil. north of this), in the forest of Retz, has a château restored by Francis I. (on the site of one burnt by the English) now a depôt de medicine, or poor-house for the district. Near it are remains of Longpont abbey church, founded in the twelfth century. General Dumas (called the French Cocles, for his defence of Brixen bridge), and Otto the statesman, were natives.]

The railway crosses the Marne three or four times to La Ferté.

TRILPORT (3¾ miles).

CHANGIS (4½ miles).

LA FERTE-SOUS-JOUARRE (5 miles), at the bridges on the Marne, (one suspension), was, in the twelfth century a *ferté* or strength, built by a seigueur called Ancoul, and in the sixteenth century was held by the Protestants, and often plundered. On a pretty island is the old château d'Ile, or La Barre, where Louis XVI. and his Queen stopped, when they were brought back from Varennes. There are several good points of view around. Population, 4,400. Trade in corn, charcoal, and meules à moulin, or mill-stones, for which it is famous. Coaches to Jouarre, (on south bank), Marigny, Montmirail, La Ferté-Gaucher, and Sézanne.

[Montmirail, (23 kil. east-south-east), on a hill by the Petit Morin, is noted for its millstones, and for a victory of Napoleon, 11th February, 1814, over the Prussians and Russians The Duc de Dudeauville has a seat here. Cardinal de Retz was a native. At Vauchamps (7 kil. east), Napoleon defeated Blucher, 14th February, 1814, after having routed his advanced guard on the 10th, at Champaubert, (11 kil. further); but at Fère-Champenoise, (24 kil. south-east of this), on the Pleurs, Marmont was finally beaten by the allies, 24th of March.—Montmort, (6 kil. north-north-east of Champaubert), has a moated brick donjon, square and flanked with turrets; with a church ornamented with good stained windows.

Sézanne (18 kil. south-south-west of Champaubert), on the Auges, which supplies mills and bleach works, was a town of *Gallia-Comata*, destroyed by Thibault IV. Count of Champagne. It was rebuilt and taken by the English, 1223; and suffered from the Huguenots and from fire; so that it has a modern well-built look, with a good church, hospital, &c. Population, 4,600.]

NANTEUIL, (5 miles). through a tunnel,

NOGENT-L'ARTAUD, (6 miles), in dept. of the Aisne, has a coach to Charly, across the Marne, through another tunnel, to

CHATEAU-THIERRY, (7 miles), a sous-préfecture of 4,700 persons, on the rocky hills of the Marne, crowned by the fine remains of a château, built 720, by Charles Martel, to hold Thierry IV., the infant son of Childeric. It has frequently suffered from war, having been attacked by the English 1370, by the Leaguers 1421, by Charles V. in 1544, by Henry of Guise 1571, (called Balafré, or gashed, like his father, from the wound he received here), the Frondeurs 1614; and especially in 1814, when it was taken and retaken, and the old bridge destroyed. This is replaced by a three-arch stone one to the faubourg across the river, where, on the promenade, is a statue of La Fontaine, (a native, 1621), whose house is still shewn here. An old fortified gate leads out to faubourg la Barre. Near the castle is St. Crépin's ancient church, with two towers; the Hôtel Dieu, founded by Philippe le Bel's queen, Jeanne, has some pictures; the hôtel Balhan, or fort of St. Jacques, and the gate and chapel of the castle, are worth notice. There are some mineral waters, and gypsum quarries. Trade in corn, linseed oil, wine, &c. *Hotels*—Du Lion d'Or, (Golden Lion); de la Sirene. Coaches to Soissons, (*see* Route 10), Neuilly-St. Front, Orbais. Good churches are seen at Essomes (thirteenth century), Chasy-l'Abbaye (built 1130); also at Mezi-Moulin and Condé-en-Brie, to the south of the railway, further on.

MEZY (5¾ miles).

VARRENNES (1¼ miles). Coaches to Fismes, Braisne, Fère-en-Tardenois.

[The last place (17 kil. north), once fortified, and taken by the Huguenots, Leaguers, &c., has, not far off, the fine ruins of Robert of Dreux's *Castle*, built 1206, consisting of parts of eight great towers, (one 60 feet high), within a wall, and joined to an outwork across the ditch, by a drawbridge, on a viaduct, built 1539, by Anne de Montmorency, 91 feet high, and 170 feet long, strengthened by tall battlements, &c. — At Braisne-sur-Vesle, (18 kil. further), are mineral waters, and a good church, which was part of an Abbey, founded 1130. — Fismes, (15 kil. north-east of Fère), in department Marne, on the Vesle, is the roman *Furis*, where councils were held 881 and 935, and which marked the borders of Austrasia. Napoleon made it his head-quarters, March, 1314.]

DORMANS (6¾ miles) at the suspension bridge on the river, has St. Hippolyte's old church, and a trade in wine, grain, &c.

PORT-A-BINSON, (5¾ miles), on the south side of the river, opposite the old castle of Châtillon-sur-Marne.

DAMERY (5½ miles), on the north side of the river, which improves as you ascend it into the champagne wine country.

EPERNAY (4½ miles), a sous-préfecture in department Marne of 6,350 souls, in a pleasant spot on the Marne, under the vine-covered chalk-hills of Champagne, of which wine this is the entrepôt for the best growths. They are distinguished as mousseux (frothy or effervescing,) and non-mousseux. The merchants live in Faubourgs la Folie and le Commerce; and the hills around are excavated for their cellars. Some houses are of timber or brick; a stone bridge crosses the river. The painted windows of the old gothic church are preserved in the new Italian one, built 1828-32. At the Hôtel de Ville is a library of 10,000 volumes, and a museum. Some derive the name from *Aquæ perennes:* Clovis gave it to the archbishops of Rheims, who fortified it. Francis I. burnt it to hinder Charles V. from taking it, and it fell to Henry IV., after a siege in which Marshal Biron was killed. Later, it belonged to the Ducs de Bouillon. Pottery, millinery, leather, &c., are made, and it has a good trade in wood and charcoal, as well as wine. *Hotels*—De l'Europe, de l'Ecu de France (Crown Piece), de la Croix d'Or (Golden Cross). Coaches to Rheims (*see* Route 17.)

AY or AÏ, (4 miles east-north-east,) where the best white mousseux wines are grown.

OIRY (3¾ miles.) Coaches to Lesmenil, and Avize (9 miles south), also noted for its wine and cave cellars.

JALON-LES-VIGNES (6¾ miles,) on the Marne, where the Somme-Soude joins.

At 8¼ miles further is

Chalons. *Hotels*—Du Palais Royal, de la Ville de Paris, de Nancy, de la Cloche d'Or (Golden Bell), de la Pomme d'Or (Golden Apple.) Population 16,000. An ancient place, chief town of department Marne, in the old province of Champagne, seat of a military division, of a bishopric, &c., in a fine meadow and wine country., on the Marne, which is crossed by a stone bridge of three arches. It was the *Duro-Catalauni*, near which Aurelian beat Tetricus, in 271, and Attila was defeated by the Romans, in 451. It is guarded by walls and moats, and has six principal gates, leading to as many roads: many of the houses are built of lath and plaster. Four churches remain.

St. Etienne's cathedral, rebuilt in the sixteenth century (on the site of a temple to Apollo,) in a rich florid style, is 360 ft. long, and has two fine spires of open work, 118 feet high, a portico in the greek style, a fine altar by Mansard, stained windows, and an ancient crypt. Nôtre Dame church, built between 1157 and 1322, is partly in the norman style, with good painted windows, and a mosaic pavement. The Hôtel de Ville, on Place d'Armes, built 1772, has an ionic façade of eight pillars, with bas-reliefs of the productions of Champagne, and portraits of natives. Hôtel dela Préfecture, built 1762, is also a good building, with a doric front. At the Ecole des arts et metiers (school of arts and trades,) is a pretty chapel and 300 pupils. The library has 22,000 volumes. The Promenade du Jard, on the Strasbourg road is well planted. There are a high school, a theatre, botanic garden, school of design, society of agriculture, priests' seminary, museum, hospitals, and immense wine stores in the chalk caves. Trade in Champagne wine, casks, wool, oil, leather, cutlery, &c. Lacaille, the astronomer was born here. The great battle above mentioned, which for a time stopped the progress of the Huns, was fought at a spot called Attila's Camp, 5 miles off, near Chape and Cuperly, with immense slaughter on both sides; Ætius the roman commander, assisted by his Visigoth allies, was successful, but their king, Theodoric, was slain.

Conveyances: by railway to Paris, Strasbourg, Epernay, &c.; by coach to Mezières, Rheims, Verdun, Chaumont, St. Menehould (*see* Route 18).

From Chalons, on the railway, you pass Vitry-la-Ville (9¾ miles); Loisy (7 miles); to

Vitry-le-François, or *Vitry-sur-Marne* (3¾ miles,) a sous-préfecture of 8,000 people, on the Marne and the canal which joins it to the Rhine, founded by Francis I., in 1545, and regularly fortified. The streets are well-built, and the houses of wood. It has an unfinished gothic church, begun by Francis I., with an old tomb; a large public place, with a fountain, &c. *Hotels*—Des Voyageurs (Travellers), la Cloche (Bell); *Café*—des Oiseaux, a well-known resort. Coaches up the Marne, &c., to St. Dizier, Vassy, Joinville, Vignory, Chaumont, Vesaignes, Langres, Montierender.

[*St. Dizier* (27 kil. east-south-east,) a sous-préfecture, in Haute-Marne, (population, 7,290) on the Marne, among woods, was besieged by Charles V. in 1544, and mostly burnt by accident 1775. It has part of an old castle, near the gothic church, and a modern Hôtel de Ville. *Hotels*—du Soleil d'Or (Golden Sun,) l'Arbre d'Or (Golden Tree.) Wood is cut and iron forged here.

Vassy or *Wassy* (15 kil. south from St. Dizier as above,) another sous-préfecture, is on the site, some say, of *Vadicasses*, burnt by Caracalla in 211. Roman coins have been found. An inscription near the hospital marks where a massacre of the protestants took place, 1562, by the Duc de Guise. Large forests and iron forges surround it. Population 2,583.

Joinville (25 kil. south-east of St. Dizier,) an old place, in a pleasant spot on the Marne, among vineyards and iron forges, under a hill, on which stood (till the Duke of Orleans pulled it down, 1790,) the old castle of the Sires de Joinville and the Ducs de Guise, where the League was entered into 1585. The Prince de Joinville takes his title hence. One of its lords was the Sire de Joinville who wrote the 'Histoire de St. Louis, IX. du nom,' which gives a charming picture of a French knight of that age and his excellent and pious sovereign.

Chaumont (44 kil. further,) is described in Route 27.]

The next stations on the rail are Blesmes (7½ miles), Pargny (5 miles), Sermaize 3¾ miles), Revigny (4 miles), and Bar-le-Duc, which is 7 miles further.

Bar-le-Duc. *Hotel*—le Cygne (Swan). Population, 12,500. Chief town of department Meuse, in a pleasant spot on the Ornain, was built for a frontier (or barrier) by Frederick, Duke of Upper Lorraine, in the tenth century, as head of the Duchy of le Barrois. High Town stands on the hill, round a fragment of the old castle (pulled down by Louis XIV., in 1670), whence there is a fine view. Low Town lies along the river, which is crossed by three bridges, and is a lively part, with good broad streets, several tanyards, cotton mills, dye-houses, &c. St. Pierre Church, on the hill, has an anatomical effigy of René de Chalons (killed 1544, at St. Dizier), with the muscles, bones, and skin displayed, by Richier, a pupil of M. Angelo. There are a hôtel de la préfecture, Hôtel de Ville, college, palais de justice, small theatre, &c. Marshal Oudinot and General Excelmans were born here. Manufactures of cottons and woollens, lace, gloves, hats, and delicious confitures (sweetmeats); trade in light wines (de Bar), iron, timber from the forests around.

Conveyances Daily, by rail, to Paris, Strasburg, &c.; by coach, to Verdun (46 kil.; *see* Route 18), Neufchâteau, &c. The Castle of Jean d'Heure, and its gardens, and Sarrasins' grotto are near.

[From Bar-le-Duc, to the north-east, you pass *St. Mihiel* (40 kil.), in a valley on the Meuse, under mountains, one carrying a ruined castle, built 1085, by a Countess de Bar. At St. Etienne's (Stephen's) abbey church is a beautiful marble of the Descent from the Cross, by M. Angelo's pupil, Richier, who lived at a house in Rue des Foxes. Population, 5,822; cotton and linen weavers. *Hotels*—Lion d'Or (Golden Lion); du Cygne (Swan).

Going down the Meuse, the next place is Verdun (*see* Route 18).]

From Bar-le-Duc, on the rail, to Nancy, you pass Longueville (2½ miles).

NANÇOIS-LE-PETIT (4½ miles). Coach to Ligny (10 kil.), a pretty place, of 3,212 souls, on the Ornain, in the middle of vineyards, with fine grounds round the old château. *Hotels*—De la Cloche (Bell); Soleil d'Or (Golden Sun).

LOXEVILLE (3½ miles).

LEROUVILLE (8½ miles). Coach to St. Mihiel (13 kil. north) as above. Viaductof 90 yards, to

COMMERCY (3½ miles), a sous-préfecture, with 4,761 inhabitants, in a pleasant fertile spot on the Meuse, well built, with public fountains, Hôtel de Ville, barracks, and riding-house. *Hotels*—De la Cloche d'Or (Gold Bell) de la Poire d'Or (Gold Pear). Coaches to Mirecourt, Epinal (*see* Route 19), Remiremont, Plombières, Bourbonne-les-Bains (*see* Route 27), Lay St. Remy.

SORCY (6 miles), on the Meuse, has traces of St. Martin's Abbey, and on a hill, near it, remains of a roman camp. Coach to Vaucouleurs, Neufchâteau (*see* Route 19). Tunnel of 570 yds., to

PAGNY-SUR-MEUSE (3¾ miles).

FOUG (3½ miles), in department of the Meurthe.

TOUL (3¾ miles), an old town and military post of the fourth class, formerly seat of a diocess, It was the head of the *Leuci*, in Belgic Gaul, in Cæsar's time, and was made a free town by the German Emperors. A bridge of seven arches crosses the Moselle. There are the old *Cathedral*, begun by St. Gerard, 965, with a fine roof and two very picturesque towers; the Hôtel de Ville, once the bishop's palace; a college, barracks, corn market, &c. Marshal St. Cyr, Baron Louis, the financier, and Admiral Rigny, were natives. Population, 7,314, who make embroidery, pottery, &c. *Hotel*—de l'Europe.

FONTENOY-SUR-MOSELLE (5½ miles).

LIVERDUN (5¾ miles), a decayed fortress, on a rock over the Moselle, with many good points of view.

FROUARD (4½ miles). At 5½ miles further is Nancy, where the branch to Metz parts off.

Nancy, *Hotels*—De l'Europe, very good, and highly recommended; du France; du Commerce; du Grand Tigre; des Halles; du Petit Paris. *Cafés*—in Place Stanislaus. Pop., 43,000. Capital of department Meurthe (formerly of Province of Lorraine) seat of a diocess, cour impériale, &c., is near the Meurthe, in a fertile plain, under some low hills, covered with forests and vineyards, and is one of the best built towns of France. It was founded in the eleventh century by the dukes of Lorraine, one of whom was René II., who obtained a famous victory over Charles the Bold, of Burgundy, in 1477, outside the town; and another was Stanislaus of Poland, who greatly improved it and left the duchy to his father-in-law, Louis XV., upon his death, 1766.

At Old Town are remains of their palace, now a barrack; also St. Epore's gothic church, which has a bas-relief (the Lord's Supper, 1582), by Drouin, a native; and the Cordeliers' church, built 1477-84, by René II., which has his tomb (1515), with those of Cardinal Vandémont (by Drouin), Antoine de Vaudémont, Philippa of Gueldres, Henry of Vaudémont and wife, and a warrior, besides Gerard I. and his wife Hadwige, in the round, or ducal chapel, restored since the ravages made in 1793. In this part of the city, too, are the Place de Grève, leading to the Cours d'Orleans, and the Porte Neuve (or New Gate), built 1785, on the Metz road, with the Place Carrière, in which stand the Cour Royale, the tribunal of commerce, and the préfecture (a large old building). The last is opposite the arch of triumph, leading to the Place Royale (or Stanislaus), the best part of the new town, which was begun by Charles III., in 1603. Here are the Hôtel de Ville, the bishop's seat, the salle de spectacle, &c., all in an uniform style; a bronze figure of Stanislaus, put up 1823, ornaments the centre, and there is a promenade out of one side, past the fountains, called the Pepinière. A large fountain occupies the Place d'Alliance.

The *Cathedral*, a modern edifice, has two low spires in its front, which is 154 feet broad and 256 feet high; a dome near the sanctuary is 51 feet across, and painted by Jacquart. Notre Dame de Bon Secours church, in Faubourg St. Pierre, on the Lunéville road, was rebuilt (1738) by Stanislaus, whose tomb by Adam is here, on the site of one founded by René over the spot where his adversary fell (1477); it has some old standards taken from the Turks. At the Palais de Justice they shew the tapestry taken from Charles the Bold's tent. St. Jean's chapel belonged to the Knights of St. John. A library of 26,000 volumes is at the Hôtel de l'Université. There are also a college, a priests' seminary, large hospitals, a deaf and dumb asylum, new barracks, collections of natural history, a society of arts and sciences and botanic gardens (both founded by Stanislaus), an exchange, &c.

Nancy is the chief head quarters of several female religious societies, as the Sisters of Christian Doctrine, Sisters of St. Charles, and Sisters of Providence, which three number about 1,000 houses in France.

Some of its *natives* are Marshal Bassompière, General Druot, Maimbourg, the historian, Hoffman, the critic, Isabey and Grandville, the painters, &c. Manufactures of cotton cloth, woollen serges, muslins, and embroidery, &c. are carried on here.

Conveyances: by rail, to Strasbourg, Metz, Paris, &c.; by coach, to Lunéville, Lyons, Mirecourt, Besançon, Colmar, Epinal, Neufchâteau, &c.; steamer to Metz (8 hours). In the neighbourhood are Liverdun (8 kil.), in a pretty spot, Bosserville (4 kil.), and its monastery; Ludres, a roman camp (9 kil.); Roville model farm (24 kil.)

[At 30 kil. north-east is *Château Salins*, a sous-préfecture of 26,000 people, on the Seille, so called after a castle built, 1342, by Isabella of Austria, near the salines or salt-works. Great quantities of salt are now got at Vic (5 kil.), Moyen-Vic (6 kil. south-south-east), and Dieuze (18 kil. east-south-east).]

From Nancy, on the rail to Strasbourg, you pass

VARANGEVILLE, St. Nicholas-du-Port (7½ miles), up the Moselle, with a fine gothic church built 1494-1544, having light pillars 92 feet high, and towers to match.

ROSIERES-AUX-SALINES (3½ miles), before which you leave on the left, Dombasle (2 kil.), where a branch of the Moselle falls into that stream, passing a ruined chateau on the top of the hill. Population 1,600.

BLAINVILLE-LE-GRANDE (3¾ miles) on the Moselle.

LUNEVILLE (5½ miles), a sous-préfecture in department Meurthe, with 12,500 people, in a fertile spot on the Meurthe where the Vezouze joins, was at first a hunting seat, and was taken by Marshal Longueville, 1638, and the fortifications pulled down. At the old palace of the Dukes of Lorraine, the Emperor Francis I. was born; it is now a cavalry depôt. There are also a large riding house, a champ de mars, a fountain in Place Neuve, and a modern church with the tomb of Voltaire's friend, Madame Châtelet. The Chevalier Bouffleurs, and General Haxo were born here. The treaty between France and Austria was signed here 1801. Trade in pottery, gloves, embroidery, wine, beer, &c. *Hotels*—Du Sauvage; de la Tête d'Or (Golden Head); du Faisan (Pheasant).

[At 28 kil. south-south-east, up the Mortagne is Ramberviller (already described); and at 30 kil. south-east, up the Meurthe, in the Vosges Mountains, is Raon l'Etape, which has a large trade in timber, and had a castle and monastery.]

MARAINVILLER (5 miles).

EMBERMENIL (5 miles).

[About 10 kil. south-west is Baccarat, on the Meurthe, under a rocky height, and celebrated for its *crystal* factory, which employs 600 hands.]

The next station,

AVRICOURT (5 miles), is not far from Blamont (15 kil.), near the head of the Vezouze, under the Vosges range (in one of whose gorges is the glass works of St. Quiren), which has a ruined castle, and gave birth to Regnier, Duke of Massa. Several lakes are near.

HEMING (8¾ miles), where the northern road from Nancy falls in.

SARREBOURG (5 miles), a sous-préfecture, of 2,600 souls, and military post on the Sarre, in a pass of the Vosges. It belonged to the Archbishops of Metz, and Dukes of Lorraine, and came to France 1661. Most of it was rebuilt after the fire of 1461. Cotton goods, paper, cordage, &c. are made.

HOMARTING (4 miles).

PHALSBOURG (5½ miles), a fortified fort, on a rock, where English prisoners were kept in the war. The citadel was built by Vauban, to command a pass of the Vosges. It was called Einartyhausen, before 1570, when the prince palatine of Velden rebuilt it under its modern name; it came afterwards to the house of Lorraine. Part of the palace is seen; besides an Hôtel de Ville of the time of Louis XIV., a college, &c. Marshal Lobau, General Gérard, &c. were born here. Excellent noyau is made. Population, 4,900. In the neighbourhood are, the fountain supplied from Hildans (8 kil. off), Kraffenthal valley, and Dabo, where Leo IX. was born (?).

LUTZELBOURG (1½ miles), near the top of the Vosges, has an old château. You pass through three tunnels to the station.

SAVERNE (6 miles), down the east slant of the Vosges (towards the Rhine), in a charming spot on the Zorn, is a sous-préfecture, in department Bas-Rhine (formerly Alsace), having 5,800 souls, and belonged to the bishops of Strasbourg, who had a seat here, now a barrack. The church has a high square tower. Copper goods are made. *Hotel*—De la Poste.

[At 6 kil. south, is Marmoutiers, with an ancient abbey church of the tenth century.]

STEINBOURG (3½ miles), on the Zorn.

[At 8 kil. north, is Neuwiller, which has a seat built by the Duke of Feltre, on the site of Herrenbourg château.]

DETTWILLER (2½ miles), lower down the Zorn.

HOCHFELDEN (5½ miles).

MOMMENHEIM (2½ miles).

BRUMATH (3½ miles), where the rail turns off from the Zorn, is the ancient *Brocomagus*, and is near the foundling hospital of Stephansfelden, founded 1220.

[At 11 kil. north-north-east, is Haguenau, on the Moder, a fortress of the fourth class, first walled round by Frederic Barbarossa, who made it an imperial town. It has two gothic churches of the twelfth and thirteenth centuries. Population 11,200, who make starch &c., and brew beer.—About 30 kil. north-north-east of Haguenau is the sous-préfecture of *Wissembourg* (population 5,200), a fortified post on the Lauter, on the Bavarian frontier, which had an abbey founded by Dagobert, and came to France by the peace of Ryswick. The old church was rebuilt 1288; at St. Jean's protestant church a bust of Luther was put up at the third centenary of the Reformation. The lines outside were taken by the Austrains, and retaken by Hoche, 1793. Landau in *Bavaria* is 12 kil. further.]

VENDENHEIM (4½ miles). About 6½ miles further is

Strasbourg, 312½ miles from Paris. *Hotels*—De Paris, near the Poste, a first-class hotel, (omnibuses to the rail and steamer); de la Maison Rouge, in Place Kléber, most comfortable, and highly recommended; de la Fleur, near the Custom House, and de Metz, in the Old Wine market, are very reasonable; de France, in Place St. Pierre-le-Jeune. *Cafés*, on the Broglie, Place Kléber, &c. The pâtés de foie gras or goose-liver pies are noted. Population, 72,000, chiefly German speaking.

Chief town of department Bas-Rhin (formerly province of Alsace), seat of a bishopric, and of Protestant and Jewish consistories, of an academy and college, &c., first class fortress, and head of a military division, in a fertile plain on the Ill and Bruche, near the Rhine and the Baden frontier. The German name is Strassburg, *i.e.* street-fort, from the street or high road over the Rhine (1½ miles east), which it commands by means of the bridge to Kehl, and which here is about as wide as the Thames, but full of wooded islands and sands. It was the roman *Argentoratum* in Germania Prima, founded by Drusus, son-in-law to Augustus; was ravaged by Attila, taken by Clovis; became an imperial free city, and established protestantism 1559, which Louis XIV. after taking the town by treachery 1681, put down, though the majority of the population (as well as of the province) are still protestant. Vauban's citadel, towards the Rhine is a regular structure of five sides, with outworks, ditches, glacis, &c., and of great strength. The town is well built, having pretty good streets lit with gas, high-roofed stone houses, (the windows covered with bars,) 47 small bridges over the Ill and its branches, seven gates, eight or ten Places, and the Contades and Robertsau promenades, with distant views of the Vosges and Black Mountains.

Holy Trinity Minster or *Cathedral*, which towers over everything else, was begun by Bishop

Wernberg, 1015, (on the site of an older, commenced 510, by King Ludwig, and added to by Charlemagne, 770), and, though helped forward by the assistance of thousands of the citizens was not finished (*i. e.* the body) till 1275; two spires over the west front were to have been exactly alike and about 550 feet high, but only the north one, built 1277-1439, is completed, 466 feet high. The front, with its statues, &c., lately restored by Ohnmacht, &c., is a sort of a screen to what is behind, 230 feet high and —— broad; a flight of steps leads up to the three great recessed portals in it, one being in each of the side towers, while the centre one, in which was a brass door (melted down at the Revolution) has above it figures of Clovis, Dagobert, Rodolph of Hapsburg, Louis XIV., and a noble stained window, 46 feet diameter.

As to the magnificent north *tower* and *spire* (which is 12 feet higher than the Pyramids), there is first the portal, then a great window, then two or three windows, then an octagon story, then the tall spire of beautifully carved open work, at the top of which are the lantern, the crown, (the highest point visitors get up to, by 635 steps), and the button supporting the cross which is 8½ feet long. The view commands a vast prospect of hills, forests, &c., on both sides of the Rhine. The names of Voltaire, Klopstock, Mozart, Lavater, Goethe, &c., are marked among those who have ascended.

In the interior, 357 feet long, you see the nave, 132 feet broad, 75 high, with 9 great clustered pillars down each side (some 72 feet round), and Dotzinger's gothic font (1442); the ancient choir, built, they say, by Charlemagne, with the high altar (over St. Sepulchre's crypt or chapel), gothic stone pulpit, restored 1824, and Silbermann's organ with 2,242 pipes (1714); and the very curious *horloge* or clock (on the pilier des Anges, with figures of angels and evangelists) of the sixteenth century, repaired 1842, by Schwilgué, (to whom a fête was given on the occasion) shewing sidereal and apparent time, the moon's changes, motions of the planets, the feasts, &c., of the calendar, &c. It is called one of the 'Seven wonders of Germany'; and should be seen at noon. Notice also monuments of Bishops Wernter and Konrad, Erwin Steinbach, one of the master builders (1318) and his daughter Sabina (who built the south porch), Moentilin an early printer, &c.; and portraits of emperors, kings, &c., in the stained windows. A profusion of grotesque and indecent figures is spread over the interior, reflecting mostly on the monkish orders.

Near it is the château royal, an old bishop's palace, built by Cardinal Rohan, and furnished with gobelins tapestry, bronzes, &c. In Rue des Frères, where the large priests' seminary stands, is St. Etienne's old church, now a magazine. Some other churches (there are 15 in all) are St. Louis, St. Pierre (with M. Schoen's pictures, and a curious wood carving), St. Jean, St. Aurélie, St. Nicholas, Ste. Madeleine, St. Guillaume (or Wilhelmer, with tombs of the landgraves Philip and Ulrich Von Woerth, 1332-44), and St. Thomas. The last, at the bridge over the Ill, used by the Protestants (who have six besides), has a high-pitched roof and low spires, with monuments of the excellent pastor Oberlin and Koch (by Ohnmacht), Schoepflin, the scholar (by Pertois), and an elaborate one by Pigalle (1797) to Marshal Saxe, in which the hero stands on the top with an eagle and other emblems about him, while France at his feet holds him with one hand and pushes back Death (who appears from below) with the other; Hercules, meantime, weeps on the opposite side. The New Church, built 1254, by the dominicans, has good stained windows, and tombs of Tauler (1361) and Blessig. There is also a large Jews' Synagogue.

The préfecture, and Hôtel de Ville (with a gallery of pictures and sculpture), the large new theatre, with its six column doric portico, and statues by Ohnmacht, the government cannon foundry, &c. are in the Broglie promenade, near the Rue Brulée, where 200 Jews were burnt, 1349. At the public library, close to the new church, are 130,000 volumes, contributed by the old convents, the suppressed Protestant university, Schoepflin, &c. (one book was printed by Schoeffer and Faust, 1466), and including a great number of MSS. and illustrations; the school of medicine has 10,000 more vols.; and there is a museum of natural history, with a collection of stained glass, &c., at the Academy near the botanic gardens. The old Hôtel de Ville, in the renaissance style, is now the chamber of commerce; a halle au blé or grain market, was built 1830, by Villot. Other buildings are the protestant gymnasium or college, the civil and military hospitals, four or five barracks (casernes), an orphan asylum, mont de piété, new boucheries or shambles near the poultry market, &c. In the old herb market is David's statue (put up 1840) of Henri Gensfleisch or *Gutenberg*, who discovered the art of printing here, which Faust and his son-in-law, Schoeffer, (a native of this city) carried out at Mayence; on the Artillery parade stands one to another native, Kléber, by Grass (1840); and near the half-timber and half-boat bridge in the Rhine, on an island is a granite pedestal to Desaix.

Other natives are Brunck, Scheffer, and Schweighauser the scholars, Andrieux the poet, General Coehorn, Marshal Kellermann, Oberlin and his father (a scholar). Rouget de l'Isle, while an engineer officer here, at the Revoluton, composed the words and music of an air which he called an offering to Liberty, but which, being sung by the patriots at Marseilles, 1792, took the name of the 'Marseillaise,' and became universally famous.

Strasbourg is the principal seat of the French Lutheran church of the Confession of Augsburg, which numbers about 250 pastors, chiefly in departments of Upper and Lower Rhine, Vosges, and Doubs. There are twenty-five in the city; a faculty of theology in connection with the body is attached to the academy, and one of their journals, the 'Revue de Théologie,' is published here.

The Manufactures comprise linen, woollen, lace, cotton, leather, hardware, and cutlery, jewellery and clockwork, paper, pottery, chemicals, &c.; and there is a good trade in corn, flax, hemp, wine, spirits, charcoal, tobacco, &c.

Conveyances: by rail to Paris, Basle, Baden-Baden, Frankfort, &c. Coaches to Barr, Belfort, Stuttgard, Munich, Constance, and all parts of Germany and Switzerland. Steamers down the Rhine to Mayence (180 miles in 9 hours, but two days back), Cologne (one day), Antwerp (two days); agent for the Rhine steamers, M. Louis Hasenclever, Quai St. Thomas, No. 14. Within a distance of 30 or 40 kil. are the mineral springs of Avenheim, Soultzbad, Holtzbad, Altwiller, Brumath, Niederbronn, &c., all of a sulphurous kind, and generally seated in some delightful valley.

ROUTE 16—*continued.*

Strasbourg to Mulhouse, Basle, &c.

Up the Rhine, by railway. Distance 141 kil. or 88½ miles; three trains a day, 3½ to 5 hours; 17, 14¾, 11, and 7½fr. 15 kil. or 33lbs. of luggage allowed. The trains stop five to ten minutes at the St. Louis custom-house, on the frontier. Terminus near Porte de Saverne; the stations are—

	kil.		kil.		kil.
Geispolsheim	11	Ostheim	3	[Branch to	
Fegersheim...	3	Bennwihr ...	4	Cernay ...	9
Limersheim..	4	Colmar	6	Thann ...	6]
Erstein.........	4	Eguisheim ...	4	Dornach......	2
Matzenheim .	3	Herrlisheim..	3	Mulhouse ...	4
Benfeld	4	Rouffach	6	Rixheim	5
Kogenheim...	5	Merxheim ...	5	Habsheim ...	1
Ebersheim ...	5	Bollwiller ...	7	Sierentz	10
Schlestadt ...	6	Wittelsheim .	5	Bartenheim .	3
St Hippolyte	6	Lutterbach ...	7	St. Louis......	8
Ribeauvillé ...	4			Basle	3

The railway passes up the valley of the Ill, which receives innumerable streams from the Vosges mountains, through its principal branches, the Eger, Andlau, Scheer, &c. Between the Ill and Rhine is the Rhine and Rhone canal, which has a branch to Bâle, and joins the Saône at Dijon.

GEISPOLSHEIM (6¾ miles,) on the Eger. Molsheim and Mutzig are 11 or 12 kil. to the west, where they manufacture ribbons, fire-arms, &c.

FEGERSHEIM (2 miles,) near the Ill and Andlau. Rosheim (15 kil. west,) in a pretty position on the Magel, is a walled town of 4,000 people.

LIMERSHEIM (2½ miles.)

ERSTEIN (2½ miles,) on the Ill. Coach to Obernai (12 kil. west-north-west,) which lies on the Andlau, above Neidernai, and is ill built, with a population of 5,100 souls, who make calicoes &c. It has an old château, and a gothic tower, called Kappelen Thurm. Further up the Vosges, you come to the Hochfeld and Odilienberg, near the Waldersbach, the scene of Oberlin's labours.

MATZENHEIM (3 miles,) on the Ill.

BENFELD (2½ miles,) also on the Ill, a small place of 2,300 souls, as old as the seventh century, but dismantled after the treaty of Munster. Coach to Barr (11 kil. west-north-west,) a protestant town of 4,600 in a delightful hollow, under the Kirchberg, Hohenbourg, Monkalb, and other heights. The old castle is replaced by a Hôtel de Ville, built 1640. Woollen mittens and socks are made. Andlau (south-west of Barr,) among vine-covered hills, is another pretty spot, near Hohe-Andlau ruined castle.

KOGENHEIM (3½ miles), on the Ill.

EBERSHEIM (2 miles).

SCHLESTADT (4½ miles), on the fertile banks of the Ill, a sous-préfecture of 10,000 persons, and an old free city of Alsace, called *Electus*, by the Romans; ruined by Attila, but rebuilt 1216, and after some changes, taken by Louis XIV., 1673, and fortified by Vauban. The chief buildings are St. George's gothic church of the fourteenth century, with a square tower 187 feet high; the Recollets' church; public library, with some early printed books; the college at the old commandry of Malta, near the round church of St. Foy; the arsenal; the fause porte or belfry-tower, in the gothic style; new corn market and tobacco factory. Martin Bucer (or Kulborn), was a native. The Giessen passes by on the north, from the Vosges mountains, which are in view. Manufactures of pottery (enamelled pottery was invented here in the twelfth century), metallic gauze, iron and copper, &c.

Hotels—du Bouc (Goat); de l'Aigle d'Or (Golden Eagle). Coaches to St. Marie-aux-Mines (*see* Route 19*a*.) St. Die, Epinal, Nancy, &c. Orschwiller (6 kil. west-north-west,) is under the fine old castle of Hohe Koenigsberg, which the Swedes destroyed after they took this town, in the thirty years' war, 1632. At Ebermunster is an old abbey of the seventh century.

ST. HIPPOLYTE (3¾ miles), in department Haut-Rhin.

RIBEAUVILLE (2½ miles), among vineyards, in a pretty valley, under heights covered by the old castles of Ribeaupierre, Giersberg and St. Ulric. St. Gregoire's church has several ancient tombs; the Hôtel de Ville is good. In the neighbourhood are remains of Nôtre Dame of Dusenbach chapel, and a famous cyclopean wall (on the sides of the Vosges,) called the Heidenmauer or heathen's wall. Near Baroche, to the south, is Hohenach castle, the tower of which commands one of the most beautiful views in this interesting country. Population, 7,200, who make linens, &c.

[At 18 kil. east-south-east, is Marcholsheim, near the Rhine, with bleach-ground and tobacco factories. Population, 2,606.]

OSTHEIM (2 miles). Riquewihr (7 miles west), among vineyards. on the Sempach, has the old castle of Reichenstein, dismantled 1209. A little south of it, on the Weiss, is the old imperial castle of Kaiserberg. And higher up the stream are the ruins of Hoh Landsberg and Plixbourg.

BENNWIHR (2½ miles). At 2½ miles further is

Colmar. *Hotels*—de l'Ange (Angel); des Deux Clefs (Two Keys); des Trois Rois (Three Kings). Population, 19,200. Chief town of department Haut-Rhin (with a tribunal, &c.), in a fine plain, near the German frontier, half way between the Vosges and the river Rhine, on the river Lauch, 1½ miles from the Ill. It is not far from the site of the roman *Argentovaria;* was an imperial free city, till given up to France, 1648, when the fortifications were razed. There are three gates, narrow streets, and many old houses; with good walks on Champ de Mars, and in the ancient pepinière, as well as in the orangery, and the cemetery of Horburg (2 kil. off). It is watered by the branches of the river and the canals of the Fecht.

The *Minster*, built 1363, is a large gothic building, with a tower about 300 (?) feet high, and an altar-piece on wood, by Schœn. Its tower commands a view over above 800 places in Alsace and Baden, &c. The Jesuit church was built 1750; the fine nave of the Dominican church is now the halle au blé (corn market); and the old protestant church is a storehouse.

Other objects of notice are the ancient maison de ville, the prefect's hôtel, the college, which includes the bibliothèque of 40,000 volumes (besides rare MSS., and a museum, which has paintings by Schœn, A. Durer, &c.); the hospital, the vast maison d'arrêt, (prison), large cavalry barracks, and public slaughter-house (abattoir.)

In the neighbourhood, are the large factories of MM. Hauseman, Hersog, &c. At Munster (20 kil. to the west-south-west), is M. Hartman's, near the old castle of Schwarzenbourg. Generals Rapp, and Rewbel, who was one of the Directory, were natives. MM. Schaller, Heintz, &c., are protestant pastors here.

Large manufactures of cottons, linens, ribbons, powder, &c.; and a trade in wine, grain, &c. Conveyances to Strasbourg, Paris, Bâle, &c., by railway; by coach to Nancy, Besançon, Lyons, &c.; Freibourg in Baden, &c. A road leads down to a custom-house and ferry on the Rhine, the passage of which is guarded by Fort Mortier, and the citadel of Neufbrisach, built by Vauban on the Rhine canal.

From Colmar, on the railway to Bâle, (up the Rhine) you pass

EGUISHEIM (5¾ miles), which has a strong six-sided tower left of an ancient château, and was the birth-place of Leo IX.

HERRLISHEIM (1½ miles).

ROUFFACH (4 miles), on the Lauch, with an old gothic church, and remains of Isenbourg castle, once a seat of the Merovingian kings. Marshal Lefebvre was born here.

MERXHEIM (3 miles), to the south-west of which is Ballon de Guebwiller, the highest of the Vosges range (4,700 feet above the sea).

Then Bollwiller (4½ miles), in a wine district; Wittelsheim (3½ miles); Lutterbach (4½ miles), where the branch to Thann turns off as below; Dornach (1 mile); and

MULHOUSE or Mühlhausen (2½ miles), a town of 20,300 souls, and a great seat of manufactures, such as cotton prints, turkey red, woollens, worsteds, muslins, yarn, silk, steam engines, spinning machines, locomotives, &c. It was an imperial city from 1268 till 1515, when it became a Swiss republic, but was joined to France, 1798. It stands partly on an island of the Ill, and on the Rhine and Rhone canal, and is generally well built, with some old houses. There are catholic and reformed churches, a synagogue, Hôtel de Ville, college, hospital, cabinets of natural history, &c., bibliothèque, various public walks, and a chamber of commerce, council of prud'hommes (joint committee of masters and workmen), and many factories, one of the largest and oldest being that of Koechlin Brothers. *Hotels*—de Paris; de la Maison Rouge (Red House); de la Cigogne (Stork); du Lion Rouge (Red Lion).

[*Ottmarsheim*, 15 kil. east-north-east, on the Rhine, has one of the most remarkable churches in this part. It is eight-sided, and believed to be remains of a Lombard basilica.]

RIXHEIM (3 miles), which has large manufactures of paper hangings.

HABSHEIM (¾ miles); Sierentz (6½ miles); Bartenheim (1¾ miles); St. Louis (5 miles), on the Swiss frontier, where baggage is searched. On the Strasbourg and Basle railway, after St. Louis,

[To the right, near the Rhine, is Huningue, which had, on a rock, one of Vauban's fortresses before 1815, when it was taken by the Austrians. It contains a good church, barracks, &c., and a monument to General Abatucci. Population 1,000.]

At 2 miles further is Basle, in SWITZERLAND.

(d) From Lutterbach, as above, a branch railway goes off, through Cernay (4½ miles), to

THANN (3¾ miles), a town of 5,900 cotton-printers, &c., on the Thur, under one of the Vosges hills, which has remains of Engelbourg castle on it. It contains several ancient houses, and St. Thibault's fine cathedral-like church, with a sculptured doorway, and a steeple 328 feet high, built 1516. Vin de Rang is produced here.

ROUTE 17.

Epernay to Rheims and Mezieres.

Distance, 106 kil. or 66 miles.

EPERNAY, by Strasbourg rail, as above (*see* Route 16). MONCHENOT (15 kil).

Rheims or Reims (12 kil.), though a sous-préfecture only (in department Marne), has a population of 44,000, is the seat of an archbishop, and one of the oldest cities in France, having been the chief town of Champagne. It stands on the Vesle, at the bottom of gently sloping chalk hills covered with vineyards, though the neighbourhood is dull. It was the capital of the *Remi* in Belgian Gaul, and called *Durocortorum* by the Romans, whose consul here, Jovinus, became a christian 366. Clovis and his Franks were baptised here 496. It was taken by Charles Martel 719, and Hugh Capet's rival, Charles of Lorraine 900; beseiged by Edward III. of England 1359, and captured 1421 by the English, who were driven out by the Maid of Orleans, and Charles VII. crowned here; as were all the French sovereigns from Philippe Auguste down to Charles X. (except Henry IV. and Louis XVIII). It was taken and retaken 1814.

Parts of the gothic walls with their turrets still remain; the streets are wide, and most of the houses one story high. Of fourteen open places, the largest is Place Royale, built 1756, which has Cartellier's bronze copy of Pigalle's Louis XV., who greatly improved this old city. Place Godinot takes it name from a canon of the last century, who built a château d' eau for supplying water, now furnished by a new reservoir (by Cordier, 1843), in Place de la Tour-du-Puits. An old fountain by Coustou, the sculptor, stands in Place St. Nicaise. One gate called the Porte de Vesle, an iron arch, leads out to the Grand Cours, a well planted walk by the river as far as Port de Laon. Close to the latter, built in the wall, is the *Porte de Mars*, a genuine roman relic; it was a triumphal arch, built by Agrippa, in honour of Cæsar Augustus, with three openings in it, and eight corinthian columns, all much worn. An amphitheatre may be traced at the Mont d' Arènes near it. But its finest ornament is the noble gothic

Cathedral, covered with a multitude of figures and ornaments, and built for the most part 1212-42, by Robert de Coucy, on the site of one founded as early as 360-400; the transept (164 feet long), was rebuilt after a fire in 1491. Length 467 feet, breadth 98 feet, height 118 feet. The beautiful font has a triple portal (the middle one being 39 feet wide), a large stained rose window, bas-reliefs of the Passion, the Judgement, Crowning of the Virgin, David and Goliah, Baptism of Clovis, and from 530 to 550 statues of various sizes, in rows, besides a row of 35 niched prelates near the top; above which rise the two towers, made of open pillars and windows, and ending in a heap of little turrets, instead of the spires which they were designed to carry. One tower (the south), a little shorter than the other, was not finished till 1480, and has the bells of la Charlotte clock, as old as 1570, with moving figures, &c. Going in you see about 90 niched statues inside the doors; the windows are richly stained with figures of apostles, kings, &c.; in the nave (which had a painted ceiling of lilies on a blue ground when Charles X. was crowned), is the very curious marble tomb of Jovinus, the roman consul, carved over with a lion hunt, and brought from St. Nicaise's church 'An VIII de la Republique,' or 1800; nine chapels surround the choir, which has a rich altar, the canopy of St. Nicaise's church, a large organ, 64 feet high, and a painting of the Israelites gathering manna.

St. Remi or Remigius' church, was built 1041-60 as part of Archbishop Turpin's benedictine abbey, being older than the cathedral, and the place where the early kings were consecrated; it is a mixture of norman and pointed in the style, and 361 feet long, with a plain front, having five portals and a rose window, between two slender towers with slated spires. It contains a modern copy of the tomb of St. Remi, ornamented by marble life-size statues of the twelve peers of France (the Count of Champagne and the archbishop are two), saved from an older tomb. Several kings and bishops were buried in this church, which has been lately restored.

The *Hôtel de Ville* (which a new street joins to Place Royale), begun 1627, and enlarged 1825, consists of a centre and wings, 290 feet long, ornamented with 68 pilasters, and bas-reliefs (at the middle) of Louis XIII. Here are placed, the cartulaire or collection of archives; the bibliothèque or library of 30,000 volumes, besides 1,000 MSS., and autographs; and a museum of pictures. A new doric palais de justice, was built 1845, on the site of the hôtel Dieu; a new covered market 1840, and an abattoir or slaughter house 1838. It has a college, priests' seminary, theatre, public baths, botanic garden, chamber of commerce, &c. A few old buildings are left, as, the hôtel des Comtes de Champagne in Rue du Tambour, hôtel de Joyeuse, near the Hôtel de Ville, hôtel de Chevreuse in Rue des Gueux, and the Maison Rouge inn (near the cathedral), on which you read, 'In the year 1429, at the coronation of Charles VII., in this inn, then called the Zebra, the father and mother of Jeanne d' Arc, were lodged at the cost of the city authorities.' At the English college for priests here the Rheims version of the New Testament was published, 1582. In the old house of Long Vêtre, in Rue de Cérès, Colbert, the statesman, was born, 1619; and in Rue du Marc, Pluche, who wrote the Spectacle de la Nature. Gobelin, who gives name to the tapestry, and Ducoudray, Marie Antoinette's counsel, were also natives. Trade in Champagne wines, corn, &c., and woollens, which are spun here. *Hotels*—De France; du Commerce; Maison Rouge (Red House), as above; du Lion d'Or (Golden Lion); du Palais, &c. Coaches to Epernay (for Paris, &c.), Laon (*see* Route 17a), St. Quentin (Route 11), Mézières, Chalons, &c.

ISLE (17 kil.), on the Suippe.

RETHEL (20 kil.), a sous-préfecture of 7,900 souls, in department Ardennes, on a hill, by the Aisne, was an old roman *castrum rectectum*, and the head of a duchy, once held by the Duc de Meilleraye, who married Cardinal Mazarin's niece. It was besieged 1650 by the Spaniards who defeated Turenne close by, then fighting for the Fronde. Condé took it four years after, but gave it up to Turenne, who was now on the court side, after changing his religion. An old tower remains. Linens and nails are made. *Hotels*—Du Commerce; de France; du Lion d'Or (Golden Lion).

[At 8 kil. west-north-west, is Château-Porcien, down the Aisne, under an old castle on a rock, which belonged to the Counts of Champagne, &c.—At 16 miles east-south-east, up the Aisne, is *Attigny*, which has traces of a palace of the early kings from Clovis, who built it 647. A council was held here 765. Witikind the Saxon was baptised 786. Charles the Simple built St. Walburges church here. It was afterwards a country seat of the Rheims archbishops, but suffered from the English and the Frondeurs, &c., so that it is now a small village of 1,600 souls.

Vousiers (12 kil. south-east of this), up the Aisne, a small but thriving sous-préfecture of 2,800 persons, near which the Prince de Ligne was killed, 1792. It was about here that a sudden panic took possession of the French under Dumouriez, who, to the number of 10,000, fled for 40 leagues before 1,200 Prussian huzzars, and for a moment threw all France into alarm.—Buzancy (22 kil. east-north-east of this) has near it the Château de la Cour, which belonged to the Rheims prelates, and a building like a mosque, called Mahomet, and built, they say, by a crusader. At 21 kil. further is Stenay (*see* Route 21).]

LAUROY (23 kil.) on the Vence.

[At 10 kil. west-north-west is Signy l'Abbaye, so called from remains of a benedictine abbey founded 1134, by St. Bernard, and endowed by a seigneur of Châtillon, to whom the saint gave a written contract, kindly promising him as many acres in heaven as he had made a donation of on earth. The original document was to be seen here till the last century.]

At 19 kil. further is Mézières (*see* Route 21).

ROUTE 17*a*.

Rheims to Laon, Vervins, Avesnes, and Mons.

Distance (to Avesnes) 118 kil., or 73 miles.

RHEIMS, as in Route 17.

BERRY-AU-BAC (19 kil.) at a ferry (bac) on the Aisne, in the old province of Champagne.

CORBENY (9 kil). At 20 kil. further is

LAON. *Hotels*—De l'Ecu (Crown Piece); de la Hure (Boar's Head); de la Barrière. Population, 9,900. Capital of department Aisne, (in the old province of La Brie), fortified town, and formerly seat of a diocess, on a rocky hill, 720 feet above sea level, in a fertile wine country, half way between the Aisne and Oise. It was the ancient *Laudunum*, and as it stands high, the air is keen, though healthy. The old walls and ramparts command a succession of fine prospects on all sides. Notre Dame *Cathedral* church, the most remarkable building, is an excellent uniform specimen of the early pointed style in France; it was built 1112-14. It has five towers, portals pierced with deep entrances (three in the west front), stained rose and other windows, and several ornamented side chapels. St. Martin's church is as old as the twelfth century, and has two good towers; the abbey of that name is now the Hôtel Dieu. Another abbey (Notre Dame, founded 645), is occupied by the préfecture, where the library of 17,000 volumes is placed. There are also the college, theatre, barracks, the citadel, on the site of a castle built by Louis Outremer and pulled down 1831, and the leaning tower of Penchée in the walls, near the Porte St. Martin. Lothaire I., St. Remi, and Marshal Serrurier were born here. It was taken by the Allies in 1814 and 1815. Clovis made it the seat of a bishop, who afterwards came to be styled Duke of Laon, &c. The caves in the rock are worth notice. Manufactures of stockings, hats, leather, nails; and a trade in corn, wine, excellent artichokes, &c.

Conveyances to Soissons, Rheims, St. Quentin, Vervins, &c,

From Laon, on the road to Mons, you pass

MARLE (22 kil.); then

VERVINS (15 kil.) on the Vilpian, a small place and sous-préfecture of 2,800 people, frequently ravaged in the civil wars of France. Henry IV, and Philip II., of Spain, made peace here, 1598. In the chapel to the hospice, founded 1570, by Jacques de Coucy, is a picture of Jouvenet (St. Charles Borromeo in the plague of Milan), and another by the same hand in the parish church.

LA CAPELLE (16 kil.) was a fortified town till 1757.

AVESNES (17 kil.) is described in Route 11.

About 40 kil. further is MONS, across the *Belgian* frontier.

ROUTE 18.
Chalons to Metz,

Distance, 146 kil., or 91 miles.

CHALONS-SUR-MARNE, as in Route 16. The next place is

L'EPINE (8 kil.) and its beautiful church.

ORBEVAL (28 kil.); to the left of which, at Valmy, is a monument to Kellerman on the spot where his heart was buried, 1820, *parmi les restes de ses braves compagnons d'armes* (with the remainder of his brave comrades) who fell in the victory which he gained here over the Prussians, 1792.

STE. MENEHOULD (8 kil.) a sous-préfecture in department Marne, and regular built place of 5,900 souls, on the Aisne, having the Place d'Austerlitz at one end and a good Hôtel de Ville at the other. The old castle was often besieged. *Hotels*—De Ville de Metz; St. Nicholas. Coaches to Metz, Verdun, &c.

CLERMONT-EN-ARGONNE (14 kil.); to the left of which (12 kil. north-north-west) is *Varennes*, memorable as the spot where, on the night of the 21st June, 1791, the unfortunate Louis XVI. was stopped in his flight from Paris, with his queen, sister, and two children.

DOMBASLE (10 kil.) in department Meuse.

VERDUN, a sous-préfecture, fortified town, with a citadel improved by Vauban, and seat of a diocess. Population, 10,577. Near the old Hôtel de Ville of Henri Quatre's time, is a bronze statue of Cheveret (a native), by Lemaire. Noted sugar plums and liqueurs are made here. In the last war, from the number of détenus, it was more than half English, with English shops 'from London.' Rue Morelle, the main street, was styled 'Bond Street;' races were held at Charnie, and there was a hunt three times a week. *Hotels*—De l'Europe; des Trois Maurs (Three Moors).

HARVILLE (28 kil.). GRAVELOTTE (23 kil.)

METZ is 24 kil. further (*see* Route 20).

ROUTE 19.
Commercy to Domremy, Epinal, Plombieres, Mulhouse, and Basle.

Distance, 226 kil, or 140 miles.

COMMERCY, as in Route 16.

VAUCOULEURS (20 kil.) on the Meuse, ascending which you pass into department Vosges, a little before

DOMREMY-LA-PUCELLE (18 kil.), a small hamlet of 316 souls, over the Meuse, on the Vosges hills, famous as the place where *Joan of Arc*, the Maid of Orleans, was born, 1412, in a little cottage, shewn by an inscription over it. Her real name, as *M.* Huldut of Nancy has shewn, was Jeanne Darc, which was altered to d'Arc when her family was ennobled by Charles VII. after her death. A school for girls, and a fountain, have been built to her honour, with a cast of the beautiful statue sculptured by Louis Philippe's daughter, Marie, which all the world is familiar with.

NEUFCHATEAU (11 kil.), the ancient *Neomagus*, is a sous-préfecture of 3,524 inhabitants, under the hills, on the Meuse, where the Meuzon joins. It has a Hôtel de Ville, and public library of 8,000 vols.

[*Contrexeville*, 18 kil. south-east, in a valley of the Vair, has some noted mineral waters. Those of Bourbonne, Plombières, &c., are in this neighbourhood.]

MIRECOURT (39 kil.), a sous-préfecture, on the Madon. Population, 5,400, Lace and musical instruments are made.

At 32 kil. further is Epinal, in the old province of Alsace.

EPINAL. *Hotels*—Du Louvre; de la Porte; des Vosges; du Lion d'Or. Population, 10,300. Chief town of department Vosges, on the Moselle, in a hollow, on the side of the Vosges mountains, 1,050 feet above the sea, with the ruins of its old castle seated on a rock higher up. The river divides it into Grande Ville and Petite Ville (joined by a stone and a suspension bridge), and the Faubourg near the canal. It is well built and provided with fountains; but the buildings are of no consequence. The large college belonged to the Jesuits; the Capuchin convent is turned into a hospital, and has large gardens round it; the parish church has a good choir. There are, besides a library of 17,000 vols., a museum, slaughter-house (abattoir), orphan asylum, cavalry barracks, the Doublat gardens, salle de spectacle, &c., and several paper works. The river makes some cascades. Many English were confined here in war time. Trade in grain, cattle, wood, &c.

Conveyances to Nancy, Mirecourt, Bourbonne-les-Bains, Plombières, Vesoul, Besançon, Mulhouse, Strasbourg.

[From Epinal, on the road to Vesoul, you pass

Xertigny (16 kil. south), among iron-works, near the head of the Saône.—At 15 kil. to the west of this is *Bains-les-Bains*, or *Bains*, in a well wooded valley on the Coucy, and so called from its warm springs, called the Old and New baths, and Fontaine de la Vache, useful as tonics in nervous and rheumatic complaints. The season is from the middle of May to that of September; there are a saloon, good lodgings, promenades, &c.; and traces of roman occupation. Population, 2,500

Plombières (16 kil. south-west), a noted watering place, among hill forests, in the valley of the Eaugronne, along which is the promenade des dames, laid out by Stanislaus, king of Poland, 1775, and leading to Moulin Joli mill, so called by the Empress Josephine. The baths are hot and cold, and are used from May to October, sometimes by as many as 1,500 people; they are for the most part saline and tonic, and are regulated by government. Bain des Dames is the site of a nunnery; Bain des Anciens, or Grand Bain, the oldest, is used by the poor; Bain Tempere, charge 40 to 70 centimes; Bain Royal, or Bain Neuf, has a salle de comédie (for balls, &c.); Bain des Romains is the most elegant. Another is called Bain des Capucins; and there are also the Fontaines du Crucifix, Savonneuses, and la Bourdeille (containing iron). Some of the waters are drunk. In the neighbourhood are Jaquot farm, the Val d'Ajou, the valleys of Erival (and its abbey) and des Roches, the Tonnazre stone, &c. They sell wood carvings and kirsch-wasser (cherry brandy) here. *Hotels*—La Tête d'Or (Golden Head); l'Ours (Bear). Conveyances, in the season, to Epinal, Besançon, Remiremont. Population, 1,400.]

From Epinal, on the way to Mulhausen (up the Moselle), you pass

REMIREMONT (26 kil.), a sous-préfecture in department Vosges, of 5,300 people, in a pretty valley under the Vosges mountains, just above where the two heads of the Moselle join. It began in an abbey for canonesses, founded 620, rebuilt in the italian style, 1751, and used as the mairie. It is well laid out, with wide streets, and fountains. The library has 6,700 vols., and there is a good cabinet of mineralogy. The Bouchot and Cave falls are near Vagney, on the Clurie (16 kil.) Trade in butter, géromé cheese, kirsch-wasser (cherry brandy), pâtés de truite (trout pie).

ST. MAURICE (29 kil.) stands under the Ballon d'Alsace, one of the highest (4,100 feet) of the Vosges, and commands a view of vast extent, taking in the plains of Alsace, the Black Forest (in Baden), the nearer Alps, &c.

[Gérardmer, 22 kil. east-north-east, is near a lake at the Valogne's head, among the Vosges hills and forests, and is noted for its cheese. Population, 5,700.]

Further on, you come to

BUSSANG, in a deep gorge of the Vosges, with 1,700 souls, and excellent mineral waters. Then to

ST. AMARIN, near the old castles of Frieldbourg and Stoenbourg.

At 29 kil. from St. Maurice is Thann, and 22 kil. beyond, brings you to Mulhouse, or Mühlhausen (see Route 16), on the Strasbourg and Basle Railway.

ROUTE 19a.

Epinal to the Ban de la Roche and Strasbourg.

Distance, 127 kil., or 79 miles.

EPINAL, as in Route 19.

GIRECOURT (15 kil.)

RAMBERVILLERS (13 kil.), a place of 4,900 souls, with a good bibliothèque of 10,000 vols.

[*St. Dié*, or *St. Diey* (24 kil. east-south-east), a sous-préfecture in department Vosges, and bishopric, on the Meurthe, rebuilt (after a fire, 1756,) by Stanislaus, King of Poland. It stands under Mont d'Ormont, and has some mineral springs, a library of 9,500 vols., and carries on a good trade. Population, 8,700.

One road leads hence, over the Vosges, to *La Poutroye* (35 kil.), on the Wass, and the lakes called Lac Blanc and Lac Noir.—At 21 kil. further is Colmar, on the Strasbourg Railway (see Route 16).

Another road brings you to *Gemaincotte* (12 kil.); and 12 kil. further east, to *Ste. Marie-aux-Mines* on the Liepvrette, in a pretty valley under the highest part of the Vosges; and so called from the mines of lead, silver, copper, zinc, and arsenic around it. It has manufactures of cotton siamoises, &c., paper, kirsch-wasser, and dye-works. Population, 11,600. Good mineral springs, but the air is sharp. At 22 kil. beyond this (past St. Hippolyte and its castle) is Schlestadt, on the Strasbourg Railway (*see* Route 16.)]

RAON L'ETAPE (16 kil.), on the Meurthe. Up a branch of it, the Plaine, (or else by way of Sennones and St. Jean du Mont), you come to

SCHIRMECK (about 36 kil.), in the Vosges.

[About 8 kil. south in the *Ban de la Roche* or Valley of Stone, (*Steinthal* in German) which divides the Vosges from the Champ de Feu mountains, are Foudai, Walbach, and Rothan, the scene of the labours of the pious and devoted pastor Oberlin. Here in a sterile spot he taught his people, who were poor and ignorant Lutherans, not only the way to Heaven, but to improve their cottages and gardens, to grow flax, to knit and weave, to establish infant and other schools, till the desert blossomed like the rose, leaving an example of what a good and earnest country clergyman may do with his flock. It was he who first opened a road across the Bruche to Strasbourg. After 59 years' residence he died, 1826, when 86 years old, and is buried at Foudai. His excellent housekeeper, Louisa Schepler, who died in 1837, lies near him.—Between the Steinthal and Schirmeck, is the Champ de Feu, a plain 3,537 feet above the sea; and close to it the Odilienberg, or St. Odili's mountain, on which are remains of a famous monastery, with two little chapels, commanding a noble view over Alsace. Hohenburg camp and castle, and an old paved way are near.]

MUTZIG (22 kil.), in a valley on the Bruche, near Donon mountain (3,315 feet high), has an old country seat of the Strasbourg bishops, now used as a powder factory. Population, 3,800. At Molsheim, a little further on, tools are made. Still further, you pass through tobacco and flax plantations; and at 25 kil. from Mutzig, you come to Strasbourg (*see* Route 16).

ROUTE 20.

Nancy to Metz and Sarrebruck.

By branch rail (from Frouard) 118 kil., or 78 miles to Fosbach; thrice a day, in 3½ to 4½ hours.

The stations from Frouard are:—

	kil.		kil.		kil.
Marbache	7	Ars-sur-Moselle	6	Herny	7
Dieulouard	6	Metz	8	Faulquemont	10
Pont-à-Mosn.	7	Peltre	6	St. Avold	11
Pagny-sur-Moselle	9	Courcelles	7	Hombourg	6
Noveant	6	Remilly	9	Cocheren	7
				Forbach	6

NANCY, as in Route 16.

FROUARD (6½ miles), towards Paris, from which it is 220 miles.

MARBACHE (3½ miles).

DIEULOUARD (4½ miles), an ancient village on a rock by the Moselle, on the site of Scarpone, or Sarpane, which the Huns destroyed (906). It has a gothic church and a ruined château.

PONT-A-MOUSSON (5 miles), a town of 8,160 souls, at the brick bridge (pont) on the Moselle, under Mousson hill, which is crowned by a ruined castle of the twelfth century. Here are a gothic church of the eleventh century, with two good six-sided towers on square bases; large cavalry barracks; part of St. Marie's old abbey; and an arcaded place (square), in which stands a house carved over with the sept péchés capiteux (seven capital sins), in the quaint coarse style of the middle ages. Marshal Duroc was a native. Charles III., Duke of Lorraine, founded an university here.

PAGNY (4½ miles) is near the fine ruins of Prény or Prigny Castle, built in the tenth century, from which the Dukes of Lorraine took their war cry of *Prigny! Prigny!*

NOVEANT (4 miles), between which and the next station are seen (at Jouy), near the river, 20 or 21 fine roman arches of the aqueduct, which went to Metz; one arch across the road is 50½ feet high.

ARS (3 miles). At 5 miles further is

Metz. *Hotels*—De l'Europe; des Victoires; du Nord, in Rue Pierre Hardi; de la Croix d'Or (Golden Cross); de France, Place de la Chambre; du Commerce; de la Ville de Paris; de la Ville de Londres; du Pelican d'Or; de l'Ours (Bear). Population 55,209. Chief town of department Moselle (in the old Lorraine), a first-class fortress, head quarters of a military division, seat of a bishopric, &c., in a flattish spot on a bend of the Moselle, where the Seille joins it at the old three-arch bridge of Pont des Bas Grilles. It was the capital of the *Medio Matrices* in roman times (whence the present name), and of Austrasie under Clovis. Afterwards it was held sometimes by the French and sometimes by the German Emperors, but was finally annexed to France, in spite of a long siege by Charles V., in 1522. At present it is a most important frontier post, and strongly fortified with works by Vauban, including the Double Couronne and Belle Croix Forts, built 1728-31. One of its nine gates, that called Porte St. Thiébaut, leads on the esplanade, near the citadel, which is laid out with walks and trees, and commands a fine prospect of the river and country, with its vineyards and woodland.

Several quays line the rivers, which are crossed by as many as seventeen bridges—as the Pont des Morts, &c.; some being very short, and old-fashioned; with water mills upon them. The Places d'Armes, de la Comédie, and Moselle, are the best squares. Most of the streets are narrow and dirty; the houses are chiefly of stone, two and three stories high, and some curiously carved.

The noble *Cathedral*, in Place d'Armes, with its flying buttresses, &c., was begun in 1014 by Bishop Thierri, but not finished till 1546. It is pierced with a great number of windows, many beautifully stained by Busch, 1526. Its length is 398 feet; width of nave, 51 feet (of the transepts, 46 feet); height of nave to the vault, 109 feet (of the transepts, 43½ feet); the two side chapels of the choir are 53 feet by 50; while the gothic spire, built in 1427, is just as high as the church is long, and carries an immense bell, weighing about 26,600 lbs. The very old font is called Cuve de César (Cæsar's tub). Several councils were held here between 590 and 1280.

Four or five other churches are of old date. One of the Knights Templars' round churches is in the large arsenal, which stands on the site of an abbey of the tenth century, and contains, besides 80,000 stand of arms, &c., a famous bronze culverin, taken at Ehrenbreitstein, 15½ feet long, 17 inches wide at the muzzle, weighs 23,717 lbs., and the shot 176½ lbs. An Ecole d'Application or practical school, for young officers from the Polytechnique, is attached to it, with a military library of 10,000 volumes, besides charts, plans, and MS. treatises. There are also extensive barracks, magazines, a military hospital,—the latter an immense building, begun by Louis XV., large enough for 1,500 patients, and which would accommodate 1,800. At the palais de justice (once the Hôtel de l'Intendance), an extensive structure, near the esplanade and the river, is the public library of 30,000 volumes (many of them early printed books), besides 800 MSS. Other buildings are the préfecture, the Hotel des Monnaies (mint), the college, priests' seminary, theatre, &c. Near the Mayen-Pont is part of an old tower, close to the Fontaine des Pucelles. For a long time it has been one of the chief seats of the Jews, who have a rabbi and a rabbinical school here. The Romans constructed an amphitheatre, and a naumachia (for sea-fights) here; but the traces are almost gone. An aqueduct went out to the south-west, of which several arches remain at Jouey (8 kil.) on the Moselle, as mentioned above. Among its eminent natives are Marshal Fobert; Generals Kellerman, Custines, and Lallemand; Bouchette, who was war minister under the convention; Barbé Marbois, one of Napoleon's ministers; Lacretelle, the naturalist; Raspail, the chemist; Mademoiselle Tastu, the poetess, &c.

Manufactures of leather, cotton, linen, woollen cloth, muslin, nails, stained papers, &c; trade in these, and wine, eau-de-vie, excellent beer and confitures, drugs, spices, &c.

Conveyances: By rail to Paris, Strasbourg, Frankfort, &c.; by coach to Thionville, Verdun, &c. By steamer—to Nancy (8 hours), 4 and 2 fr.; to Thionville; to Trèves (7 hours), 10 and 5 fr.; Coblentz, 25 and 18 fr. Omnibuses to the pretty village of Moulins, 30 cents. (3d). In the neighbourhood of Metz are also the rock of Roche-Rudotte, in the valley of Mance; the Château of Montigny-les-Metz; the cascade on the Digue of Wadrineau, &c.

From Metz, on the railway to Forbach (towards Frankfort), you pass

PELTRE (4½ miles).

COURCELLES (4½ miles).

REMILLY (5 miles).

HERNY (4½ miles).

FAULQUEMONT (7 miles).

ST. AVOLD (6½ miles), a pretty little place of 3,600 population, with some mineral springs, and cloth manufactures.

HOMBOURG (4½ miles) or Hombourg le Bas, at the bottom of a hill which has the ruined château, at the top, of Hombourg l' Evèque.

COCHEREN (4½ miles).

FORBACH (3½ miles), the last place before the Prussian frontier, with a custom-house, and remains of a château fort on Selosberg hill, which the town is built on. Population 4,350; who make pipes, glass, and hardware.

[At 16 miles to the south-east is *Sarreguemines*, a sous-préfecture of 5,400 souls on the Sarra, where the Bliëse falls in, which was called Guemonde and had a capuchin convent founded by Duke Leopold, 1621, now turned into the sous-préfecture, college, &c. It is noted for tabatières en carton (pasteboard snuff-boxes), of which 100,000 doz. are sold; gold pottery is also made. *Hotel*—Couronne d' Or (gold crown). The glass works of St. Louis are near. At 39 kil. further is the strong fortress of *Bitche* which commands the wooded forest of the Vosges mountains, and stands 1,292 feet above the sea; it is considered almost impregnable. The village below contains a population of 4,200. About 30 kil. to the north is Deux Ponts in BAVARIA.]

At 9 kil. beyond Forbach is Sarrebruck (in PRUSSIA), whence the rail continues to Mayence and Frankfort.

ROUTE 21.

Metz to Thionville (TREVES, LUXEMBOURG), Montmedy, Sedan, Mezieres, Rocroi and Mons.

Along the north-east frontier; distance to Mézières about 177 kil., or 110 miles.

METZ, as in Route 20.

MONDELANGE (17 kil.) on the Moselle.

[19 kil. to the west is *Briey*, a small sous-préfecture, on a hill-side over the Wagot, a branch of the Orne.]

THIONVILLE (11 kil.) a fortified port of the third class, where Pepin l'Heristal had a seat, in a flat part of the Moselle. After being held by the Spaniards it was taken by Condé 1643; the Prussians took it 1792, and held it again 1815. It has many old houses of the sixteenth century; a Place d'Armes, surrounded by barracks, and a manége for cavalry; a large parish church; halle au blé (corn market); works for steam-engines; a college, botanic gardens, &c. The old covered bridge on the Moselle, was re-built of stone, 1844. Large distilleries and sugar works are carried on in the neighbourhood. Population 6,850. *Hotels*—Du Luxembourg; du Commerce. About 35 kil. to the north is Luxembourg, in HOLLAND.

[Hayange, 10 kil. west-north-west, is an industrious village in a pretty spot, on the Feusch, among ironworks and mines.]

LONGWI (45 kil.) or *Longus-vicus*, on the Belgian frontier, including the Basse (lower) Ville on the Chiers, and Haute Ville on the hills above, strongly fortified by Vauban. It belonged to the Dukes of Lorraine till the French acquired it 1679; and was taken by the Prussians 1792. General Mercy, who fell in battle 1659, was a native.

[*Sierck* (19 kil.) the last place near the Prussian frontier, at the bottom of the hills on the Moselle, commanded by an old château, from which there is a good prospect. Further down the river are the lines of Künsberg, where Marlboro' was stopped by Villars. At 26 kil. beyond it is Sarrebourg in PRUSSIA; and Treves is about 8 kil. past it.]

LONGUYON (16 kil.) on the Chiers, has ironworks, where fire-arms, &c. are made.

[The direct road to Metz from this leads past Etain (25 kil. south-south-east), on the Ornes, in the middle of the fertile plain of Voëvre, which belonged to St. Euchane's abbey at Trèves in the seventh century, and was given up to the duke of Lorraine by the peace of Ryswick 1697. It has a good Hôtel de Ville. About 18 kil. west south-west of it is Verdun; and Metz is 40 kil. east-south-east.]

MONTMEDY (23 kil.) a sous-préfecture in department Meuse, of 2,700 souls, and one of Vauban's fortified forts of the fourth class, irregularly built on the Chiers—the upper town being placed between two hills (mons medius). It was taken by France, 1657. Trade in pottery (made by gypsies, called 'Bohemians'), leather, hosiery, &c.

[At 7 kil. to the north is Aviethe deserted gothic church, with some elegant carvings, and light spires; near it is a small chapel, having a pretty spire porch in front. Many traces of roman possessions were found in 1823.—To the west-south-west, 15 kil. is Stenay, an old place on the flats of the Meuse, called *Satanacum* when the kings of

Austrasie had a seat here. Louis XIV. in 1648 gave it to Condé, and captured it a few years after from the leaders of the Fronde, who made a treaty with the Spaniards here. There are large cavalry barracks, and forges turned by the stream.]

CARIGNAN (22 kil.) on the Chiers (which joins the Meuse above Sedan) was called Ivoi, and belonged to the families of Soisson and Penthièvre. It was given up to France at the peace of Ryswick 1698, having been part of Luxembourg before.

SEDAN (21 kil.) up the Meuse, a sous-préfecture with 14,700 people, and fortified town of the third class, in a flat spot. It had a castle in the ninth century belonging to the archbishop of Rheims, which came to the ferocious De la Marck, the Wild Boar of Ardennes, in the seventeenth century, and then to the Ducs de Bouillon. Turenne was born 1611, in the old château, a site marked by a stone; a bronze of him by Gois, stands near the Hôtel de Ville. He was brought up at Bazeilles, outside the town. Sedan is well-built, of stone and slate, but the water is so bad that the people are subject to goitres in the neck. There are a library, a theatre, three barracks, one being for cavalry, a well-supplied arsenal and magazines, and a military hospital, on a hill 130 feet above the river. A large tree called Trois Frères, stands on the Garenne promenade. Trade in grain, medical plants, leather, and the weaving and dyeing of cloth of noted quality. *Hotels*—De la Croix d'Or (Golden Cross); de l'Europe; de Turenne. Conveyances to Mezières, Verdun, Rheims, &c.

At 22 kil. farther is

MEZIERES. *Hotels*—Du Palais Royal; des Postes. Population 4,900. This small, dull, capital of department Ardennes, and a military post of the second class, close to the Belgian frontier, is on a bend of the Meuse, in a pleasant hilly spot, surrounded by Vauban's lines and a citadel. It is as old as 847, when a castle was built here, which the counts of Rethel, took possession of. Among the few buildings worth notice are, the old gothic church, built 1412-1506, which has a good portal, a high vault, painted glass, and an inscription, 'feliciter,' put up when Charles IX. married his wife here, 1570. At the Hôtel de Ville, built 1722, is the flag of the Chevalier Bayard, 'sans peur et sans reproche' who with 2,000 men defended the town against a force of 40,000 Austrians, in 1521, when bombshells were used for the first time: this flag is carried in procession every 27th September. It also stood a seven weeks' siege in 1815, after Waterloo. The Hôtel Dieu was built 1746. About 4,000 volumes are in the public library. Leather, serge, &c. are made. Conveyances to Sedan, Givet, Rheims, Verdun, Metz, &c.

From Mézières, on the road to Namur, you pass *Charleville*, by a short road only ½ kil. long, leading over a suspension bridge on the Meuse. It was built by, and called after Charles, duke of Nevers and Mantua, 1606, and has a pretty walk at Petit Bois, a college or school, hospital, theatre, and bibliothèque of 24,000 volumes, with a museum of natural history. A castle stood on Mont Olympe between 1639 and 1689. Population 9,400, who make nails, fire-arms, iron gooods, and trade in slate, coal, marble, grain, &c.

RIMOGUE (15 kil.)

ROCROY (11 kil.) or Rocroi, a fortress of the fourth class, with a frontier custom-house or douane, on a plain 1,190 feet above the sea, where the great Condé, when Duke of Enghien and only twenty-two years old, gained his famous victory over the Spaniards, &c., 19th May, 1643. The town stands among the forests of Ardennes, and was founded by Francis I. Population 3,600.

From Rocroi, it is about 120 kil. to Valenciennes, by way of Bellevue, La Chapelle, Avesnes, and Landrecy, described in Routes 11 and 13; or it is about 80 direct to Mons, in BELGIUM.

FUMAY (16 kil.) on the Meuse, is noted for its ardoisières or slate works, in the mountains here, through which the river has made a deep cutting. An old castle stands upon it. Merinos, flannels, steam engines, glass, &c. are made. Population 3,400. It was the centre of a little neutral spot, joined to France 1770.

GIVET (22 kil.) a fortified town on the Meuse, close to the Belgian frontier, in a hilly and rather picturesque spot, is composed of Petit Givet, at the end of the stone bridge, and Grand Givet, with Charlemont fort at the other end, the latter being on a high rock. It was used as a depôt for English prisoners in the war, when the Rev. R. Wolfe voluntarily laboured among twelve hundred of them, preaching the gospel, forming schools, &c., as related in his work, 'English Prisoners in France.' It has the churches of St. Hilaire and Notre Dame, a library of 5,000 volumes, and chamber of manufactures. Population 5,900. Pottery, pipes, and iron goods are made. In the neighbourhood is the old château of Mont d'Hano (near Vireux Wallerand,) and up the river, the high slate cliffs, called the Dames de la Main. Boats ascend it to Mézières. *Hotel*—Du Mont d'Or.

[Further down the river are Dinant and Namur in BELGIUM; and 23 kil. to the left is Phillippeville, on the road to Waterloo and Brussels.]

SECTION IV.

ROADS TO THE SOUTH-EAST;

IN CONNEXION WITH THE PARIS AND LYONS AND MEDITERRANEAN RAILWAYS, (CHEMIN-DE-FER DE PARIS A LYONS,) SUPPLYING MELUN, FONTAINEBLEAU, TROYES, AUXERRE, DIJON, BESANÇON (AND GENEVA), CHALONS-SUR-SAONE, LYONS, ST. ETTIENNE, GRENOBLE, (CHAMBERY, TURIN, NICE, &C.,) VALENCE, AVIGNON, MARSEILLES, TOULON (CORSICA), NISMES, MONTPELLIER, CETTE, NARBONNE, CARCASSONE, PERPIGNAN, ETC. ROUTES TWENTY-FOUR TO FORTY-EIGHT.

ROUTE 24.

Paris to Chalons-sur-Saone.

Embarcadère or station in Boulevard Mazas, near Rue de Bercy and Pont d'Austerlitz. Omnibuses to all the trains from various points: central office, 21, Rue de Bouloi. First opened 1849, and through to Chalons in 1851. It is in the hands of the government. Distance 388 kil. or 239 miles. Four trains a day, in eight to twelve hours. $39\frac{3}{4}$, $29\frac{3}{4}$, and $21\frac{3}{4}$ francs.; baggage allowed, 30 kil. or 66 pounds. Buffets for refreshments at Montereau, Tonnerre, Dijon. The 8 p.m. Paris train reaches Chalons in time for the 5 a.m. fast steamer to Lyons, in six hours: another steamer at 10 a.m. A fast steamer leaves Lyons at 4 a.m., corresponding with the Avignon railway to Marseilles and Montpellier, so as to reach them the same day: a second steamer at noon. From Chalons the route to Geneva is shorter by 25 kil. than that by Dijon, and is travelled by Caillard's fast coaches from the Hôtel du Parc.

The stations are—

	kil.		kil.		kil.
Villen-St.-G.	15	Pont-sur-Yn.	11	Les Laumes,	14
Montgeron...	3	Sens	11	Verrey	22
Brunoy	4	Villen-s-Yon	14	Blaisy-Bas ...	11
Combs-la-V.	4	St.-Jul-du-S.	8	Malain	8
Lieusaint ...	5	Joigny	11	Plombières ...	14
Cesson.........	7	Laroche	9	Dijon	5
Melun	7	Brienon	8	Gevrey	11
Bois-le-Roi...	6	St. Florentin	9	Vougeot	6
Fontainebleau	8	Flogny.........	11	Nuits	5
Thomery ...	5	Tonnerre ...	13	Corgoloin ...	6
More - St. -		Tanlay.........	8	Beaune	9
Mamés......	5	Ancy-le-Frn.	14	Meursault ...	7
Montereau...	10	Nuits-s.-Rav.	6	Chagny	8
Villen - la -		Aisy	8	Fontaines ...	6
Guyard ...	11	Montbard ...	10	Chalon	16

The station is a large pile of stone, 720 feet by 262, with a hangar or starting-place 138 feet wide. Leaving this, outside the barrière de Bercy, is La Grande Pinte, among wine, spirit, and oil warehouses, which continue to Bercy, where a suspension-bridge crosses the Seine. The railway passes through the gardens (laid out by Le Nôtre), to the château of the time of Louis XIV. At Charenton, near the new fort, it crosses the Marne (which joins the Seine a little below), by a five-arched viaduct resting on an island, and not far from the old ten-arch bridge to Alfort, (four are of wood). Charenton is in a pleasant healthy spot, and has a country-seat, which belonged to Henry IVth's mistress, Gabrielle d'Estrées, and an excellent lunatic asylum for four hundred persons, founded as far back as 1644. Alfort is noted for its Government veterinary college, founded 1766 by Bourgelat.

[*Vincennes*, to the east (6 miles from Paris,) in a forest, where nine roads meet, is remarkable for an ancient château, now strengthened and repaired, and made a depôt of artillery for the capital. It was built in 1337, by Philippe of Valois, on the site of Louis le Jeune's country seat, (as old as 1137). Henry V. of England died in it in 1422. Louis XI. lived here, and, as usual, made it a state prison. Charles IX. died in it, as did Cardinal Mazarin (1661), and here the Duc d'Enghien, was brought from across the frontier, tried, and shot by Napoleon's order, 20th March, 1804. A marble pillar in the ditch marks the spot ('Hic cecidit,' here he fell). Louis XV. lived here when young; Mirabeau was a prisoner here; the ministers of Charles X. were also sent here; and lately it was the residence of the duke of Montpensier. Here Thiers, Changarnier, Cavaignac, &c. were confined on the memorable 2nd December, 1851. It is a moated space 4,115 feet by 656 feet, with remains of towers on the walls; and includes three or four courts; the tall square donjon, with round towers and turrets at the corner, (now a powder magazine) and la Sainte Chapelle, a later pointed building of the sixteenth century (begun 1379 by Charles V.), having three spires, the Duc d'Enghien's tomb, good traceried windows, stained by J. Cousin, in which you see the devices of Henry II. (an H.), and Diana de Poictiers (a crescent). The beautiful armoury is worth seeing; admission by ticket on Saturday. A great fête is held in the woods August 15th. Under its trees the excellent St. Louis used frequently to administer justice to his people. To the south of it is St. Maur-le-Pont, on the right bank of the Marne, near a canal of 3,640 feet, which cuts off a bend of that river, tunnelled through the rock.]

Leaving Choisy-le-Roi, on the right, across the Seine, you come to

VILLENEUVE-ST.-GEORGES (9½ miles), on the Seine, where the Yères joins (crossed by a three-arched viaduct), among many country seats. That of Beauregard, on a hill, commands a fine view. Coaches to Draveil, Vigneux, Limeil, Boissy-St.-Leger, Valenton.

[Boissy (5 kil. east), is on a hill covered with vineyards and country houses, in department Seine-et-Oise. Grosbois château is near it].

MONTGERON (1¾ miles), in Senant forest, has a large château; and coaches to Crosne l'Abbaye and Valée d' Yères. A large viaduct crosses the valley of the Yères, leading on to

BRUNOY (2½ miles), which stands in the forest, and had a château of Louis XVIII., who gave an estate here, with the title of Duc de Brunoy, to our great Wellington, one of his many well-earned rewards, though scarcely heard of till his death. It stands on the site of a favourite seat of Phillippe de Valois, and has a church of the thirteenth century. Talma had a house here. Coaches to Quignes, Chaumes, and to *Brie-Comte-Robert* (9 kil. east-south-east), the old capital of Brie, in a marshy but fertile spot, founded in the twelfth century by Robert de Dreux (brother of Louis VII.), who built the old ruined castle or Tour-de-Brie. Robert II. built St. Etienne's gothic church, which has some old tombs; the hôtel dieu is nearly as old. Charles VII. took it from the English, 1440. Brie cheese, pens, tiles, &c. are made, and there is a good trade in grain. Population 2,800.

COMBS-LA-VILLE (2½ miles,) on the Yères.

LIEUSAINT (3 miles).

CESSON (4½ miles). Coach to Seine-Port, on the Seine. At 4½ miles further, an iron viaduct of three arches, each 131 feet span, leads over the river to Melun.

MELUN. *Hotels—De* France; de la Galère (Galley); du Grand Monarque (*i. e.* Louis XIV.); du Commerce. Population 6,900. Capital of department Seine-et-Marne, and the *Lodunum* of Cæsar, in a pleasant spot on the Seine, which winds round an island here, on which the oldest part of the town with its broad quays is seated. Two bridges, one called the Pont-aux-Moulins (Windmill bridge), on several irregular arches, joins this part to the quarters on the right and left banks; the latter being the best built, and

PASS OF
VIRON

called St. Aspais, after an old solemn-looking gothic church, which has some excellent stained windows. It stands on Grande Place, near the préfecture, which, with the ancient clock tower, was part of St. Pierre's benedictine abbey, of very early date (when Clovis took the town in 494, it had several convents, &c.), but damaged by the normans in their invasion, and finally ruined by Henry IV. in the wars of the League. On the Ile, you see the house of detention, for this and four other departments, an enormous square pile, with two towers, &c.; and the site (built on since 1740) of the château or palace of the early French kings, where Philippe I. and Robert died, and Blanche, mother of St. Louis, kept her court; Isabella of Bavaria fled to it when driven out of Paris. There are a palais de justice in an old convent, a library of 10,000 volumes at the préfecture, a theatre, large barracks, &c. The English held possession between 1420-30; and Bishop Amyot, grand almoner of France, and the translater of Plutarch, was born here 1513. Trade in grain, wine, cattle, Brie cheese, &c. Conveyances: by rail, to Paris, Fontainebleau, Troyes, Auxerre, Dijon, &c.; by steamer to Paris, Montereau, &c.; by coach to Nangis, Provins, La Chapelle, Gentière, Mormant, Champeaux, Blendy, Morsenay, Milly, Malesherbes, Vale[illegible]-le-Chatelet.

[*Nangis* (23 kil. east), in a fertile hollow of the Brie country, has a population of 2,200, who trade in corn, butter, cheese. Two towers of the château of its marquises remain, besides an ancient gothic church. Napoleon defeated the allies here 1814. At 21 kil. further is Provins (see Route 26). Near Mormant (10 kil. north-west of Nangis), which has a good spire church, are the old moated châteaux of Bressey and *Grange-Bleneau*. In the latter Lafayette lived, and was visited by Fox, who planted the ivy over the gateway. It has portraits of Presidents of the United States, and of Franklin, Kosciusko, Bailly, Rochefoucauld, &c., besides the flag of the States, given to Lafayette in his last voyage to America.—Malesherbes (30 kil. south-west of Melun), in a marshy part of the Esonne, under a hill covered by a fine château.]

From Melun, on the rail, to Dijon, you pass, Bois-le-Roi (3¾ miles), at the border of the royal forest of Fontainebleau. The châteaux of Pény (finely seated) and Rochette; then

Fontainebleau (5 miles), remarkable for its château, where Napoleon abdicated 1814, standing near the town, which is a sous-préfecture, in department Seine-et-Marne, in a hollow of the forest, with 8,200 souls. It is well built, and has an Hôtel de Ville, a church, built 1624, the palais de justice in Place du Marché, with the bibliothèque of 28,000 vols.; two hospices founded by Anne of Austria and Madame de Montespan; a château d' eau or reservoir in Rue Bawer, for supplying the fountains; and the obelisk to the south built 1770 when Louis XVI. was married.

The *Château* or *Palace* is an irregular pile composed of five or six courts in different ages and styles, chiefly of brick and high-roofed; joined together by galleries, and adorned with wall paintings, Gobelin tapestry, china, &c. It originated 1162-9 in a hunting seat of Louis VII., called *Fontaine de Belle eau*, after a spring here; though some explain it Fontaine-Bleaud, from a dog of that name. Philippe-le-Bel died in it, Francis I. greatly improved it; it was the favourite seat of Henry IV.; Louis XIII. was born here, as was Henry III.; the great Condé died here, 1686, the year after Louis XIV. signed here the Revocation of the Edict of Nantes; Louis XV. was married here, 1734; Napoleon too here married Marie Louise, 1810; signed the concordat with Pius VII. (who was here a prisoner), 1812, and abdicated 1814; and here the late Duke of Orleans was married 1837, since which the château has been restored in part. A gate called the Entrée d' honneur, in Place Ferrare (from which a railing 340 feet divides it), leads into the first court, or *Cour du Cheval Blanc*, so called from the plaster cast of M. Aurelian's horse at Rome; it is the largest court, and since Napoleon took leave of his guard in it, is commonly styled *Cour des Adieux*. The *Cour de la Fontaine* opens out to the gardens, and has on one side the Salle de la belle Cheminée; here Charles V. was lodged with his suite, 1539; it has the apartments of the Queen-Mother, and of the Duke of Orleans. *Cour Ovale* or du Donjon, the most ancient, is long and narrow, and entered by the Porte Dorée (with its frescos), from the Allée Maintenon; another gate is called Porte Dauphin, in memory of the birth of Louis

XIII. It includes a balcony on 45 pillars, with several rooms or salles, as the salle de bal or gallery of Henry II., with pictures; the salles du trône and du conseil; a library of 30,000 vols. in Francis I's chapel, whose gallery of frescoes by Rossi is here; a small plain cabinet, where Napoleon signed his abdication; the gallery of Diana, 1600, and its pictures, by Pujol, &c. In the *Cour de l'Orangerie*, is the gallerie des cerfs (ornamented with stag heads), where Christiana of Sweden put her servant Monaldeschi to death, 1657. She lived in the next court, *Cour des Princes*, the smallest of all. The last, or Cour des Cuisines, has the kitchens, &c., and was built 1609, and contains a fountain with bronze mascarons or grotesque marks on it. The chapel was built 1529, by Henry IV., on the site of St. Louis's, and is richly decorated. Statues, besides jets d'eau, are dispersed over the gardens, especially a Telemachus by Canova, which was Napoleon's favourite; the parterre du Tibre is the oldest; the new one on the south side has a large pond or étang full of carp, and some waterfalls at the end where the canal goes off through the park, towards the old church of Avon (where a stone records that *Ci-git* MONADELXI.); the park contains a Jardin Anglais, a labyrinth, &c., and the royal treille or vineyard.

You walk from the town directly into the *Forest*, which is spread over an extent of 35,000 acres, on a white sandstone rock, with a very irregular surface. It is pierced by scores of sentiers or paths; and is full of strikingly picturesque sites, some parts being green and well wooded, with magnificent shady alleys of oak, beech, &c., nearly 100 feet high, and groves of fir; others bare and rugged, or covered by patches of heath and broom. The whole has been throroughly investigated by M. Denecourt, an enthusiastic resident, who has published an excellent plan, and about a dozen numbers of the 'Délices de Fontainebleau,' containing minute itineraries of the best promenades, and points of view, as the Rocher d' Avon, Chêne des Fées, Mont Ussy, the Gorge de Franchard, and its hermitage, where people spend Whit Tuesday, the Gorges d' Apremont, and aux Loups, the Vallée de la Solle, Calvaire, La Croix du Grand Veneur, &c.

Trade in wine, fruit, paving stones, ornaments in juniper wood, called genèvrines, &c. *Hotels*—De France, near the château; du Lyon, in Rue Royale; de l'Aigle Noir. A steamer runs on the Seine to Paris. Coaches to Nemours, Beaumont, Montargis, Château Landon, Gien, Briare, Cosne, Sancerre (*see* Route 25).

A fine curved viaduct leads into

THOMERY (3⅝ miles), near the Seine, but still in the forest; it is noted for its choice Fontainebleau or chasselas grapes. Another viaduct leads to

MORET ST. MAMES (3 miles), on the Seine, where the Loing falls in, having parts of its ancient walls and castle, and old church, built by Louis VII., and dedicated by Becket when a refugee at Sens. Henry IV's son, Antoine de Bourbon, killed 1652, at Castlenaudary, was Count of Moret. The Allies took it 1814.

MONTEREAU (6¼ miles), on the river, where the Yonne joins it, is the site of the roman *Condate*, under a hill which has the château of Surville (*i. e.* Above town) on top, commanding a fine view of both rivers, their bridges, &c. Napoleon beat the allies here 1814; and in the church is the sword (or a wooden copy) of Jean Sans-Peur of Burgundy, who was murdered on the old bridge over the Seine, by Charles the Dauphin, for having killed his father. Till the Revolution, they used to shew his head, with a gash in it. When Francis I. saw it, he observed that it seemed to be a very large hole. 'Yes,' said a canon, 'it ought to be, for the English entered France through it,'—the murder being followed by a civil war, which encouraged them to invade the country. Population 5,000, who make good tiles, porcelain, and pottery, one work being in the Recollets' convent. The branch railway to Troyes turns off here (*see* Route 26).

Coaches to Cannes, Mizy, Barbey, Marolles.

VILLENEUVE-LA-GUYD (6¼ miles).

PONT-SUR-YONNE (6¾ miles), at the bridge on the Yonne, in a pretty wine country.

SENS (7½ miles), a sous-préfecture, in department Yonne, seat of an archdiocess, and the old capital of the *Senones* in Cæsar's time, to whom they made a bold resistance. It stands in a pleasant spot on the Yonne, near where the Vanne joins; is well built, and watered by little brooks running through the streets, and is enclosed by remains of walls (used as promenades) built by Charles V., on the top of those built by the Romans, on courses of large rough stones. Its gates are all ancient-looking. Roman ways are traced in the neighbourhood, besides an amphitheatre. A council under St. Bernard met here, 1140, and condemned the works of Abélard, and here Pope Alexander sought refuge 1163, as did Becket the year after. It was besieged by Henry IV., in 1590, and taken bythe Allies, 1814.

St. Etienne's *Cathedral* is a fine structure in the early gothic style, replacing one burnt 970, which was built by St. Savinien on the site of a Pagan temple. It has three porches and two towers, a large and richly decorated choir, rose and other windows stained by J. Cousin, a native; a marble mausoleum of Louis XVI., by Coustou, with figures of Time, Conjugal Love, Religion, &c.; the chapel of the Virgin; that of St. Savinien, with a bas-relief of his martyrdom; the beautiful bas-relief, nearly fifty feet long, round Cardinal Duprat's tomb, and the primate's throne. In the chapter-house they shew Becket's mitre and other parts of his dress, besides portraits of all the prelates. The chapel of the Hôtel Dieu deserves notice for its vaults, &c.

At the Hôtel de Ville, which is in the renaissance style, is the museum, containing the original MS. of the Office des Fous, a festival, like that of the boy-bishop, held here till the sixteenth century. The public library of 12,000 volumes is placed in the college. There are a priests seminary, a nunnery in St. Columbe's abbey, a salle de spectacle on the esplanade, baths, &c.. No. 102, in Rue Dauphine is an ancient timbered house, with a carved genealogy of Jesus Christ on the face of it. Outside the town is the old château de Fleurigny; the hermitage of St. Bon stands on a hill, 328 feet above the river. Razors and other steel goods are made, besides leather, &c.; it has a good trade. Population, 10,100. *Hotels*—De l'Ecu (French Crown); de Paris; du Grand Cerf (Great Deer). Coaches to Courtenay (22 kil. south-west; *see* Route 25). Château Renard, Villeneuve l'Archevêque. Troyes (*see* Route 26), is 34 kil. further.

[Rigny de Féron, 25 kil. east-north-east, up the Vannes, is remarkable for a church with a fine window, stained by Cousin, with the genealogy of Christ, and the life of St. Martin. Cardinal de Bérulles was a native; he takes his name from a village to the south-east, which has one of the best built churches in the department.]

VILLENEUVE-SUR-YONNE (8¾ miles), or Ville-le-Roi, a pretty place on the Yonne, was built by Louis VII. in 1163, and has the tower of a royal château left, two gothic gates of thirteenth century, and a church partly as old, and 220 feet long, with a renaissance portal. Population, 5400.

ST. JULIEN-DE-SAULT (5 miles), on the river, opposite Ville-Vallier.

JOIGNY (7 miles), a sous-préfecture at the bridge on the Yonne, takes its name from Flavius Jovinus, the roman founder. It is steep in some parts, but has good points of view, and a long quay on the river. The Hôtel Dieu was built by Jeanne de Valois, and the half-ruined château by Cardinal Gondi, of the fifteenth century, includes St. Jean's church, on the hill. The law court (tribunal) is placed in St. Andre's old priory chapel. Population, 6,100. The branch rail turns off here to Auxerre (17 miles), and Clamecy (*see* Route 28). Coach to St. Amand-en-Puissaye.

LAROCHE (5½ miles), Brienson (5¼ miles), are the next stations.

ST. FLORENTIN (5¼ miles), on the Armançon, where the Armance joins, and where the Canal de Bourgogne goes off by an aqueduct over the latter, is in a pleasant spot, with good prospects, especially from a hill near the priory. The church was begun 1376, on the site of a rural château, and has some stained glass, with a good choir, &c. Coaches to Chailly, Ervy, Chablis, and Troyes (*see* Route 26).

[Ervy (13 kil. east-north-east) on a rocky height above the Amance, in department Aube, commanding a fine view around, has some old houses and a porte or gate of its ancient walls.]

FLOGNY (7½ miles), near the Armançon, which has a roman camp on its banks.

[At Pontigny, 10 kil. to the south-west, on the Serain, which a bridge (pont) crosses, is the fine gothic churchof the cistercian abbey (founded 1114), 310 feet long, 71 wide, and 67 high.]

TONNERRE (8 miles), a sous-préfecture of 4,500 people, in a fertile wine country, on a rocky hill over the Armançon, belongs to the Marquis de Louvois, whose old château was the seat of Margaret of Sicily, St. Louis' sister-in-law, and founder of the rich hospital here for the sick. It has on the face a large gnomon or dial, placed there 1786, by Ferouillat, a monk of St. Nicholas' old abbey, which was founded 980. Parts of the town walls remain. The best promenade is the Pâtis. In Faubourg Bourberreau a spring called Fosse Dionne, falls into a basin 42 feet diam eter. St. Pierre's church, near the hospital, over the town, has a gothic clock tower, and carved effigies of Marguerite, and the Marquis de Louvois, who was Louis the Sixteenth's war minister,—the latter by Girardon. There is a large horse market (marché-aux-chevaux) here. It was sacked by the English, 1359, and ravaged by the plague 1569 and 1632. The Chevalier d'Eon was a native. Trade in white and red wine, forcemeats (andouillettes), snails, stone for sculpture, &c. *Hotels*—De Lion d'Or (Golden Lion); de la Poste. Coaches to Chablis, Chaource, Avallon, Auxerre, Les Kiceys, and Troyes.

[*Chablis* (12 kil. west-south-west), on the Serain, is noted for its white wines, and stands near traces of a roman way to Auxerre. Population, 2,000.]

TANLAY (5 miles), has the fine château of the Marquis de Tanlay, one of the best preserved in this part of France, and a specimen of the renaissance style, which succeeded the gothic. It was begun (on the site of an earlier) 1550, by François de Coligny, brother of the admiral who was killed on Bartholomew's day, and finished 1642, from designs by Le Muet, having cost about four million francs. It forms a high roofed quadrangle, with low round domed towers at each end of the open side, and a gateway in the middle. In the interior is a large picture gallery, with frescos of the leaders of Coligny's day; also a highly decorated chapel; and the grounds comprise gardens, avenues, a canal, château d'eau (water works), park, &c.

After passing the two tunnels of Lezine and Passy (about 1,740 and 3,280 ft. long), you come to

ANCY-LE-FRANC (8¾ miles), among forests and forges, on the Armançon, with a fine château belonging to the Marquis de Louvois, built between 1555 and 1622, from the designs of Primaticcio; a square pile with paintings at each corner, and decorated with frescos from the Pastor Fido, by Nicolo del Abate. Coaches to Chatillon (36 kil. east; *see* Route 26), Avallon (34 kil. south-west; *see* Route 28).

NUITS-SOUS-RAVIERE (3¾ miles). Coaches to Bourbons-les-Bains, Chatillon, Chaumont, Bar-sur-Aube, Langres, Bar-sur-Seine, Froyes (*see* Routes 26 and 27).

AISY-SUR-ARMANÇON (5 miles).

MONTBARD (6 miles), a pretty spot on the Brenne, in department Côte d'Or, the birthplace of Buffon and Daubenton. The château of the former stands among gardens and avenues, on the hill, at the top of which are the walls of the great naturalist's study, called the tower of St. Louis. Population, 2,400. Coaches to Semur, Saulieu, Autun (*see* Route 28), Avallon, Chatillon, Chaumont, Langres, Neufchâteau (*see* Route 19).

[*Semur* (14 kil. south), on a picturesque granite rock over the Armançon (crossed by a high one-arched bridge, and another), is a sous-préfecture of 4,200 souls, and was the old fortified capital of the *Auxois* district in Burgundy, to which Henry IV., in the troubles of the League, 1490, transferred the Dijon parliament. It is divided into three parts, the Bourg, the Donjon, and the Château; the last is now a barrack, and the four great towers of the donjon are close to the bridge. Notre Dame church, built 1065, by Robert I., 213 feet long, has a triple portal between square towers in the front, an ancient pulpit, and bas-reliefs over the west porch, of the death of the founder's predecessor, Dalmace, whom they say he poisoned. A manuscript of the eleventh century is at the library; which contains 15,000 volumes; there are a college, theatre, new abattoir, &c. Salmasius was a native; his defence of Charles I. produced Milton's '*Defensio pro populo Anglicano*.' Several falls of the river are near, and at Mont-Auxois is a roman camp. Druggets and coarse woollens are made; trade in wine, cattle, corn, fruit, honey, &c. *Hotels*—De la Côte d'Or; du Dauphin.

Saulieu (25 kil. south-south-west of this), an old walled-up place, among woods and lakes, having two ancient churches, with traces of a roman temple, and a way to Autun. Vauban was born at St. Leger-de-Foucheroise, near this.]

LES LAUMES (9 mls.), is near Alise-St. Reine, the *Alesia* of Cæsar, which Vercingetorix held for seven months against him. St. Reine abbey has good sulphur baths, and is not far from Flavigny dominican priory, lately established by Abbé Lacordaire. Coaches to Semur, Saulieu, Avallon, Vitteaux, and Pouilly.

[Vitteaux (10 kil. south), a pretty little place

[on the Brenne, among vineyards, rocks, and woods, with an old château, razed 1638. Woollens are made, and it is noted for its prunes, &c.]

VERREY (13½ miles) has a fine château, used for a department school of agriculture. Coaches to St. Seine and Vitteaux.

[*St. Seine*, or *Seine l'Abbaye* (— kil. north-east), in a deep valley among the hills, has a good church, which belonged to a benedictine abbey, founded, 525, by Seyne, son of Comte de Mémont.]

BLAISY-BAS (5½ miles), a small village, remarkable for its *tunnel*, opened 1849, after 3½ years' labour, as many as 2,500 men being sometimes employed by the contractor, M. Debains. Its length is 4,100 metres (13,452 feet, or 2½ miles), and it runs through a mountain, 1,940 feet above the sea, or 643 above the railway. Though the tunnels of Mauvage (on the Rhine and Marne Canal) and La Nerthe (on the Avignon and Marseilles Railway) exceed it by a length of 500 or 600 metres, this is on a larger scale, and is, in truth, one of the greatest works of the kind in Europe. The cost was above £400,000. It falls towards Dijon, in approaching which the country is so hilly that the line is a succession of tunnels and viaducts. Five tunnels have a length of 2,624 feet; and of nine viaducts, four are 660 to 1,080 feet long, and two on a double row of arches. Coaches to Sombernon (which has remains of a fine castle of the dukes of Burgundy), Commarin, Arnay-le-Duc, Autun (*see* Route 28), Pouilly, and Vitteaux.

MALAIN (5 miles), the next station, is approached by a viaduct 65 feet high. That of Combe-de-Fain, on a double row of arches, is 147 feet high.

PLOMBIERES (4½ miles), in a pleasant spot, has a good church, and a country seat of the Bishop of Dijon, which is 2¾ miles beyond, through deep cuttings in the rock. The terminus commands a view of the mountains of Côte d'Or, and the pinnacles and towers of the old city of

Dijon. *Hotels*—Du Parc, a first-rate house, and highly recommended; de la Cloche; de la Galère; du Lion d'Or; du Chapeau Rouge; du Geneve. *Cafés*—Thibault, in Rue de la Liberté; Jussaume, near the theatre; de la Comédie, &c.

French Protestant Chapel, Rev. A. Pertuzon. Bankers, Dunnoyer and Co., Marion and Co.

Population, 28,000. A fine old town, the capital of department Côte d'Or (formerly of Burgundy), seat of a bishopric, a university (or college), a military division, &c., and centre of the Burgundy wine district; is in a rich plain on the Ourche, where the Suzon joins it, not far from the Côte d'Or hills. It was the roman *Dibio*, and after being a separate lordship, came to the dukes of Burgundy, who resided here, in what is now the museum. The streets are irregular, but clean and well-paved; the houses of stone, seldom more than two stories high. Water is brought to a reservoir from a distance of 15 miles. There are five gates in the old walls, which are planted, and surrounded (outside) by handsome public walks, such as the Retraite, Creux d'Enfer and its fountain, Cours Fleury, the Marronniers, near the Guillaume Gate, the Jardin d'Arquebuse or botanic garden (where there is an enormous poplar, 25 feet round, planted 1550), and the Parc, laid out by Le Nôtre, near the Ourche. The chief buildings are—

St. Benigue's *Cathedral*, a gothic pile of the twelfth century, 227 feet long, by 93 wide, and 89 high, having a good wooden spire, 328 feet high; the martyrdom of Stephen over the portal (by Bouchardon), and the tombs of Philippe le Hardi and his son, Jean sans Peur (whose bodies were discovered in good preservation, 1841).

The old cathedral of *Notre Dame*, built between 1252 and 1334, is 151 feet long, and includes a good porch, from which the statues have been torn away; a well-balanced roof, a group of the Assumption (by Dubois). The ancient clock made by Jacques Marques, a Dutchman was given by Philippe le Hardi in 1382. St. Michael's church, of the sixteenth century, is a mixture of gothic and italian (or renaissance) styles, about 200 ft. long, with a portal by H. Sambin. St. Anne's, at the orphans' hospital, has a dome 52 ft. across.

Le Palais des Etats, in Place d'Armes, which belonged to the dukes, and was afterwards used by the provincial states, has been new fronted. What remains of the old palace are the great tower (now the observatory), finished by Charles the Bold, the guard-room, the kitchen, and carved mantel-piece, 30 feet high. Here are kept the archives of the duchy, a cabinet of natural history, a library of 45,000 vols. (besides 630 MSS. and 2,400 medals), and a museum, which includes pictures, the cup of St. Bernard (who was born at Fontaines, 2 kil. off), and the fine effigies of dukes Philippe and Jean, which before the revolution stood in the Chartreuse convent (on the Saumur road). The préfecture and palais de justice are large buildings; the theatre, in Place St. Etienne, is another, being 200 feet by 70, with a portico of eight pillars. St. Etienne's old church is a market. The public baths are in Place d'Armes. There are besides a general hospital, cavalry barracks, a college, school of arts, botanic garden, &c.

Bossuet (Bishop of Meaux), Crébillon, Piron, Daubenton, the Duc de Bassano (Maret) were natives. Trade in wine (Chambertin, Beaune, Vougeot, &c.), grain, wool, leather, vinegar, good mustard, &c.; a few woollens, cottons, and silks are made.

Conveyances, by railway, to Paris, &c., and to Chalons (thence by steamer to Lyons, in all 18 hours). Coaches to Nancy (*see* Route 16), Mulhouse (28 hours, Pontarlier, Besançon (*see* Route 30; a railway is projected in this direction), Gray, Dôle (*see* Route 29), Geneva.

[*Gray* (50 kil. north-east), up the Saône, where it becomes navigable, is a sous-préfecture of 6,600 persons (department Haute-Saône), on a hill-side, and was the favourite seat of Philippe-le-Long's wife, Jeanne, where as many as ten religious houses were founded. It was fortified, 1420, and suffered cruelly in the civil wars; the streets are crooked and old fashioned. Parts of the castle are left; and it has also a good bridge and quay, to which steamers from Dijon come; a Hôtel de Ville, built 1568, a library of 6,000 vols., salle de spectacle, and a very superior mill, with 14 wheels, for grinding corn, oil, tan, &c. *Hotel*—Du Sauvage.

At 18 kil. north-west of it is Fontaine-Française, marked by a pillar, where Henry IV., with a small force, fought the Duc de Mayenne, with 18,000, in 1595.]

From Dijon, on the railway to Chalons-sur-Saône, near the Côte d'Or hills, and through the Burgundy wine district, you pass La Baraque and

GEVREY, or GIVRAY (6¾ miles), in a picturesque valley, near the vineyards of Chambertin, Chambolle, Morey, Gilly, &c.

VOUGEOT (3¾ miles), where the finest Burgundy wine is made, 6 to 8 fr. a bottle.

NUITS (3¼ miles), on the Mezin, under Côte Nuitonne, with its two churches, is near the vineyards of Romanée, Richebourg, St. George's, Musigny, &c.

CORGOLOIN (3¾ miles).

BEAUNE (5¼ miles), a sous-préfecture, under the Côte d'Or, and centre of the wine trade, with 11,500 people, on the Bouzoize, having Chancellor Rollin's hospital, founded 1443, in the gothic style (with a court, &c.); also a library of 25,000 vols. and museum, two old churches, a belfry of the fourteenth century, a corn market (halle au blé), the fountain of Aigue, public gardens and baths, a theatre, &c. Monge, the mathematician, was a native. *Hotels* — De France; du Commerce; du Chevreuil.

The vineyards of Pomard, Volnay, &c., are near. Coaches to Nolay, Autun, Moulins, Arnay-le-Duc, and Bligny.

[*Nolay* (18 kil. south-west), in a white wine country, at the bottom of a narrow valley, has a good spire church, and the tower of its old château. On the promenade is la Journée fountain; and at Bout-du-Monde (End of the World), at the source of the Cusanne (4 kil. off), is the fine fall of Menevault, 66 feet down into a rocky hollow below. On Chatillon hill a roman camp is seen. Population, 2,000.]

MERSAULT (4½ miles), has some noted white wine vineyards, and a spire church.

CHAGNY (5¼ miles), on the Deheune, and the Canal du Centre, under which the railway is carried by a tunnel. Coaches to Digoi (*see* Route 51), Genelard, Blanzy, St. Berain, St. Leger, and St. Creuzot.

FONTAINES (1¾ miles); and 8½ miles further is CHALONS-SUR-SAONE, where the Lyons railway terminates for the present. It will be extended to the latter city in 1854.

Chalons-sur-Saone, or CHALON, as it used to be called. *Hotels*—Du Parc is first-rate, and is strongly recommended; des Diligences, near the Quay, a very good house, and well situated; des Trois Faisans; du Chevreuil. Population, 16,000. A sous-préfecture in department Saône-et-Loire, and an ancient place, in a good situation for trade, being on the Saône, where it is navigable to Lyons, and whence the Canal du Centre (cut in 1791) proceeds to join the Loire at Digoin. It is Cæsar's *Cabillonum*, a town of the *Ædui*, which he made a roman granary. Both Augustus and Constantine visited it. Attila took it after a siege, 451; and the Saracens, in 732. It suffered in the wars between Louis XI. and his restless vassal, Charles the Bold, who held it as part of Burgundy, the vineyards of which begin about here. Charles IX. built the citadel here. 1563. In the wars of the League it was the Duke of Mayenne's head quarters. The Austrians took it, 1814. The soil is very fertile; the broad quay offers a rather good view; and they say the Dauphiné Alps, though 120 miles off, may be seen (?) A stone bridge of 5 arches, with its piers carried above the top, in the shape of pyramids, joins St. Laurent, on an island in the river, where there is an old hospital (1528) with public baths attached, and a promenade.

The head church, or cathedral (once the seat of a bishop), is of the thirteenth century, with two modern towers, and is about to be restored. There is another church (St. Pierre), a new Hôtel de Ville, bibliothèque of 10,000 vols., palais de justice (law court), salle de spectacle, a pretty cemetery, a fountain, with a figure of Neptune, in the Place de la Beaune (which has an old gate near it), a college, and a granite obelisk, in Grand Rue, on the canal. At 2 kil to the east is the church of St. Marcel's abbey, where Abélard died.

Manufactures of silk hose, hats, leather, oil from cole-seed (for which there are crushing mills), bricks, tiles, beet-root, sugar, white beer, barges, and écailles d'ablettes, for mock pearls. Trade in these, Burgundy wine, grain, timber, &c., which find their way there as an entrepôt for the north and east of France.

Conveyances by rail to Paris, Dijon, &c.; by coach to Lons-le-Saulnier (*see* Route 31), Charolles, Marcigny, Roanne, Vichy, Moulins, Nevers (*see* Routes 33 and 51); and to Lyons (viâ Macon), near the course of the Saône, when the river is not navigable, in 16 hours (about 160 kil). But the best way of going to Lyons is by steamer, five of which run down daily, in 7 to 8 hours, for 6 and 8 fr.; the return, being against stream, takes 12 to 14 hours. The banks are flat at first, but cultivated with fruit trees and vineyards. Barges traverse the stream all day long. The railway will take the direction of the road.

From *Chalons, down the Saône*,* you pass St. Remi, St. Loup, and its old castle; Marny and its paper mills; Ormes, which had a bridge in Roman times; Senecey (18 kil. by road, in the interior), with its iron works, and ruins of Château Ruffey.

TOURNUS (10 kil.), an ancient town of 5,400 population, on the west, at the new suspension bridge on five piers, having an Hôtel de Ville, with a black granite pillar in front, and a hospital of the thirteenth century, an old half Norman church near St. Philibert's Abbey, founded 875, &c., and a slab (over the house where he was born, 1725,) to J. B. Greuze the painter.

Manufactures of pottery, leather, beer, sugar, &c. *Hotels*—De l'Europe, du Sauvage.

UCHIZY, on the west, is said to be peopled by descendants of Saracen settlers.

ST. ALBIN (16 kil.), on the west, near Fleurville bridge, and nearly opposite Pont de Vaux, which is a pretty village in La Bresse, or department Ain, noted for its capons.

[To the west of St. Albin, about 5 miles in the interior, is *Cluny*, which has the cloisters, abbot's house, a chapel, and two towers of the famous Benedictine abbey, the head of that order, which was destroyed at the revolution, 1789. The church was 600 feet long. It was rich in MSS., and the revenue was 70,000 livres.]

At 14 kil. further is

MACON. *Hotels*—Du Sauvage, de l'Europe, des Champs Elysées. Population 12,000. This chief town of department Saône-et-Loire, on a low hill, in a fertile spot, was once the roman *Matisco Æduorum*, seat of a diocess, and of a county called the Mâconnais, which was sold by the Burgundian dukes to France, 1241. It was ravaged by the Huns and other invaders, and suffered in the religious wars of 1562 from both parties. The Austrians took it 1814 after a little fighting; Napoleon was received 15th April, 1815. Like all old towns, most of the streets are narrow and dirty; but it has pretty walks and good prospects in the neighbourhood. From the 12-arch bridge leading over to St. Laurent, and lately altered and improved, you may even see Mont Blanc; the bridge itself replaces a Pont Jud, built, they say, by the Jews whom Philippe le Bel expelled.

St. Vincent's new church, in Place d'Armes on the hill, of brick and stone, was built 1810-16, and stands opposite Soufflot's hospital, built 1758-

* See Kauffman's *Bords de la Saone*, for fuller particulars.

It replaces the old cathedral church, demolished 1793, except the two octagon towers (visible all round), and parts of the front and cloisters. St. Peter's church belonged to the Cordeliers convent, now used by the gendarmerie. The préfecture is on the site of the citadel (pulled down 1585), and was the bishop's palace. The public library and theatre are at the Hôtel de Ville, the old seat of the Counts Montrevel. There are two hospices for incurables and orphans, a palais de justice in pretty grounds, and some old houses in Rue de l'Oratoire. One of the best buildings is the hôtel de Senecey. The Mâconnais women wear a peculiar headdress. About 3,000 roman coins were found here 1764, with a few marbles; and a roman way may be traced towards Autun. *Lamartine*, the republican statesman and poet, is a native, and has a seat at St. Point (12 kil.), in a beautiful spot among the Charolais hills, near an old castle. Pottery, leather, &c. are made; trade in wine (from Thorins, Moulin-à-Vent, Romanêche, which was a roman station, &c.), grain, cattle, timber, &c. Conveyances, by steamer, to Lyons, Chalons; by coach to Moulins, Bourg, (35 kil.), Ville franche, Cluny.

St. Romain (16 kil.) at the suspension bridge on the river, nearly opposite Thoissey, in the Dombes (to the east); while to the west of it is Romanêche, which has a manganese mine, and is noted for wine called Moulin-à-Vent (Windmill). The Jura mountains come into view on the west.

Belleville and Montmerle bridges appear next,—the latter place having an old castle, and the former an old church.

[To the right of Belleville, in the interior, is Beaujeu, with remains of an old château on the hill above it, once the seat of the lords of the Beaujolais.]

Then the Iles de Guerrein, the bridge of Beauregard, and another at the mouth of the Morgon, up which river, a little to the west, is

Villefranche (38 kil. from Mâcon), a pretty sous-préfecture of 7,100 people, among vineyards and good points of view. It was founded by Humbert, Count of Beaujolais, who, they say, granted his vassals land at three derniers a fathom, and the privilege of beating their wives. The latter are good-looking, however, and noted for their liveliness. The Gothic church is good. [illegible] are made. *Hotel*—Le Faucon.

Anse (5 kil.), below St. Bernard bridge, in a beautiful country, proverbial for its fertility, has a church, on the site of Augustus Cæsar's palace.

Trevoux (3 kil.), on the west, at the new suspension bridge, a sous-préfecture, with an island in front, and remains of a castle on the hill; also the house where the Jesuits printed their Journal de Trévoux and Dictionnaire de Trévoux; and the old palace of the Parliament of Dombes. The terrace commands a fine prospect. Trévoux, some say, comes from *Tres viæ*, because three roman roads met here. Septimus Severus defeated Albinus near this in 171. Further on, you leave on the right Mont d'Or (1,000 feet high), so called from its rich appearance in autumn, and having a view which takes in the fine plains of Burgundy and Lyonnais, and the Dauphiné Alps.

Neuville, on the west, has a suspension bridge. Rochetaille, on the west, near Couzon bridge, has a cutting (taille) through the rock, made by Agrippa for his roman way, and part of an old château.

Four islands, called Iles d'Albigny, come next.

Mont Cindre, on the right, has a hermitage on the top, whence there is a fine view of the valley of the Létra. St. Cyr and St. Didier have quarries which abound with fossils. Another bridge joins Collonges to Fontaine, on the left. Below this is St. Rambert's very ancient abbey church, on Ile Barbe, which has a suspension bridge to each bank of the Saône

Three more bridges bring you to the suburbs of Lyons, which is 31 kil. below Villefranche, in a fine spot, something like the Avon, at Clifton, where the Saône falls into the Rhône.

Lyons or Lyon. *Hotels*—De l'Univers, near the post-office and steam-packet station, a first-class hotel, highly recommended: Mr. Glover is an Englishman; de l'Europe; de Provence, in Place de la Charité; du Nord, in Rue Lafont; de Marseille, on Quai St. Antoine, with a fine view; de Paris, on Quai Peyrollerie, near the Saône steamers; de l'Hermitage, Place de la Préfecture, &c. *Cafés*—Perle, Jeune France, Rhône, Neuf-Four, Lyon, Bertheoux, &c., many being in Place des Célestins; also Casati, Poulet, Toriani, &c. for chocolate, a cup of which, taken before dinner (2 o'clock), is ½ fr.; dinner, 2 to 3 fr. The small loaves, cakes (brioche), beer, pork, sausages, and river fish are noted.

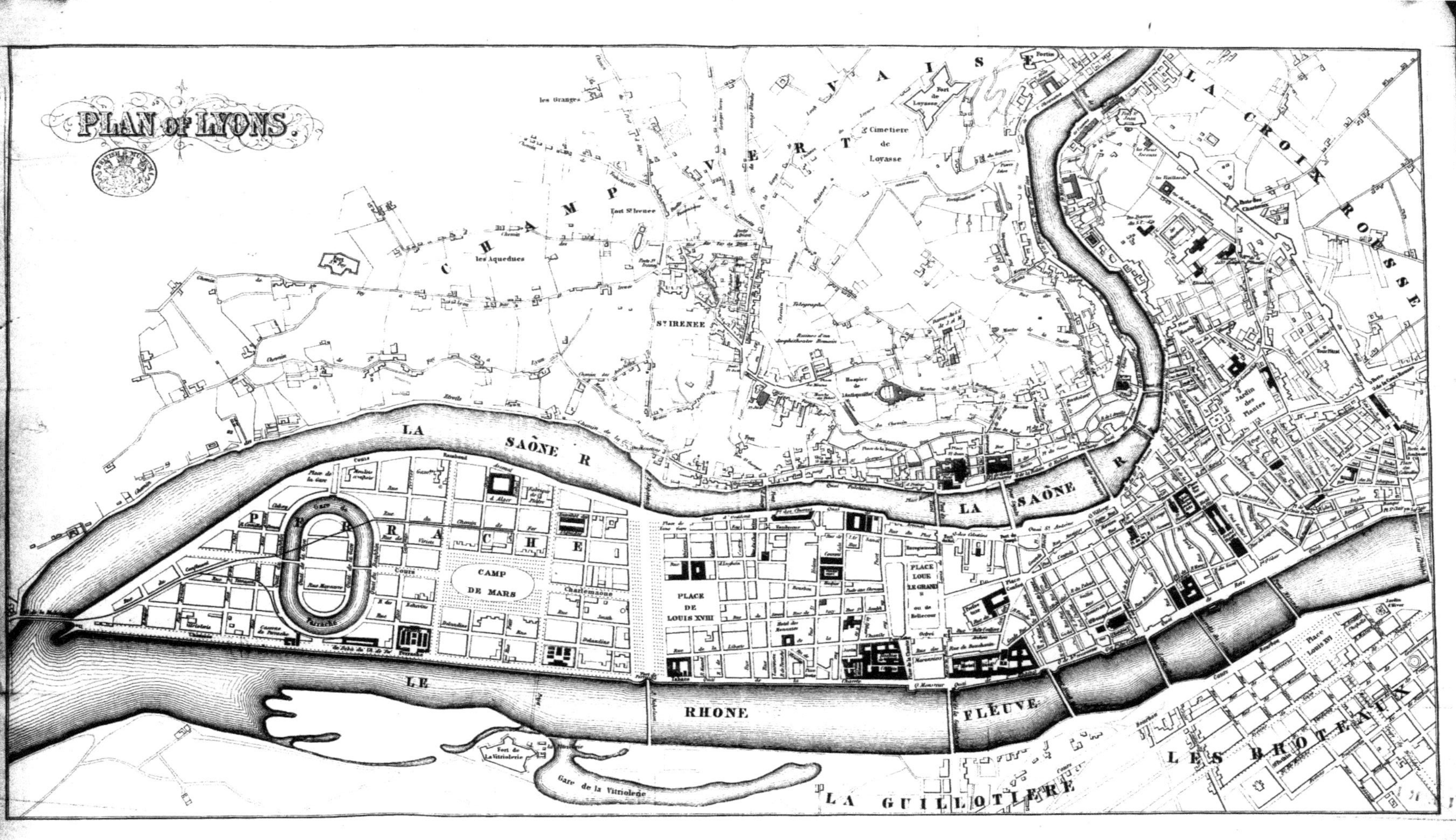
PLAN OF LYONS
CHAMP VERT
VAISE
LA CROIX ROUSSE
LA SAÔNE R
LA SAÔNE R
LE RHONE FLEUVE
PERRACHE
CAMP DE MARS
PLACE DE LOUIS XVIII
PLACE LOUIS LE GRAND
St IRENEE
les Aqueducs
les Granges
Fort de Loyasse
St Cimetiere de Loyasse
Jardin des Plantes
Place Louis XVI
LES BROTEAUX
LA GUILLOTIERE
Gare de la Vittiolerie
Fort de la Vitriolerie

Omnibuses run to most of the best points of view near the city, and to several pretty villages round it; such as Oullens, Charbonnières and its springs (8 kil.), Mont Cindre near St. Cyr, St. Bonnet-le-Froid (16 kil.) on a hill, Ecully, &c.

Malle-postes, diligences, &c. go out to Paris (33 hours); or 18 hours by steam and rail. Chambéry (15 hours); Turin (39 hours); Milan (72 hours); Genoa, Marseilles (20 hours); Toulouse, Bordeaux (38 hours); Geneva (13 hours); Clermont-Ferrand (20 hours); Strasbourg, Grenoble, Valence, Besançon, Nantua, Bourg, Annonay, Aix-les-Bains (11 hours); Trevoux, Roanne, Tarare, Beaujeu, St. Symphorien, Montbrison, Montluel, Neuville, Mulhouse (33 hours); Vienne, Coudrieu, Chavanay, Pelussin, Serrière, Le Péage, St. Vallier, Tain, Romans, Le Puy, &c.

By rail to St. Etienne in 4 hours.

By Steamer down the Rhône, daily, to Valence (5 hours); Avignon (12 hours); Arles, Beaucaire, corresponding with places on both sides of the river, as Nismes, Privas, Aubenas, &c. Prices to Valence 7½ and 10 fr., Avignon 15 and 20 fr., Arles 18 and 23 fr. From Arles to Marseilles, by sailing boat in 5 hours for 5 fr. But this part of the journey is superseded by the rail, which takes you from Avignon to Marseilles in 3 hours.

By steamer, up the Saône, by Macon to Chalons, in 10 hours, 6 and 8 fr.

Post-office in Place Bellecour.

Chapel Evangelique, in Rue de l' Arbre Sec, where the English service is read on Sunday afternoons. MM. Buisson, Aeschimann, Illaire are French Protestant pastors here.

This old and populous city is the capital of department Rhône, head of a military division, seat of an archbishopric, of the silk trade, &c., on the grand route to Marseilles and Italy, in a fine spot at the junction of the Saône and Rhône, in a circle of hills crowned with country seats, vineyards, and mulberry trees. Great part (the Bourg) stands on the tongue of land between rivers,—the Saône stealing quietly by and losing itself in the Rhône, which rushes past with a strong tide towards the Mediterranean. The point where they now join (Mulatière bridge, which the St. Etienne rail passes over) is some distance south of the old junction (near Ainay bridge), and the land thus reclaimed and called Perache, after the architect who effected it by turning the course of the Saône, is laid out and partly built on; it includes the Cours de Midi, Champ de Mars (where an equestrian statue of Napoleon was placed, 1852), the rail terminus, &c.

The roman city, founded 47 B.C. by Lucius Munatius Plancus, the consul, and called *Lucidunum*, and *Lugdunum* after him, occupied the west side of the Saône (which was not crossed till the ninth century), on the hills of St. Sebastian and St. Just, where Fourvière's church stands. Great roads made by Agrippa went hence to the north, (through the Pierre Scisse or Rochetaille *i. e.* cut rock), and to Spain, Marseilles, and Italy; Marc Antony constructed the aqueducts, of which there are remains on Mont d' Or, at Pilat, and other places. It was taken by the Huns, and by the Saracens (725); became the capital of Burgundy; and was at length held by its archbishops. The people began to choose their magistrates 1195. Philippe le Bel incorporated it with France, 1310. It suffered much from the religious wars of the sixteenth century when the Protestants of the Cevennes were hunted down. One of their leaders, the Baron des Adrets, took it by surprise 1562. But it revived upon the issuing of the edict of Henry IV. as mentioned below. A pestilence, 1628, carried off 35,000 people in three months. At the revolution it sided with the Girondists, and was dreadfully punished by the revolutionary leaders who, in 1793, sent against it an army of 60,000 men; after a siege of three months it yielded, and the scenes which followed by order of the infamous Collet d' Herbois and Couthon, were as bloody and terrible as the Noyades at Nantes (see *Alison's History*). The Austrians took it 1814, and carried the keys to Vienna; it opened its gates to Napoleon, 1815, during the hundred days; and was the scene of insurrection, 1831–34, at the cost of hundreds of lives.

Lyons proper, with Fourvières, St. Foy, &c., contains a population of 160,000; La Guillotière and Le Broteaux, on the east or left bank of the Rhone, the richest quarters, 34,000; Croix Rousse and St. Paul, to the north, where the weavers live (the master manufacturers, in St. Clair), 20,000; Vaise, to the north-west on the Saône, 8,000: making a total of 222,000. The people are intelligent and jocose, fond of nick-names, arguments, and fighting (as the events of 17

1831-4, prova); but they are small-sized, and as poor and miserable as the Spitalfields weavers, who are their cousins, by a few removes, being descendants of the Protestant exiles driven out of Lyons and other parts of France in 1685, at the revocation of the Edict of Nantes. This edict, when passed by Henry IV., 1598, brought peace to the French Protestants, and especially to Lyons; but its revocation by Louis XIV., sent 100,000 families into foreign countries, and so reduced the city that a century after (1787); there were but 7,500 workmen in it. This act of wicked folly made Christiana of Sweden say that Louis XIV. had cut off his left hand with his right.

The silk trade was first introduced by Italians in the fifteenth century, who fled from the civil wars of their own country. Colbert encouraged the planting of mulberries; ferrandines were invented 1630, by Ferrand; poplins about 1700; velvets and moirées 1730; and the jacquard loom 1815. Other staple trades are dyeing, hat making (45,000 yearly); gold and silver work, and bijouterie (trinkets), to the value of 12 million francs; chemicals and varnishes, stained papers, beer and liqueurs, soap, tanning, steam-engines, and machinery,—water power for the works being close at hand. Design is promoted by the école des beaux arts (school of fine arts), founded 1805, by Napoleon, under five professors; and by another institution (école des arts et metiers, *i.e.* practical arts and trades) called La Martinière, which is self-supporting (?) A conseil des prud'hommes, *i.e.* a standing committee of masters and men, settles disputes about wages, &c.

One of the best views of the city is from the heights of La Pape, near the Strasbourg road, where you see it spread below you, with its rivers, quays, bridges, and faubourgs, and catch a prospect of the country, with the Dauphiny Alps and even Mont Blanc in the distance (100 miles away). Another view may be had from the telegraph over St. Irenée, or from the church of Fourvières, at the belvedere or observatory, above the west bank of the Saône, and reached by Tilsit or Palais bridges. Go also to Quai St. Clair, and to Guillotière bridge, at night, when the city is lit up. About 18 forts strengthen the points around, most of them built since 1831-4, when the insurgent weavers, &c., were put down by the soldiery with great bloodshed. The largest are Forts Caluire, Montessuis, Broteaux, Villeurbanne, Irenée, &c.

Broad quays, as usual in French ports, line the river banks, the best of which are — Quais St. Antoine, des Celestins (near the theatre and cafés), d'Angoulême, and de l'Hôpital (on the Rhône), St. Clair, &c.: there are 28 in all. The Rhône is about 660 feet broad on the average, and crossed by six bridges, which are (beginning from the north), St. Clair, suspension bridge; Morand, of wood, built 1774, leading to Broteaux; la Fayette, foundation on stone piers, 700 feet long; l'Hôpital, suspension, opposite the general hospital; la Guillotière (having a good prospect), the oldest and longest, being 1,617 feet from end to end, on 17 stone arches (when first built, 1190, it had 20), of which 8 are usually in the water; Napoleon, suspension, the latest built. Eleven or twelve bridges cross the Saône, which is from 330 to 500 feet broad. Beginning at the south, where it joins the Rhône, we have the two Mulatière bridges—one being used for the railway; the Napoleon; Ainay, near that church; Tilsit, one of the best, on 5 arches, 393 feet long; du Palais, near the palais de justice; du Change, rebuilt since 1840; Feuillée, very elegant, with lions at the ends; Sérin, to Vaise; Verrerie; Gare, suspension; and the suspension bridges of the Barbe. Some, as la Guillotière, are longer than there would seem to be need of, on account of the floods, which swell both streams after continued rains. Inundations are recorded in 592, 1570, 1602, 1611, and especially 1840, when boats floated in Place de Bellecour, Place des Jacobins, and les Broteaux. By means of its rivers and the canals which fall into them, Lyons communicates with all the great towns.

The houses are in general high, but the streets narrow and badly paved; so that however pleasant the town looks in summer, it is shocking in rainy or snowy weather, when, from its situation, it is very misty. Some of the oldest houses worth notice are in Rue St. Jean, Rue Lainerie, Rue de la Poulaillerie (old Hôtel de Ville), Rue Mercière, Rue St. Guze, (commandery of Malta); also on Quai de Flandre (house of Roi de Ribauds), Quai Fulchiron, Place d'Albon. The Passage de l'Hôpital is a covered way or arcade of modern date.

There are several public places or squares. Place Bellecour, 1,017 feet by about 690, fills 15 acres (Lincoln's Inn is 13½), and has a bronze of Louis XIV., by Lemot, put up 1828, to replace one thrown down, 1793, by Couthon, the terrorist, who also ordered some of the best houses here to be razed. Place de Terreaux is small, but marked by the Hôtel de Ville and the palais des arts. Here Cinq Mars and De Thou were executed, 1642, for conspiring against Richelieu; and the guillotine was set up 1794. Place du Meridien or des Cordeliers, a good point of view, has a column 70 feet high, with a channel in it shewing the direction of the meridian, and a figure of Urania on the top, put there 1768, by Payet. In Place des Célestins stand the theatre, &c.; Place du Change has the protestant chapel; Place Sathonay, so called after a mayor, is opposite the Jardin des Plantes (botanic gardens). Place Louis XVIII., near Cours de Midi, at Perache, and Place Louis XVI., at Broteaux, are both large and square; Place de Perron, on a point of Croix Rousse, has a statue of the Homme du Peuple (man of the people); and Place St. Jean, near the cathedral, contains a fountain group of the baptism of Christ, by Bonnaissieu. There are few other fountains worth remark. A long promenade is laid out in Avenue Perache, on the Rhône.

Of the eighteen churches, the *Cathedral* of St. Jean is the first. It stands on the west side of the Saône, where the Roman city was begun. The oldest part is of the twelfth century; it has a high front, with three deep doors in it, ornamented with statues; a rose window, and low towers at the outer corners. There are also two other towers, a nave 260 feet long, stained windows, a large high altar, several side chapels (the Bourbon chapel being richly carved), and a curious superannuated clock, made by Bâlois, 1598, which showed the saint days, changes of the moon, &c., besides having figures to strike the chimes, and a cock to crow the hours. Notre Dame de Fourvières, near it and the observatory on the hill, whence the view is obtained, stands on the site of Trajan's *Forum Vatus*, and is full of offerings to an idol of the virgin, which adorns it. It was built 1192, and partly ruined 1562. St. Irenée has a crypt where Irenæus was buried.

Ainai or Ainay abbey church, on the site of Caligula's Athenæum, to which Juvenal refers, has the granite pillars of a small temple, built here by Augustus, and below is the dungeon where the martyrs Pothinus and Blandina were confined. St. Nizier is large, and a good specimen of flamboyant gothic of the sixteenth century, having a lofty vault, the virgin chapel, with her statue by Coysevox, a tall spire, &c. St. Paul, a small pretty gothic church, replaces one built by Charlemagne. The Chartreux church, founded by Henry III., on Croix Rousse Hill, has a good dome by Servandoni, a well-proportioned choir, and a fine marble altar. St. Bonaventure's, or the Cordeliers church, built 1326–1468, has a good front, but is most remarkable for being the scene of many events in the history of Lyons. At St. George's there is a tall spire. The protestant chapel, built 1747, was used as an exchange till 1804. A chapel in the form of a pyramid occupies the place where the massacres of 1793 took place at Broteaux.

The new *Palais de Justice*, on the Saône, by Baltard, has a colonnade of twenty-four pillars, and is adjacent to the old one, which was the seat of the Counts of Roanne, now a prison. The hôtel de la préfecture, in Place Confort, is, with some alterations, part of the Jacobin convent. A better building, and one of the most uniform of this class, is the *Hôtel de Ville*, built 1646-55, by S. Maupin, in Place des Terraux; in the front, 157 feet long (and restored by Mansard, 1702), are a bas relief of Henry IV. on horse, and figures of Hercules and Pallas. The wings, with their high roofs, are 383 feet long down to Place de la Comédie, and include two courts, over the first of which the club-room rises 141 feet high. In the vestibule are Coustou's bronze figures of the Rhône and Saône; one mounted on a roaring, the other on a quiet, lion, as characteristic of the two rivers. Blanchet's wall paintings are seen further on up the grand staircase, which is admired for its construction. The archives are placed here, and it has also a curious collection, made by M. Rozaz, of medals, proclamations, caricatures, pamphlets, &c., between 1789 and 1840. Opposite the Hôtel de Ville stands the

Palais des Arts, a large square 334 feet long, with a figure of Apollo in the midst, built 1667 by Valsinière, on the site of St. Pierre's benedictine convent, (of which the cloister and chapel remain); it includes a gallery of 500 pictures, chiefly by Flemish and Lyons artists, one being a view of the old bastile, on Pierre Seisse (pulled down 1789); roman mosaics and other marbles, especially the bronze tables of the emperor

Claudius (a native); museum of medals, silk, machines, subjects of natural history, works of art; busts of natives, a portrait (in *silk*) of Jacquard, &c. The *Jardin des Plantes* (Botanic Garden) in Place de Sathonay, on the site of a roman naumachia (where marine fights were displayed), has a bust of Abbé Rozier,—an orangery, &c., and commands a good prospect of the city. At the public *Bibliothèque* on Quai du Rhône in part of the old convent of Trinity, is a rich collection of 100,000 vols. and 8,000 MSS.; one room is 164 feet long. The college is close to it.

Among the Charitable Institutions are, the General Hospital or *Hôtel Dieu*, a vast pile on the Rhône, first founded, they say, by Childebert, in the sixth century, but re-built with its large dome, &c. since 1793, by Soufflot; it contains 1,800 beds. To the south of it is the hospice de la Charité, as large if not a larger building, founded 1617, for 400 poor people, besides orphans, &c. Behind this is an excellent military hospital; the hospice de l'Antiquaille, for 600 incurables, lies on the west side of the Saône, on the site of the roman emperor's palace, afterwards of a monastery. A depôt de mendicité stands on the east bank, on the site of Chazeaux convent. There is an old hospice (asylum) on Quai de Flandre. At the Mont de Piété, pledges are taken for loans, under proper regulations.

The *Grand Théâtre*, near the Hôtel de Ville, is large and plain; another is on Quai des Celestins. There are baths in all parts of the city, the largest being opposite the college. A cemetery, large and well planted, at Fourvières. The douane (custom-house) and salt stores are near Tilsit bridge; veterinary school and large barracks at the ends of Serin bridge. School of arts et metiers (arts and trades), near the Saône, above Du Change bridge; the government tobacco factory on Quai du Rhône; the new prison of St. Joseph at Perache; a pepinière or nursery of trees, &c. near Vaise. The corn and wine markets are also worth notice, as well as the large hotel des monnaies (or mint). Of institutions for promoting science, &c. there are the Academies of sciences, belles lettres and arts; agricultural, Linnean, and medical societies. There is also a 'condition des soies,' or test house for silk. On Quai de Flandres is a wooden figure, replacing an older one, of the homme de la roche, in honour of Jean Cleberg, a benefactor to the town; a tour de la belle Allemande (tower of the beautiful German) at Rochette opposite Vacques, is said to commemorate his wife. Further up the Saône, in a charming spot, is Ile Barbe, an island covered with trees and the buildings of St. André's old abbey, Charlemagne's house (?), a church, &c., and joined to the main land by suspension bridges. The Lyonnois always visit this at Easter and Whitsuntide. At Fort de la Motte, on the east side of the Rhone, Henry IV. was married to Marie de Medici. The Fountain de Rozet, near Roche Cardon, in the neighbourhood, stands in a wood, which Rousseau used to frequent. On a little brook behind St. Foy, are remains of a roman aqueduct. Pavements, &c. are occasionally found; one as late as 1843, in Rue Jarente.

Some of the eminent natives, are the emperors Caracalla and Claudius; Philibert de l' Orme and Perache, the architects; Coustou and Lemot, the sculptors; Jussieu, the botanist; Louise Labé, or la belle Cordière, a poetess of the time of Francis I.; J. B. Say; Jacquard; Marshal Suchet, &c. Herod, the tetrarch, was banished to Lyons by Caligula, A.D. 43.

ROUTE 24—*continued.*

From Lyons down the Rhone.

This river is navigable with difficulty above the city. The descent is easy and rapid, though obstructed by sand banks; to Avignon (about 150 or 160 miles), 12 hours is allowed; but to ascend it against the current takes 45 hours; a barge 14 days. A number of suspension bridges cross this beautiful stream, which flows with a rapid, winding course, and a breadth nearly uniform to Avignon; between hills covered with cornfields, vineyards, mulberry trees, &c., and crowned by the picturesque remains of many old feudal castles. Many parts of it resemble the Lower Rhine in character. It divides the departments of Isère, Drôme, and Vaucluse, from those of Ardèche and Gard, which formerly comprised the provinces of Dauphiné, Vivarais, &c. Coaches as well as steam-boats, run along both sides of the river; and the St. Etienne Railway follows the west bank as far as Givors. The places on or near it* are as follows (distances being reckoned from Mulatière Suspension Bridge):—

Above Mulatière Bridge, is St. Foy (on the west), and its heights, crowded with country seats, and commanding extensive prospects.

Oullins (3 miles from Lyons), on the west, another pretty spot, having a college, which was a seat of Cardinal de Tencin; a church, where Jacquard is buried; and the Château du Perron, which now belongs to the General Hospital at Lyons. Thomas, a writer of the last century, died here, 1785.

St. Genis Laval, behind the above, has an old seat of the archbishops of Lyons, where Clement V. received the homage of Charles of Anjou.

Feyzin (4 miles), on the east, opposite Irigny, is the first village in Dauphiny, and has a college and a seat of the Comtesse de Brison-Chaponay, whom Josephine and her daughter visited here before the revolution. Guillaume de Peyrat, almoner to Henry IV., was a native.

Solaise (6 miles), on the east, opposite Vernaison, has a roman miliary, or mile-stone, standing on the ancient way to Vienne, with the figures VII. on it. Several islands stand in front of Vernaison, and Charly (on the west) behind it.

[St. Symphorien d'Ozon, 2 miles south-east of Solaise, has part of an old castle of the counts of Savoy, who fortified the town in 1200.]

Millery (7 miles), on the west, with Galée château, which belonged to the brother of President Moulceau, one of Madame de Sevigné's correspondents.

Grigny (8½ miles), on the west, was the site of a monastery of some note, and has remains of the fine château of the Moulceau family. Opposite it is

Ternay, with a château which belonged to Marshal Bourg, of the time of Louis XIV., and St. Mayeul's excellent priory church, founded in the twelfth century, but much disfigured.

Givors (11 miles), on the west, where the canal comes in, and St. Etienne railway turns off, has a bridge, large glass works, foundries, &c., and a trade in coal. It is at the mouth of the Gier, which makes a basin 880 feet long. A large new church is in the grecian style. Population, 10,000

Loire (13 miles), on the west, with Ile Blanche and other islands in front, is nearly opposite Seyssuel or Chasse, which gives name to the Seyssuel or Seyssel stone, and the Saxeolum wines, which Pliny speaks of. There are ruins of a château of the Vienne archbishops.

Vienne (17 miles, or, by road, 28 kil.), a very old town, a sous-préfecture in department Isère, and once the seat of a diocess, is at the Gère's mouth, at the suspension bridge to St. Colombe, in an amphitheatre of vine-covered hills. It was the *Vienna Allobrogum*, or chief town of the Allobroges, and came to be an important roman city; but it declined after the Burgundian kings sold it to the archbishops. The Gère turns many mills for linen, cotton, iron, paper, glass, hemp, &c. Traces of roman works are on Mont Pipet, Mont Arnauld, Mont Salomont, &c., the last having remains of a middle age castle. The *Musée*, where many roman marbles, inscriptions, &c., are collected, was itself a temple to Augustus, afterwards used as a church; it is something like the Maison Carée at Nismes, and has a library of 6,500 vols. Near the theatre is an ancient portico, now called the arche de triomphe, or 'arcade du forum.' Outside the Porte d'Avignon, is the Aiguille (needle), a pillar of unknown history, 52 feet high. Remains of quays on the river, of aqueducts, of an amphitheatre, &c., have been noticed.

The large *Cathedral* church of St. Maurice, near the river, is partly of the thirteenth century, the latest addition being 1515; it has two towers, a sculptured portal, a high vault on 49 pillars, a tomb of a King Bozon (1200), a fine altar by Slootz, &c. In 1312, a council met here to pronounce against the knights templars. St. André-le-Bas church, which was partly made out of a roman temple, was the burial place of the Burgundian kings, as far back as 993; it has a norman-built tower, and some ancient cloisters. There are remains of St. Pierre monastery, founded in the sixth century; also an old college of the Jesuits, a corn market, two hospices, &c.; with a house in the renaissance style (in Rue Marchande). Archelaus was banished from Judæa to Vienne, by Augustus, in the year 9, A.D.; and to this place also, Pontius Pilate was banished, by Tiberius, about 38, A.D.

* See L. Dignoscyo's *Carte Topographique du Cours du Rhone, de Lyon à la Mer.*

At Pont l'Eveque, on the Gère, lead mines are worked. The new quay is about 1,600 yards long; steamers run hence to Lyons, besides those from Avignon. Omnibuses start to meet the trains on the St. Etienne Railway, at Givors. The road to Grenoble is 86 kil., by way of La Detourbe, La Frette, &c. Population, 18,000. *Hotels*—Du Louvre; d'Ombrie; de la Table Ronde; du Parc.

St. Colombe, opposite Vienne, and St. Romain-en-Gal, near the former, both abound in roman traces which turn up now and then. Three roman bridges, they say, at one time joined St. Colombe to Vienne; it was afterwards noted for its religious houses. In the Cordeliers convent, which still exists, Philippe le Bel and Philippe de Valois staid at their visits to Vienne, 1311 and 1343.

St. Cyr (18 miles) on the west, is nearly opposite to the old church of Nôtre Dame de l'Ile, which belonged to a priory of the twelfth century, the cloisters of which are standing.

Ampuis (20½ miles) on the west, opposite Vaugris and Montagne de Marcon, was known as *Ampucius* in the sixth century, and has a seat of the old family of Maugiron. The red wines of Côtes Rotie grow here, and at Tapin (1 mile further); and it is known also for its apricots and melons. Mont Pilas in the distance, 3,500 feet high, is round topped, and frequently covered with snow.

Condrieu (24 miles) on the west, is noted for its white wines. The people (4,000) are sailors and bargemen. It was founded by Archbishop Reynaud in the twelfth century, and gave origin to the families of Cardinal d'Arces and Marshal Villers. A suspension bridge leads over to Les Roches, a village of 2,000 souls, behind which are St. Clair, Clonas, Auberive (on the Marseilles road), &c.

St. Michel (25 miles) on the west; St. Alban (26 miles) on the east, with St. Maurice behind it; Chavanay (27 miles) on the west again.

St. Pierre (29 miles), and Limony (31 miles), both on the west, are known for their wines. At 2 miles from the east bank is le Péage de Roussillon, on the Marseilles road.

Charnas (32½ miles), on the west.

Serrières (33½ miles), on the west, was ravaged by the cholera 1832, and the floods of 1840-1. It has a good trade in wine and timber. A suspension bridge joins it to Sablons, a place in department Isère, which has an old château, and Peyraud (35 miles), on the west, opposite the little river Dolon, which runs up to Charnas.

St. Rambert (36½ miles), on the Marseilles road.

Champagne (37 miles), has a curious norman-style church, half fortified, once part of a benedictine abbey, founded by the Dauphins, and built out of a roman temple. It is covered with quaint carvings.

Andance (39 miles), on the west, which was ravaged by both sides in the religious wars of 1575, stands among vineyards, and is joined by a suspension bridge to Andancette, which has a tower of the old chateau of the Counts of Graisivaudan. The roman *Figlinæ* is near this, as proved by traces of a bridge, aqueduct, &c. After passing Chauvet mill, and the telegraph opposite Silon, you come to

St. Vallier (43 miles), on the east, at the Galaure's mouth, a place of 3,000 souls, who make silk and pottery. It has a roman pillar, and belonged to the brother of Diana de Poictiers. The gothic chateau on the cliffs, with large gardens laid out by Le Nôtre, is the seat of M. de Chabrillan. The old château des Rioux, to the north, is used as a factory for chemicals; that of St. Barthéleme de Vals, up the Galaure, stands in a narrow gap called Roche Taillée. A suspension bridge leads over to Sarras; and thence a road goes to Annenay, on the St. Etienne rail. *Hotel*—l'Ecu (Crown-piece).

[*Annonay* (21 kil. west-north-west), an old town in the Ardèche among rocks, and on the Deune where the Cause joins it, is the roman *Apnoneum*, and is noted for manufactures of gloves, excellent paper, and white silk. Mulberry trees are planted all round it, and the ruins lined with factories. Some of the latter belong to the Montgolfiers, of the same family as the brothers Joseph and Stephen (natives), who went up in their first balloon here, 5th June, 1783. An obelisk to them stands in Grande Place. It has a suspension bridge, and a library of 12,000 volumes. Population 10,000. Boissy d' Anglas, president of the Convention, was also a native. *Hotels*—Du Midi; du Nord.]

Ozon (44 miles); then Ponsas (45 miles), on the east, which has a ruined tower of Château

Pilate, so called after Pontius Pilate, who they say drowned himself here, after his banishment to Vienne.

SERVES (46½ miles), on the east, opposite Arras.

VION MILL (48½ miles), on the west, opposite Erome and Gervaud.

CROZES (50 miles), on the east, behind the Coteau (hill) de l'Hermitage, where the famous Hermitage wine is grown, so called from a hermit's cell at the top.

TOURNON (51½ miles), on the west, below the Doux's mouth, a sous-préfecture in department Ardéche, has at the mairie, remains of the old castle of the Comtes de Tournon (one of the most ancient names in French history,) and the Ducs de Soubise. Cardinal Tournon, prime minister under Francis I. and three other kings, and whose life was written by Henry Ternal a native of this town, founded a college here 1542, which was the first held by the Jesuits in France, attracted many scholars, and was not given up till 1766. It has fine gardens round it. The castle is near the suspension bridge to Tain, built 1825, by M. Seguin, being the oldest in the country. Population 4,600. *Hotels*—L'Assurance; du Louvre.

A road here to St. Agreve and Le Puy.

TAIN, opposite the above, is the roman *Tegna*, and has, in the Place du Tauribole, an altar, found in the sixteenth century at the top of the Coteau de l'Hermitage, which is close by. Trade in wine, silk, grain, &c. Population 3,000. The church was part of the benedictine priory in which Charles the Dauphin was married to Jeanne de Bourbon 1350. Excellent grey granite is quarried at Pierre Aiguillon. Conveyances go to Romain and Grenoble on the Isère.

MAUVES (54 miles), on the west, with a mill in front, and several islands.

LA ROCHE (55½ miles), on the east, opposite Glun, in Ardèche, carries on a trade in wine, wax, shot for sportsmen, and is named after a rock, crowned by the old castle of a feudal seigneur, who used to take toll of passers by.

CHATEAUBOURG (57 miles), on the west, has a château, lately restored, once held by Barjac de Pierregourde, who figures in the civil disputes of this part. Mont Blanc (80 miles off), is seen here.

CORNAS (58½ miles), on the same side, opposite the mouth of the Isère, is noted for its red wines. To the south of it are the heights of St. Peray and its old castle.

VALENCE (61 miles), or by road (101 kil.) *Hotels*—De la Poste; du Commerce; de la Croix d'or (Golden Cross); de l'Europe. Population 12,000. The *cafés* are in Place d'Orleans, &c. Chief town of department Drôme, (in the old province of Valentinois in Lower Dauphiné), seat of a diocess, &c., and of an artillery school where Napoleon studied 1785; standing on the east bank, about half way (or five hours run) to Avignon, with a large suspension bridge, built 1828. It was the capital of the Sigalauni, and called *Valentia* by the Romans, who have left remains of pavements, &c. Like other old places it suffered from the Visigoths, Huns, and subsequent invaders. After being held by the bishops as a county, it became the head of a duchy, which was united to the French crown under Charles VII. Protestantism took root here from the first; so that in the religious wars the Baron des Adrets made it his head quarters, after slaying the roman catholic governor at his own door; here also Pius VI. died a prisoner 1799.

The streets are narrow and dirty; parts of the old fortifications are left, as well as the citadel, which commands a view of St. Peray castle, and the mountains of Vivarais opposite. Another view is had from the Polygon or Champ de Mars. In Place aux Clercs stands a monument to General Championnet, a native. Near this in Grande Rue, you see at M. Auriel's library, a curious half gothic house, with statues, heads, and other carvings about it. Bonaparte lived at No. 4 in the same street.

St. Appollinaire's *Cathedral*, having been often burnt and restored, is a mixture of various styles, between 1098 and 1604; it is marked by a tall square block tower, burnt 1822, and rebuilt 1838; and it holds a marble cenotaph to Pope Pius VI., with his heart and Canova's bust, besides a painting of St. Sebastian, by Carracci, &c.; among the side chapels, is that called the Pendentif chapel, a small square building, with a hanging vault on four piers, built 1480, by Canon Mistral, in the renaissance style, and having the arms, &c. of his family, with many good carvings. The bishop's palace is ancient; a handsome palais de justice was built 1826; the library contains 15,000 vols.; there are a gothic theatre, baths, &c.; one of the Scaligers was, by some accounts, professor of the university here, before its removal to Grenoble. About 1661, Racine in a letter to Fontaine says, when he travelled south of Lyons, the Provençal pâtois prevailed to such a degree, that he could neither understand the people, nor make himself intelligible to them. The women are rather noticeable for their good looks and liveliness. L. Joubert, the physician, and Comte de Montalivet, were born here. Trade in silk, leather, wine, olive oil, &c. Conveyances by steam, up and down the Rhone, to Lyons, Avignon, &c.; by coach to those places, also St. Etienne, Grenoble (*see* Route 35), Privas (Route 41), Montelimart, &c. For road to Gap, *see* Route 37.

The beautiful suspension bridge leads over to Guilheraud (1 mile west), and the château de Crussol, the old ruined seat of Geraud Bastet and his descendants, finely seated on the cliffs; the gables of the keep are called the Cornes de Crussol, by sailors. About 1 mile further is *St. Peray*, known for its light, sparkling wine, and stone quarries. In the latter, were found, in Louis the Dauphin's time, the bones of 'a man 23½ feet long,' most likely a fossil of the saurian tribe. Beauregard château, which was a prison, is now turned into a wine store.

Soyons (64 miles), on the west, with three islands, has a slanting tower left of its old castle, and was once noted for its abbey founded in the twelfth century, but moved to Valence.

Charmes (67 miles), on the west, a little way up the small river Embroye, and opposite Ile St. Marcel, has on the rocks behind it the ruined chapel of a castle, one of the many which lined this river in feudal times.

Beauchatel (69 miles), on the west also, and on the river Eyrieux, is so called after a castle which belonged to the bishops of Valence, and has a wire suspension bridge across its little but rapid stream.

La Voulte (71 miles), on the west, is behind a group of islands, called Ile de Roussillon, de Tintebat, de la Baraque, &c. Population 2,000, engaged in the foundries, &c., which now occupy the rather fine remains of a castle (called *La Vôlta* in the romance language, because the Rhone *turns round* the rock it stands on), of the house of Lévy and the princes of Rohan. There used to be in the old chapel a picture of the Virgin appearing to one of the Lévys with his cap in his hand; a label out of his mouth, was inscribed '*Je vous salue, ma cousine*' (I salute you cousin), to which she answered, '*Couvrez vous, mon cousin*' (Cover yourself, cousin!)

Livron is 3 miles up the Drôme (on the east), which at 73 miles, falls into the Rhone. It stands on the Marseilles road, and has a population of 4,000, with some part of a château besieged by the roman catholic leader, Bellegarde, and demolished by Louis XIII.

[Loriol, one mile south of it, on the same road, is chiefly supported by the carrying trade along this route. It is the roman *Aureolum*, founded, some say, by Aurelian. Faujas, the naturalist, died at his house of St. Fond, 1819.]

Le Pouzin (74 miles), on the west, at the L'Ouvèze's mouth, where the road to Privas, Aubenas, &c. turns off (*see* Route 41), suffered much in the religious wars of the time of Louis XIII, and was taken after a long siege by Montmorency, 1628.

Baix (77 miles), on the west, a little beyond the Payre's mouth, was another of the protestant strongholds, and the birth place of Archbishop Audibert de Lussan. Several islands face it.

Cruas (81 miles), on the west, behind another group of islands, has a norman parish church (partly washed away), as old as 1095, and once part of the more ancient abbey of St. Benoît, Opposite it are the hamlets of Logis Neuf, Concourde, &c., and the half ruined town of Lèn, on a stream of that name, so called after a princess Bélène, who retired here a leper.

Meysse (84 miles), on the river Lavezon, on the west, has a quarry of gun flints.

Ancone (86 miles), on the east, below Ile Blanc, the ancient *Ancunum*, taken by storm by Lesdiguières, 1586, when the fortifications were reduced. A little below it, a bridge leads over Rochmaure, and its old basalt castle, on a lava cliff, 320 feet high, once the seat of the Adhémars, and a stronghold of the catholics. About 2 miles inland from Ancone is

Montelimar (47 kil. from Valence), a sous-préfecture (of 9,450 souls) in department Drôme, on the rivers Roubion and Jabron, and the Marseilles road, in a fertile spot, cultivated with vines, mulberries, olives, oranges, &c., having some ancient gothic ramparts and gates, and a château now turned into a citadel. It belonged to the Adhémars till 1198; was dreadfully injured in the religious wars; and gave birth to, among others, D. Chamier, a protestant minister, who was shot defending a breach at Montauban, 1621, and who, therefore, according to the catholics, died *canonized*. There was a fight on the bridge, with the Duke of Angoulême's troops, 1815. It has a good mineral water, and a trade in Nougat cakes (of honey and almonds), fruit, wax, oil, grain, cattle, morocco leather, &c. *Hotels*—Du Palais National; des Princes. The roads to Dieu le Fit, Château Grignan, Nions, &c., turn off to the east.

[At 25 kil. east is *Dieu le Fit*, (*i. e.* God made it), an industrious little place, at the Jabron's head, noted for its mineral waters, useful in bilious and other complaints; linen, cotton, and silks are made. A curious grotto, called by the good English name of 'Tom Jones,' near it, has a high vault, and many beautiful stalactites. Population, 4,000.]

LE THEIL (89 miles), on the west, at the bridge below Luizene island, was taken and reduced by Louis XIII. in 1632, and is noted for its pottery; near it are the Marquis of Joviac's seat (with a gallery of roman inscriptions), the Roches des Dames (at Aps), where they say some of the persecuted Albigenses were hid, and Melas on the river Frayol, which runs into the Rhône a little south.—Passing Barquassa, Gastor, and other islands, you come to the cliffs of

VIVIERS (94 miles), on the west, the old walled capital of the Vivarais, now seat of a bishopric, with 2,500 people (once it had 15,000). It grew out of a roman town called Alps or Aps on the Escontaye, which runs up by it; but decayed after the religious wars here. The choir and tower of the cathedral, standing over the town, are gothic; the nave is more modern. The bishop's palace is a fine building, with good grounds about it. Richelieu visited the place in his ascent of the Rhône, 1642, with his two victims, Cinq Mars and De Thou. A road to Villeneuve de Berg goes off to the west. Opposite it is

CHATEAUNEUF-DU-RHÔNE, on the slope of the hills, having part of a roman camp and various marks of a decayed town. It gave birth to an adventurer called the marquis de Courbon, who led the Venetian armies at the siege of Negropont, and fell only thirty-nine years old. The river from this part is less hilly on the banks, but more winding in its course and broken with islands.

DONZERE (96 miles), on the east, opposite Ile Toncheloz, was given to the bishops of Viviers, 877, who had an abbey here, and built a château of the sixteenth century, of which there are some fragments. They were styled princes of Donzère. It commands a view over the plains of Vaucluse, and is noted for its red wine. Population, 1,500. A large group of islands (2 miles long), called the Margiries, divides the Rhône into two branches below this.

[At 15 kil. east, up the Berre, are the remains of the fine *Château de Grignan*, half demolished at the revolution, and remarkable as the residence of Madame de Savigné, who has made it known by her charming letters, and died here 1676. It stands on a rock above the town, with many windows and a wide terrace round it, and became the head of a comté, 1550. Frederic Barbaroussa once resided in it. The plain church contains the tomb of Madame.]

BOURG-ST.-ANDEOL (102 miles), on the west, has a large and good church, built in the tenth century by the bishops of Viviers, on the site of the relics of St. Andéol, a disciple of St. Polycarp. It was one of the chief seats of the bishops, and had many convents before the revolution. Population, 4,500. At the fountain of Tournes, is a grotto, with a carving of Mithras sacrificing the bull with his dog, an altar, and traces of an inscription. A suspension bridge leads over to the east bank, two miles from which is

PIERRELATTE, on the Marseilles road, with a trade in wine, silk, fruit, and grain. It had a castle on the rocks (pierre), 300 feet high, taken by the Baron des Adrets, with great bloodshed. Population, 3,550.

ST. MARCEL (105 miles), on the west, 1 mile inland, in the Ardèche, has a part of the old seat of the Bernis family, where a cardinal of that name was born, 1715. Population, 3,000.

[At 6 miles east-south-east is *St. Paul-Trois Châteaux* (or three castles), a very old place under a hill, and the capital of the Tricastins, when the Romans came in, who called it *Augusta - Tricastinorum*. Remains are seen of an amphitheatre, of a wall (in St. Jean quarter), mosaics, bas-reliefs, and a gate (one of three), called Fan Jou, *i.e.* Fanum Jovis, because it was part of a temple of Jupiter. Many fossils are collected near this.]

To the left is St. Just and its church, in a richly cultivated spot. Nearly opposite it, and as far inland from the east bank is

PALUD, on the Marseilles road, the first place in department Vaucluse, and once a fortified town belonging to the knights templars, with a spire church. A road goes off to Nions.

PONT ST. ESPRIT (109 miles), on the west, below the river Ardèche, which falls in here, and gives name to the department, is a dirty place of 4,500 people, with a citadel, and a remarkable stone-bridge of twenty-six arches, 2,622 feet long, built 1263-1309, by a brotherhood of masons, &c., called the Frères du Pont, with subscriptions collected in Holy Ghost (St. Esprit) chapel, hard by. The centre arch is 108 feet wide. The town was occupied by both parties in the religious wars in the time of Louis XIII., and sacked by the Baron des Adrets. Roads go out to Barjas and Mende, and also to Nismes. Route 37*a*, to Gap, turns off here.

MONTDRAGON (111 miles), about 1½ miles inland, on the east, standing on the river Lez, under an old castle on the rocks, was held by the archbishop of Arles, with the title of prince.

MORNAS (114 miles), on the east, nearly opposite St. Etienne-de-Sorts, is an ancient place, with a ruined castle, which was taken in 1562, by one of Des Adret's fierce captains, Dupuy-Montbrun, and its defenders forced to jump from the rock on the pikes of his soldiers. Their bodies were then put in a boat to float down the river, with this notice to the people of Avignon, 'Pass the bearers, as they have paid their passage at Mornas.' To the right of it is

PIOLENC a small fortified port, with a ruined castle near its church, in a spot abounding with wine, corn, fruit, &c.

CODOLET (119 miles,) on the west, near the Cèze's mouth, is known for its wine, and had the château of the marquis d'Ancèsune-Cadart, who received Louis XIII. here, in 1662. A few grains of gold have been picked in the little stream. On the opposite side of the Rhone, 4 miles inland, and near the river Aigues (which falls in a little above), is

ORANGE (98 kil. from Valence), in a well-watered plain. Though but a sous-préfecture in department Vaucluse, with 9,300 souls, and much decayed, it was the *Arausio* of the Romans, who placed the second legion here, and have bequeathed a famous arch, and a theatre to present times. It was also the seat of an archbishop; but an Englishman will be pleased to look upon it as having once belonged to our great deliverer, William, prince of Orange, through his ancestor, René de Nassau, who succeeded to the principality on the death of his uncle, Philibert de Chalon, 1530. After the death of William III. it was seized by Louis XIV., but the title and arms are still borne by the eldest son of the king of Holland.

It has narrow straight streets, with several fountains, and a new college, near which is the greatest curiosity, the roman *Triumphal Arch*, called the 'Arch of Marius,' though the founder and date are uncertain. It stands across the Lyons road, on the north side of the town; is nearly square, 70½ feet wide, and 64 feet high, with a centre arch and two side arches, supported by corinthian pillars, and carved with bas-reliefs (different for each face), of fruits, cornucopiæ, syrens, ships, military trophies, &c. A museum of roman marbles, &c. has been collected near it. The roman *Theatre*, called the 'Cirque,' rises over a hill to the south, close to the remains of the old citadel. It is well preserved, and makes a large half-circle, with two rows of arcades, and a heavy wall across it, formed of great blocks, joined without mortar, 334 feet long, 120 high, and 13 thick. It would hold about 6,000 persons. You may see in the wall, above the cornice, the holes for the poles which the awning was spread upon. There is also a museum here for roman remains; and parts of baths and acqueducts are noticed elsewhere. Trade in silk, wool, oil, scented wines, truffles, &c. Roads strike off west to Vaison and towards Mont Ventoux.

[At 22 kil. south-east is *Carpentras*, a sous-préfecture, with a population of 10,200, under Mont Ventoux, over the deep ravine of the Auzon, in a fertile spot. It was *Carpenteracte* and Forum Neronis of the Romans, who settled a colony here; was pillaged by Crocus, the Pomeranian leader, in 266; by the Lombards, Saracens, &c., but revived under the encouragement of popes Clement V. and Innocent VI. The former began the aqueduct, 10 kil. long, from Mont Ventoux, finished 1720-34, part of which, 2,790 feet long, crosses the river on forty-eight arches. It has its old turreted walls and four gates; that of Porte d'Orange carried a great tower. There are good walks outside in the faubourgs, with delightful prospects.

The fine façade of the hospital was built in 1751. The gothic cathedral church includes a tower of Charlemagne's time, and pillars (in the front), brought they say, from the temple of Diana, at Venasque. Near the palais de justice (which was the bishop's seat), in the Place, is a very much decayed roman *arch of triumph*. The public library, given by bishop Inguimebert, comprises 22,000 volumes and 2,000 MSS., many of which belonged to Peyresc, the scholar, besides engravings, paintings, 6,000 medals, antiquities, &c. There are also a large lavoir publique or baths, theatre, new prisons, market halls, &c. Trade in spirits, wine, essences, oil, fruit, silk, &c. *Hotels*—Du Nord; de l' Europe.

At 12 kil. north-east, is Bedouin, where the ascent to *Mont Ventoux* begins: it takes from four to five hours to reach the top (10 kil.) which is about 2,200 yards above the sea level (the highest in all this quarter), and looks like a cone placed on a dome. The north side, on the Drôme border, is steep and almost inaccessible. At the summit (covered with snow three-parts of the year), is a chapel, near a lake, whence there is a splendid panorama, which takes in the Rhône, the Alps, Cevennes, &c.]

CADEROUSSE (122 miles) on the east, just past the large island of Piboulette, which is noted for its fertility, was given by Pope Alexander VII. to the Dukes of Avignon, and now belongs, with a handsome seat, &c., to the Duke of Gramont-Caderousse. Population 3,000.

MONTFAUCON (123½ miles), on the west, with St. Geniés-de-Comolas behind it, on the Avignon road.

ROQUEMAURE (125½ miles), on the west, past Ile de Lers, and so called from the dark colour of the cliffs (as in the latin *maurus*, a Moor), is, according to some, the spot where Hannibal crossed on his way to Italy, 218 B.C., and is further noted as the place where Clement V. (on his way to his native town, Bordeaux) died in 1314. He was hardly dead, when his attendants went off with everything they could lay their hands on, leaving his very body half-burnt by a torch which fell on it. Trade in wine, eaux-de-vie, olive oil. Population 5,000. About 1½ mile to the left, the suburb of Sauveterre carries in its name (Safeground) the memorial of a fortified retreat against robbers in old times.

CHATEAUNEUF-DU-PAPE (127 miles), opposite Ile d'Oiselet, on the heights to the east, has part of a country-seat of the Popes, when they reigned at Avignon.

SORGUES, on the east, a little way up the Ouvèze or Sorgues, which falls in here (130 miles), is the place next to Avignon, towards which the Rhône makes a bend, dividing into two parts round the large Ile de la Barthlasse. Sorgues, with a population of 3,000, stands in a wide plain, on which Cneias Ænobarbus defeated the Celtic barbarians. It has a curious old four-arch bridge, and the walls of a seat of the Counts of Toulouse, which Urban V. enlarged for a country house.

AVIGNON, where the railway begins again, is 134 miles from Lyons, and to the Mediterranean is about 50 miles further.

Avignon. *Hotels*—De l'Europe (highly recommended); St. Yves; du Palais Royal; du Bras d'Or (Gold Arm). Population 33,786.

This old city of the Popes, chief town of department Vaucluse, seat of an arch-diocess, &c., is in the valley of the Rhône, where the Durance joins it, in a country of orchards, vineyards, mulberry, and olive grounds. The Romans, when they colonized it, called it *Avenis*. It afterwards came to the Burgundians, Ostrogoths; was for awhile kept by the Saracens; and at length was divided between the counts of Provence and Toulouse. Louis VIII. took it after a siege, 1226, for supporting the Albigenses. Pope Clement V. (a Frenchman) came to live here 1309, and in 1348, Clement VI., the antipope, bought it of the Countess of Provence. The last resident Pope was Benedict XIII, whom the French drove away 1408; but it was garrisoned by his successors under a vice-legate till 1791. The inquisition was established, but while the Pope held the town, the river belonged to the King of France, who kept him in check at Villeneuve. It lies almost entirely within the machicolated walls which are strengthened with ramparts and towers; and have a cour or promenade round them commanding very pleasing prospects of the country, the green islands of the Rhone, Provence, the Alps, &c. Houses of stone, but the streets narrow and winding. Rue de la Ferraterie is the most bustling; Rue Calade contains several fine buildings. The quays are large; the Jews live in the Juiverie. A long wooden bridge leads over the Rhône, near remains (three or four arches) of a stone one, built by St. Benezet; another on boats has been replaced by a suspension bridge to Villeneuve-lés-Avignon.

The *Cathedral*, called Nötre Dame des Doms, on the Rocher des Doms, which is mounted by steps, was rebuilt by Charlemagne. It has monuments of Archbishop Libelli, Pope John XXII., and the brave Crillon, who was a native, and whose hotel remains; with the papal (now archbishop's) marble throne. Close to it is the large *Palace* of the Popes, an irregular gothic pile, now used as a barrack and prison. Rienzi the 'last of the Tribunes' was kept a prisoner here by Clement VI. It has traces of frescos by Giotti, the salle de la question (where heretics were tortured), and the Glacière tower whence the revolutionary mob threw their prisoners, 1791. St. Pierre's Church, has a good front, built 1512, and a black marble pulpit. There are sixteen other churches; at one time it had sixty, and as many religious houses. A piece is left of the Cordeliers' church, which had the tomb of Petrarch's Laura de Sade, whom he first saw here, 1327. A cypress marks the spot. Hôtel de Ville, was the Pope's Mint, built by Paul V. Near it, on Place d'Oulle, Marshal Brune was killed by the royalists, 1815. Other buildings are the Hotel des Invalides (for soldiers) formerly a religious establishment; the public Library, of 42,000 vols. and 500 MSS., near St. Martial's church; the Museum Calvet (so called after the founder) with roman and other inscriptions, medals, sculptures, the Inquisition seal, rare books, pictures by italian and dutch masters, the Vernets, &c., and a cabinet of natural history, &c.; the botanic garden, theatre, barracks, mont-de-piété, lunatic asylum (hospice des alienés) where the ivory crucifix, 26 inches long, which was in Misericorde church, is placed; the Jacquemart clock-tower near the theatre; priests' seminary, &c. The women are handsome.

Villeneuve-lès-Avignon, across the new bridge, has the old fort and abbey of St. André, the Chartreuse convent on a rock, with the ruined church. Population 5,564.

Manufactures of silk, madder, (first introduced by a person whose statue is near the cathedral), leather, &c.; several dye-houses; a trade in grain, &c., the produce being taken down to Marseilles.

Conveyances: by rail, to Nismes, Arles, Marseilles, Montpellier; by steamer and coach to Valence, and Lyons (being against the stream, the steamer takes three or four days to go up). The new road to Geneva by the plains of the Bresse is open, by coach to Carpentras, Digne, &c. A caleche may be hired to Vaucluse (17 miles) there and back, 22 fr., including the driver (*see* Route 38). Senany Abbey and Pont du Gard (*see* Route 43) are near.

The railway from Avignon, down the Rhône to Marseilles, is part of the incomplete Lyons and Mediterranean line. The stations are—

	kil.		kil.		kil.
Rognonas	6	Raphèle	9	Rognac.........	6
Cadillan	6	Saint-Martin	7	Vitrolles	4
Tarascon	9	Entressen ...	13	Pas des Lan-	
[To Nimes 30]		Constantine.	4	ciers	5
Ségonnaux ...	3	St. Chamas..	5	L'Estaque	8
Arles	7	Berre	15	Marseilles......	10

Leaving Avignon, you pass ROGNONAS (5 miles), Cadillan (4½ miles); then

TARASCON (5 miles) where the Nismes rail joins (*see* Route 43). It is an old fortified town of 10,967 inhabitants, at the suspension bridge to Beaucaire, having a fine ruined castle (Château du Roi René) on a rock above the Rhône, a good church of the 11th century, a palais de justice, Hôtel de Ville, library, theatre, ship-yard, &c.; and a trade in silks, wine, oil, eaux-de-vie. *Hotel*—Des Empereurs.

[*St. Remy* (13 kil. east), in a fine spot on the Real canal, has roman remains about 50 feet asunder; one being part of a triumphal arch, the other a mausoleum of beautiful design.]

SEGONNEAUX (3⅜ miles).

ARLES (5 miles), a town remarkable for its roman remains and its beautiful women, is a sous-préfecture, in a marshy but cultivated spot at the head of the delta of the Rhône, about 24 miles from the Mediterranean, to which a canal runs down as far as Port de Bouc. It was the roman *Arelate*, a port of great trade, which Constantine improved and called Constantina. It fell to the Goths, and after Charlemagne's time was the head of a sort of kingdom; then became subject to the Emperors of Germany, and was given up to France in the time of Charles VI. It stands on a rock; the streets are irregular and narrow; a bridge of boats leads to Trinqueville, which Constantine founded. Place Plan de la Cour is shaded with trees. In Place Royale, is the Hôtel de Ville, built by Mansard, in the corinthian style.

St. Trophime's *Cathedral*, begun 626 by St. Virgilius, has a large and highly decorated portal of the twelfth century, with columns, niches, grotesque sculptures, and a fine cloister adjoining the old palace of the archbishop, with an ancient *obelisk* in the middle of it. This is a single block of plain granite, 50 feet long, and was brought here by the Romans, but remained on the ground till set up, in 1676, to the honour of Louis XIV., with a pedestal and lions, and a globe and sun for an apex, added to it, making the total height 65 feet.

The roman *Amphitheatre* is in pretty good condition; it is an oval, 338 feet by 460, in three stages of about sixty arches each, chiefly in the composite style; it had four principal entrances, with upwards of forty rows of seats, and would hold above 2,500 persons. Two later towers have been built on it. Near it and the old house of La Miséricorde are some arches of a theatre, now called the Tower of Roland, with two columns of breccia marble on the site of the stage, remains of seats, and a gate not far off. In Place St. Lucien, or du Forum, are two granite pillars of a Temple of Minerva, and some other fragments. Ruins of an aqueduct are also seen. The Tour de la Trouille, near the old houses of the Grand Prior of Malta, was built, they say, by Constantine.

St. Anne's church, now the museum, has a good collection of bas-reliefs, busts, altars, gravestones, &c. The public library contains 12,000 volumes. There is a school of navigation, a college, &c. Good walks on the Lice promenade by the Graponne canal. Notre Dame de Grace church, with its eight-sided steeple, stands in the old roman cemetery, called Eliscamp (Campus Elysius), where many ancient gravestones remain, on a hill outside the town, now occupied by railway work-shops. On another hill are the ruined church (partly as old as the tenth century), and cloister, the machicolated tower (built 1369) 85 feet high, and St. Avir (or Crucifix) chapel (in shape of a greek cross, built 1019), belonging to the abbey of Mont Majour. Races are kept up. Constantine's son was born here.

Hotels — Du Nord; du Forum. The *Cafés* are in Place des Hommes. Manufactures of silk, soap, brandy, and good sausages; and a trade in corn, wine, oil, manna, salt, wool, cattle, horses, &c. Conveyances: by rail to Marseilles, Avignon, Nismes, Montpellier; steamer to Marseilles.

The *Camargue* or delta of the Rhône, below Arles, is a salt marsh, full of lakes, where the pelican, flamingo, and beaver breed, and vast numbers of horses and cattle are pastured. One part of it, called the *Crau*, is a desolate flinty plain, across which the mistral blows with terrible keenness.

The next stations on the rail are—

RAPHELE (5 miles) with the very old Castle of Baux on the left; St. Martin (5 miles); Entressen (7½ miles); Constantine (3¼ miles). The great Marseilles aqueduct is seen now and then.

ST. CHAMAS (3 miles) a small port on the Touloubre, having a genuine roman bridge of one arch, 70 feet long (besides the cross arches at each end). There is a government powder factory, and an old church on the ridge which divides the town in two.

BERRE (8¾ miles) in a pleasant but marshy spot on the lagoon, or Etang de Berre, with a good trade in oil, almonds, figs. At the mouth of the lake is the fishing port of Martigues, with a population of 7,500.

ROGNAC (3¾ miles), on the same lagoon, where the Aix road turns off. Then Vitrolles (2½ miles); Pas de Lanciers (3 miles); L'Estaque (5 miles), near the roman pyramid of Pennelle; on to Marseilles, which is 6 miles further, and is approached by La Nerthe tunnel, 15,140 feet, or nearly 3 miles long. The terminus commands a view of the town and Mediterranean.

Marseilles, or MARSEILLE. *Hotels*—Des Colonies, Rue Vacon, a first-rate house, and highly recommended; des Ambassadeurs, Rue [illegible]santly situated, very comfortable [illegible]ate; Hôtel Bristol, Rue Saffron, a [illegible]table, good house, and the host intelligent [illegible]d obliging; des Empereurs, in Rue Canebiere; d'Angleterre, reasonable and comfortable; des Princes, in Rue Beauveau; and many other hotels. *Cafés*—De l'Europe, in Place de la Comédie; de l'Univers; des Milles Colonnes, in Rue Vacon; &c. Dinner, 3 to 5 fr.; table d'hôte, 2½ to 3fr.; bed, 1 to 1½fr. A cup of excellent coffee or chocolate, 60 to 75 centimes. Population, 170,000.

English consul, A. Turnbull.

English service at the church, Rue Silvabell, No. 100, by the Rev. M. J. Mayers, at 10½ a.m. and 3½ p.m. Rev. MM. H. and J. Monod, and M. Beziès are French Protestant pastors.

Post-office in Rue Jeune Anacharsis.

The traveller for Marseilles direct should, on landing at Boulogne or Calais, have his passport *visé* for this place at once, to save delay when applying for it at Paris; he will receive a provisionary passport, costing 2 fr. From London it is about 880 miles; from Paris, 550; from Lyons, 225. Time from London, 73 hours; namely, by rail to Dover, boat to Calais, and rail to Paris, 12½ hours; rail to Chalons, 9¾ hours; boat to Lyons, 7 hours; boat to Avignon, 10 hours; rail to Marseilles, 5½ hours; allowing 11 hours at Paris, ½ hour at Chalons, and 18 hours at Lyons. Fare: first class, £6; second, £5 0s. 5d.; third, £3 0s. 8d.

This large city is the capital of department Bouches du Rhone (which was part of Provence), head quarters of a military division, seat of a bishopric, &c., a consulate, and the chief port and packet station in the Mediterranean; in a gulf, about 27 miles east of the delta, or mouths (bouches), of the Rhone, and 450 miles from Algiers, the settlement of which has greatly stimulated its prosperity. It is the oldest place in France, or western Europe, having been founded as far back as 600 B.C., by Greek settlers from Phocæa, under their leader Euxenus, and called *Massalia*, or *Massilia*. From hence they also colonised Nicea (Nice), Antipolis (Antibes), Agatha (Agde), and other little republics; while the mother country increased in power and fame, in spite of the jealousy of Athens and the Carthaginians. It was taken by Hanibal, punished by Cæsar for siding with [illegible]mpey, ravaged by the Visigoths (A.D. 483), the Burgundians, Ostrogoths (588), the Saracens (735), and came to the Counts of Provence, 1257. Alphonso of Arragon sacked it 1421, and held it for two years, but it revived under good king René of Anjou, who died here, 1480. In his time it was noted for its soap and glassworks, its furs and hides. Under Louis XI. it became part of France; the Duke of Guise occupied it for Henry IV.; Louis XIV. entered it through a breach in the walls in token of his displeasure for its resistance to him, and curtailed its political rights. It was ravaged by the plague 1530, and again in the great plague of 1720-21, when 40,000 or 50,000 out of 90,000 were carried off, and Bishop Belzunce, Chevalier Rose, and others, exerted themselves so admirably. At the revolution it supported the Girondist party with great fervour, and was, therefore, visited with the bloody vengeance of the Terrorists, who sent Fréron and Barras here. The famous Marseillaise song, to which it gives name, was composed at Strasbourg, by Rouget de l'Isle, 1792.

As seen from Viste hill, for example, on the Aix road, it appears most happily placed in picturesque and convenient spot, at the bottom of a natural inlet, which opens right out to the Mediterranean; limestone hills rising gradually all round to a height of — feet in some parts, with a clear and beautiful sky overhead. Thousands of bastides (as they call the country seats here) dot the sides of this amphitheatre, and there are numerous gardens of vines and olives, but the soil being white and dry, it is excessively hot in summer; then gnats and mosquitos bite, the keen north-west mistral blows, and perhaps a scorpion may be found in the bed. The town surrounds the harbour like a horse-shoe, the oldest part, with its narrow dirty streets, being on the north side, while the modern and better built quarters are on the east and south. The Rue de Canebière and Allées de Meilhan nearly mark the line of division, while the boulevards shew the extent of the old town and the site of the ramparts, taken down 1800. These offer the best promenades; there are others in Cours Bonaparte (near the arsenal, the Hôtel Bacri, the Cirque Olympique), and Grand Cours, which joins Porte d'Aix to Rue de Rome, leading on to Grand Chemin de Rome, Place Castelane, and by the Prado beyond, to the sea side.

Most of the Places or squares are ornamented

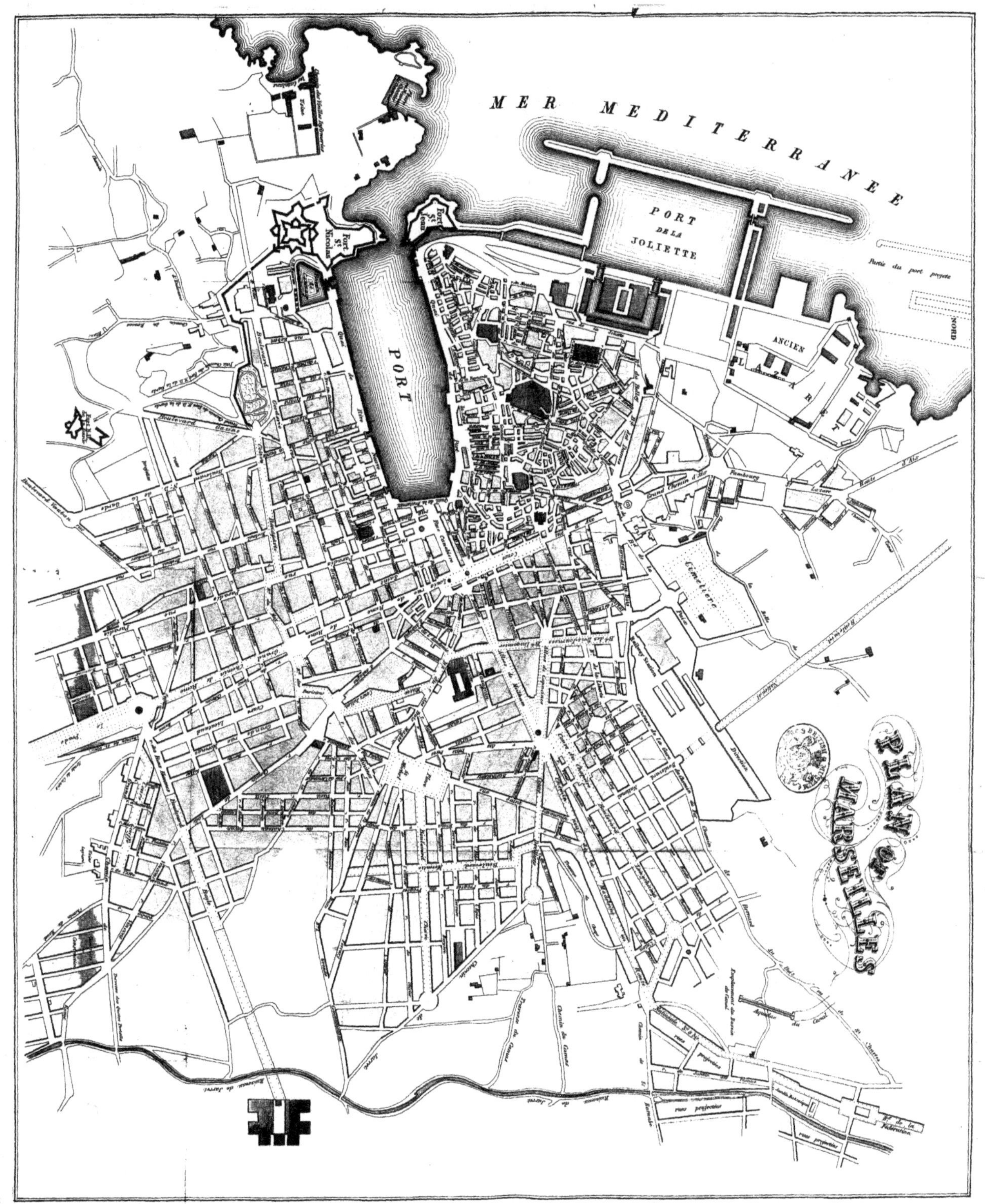
MER MEDITERRANEE
PORT DE LA JOLIETTE
PORT
ANCIEN LAZARET
PLAN DE MARSEILLES

with fountains (supplied by subterranean cuts from the Huveaume, &c. and the great canal from the Durance). That of Porte Paradis was raised to those excellent persons who attended on their townsmen in the great plague; one in Rue d'Aubagne is actually dedicated to 'Homer, by the *descendants of the Phocæans*;' another stands in Place Royale, the largest square in the city. That in Place des Fainéants is a black marble obelisk, 28½ feet high, on four lions; the Fontaine de Puget, in Rue de Rome, is a little pyramid before the old house of this Marsellaise architect, whose works served to adorn his native city, but were swept away after the revolution. He was known in England by having built Montague House, the old British museum. Place de Lenche was the site of roman baths.

The large corinthian triumphal arch at the Porte d'Aix was begun 1823, in honour of the Duc d'Angoulême, but remains unfinished.

The *Harbour* is an oblong of about 3,080 feet by 980, or about 70 acres, and is extremely safe, though the mouth is narrow. It is generally crowded with shipping, of which it will hold 1,200, with water deep enough for those of 600 tons. A great disadvantage is, that the ebb and flow of the tide being very small, the stench of the sewers opening into it is constantly felt. It is lined with narrow quays, where all the costumes and languages of the Mediterranean may be witnessed. On the south side, or Rive Neuve, or Commerce, are the mast-house, the douane and magazines, with a canal running round them, the place-aux-huiles (oil stores), ship yards, stores for soap, bones, &c. Along the opposite side, or Boutique, you see the Place du Cul de Bœuf, the Consigne or board of health, the fish market and cafés, the Hôtel de Ville, stamp office, bazaar, shops for ship-chandlery, &c., and Fort St. Jean. A wet dock, or Bassin de Carenage, lies just outside the harbour, on the south.

The *Hôtel de Ville*, a small building, has bas-reliefs on its front, with a bust of Louis XIV., and a latin inscription; on the staircase a statue of Liberty, and some pictures in the hall. The ground floor is used for the Bourse or exchange.

The *Préfecture*, in Place St. Ferreol, on one side of a wide court, has two façades, and is one of the largest public structures in the city. Near the old prisons is the palais de justice, with nothing particular to distinguish it. The new prisons, built 1823, are at Aix.

Among the market-places or Halles, are the vieille poissonnerie, the halle Puget, and halle neuve (new), rebuilt 1801, on the site of an older one. A large boucherie, or shambles, stands on the sea, between the anses (bays) de l' Ourse and de la Joliette,—the latter, they say, named after Julius Cæsar. Here a new port is making, inside a breakwater and two moles; but it is reported to be dangerous with unfavourable winds. Not far from this, at the entrance of the town, is Porte Joliette, one of the few pieces of antiquity here, but much decayed, and used as the bureau of the Octroi.

Most of the churches are plain buildings; that of De la Major, or the *Cathedral*, near the Anse de l' Ourse, is the most ancient; it replaces a temple to the 'great goddess Diana,' whose worship the Greeks brought here, and is a tasteless mixture of various styles, with a front spoilt by the plasterer; a bas-relief of St. Lazarus is of the eleventh century, and there is a good organ. St. Victor, one of the oldest, near Fort St. Nicholas, stands over the burial place of an early martyr, which became the site of a rich abbey; it has crypts of the eleventh century, and Pope Urban's two towers built 1350; with an image of the Madonna, to which the people come to pray in long seasons of drought. St. Vincent de Paul is in the Allées des Capucins; near the Cours Italien is Notre Dame du Mont, re-built 1822, except its old clock tower. That on Mont Carmel has a good prospect. A new circular church stands close to the Flèche des Accoules, which is the tall romanesque clock-tower of a large church, pulled down at the revolution, with another at a little distance from it. The Chapelle du Château Babon belonged to a castle on the site of Fort St. Jean. A pretty chapel of the seventeenth century, called the Madeleine or Chartreux, outside the town, has a good nave, and light campanile towers. There are Protestant and Greek churches, a synagogue, &c.

Hôtel Dieu or Hôpital du St. Esprit, behind the town-hall, was founded 1188, and is a large irregular mass in the heart of the old city, having beds for 560 and a chapel built 1600. *La Charité*, near Place de l' Observance, and founded 1640, for 850 old people and orphans, forms a court, in which stands an oval chapel by Puget, with a dome. Among other charitable institutions are the two hospices of St. Joseph and St. Lazare, the asylums for aliénés (lunatics) and for the deaf and dumb (sourds-muets.)

Most of the learned societies are established in the old convent of the Bernardines (in Cours de Marché, near the Champ de Mars), which has several long galleries in it, a tower, and a cruciform church crowned with a dome. Here are the academy of sciences and belles lettres; a large public bibliothèque or library of 60,000 vols. and 1,270 MSS., in a room 130 feet long, open Mondays, Wednesdays, and Fridays; cabinets of roman and greek antiquities, and of medals and natural history; a picture gallery in the old chapel, of about 140 paintings of the French (89 specimens), Italian, and Flemish schools; the college or high school; and schools of design and architecture, &c. A school of navigation is fixed in the observatory, which has a fine prospect. The jardin des plantes or botanic garden, in the Chartreux quarter, opened since 1810, has many exotics, including an orangery.

In Place Royale is the *Grand Théâtre* like the Odéon of Paris, built 1787, with a front of six columns. Théâtre Français stands near the Allées des Meilhaus. There is a concert-hall; another place of amusement is the Montagnes Russes. Baths in the Prado, &c.: sea-baths on the bassin d' Aren, to the north of the town; charge 1½ fr., including the omnibus; lodgings 6 to 7 fr. a day.

The gendarmerie barracks are near Places de la Porte d'Aix and du Terras. The arsenal stands in Cours Napoleon, not far from his column and the road to Fort Notre Dame, the most commanding point above the city. It is so called from a pilgrim's chapel of the thirteenth century, round which Francis I. built the fortress, and is still crowded with a multitude of curious votive gifts from sailors, &c.; at the Fête Dieu, the image of the Bonne Mère is carried in procession. The prospect here is a beautiful panorama of the city, the coast, the sea, and islands off the town. Fort St. Nicholas, lower down, opposite Fort St. Jean, was built by Louis XIV., and has been lately restored. Tour Carrée (Square Tower) was raised by king René.

About two miles west of the harbour is the Ile d'If, and the fort of Francis I., in which Mirabeau was confined; a little beyond it are two larger islands, Pomègue and Ratoneau, with batteries on them, and joined by a causeway 980 feet long, making the quarantine port of Dieudonné (God-given) for 200 vessels. Here Cæsar's fleet anchored when he took Marseilles; and in the present day, when a foolish man forgets himself, they call him Roi de Ratoneau, in allusion to a story of a poor lunatic soldier, who assumed the title of king and turned the guns on his comrades in 1765.

For sanitary purposes, there are a lazaret (lazaretto) of 50 acres, between Points de la Joliette and St. Martin, where infected persons are fumigated; and the Consigne or quarantine office in the harbour. The latter has Puget's bas-relief of the Plague of Milan, Gerard's picture of the Great Plague of Marseilles, Vernot's picture of the Cholera, &c. A large cemetery is laid out beyond the city. An abundant supply of water is now brought in by the great canal lately cut from the Durance, 25 miles off. It is the work of M. Montricher, and passes through several tunnels, and, by the great aqueduct of Rochefavour (1,200 feet long), over the Arc, coming into the city at a point 400 feet above the sea.

The custom duties of this port are a fourth to a fifth of all France; the imports include hides, tallow, dried fruits, sugar, coffee, olive oil, cotton wool, lead, bones, &c.; and among the articles made or exported are salt meat, salt fish, fruit, almonds, wine, refined sugar, molasses, madder, oil, sulphur, soap, candles, chemicals, liqueurs, essences and perfumes, printed woollens and cottons, morocco leather, tobacco, hats, glass, porcelain, china, coral ornaments, anchovies, &c. Steam engines are made by Taylor and Sons.

In the suburbs are the villages of St. Genie, Capelette, St. Pierre, La Madeleine, Chartreux, St. Charles, Barthelemi, St. Just Passet, Belle de Mai, Bon Sécours, Canet, and others, some of them seated on the little rivulets Huveaume, Jarres, Plombières, and Aygalades. The last has an old castle on it; and on the Huveaume is the aqueduct of Ville-a-la-Pomme, with the château Borelly, a fine seat near the sea, built by a Marseilles banker. Further off is the Madrague de l'Estagne, where the large tunny fish is caught; near it a part of a roman aqueduct may be seen, also the Bouido which spouts up after rain, and

MARSEILLES
LYON
AVIGNON

the Maoupasset, a seat of le bon Roi René, where they show some of his paintings. Wild fowl swarm in the Etang (lake) de Martigue; and at Christmas crowds of sportsmen go out to shoot wild ducks.

Puy de Mimet, 12 kil. north-east of the city is noticeable for the experiments made there by Baron Zach, the astronomer, for measuring the density of the earth. It has a grotto much frequented for views about it.

White, red, and muscadel wines are produced in this corner of France. The language is a mixture of French and Provençal (a corrupt Latin), with a tincture of Greek and Celtic.

Pytheas, an early navigator who sailed to Britain and Iceland and to the Baltic from this place, was a native of it; in modern days it reckons Puget the sculptor and painter, and Barbaroux, a member of the Convention.

Conveyances.—By railway to Arles, four times a day, in 2 to 2¾ hours, (see *Bradshaw's Continental Railway Guide*). Thence to Avignon, Nismes, Cette, &c. Omnibuses run from the great thoroughfares to the station near the Arche de Triomphe. By coach daily to Aix, Avignon, Lyons, &c,; to Toulon, Nice, Draguignan, Aix, Nismes, Martigues, Barjols, Brignolles, Manosque, Briançon, &c., on the routes to all the chief towns.

By steam (see *Bradshaw's Guide*) to Arles up the Rhône, and to every part of the Mediterranean. The English naval steamers, with mails on the 8th and 26th of each month to Malta, for the Ionian Islands, and Alexandria, 1st class, £8 2s.; 2nd, £4 10s.; 3rd, £2 14s., including provisions and every charge; passage in about 70 hours. Office in Rue Haxo, No. 9.

The Anglo Italian Company's Screw Steamers join from Italy, on the 15–17th, and proceed to Liverpool. calling at Gibralter, on the 17–20th. Office, 12, Rue Jeune Anacharsis.

The French mail steamers of the messageries nationales, start on the *Italian* Line (by Genoa, Leghorn, Naples, Messina,) to Malta, 9th, 19th, and 29th of each month. taking 6 days, and corresponding with the Levant packets from Malta on the 5th, 15th, and 25th; on the *Levant* Line (by Malta, Syra, Smyrna,) to Constantinople, 1st, 11th, and 21st of the month, in 11 days, corresponding at Syra with the Italian packets; on the *Greek* Line (by Malta, Syra, Athens, Naupia, &c.) 1st, 11th, and 21st of the month, in 12 days; on the *Egyptian* Line (by Malta) to Alexandria, 4th and 23rd of the month, in 8 days; on the *Syrian* Line, every 20 days, in connexion with the Constantinople and Egyptian Lines, taking the round of Rhodes, Alexandrette, Latakia, Tripoli, Beyrout, and Jaffa, between Smyrna and Alexandria, (12 days). On the return there is 5 days quarantine at Smyrna.

The United French, Sardinian, and Neapolitan Line starts every other afternoon; they are dear, crowded with goods, and uncivil, the Neapolitan boats being the best managed. They carry English engineers, and take 18 hours to Genoa, 10 to Leghorn, 12 to Civita Vecchia (for Rome), 14 to Naples. Enquire if there is a quarantine anywhere, or you may be kept on board for 6 days.

French mail steamers to Bastia (26 hours), and Ajaccio (22 hours), weekly. Steamers alsoto Cette (8 hours), twice a week; to Nice (12 hours), weekly; to Algiers, every five or six days; to Oran, twice a month; to Cadiz (by Barcelona, Valentia, Alicante, Carthagena, Almeria, Malaga, Algesiras) in 8 days, about once a week, in French and Spanish boats. Offices, 26, Rue de Breteuil; and 29, Rue Montgrand.

ROUTE 24, *continued.*

From Marseilles, on the road to Toulon and Nice, you pass

Aubagne (17 kil.), a town of 6,200 souls, on a hill by the Huveaume, with a ruined château and a roman bath in the neighbourhood. The Abbé Barthelemy, who wrote the Travels of the Jeune Anacharsis, giving an account of ancient manners and customs, was a native.

[At 5 kil. to the north-west, is the picturesque village of Allauch, having remains of towers, walls, &c., belonging to a much older place.—At 7 kil. to the south-south-west, is Cassis, on the coast, the *Carsicis Portus* of Antonine's Itinerary, with a good port. It has a trade in coral, fruit, and Muscatel wine.—Cistal (the greek *Citharistes*) lies to the east; and beyond it is the site of *Tarentum*.—At 8 kil. to the north-north-east, is Roquevaire, on the Huveaume.]

Cujes (12 kil.) has an old country seat, in a fertile spot.

Le Beausset (14 kil.) has a trade in oil and wine.

Ollioules (9 kil.), in a wild, deep pass, called the Vaux d'Ollioules, with a ruined castle over it.

Toulon (7 kil.), the chief naval station in the Mediterranean, and a maritime sous-pré ecture (in department Var), on a fine circular harbour or bay, with a roadstead outside, and a line of hills behind. It is as old as the tenth century; was taken by Charles V., in 1526; fortified in the seventeenth century; besieged by Prince Eugene, 1707; and blockaded by the English fleet, 1793, when 42 ships were burnt or taken, and 15,000 royalists received on board, as the republicans entered it, after a three months' siege, their success being due to the skill of Bonaparte, then a young officer of artillery. It is strongly fortified, and defended by batteries on all the commanding points, as Fort la Malgue (a fine view), Faron, Eguillette, Ballaguier, Napoleon, &c. Rue de la Fayette is the best street, the rest being mostly narrow and crooked. It has a Hôtel de Ville, with carvings by Puget, whose house is behind it, in Rue de Rome; two or three churches; the seat of the maritime préfecture, in Place d'Armes; a college, and bibliothèque of 8,000 vols.; botanic garden, salle de spectacle, &c.

The *Port* includes the mercantile dock, with its wide quay, and the naval dock yards, the largest of which extends over 55 acres. It contains several building slips, two of which, covered over, are 300 feet by 65½; workshops, forges, masthouse, rope and sail lofts; a general magazine, 328 feet by 56, and three stories high; the naval arsenal; a park of artillery; a salle d'armes, or armoury; a corderie, or ropehouse, on 68 arches, about 1,100 feet long, begun by Vauban, and finished by Riquet, the planner of the Languedoc canal; a naval artillery school, founded 1822, with laboratories, models, library, &c.; and a naval museum, arranged in three great classes, viz., models of ships, machines, and general objects. There is a large bagne for 4,000 forçats or convicts, chained two and two, some living on board the hulks. A large naval hospital at St. Mandrier, has 2,000 beds. Capes Sicie and Sepet are two oints or look-outs, well known to the English fleet in the last war.

Hotels—De la Croix d'Or (Golden Cross), in Place au Foin; de la Croix de Malte; du Lion d'Or. Population, 46,000. Trade in wine, eaux-de-vie, oil, capers, dried raisins, almonds, oranges, figs, &c Conveyances to Marseilles, Hyères, Ciotat, Brignolles, Aix, Draguignan, &c. Steamers to La Seyne, across the harbour, hourly; to Algiers, 8th and 28th of the month, in 32 hours (120 leagues).

The road here turns *via* Cuers (23 kil.), Le Lac (30 kil.), &c., to Frejus, Cannes, and Nice, described in Route 34.

Hyeres (18 kil. from Toulon), near the marshes of the sea coast, but with a soft climate, is on the slant of an amphitheatre, sheltered from the north by hills nearly 1,000 feet high. It has orange and citron gardens, and a few date trees, with olives, mulberries, vines, fig, pomegranate, myrtle, &c. From Place de St. Paul, near that church, is a view of the Mediterranean, taking in the Iles d'Hyères, the ancient Stœchades; in Place Nationale stand a pillar to Massillon, the preacher, who was born here, and the statue of Charles, Count of Provence. In the old town are remains of a castle. At the seat of M. Denis is a collection of roman antiquities, chiefly from the site of Pomponiana. There are a Hôtel Dieu, sea baths, a Maison de Santé for invalids, with several lodging-houses and restaurants. *Hotels*—De l'Europe; des Ambassadeurs, &c. Population, 10,000. Trade in wine, oil, and fruit.

St. Tropez (45 kil. further to the east) is a pretty fishing town on the Gulf of Grimaud, which makes a good harbour for it. Traces of the roman *Heraclea Caccabaria* are found in the shape of inscriptions, columns, coins, &c.—About 30 kil. beyond it is Frejus (*see* Route 34).

From Marseilles to Corsica.—As a part of France, containing the birth-place of the Bonapartes, it may be useful to give a short description of one or two routes in this island. Steamers start from Marseilles every Tuesday, for Bastia (26 hours), returning on Friday; every Friday, for Ajaccio (22 hours), returning on Tuesday, Fares, 50 fr. and 30 fr., exclusive of provisions, which are 6 fr. and 4 fr. a day. A run of 170 to 180 miles to the south-east, brings you to the Gulf of Ajaccio, the most southern but one of several good, open bays, on the west side of Corsica, such as St. Florent or Fiorenzo, Calvi, Porte, Sagone, Valinco, &c.

AJACCIO (pronounced Ayacheeo), the capital of Corsica, under a rugged line of hills, which shelter it from the east and north, is the seat of the préfect, bishop, &c., and is further distinguished as the place where Napoleon Bonaparte was born, 15th August, 1769, according to the register, preserved here. Population, 9,000.

It was called *Urcinium* by the Romans, being noted for making earthern wine-bottles. Before 1345 it stood lower down, in a marshy site, where remains of buildings may be still seen. The citadel was built in 1554, by Marshal de Thermes. Except two good streets, the rest are narrow and dirty. Among the public buildings are the préfecture, cathedral, with a tower and dome, a college, library of 15,000 volumes, navigation school, salle de spectacle, botanic garden, &c. There is a fine promenade by the sea-side. *Napoleon's house*, which still belong's to his mother's family, the Ramolini, is a plain three-storied building, though one of the best in the town, in a little court in Rue Charles. They show a small cannon, about three feet long, and thirty-two pounds weight, which the future soldier used to play with. At the age of ten, his father, Carlo Bonaparte, a noble by descent from a Tuscan family, and assessor to the law courts of Ajaccio, sent him to the military school at Brienne. Curiously enough, his first piece of active service, as lieutenant of artillery, was to attack his native town (February, 1793), which Paoli held against the Convention. He removed his family to Marseilles in May, when the English took Corsica. Here were born also, his brothers Lucien (1775), Prince de Canino; Louis (1802), king of Holland, and father of Louis Napoleon, by Hortense Beauharnois; Prince Jerome (now Governor of the Invalides); and his three sisters Eliza (Duchess of Lucca), Caroline (who married Murat), and Pauline (Princess Borghese). Joseph, king of Spain, was born at Corte (*see* below). His father, Carlo, and mother, Letizia (1750), were also natives. Another native was Pozzo di Borgo, the Russian statesman; his and Napoleon's family belonged to the two opposite parties, which divide this island.

In the neighbourhood are the oriental tombs of a colony of Mainote Greeks, settled here by the Genoese, 1676. The climate is very mild, but the summer hot and unhealthy. Trade in oil, wine, coral, &c.

The only good road is that to Bastia, about 140 kil. or 76 miles long, made by the French soldiers. There are no inns, except in two or three towns on the coast; but decent lodgings may be found at the convents, and the villagers are hospitable. In the interior, brigandage is not uncommon, and it is therefore unsafe to go alone, or unarmed.

Travelling is by mule, as best suited to the ground, which is up and down rugged mountains of granite and limestone, crossed by deep gorges, with brawling rivers at the bottom; and through vast forests of pines, (which the French use for their navy) oaks, chesnuts, cork, box, arbutus. In the lower parts and near the coast, are groves of olives, orange, lemon, figs, almonds, &c., and thick underwood, called makis. The chesnuts grow to an immense size, and yield the chief food for the natives, who live by keeping flocks and herds, and are too proud to work; this is left to the women, or to the industrious Italians, who came over every year, to the number of 6,000. It is the latter who cultivate the flax and tobacco, tend the vines, pomegranates, and other fruit trees, and collect the bitter honey and wax for exportation. But though so indolent, the Corsicans are a quick and intelligent race, always ready to fight for their liberties, strong friends and strong enemies, and free and inquisitive in their manners. One of their chief amusements is boar-hunting; their war-dance is attended with much thumping and gesticulation. Like the Scottish highlanders of old, they use arms, and are prone to indulge in the *vendetta* or private revenge, which they transmit from father to son. The men dress in a cap with a short brown jacket and breeches; the women much in the italian style. Their language is Italian, with a mixture of moorish and spanish words. They are all devout Roman catholics, believing, of course, that there can be nothing good out of their church. When Boswell travelled here (1765), he relates, "That while stopping to refresh his mules, a strong black fellow in the crowd cried out, '*Inglese! sono barbari; non credo in Dio grande.*' (The English are heathens; they don't believe in the great God). I said to him, 'Excuse me, sir, we do believe in God, and in Jesus Christ too.' '*Um*,' said he, *e nel Papa?*' (And in the Pope?) 'No,

'*E perchè?*' (And why?) This was a puzzling question in these circumstances, so I thought I would try a method of my own and very gravely replied, '*Perchè siamo troppo lontani.*' (Because we are too far off)." An ingenious argument, which, he adds, perfectly satisfied the querist.

The road out of Ajaccio, leads up the Gravone, which enters the Campo del Oro, a fertile pass between the main line of mountains, which run nearly north and south through the island. The first stage is Carazzi (18 kil.), having, some distance to the right of it (beyond the Prunella), Cauro, with a fine prospect of Ajaccio.

Bocognano (22 kil.), near the head of the Gravone, is under Mont d' Oro (or Gradaccio), the *Mons Aureus* of Ptolemy, in Vezzacona forest, at the centre of Corsica, a granite peak, 8,700 feet high, covered with snow nearly all the year, and whence there is a noble view of the whole island, of Sardinia and Elba, and even of the coasts of Italy and France. Mont Rotondo to the north, is seen, 8,766 feet high, the highest point in the island; to the east is Mont Capella, and to the south, near Porta Vecchio, Mont Calva. Several of the lower peaks are mica slate; and iron and asbestos have been found. A bye road turns off to Bastelina, near the head of the Prunella, with a population of 2,000.

Vivario (21 kil.), leaves Mont Rotondo on the left, with its lakes near the top, frozen all the year round.

Corte (23 kil.), on a rocky height of mica, where the Restinoga falls into the Tavignano, was the seat of Pascal Paoli's government, when Boswell visited him at his country house, Sollacaro, a little way off, the old seat of the Colonna family. This virtuous patriot was born at Saltretta, the son of Giacinto Paoli, a leader in the first revolt against the Genoese, when the Corsican assembly met here and proclaimed their independence, 1755. P. Paoli was chosen their general and leader under the protection of England, whither he retired when the Genoese sold the island to the French, 1768-9; he came back in 1794-6, when it was again held by the English, as part of the British empire, under Sir G. Eliot, as viceroy; but returned to England and died there 1807. He founded an university at Corte. The castle is perched on a rugged and inaccessible rock, and was only taken by the French, by starving the garrison. Population 3,800. Here Napoleon's eldest brother, Joseph, was born, 1768.

The Tavignano falls down to the east coast at the Tour of Aleria. At Bozzo, near Corte, the first revolt against the Genoese broke out 1729, when the collector seized the goods of a poor woman for five pence taxes.

Monte Albano (12 kil.).

Ponte Leccia (9 kil), at the bridge on the Golo, on the banks of which the Corsicans beat a superior force of the French under Marbœuf, 1768; but in the next year they were finally defeated at Pontenuovo.

Lucina (13 kil.), near the Golo's mouth and the east coast.

Biguglia (10 kil.), is close to a narrow lagoon of the same name, 8 miles long, and abounding with fish. To the left of it, is Murato, with a church shaped like a turkish mosque.

Bastia (9 kil.), the military head quarters of the island, and a fortified town, is opposite Italy and Elba, 35 miles from the latter, and upwards of 200 miles east of Marseilles. The English bombarded it 1745, and took it 1794, Nelson aiding in the Agamemnon. It stands at the foot of some hills, on a little bay, which, with the help of a mole, makes a harbour for small craft, defended by a citadel in Terra Nuova, or New Town. At the mouth is the *Leone rock*, a piece of limestone, washed by the sea into the shape of a sitting lion, with his head raised, and serving as a breakwater. The houses are in the Italian style, and amongst the best buildings are the old cathedral church; Ste. Croce chapel, a pretty structure; a palais de justice, college or high school, gendarmerie barracks, &c. Population, 10,000. Trade in wine, timber, cattle, tobacco, soap, wax, liqueurs, &c. There is a fine view of Elba, Pianosa, Capraja, Monte Cristo, and the Tuscan Coast.

A narrow peninsula, 7 miles by 22, stretches from hence, north to Cape Corte, (the ancient *Sacrum*), traversed by a ridge which is 4,540 feet high at Mont Stella, about the middle of it. On the west side of it, at 10 kil. west of Bastia, is

St. Florent or St. Fierenzo, which is well built, but unhealthy, with a good harbour or road, where the English squadron used to anchor in the war. To the north of it are the towers of Farinole and Negro. Further on are the towers of Sisco, and of *Seneca*, the latter on a sharp peak, and so called after the roman philosopher, who was exiled here by Claudius, and wrote his treatise on Consolation, for amusement. He mentions the scorching heat of summer, and the sirocco winds which bring sickness. Another called tramontona, blowing from the mountains, brings snow; and there is a fierce gusty wind ealled the lion wind. Near Cape Corte is Porto Centuro.

(*a*) A coast road from St. Fierenzo, leads past Monte Arazza to Ile Rousse or Isola Rossa (45 kil. from Bastia), a little town of 1,100 people, founded by Paoli, opposite an island of the same time, and now turned into a fortified post.

CALVI (about 20 kil. further), on a rocky point in the Gulf of Calvi, has a good harbour, and an old castle which Marshal de Thermes attempted without success. Population 1,400. A winding road of about 60 kil., which sometimes bends deep inland, under Monte Pagliarba, Rotondo, &c., brings you to

CARGESE, on the Gulf of Sagone, which belongs to about 700 descendants of the Greeks, whom the Genoese brought over in 1676, and is the best cultivated spot in the island. One of their little hamlets was called Paomia. The natives shewed the most cruel jealousy towards them. At first they used the greek, but since 1822, the roman liturgy. A convent of St. Basil, founded by them, was abolished by the Genoese.

At 30 kil. further on is Ajaccio, described above. About 40 kil. beyond it is

SARTENE, near the river Valinco, which runs into that gulf, having a population of 2,800. At 30 kil. from this is

BONIFACIO, a fortified town of 3,000 souls, at the south end of the island, on the Strait of Bonifacio, which divides Corsica from Sardinia. It is thought to be the site of Ptolemy's *Pallae*, and was founded by a Count Boniface, from Pisa. Alphonso of Arragon besieged it 1420, and the French took it 1553. Trade in coral, wine, and oil. The islands of Perdullo, Cavallo, Lavazzi, &c., lie in the strait, which is 5 miles broad across to Point Longosardo. The coast road from this turns north past Gulf de Santa Manza, to

PORTE VECCHIO or Old Port (22 kil), on the bay of the same name, which makes a safe, deep harbour, 5 miles by 1½, in the midst of an unhealthy marsh, which, however, yields good salt. It is the *Œlistum* of Ptolemy, and is fortified. Pearl mussels are found; and granite worked in the neighbouring hills, which at Mont Calva are 5,130 feet high. It has a trade in the red wine of Sari, &c. Population 1,800.

After this, you pass the towers of Pinarello, Fuello, Salenzara (at the mouth of a stream which comes down from Sari), Seposa, &c., which belong to a chain raised in past times by the Genoese, for securing their conquests, and for defending the coast against pirates, and come to Tour d'Aleria, at the mouth of the Tavignano (60 kil. from Porte Vecchio). This marks the site of a tower founded by the Dictator Sylla, now half a mile from the sea. A little north of it, at the Tour de Diana, is part of a temple, built by Marius, when he founded Mariana, between two lagoons or sea lakes. Monte Capella, 6,750 feet high, lies to the west. The road hence passes Ste. Luciana, Tour S. Pelegrino, &c. for 60 kil. to Bastia, again. So that the circuit of Corsica by this road is upwards of 370 kil. or 230 miles. Its greatest length is about 130 miles, and breadth 53; area, 3,380 square miles; and total population, 200,000.

Ptolemy called it *Coornos*. It was occupied in whole or part by all the nations who figure in the history of the Mediterranean, the Greeks, Carthagenians, Romans, Saracens, &c., and at length by the Genoese, who however held but a nominal possession for 400 years, till 1729, when the natives revolted, and in 1734 placed a german adventurer, Theodore de Neuhoff, on the throne. Being obliged to fly, he mortgaged his little 'kingdom' to pay his debts, and died in London 1746. The French who had at various times come to the assistance of the Genoese, acquired possession of it, as above mentioned, after 1769.

ROUTE 25.

Melun to Nevers.

Distance, 179 kil., or 111 miles. A railway is projected in this direction.

MELUN and FONTAINEBLEAU, as described in Route 24.

NEMOURS (16 kil.) in a hollow, on the river and canal du Loing, has the old castle of the Ducs de Nemours, now used for a public library (3,000 vols.) &c. It belonged to the Armagnacs and Gaston de Foix, before it came to the Orleans family. The bridge was built by Peyronnet. Population, 3,000. Near it is Bignon, where Mirabeau was born, 1749.

CROISIERE (13 kil.).

MONTARGIS (19 kil.), a sous-préfecture in department Loiret, with 7,200 population, on the Orleans canal, where those of Briare and Loing join it, grew out of a royal castle built on a hill (mont) on the site of a roman camp. One of its seigneurs was Pierre de Nevers, who married the sister of Yolande, emperor of Constantinople. It was nearly taken by Warwick, 1427, but relieved by Dunois. Most of the town was built after 1527, when a fire burnt all but four houses. St. Madeline's large old church was begun by Henri II. The great castle was nearly all pulled down 1810; one of its frescos was a painting of the famous Dog of Montargis, who, in the presence of Charles V, fought and vanquished the murderer of his master, Aubrey de Montdidier, who was killed in the forest of Bondy. P. Manuel, a member of the Convention, Girodet Trioson, the painter, and Madame Guyon, whose religious poems were translated by Cowper, were natives. *Hotels*—De la Poste, de la Ville de Lyon, de l'Ange.

[At 25 kil. to the east is the old family seat of the Courtenays, on the Clare, which came to the Fontenelles in 1773].

NOGENT-SUR-VERNISSON (17 kil.), on a small branch of the Loing. About 4 kil. from it is the Château of Chenevière, including remains of a roman amphitheatre, made of great blocks of stone. At 7 kil. east-south-east of it is *Chatillon-sur-Loing*, which has the ancient castle where the great Huguenot, or Protestant, leader, Admiral Coligny, was born, his mother being sister to the Constable Montmorency. After Bartholomew day his body was taken to Chantilly, and is now in Paris. A collegiate church was founded here by the Archbishop of Sens

LA BUSSIERE (12 kil.) has a château of the fifteenth century, with a view of the Loire.

BRIARE (12 kil.), where the canal from Montargis falls into the Loire, is on the north bank of this river, on the road from Orleans to Nevers (*see* Route 50*b*). The canal, the oldest in France, was begun by Sully, and finished 1740. Population, 3,300. Trade in wine, wood, charcoal, building stone, &c.

COSNE (31 kil.), a sous-préfecture, up the Loire, of which it has a beautiful prospect, and several iron forges round it. Population, 5,987.

LA CHARITE (20 kil.), a pretty place of 5,086 souls, on the Loire, which is crossed by a fine bridge.

Further up the river (25 kil.) is NEVERS, as in Route 51.

ROUTE 26.

Montereau to Dijon.

By railway from Montereau to Troyes, thence to Bar-sur-Seine, &c. Opened 1848; 100 kil. or 62 miles from Montereau, up the Seine. Four trains a day, in 3 to 6 hours. The stations are—

	kil.		kil.		kil.
Chatenay	13	Nogent	7	St. Mesmin	6
Vimpelles	8	Pont-sur-Seine	9	Payns	7
Les Ormes	3	Romilly	9	Barberey	7
Hermé	10	Mesgrigny	12	Troyes	9
Melz	4				

MONTEREAU, as in Route 24. A viaduct bridge of four arches, each 79 feet span, crosses the Yonne. Another of three arches carries the railway over the Seine, a little further on, near St. Germain.

CHATENAY (6¾ miles).

VIMPELLES (5¼ miles). Coaches to Donnemarie, and Bray, on the south bank of the Seine at the bridge to Mony.

LES ORMES (2 miles). Coach to Provins.

[*Provins*, 11 kil. to the north-north-east, a sous-préfecture in department Seine-et-Marne, in a fertile spot, on the Voulzie and Durtein, on the side of a hill, has many middle-age remains of wells and buildings, having grown out of a royal castle, founded before 1120. It suffered much in the civil and religious wars. In Upper Town are the walls, traces of the château, and St. Quirian church, which has a good choir, cupola, &c. Near it stood till lately the Tour de César, built in the thirteenth century. The two old gates of St. Jean and Jouy lead down to Low Town, where the modern houses are, surrounded by walls, with two churches; the old Cordeliers' convent, now the hospital, founded by the Counts of Champagne, 1050; and mineral spring under a bath house, useful in all cases of debility, &c. Part of the old town is excavated into caves and underground passages. The rivers turn many corn-mills and dye-works. Population 6,200. Trade in grain, wood, leather, and confectionery made from roses, grown here—the true seat of the Provins (not Provence) rose. *Hotels*—De France; de Fontaine.

About 17 kil. to the north, near Louan, are the fine and extensive ruins of Montaguillon in a forest.]

HERME (4 miles) and Melz (4½ miles) are the next stations; beyond which a viaduct in three parts, 216 feet long, crosses the Seine near Bernières château.

NOGENT-SUR-SEINE (3¾ miles), a sous-préfecture (in department Aube) of 3,600 persons, on the Seine, opposite the weir or fall, where it becomes navigable. It belonged to St. Denis's abbey, and came at length to the family of Cardinal de Noailles. The allies, under Prince Schwartzenburg, took it by storm when held by Bourmont in 1814, when the Hôtel de Ville and a bridge were destroyed. The large church was built between the reigns of Charles VI. and Henry II.: the tower has a turret (built 1521-42) with a figure of St. Laurent on top. Trade in millinery, grain, charcoal, leather, rope. *Hotels* — Du Cygne d'Or (Golden Swan); du Signe de la Croix (Sign of the Cross).

[About 8 kil. east-south-east, on the Ardasson, are remains of the monastery founded 1123 by Abélard, who fled here from his enemies, and called it *Paraclete* (*i.e.*, comforter); which became a convent under his wife Heloise, where they were both buried. Their bodies remained here till removed to the Père la Chaise about 1793, and placed under the monument brought from Abélard's first grave (at Chalons-sur-Saône); a pillar set up by General Pajol marks where they lay before this change.]

PONT-SUR-SEINE or Pont-le-Roi (6¾ miles), in a pretty spot on the Seine, where the Aube joins, had a hunting château of the Counts of Champagne, built by Le Muet, in which Napoleon's mother lived; but being burnt by the Russians 1814, was rebuilt by Casimir Perier, 1830, in the italian style. Population 1,950. In the neighbourhood is a large dolmen or cromlech, of one great stone on three or four others; besides others lying about, called by the people Tombeaux romains (roman tombs).

Coach to Villenauxe.

[*Villenauxe* (9 kil. north-north-west), noted for its white wine and vinegar, is on a branch of the Seine, and was once fortified. The benedictine monks of Nesle la Réposte abbey (founded 501) came here in the sixteenth century and rebuilt their church of the original stones, as it now stands—a large and elegant structure, having a light spire, beautiful stained windows of the sixteenth century, when the art was perfected, and, among other carvings, a curious one in the porch, of a web-footed queen, supposed to be Clothilde.]

ROMILLY (6 miles), in a fertile hollow on the Seine, has a beautiful château on the site of an old moated fortress. Needles, &c., are made. About 2 kil. west-north-west are two arches of the cistercian abbey of Scellières, where Voltaire's body (having been refused burial by the Paris clergy) lay from 1778 to 1791, when it was moved to the Pantheon. A stone with AV on it marks the spot. Coach to Sézanne. (*see* Route 16.)

MESGRIGNY (7¼ miles) is reached by a viaduct across the étang or lake. Coaches to Arcis and Sézanne.

[Méry-sur-Seine, a short distance off, is a small decayed town, on the Seine, frequently attacked in earlier times, and finally burnt by Blucher 1814.

Arcis-sur-Aube, about 21 kil. east, a sous-préfecture, in department Aube, of 2,800 souls, on the Aube, where it is first navigable, was burnt in the defence made by Napoleon, with a small force against 80,000 Austrians in 1814. A small suspension bridge, 56 feet long (cost 600 fr.) leads to Dampierre, where the general of that name is buried, and which has a château built, 1671, by Mansard. The views from the hills around command good prospects. Danton was born here.]

ST. MESMIN (3¾ miles), Payns (4½ miles), and Barbery (4½ miles), bring you to Troyes (3 miles), at the Mail de Prelize terminus.

Troyes. *Hotels*—Des Courriers, in Grande Rue; du Commerce, Rue Notre Dame; de la Croix d'Or (Golden Cross); de la Fontaine; de France. Population, 25,000 at one time it had

50,000. Capital of department Aube (formerly of province of Champagne), seat of a bishop, a society of agriculture, &c., in a wide and fertile plain (dotted with country houses), on the Seine which divides itself here into several canals; though for drinking, the water is entirely drawn from wells in the chalk. It was the head town of the *Tricases* or *Trecæ*, whence the modern name. Attila threatened it, 451, and the Normans pillaged it, 889, a few years after the meeting of Pope John VIII. and Louis le Bégue about the succession to the imperial crown. Under its count, Thibault IV., in the twelfth century, it became a great place for trading fairs; and hence we get the *troy* pound of twelve ounces. It was held by the English after the treaty of 1420, by which Henry V. married Katharine, daughter of Charles VI., and was to succeed to the French crown; but Charles VII. took it, 1429. The parliament of Paris was sent here, 1787. Napoleon made it his head quarters, 1814.

On the top of the old walls, built by the romans, but much altered, is a promenade called the mall; in them are the Hector, Andromaque, Paris, and other gates, fancifully named in remembrance of old Troy. The Porte St. Jaques, near the bridge, is flanked by two low-peaked gothic towers and turrets. Close to the Porte de Paris was a royal château, burnt in the great fire of 1524, along with a second, which belonged to the counts of Champagne, and another, which stood hard by the Cordeliers convent,—which make some derive the name from *tres arces* (three castles). The streets are full of old houses of carved and plastered timber, with their gables fronting you, as ancient as the sixteenth century for the most part. Among its eight churches is

St. Etienne *Cathedral*, begun 1208-25 (on the site of one as old as 872), and carried on till the west front was built, about 1506-20. This front has a good tower, 204 feet high (there were to have been two), and a fine stained rose window. It is 371 feet long, and 164 wide through the transept, the nave, exclusive of its five aisles, is 34 feet wide and 96 high, ornamented, like the choir, with windows of the thirteenth century, finely stained with portraits of kings, counts, bishops, saints, &c., all in costume. St. Urban's beautiful collegiate church was built in the thirteenth century, by Pope Urban IV., a son of a tailor here, whose trade is painted in one of the windows. Excellent stained windows are seen in Ste Madeleine's ancient church of the eleventh and sixteenth centuries, and a well-carved rood-loft (by J. Galdo, 1518), one of five for which the city was noted; also in St. Pantaleon's, which has besides twenty statues close to its pillars. St. Nicholas offers a good portal; St. Jean an altar-piece of the baptism of Christ, by Mignard (a native); St. Remy a bronze crucifix, 3½ feet high, by Girardon (another native).

The Hôtel de Ville, built 1624-70, by Mansard, has a good front, with busts of natives, and Girardon's medallion of Louis XIV. At the bibliothèque are as many as 55,000 volumes, and 5,000 MSS., in a room 164 feet long; and specimens of glass, painted by Linard Gouthier, with scenes from the life of Henry IV. In the musée is a gallery of pictures and a collection of minerals, &c. Two tombs of Henry I. and Thibault III. (1180-1200) are placed at the bishop's house. Other buildings to be noticed are the old timbered abattoirs or shambles, wine and corn halls (the latter has a fine timbered roof), the college, seminary, theatre, the Vouldry pepinière or nursery, &c. The manufactures are a chalk preparation, called blanc d'espagne (Spanish white), cotton stockings and caps, linen, paper, &c.

Coaches to Bar-sur-Aube, Bar-sur-Seine, Bourbonne-les-Bains, Brienne, Chalons-sur-Marne, Chaource, Chatillon, Chaumont (*see* Route 27), Epinal (Route 19), Ervy, Estissac, Langres, Nancy, Receys, Vandeuvre, Vesoul (Route 27).

ROUTE 26—*continued.*

From Troyes, you proceed by road to

St. Parre-les-Vaudes (19 kil.), up the Seine.

Bar-sur-Seine (14 kil.), a sous-préfecture of 2,500 persons, in a fertile valley among vineyards on the Seine (crossed by a stone bridge), below the junction of the Ource and Laignes, was a large place in Froissart's time (1359), when the English burnt '900 bons hôtels' (houses). It has a good gothic cross-shaped church, with large windows, and walks by the river. On St. Germain's hill, to the west, is (besides traces of the castles) the pretty rustic chapel of Nôtre Dame, founded 1070, by Simon de Valois. *Hotel*—Du Cheval Blanc (White Horse). Trade in wine, wool, cutlery, paper, &c.

[At 19 kil. west-south-west is Chaource, once fortified, near the head of the Amance, which turns several mills. The old gothic church is covered with inscriptions, pretending that it existed before 654. Amadis Jamyn, a poet of the sixteenth century, was a native.]

MUSSY-SUR-SEINE (19 kil.), in a forest, on the Seine, was a country seat of the bishops of Langres.

[About 10 kil. west, in the valley of the Laignes, are Ricey Haut, Ricey Haute-rive, and Ricey Bas, three places founded, they say, by industrious Swiss settlers, with good spire churches, and noted for wine, which is exported to the north and to Belgium. Population, 3,564.]

CHATILLON-SUR-SEINE (16 kils.), a sous-préfecture of 4,800 persons (department Cote d'Or), in a hilly but healthy spot on the Seine, where the little Douix joins. It was one of the first seats of the Dukes of Burgundy, and in 1814 noted for the conference between Napoleon and the allies. Among the buildings are the Hôtel de Ville, in the old benedictine convent, St. Nicholas' church, of the twelfth century, a chapel which belonged to the ducal castle, a library of 7,500 volumes, a college, hospital, &c., and a large château (at Chaumont), built by Marshal Marmont, who was born here. A roman way to Auxerre is noticed. Trade in iron, wood, wool, paper, &c. *Hotels*—Du Commerce; de la Côte d'Or. Coaches to Dijon, Ancy-le-Franc, on the Lyons railway.

AISEY-LE-DUC (14 kil).

AMPILLY (14 kil.), Chanceaux (15 kil.), St. Seine (12 kil.), and Val-Suzon (10 kil.), in a deep Alpine valley, are the next places; and

At 53 kil. further is DIJON (*see* Route 24), on the Lyons railway.

ROUTE 27.

Troyes to Chaumont, Vesoul, Basle.

Distance, 329 kil., or 204 miles.

TROYES, as above, in Route 26.

MONTIERAME (19 kil.) on the Barse, past the forest of Lusigni.

VENDEUVRE (13 kil.), among hills and vineyards, at the Barse's head, has an ancient château, which belonged to Henry of Luxembourg, 1614, and a church, with this pretty inscription to a woman (1599): '*qui ami bien, tard oublie*,' (he who loves best, forgets latest). It has a good trade in sheep and cattle. The ground is so strong that it takes 8 or 10 horses to the plough. In the charming valley of Val-suzenay is a pilgrims' chapel, where a fête is held on the 8th of September.

BAR-SUR-AUBE (21 kil.), a sous-préfecture of 4,200 souls, in a fine spot among the vineyards of the Aube, belonged to the early kings of France, and was noted for its trading fairs, attended by the Dutch, Germans, &c. Besides remains of a castle on Châtelet hill, it has a hospital of the eleventh century, two ancient churches, and a stone bridge, over which Charles VII., in 1440, threw his rebellious subject, the Bastard of Bourbon, tied up in a sack. In 1814, Marshal Mortier here defeated the Austrians, who a little after defeated Oudinot. Trade in white wine, eaux-de-vie, corn, wool, wood, &c. *Hotels*—De la Poste; du Mulet; de la Pomme d'Or (Golden Apple). Coaches to Troyes, Chaumont, Basle.

[At 22 kil. north-north-west is *Brienne-le-Château*, so called from the fine seat built by Louis its last count, and noted till 1790 for the military school in the Minimes convent, to which the young Corsican, *Napoleon*, 1779-84, was sent as a king's pensioner. Nothing is left of it. In 1814 the Allies were defeated here by Napoleon, who, however, was nearly killed by the lance of a Cossack.

At 12 kil. south-south-east of Bar, is *Clairvaux*, up the Aube, now a central house of correction for 2,000 prisoners from thirteen departments; but once famous for the cistercian abbey founded 1105-14, by Hugh, count of Troyes and St. Bernard. It had the capacious Tun of Clairvaux, which held 2,000 hectolitres (each 24 gallons) of wine; smaller casks held 250 to 1000 hect. Straw hats, gloves, &c. are made. A little north-west, in the forest, is Arconville, a great heap of stones, or cairn, gradually made by the contribution of passers by, on the spot where a Huguenot was killed in the wars of the League.]

COLOMBEY-LES-DEUX-EGLISES (15 kil.), in department Haute-Marne.

[At 12 kil. north-north-east, is Cirey château, where Voltaire lived with the Duchess de Châtelet. About 12 kil. north-west of this stands Tremilly, the old moated seat of the Tremouilles, flanked by two pyramidal towers, &c., now belonging to the Broglie family.]

JUZENNECOURT (8 kil).

[About 18 kil. south is Château Villain, on the Anjou, which belonged to the Orleans family, and was one of the finest seats in Champagne, before the revolution.—Arc-en-Barois (12 kil. south-south-east) higher up the Anjou, was a fortified town in Burgundy, and latterly the property of Madame Adelaide d'Orleans.]

At 17 kil. further is

CHAUMONT, or Chaumont-en-Bassigny. *Hotels*—De l'Ecu-de-France (French Crown-piece); de l'Arbre d'Or (Golden Tree); de la Poste. Population, 6,000. Chief town of department Marne, on a ridge of the Marne where the Suize joins. It grew out of a castle built by the Counts of Champagne, was fortified by Louis XII., and is known for the treaty signed here by the Allies against Napoleon, 1814. Some parts of it are well built; but there is little worth notice. Among the buildings are the Hôtel de Ville, which has a bust of Henry IV.; the palais de justice, the college, with a good portico to the chapel, library of 35,000 volumes, and cabinet of natural history, hospital, theatre, fountains, made by Cordier de Béziers, and a triumphal arch begun by Napoleon, but finished by Louis XVIII. Bouchardon, the sculptor, and Lamoise, the Jesuit, are natives. Manufactures of druggets, gloves of good quality, cutlery, &c. The falls of the Marne are 1 kil. off.

Conveyances, by coach, to Troyes, Dijon, Epinal, St. Dizier, &c.—It is 111 kil. to Nancy, *viâ* Neufchâteau.

From Chaumont, up the Marne, on the road to Vesoul, you pass

VESSAINES (17 kil.).

LANGRES (18 kil.), an ancient town, sous-préfecture, bishopric, &c., and seat of the cutlery trade, on a hill side by the Marne, which here runs through a cultivated plain, 1,457 feet above the sea, on which that river, with the Aube, the Meuse, &c., take their rise. It is the roman *Langonum*, and there is yet a triumphal arch in the west wall, built about 240, by the Emperor Gordian. The old romanesque cathedral of the eleventh century, has a modern front, and a fine view from the top. A library of 30,000 volumes at the Hôtel de Ville, and a museum at St. Didier's old church. It has two theatres, a college, priests' seminary, &c. A walk through the Belle Fontaine promenade leads to the Fontaine de la Grenouille, among large trees. Diderot was a native. The cutlery made here is of a superior kind. *Hotels*—De la Poste; l'Europe, &c. Population, 8,700.

[*Bourbonne-les-Bains* (42 kil. north-east, *viâ* Montigny), in department Haute-Marne, in a pleasant spot where the Apance and Borne meet, is noted for its baths, called La Fontaine and Grand Bassin, useful in cases of rheumatism, paralysis, scrofula, &c., and much frequented between June and October. It has a military hospital, with 500 beds, and an establishment for civilians, containing 50 baths, besides assembly rooms, &c. Both the baths and living are moderate. Population, 3,900. *Hotels*—Du Commerce; des Vosges.]

FAYL-BILLOT (27 kil.) has a good cutlery trade.

PORT-SUR-SAONE (24 kil.), on the Saône, has a trade in iron, cattle, &c., and remains of a castle on an island near the bridge.

At 13 kil. further is

VESOUL. *Hotels*—De la Madeleine; de la Cigogne (Stork); de l'Aigle Noir (Black Eagle). Population, 6,000. This small capital of department Haute-Saône (once part of Franche Comté) in the valley of the Durgeon, belonged to the Besançon archbishops, the Duke of Burgundy, &c., and after suffering in the wars of the sixteenth and seventeenth centuries, was joined to France by the peace of Nimwegen, 1678. The old walls are gone, as well as its impregnable castle, which stood on La Motte, a peak 1,320 feet high to the top, covered with vineyards, and commanding a noble prospect. Most of the buildings are modern,—the oldest being the church, built about 1750, with a square tower, and an ancient tomb. The préfecture was built 1822; in the library are 23,000 vols., with a museum; there are also public baths, a salle de spectacle, cavalry barracks (built 1777), a priests' school, pepinière or nursery, &c. Trade in wine, grain, &c.

Coaches to Paris, Besançon, Dijon, Lure, Epinal, Mulhouse, &c. Fossil bones have been found in the grotto of Trou-de-la-Baume, near Echenos.

[*Villersexel* (20 kil. east-south-east), on the Oignon, has the fine château of the Marquis de Grammont,—a family whose castle was formerly on the Montagne de Grammont (within view), and who founded a hospital here, 1769, as well as the ancient abbey of Vieux-Croissant.

Luxeuil or Luxen (30 kil.), is another place for mineral baths, in a plain under the Vosges, covered with wood. It was known to the Romans, as proved by an inscription at the Hôtel de Ville, in the Rue des Romains, where the baths stand in the midst of fine grounds, under the names of Bains des Femmes, des Hommes, &c. They are of the same quality as those of Plombières. It has a college, and old benedictine abbey. Population 3,800. Trade in hams, cattle, wine, grain. *Hotels*—Du Lion d' Or (Golden Lion); Lion Vert (Green Lion).]

CALMONTIER (11 kil.) on the Durgeon, near several grottoes and falls.

LURE (18 kil) a sous-préfecture, in department Haute-Saône (population 3,250), on the wide marshy plain of the Oignon, was once a strong place, and had an abbey of the seventh century, parts of which, in the Grand Rue or High street (where many large houses are seen) are used for the mairie, theatre, &c. The college is a large building, as is the Hôtel de Ville, built 1836. Frequent markets and fairs are held.

CAMPAGNEY (18 kil.) on the Rohain, a mining village of 3,100 souls.

[*Hericourt* (16 kil. south) on the little river Luzenne, a bustling village of 3,000 person s chiefly Protestants, who use the nave of the church, while the Catholics take the choir. It has several old houses, and the castle of the dukes of Wurtemburg, who obtained it 1561, along with Montbeliard.]

BELFORT, or Béfort (14 kil.) where the road from Besançon (*see* Route 30) and five other high roads fall in, making it a good place for trade, is a sous-préfecture of 5,500 souls, and a first class fortress, in a healthy part of the Savoureuse, between the Vosges and Jura mountains. It has three gates and faubourgs, and is divided into High and Low town. The church was built 1728; there are a good Hôtel de Ville, a college, and a library of 20,000 vols.; also a military hospital and barracks. On the rock above is the castle (bel fort), built 1228, and held by the Austrians till given up to France by the treaty of Munster, when it was fortified by Vauban, being the first on his system. Another rock to the north is crowned by a ruined tower, called Pierre Miotte. Trade in wine, eaux-de-vie, excellent kirsch-wasser, cheese, iron, brass, copper, &c. *Hotels*—De l'Ancienne Poste; du Sauvage; du Commerce. Coaches to Mulhouse (on the Strasbourg rail), Basle, Besançon, Lyons, &c.

CHAVANNES-SUR-L'ETANG (15 kil.) on the Rhine and Rhône canal.

ALTKIRCH (19 kil.) a dull sous-préfecture, of 3,400 souls, on a hill-side by the Ill, with ruins of a château built by the Counts of Ferrette, and made the seat of the Dukes of Austria when Alsace belonged to them. Trade in pottery, hemp, ribbons, wine, cattle, &c. *Hotel*—De la Tête d'Or (Golden Head.) Coaches to Basle and Mulhouse.

[*Ferrette*, or la Ferrette (15 kil. south-south-east) has the picturesque remains of its old castle on a rock above it, near a branch of the Ill, not far from the Swiss border. Its name occurs in 'Anne of Geierstein;' and it has a well, they say, nearly 640 feet deep.—*Lucelle*, 9 kil. south-west of this, near Suitz island, had a cistercian abbey burnt 1524; to which was attached the castle of Lœwenbourg, a ruin on a hill near. That of Blomont, burnt by the Baslese 1449, is on another hill.]

LOCH-WURTH (13 kil.)

ST. LOUIS (15 kil.) with a frontier custom-house, on the Strasbourg and Basle rail.

At 5 kil. further is Bâle or Basle in SWITZERLAND.

ROUTE 28.

Joigny to Auxerre, Clamecy, Avallon, Autun, and Chalons-sur-Saone.

By rail to Clamecy, and thence by road.

JOIGNY, as in Route 24, on the Lyons rail.

Ascending the Yonne you come to

BASSON (10 kil.) on the branch rail.

APPOIGNY (4 kil.)

And 8 kil. further is

Auxerre. *Hotels*—Du Leopard; de Beaune; du Faisan (Pheasant). Population 11,439. Capital of department Yonn e, and seat of a diocess is an ancient town on a healthy slope in the Burgundy wine country. It was called *Autissiodurum* when Cæsar took it, A.D. 521, and had a bishop as early as 273. The Yonne makes a port for the conveyance of produce, opposite an island covered with trees and mills. The streets are in general narrow. There are good prospects from the boulevards.

The fine *Cathedral* dedicated to St. Etienne (Stephen), on the hill, built between 1035 ard 1548, is 328 feet long, 111 feet high to the vault, with a tower (the last built) 195 feet high. It is chiefly in the flamboyant (pointed) style, and much admired for its regularity, fine portals, ornaments, columns, figures, &c., and especially the large number of richly stained windows. The altar is simple but grand, and has near it figures of the patron Saint, Bishop Amyot, the translator of Plutarch, and Bishop Colbert, brother of that minister. St. Eusebius' and St. Peter's churches bear marks of the romanesque style, corresponding to our norman. St. Germain's Abbey (now part of the Hôtel de Ville) covered the relics of above sixty saints, including the one also commemorated by the Parisian church of St. Germain l'Auxerrois, and it holds the tombs of the old counts.

Hôtel de la préfecture was the bishop's palace. At the bibliothèque, or public library, are 15,000 vols., 200 MSS., and Baron Denon's collection of medals, &c. The clock tower, on a gate near the old house of the dukes of Burgundy was made 1670, and marks solar and mean time, with the changes of the moon. There are also a large foundry, hospital, college, theatre, baths, barracks, and botanic garden. Trade in wine, as *petit vin d'Auxerre* (used to flavour Burgundy), *Chablis* (white), *Côte de la Chênette* and *Côte de la Mègrène* (both red); timber for casks, a few woollens, &c.

Conveyances, daily, by rail, to Paris, Dijon, Lyons, &c.; by coach, to Toucy, St. Fargean, St. Sauveur.

[*Toucy* (18 kil. south-west) on the Onane, was the place where Hugh Capet's brother, St. Héribert, built a château and died 995. At Mainfron is a mineral water.—At 13 kil. south-west of this is St. Sauveur, in the beautiful country of Puisaye, having a château, an ancient tower, and the ruins of Moutier Abbey.—At 10 kil. further to the west, towards the Loire, stands the fine château of St. Fargeau, in the midst of a great park. It was founded as far back as 980, but has been rebuilt, having passed through the hands of René d'Anjou, Gaston, Duc de Montpensier, &c., and now belongs to the Marquis de Boisgelin.

Vermenton (18 kil. south-south-east of Auxerre) in a pretty part of the Cure, under a hill, has an old church, with a remarkable recessed porch, having in the arch, God the Father, in the midst of angels, apostles, bishops, &c.; while below, on pedestals, are larger figures of the Son, the Virgin, a saint, and four crowned persons.]

From Auxerre, along the rail you pass on to Courson (20 kil.), Coulangis-sur-Yonne (7 kil.), and

CLAMECY (9 kil.), a sous-préfecture in department Nièvre, of 5,734 inhabitants, on the Yonne and Beuvron, with a good trade in wood, charcoal. &c. Near it are the Villette paper factories. The rail, which ends here at present, is to be carried on to Nevers, following the Yonne and the canal du Niverrais. Coaches to Varzy, La Charité, Premery, and Nevers.

[Varzy (15 kil. south-east), under a vine-covered hill. La Charité, 36 kil. beyond, as in Route 25. Hence it is 23 kil. up the Loire to Nevers; and 45 kil. to Bourges (*see* Route 51).]

From Clamecy, on the way to Chalons, you pass

VEZELEY (18 kil.), having the very ancient Madeleine church, which belonged to the abbey founded in the ninth century by Gherard de Roussillon, where St. Bernard preached a crusade before Louis VII., in 1145. T. Beza, the reformer, was a native.

AVALLON (16 kil.) a sous-préfecture of department Yonne, in a charming valley on the Cousin' was the roman *Aballo*, and had a castle of the dukes of Burgundy. Petit Cours, the site of a roman camp, offers a fine prospect. Population 5,569. The church has a curious porch.

[At 20 kil. to the left are the famous caves of Arcy-sur-Cure, which include several chambers, the largest being above 1,200 feet. They are visited in dry weather, about August or September.]

The next places are

SAULIEU (39 kil.) Arnay-le-Duc (28 kil.), Ivry

(17 kil.); and 40 kil. further is Chalons-sur-Saône, on the rail (*see* Route 24).

From Clamecy (as above) by a more direct way to Chalons you pass

CHATEAU CHINON (about 130 kil. or 84 miles from Avallon), a small sous-préfecture, on a mountain about 1,900 feet above sea level, in the midst of woodland, near the source of the Yonne. The air though healthy is sharp and cold.

Autun (37 kil.) on the Arroux, where seven roads meet, is a sous-préfecture, in department Saône-et-Loire, a bishopric, &c., remarkable for its roman remains. You may also reach it by way of Beaune, on the Lyons rail, from which it is 50 to 60 kil. It was the roman *Bibracte* or *Augustodunum*, one of the chief places in Gaul, and was burnt by the Saracens about 730. The present town is on a slope, under three hills (Mont Drad or Druid, Mont Jeu or Jove, and Mont Cenis which has a lake supplying the town with water) occupying about one-third of the old site, within the ancient walls, which are solid and entire in most parts, and about 3¼ miles round.

Two gates out of four are left, of arches on arches, with pilasters, &c. One is Porte St André close to St. Andrew's Church; the other and the best, Porte d'Arroux, or *Porta Senonica*, is 53 ft. by 46, and leads over the river, past the site (circular) of the Temple of Pluto to the mouth of the Tarenai, which joins the Arroux here, and is crossed by a sort of bent *Roman Bridge* or causeway of 17 arches, above 300 feet long. Between this and the bridge of St. Andoche, on the *Chaumar* or Campus Martius, stands another relic, the *Temple of Janus*, a square pile, of which three sides remain, 56 feet long, 72 high. The Marchau is the Martiale Forum at the centre of the old town where the two leading roads met. Place de Ladre in the Ville, or lower town, has around it the sites only of the Emperor's palace, the temples of Hercules, Apollo, and Minerva, the baths, the Menian schools, &c.

In the upper town, or Château (where the capitol stood), is St. Lazare, or Lazarus Cathedral, having a fine crocketed spire, four quaintly carved pillars in the entrance, a good cheir, statues of President Jeaurin, &c. An ionic fountain adorns the place (square) in front. Other buildings are the priests' seminary, a large pile; the college and public library, having many rare books, a museum, &c.

The tower of Francis I. is a ruin; the ruins also of the roman theatre and amphitheatre are visible, inside the old walls (to the east) and traces of the naumachia (a hollow), lie without. On a hill to the south, called Champ des Wines, is the *Pierre de Couard*, a kind of stone pyramid, 72 feet by 59, and 65 high. A collection of above 3,000 roman coins is at the Mairie. Population 9,921. *Hotels*—De la Cloche (Bell); de la Poste; de la Ville de Lyon. Carpets, rough bed coverlets, &c. are made.

Conveyances, daily, to Chalons ;Dijon, Nevers (on Orleans rail).

ST. LEGER (31 kil.).

CHALONS (20 kil.) as in Route 24.

ROUTE 29.

Dijon to Dole, Poligny, Lons-le-Saulnier, Lausanne, Geneva.

Distance, 181 kil., or 112 miles.

DIJON, as in Route 24.

GENLIS (16 kil.), on the Tille.

AUXONNE (14 kil.), on the Saône, a military post of the fourth class, fortified by Vauban, 1675. Population, 4,700. It has an arsenal, barracks, powder magazine, &c.; and it was here that the sledges were made for Napoleon, when he carried his ordnance over the Great St. Bernard, in the winter of 1800.

[St. Jean de Losne (16 kil. south-west), an old village, in a green spot, down the Saône, where the Canal de Bourgogne falls in, and near the mouth of the Canal du Rhône au Rhin. It sustained a hard siege in 1636.

Seurre, 14 miles south-west of this, lower down the Saône, where it becomes navigable, has a population of 3,100, and a good trade in grain, wood, charcoal, &c.]

DÔLE (16 kil.), a sous-préfecture in department Jura, pleasantly situated on the Doubs, near the Canal du Rhône au Rhin, with some fine prospects round it. The streets are steep. It has remains of a roman amphitheatre and aqueduct, an old Hôtel de Ville, Vergy tower (near the prison), the college de l'Arc (which belonged to the Jesuits), a library of 6,000 vols., with a museum of paintings, by natives of Franche Comté, of which this town was the capital. It was given up to France in the time of Louis XIV. Iron and coal are found here.

Hotels—De Paris; de la Ville de Paris; du Commerce.

At 48 kil. east-north-east, is Besançon (*see* Route 30).

MONT-SOUS-VAUDREY (18 kil.), a pretty little place, where the road to Lausanne turns off (36 leagues, or about 90 miles, *viâ* Pontarlier, for which *see* Route 30).

[*Sallins*, on this road, 48 kil. from Mont-sous-Vaudrey, is a town of 7,000 souls, in a rocky gorge among the mountains, at the head of the Furieuse, and has been rebuilt since the great fire of 1825, by a contribution of two million francs from all parts of France. It is noted for the government salt works (salines), an immense pile above 900 feet long, where salt is boiled for the brine springs in the gypsum, which corresponds to the new red sandstone of Cheshire. There is a good trade in wine, wax, honey, and cheese. Mont Poupet, near it, is 2,490 feet above the sea.]

POLIGNY (19 kil.), a sous-préfecture, and the latin *Castrum Olinum*, at the head of the Golantine, in a gap under the Jura mountains, having several fountains and mills, a saltpetre work, part of an old fort, and of a roman way called Chemin Pavé. Population, 5,900. A little north of it is Arbois, where Pichegru was born.

Lons-le-Saulnier is 30 kil. south-west of Poligny (*see* Route 31).

[*Pierre* (30 kil. west), near the fine moated château of Thiard or Thyard, built 1672. It consists of two courts, and contains among other rooms, the cabinet de l'Empereur, in which are Napoleon's writing desk and bureau.]

CHAMPAGNOLE (22 kil.), in a pretty spot on the ascent of the Jura, under Mont Rivel, on the Ain, which turns mills for making wire, &c.

ST. LAURENT (28 kil.), at the top of the Jura range, has a douane or custom house, and an old castle commanding a wide prospect. *Hotel*—l'Ecu. Thence down to

MOREZ (12 kil.), in a narrow gorge of the Bienne, lined with mills and forges. Population, 3,200. Clock work, tourne-broches (jacks), pins, nails, cotton thread, &c., are made; and there is a good trade in Gruyère cheese, timber, wine, &c.

LES ROUSSES (3 kil.), on a lake near the Swiss frontier, in the highest part of the Jura mountains, which may be ascended for the prospect. The last French custom-house is here; and here also the rivers divide, some towards the North Sea, others towards the Mediterranean. Here the road turns off to Noyon, on the Lake of Geneva.

LA VATTAY or Lavatay (5 kil.), a small collection of chalets, from which there is a short cut towards Gex, through the narrow defile of *Monts Faucilles*, which brings you to the south side of the mountain, and all of a sudden discovers one of the *grandest prospects* in Europe, taking in the Lake of Geneva, Mont Blanc, part of Savoy, &c. The traveller must look out for this by all means; especially towards sunset.

GEX (15 kil)., a small sous-préfecture (in department Ain) of 2,900 souls, at the bottom of Mont St. Claude, on the Jornans, between the Jura mountains and lake of Geneva, of which it commands a fine view, as well as of the Alps, the Jura chain, &c. Gruyère cheese, watches, &c. are made. *Hotels*—De la Poste; des Etrangers; du Pont d'Arche.

[About 28 kil. to the west-north-west is *St. Claude*, another sous-préfecture (in department Jura), and a seat of a diocess, in a picturesque valley in the Jura range, where the Bienne and Tacon join. The cathedral is not remarkable. Many small articles in bone, ivory, wood, as well as buttons, musical instruments, nails, copper goods (quincaillerie), &c., are made. Population, 6,000. Round it are some objects worthy of notice, as the falls of Flumen and Queue du Cheval (*i.e.* Horse Tail), Foules cave, the intermittent springs of Noire Combe, the Pont de la Pile on the Ain, and the pass leading to Tour-du-Meix.—Sept-Moncel (12 kil.) is noted for its cheese, and manufacture of stone carvings.]

FERNEY, or FERNEY-VOLTAIRE (12 kil.), on the *Swiss* side, is a small village of watch-makers, on a beautiful part of the Geneva lake, formerly the residence of Voltaire, from 1759 to 1778. They shew his sitting-room and chamber; portraits of him, of Frederick the Great, Catherine II. (in tapestry, worked by herself), Franklin, &c.; also a pyramid (which once held his heart), set up by the Marquise de Villette, his adopted daughter, with the words '*Son esprit est partout, mais son cœur est ici*' (his spirit is every where, but his heart is here). The theatre is gone, but the church he built, 'Deo erexit Voltaire,' remains. Mont Blanc is in view.

At 6 kil. further is GENEVA, to which omnibuses run.

ROUTE 30.

Dole to Besançon (LAUSANNE, NEUFCHATEL), Beaume, Belfort (BASLE, STRASBOURG).

Distance (to Belfort) 146 kil., or 91 miles; to Lausanne about 120 miles; to Neufchâtel about 107 miles.

DOLE, as in Route 29.

ST WIT (28 kil.)

At 18 kil. further is

BESANÇON. *Hotels*—National; de Paris; de France. Chief town of department Doubs, a first class fortress, seat of the sixth military division, of a college, archbishopric, academy of sciences, &c. Population, 29,167. This fine old town, one of the strongest and best built in France, in the old province of Franche Comté, and the centre of its watch-making trade, is the *Vesontio* of Cæsar, on the Dubis, now the Doubs, which still surrounds it exactly as in his time, *ut circino circumductum, pene totum oppidum cingit* (girdling it nearly quite round, as if drawn with a pair of compasses). It stands in a fertile valley, bordered by vine-covered hills, strengthened by forts commanding the approaches. Upper Town, or La Ville, is the site of the old city where Vauban's citadel stands on a mass of rocks in the peninsula made by the river, over which an old bridge, resting on great piers, made by the Romans, crosses to the Lower Town. The streets are broad and well built, and the promenades ornamented by fountains; one of them is a nymph, with the water flowing from her breasts. Le Chaumars (Campus Martius) on the river, is the longest walk; another is the garden of Cardinal Granvelle's old palace. There are six gates.

La Porte Noire (Black Gate), is a roman triumphal arch, with two columns, and some statues left. There are also remains of an amphitheatre, baths, incriptions, &c. St. John's cathedral, of the eleventh century, has pictures by Vanloo (the Resurrection), Fra Bartolemeo (a St. Sebastian), Del Piombo (Death of Sapphira), and others. St. Madeleine's church has a fine portal, built 1830. St. James' was built 1707. At St. Francis Xavier's are several pictures.

Other buildings are the préfect's hôtel; the law college and its garden, founded by the Granvelles; the palais de justice, near the préfecture, built 1745-49; large caserne, or barracks; the salle de spectacle, with a doric portico of six pillars; public library of 50,000 vols. and some rare MSS.; the Musée Paris, founded by M. Paris, a native, having many coins, paintings, antiques; museum of natural history, and St. Jacques' hospital.

Cæsar calls it the first town of the *Sequani*, in Belgic Gaul. It was taken by Attila, fifth century; afterwards became part of Burgundy, and an imperial city, till given up to Spain, 1648, and to France (with Franche Comté), 1678.

Here Hecker and Struve organised their disastrous revolution of Baden in 1849. Among the natives are Charles Nodier, Victor Hugo, Suard, General Moncey, M. Droz, &c. Rev. M.M. Miroglio and Sandoz are French Protestant pastors here.

Manufactures of watch and clock-work, hats, druggets, carpets, coarse woollens, thread, yarn, &c. The canal from the Rhône to the Rhine passes by. Conveyances to D le, Dijon, Lyons, Monbéliard, Colmar, Strasbourg, Berne, Lausanne, Geneva, &c. In the neighbourhood are the château de Montfaucon, built by Louis XI.; and near Boussières, down the river, are the large caverns, or grottos, d'Oselles, 2,620 feet long.

From Besançon, on the road to Belfort, you pass

BEAUME-LES-DAMES (31 kil.), a pretty souspréfecture, on the Doubs, under five peaks of the Jura, on one of which is a ruined castle of the dukes of Burgundy, destroyed 1476.

[At Chaux-les-Passavant, 9 kil. south, is one of those remarkable subterranean glaciers which are met with in various parts of the Jura range.]

MONBELIARD (49 kil.) is a thriving place of 4,767 souls, in the fertile valley of the Allan, which is overlooked by a feudal tower; and is the birth-place of the great *Cuvier*. Watchmaking, &c., are carried on. *Hotels*—Du Lion d'Or (Golden Lion); de la Balance.

At 20 kil. is Belfort (*see* Route 27), on the road to Basle, Colmar, and Strasbourg.

(a) From Besançon, on the hilly road to Lausanne, you pass

Ornans (27 kil.), in the picturesque valley of the Loue, which is crossed by two bridges. To the north-west, on a high point, stands the old castle of the dukes of Burgundy. Paper and cherry brandy (kirsch-wasser) are made here, and cheese like the Gruyère. Population, 2,982. There is a broken fall, called Syratu, nearly 600 feet down altogether. In the neighbourhood are the grottos of la Brème, Beaumarchais, Bonnevaux, &c.

La Grange d'Aleine (16 kil.), has near it, on the left, the source of the Loue, issuing out of a cave, in a precipice 340 feet high.

Pontarlier (17 kil.), a border town and sous-préfecture, of 4,707 population, under the second chain of the Jura mountains, at a height of 2,700 feet above sea, is well built, and has a college, barracks, Hôtel de Ville, library, &c.; with manufactures of iron, paper, tools, leather, wormwood, &c. General d'Arçon, who made the floating batteries at the siege of Gibraltar, was born here. *Hotels*—Des Voyageurs; National, &c. Conveyances to Lausanne and Neufchâtel (in Switzerland), passing *Fort de Joux* (4 kil.), near the defile of La Cluse, on a precipice about 640 feet high, where Mirabeau and the unfortunate Toussaint l'Ouverture were confined. Neufchâtel, on that lake, is 16½ leagues (about 66 kil.) to the north-east, down the picturesque Val Travers.

[The Doubs rises under Mont Rixon, in the Jura range, 3,120 feet above the sea, and about 30 kil. south-south-west of Pontarlier. —At 25 kil. north-east of this town, near Mórteau, in a rocky defile, only 32 feet wide, it tumbles over a fine fall, called the *Saut-de-Doubs*, about 86 feet down.]

About 25 kil. and 4 Swiss posts further, *viâ* Jougne and Orbe, is Lausanne, on the lake of Geneva.

ROUTE 31.

Chalons-sur-Saone to Lons-le-Saulnier and Geneva.

Distance, about 154 kil. or 96 miles.

Chalons, as in Route 24.

Louhans (about 25 kil.), a sous-préfecture of 3,800 people, in a fertile plain, on the Seille, with a good trade in corn, poultry, &c., and manufacture of iron. The houses are old, and there are traces of roman possession. *Hotel*—Du Cheval-Blanc (White Horse).

[Cuiseaux, 32 kil. south-east of it, among the Jura mountains, has a large church, with many eccentric carvings about it.]

At 27 kil. further is

Lons-le-Saulnier. *Hotels*—Du Chapeau Rouge (Red Hat); Jacquinot; Robert; &c. Population 8,500. Capital of department Jura, (formerly in province of Franche Comté), in a hollow or gorge of the Jura mountains, covered with vineyards, is noted for its salt springs, which were worked by the Romans, from whence it received its name, *Ledo Salinarius*. The ground is so undermined that there are few large buildings. The church is on Place d'Armes, which has a fountain and a pedestal, which till 1830 bore a statue of Pichegru. Covered galleries or arcades line the principal street, which is lit with gas. There are a college, a library of 3,000 volumes, a museum, theatre, &c. General Lecourbe was born here. At the north end of the town, near the old castle of Montmorot, are the Puits des Salines (salt springs), rising into a great pit 65 feet deep, whence the brine is carried by pumps and wooden gutters to vast buildings for filtering and boiling it. About 20,000 quintals (of 100 lbs. each) are made. There is a good trade also in iron, wood, wine, eaux-de-vie, Gruyère cheese, &c.

Conveyances to Châlons, Maçon, Bourg, Lyons, Dôle, Besançon, Dijon, Geneva, &c. In the neighbourhood are, the old abbey of Baume-les-Messieurs under the fine Roches de Baume, the very old church of Coldre near a well preserved roman camp, the château du Pin where Henry IV. once stayed, the château d'Arlay which belonged to the Prince d'Aremberg, and the fall of Poitte (15 kil.) on the Ain (about 53 feet down).

From Lons-le-Saulnier, on the road to Geneva, you pass Clairvaux (23 kil.) at the bottom of a pretty valley, near a lake.

St. Laurent (26 kil.) is the next place, (*see* Route 29), beyond which is Geneva.

ROUTE 32.

Macon to Bourg, Nantua, Geneva, and Chambery.

Distance, to Geneva, 149 kils. or 93 miles; to Chambéry, 128 kils, or 79 miles.

Macon, as in Route 24.

LOGIS-NEUF (16 kil).

At 16 kil. beyond is

BOURG, or Bourg-en-Bresse. *Hotels*—Du Palais; de l'Europe; du Nord; du Griffin. Population 10,500.

The chief town of department Ain (formerly La Bresse), in a fine spot on the Reyssouse, was founded in the thirteenth century by the dukes of Savoy, and given up to France 1350. It is on the whole well built; having some fountains, one of which is to the memory of General Joubert; a statue of Bichat the surgeon, by David, in the Bastion promenade; Nôtre Dame church, in the gothic and renaissance styles; the Hôtel de Ville; the halle au blé (corn market), a circular building; public library of 19,000 volumes; college or school; museum of antiquities; and a large hospital outside the town. Near the last is the fine church of *Brou*, built in the fifteenth century by Margaret of Austria, whose motto 'Fortune, fortune, fortune' is repeated all over it. It contains many specimens of arabesque and other carvings, stained windows, and tombs of the dukes of Savoy, whose castle was at Bourg, besides eight or nine religious houses. Lalande the astronomer was born here.

Manufactures of linens, cotton thread, silk stockings, leather; and a trade in wine, corn, live stock. Good poultry is got here.

Conveyances to Lyons, Besançon, Maçon, Châlons, Strasbourg, St. Claude, and Geneva.

From Bourg, on the road to Geneva, you pass

PONT-D'AIN (20 kil.) under a mountain, which has a castle of the dukes of Savoy on it.

CERDON (13 kil.) under precipitous mountains, is near the fine fall of Marcelin, close to the old castles of Labatie and St. Julien; and not far from the great fall of the river Fogue in a wild spot.

NANTUA (19 kil.) a sous-préfecture, &c., of 3,701 souls, on a lake between the mountains in the Jura chain, having a lombard church, where Charles the Bold was buried. Fine trout are caught in the lake. Trade in shoes, muslins, woollens, tapes, thread, &c. *Hotels*—Du Nord; de l'Ecu (Crown-piece); d' Angleterre.

BELLEGARDE (25 kil.) at the Swiss border, is among the rocks on the Rhône where the Valserine joins it. Every one coming into France is strictly searched here by the custom-house officers

At 40 kil. further is Geneva.

(*a*) From Bourg, on the road to Lyons and Chambéry, you pass

PONT D'AIN (20 kil.) as above, where the road to Lyons, parts off by

MEXIMIEUX (22 kil.) a town of 2,300 souls, with a good trade.

[About 12 kil. east of it, across the Rhône, at Balme, is the large and curious grotto of Nôtre Dame.]

At 35 kil. beyond it, past Montluel, is Lyons (*see* Route 24).

ST. RAMBERT (21 kil. from Pont d'Ain) is on the Albarine, among mountains, with 2,600 souls, employed in the manufacture of linens, damasks, silks, velvet, and paper. A pass 20 kil. long leads between steep cliffs on both sides, on to

BELLEY (33 kil.) a sous-préfecture and bishopric, on the Furan near the Rhône, which is crossed by a suspension bridge for the high road into Italy across the frontier. It was rebuilt after a fire in 1385 by the dukes of Savoy, and given up to France with the district of Bugey 1609. The cathedral has two pillars of a temple to Cybele, and a good clock tower. Le Camus the friend of St. Francis de Sales held the diocess. There are a public library, Abbé Greppo's cabinet of medals, &c., and the college where Lamartine was educated. *Hotels*—Loyola; Tissot. Several lakes, grottos, mountains, &c., are in the neighbourhood.

At 22 kil. further is Chambéry in SAVOY; where the projected rail from Lyons and Grenoble will pass on to Turin.

ROUTE 33.

Lyons to St. Etienne, Montbrison, Roanne.

By railway, 140 kil., or 87½ miles; four trains daily, in about two hours.

Starting from Perrache you pass over the Saône, at Mulatière bridge, to Pullins (2 miles); Trigny (4½ miles); Vernaison (1¾ miles); La Tour (¾ mile); Grigny (1¼ miles); Givors (3 miles); all of which lie on the Rhône, and are described in Route 24. The railway turns off here to

BUREL (5¾ miles); Gouzon (2¼ miles).

RIVE-DE-GIER (1½ miles), a manufacturing town of 12,000 souls, on the Gier, where the canal to Givors ends in a large basin, is at the middle of the best coal field in France. They make glass, steel, machinery, railway carriages, silk, &c. here. Some distance to the right, at Champonost, are to be seen as many as 90 arches (?) of a roman aqueduct. The next stations are

GRANDECROIX (2½ miles), and

ST. CHAMOND (3¾ miles), under a cultivated hill, where the Janon joins the Gier. Population, 8,300. It is well built, and has two churches, a college and library, public baths, and a ruined château, with many foundries, cotton and silk mills. Ribbons, lace, nails, copper goods, &c. are made. *Hotels*—Du Chapeau Rouge (Red Hat); la Tête d'Or (Gold Head). Many fossil plants, of the usual tropical character, are found in the coal mines.

TERRENOIRE (4¼ miles); then through a tunnel of 4,900 feet, to St. Etienne (2½ miles).

St. Etienne. *Hotels*—Du Nord; de France; de la Poste; de l'Europe; de Milan (on Grande Place); de la Paix (Peace). Population, 46,100, or 60,000 with the suburbs. (In 1804 it was only 24,000.) A sous-préfecture in department Loire, on the Furens, with little to recommend it beyond its manufactures of fire-arms, tools, cutlery, hardware, and ribbons, which are some of the most important in France. It stands on a rich bed of coal and iron, and the river turns above a hundred factories of various sorts. Gr ndstones are quarried in the neighbourhood, of the white sandstone of which the houses are built. The Hôtel de Ville, in the Grande Place, is a large pile, including the bourse (exchange), chamber of commerce (conseil de prud'hommes), museum of minerals and practical arts, and a bibliothéque of 5,000 volumes. The church is of the eleventh century. There are bridges, a school of mines, a college, the government gum factory, a salle de spectacle (theatre), gas works, &c. The ribbons are of great beauty, and worth upwards of 45 million francs yearly. About half-a-million tons of coal are exported.

Conveyances: by railway to Lyons in 2¼ hours, four times a day; Roanne in 4 hours (twice); Montbrison in 1 hour (twice). By coach to Marseilles (25 hours), Le Puy, Clermont, Valence, &c. A branch railway (20 kil. long), for goods, coal, &c., goes from St. Etienne to Andrezieux.

[Across the ridge dividing the basins of the Loire and Rhône lies

Bourg-Argental (28 kil. south-east), which stands in the valley of the Deune, under an old castle, and is noted for its white silk.

Annonay (*see* Route 24) is 15 kil. further.]

From St. Etienne, on the railway to Montbrison and Roanne (a succession of inclined planes only), you pass

LA RENARDIERE (11½ mls), St. Galmier (3¾ mls).

MONTROND (5½ miles), a little place on the Seine, 15 kil. from Montbrison (to which there is a coach), having the ruins of an old castle, with another called Bellegarde not far off.

[MONTBRISON. *Hotels*—Du Nord; du Centre; du Midi (the South). Population, 6,000. All the trains stop at Montrond for this town (fare 1 franc), *viâ* which there is a correspondence with Clermont (*see* Route 52). It was chosen for the capital of department Loire, on account of being near the middle of it, and stands on the Vizezy, under a volcanic rock, which carries some remains of a castle built by the counts of Forey, and gives name to the place. The old town walls are gone; it is ill built; the only edifice worth notice being Notre Dame cathedral *Church*, founded 1205, by Guy IV., Comte de Forey, whose marble effigy, with a lion at the feet, is inside. It is a plain gothic building, having but one tower completed, and a lofty vault. St. Maurice church has a dome. The préfecture belonged to the brethren of the Oratory; a library of 15,000 volumes is at the college. There are a corn market, a salle de spectacle, barracks, a hospice, &c. Charles VII. signed a treaty here with the Duke of Savoy. It was ravaged by the Calvinist leader, the Baron des Adrets, 1562. In the neighbourhood are three mineral springs, on the river, one called the Hospital being the most useful.

Conveyances to Lyons, Roanne, St. Etienne, Clermont-Ferrand, &c.

About 2 kil. south of Montbrison, at *Moignt*, is a round building, about 130 feet diameter, faced with pilasters, and commonly called the palace of the Saracens. It is supposed to be the site of the roman *Mediodunum*. Further south (21 kil. from Montbrison), is St. Bonnet-le-Château, near Agrippa's roman way, on the top of a hill, where stood the camp of Varus, afterwards styled Château-Vair.]

FEURS (7½ miles), on the Loire, is the old capital of *Forrez* and the site of the roman *Forum Secfusianorum* of which traces are seen in parts of the church, a mosaic, &c. in a house hard by, besides parts of columns, aqueducts, &c. There is a bronze statue to Colonel Combes, who fell at Constantine, in Algiers. Population 2,900. Mont Lezore, a basalt hill, is near

BALBIGNY (5¾ miles); then come Neulize (6¼ miles), on a double inclined plane; St. Symphorien de Lay (3 miles), which has parts of its old walls, and cotton factories; and L' Hospital (4½ miles); and at length the terminus at

ROANNE (5 miles), the roman *Rhodumna*, and a sous-préfecture in department Loire, on that river, with 13,000 people, and a good trade by water and rail in wines (called Renaison, St. André, &c.), cotton, grain, iron, charcoal, and other products. It has a good bridge over the Loire, a large church, baths, a theatre, and a library of 10,000 vols. at the college. Conveyances to Moulin, Clermont, &c.

ROUTE 34.

Lyons to Chambery (GRANDE CHARTREUSE), Grenoble (TURIN), Gap, Digne, Cannes, Nice (and GENOA).

Distance to Grenoble 98 kil., or 61 miles; to Nice, about 422 kil., or 262 miles.

LYONS, as in Route 24.

BRON (10 kil.), in department Isère; and St. Laurent des Mures (8 kil.), a village of 1,200 people, so called after the mulberry trees here.

LA VESPILLIERE (11 kil.), in a pretty spot, with an old château.

BOURGOIN (12 kil.), on the Bourbre, where the road to Chambéry turns off, has 4,400 souls, and manufacturers of cotton, linen, paper, leather, &c.

[From Bourgoin, on the way to Chambéry, you pass

LA TOUR DU PIN (15 kil.), a sous-préfecture with 2,700 people, on the Bourbre, with a trade in wine, grain, leather, &c.

GAZ (8 kil.), where the road from Grenoble and Voreppe crosses the Rhône towards Belley on the other side of it.

PONT DE BEAUVOISIN (10 kil.), on the Guiers, which is covered by a single-arched bridge, with the French and Savoy douanes at the ends. Population, 3,800 (part in both countries). The Chaille pass leads on by Les-Echelles-de-Savoie (15 kil.), St. Thibault-de-Cour, (12 kil.), Chambéry (12 kil.), and over Mont Cenis to Turin, in ITALY. At Les Echelles-de-Savoie there is a way south to St. Laurent-du-Pont, from which the Chartreuse may be visited (*see* Route 34*a*).]

From Bourgoin, as above, on the Grenoble road, you pass

ECLOSE (11 kil.), near which the road from Valence fall in.

LA FRETTE (15 kil.), where the fierce Huguenot leader, the Baron des Adrets, was born and where he died.

RIVES (13 kil.), on the Furens, at the edge of a pretty valley, where manufactures of linen, paper, iron, steel, are carried on. Population 2,420. Château d' Alivette is near. Soon after this, you come into a beautiful part of the Isère, called the valley of Grésivaudan, richly cultivated.

VOREPPE (14 kil.), where sand for glass, &c. is got, and where conveyances are taken for Grande Chartreuse, which turns off here (*see* Route 34*a* below). Population 3,100. At 12 kil. further is

Grenoble. *Hotels*—Des Trois Dauphins (in Rue Montorge), where they show the room in which Napoleon lodged on his return from Elba, when the garrison of 7,000 men joined him; des Ambassadeurs; de l'Europe, in Place Grenette. Table d' hôte 3 fr., déjeuner à la fourchette (meat breakfast), 2 fr. *Cafés*, Mabout, in Place Grenette; Mille Colonnes. Population, 29,000.

An ancient fortified town, chief place of department Isère, head of a diocess, and of a military division, finely seated on the rapid Isère (which cuts it in two), under a hilly ridge 900 feet above sea, called Mont Rachel. The best view of it is from this ridge, which commands also a propect of 30 leagues, and even of Mont Blanc. The Drac joins the Isère, near the town. The old province of Dauphiné, of which it was the capital, took its name from the *dolphin* or Dauphin, borne in the arms of its old counts and their successors, the eldest sons of the reigning kings.

It was called Cularo by the Romans, till the Emperor Gratian changed it to *Gratianopolis*, whence the present name is derived. The oldest part is St. Laurent on the north bank, where the old wall stood, below the ridge just mentioned, which carries the new citadel on it, enclosing a piece of the old Bastille. Two bridges (one a suspension bridge) join this to the Bonne or largest half on the south side, which has some good houses (on the quays) and streets; in general, the streets are narrow. It has seven gates, with many fountains; and is lit with gas.

Among the promenades and objects worth notice, are Place Grenette; Place Notre Dame, and its cathedral, a gothic structure of no mark; Place St. André, containing a bronze statue of the famous Bayard, and a church which held the tombs of the Dauphins, whose old gothic palace is now the palais de justice, opposite; the cours, towards Pont de Chaix; the Porte de France; and the public gardens (with a figure of Hercules), near the quai and the préfecture, which belonged to the Constable Lesdiguières. The crypt of St. Laurent's church, which dates from the sixth century, is in that quarter. At the bishop's palace is another (?) room, once occupied by Buonaparte. The college or high school, the public library of 60,000 vols. and 600 MSS, are in the same building with the museum, which besides pictures, minerals, &c., has statues of Condillac, Mably, Vaucanson, who were all natives, as were Casimer Perier, Barnave, Rollin (?); as well as one of Bayard 'le chevalier sans peur et sans reproche' (the knight without fear or stain) who was born near here. There are an artillery school, schools of medicine, &c., two priests' seminaries, theatre, &c. The fortifications as planned by Vauban and General Haxo, render this frontier town a place of great strength. It is liable to inundations in wet seasons. Rev. M. Fermaud is protestant pastor here.

Manufacturers of good gloves, cottons, cheese, liqueurs, leather; and a trade in marbles, fir timber, walnut tree (for furniture), &c. Two citizens here, in the year 1853, invented a machine which sews gloves perfectly, and is likely to produce a complete revolution in glove-making. Hitherto the manufacturers have not been able to supply the demand for want of workmen.

Conveyances to Lyons, Valence, Marseilles, Gap, Briançon, Aix, Turin, Nice, Chambéry, &c. Several excursions may be taken from this point, among which are that to Sassenage (10 kil. west), a charming spot among hills, woods, and waterfalls, with large grottoes; to Grande Chartreuse (*see* Route 34*a*); also the valleys up and down the Isère, Drac, &c., the mineral springs of Uriage (10 kil. east-south-east, near an old château), Allevard (30 kil. in a fine spot), de la Motte, and Bayard's château.

[From Grenoble, on the road to Chambéry you pass (by the old roman way, up the Isère), Lumbin (20 kil.). Fort Barraux (about 16 k.), a frontier post on the Isère, to defend the pass. Opposite it, on the right or east bank of the river, are remains of *Bayard's Château*; they stand on a height, and include the court, terraces, stables, &c., and the room where the hero was born, 1476.—Allevard, not far from this, is noted for its iron and steel works.—Chafareillan (4 kil.) has a custom-house.—At 15 kil. further, is Chambéry, in SAVOY. By this pass, or by Mont Genèvre, it is thought, Hannibal invaded Italy, 218 B. C.]

From Grenoble, on the direct road to Marseilles, you pass (by a hilly route)

VIF (16 kil.); Monestier de Clermont (18 kil.); Lalley (31 kil); Croix Haute (11 kil.); Serres (15 kil.); to Sisteron (33 kil.), on the road from Gap to Marseilles (*see* Route 24).

From Grenoble, on the road to Gap (87 kil.) and Nice, you pass (up the Drac, with Claix and its single-arched bridge of 140 feet on the right, and the mineral waters of St. Martin d'Uriage on the left) to

VIZILLE (18 kil.) an old military station on the Romanche, with a château built 1610-20, by the Constable Lesdiguières, nearly burnt, 1825, but since restored by the family of Casimir Périer, the French statesman, who have established a print factory in it. Here the States of Dauphiné met, 21st July, 1788, to address Louis XVI. previous to the revolution. Population, 3,100.

LAFFREY, or Lafrey (7 kil.) is near the spot where the troops sent from Grenoble to capture Bonaparte on his way to Paris, 1815, came over to him, upon his crying out 'If any one wishe to kill his emperor, let him fire,' at the same time opening his breast to them, as represented in the well-known picture of this scene. Labedoyère (who was shot for it), joined him soon after. All this road is full of recollections of his march.

LA MURE (14 kil.), a village of 3,500 nailmakers, &c.

SOUCHONS (11 kil.) in a deep valley, near Mont

Aigistie, which is 6,560 feet above sea level, and strikingly shaped.

[To the east is *La Salette* mountain, noted in the present day for a pretended appearance of the Virgin Mary, in September, 1846. She shewed herself, they say, to two shepherd children of the country, on a rock, now marked by the prints of her feet, and by a 'miraculous' spring, the water of which is sold to pilgrims, who flock here, and for whose use a chapel has been built. This trade, however, having interfered with the claims of Notre Dame de Fourvières, &c., the dignitaries of Lyons and Gap have pronounced against it.]

Corps (14 kil.), and La Ginguette-de-Boyer (14 kil.). At 23 kil. further is

Gap. *Hotels*—Du Nord; de Provencé. Population, 8,800. The chief town of department Hautes-Alpes, seat of a diocess, &c., in the old province of Dauphiné, was the roman *Vapincum*, afterwards the capital of Gapençoise, which belonged first to the Counts of Forcalquier, then to the bishops. It stands on the Bonne and Laye, about 2,400 feet above sea, in a fertile hollow, among hills; some bare, others covered with vineyards. The streets are narrow and poor. It has a small gothic cathedral, a protestant chapel, priests' seminary, library and museum, good barracks, a cistern against fire, and the marble effigy (by Richier), of the Constable Lesdiguières (who was born at St. Bonnet, on the Drac), at the préfecture. Napoleon stopped here on his way from Elba. Farel, the reformer, was born at Fareau or Farel (12 kil.) to the north of this, on the Buzon, under Bayard's mountain. A few cottons and linens are made, and a trade carried on in grain, cattle, wine, leather.

Conveyances to Embrun, Briançon, Grenoble, Aix, Marseilles, Nice (237 kil.), &c.

From Gap, on the road to Digne and Marseilles, you pass

La Saulce (17 kil.) on the Durance, with a mineral spring.

Sisteron (30 kil.), an ancient place and sous-préfecture, at the bottom of a narrow pass, commanding the valleys of the Durance and the Buech (which join here), and the old way into Provence. It was the roman *Secustero*, and was sacked 1562. It is walled in, and defended by a citadel on a high rock, near the bridge; on another is perched the faubourg of La Baume. It has an old church, a college, and a pretty walk near the Porte d'Aix. Population, 4,400. *Hotel*—Du Bras d'Or (Golden Arm).

The road to Marseilles parts off to the right. At 40 kil. to the left you come to

Digne. *Hotels*—Du Petit Paris; du Grand Paris; des Empereurs. Population, 5,000. The roman *Dina* or *Dinia*, capital of department Basses-Alpes, in Dauphiné, seat of a bishopric, &c., on the Bléone, which runs swiftly by to the Durance. The oldest part, with its narrow steep streets, is on a rock, below which is the Boulevard Gassendi (so called after Gassendi, born in this neighbourhood), where the best houses are placed, with a fountain; another is in Cours des Arrêts Notre Dame church is above the town, near the prison. The préfecture was the bishop's palace; other buildings are the library of 3,000 volumes, college, seminary, barracks, theatre, &c. Some remains of the old cathedral, with traces of wall painting, are on the Barcelonnette road (to the north). About 2 kil. off are some mineral springs, useful in rheumatism, paralysis, &c. The Bignolles prunes are grown round this place.

Conveyances to Marseilles, Avignon, Toulon, Nice (150 kil.), &c.

From Digne, on the road to Draguignan, you pass

Barreme (29 kil.).

[About 30 kil. to the left is Annot, and its grottoes, near the Savoy border.]

Castellane (25 kil.), an old town and sous-préfecture in department Basses-Alpes, in a defile of the mountains, on the Verdon, which is crossed by a bold one-arched bridge. The cliffs on which Notre Dame chapel stands, have a noble view of the Mediterranean. Parts of the ancient walls are left.

[Grasse (*see* below) is 52 kil. to the south-east, on the direct road to Nice.]

Camps (16 kil.); and 25 kil. further is

Draguignan. *Hotels*—De la Poste; Roquemaure. Population, 8,800. A small town, the capital of department Var, in the old province of Dauphiné, founded in the fifth century, and standing on the Pis, or Nartubie, under Malmont hill, in a fertile plain bordered by an amphitheatre of hills covered with vines and olives. The climate is soft and healthy; the walks around are beautiful. Before the revolution it had several convents, and the palace of the bishop of Frejus. At present the buildings worth notice are the square clock-tower on the hill, the hospital in a pretty situation, the palais de justice, and the fountains; there are also a library of 15,000 volumes, a museum of medals and pictures, and a well-planted botanic garden. Trade in olive oil, woollens, leather, stockings, pottery, soap, fruit, spirits, wine, wax, &c. Good stone is quarried.

Conveyances, daily, to Toulon, Aix, Marseilles, Antibes, Nice, &c.

From Draguignan, on the road to Nice, you pass

LE MUY (12 kil.), which is near some granitic rocks, with chapels on them, but is noted for a castle, where some Provençal gentlemen conspired to take Charles V. at the head of his army. They smashed his coach with a machine, but were all killed, the emperor escaping on horse-back.

FREJUS (15 kil.), the seat of a diocess, in a pleasant open spot near the mouth of the Argius, on the Mediteranean, was the *Forum Julii* (whence the name comes) of Augustus Cæsar, who made it a colony for the third legion, and the station for the fleet taken at Actium. Its decay was completed by the ravages of the Saracens, &c., and the filling of the port.

St. Etienne's norman cathedral of the twelfth century has some roman stones in it, and an eight-sided bapistery on granite pillars: the bishop's house is gothic. Various proofs of the ancient importance of Frejus are left; among these are—parts of the walls; an oval circus of stone and brick (about 650 feet round); and the Porte Dorée or gold gate which led to the harbour (another was called Cæsar's gate, and there were two besides), where a quay or mole may be traced, and two granite posts and a pharos or lighthouse are seen. The harbour was about 1,600 feet square, but is now a swamp, with an étang or pool in the midst; a canal of 2,500 yards led down to the sea. An aqueduct on one and sometimes two rows of arches, 18 or 20 miles long, brought water from the Siagne to the north-east, to the port and town; parts of it still exist. At Villeneuve farm (2 kil.) are remains of a temple; another to Diana, stood on Estérel hill. In some rocks, overlooking the sea, is the grotto of St. Honorat, founder of St. Serin's abbey. An italian patois is spoken.

At St. Raphael's fishing village, to the south-east (2 kil.), near St. Tropez, Napoleon landed from Egypt October, 1799, and here he embarked for Elba 1814; he would have landed here in 1815 but for the wind. Julius Agricola (the father-in-law of Tacitus), and Abbé Siéyes the constitution maker, were born here. *Hotels*—Du Midi; de la Poste. Population, 3,200.

L'ESTEREL or L'Estrelle (14 kil.) is near the sea, under the range of broken porphyry hills called les Maures (after the Saracens or Moors), which shelter this part like Undercliff in the Isle of Wight, and contribute to the softness of the climate. They are covered with cork, arbutus, and other trees; "and exhibit all the grandeur of the Alps with all the beauty of cultivation, every variety of prospect, hill and dale, and wood and rock, and the distant sea."

CANNES (19 kil.), a pretty port under the hills, on a bay of the Mediteranean, near which (marked by a pillar) Napoleon landed 1st March, 1815, from Elba, with his little army of 800. It stands on the site of *Oxibia*, which the Saracens destroyed. The quay is planted, and the old church is perched on a rock near an old gothic château. Lord Brougham's seat, Villa Louise, stands in a fine, dusty spot, among orange, citron, and other trees. There are gardens of heliotrope, hyacinth, and other sweet smelling flowers. Trade in perfumery, sardines, anchovies, fruit, wine, oil. *Hotels*—De la Poste; du Midi Pinchinat (near the sea).

In front of the bay are the well-wooded Iles de Sérins, including Ste Marguerite, with a tower in which Richelieu confined the man with the Iron mask (an Italian named Matthioli; his mask was really velvet), and St. Honorat, in which are a tower (commanding a noble view), chapels, kitchens, the refectory, &c., of an abbey founded by St. Honorat, bishop of Arles, in 410.

[At 16 kil. to the left is *Grasse* (90 kil. east of Draguignan), an ancient town and sous-préfecture in department Var, among gardens of oranges, lemons, roses, and scented flowers, with a population of 11,300 souls, who distil essences, make perfumery, &c., and trade in organgine, liqueurs, soap, olive oil, fruit, marble. Some say it was founded by Crassus, others by a Jewish colony from

Sardinia, in 585. Napoleon bivouacked hard by on the rock of Ribes (near the fall) on his way to Paris, 1815. There are beautiful prospects, especially from the obelisk in Place du Cours, taking in the Alps and the Mediterranean, as far as Corsica (90 miles). The church is large but plain, with an old gothic tower near it; in the chapel to the hospital are three pictures by Rubens; the library contains 6,500 vols.; the salle de spectacle is modern. Traces of a palace built by Jeanne, countess of Provence, are seen; besides a roman tower (?) near the Hôtel de Ville, and St. Hilaire's old chapel.

Hotels—De la Poste; des Ministres.

Mons, 18 kil. west-north-west of this, has a remarkable grotto, with many winding passages in it.]

ANTIBES (12 kil.), the next place to the Piedmont frontier, is a port and military station, in a fine spot under the Maritime Alps, with a jetty made by Vauban. This was the first place summoned by Napoleon, when he landed from Elba; and failing to win over the commander, he struck into the country over the hills, towards Gap. It was planted by the greek colonists of Marseilles, like many other towns along this beautiful shore, and used by the Romans. It has a church on the site of Diana's temple, two roman towers, traces of a roman theatre, an inscription at the corner of a street, a marble fountain with Louis XIVth's name on it, and a pillar to Louis XVIII. Flowers of all kinds are grown for essences and perfumery, in which there is a trade, as well as in wine, olive oil, oranges, figs, fruit, tobacco, fish, &c *Hotel*—De l'Aigle d'Or. Population 5,000.

At 22 kil. further you come to the custom-house of St. Laurent-du-Var, at the bridge (262 feet long) over the Var, which divides France and Piedmont.

NICE, 2 miles beyond, in ITALY, is a town of 30,000 souls, where many English spend the winter. From this it is about 70 leagues to Genoa, and about the same distance to Turin.

ROUTE 34*a*.

Grenoble to Grande Chartreuse.

GRENOBLE as in Route 34, from Lyons.

VOREPPE (12 kil.), in the same route, where the way to La Grande Chartreuse turns off. It takes about six hours to reach it, by mule, which may be hired for 5 fr. there and back.

Passing through the valley, covered with fir, &c. on one side, you come to La Placette (1½ hours); then to St. Laurent du Pont (1¾ hours), about half-way from Voreppe (10 miles), on the little mountain stream of Guiers-Mort, up which the road lies. At Fourvoirie (½ hour), the pass suddenly narrows at a rustic bridge, thrown across the stream. A gateway leads on to the rugged path made by the monks through this defile, which is lined by cliffs several hundred feet high, covered with trees, and is so narrow and obscure that you can hardly see the sun, the river all the while foaming at the bottom. After Pont Peraut bridge (3½ hours) is crossed, you come to a second gateway. and a pointed rock called the Aillette or Aiguillette, from which the pass widens up to the spot where the monastery stands in a circle of forests and irregular peaks, 4,270 feet above the sea.

La Grande Chartreuse (1½ miles), the head of that monkish order (of which Charter House in London was a branch), was founded in 1084, by St. Bruno, from the mistaken notion that he would find purity of heart and love to God and man, in flying from his duty to society to a life of useless contemplation. The present pile is of a much later date, an irregular collection of high-roofed buildings. One long gallery leads to the general's apartments, church, kitchen, refectory, &c.; another to the cloisters, chapter-house, and cells for about sixty brethren and servitors. Higher up the stream is a chapel, which was St. Bruno's cell. The monks dress in white or brown; they take one meal a-day, with a light supper, alone, but on sundays and holidays they meet in the refectory, one reading while the others eat.

Strangers are kindly treated, and may find eggs, fish, fruit, and sweetmeats, with a good bed, for which it is usual to give them 4 francs a-day; women being lodged outside the precincts. They make excellent vegetable elixir and eau de melisse, distilled from the plants around; also tooth-powder, and mineral paste called boule d'acier. You come back on the same road, or round to Grenoble, by Sapey, in six hours.

ROUTE 35.

Grenoble to Valence,

DOWN THE ISERE.

Distance, 92 kil., or 57 miles.

GRENOBLE, as in Route 34.

VOREPPE (12 kil.), in the same route, where the way to GrandeChartreuse turns off (as above, Route 34*a*.) The road to Valence is direct to Tullins (12 kil.), or else through Rives (13 kil.), on the Fure or Fures.

TULLINS (14 kil.), in a rich valley, where various manufactures flourish. Population 5,000.

ST. MARCELLIN (22 kil.), a sous-préfecture, with a population of 3,450, on the Isère, in a fine country.

LES FAURIS (14 kil.), where a road turns off by the suspension-bridge over the Isère, on to Pont en Royans, so called after a bridge, said to be roman, thrown across the torrent of the Bourne.

ROMANS (12 kil.), in a pretty spot on the Isére, across which is a bridge to Péage. It was founded in the ninth century, and has parts of its old walls left, with a church of the tenth century. Here Humbert II., the last native dauphin, made over his dominions to Philippe of France, 1349. Population 10,000. Tanning in various shapes is the chief employment, and it is also noted for its wine, truffles, liqueurs, &c.

[About 16 miles to the south-east, is the castle of La Chartronnière, in the beautiful alpine valley of St. Jean en Royans.]

At 18 kil. further is Valence, on the Rhône (*see* Route 24); and Tournons is about as far off, but higher up the river.

ROUTE 36.

Grenoble to Briançon and Turin.

Distance to Briançon, about 110 k., or 68 miles.

GRENOBLE, as in Route 34. From this, you pass by Bonaparte's noble mountain road into Italy, (begun 1804, and now completed).

VIZILLE (18 kil.), as in Route 34; then

LIVET (5 leagues), on the Romanche.

BOURG D'OYSANS (2½ leagues), on the same river, in a rich mountain valley, has 3,400 people and is near Mont de Lens.

[Up the valley of the Veneon, to the south-east, past St. Christophe and La Bérande, brings you to Mont Alle-Freide or *Mont Pelvoux*, the highest peak in France, 14,000 feet above the sea, and covered with glaciers.]

The road goes on through the wild and deep alpine passes of Infernets and Malval (through a tunnel of 234 yards in one place), to

GRAVE-EN-OYSANS (6 leagues), near several falls.

VILLARS OR VILLARD D'ARENE (1 league), near another deep pass of the Romanche, and at the bottom of the

COL DE LAUTERET (1 league), a pass which is 6,850 feet above the sea, commanding a fine prospect. It has good pasture, and near the top stands the small hospice of the Madeleine, founded for the benefit of travellers in the eleventh century, by the Dauphin Humbert II.

LE LAUZET (1 league).

MONESTIER (2 leagues), in a fertile valley on the Guisanne (one of the heads of the Durance,) has some excellent warm sulphur springs, which are used in the season. Population 2,600.

BRIANÇON (4 leagues), a sous-préfecture in department Hautes-Alpes, and a very strong military frontier town of the first-class, on the Durance, where the Guisanne and Clarée join it, stands (about 5,900 feet above the sea), in an amphitheatre of heights, crowned with seven forts, the highest of which is 2,300 feet above the lower ones. Zig-zag ways lead to them, and they communicate by tunnelled galleries. A triple line of walls surround it; the streets are very steep and irregular; a bridge of 130 feet span crosses the deep bed of the Clairée, built 1634. It was the roman *Brigantium Vians*, and forms the key of France on this side of the Alps. Population 4,350. Trade in hams, mules, sheep, &c. The manna was considered one of the 'wonders' of Dauphiné. *Hotel*—De la Paix.

From this you come to La Vachette, at the foot of *Mont Genèvre* (11,790 feet high), on the other side of which rises one head of the Po. Thence

BOURG MONT-GENEVRE (2 leagues), a small place of 400 souls, where the douane or frontier custom-house is placed. There is a pillar to Napoleon here, 65 feet high, and a hospice founded by Humbert II., and rebuilt 1804. By this route Charles VIII. entered Italy, 1494, and Belleisle and his army, 1747. The first place on the *Italian* side is Cesanne; on to Turin is 26 leagues from Briançon.

From Briançon, as above, you pass

LA BESSEE (17 kil.), near the Val Louise (which leads up the lofty Mont Pelvoux, to the west), and near also a cave called Baume des Vaudois, where 3,000 of these suffering worthies were smothered or slain by Charles VIII., in 1488.

LA ROCHE (7 kil.), leads into Val Fressinière, where Felix Neff is buried. He lived chiefly at La Chalp in Val d'Arvieux.

PLAN DE PHAZY (10 kil.), on the Durance, where the Guil joins it, is near Mont Dauphin, which has a strong frontier fortress, by Vauban. Up the Guil, through the valley of Queyras you come to Guillestra, where English prisoners were confined in the war. Then to Veyer and the deep gorge of Chapelue. Further on, to the village of Ville-Vieille, opposite the Fort de Queyras, which stands most picturesquely on a peak by itself in the midst of snowy heights.

VAL D'ARVIEUX, Val Veran, &c., which stretch around this, are consecrated by the labours of *Felix Neff*, among the Protestant Vaudois (*i. e.* valley people), who have for ages made this desolate region their asylum. He was like Fletcher, while Oberlin in some respects resembled Wesley. At the head of the Guil are Aiguille, Abries, Ristolas, and Mont Viso and its glaciers, 13,840 feet high, on the *Italian* border, round which are passes into Piedmont to La Torre, &c., the 'ancient fold' of the Vaudois.

At 16 kil. further is

EMBRUN, as in the Route below (36*a*).

ROUTE 36*a*.

Gap to Embrun.

Distance, 31 kil., or 19 miles.

GAP as in Route 34.

CHORGES (7 kil.) was a town of the Caturiges, and has traces of a roman fort, with other signs of their occupation, and a church on the site of a temple of Diana. Here a road of 17 leagues turns off to Gap, *viâ* St. Vincent, where the road to Barcelonnette joins it.

[*Barcelonnette* (about 36 kil. from Chorges) is a sous-préfecture in department Basses-Alpes, on the Ubaye, and is one of the prettiest and best built places in this part. It was founded 1230, by Raymond, Count of Provence. In the Place, near the old clock-tower, is a fountain in honour of Manuel, with an inscription from Béranger, the poet, signifying that 'arm, head, and heart, were all found in him.' Population, 2,300. *Hotels*—Lions; Maurin.]

A road leads hence across the *Savoy* border, for about 65 leagues, on to Genoa.

EMBRUN (24 kil.), a sous-préfecture and fortified town, among the hills, on the top of a rock, over the Durance, and called by the Romans, *Ebrodunum*. It was the seat of an archbishop, and has Nôtre Dame gothic cathedral, which bears a good norman spire, and had the image of our Lady of Embrun, so much reverenced by her pious servant, Louis XI. The palace, now a barrack, is close to the old tower called Tour Brune. A house of correction supplants the seminary for the Jesuits. Trade in wine, fruit, cattle, &c. Population, 4,500.

CHATEAUROUX (8 kil.), a village in a fine spot where the Grave falls in. Still ascending the Durance, you come to Mont-Dauphin fort (16 kil.), and La Roche, to the left of which towards Monte Viso, a road passes leading to Val de Queyras and Val d'Arvieux, the ancient settlements of the Protestant Vaudois, where Felix Neff laboured (*see* above, Route 36). By way of Briançon, the distance from Embrun to Turin over the Alpine passes is about 40 leagues.

ROUTE 37.

Valence to Gap.

Distance 142 kil., or 88 miles.

VALENCE, as in Route 24.

LA PAILLASSE (9 kil.), down the Rhône.

CREST (16 kil.), on the Drôme, the old capital of the Valentinois, under Roche Courbé hill, had a castle, which took part with the Albigenses against Simon de Montfort, of which there are fragments. Population, 5,000. General Digonnet was a native. A little further on is Aouste, the roman *Augusta*.

SAILLANS (15 kil.), up the Drôme.

[About 13 kil. south is the picturesque hermitage of Félines, in a very solitary spot, reached by 50 steps in the rock.]

POULAIX (7 kil).

DIE (9 kil.), on the Drôme, a sous-préfecture of 3,900 souls, among the mountains, was the *Dea Vocontiorum* of the Romans, who left some relics, which are collected at the old bishop's house. Porte St. Marcel, a triumphal arch, in the ancient walls on the Gap road, is worth notice. It was the head of the Diois comté (joined to Dauphiné, 1189), and seat of a diocess till the time of Louis XIV., when the cathedral church (ruined in the religious wars) was rebuilt; length 265 feet by 75 broad, without a single pillar. Trade in silk, oil, fruit, and excellent white wine, called Clarette de Die. *Hotels* — St. Dominique; des Trois Faisans (Three Pheasants). Coach to Valence and Gap

[In the neighbourhood are, Montagne de Glandasse (2,620 yards high), where the bear, chamois, white hare, &c., are found; But de St. Genie (1,650 yards), Montagne de Fordurles (near St. Julien, 10 kil. off), on which is a grotto and lake where a June cattle fair is held; Montagne de Solore, and its grottoes; the *Mont Inaccessible* (10 kil.), which only the chamois can reach, but which a Sieur de Domjulien scaled 1492, by the help of ropes, to please Charles VIII, and planted crosses on the top.—Bouvante, 20 kil. north-east, is a fine spot among the mountains of the Royanais, near the head of the Bourne.]

AIX (6 kil.), on the Drôme, where the Bes joins from above Chatillon, which has caves no one can descend, because of the carbonic acid gas given out.

LUC (10 kil.), the ancient *Lucus-Augusti*, has a roman tomb for its public fountain.

RAURIERES (10 kil.), still on the Drôme, is the only useful pass through the mountains here.

LA BAUME-DES-ARNAUDS (12 kil.), in department Hautes-Alpes, so called from a grotto near it, and a fine cascade, down which the water falls 70 or 80 feet.

ASPRES-LES-VEYNE (18 kil).—Veyne (6 kil.) on the Buech.—La Roche-des-Arnauds (12 kil.)

At 12 kil. further is GAP (*see* Route 34).

ROUTE 37*a*.

Pont Esprit to Gap.

Distance, 133 kil., or 83 miles.

LA MOTTE, opposite Pont Esprit, on the Rhône, as in Route 24.

TAZE (10 kil. east) is on the Leren; Tulette, 8 kil. further; St. Maure, 6 kil. beyond this, on the Aigues.

NYONS or Nions, 10 kil. higher up the Aigues or Eygues, is a sous-préfecture (population 3,400), in department Drôme, and the ancient *Neomagus*, finely seated over the beautiful valley of the river, under the Col de Devoz, Mont de Vaulx, and Mont de Garde Crosse. It had a château of the Dauphins, and made in 1622 against the Duke of Savoy, a worthy defence, headed by the daughter of Marguerite de Charce.

The town proper, called the Halles, from an arcaded building here, is divided from the Bourg and forts (where the castle stood) by old walls and gates; in the lower part, at the defile of Pilles, a very old, if not roman, bridge, crosses the river, by a single stone arch 127 feet wide, 65 high, having a square tower in the midst.

The valley of the Aigues is like a garden all the way to the Rhône, between high hills, covered with vineyards, olive yards, mulberry grounds, &c. It is remarkable for a healthy wind called Vent Pontias, blowing down the valley from the mountain of that name at the head of it every day till noon, when it is succeeded by another blowing up it, called Vésine, more hot and enervating. A road turns off to Carpentras.

[Nollans, 20 kil. south, in a picturesque ravine on the Ouvèze, under Chatelard and other mountains. It has a sulphur spa, &c.—Vaisons, a little lower down the Ouvèze, in department Vaucluse, is the roman *Vaisio*, with remains of a circus, aqueduct, temple, a good bridge of one arch, &c.]

PILLES, 8 kil. past this; then Villependrix, 8 kil.; Remusat, 7 kil.; Rozans, 14 kil., at the head of the Aigues, in department Hautes-Alpes; then Montelus, 14 kil.; and Sevres, 9 kil.; from which to Veyne is 15 kil., beyond which is Gap (24 kil.), as in Route 34.

ROUTE 38.

Avignon to Vaucluse and Digne.

Distance, about 141 kil., or 88 miles.

AVIGNON, as in Route 24.

[Château-Renard, 16 kil. south-east, on the south side of the Durance, is so called from an old castle which commands a noble range of view. — Further up the river is Orgon once a roman settlement, with old walls and two or three castles round it.—On the opposite or north bank, is another roman station, Cavaillon, in a fertile spot, where vermicelli, silk, &c., are made. — Still higher up the river is Cadenet, 19 kil. south of Apt, near the remains of a roman station; the font in the church is roman.]

L'ISLE (20 kil.) on the Sorgues (noted for its eels and trout), 8 kil. to the left of which is

VAUCLUSE, at the head of a deep cleft (vallis clausa) in the limestone of Mont Ventoux, where the Sorgues takes its rise, in precipices 500 feet high, either trickling down from many parts of the rock (as in summer), or falling like a cataract, from an arched cave (over-shadowed by a fig-tree), into the dark pool or *Fountain of Vaucluse* below. Petrach describes it in his letters, and they shew his little country seat on a hill to the right. An ugly pillar stands close to the pool.

Apt (35 kil.), a sous-préfecture of 5,707 souls in department Vaucluse, on the Cavalon, founded by Cæsar, as *Apta-Julia-Vulgientes*. Old walls run round it, and it stands in a valley among vines and olive yards.

Cereste (16 kil.)

Forcalquier (20 kil.) another old place, once the capital of the Memini, now a sous-préfecture in department Basses-Alpes. Population 3,036.

About 50 kil. further is

Digne (*see* Route 34) up the Durance.

ROUTE 39.

Marseilles to Aix and Digne.

Distance, 140 kil., or 87 miles.

Marseilles as in Route 24.

Le Pin (15 kil.) near Viste or La Vista Hill, which commands a noble prospect of Marseilles.

Aix (14 kil.) a sous-préfecture in department Bouches-du-Rhone, seat of an archbishopric, academy, &c., and a watering place, was founded as the roman *Aquæ Sentiæ*, by C. Sextius Calvinus, about 124 B.C., and became the capital of Provence, under the Troubadours.

It stands near the Arc, in a fertile valley separated by hills, to the north and south, from the Durance and the coast; Mount Victoire lying to the east. The old square shaped town, with its dirty streets, half-ruined walls, and six gates, is on one side of the Cours Orbitelles, or High Street, which has David of Angers' statue of King René, three fountains (one of warm water), and the statues of Portalis and Simeon, placed there 1847. Outside the town are the mineral springs, called the Fontaine de Sextius, with a bathing house; the season for using them is from May to October; and they are beneficial in cases of rheumatism, paralysis, skin diseases, &c. Fountains and granite pillars ornament the principal squares; Place des Précheurs has an eagle on the top; that in Place de la Madeleine, an eagle and four lions, with medallions of Caius Sextus, Charles III. count of Provence, Louis XV. and Louis XVIII.; another called Fontaine des Quatre Dauphins, in the Corso, spouts out warm water for the use of the washerwomen.

The *Cathedral*, dedicated to St. Sauveur, is composed of a romanesque aisle of the eleventh century, a gothic nave of the fourteenth century, with a front and tower of the same date (the carved cedar doors are later), another aisle of the seventeenth century, a large and well-shaped choir, built 1285, and the ancient cloisters of the eleventh century. The old *baptistry*, with its eight large granite pillars, was, they say, part of a temple to Apollo; there are also a sarcophagus (in St. Mitre's chapel) with bas-reliefs of Christ preaching, a painting of the Virgin and Child, with portraits of King René in it, sculptures by Cleastel, and two lions from René's throne, monuments of archbishop Pénard and Fabri di Piersac, an equestrian figure of St. Martin, an old niched image of the Virgin, held in great veneration by the superstitious, &c.

At St. John's gothic church, which belonged to a priory of Malta, and was built 1231, by Raymond Berenger IV., are the tombs of the counts of Provence (restored 1828), some paintings, and a good clock-tower 213 feet high. St. Madeleine is 200 feet long, and adorned with various paintings, one being by Albert Durer.

There are five or six other churches and chapels. At the Hôtel de Ville, built 1668, are Coustou's statue of Marshal Villars, and a large and valuable library of 100,000 vols., chiefly the gift of the Marquis de Mejanes, and 1,100 MSS., with busts and urns; that of Vauvenargues is by Ramus, a native artist. Near it is a clock tower built 1512, with a clock and figures moved by machinery. The old priory contains a museum of roman and greek antiquities, besides a gallery of pictures, among which are Gros's Night of the 20th March at the Tuileries, Forbin's Siege of Granada, &c. Opposite the fountain of St. Louis, is the school of arts et metiers (trades). The new *Palais de Justice* is a large building, worth notice, with the prisons close beside it, standing on the site of the old seat of the Counts of Provence, where the parliament of Aix used to meet. It has also public granaries, barracks, three hospices, a salle de spectacle, college, &c.

Among the eminent men it has produced are Adamson and Tournefort the naturalists Vanloo, Forbin, and Granet the painters; Marquis d'Argens (brother of President Boyer), the friend of Frederick the Great; Entrecasteaux, the navigator; and General Miollis. It still enjoys a reputation for learning and the arts. Pope Alexander V. founded a university here 1409.

Trades in almonds, wine, eaux-de-vie, excellent olive oil, silk, coral, prints, confitures (sweetmeats). *Hotels*—Des Princes; de la Poste; du Midi, &c. Population, 24,500.

Conveyances to Marseilles (4 hours), Toulon (8 hours), Nice, Draguignan, Nismes, Avignon, Lyons, &c. At about 1½ hours distance up the Arc, is the large aqueduct of Roquefavour 1,230 feet, carrying the Marseilles canal over the Seine.

[At 18 kil. to the west, at Labarben is the fine old château of the Forbins.—The beautiful château of Roque Antheron is 21 kil. to the west, near the Durance.—Mimet, 12 kil. to the south-east, has a curious gothic church, 190 feet long, on the top of Puy-le-Mimet.—On or near the Infernets, a stream to the north-east, are the following:—

Tholonet (4 kil.), a charming country spot in the valley of the stream, where signs of roman occupation are detected.—St. Marc (5 kil.) a little higher, has an old château fort in the pass of Vauvenargues, and the tower of Les Signeaux, on a plain 1,300 feet high.—Further up is Vauvenargues (11 kil.) at the bottom of *Mont Victorie*, so called from the famous victory of Marius over the Teutons, 125 B.C. It has a castle of the fourteenth century, with an hermitage at the top of the mountain, 3,420 feet high, where a fête is kept 24th April.—Beyond this Puyloubier (16 kil.) which enjoys a fine view of Mont Victorie, and has the grotto or hermitage of St. Ser.]

PEYROLLES (21 kil.)

[*Barjols* (20 k. east), in a picturesque spot, frequently visited by sketchers. It stands in an amphitheatre, among woods and waterfalls, and has manufactures of paper, wax, leather, with a trade in olive oil, fruits, &c. Pop. 4,000.]

ST. PAUL-LES-DURANCE (13 kil.) near Mirabeau's family château where he lived when a boy.

[About 18 kil. to the north of it is *Manosque*, on the Durance, a town of 5,700 souls, who carry on a good trade in olives, oil, truffles, eaux-de-vie.]

GREOUX or Bains-de-Gréoulx (18 kil.) has some useful mineral springs, known to the Romans, and frequented from May to September.

RIEZ (20 kil.), the *Abece* of the Romans, on the Ouvestre, under high hills, in a fertile spot, has some antiquities, as a group of four corinthian pillars, near another of eight columns, all of granite. Trade in wine, fruit, &c. Pop. 2,900.

[About 15 kil. to the east is Moustier, in the midst of a chain of rocky heights and partly built on the bridges which carry the road over the torrent in a deep valley below. At the head of this gorge, behind the village, some one has suspended an iron chain across from peak to peak, 417 feet long, with a star hanging from the middle. The intention of it is not known.]

ESTOUBLON (19 kil.)

DIGNE is 20 kil. further. (*See* Route 34.)

ROUTE 39*a*.

Toulon to Draguignan.

Distance, 85 kil. or 51 miles.

TOULON, as in Route 24.

CUERS (21 kil.), a pretty place among vines and olives.

[*Brignolles* (2 kil. north), a sous-préfecture in department Var, with 5,600 people, in a fertile and healthy spot on the Carami, was once the second city in Provence, and carries on a trade in prunes, fruit, oil, soap, wine, liqueurs, &c. Raynouard a writer on the poetry of the Troubadours was born here. *Hotel*—De la Cloche Argent (Silver bell).]

CARNOULLES (12 kil.), has on its right, Garde-Freinet, among the mountains, where the Saracens built the stronghold of Freinet or *Fraxinet* about 890, which they kept till driven out by Guillaume of Provence in 973. It stood on a point of difficult access, where traces of it may yet be seen.

LE LUC (16 kil.), near a factory of Bohemia crystal glass. It is noted for its chesnuts.

[Salernes, 20 kil. north-north-west, near the picturesque valley of Barthélmy, has an old moorish castle on the rocks.]

VIDAUBAN (12 kil.), a pretty place among cork trees, &c., on the Argens, which at St. Michel's chapel on the road to Tholonet, falls over a rock in fine cascades.

From this it is 24 kil. to Draguignan, (*see* Route 34), *viâ* Le Muy.

ROUTE 40.

St. Etienne to Le Puy, Mende, Albi, and Toulouse.

Distance, 410 kil. or 244 miles.

This route runs through Auvergne, and the

romantic country at the head of the Loire, Lot, &c., little known to ordinary tourists.

ST. ETIENNE, as in Route 33.

By a hilly road you come then to

FIRMIGNY (12 kil.), among coal mines, silk factories, &c.

MONISTROL (17 kil.), between two valleys, having remains of an ursuline convent, and the country seat of the bishops of Puy, now a ribbon factory. Population 4,550.

YSSINGEAUX (20 kil.), a sous-préfecture in department Haute-Loire, with a population of 7,700.

After 28 kil. more, through the volcanic country of Velay, you come to

Le Puy, 77 kil. or 48 miles from St. Etienne, *Hotels*—Du Palais Royal; de Milan; des Ambassadeurs; du Commerce. Population 16,000. Capital of department Haute-Loire, (formerly of Velay in Auvergne), seat of a diocess, &c., near the roman Reussio, was at one time called Ville d' Anis, and then *Puy* or *Puech, i. e.* a peak, from the volcanic mountain, on whose north and west sides it lies, sloping in a remarkably picturesque way towards the Borne, which valley joins those of the Dolaison and Loire close by. This conical peak, in the midst of a circle of other rugged volcanic hills covered with vineyards, &c., is 2,484 feet above the sea, or 460 above its spreading base; from which the lava-built houses with their tiled roofs rise in tiers, past the Cathedral, the gardens of the seminary, &c., to the top called the Roche de Corneille, and crowned by the ruined castle. From the Pont St. Jean, the top offers a rough likeness to Henry IV., with his aquiline nose, moustache, and beard. On the east of Mont d'Anis, is a sharp peak of volcanic breccia, nearly 300 feet high, called L'Aiguilhe or *L'Aiguille* (the needle), on which is the little spire chapel of St. Michel, seemingly inaccesible, but reached by a spiral of 218 steps, and built in the norman style of the tenth century. Below, between the peaks, is the 'temple of Diana,' a little seven-sided norman built chapel of St. Clair, now used as a barn or a theatre. From the position of the town, the streets are too irregular and steep for carriages; they are paved with lava. One old gate has great machicolated towers on each side. A flight of 120 broad steps brings you up to the

Cathedral, which stands with its back to the rock, and is built of lava, in a half norman style; it has two pillars of red porphyry in front, an isolated pyramidal spire and low towers, a nave of three aisles on great pillars, good carved pulpit, a painting of the Innocents, a carving on wood of St. Andrew's martyrdom, and an altar of divers colours, on which stands an ebony image of the Virgin in gold brocade, brought they say from Egypt, by St. Louis on his return from the Crusades 1254; a gift which produced many pretended miracles, besides an abbey and convents, and many royal visits. The bishop was by custom, president of the States of Velay.

A large priests' seminary and the hospital stand near the cathedral; at the college, (which has a chapel with an italian front) is a library of 5,000 volumes. St. Laurent's great church in Lower town, near the bridge, contains the modern effigies of Duguesclin, copied from those destroyed by the Baron des Adrets when he and his fierce calvinists attacked the town. A new Hôtel de Ville is in Place des Breuil; and at the museum is a collection of pictures, roman antiquities, minerals, and fossils.

Manufactures of blond and cotton lace, woollen goods, leather, skins for wine bottles, muleteers' hats, and bells, &c. Coaches to Clermont, St. Etienne, Mende, &c.

Among the various objects of notice in the neighbourhood (of which the Roche de Corneille commands a fine prospect,) are the Orgues d'Espalley (west), the châteaux of Polignac, St. Vidal, and Loudes (north-west), château of Ceyssac (south-west), Roche Rouge or red rock (east), the cavernes le Fées, the lac de Limagne, and numerous volcanic peaks.

[*Polignac* (3 kil.), a village near the Borne, round the base of a basalt mass, crowned by the fine keep and round towers of the ruined castle of the Polignac family, which stands on the site of a temple of Apollo (Apollonicum, whence the present name), and was destroyed at the revolution. Its seigneurs were styled 'Kings of the Mountains'.—At 18 kil. beyond this, up the river, near Allègre, is the Cratère or Dôme de Bar, a perfect crater, 1,590 feet diameter and 127 deep, the sides being planted with beeches.

Orgues d'Espally (2 m. west of Puy), on the Borne is a striking pyramidal mass of basalt pillars like the pipes of an organ (orgues), at the top of which are traces of a château, where

Chas. VII. was proclaimed by the states, 1424. One of the best views of le Puy is got here.

At 30 kil. south-east-by-south of le Puy is *Mont Mezenc*, in the Cevennes, the highest of the volcanic range of Ardêche, (1,940 yards above the sea,) at the head of the Lignon, Gazelle, Erieux, &c., and not far from the Gerbier de Joncs (1,710 yards) at the Loire's head. Mont Mezenc has the two fine falls of la Roche and la Baume on the west side, 82 and 98 feet down; and commands one of the noblest views in France, taking in the French and Swiss Alps, &c.]

CHACORNAC (14 kil.). About 3 kil. west of this, is Bouchet lake, in the crater of a volcanic peak, 14,760 feet round, and 92 deep.

LANDOS (8 kil.).

PRADELLES (8 kil.), where a road turns off to Aubenas in Ardèche (*see* Route 41).

LANGOGNE (6 kil.), on the Allier in the Cevennes, where another road turns to Alais and Grand Combe (*see* Route 44), is on one of the highest places in the department of Lozère, and has a church which belonged to an abbey of the tenth century, founded by the Viscounts de Gévaudan. A roman camp, is traced on Mont Milan.

[Grandrieux (18 kil. west-north-west), is near Agrippa's roman way from Lyons into Spain, and has an old square tower.—Naussac (6 kil. north-west), lower down the Allier has remains of a château, which the excellent Belzunce, bishop of Marseilles, at the plague of 1722, used to visit. It belonged to Chambons abbey.]

CHATEAUNEUF-RANDON (19 kil.), on a rocky height, belonged to the Lords de Gévaudan and was defended by the old castle of Randon, which the English held 1380, when given up to Duguesclin who died in the meantime, and to whom a pillar was set up at Bitarelle 1820. He was for his time, a gentle soldier, and on his death-bed, desired his people to remember, that wherever they made war, churchmen, women, children, and the poor were not their enemies.

At 19 kil. further is

MENDE. *Hotels*—Du Pavilion; Crey; Rosier, &c. Population, 5,600. Chief town of department Lozère, seat of a bishop, &c., in the fertile valley of the Lot, among the Margeride (a range of the Cevennes) mountains, one of which, Mont Mimat, 3,600 feet above the sea, or 650 above the town (to which it gave name), has the hermitage of St. Privat, who was martyred here by the Vandals. He is called the apostle of the Gabals, or people of Gévaudan. The streets are narrow and crooked, but ornamented with many fountains. Country houses are perched on the hills around.

The *Cathedral*, with two tall gothic spire towers (one slender and well carved), stands on the site of St. Privat's grave. At the old episcopal palace, now used for the préfecture, is a gallery of pictures, some by Bénard. The library contains 7,000 vols. There is a college, a priests seminary, &c.

[In the neighbourhood are the following:—Pont Gothique, a bridge of four pointed arches, besides a ruined one.—Lanuéjols (7 kil. east), near the Lot, with its fine roman mausoleum, about 25 feet square, with corinthian pilasters, &c., on each face.—Bagnols (9 kil.), and the sulphur springs, higher up the Lot. — St. Julien - de - Tournel, 8 kil. higher up, has a seat of the lords of Gévaudan. Lead mines were worked here by the Saracens.—Villefort (21 kil. east-south-east of this), in the narrow valley of the Devêze, is noted for its lead mines, and is an entrepôt, for the wine, silk, salt, oil, grain, &c., of this mountain region.—The ruins of Alène (12 kil.)—Mont Lozère (10 kil.) about 4,900 feet high, in the forests of which the wolf is hunted.]

From Mende, on the road to Rodez and Albi, you pass

BARIAC (9 miles), on the Lot; 10 kil. to the north-west of which is *Marvejols*, a sous-préfecture of nearly 4,000 people, in the valley of the Colagne; it was nearly destroyed by the royal forces under the Duc de Joyeuse, 1586, but restored by Henry IV, and well built. The springs about have a good dyeing quality.

CHANAC (7 kil.), on the Lot, has remains of druid stones near it, and, upon the cliffs above, an old château of the bishops of Mende.

[8 kil. to the north-east, on the Colagne, at Chirac, are several other druid monuments, and a spot called Cimetière des Anglais, where the English were defeated in the fourteenth century.]

LA CANOURGUE (10 kil.), in a fertile valley,

where the serge stuffs of Canourgue are made, has remains of an ancient fort of St. Amand; and much roman pottery was found, 1829.

[5 kil. to the north of it, is the church of St. Salmon, built by Pope Urban V.; a bridge over the Lot, leads to the village of Mont-Jèzieu, so called because a colony of Jews were settled here before the fourteenth century.]

SEVERAC (20 kil.), in department Aveyron, is on the Biaur, above which is the old château of its marquises, built in the seventeenth century, square, with corner towers.

MILHAU, or Millau (30 kil.), a sous-préfecture in Aveyron, of 9,500 souls, in a pretty part of the Tarn, suffered in the Albigensian wars, and was one of the first to accept the reformed faith in 1534, when the marriage of the Benedictine prior with the Abbess of Arpajouie took place here. General assemblies were frequently held in the town, and it is still chiefly protestant; the pastors being the Rev. MM. C. Boube and F. Maffre. The stone bridge was re-built 1817; a suspension bridge is of later date; there are good walks about. Good ewe-milk cheese (called Roquefort), gloves, vellum, thread, &c., are made. Generals Sarret and Solignac were natives.

At 55 kil. to the north-west is Rodez (*see* Route 52). The road to Montpellier turns off to the south-east (Route 45 *a*).

ST. AFFRIQUE, or St. Fric (28 kil.), a sous-préfecture of 6,800 persons, in a rocky part of the Sorgue, has many old gothic houses, and parts of the walls, built 1357, but which Louis XIII. dismantled for its attachment to protestantism. An old hospital is used for the mairie, and stands opposite the new palais de justice. The neighbouring hills are covered with vineyards and orchards. Good cloth is made, and it has a trade in cheese, wool, &c. Rev. MM. Mason and Amicel are protestant pastors here.

[At 12 kil. south-south-east, are the warm mineral sulphur waters of Silvanès (104° temperature), which are used from June to September.—About 6 kil. south-west of this, near the little village of Pont-de-Camarés, on the Dourdon, are the cold 'eaux-gazeuses,' or carbonic acid gas springs of Andabre and Prugnes, which taste something like soda-water.]

ST. SERNIN (32 kil.), on the Rance, at the bottom of a circle of mountains.—About 16 kil. south-east is Belmont, on the slant of a rock over the Rance, with a good spire to its church.

LA FRAYSSE (24 kil.), in department Tarn; 23 kil. beyond which is

ALBI (*see* Route 52). — Toulouse is 72 kil. further.

ROUTE 41.

Valence to Privas and Alais.

Distance, 132 kil. or 82 miles; through the silk country of Ardèche, and among the Cevennes.

LE POUZIN, on the Rhône, where the Ouzève falls in.—At 12 kil. up the stream, (or 39 kil. from Valence, *vià* La Voulte,) is

PRIVAS. *Hotels*—Du Nord; de la Croix d'Or (Golden Cross); du Lion d'Or; du Commerce. Population, 5,000. This small capital of department Ardèche (the old *Vivarais*), in a hilly spot, where two little streams join the Ouzève, among vineyards and silk works, was an old fortified town, taken, for its attachment to protestantism, in 1629, after eight weeks' siege, by Louis XIII., the walls razed, and the garrison put to the sword. Some old houses are seen, and the modern streets are well laid out. It contains a catholic church, protestant temple (on the castle site), palais de justice, with a four-column portico; college for 200; bibliothèque of 2,000 vols.; large new prison, and hospital. Silk goods, leather, oil, spirits, &c., are made. Rev. S. Vincens is protestant pastor.

[*Antraigues* (20 kil. west-south-west) is finely seated at the Volane's head, among forests of chesnuts, &c., on masses of basalt and beds of lava, which were thrown out by the neighbouring volcanoes; especially one called Coup d'Aisac, having a regularly shaped crater, now filled up by trees. The mountains of Mezenc, Gerbier-de-Jones, and other peaks of the Cevennes are in view.]

AUBENAS (30 kil.), a depôt for the silk trade of the Ardèche (population, 4,800), among the volcanic peaks of the Coiron mountains, covered with vines, olives, mulberries, &c., standing on a hill over the river Ardèche, above which rise its spire and domed churches, and the towers of its Hôtel de Ville, once a castle of the Ornano and Harcourt families. Parts of the town walls remain; and the college and hospice deserve notice. Silk and cotton are spun, and paper, &c.,

made; trade in silk, leather, corn, wine, oil, chesnuts, &c.

[*Vals* (5 kil. north-north-west), up the Volane, which makes several falls, in a most picturesque spot, is noted for its tonic mineral waters; and is near the Pont de Bridon, where the lava beds and basalt rocks, above mentioned, begin. The waters are drunk between June and September.—At 14 kil. north-west is Thueyts, round which, and Mont Pezat, are vast beds of lava, &c., and volcanic ranges, which rise towards Mezenc and the source of the Loire.]

St. Etienne-de-Boulogne (3 kil.), has the fine ruins of one of the feudal castles of the Vivarais district.

[At 10 kil. east-south-east, is Villeneuve-de-Berg, originally a fortified tower of the monks of Mazan, who built the town in Philippe le Hardi's time. There is a pillar to Olivier de Serres, a native, who wrote the Thèatre d'Agriculture, and first planted the mulberry; the learned de Gebelin was also born here. Population, 2,600.]

L'Argentiere (10 kil.), out of the road, in the deep, rocky valley of Ligne, is a sous-préfecture of 3,000 souls, and so called from the lead mines (from which silver, or *argent*, is extracted), worked here since the twelfth century. The old gothic church is light, and rather elegant; and there is an ancient castle on the cliffs. Trade in silk. Near it is a grotto, including several caves.

[St. Laurent des Bains 27 kil. north-west, has some excellent warm sulphur waters, in a wild and rocky, but healthy spot on the Borne.—Jaujac, 14 kil. north, of Argentière, lies among volcanic peaks in department Ardèche, and near Ardèche river.

Joyeuse (8 kil.), on the Drobie, a branch of the Ardèche.

[Below Ruoms (7 kil. east-south-east), is a wild, rocky part of the Ardèche (especially at the junction of the Voisin), where the river worms itself through caves and around masses of rock of the most fantastic shape (some regular cubes); while the banks on both sides in one part rise at an angle of 45° by immense steps, made by the wearing away of softer masses of rock.—At Vallom (which has a famous stalactitic grotto), 7 kil. lower down, are two curiosities—the fall of *Ray Pic* (122 feet down, over a basalt rock), under the curve of which you may take shelter in rain, like the Hepste fall in Brecknockshire, and which freezes in winter; and the remarkable *Pont de l'Arc*, a rugged, natural bridge, of hard, grey limestone, stretching in one arch across the river, about 173 feet span, and 96 high, the irregular roadway being above 200 feet above the water, and 40 feet wide. It has been used from roman times; Louis XIII. built a fort to command the pass; and cottages stand hard by it. In the neighbourhood is the Gouffre (or gulf) de la Goule, a savage valley or pass between the Usège mountains.]

Jalez (11 kil.), near the Chassezac, where the road to Villefort and Mende, in Lozère, turns off.

St. Ambroix (12 kil.), on the Cèze, in department Gard.

At 19 kil. further (south-west) is Alais, on the Nismes railway; or 34 kil. to the south-east is Uzes, whence it is 20 kil. to Nismes (*see* Routes 43 and 44).

ROUTE 43.

Avignon to Beaucaire (Pont du Gard), Nimes, Montpellier, Cette, Narbonne (Toulouse), Perpignan, and Spain.

Distance, about 140 kil. to Montpellier, and 140 more to Perpignan; making about 280 kil. or 174 miles.

By rail to Tarascon, Nîmes, Montpellier, Cette; four trains a-day, but not through; and not faster than 18 or 20 miles an hour. There is a delay, therefore, at some of these places.

Avignon, as in Route 24.

Tarascon (21 kil.) in the same route, whence the branch line to Nîmes turns off, on a viaduct across the Rhône, the banks of which so far are picturesque. About twenty stations hence to Montpellier.

Beaucaire (— kil.) across the Rhône, which has an old Provençal castle on the rocks above, is noted for a commercial *Fair*, lasting from 22nd to 29th July, and attended by merchants from all parts of the Mediterranean. As many as 300,000 people are sometimes collected. The old carved Hôtel de Montmorency deserves attention. An old bridge of boats here has been replaced by Challey's noble suspension bridge, hanging on four bends, each 426½ feet long. It is the largest in France, and ranks next to Menai, which is itself second to that of Fribourg, by the same architect (Challey).

The Aurelian way to Nimes and Spain went through this place, the ancient *Ugarnum*. A canal runs down to the sea below Aigues Mortes, in connexion with the Canal du Midi.

[At 16 kil. north-north-west, and 31 west of Avignon, by road to Nimes, you pass La Foux, on the Gard or Gardon, 1 kil. from the

Pont du Gard, a noble roman remain, being part of the great aqueduct (17½ miles) which carried the waters of the Aure to Nimes; and looking like a screen across the valley. It is a mass 640 feet long and 138 high, of three rows of arches, one over the other,—the lowest, a row of 6 arches; the next, 11 of the same size; the third, 25 small arches, having the water way above, where it ran 6½ feet wide and deep. It was used as a road before a bridge was built, 1747, close to the bottom of it. Being half-way between Avignon and Nismes, it is common for pic-nic parties from both towns to meet here to pass the day.]

Nismes or Nimes, 30 kil. from Tarascon by railway. *Hotels*—Du Luxembourg, on the Esplanade; du Midi (the South); de Paris; du Louvre; de l'Europe; du Gard. *Restaurant*, Durand's, in Rue Notre Dame; the *Cafés* are in Grand Cours and in the Esplanade. Population 60,000, one-third of whom are protestants: there are 150,000 in the department.

This old city, the capital of department Gard (part of Languedoc), seat of a bishop, a protestant consistory, a college, &c., is most remarkable for its monuments of antiquity, such as the amphitheatre, tower, maison carrée, &c., and stands in the dusty, unattractive, though fertile plain of the Vistre, near the Garrigue hills, or beginning of the Cevennes range. Some think it was founded by the Marseilles Greeks; the Romans, however, who took it 121 B.C., and called it *Nemausus*, were its greatest benefactors, and, under Agrippa, built the baths, aqueduct (from Pont du Gard), &c.; while Antonine, whose ancestors were natives, constructed the amphitheatre. It was then two or three times larger than now. The Vandals (407), Saracens (720-7), and others, so reduced it by their ravages, that, in 1336, it had but 400 souls. It was a sort of republic, under consuls, &c., from 1226 till 1555, when it was finally joined to the crown. Charles VII. took it 1420.

The old town or Cité is a heap of small dirty streets, surrounded by the Grand Cours and the faubourgs of the modern town; this Cours, on the site of the boulevards, is well planted, and set off with delightful gardens. The best view of Nismes is from the hill near the barracks, or from the Tour Magne, which overlooks a vast range of country. Many of the lowest streets are named after emperors and noted men, as Adrian, Vidal a judge, Baduel and Petit the scholars, Saurin the divine, Traucat who planted the first mulberries here, &c. Its later buildings are not of much consequence.

The cathedral, in the cité, is an irregular pile, with bits of all styles in it, from the byzantine downwards; the oldest part near the tower being of the eleventh century (the base, they say, was part of a roman temple); the rest belongs to the sixteenth and seventeenth centuries. It contains a picture of the Baptism, and tombs of Fléchier and Cardinal Bernis. St. Paul's, in Place de la Madeleine, is a modern building, in the byzantine style. The churches of the college, and of St Bandile, are also seen, the latter having a good façade. There are two protestant churches, Grand and Petit Temple (a protestant church was founded as early as 1559 by G. Moget); and a synagogue in Rue Rousny. An Hôtel Dieu, founded 1313 by Raymond Rossi, was rebuilt 1830; Richard's large hôpital, for old people, foundlings, and lunatics, was founded 1686, and enlarged 1811. The palais de justice, in the classical style (after the Propylea at Athens), was built 1826, on the site of Plotinus's roman basilica, near the railway station and Cours Feuchères. Maison centrale de detention (house of detention) on the site of Vauban's citadel and Fort de Rohan, serves for 13 departments, and has room for 1200. The bibliothèque of 40,000 volumes and MSS., is connected with the cabinet of natural history; on the site of Recollet's convent is the theatre, by Meunier, with an ionic portico. Not far from this is one of the great antiquarian treasures of the city, the

Maison Carrée (*i.e.* Square House), the common name of a beautiful temple, founded either by Augustus or Agrippa (the inscription being gone), and thought to have been part of the public forum. At one time it was used as a church (St. Etienne), then as the Hôtel de Ville (eleventh century), then as a stable (by one Brueys), and latterly as part of the Austin convent; but it is now restored with great care, and occupied as a museum and picture gallery, in which are Delaroche's 'Cromwell' and Sigalon's Nero.' It stands inside a railing on a stylobate or basement, 21½ feet high, to which fifteen steps lead; it is 82½ feet by 40; and is surrounded on three sides by fluted corinthian pillars, having rich capitals, with a well-carved cornice and freize; of the pillars ten are in the north portico (six in front), and the ten down each side are (some of them) half let into the wall, but not at *equal* distances. The door under the portico, 9¾ feet by 9½, leads into the temple itself, which is 52½ feet by 36, and 36 feet high, and lit from the roof. Cardinal Alberoni was so charmed with this work that he said it ought to have a gold case; and Colbert and Napoleon thought of transporting it to Versailles. It is open to the public on Sunday, but may be visited at any time by strangers.

The Arènes (arena) or *Amphitheatre*, the best preserved one existing, after that at Verona, stands in an open space, and is an oval, lying east and west, 437½ feet by 332½; 226½ feet by 124½ inside; 1,175 feet round; 70 feet high (inside the ground is 7¾ feet lower). It is composed of two rows, of sixty equal arches each, in a plain tuscan or doric style, with a cornice between the rows, pilasters between the arches in the first row, and pillars between those in the second; these arches communicate with the corridors and passages leading inside. Four principal entrances front the points of the compass, that on the north being distinguished by a pediment and two carved bulls. On the north-east side you may trace bas-reliefs of fighting gladiators, and the story of Romulus and Remus suckled by the wolf; and round the top (which is broken in the east) are holes for the poles, which the awning was spread on. In the inside are remains of the 32 rows of seats (16 or 17 may be traced), made of enormous stones, and ranged in four divisions according to the rank of the sitters, who came in and out by the passages or vomitories. It may have held from 18,000 to 20,000 when full; and was used, not only for the inhuman gladiator combats, but for naumachia or sea-fights, water being brought by the great Pont du Gard aqueduct. Machiolated towers were at one time added, and it was turned into a castle, to which the church of St. Martin was added (inside) in the eleventh century, but this and the houses piled against it have been long removed, and it is now taken proper care of. Wild bulls from the Camargue are sometimes baited here. A fine moonlight view may be enjoyed from the hills to the north.

At a beautiful spot, near Place de la Bouquerie, called Jardin de la Fontaine, after a spring which rises at the Creux de la Fontaine and supplies the town, are the fine remains of the

Temple of Diana, built by Augustus and ruined by Charles Martel, after driving out the Saracens. It is used as a bath; the great aqueduct came in here, into a château d'eau, or reservoir, lately discovered. M. Crespon has a museum of natural history here. Beyond this, on Mont Cavalier, is the *Tour Magne* (Great Tower), a conspicuous mark for the city, and commanding a great sweep of view; it is a ruin, six-sided at bottom and eight-sided above, where it narrows, about 110 feet high (might have been 130 once), and 65 feet through at bottom,—the top is less than half as much; built of rough stones, with an arched base pierced with windows, and remains of four ionic pilasters on one side, in the upper story. There is no staircase or roof. Some think it was a roman watch tower, others a mausoleum. Behind the cypresses here was the burial ground, where urns, amphoræ, pottery, and bones have been found.

Out of ten roman gates in the ancient walls, two are left. Porte de France, near the hospital, on St. Gilles road, is a single plain arch, 22½ feet high, 13½ wide, with round towers at the sides. Porte d'Auguste, on the Domitian way, or road to Rome, is more ornamented than the other, and was built in the year 7 B.C., along with the wall, as an inscription to Augustus testifies; it has four arches through it, two large and two small, with an ionic column between two corinthian pilasters on the face.

Among the buildings which have disappeared were the capitol, on the site of the gendarmerie; the baths, in Porte St. Antoine; basilica, where the palais de justice now stands, &c. Charles VI. built a castle near Porte des Carmes; pulled down 1693. Several protestant martyrs were burnt 1551, in Place de la Salmandre (the crest of Francis I.); and on Place de Boucaire, the Camisard leaders were burnt, 1705. Besides the college, there are a large priests' seminary, and schools of the brothers of christian doctrine; also protestant schools, with an orphan home and a normal school. The protestant cemetery is on the Alais road, with '*Après la mort, le jugement*' (after death, the judgment) over the gate; beyond it are the stone quarries in the Garriques hills. Tertiary fossils are found on Puy d'Autel, a hill the south-west, towards St. Cesaire, where the telegraph stands.

Of the three railway stations, or embarcadères for Alais, Beaucaire, and Montpellier, that for the last is the best, and is 328 feet long. The people are rough and independent in their manners, and divided into two distinct religious and hostile parties; wheat is thrashed in the open air by horses; and the plough, or charrue, still keeps its classic shape. Though the climate is better than that of Marseilles, it is still too cold and exposed to the mistral and vent-de-bise for persons in weak health (Lee's *Companion to the Continent*.)

Among its natives are Nicot, who brought tobacco into France (called Nicotina, after him), and *Guizot*, the statesman; Reboul, the baker-poet, is a resident; Cavalier, the Camisard leader, was also a baker. Eleven protestant pastors are stationed here. The Rev. F. Gouthier, whose life has been written by his nephews, the Villemins, laboured here for 9 years.

The manufactures are shawls, gloves, silk goods, cotton, carpets (at Flessier's factory), pianos, steam engines; there is a trade also in grain, wine, eaux-de-vie, olive oil, drugs, essences, &c.*

Conveyances,—by rail, to Beaucaire (1 hour), Avignon, Marseilles, &c., to Alais (2 hours), to Montpellier (2 hours). By coach to Toulouse and Marseilles (malle-poste), Lyons (26 hours), Montpellier, Perpignan, Uges, Clermont, Sommières, &c. Carriages to Pont du Gard, 12 fr. there and back.

[At 4 kil. south is Caissargues, which has good fishing in the Vistre, and had a castle, pulled down 1574. Names ending in *argues* are common here, and are derived from *ager*, a field, as in this name—Cassii ager, *i.e.*, Cassius' field, or farm.—About 15 kil. further on is

Gilles-les-Boucheries, in a wine country, on a rock, near the Canal de Beaucaire, and so called after *St. Gilles* abbey, of which the highly carved romanesque church of the twelfth century remains, having behind it St. Gilles' screw, or spiral staircase. The knights templars had a priory here. Distilling, &c., are carried on. Raymond, Count of Toulouse, was absolved here by the pope's legate after being scourged, 1209, and here Clement IV. was born.—Nearly 30 kil. further south, among the sand hills at the mouth of the Petit Rhône, is Les Saintes Maries, and its ancient fortified church, with towers and battlements, and curious carvings, and four paintings on wood, by King René.]

From Nismes, on the railway to Montpellier, you pass (stopping at fourteen stations)

UCHAU (12 kil.).

[12 kil. south of it is Vauvert, *i.e.*, Valée-vert (or green valley), the centre of the wine district in this quarter, and once the site of a château, visited by St. Louis, &c., and pulled down, 1628. An old castle (Beauvoisin) of the templars is near.]

The road is crossed by a roman bridge over the Vidourle, about 12 kil. from Uchau.

LUNEL (14 kil.), a town of 6,200 souls, trading in muscat or sweet wines, liqueurs, eaux-de-vie, fruit, grain, &c.. and standing among vineyards and oliveyards. It had a famous synagogue in the sixteenth century, and walls, which Richelieu razed, 1632. *otels*—Du Palais National; du Grand Soleil (Sun).

[At 12 kil. north, is *Sommières*, a thriving place of 3,600 persons, on the Vidourle, under an old castle, and having large manufactures of flannel, cloth, &c. Not far off is Ville Vieille (*i.e.* Old Town), where a roman bridge and other antiquities have been discovered by M. E. Dumas, an eminent geologist here. *Hotel*—Du Soleil d'Or (Golden Sun).

To the south of Lunel, at 3 kil., is Marsil-

* See *Tableau pittoresque, &c., de Nismes, et de ses Environs*, by Rev. E. Frossard.

largues, in a dull spot, on the Vidourle, noted for its wines and alcohol, and having a castle built 1623, with Diana of Poictier's cypher upon it,' and many portraits of the Calvisson family, to whom it belongs. Ferrades, or baiting and marking the wild bulls from the Camargues, is a great sport here.—At 12 kil. further south, on the salt marshes near the sea, is

Aigues-Mortes, on the Grand Roubine and other canals. At first there was a benedictine abbey, called Psalmodi here (restored 788 by Charlemagne), of which the gate tower is left. In 1248, St. Louis built a castle and the Tour de Constance, which is 94 feet high, besides a turret of 35 feet on top; walls were added by his son Philip, and the place now offers a complete specimen of a fortified town of that age, with its towers, battlements, machicolations, ditches, &c. Louis XIV. confined some unhappy protestants in the Constance Tower for 35 years; another is called Tour des Bourgignons, from a massacre made by the Dauphin's troops, 1421, when the fort was held by the Burgundians, whose bodies were thrown here. The clock-tower is of the thirteenth century. A canal led down to the Grau-Louis, or harbour, on the Mediterranean, whence St. Louis (Louis IX.) embarked for the crusades, 1270, and where Charles V. landed for his interview with Francis I., in 1538. At Peccais, about 2,000 men are employed in the salt works. Fevers and mosquitos are the torment of this part.]

COLOMBIERES (10 kil.), among rocks of the Carroux, in a pleasing spot, near Pont-du-Verdier, a bridge of one arch from rock to rock.

At 13 kil. further is

Montpellier. *Hotels*—Nevet, on the Esplanade; de Londres (formerly des Ambassadeurs); du Midi (the South); du Cheval Blanc (White Horse), for commercial travellers. Living, 5½ to 6½ fr. a-day. Several *Cafés* and *Restaurants* in Place de la Comedie. Population, 40,500. Capital of department Hérault (part of the province of Languedoc), seat of a military division, of a bishopric, &c., on a rocky hill, near the Mosson, about 4 kil. from the Mediterranean, was founded in the eighth century, when Charles Martel destroyed Maguelonne (which the Saracens held), and under the name of *MonsPossulanus* became noted for its commerce and school of medicine. The latter appears to have gained for it the reputation of being a peculiarly healthy spot for invalids, though other places along this shore are as healthy and more beautiful. Matthews, in the 'Diary of an Invalid', says, 'It is true there is almost always a clear blue sky, but the air is sharp and biting, and you are continually assailed by the *bise* (north wind) or the *marin*. The one brings cold, the other damp.'

One of its counts married a daughter of a king of Arragon, whose descendants sold it to Philip de Valois. It was taken by Louis XIII. as a stronghold of Huguenots, to keep whom in check he built the citadel at one end of the hill, 167 feet above the sea, whence there is a fine view of the cultivated gardens, vineyards, woods, and country around,—the sea, Mont Canigou in the Pyrennes, and the Cevennes being visible. At the other end is *Place de Peyrou*, a large, regular, well-planted square, built by Daviler. Here stand Dorbay's triumphal arch to Louis XIV. in one corner, his bronze statue in the centre, and a six-sided domed château d'eau, faced with corinthian pillars, to which the water from St. Clements is brought by an aqueduct, eight miles long, begun 1753, by H. Pitot, and distributed to 29 fountains in the town—one of which, in Place de la Comedi, has a group of the Graces. This aqueduct is mostly under ground, but near the city, it runs on an imposing double row of arches (183 arches in one row, 53 in the other), and at one point is 92 feet high.

At a house in Place de Peyrou, is the *Musée Fabre*, a gift of Baron Fabre (pupil of David, and who died 1837) to his native town; it includes prints, sketches, medals, statues, paintings (about 490) of the French, Italian, and Dutch schools, and 25,000 books, of which 15,000 belonged to his friend Alfieri; and is open thrice a-week. Many of the paintings are worth notice; one among them is Sir J. Reynolds's 'Young Samuel,' a beautiful specimen. A school of design is connected with it.

St. Piere's Cathedral is the largest and ugliest of all the churches, of which there are four or five; it is 180 feet long, and has three towers, a porch curiously resting on two cylindrical pillars with conical tops, ten side chapels, Santarille's statue of the Virgin, and paintings by Bourdon ('Simon Magus'), Jean de Troy ('Healing of the cripple'), and Ranc ('Power of the Keys'). Nôtre Dame des Tables church, which belonged to the Jesuits, is now the college.

Near the cathedral is the ancient machicolated *Ecole de Médecine*, first founded, they say, by the Arabs (or Saracens), and seated in what was the bishop's palace. Among the objects in it worth notice are, busts and portraits of eminent professors from the thirteenth century (besides a bronze of Hippocrates brought from Cos); the patched robe in which licentiates are dressed, once worn by Rabelais; the lecturer's seat in the amphitheatre (which holds 2,000); a marble piece of antiquity from Nismes; a library of 40,000 vols., and 600 MSS. in various languages, including Tasso's plan of his 'Jerusalem Delivered,' and Queen Christina's papers; and a room of anatomical models in wax, chiefly from Italy, but some by Delpuech. The *Botanical garden*, where De Candolle lectured, is in this neighbourhood, and was begun by Richier de Belleval 1593, in the time of Henry IV.; it contains 8,000 plants, many being rare exotics, and one, a cyprus called the Tree of Montpellier. In one corner is a tablet to Narcissa, supposed to be Young's daughter-in-law, Mrs. Temple; she died of consumption, and was buried here, but the body was afterwards moved to Lyons, to escape the bigoted fury of the populace. This town is still reckoned a great catholic stronghold; and the hatred of both parties is so great that they use different cafés and will hardly meet in society.—(Trollope's *Impressions of a Wanderer*).

St. Eloi's hospital, with 500 to 700 beds in it, was founded as far back as 1183; the hospital for incurables was built 1682; an asylum for insenses (lunatics), is near it. There is a prison for 450 on the solitary system, opened 1844; also a new palais de justice. The public bibliothèque has 7,000 vols.; the theatre on the citadel esplanade, is generally used as a bourse or exchange; the chamber of commerce is at the Hôtel St. Côme; the Tour de l' Observance serves as a telegraph.

Among a long list of natives are, James, King of Arragon, Count Daru and Cambacères. Rev. MM. Michel, Rognon, Corbière, are protestant pastors here. Manufactures of linen and cloth, liqueurs, chemicals, verdigris, refined sugar, leather, &c.; and a trade in these, with wine, fruit, olive oil, &c.

Conveyances: by rail, to Nismes, Marseilles, Cette, &c.; by coach, to Paris (malle poste in 47 hours), Toulouse, Perpignan, Rodez, Clermont, &c.

Up the little stream of the Verdanson, you come to the fountain of Jacques Cœur, Charles VII's goldsmith. Several decayed ports are along this coast, which is lined with low marshy lagoons or étangs.

[At 10 kil. south, on one of these étangs (de Thou) is the old church of Maguelonne, a mixture of the arab or norman, and the gothic, begun in the seventh century, and altered 1054. It is now a barn. The town was ruined in the 8th century by Charles Martel.]

(*a*) From Montpellier, on the rail, to Cette (17 miles long), trains go in less than an hour, the first starting at 5¾ a.m. to catch the steamer for Agde, whence the ascent by canal to Toulouse is made (p. 122). Fares, 2fr. 20c. and 1½ fr.

VILLENEUVE (7 kil.); Maureilhan (8 kil).

FRONTIGNAN (7 kil.), noted for its sweet wine, which is raised in what appears a most uninviting spot.

CETTE (7 kil.), a port, with 19,900 souls, on a flat piece of land under a chalk hill (590 feet high, outside the lagoons), in the Mediterranean, founded by Louis XIV., to complete the navigation of the canal du Midi. The harbour is made by two moles, (one 1,970 feet long), strengthened by forts at each end and a citadel and will hold about 400 sail, which may go in and out at all times, an advantage enjoyed by no other port in this quarter. This renders it the best starting point for Algeria. It has baths, &c., and there are salt works on the étangs, which are traversed by causeways and canals towards the Rhône, and towards the canal du Midi. The Duke d' Angoulême made his escape on board a ship here in 1815, when pursued by Napoleon. Good water is very scarce. Trade in wine, eaux-de-vie, fruit, salt, soap, perfumes, liqueurs, grain, timber, &c., and especially 'made wines of all kinds and qualities' for the foreign market. *Hotels*—Du Grand Galion; de la Souche.

Conveyances: by steamer to Marseilles, daily, in ten to twelve hours; twice a day to Meze, Marseilles, and Agde, and (by barge) up Canal du Midi to Toulouse, in thirty-six hours, for 19½ fr., 13 fr. and 7½ fr. according to class; to Algiers, on the 2nd, 12th, and 22nd of each month, in thirty-four hours.

ROUTE 43—*continued.*

From Montpellier, on the malle-post road to Carcassonne, Perpignan, and Toulouse, you pass

FABREQUES (11 kil)., to the right of which is Piguan, with an old castle of the eleventh century, and the ancient half-moorish abbey church of Vignogoul, older than the twelfth century.

GIGEAN (8 kil). A little further on to the left is Balarue, and its warm springs, with a temperature of 90°. 'They have a high reputation in rheumatic, and especially in paralytic cases.' (Lee).

MEZE (12 kil)., a small port on the étang de Thau (having Cette outside) with 4,800 persons, where the old seaside road to Béziers turns off. Here are the old church and cloisters of Vallemagne abbey, built in the twelfth century.

PEZENAS (18 kil)., a town of 7,700 souls, on the Hérault, where the Peine joins it, in a pleasant and healthy spot, is the roman *Piscennæ*, which Pliny praises for its wool. Simon de Montfort held it at one time; but when visited by Richelieu 1629, it belonged to Montmorency, whom he soon after beheaded. Its old château commands a fine view of the beautiful country around. The black nuns' church is now the salle de spectacle; that of the grey nuns is an eaux-de-vie distillery; and the Hôtel de la Paix occupied that of the white nuns. At M. Brun's house is the barber's chair in which Moliere, who made his debût here, used to be shaved. A large weekly market is held for eaux-de-vie, wine, dried fruit, &c.

LA BEGUDE-DE-JORDY (10 kil).

[At 13 kil. to the north is Gibian, which has a mineral spring, and remains of a roman aqueduct to Béziers. Near it is Casson convent, a large building. About the same distance to the south is

Agde, a port of the fourth class, near the mouth of the Hérault and the Canal du Midi (in Etang de Thau); it is a most ancient place, the greek *Agathe* (which means good or beautiful), founded before Christ by the Marseilles colonists, in a fertile spot, covered with lava from the extinct crater of St. Loup. It is nearly built of lava, and styled the Ville Noire (Black Town), in consequence. The harbour will admit 300 ton ships. An old gothic cathedral, of basalt, has a fine altar piece, and was the seat of a diocess in the fifth century. The strong fort of Brescou, in the rocks, protects the town. A suspension bridge hangs over the river. Population, 8,800.

The *Canal du Midi* (*i. e.* of the south), or *Canal du Languedoc*, was cut 1667-81, in the time of Louis XIV., by Riquet-de-Bonrepos, according to the plans of Andréosi. It begins at Agde at the south end of Etang de Thau, and passes Béziers, Carcassonne, &c. to the Garonne, a little below Toulouse, where that river is navigable to the Bay of Biscay; so that a complete water communication is thus opened between the latter and the Mediterranean. Length about 152 miles, with 64 locks, about 100 bridges, and 55 aqueducts; it is 66 feet wide. The tunnel of Mal-pas, is 567 feet long. Good barges ascend it. "There is an airy and comfortably fitted up little cabin, in which, or on the roof of which, one may sit at pleasure, and be drawn along without jolt or dust, by four horses at the rate of six or seven miles an hour." But this conveyance is tedious from the number of locks and turnings. The proposed Bordeaux and Cette railway follows this route.]

BEZIERS (12 kil)., a sous-préfecture of 18,000 souls, and the roman *Biterra*, finely seated on a rock 200 to 260 feet above the Orb and the Canal du Midi, in a beautiful country. It is one of the most thriving seats of the *brandy* trade. The main street runs up to it through a ravine. A few roman antiques are worked into its old wall, parts of which, however have been pulled down to make room for houses, a theatre, and boulevards. It was one of the chief towns of the Albigenses, when the 'triple tyrant,' Innocent III., proclaimed a crusade against them in the thirteenth century, headed by Simon de Montfort, and 60,000 were slaughtered here.

The old castle-like *Cathedral*, with its great tower and turrets, has a good nave and choir, and several stained windows; near it are water works by Cordier, and the old bishop's palace, now the sous-préfecture, with a noble prospect. Madeleine and Aphrodise churches are worth notice, the latter being so called after the patron saint who came here, they say, as early as 250, on a camel. The figure of 'Pépuzac' the traditional founder of the town, is pointed out. There are large factories for casks, made of beautiful oak imported from Rome. The marché aux grains was once a church; that for cattle is the site of the citadel; a public library of 5,000 vols. was begun by the Jesuits 1637. A walk may be taken to the locks on the canal; silk stockings, gloves, eaux-de-vie, liqueurs, confitures, glass, paper, soap, &c. are made; and there is a trade in white, red, and muscatel wines, fruits, &c. The figs of Puissalcon, the Neflès figs, and the game pâtés of Laurens, are all noted. *Hotels*—De la Croix-Blanche (White Cross of the Crusaders); du Nord; de la Poste.

At 27 kil. beyond is Narbonne, whence it is 59 kil. to Carcassonne, and 93 further to Toulouse (*see* Routes 47 and 50).

Narbonne, a fortress, sous-préfecture of 12,000 population, in department Aude, and once seat of an archbishop, in a fertile plain, on a cut from the Aude to a lagoon called étang de la Roubine, on the Mediterranean, which is three leagues distant. It stands on the old Aurelian way, and was colonized in the 636th year of Rome, by Lucius Crassus, as *Narbo Martius*, the capital of Gallia Narbonensis. The Visigoths made it their capital when their leader married the sister of the emperor Honorius 414; in 752 it was incorporated with France by Pepin. Many roman inscriptions are let into the ramparts. Pont des Marchand is part of the ancient Pons Vetus or old bridge.

The streets are narrow and crooked; walks in Plan des Barques, and the Allée des Soupirs, on the canal. St. Just's cathedral church, consisting of a large choir only, is a fine gothic specimen, begun 1272, having flying buttresses, two towers, a vault 131 feet high, with slender pillars and painted windows, besides monuments of bishop De la Jugie, and a soldier named Lasbordes (black marble, in armour of 15th century), with a carving of the Assumption. Two popes, Clement IV. and VII., were priests here. There are six other churches, St. Paul's being as old as 1229, and large; while St. Sebastian's has many roman stones in it. At the archbishop's old place or castle, with an ancient square tower rising over it, Louis XIII. gave up Cinq Mars to the vengeance of Cardinal Richelieu. The museum contains several roman remains, and the public library. Trade in wines, honey, wax, olives, corn, cloth, &c. *Hotels*—De France; de la Dorade.

Mont Laures to the north-west, has traces of a country seat of the emperor Augustus.

From Narbonne, the next place is

Sijean (21 kil.), near the coast and Etang de Sijean; not far from which Charlemagne defeated the Saracens 737.

Leaving Leucate, a roman station, on the left, and the lake which it stands at the head of, you come to

Salces (26 kil), which was the ancient *Salsulæ*, from its mineral waters, and has a round donjon tower built by Charles V., surrounded by low walls, with towers at corners, ditches, &c. White wine to imitate Tokay is made.

Rivesaltes (7 kil). It stands in the fertile plain of the Aigly, having a population of 3,740, and a good trade in muscatel wine.

[At 16 kil. west up the river, is Estagel, a pretty place, with a trade in wine, oil, spirits, bees, cattle; where Arago, the astronomer, and his brother Jacques, the circumnavigator, were born. Nôtre Dame des Peines hermitage is near, on a rock. Grey marble is quarried.—Further up (16 kil), is St. Paul de Fenouillet, among mountain rocks, on which three old castles are seen; it has a mineral spring, and the grotto hermitage of St. Antoine de Galamus.]

At 8 kil. further is Perpignan, on the Aurelian way, which still forms the high road into Spain.

Perpignan. *Hotels*—De l'Europe; du Petit-Paris; du Luxembourg; des Ambassadeurs; du Midi (the South). Population, 20,000. Chief town of department Pyrenées Orientales (or East Pyrenees), seat of a bishop, a fortress of the first class, &c., was formerly the capital of Roussillon, a province held by the Visigoths, between the fifth and eighth centuries, then by the king of Arragon till it came to France, 1659, by the treaty of the Pyrenees; but the people are almost spanish in their manners, appearance, and language.

The town stands on the Tet, 11 kil. from the

Mediterranean, in a wide fertile plain, terminated by the Pyrenees and the Spanish frontier to the south (25 kil), Mont Canigou to the south-west (35 kil), and the Corbières to the north. There is a seven-arched bridge over the Tet, whence there is a good prospect; and another of one arch over the Basse, which is a branch of it. Gardens of vines olives, pomegranates, oranges, &c., are seen outside the brick ramparts; the streets are narrow, dark, and paved with pebbles, and the houses spanish looking, having wooden balconies, &c. Outside porte Notre Dame is the ancient brick château of Castillet, on a high rock, now used as a prison; it is machicolated, and in the moorish style. Porte Canet leads out to the Blanqueries, where the tanners live. Place de la Loge, where the Hôtel de Ville stands, is so called from an old carved gothic building; in Place de la Liberté was the Jesuits convent, destroyed at the revolution. Near the church of St. Jean le Vieux (the old), built in the eleventh century, cross-shaped, with a square tower, is the

Cathedral of St. Jean, begun by the kings of Majorca (who held the town from James I of Arragon in the thirteenth century), and finished by Louis XI (who took it in 1474 from Jacques II). Length, 254 feet; breadth, 64; height 92, the vault being unsupported by pillars; it has a good screen of white marble. The old churches of the Cordeliers, Carmelites (on the esplanade,) and Dominicians, deserve notice.

The *Citadel*, on a slight rise above the town, built by Vauban, includes a large place d'armes, barracks, and the donjon castle of the Comtes de Rousillon, &c., consisting of eight square towers joined by high walls; besides an old chapel which serves for the magazine. A library of 14,000 vols. and a museum are placed in the old university buildings, founded by Pedro, of Arragon, 1349; there is a pepinière or nursery, besides public baths, theatre, a college, priests' seminary, two hospitals, &c. At the Jardin de Pharmacie is a virginian tulip tree, planted 1769, sixty feet high. Since 1800, a government bergerie for breeding merino sheep has been established here. H. Rigaud, the painter, and Madame Tastu, the poetess, were born here.

Linen and woollen stuffs, playing cards, bricks, oil, eaux-de-vie, &c., are made; and there is a trade in cork, wine, iron, &c. Coaches to Narbonne, Toulouse, and to Spain, for which the Spanish consul will *visé* the passport for 5fr.

VILLEMOULAGNE (13 kil.).

[*Elne* (10 kil. east), near the Tech, once strongly fortified, has a romanesque church of the eleventh century, with two towers, &c.]

LE BOULAU (8 kil.), on the Tech, where Route 43 *b*, to Mont Canigou, turns off.

[At 22 kil. east is *Port Vendres*, on the sea, near Cape Bearn, the *Portus Veneris* of the Romans, surrounded by hills, and improved for deep vessels by Louis XVI, to whom there is a pillar of Rousillon marble, 108 feet high. It is a fourth class fortress. A pass leads south by the Col de Banyuls and the coast to Rosas, in Catalonia.—Collioure to the north of it, is another port, fit for small craft only, with a population of 3,300, the *Cauco-Illiberis* of the Romans, rebuilt by the counts of Roussillon.]

L'ECLUSE (5 kil.), the old *Clausuræ*, with a decayed fort.

BELLEGARDE (5 kil.), a fort, on the very frontier, to defend the pass of the Pyrenees here called Col de Perthus. The town, built 1674 by the Spaniards, was surrounded with bastions by Louis XIV, in one of which General Dugommier, killed 1794 in the spanish war, was buried; but his remains with those of General Dagobert are now at Perpignan. Here Pompey, on the Summum Pyrenæum, built a column stating that from the Alps to the further end of Spain he had reduced 867 cities to the roman rule; which, with the altar, added by Cæsar, is gone. At 24 kil. further is Junquera, the first town in *Spain*, on the road to Figueras and Barcelona.

ROUTE 43*a*.

Perpignan, up the Tet, into Spain.

Distance, about 72 kil. or 43 miles.

PERPIGNAN as above, in Route 43.

St. FELIN (12 kil.) on the Tet.

ILLE (13 kil.), a small town at the end of the plain of Perpignan, surrounded with old turretted walls, and once noted for peaches and other fruits. The church is built of rough marble.

VINCA (8 kil.), where a stream from Mont Canigou falls in, passing Valmanya (11 kil. south), a mining village, by which the mountain may be ascended, by a good climber, and a descent made to Arles on the opposite side.

PRADES (16 kil.), a small sous-préfecture (population, 3,200), in a fertile hollow of the mountains, built 844; having a college, hospice, a good church, and (near it) remains of St. Martin de Cuxa abbey. Trade in corn, wine, wool, hemp, &c. The Canigou is reached about 12 kil. south, by way of Taurinya.

[At 6 kil. north-north-west is *Molitg* or Moligt a small place (population, 600), in a gorge of the Castillane, noted for its twelve warm springs (temperature 90° to 100°), useful for indigestion, ulcers, chronic muscular complaints, nervous diseases, and frequented July to September; board, 3½ to 4½fr. a day.]

VILLEFRANCHE (5 kil.), a third class fortress, in a deep gorge at the bottom of the cliffs which hem in the Tet, here lined by two streets of red marble houses. It was built by Vauban for Louis XIV, who, they say, confined some of his court ladies here. On the south side, beyond the ramparts, is Coba-Bastère grotto. Population, 700.

[To the south, up the valley of the Conflent, is Vernet (8 kil.), a pretty village, known for its hot springs. About 3 kil. higher up the side of Mont Canigou, on a rocky height, are the picturesque remains (a good tower, &c.) of St. Martin's abbey, founded in this desolate spot, 1101, by Guiffred, Comte de Cerdagne and Conflent,to expiate the murder of his nehpew. In winter it is covered with snow, and inhabited by wolves.]

OLETTE (9 kil.), where two streams join the Tet.

THUES-EN-TRAVAILLS (5 kil.) has several hot sulphur springs, one of which, the Cascade, is as high as 160° temperature.

FONTPEDROUZE (5 kil.), in a pretty part of the Tet, near a fall, and several good points of view.

MOUNT-LOUIS (5 kil.), as in Route 48; beyond which is the head of the Segre, and Bourg-Madame, on the *Spanish* frontier.

ROUTE 43*b*.

Perpignan, up the Tech, by Mont Canigou, into Spain.

Distance, 51 kil. or 34 miles.

PERPIGNAN, as in Route 43, above.

LE BOULAU (21 kil.), in the same route.

CERET (8 kil. south-west of Le Boulau), up the Tech (above the curious one-arch bridge, 149 feet span from rock to rock, 80 from the water, only 14 broad, built 1336), is a sous-préfecture of 3,519 souls, and an old place with modern faubourgs beyond the old walls. It has a large public fountain, and St Fereol hermitage is near. The commission met here 1660, to settle the boundaries of France and Spain.

FORT-LES-BAINS (7 kil.), so called from a mountain fort, and the sulphur springs below, used by patients afflicted with rheumatism, paralysis, &c. Fish and game are plentiful. There is a military hospital here.

ARLES-SUR-TECH (5 kil.) has the ancient church of St. Benoit's abbey (founded 778), in the porch of which is the grey marble tomb of two saints, brought from Rome in the eleventh century. Population, 2,000.

[About 5 kil. west-north-west, up a branch of the Tech, is Corsavy, near a precipice 886 feet down; whence it is almost 10 kil. by mule-paths and serrated ridges, and hard climbing to the top of

Mont Canigou, the highest peak of the East Pyrenees, 1,454 toises, or 9,298 feet above the sea, and visible 30 leagues round. It is covered with snow seven months in the year, and shews signs of having been worked for minerals. The mountains in this quarter are not bare, but edged with forests of pines, oak, ash, chesnut, cork, &c.]

LE-SAUVEUR-LE-TECH (8 kil.).

PRATS-DE-MOLLO (5 kil.), a small fortified mountain post, strengthened by old gothic walls, and La Garde fort, built by Vauban. Population, 3,500. A path leads over the ridge of the Pyrenees to Campredon, on the *Spanish* side (18 kil.) on the river Ter. To the west, near the head of the Tech, are the warm mineral waters of La Preste close to the grotto of Britchos, and quarries of veined marble and breccia.

ROUTE 44.

Nismes to Alais, Grand Combe, Florac, Mende, St. Flour, & Clermont.

Distance, about 322 kil. or 200 miles, through the hilly and interesting districts of the Cevennes.

By rail from Nismes to Alais; 30 miles or 49 kil. in 1¾ hours; twice a-day. The rail passes several rocky trenches, and has four tunnels (one 1,300 feet long), and some well constructed bridges and viaducts.

NISMES, as in Route 43.

[At 20 kil. north-north-east is *Uzès*, 14 kil. north-west of Pont du Gard, a sous-préfecture of 6,200 souls, on the olive-covered rocks above the Auzon. It is the roman *Ucetia* which had a temple to Augustus, and sent a bishop to the council of Arles 455 A.D. In 1560 the bishop and all went over to the reformed faith, for which Louis XIII. garrisoned it and razed the walls. It was latterly a duchy in the Crussol family (first peers of France), whose old château remains, with high walls and corner towers, like the bastile at Paris; the chapel has stained windows, and tombs of the dukes from 1660. St. Therri's cathedral was burnt 1611, except the fine circular romanesque tower of six stages (once, eight, they say) to which a modern church is added, with a portrait of Cardinal Pacca. St. Etienne's was the Jesuits' church. An ancient crypt, in another part, has an ill-made figure of Christ crowned, with the stigmata. The large bishop's palace is now the préfecture, with a beautiful park behind. A little beyond is the house where Racine lived, 1661–2, when studying theology here; it has a fine prospect over the valley of Gisfort, in which is a grotto called Temple des Druides, with a dolmen close by; also the Tournal tower and the Fontaine d'Eure, which supplied the great aqueduct to Nismes. Many roman inscriptions have been found. A few silk goods are made. Revs. MM. Saussine, Dumergue, and Roux, are protestant pastors here.

Conveyances to Nismes, Alais, &c.]

MAS-DE-PONGE (6¼ miles).

FONS (5¼ miles).

ST. GENIES (3¾ miles).

NOZIERES (2¼ miles).

BONCOIRAN (1¼ miles) on the Gardon, which floods it sometimes, is a small village, with some mills, gothic looking houses, and an old château with a square tower, on a rock.

NERS (1¾ miles) on a hill, overlooking the fine valley of Beau-rivage, on the Gardon, with the Cevennes in the distance.

VEYENOBRES (1¾ miles) on a hill side.

ST. HILAIRE (4½ miles).

Alais (3¾ miles) a sous-préfecture in department Gard, of 17,000 people, and a thriving town, among coal and iron mines, under the Cevennes mountains, where the Cèze meets the Gardon d'Alais and Gardon de Mialet. It had a leper's hospital for the crusaders in the time of St. Louis, and was held by the English when given up 1422, to Charles VII. Having become a head quarters of the French reformed church (which held a synod here, 1620, under Dumoulin), it was besieged and taken by Louis XIII., who razed its walls. Louis XIV. built a citadel, and sent a bishop to bring them back, but without success. The fort is now a law-court; there are a gothic cathedral church, a library of 3,000 vols., silk mills, &c.

In the neighbourhood are the pretty walks on the Gardon, the hermitage, part of a convent, the sulphur mines of St. German de Valgagne; by another way, in the valley of the Calaigon, you pass the Tour de Fare belonging to General Meynadier, and part of Puech-de-Cendras abbey, burnt by the Camisards, who were hunted down in the religious wars of 1704. Some mineral springs here are useful as tonics and in skin diseases. Revs. MM. Gaillard, Dubois, E. Dhombres, are protestant pastors here.

Hotels—Du Luxembourg; du Commerce; du Louvre.

A railway of 10 miles (1½ hours, thrice a day) goes on past Les Tamaris to La Lavade and La Pise, in *La Grand' Combe*, the centre of this coal and iron district, the mines of which are in the hands of a company. Coal (houille) is plentiful, both anthracite and inflammable, and is worked by means of galleries; the steam-engines were made in England, and brought here by way of Cette; several english workmen are employed in the mines and iron-foundries. The coalfield reaches to St. Ambroix (20 kil. north-east of Alais) on the Cèze, a fine spot among the rocks, with many silk mills.

The road hence to Privas and Valence, is described in Route 41.

[At 10 kil. south-west of Alais is Anduze, the roman *Andusia*, a picturesque town near the fine château of Tornac (a key to the Cevennes), where the Camisards began to rise against their oppressors in the time of Louis XIV., and where also Marshal Villars made proposals of peace to their chief leader, Jean Cavalier. They were eventually subdued by the Duke of Berwick, 1705.

On the west is the fine valley of St. Jean de Gardonnenque. The rugged rocks of granite, grau-wacke, limestone, gypsum, &c., are worth notice; *quercus coccifera*, an oak yielding a beautiful dye, abounds here.

To the south-west is the castle where Florian the French novelist was born; also Sauve, on the Vidourle, where fourches or wooden pitchforks are made, and lead mines worked; La Salle (population 2,120) which has silk mills on the Gardon, and gypsum quarries; St. Hippolyte (population 5,200) near the head of the Vidourle, with a protestant temple, built out of the fort erected to overawe that faith, which fort was formerly the château of the seigneurs; and Le Vigan (see below). Revs. MM. Boissière and Dussaut, are protestant pastors at St. Hippolyte.]

MIALET, 10 kil. west of Alais, is noted for its mountain caves, in which bones have been found; and was the birth-place of Roland, the Camisard leader in the religious wars, who used to hide here, and who, being captured by Villars, was burnt alive at Nismes. At 5 kil. further is

ST. JEAN DU GARD, on the coach road to Nismes, in a fine part of the Garden d'Anduze, where silk goods, millinery, &c. are made.

[*Le Vigan* (25 kil. to the south-west) is another charming place (and sous-préfecture, of 5,200 souls) on the Arre, near Mont l'Eperon in the Cevennes, surrounded by country houses of the Nismes and Montpellier gentry. A gothic bridge crosses the river; there are catholic and protestant churches, cotton and silk thread mills; and, on the principal place, a bronze of d'Assas, a young captain of an Auvergne regiment, who fell at Clostercamp in Flanders, 1760. Making a reconnaissance at night, he suddenly came upon the enemy who were advancing to surprise the French, and threatened to shoot him if he spoke. Without hesitation he rushed on them shouting '*A moi Auvergne, ce sont les ennemis*' (after me soldiers, these are the enemy!) and fell, pierced by scores of balls. His last words are cut on the statue. Revs. MM. Dhombres, Colombier, and Bonquier, are protestant pastors.

A hill near château Marave offers a fine point of view. There are mineral waters at Cauvalet; and, up the Arre, you come to the coal mines, which Mr. Hammond, an Englishman, is working.

The road from Le Vigan to Montpellier, is described in Route 45.]

LE POMPIDOU (30 kil.) on the Gardon, under the ridge of the Cevennes, which divides the departments of Lozère and Gard.

[Cassagnas, about 10 kil. north-east, with its caves was one of the head quarters of the Camisard leaders.]

FLORAC (23 kil.), a sous-préfecture in department Lozère, of 2,300 souls, in the valley of the Tarn, where the Tarnon and Minente join it, among the Hautes Cevennes. It began in a castle of which a part of two low battlemented towers are left; and has but one main street, with a church, a protestant chapel (Rev. Mr. Alberic, pastor), palais de justice, &c. The sides of the rock are covered with vines, chesnuts, and oaks.

About 12 kil. up the Tarn is Pont Montvert, under Mont Lozère, where the Camisards murdered the priest Chayla, 1702, a cruel persecutor of the protestants, for which their leader was burnt alive. Pope Urban V. was born at Grizac near this.

ISPAGNAC or Hispagnac (9 kil.) on the Tarn, in a pretty valley, near the high, cold, and dreary plain, called the Causse de Sauveterre, 2,870 feet above the sea.

[Quezac, nearly opposite it, is noted for its mineral water, and a gothic bridge and chapel, built by Pope Urban.—St. Enimie, 11 kil. further down the Tarn, in the midst of wild and rugged peaks, grew out of a monastery to St. Bennet founded in the seventh century, by a daughter of Clotaire II.—St. Prejet, 20 kil. still further down the Tarn, at the bottom of a defile, 1,900 feet deep at the Pas de Souci, where it is so narrow that a bridge might be almost run across.—Megruies, 20 kil. south-east of this is noted for three large caves.]

At 28 kil. further, passing Molines, is Mende, (*see* Route 40); beyond that is St. Chaley (48 kil.)

and St Flour (30 kil.) on the Clermont road, as in Route 52.

ROUTE 45.

Montpellier, up the Herault, to Mende.

Distance to Le Vigan, about 51 kil. or 32 mls.

MONTPELLIER, as in Route 43.

MONTFERRIER (6 kil.) a little to the east of the road, makes a pleasing appearance, being on a volcanic peak about 140 feet above sea, on or round which are grouped an old château of its marquises, a park stretching to the Luz, mills, &c. Another lava peak, Valmahargues, is to the west.

ST. GELY (5 kil.)

[At 5 kil. to the east is Prades, at the head of the Lez, which has its source in a ravine (something like Vaucluse), behind the castle of Restinclières.]

ST. MARTIN (12 kil.)

ST. GUILHEM-LE-DESERT (7 kil.), in a deep gorge of the Hérault, among the rugged limestone peaks of the Cevennes range, is under the large old castle called the Géant, which belonged, they say, to the giant Gallone, who fought with St. Guilhem. In one part is a primitive suspension bridge, in the indian style, running from cliff to cliff, about 127 feet long.

ST. BAUZILLE-DU-PUTOIS (6 kil.), a small village on the Hérault, is remarkable for a succession of caves in the limestone, called (in the patois of this part) Baouma de las Doumaïselas, or the ladies' cavern (another name is the grotto of the Ganges), full of stalactites and stalagmites of all shapes.

GANGES (5 kil.), further up the Hérault.

LE VIGAN, on the Arre, is about 10 kil. north-west of this (*see* Route 44). St. Hippolyte about 15 kil. east; and St. Jean du Gard about 20 kil. north of St. Hippolyte.

From St. Jean the road to Mende is as in Route 44, where these places are described.

ROUTE 45*a*.

Montpellier to Lodeve, Milhau, and Rodez.

Distance (to Milhau) 121 kil. or 75 miles.

MONTPELLIER, as in Route 43.

LA BARAQUE-DE-BEL-AIR (12 kil.)

GIGNAC (18 kil.) on the Hérault, which a curious bridge crosses, has a good church, a square tower, and the chapel of Nôtre Dame on the heights, thought to have been a temple of Vesta. A little higher up the river is Aniane, where St. Bennet was born; the old abbey, founded 782 by a count of Maguelonne, is here.

LODEVE (24 kil.), a sous-préfecture, with 10,800 population, on the Ergue (a branch of the Hérault), in a pretty valley at the foot of the Cevennes mountains, which are cultivated to the top. The old church of St. Fulcran (a cathedral till the revolution), which was part of St. Sauveur's abbey, has a great square machicolated tower, with turrets, &c., and was fortified against the Albigenses, when the town was walled round. It has a mineral spring, and the Juifs' (Jews') grotto. Cardinal Fleury and General Lagarde were born here. *Hotels*—De la Croix Blanche (White Cross); du Cheval Vert (Green Horse)

[Clermont-Hérault, 15 kil. south-east, near the Ydriomel, is an industrious town of 6,200 people, who make cloth, cotton, &c. It has an old castle, and a gothic church with a fine rose window.]

ST. PIERRE-DE-FAGE (15 kil.)

LE CAYLAR (13 kil.), on a plateau above the source of the Legerce, has remains of old walls. A charming path, called the Escalette road, leads to several fine points of view, near the source of the Ergue.

LA CABALERIC (22 kil.)

MILHAU (17 kil.), already described (*see* Route 40), where the roads to Mende and Albi divide off.

[About 23 kil. south of Milhau, is Nant in the beautiful valley of the Dourbie, where it joins the Tarn, in a spot remarkable for the Poujade and other grottoes.]

BOIS DU FOUR (21 kil.)

PONT DE SALARS (26 kil.)

RODEZ is 25 kil. further, as in Route 52.

ROUTE 46.

Beziers to St. Pons, Castres, (ALBI,) and Toulouse.

Distance, 172 kil. or 107 miles.

BEZIERS, as in Route 43.

ST. CHINIAN (27 kil.), a small place of about 3,400 souls, where cloth and eaux-de-vie are made. Large stalactite caves are in the limestone hills near it.

[About 18 kil. to the south-west is *Minerve*, an ancient place on the Brian and Cesse, in a wild rocky spot, where the bloody Simon de Montfort and his crusaders burnt about 4,000 of the Albigenses. On the Cesse are the large grottoes of Baume de la Coquille, so called because of an enormous shell-like stalactite in it, full of water.—At Bize, 16 kil. lower down the Cesse, in the valley of Fons, many bones have been found in the caves.]

St. Pons-de-Thomieres (23 kil.), a sous-préfecture of 6,270 people, in a pretty valley of the Jaur, among the mountains, has a fine old church, built of marble; and, at the head of the river (which falls into a natural basin), another old church of Charlemagne's time; a gothic tower on a rock, and two great elms, making a very picturesque group.

St. Amans-la-Bastide (25 kil), on the Thore.

[At 25 kil. south is Caunes, in department Aude, with good marble quarries, and remains of a hermitage in the rocks near them.]

Castres (27 kil.), a sous-préfecture in department Tarn, on the river Agout, which divides it from Villegoudon, has beautiful promenades called Lices (lists, where tournaments were held), with an Hôtel de Ville, built by Mansard, (where the public library of 7,000 vols. is placed), barracks for cavalry, public gardens, and the church of St. Benoit (formerly the cathedral), which contains paintings by Ridals, Lesueur, and Coypel. Among the natives was Rapin, who wrote the History of England. A logan stone is to be seen in the neighbourhood. Population 16,418.

Rev. MM. Dejean and Dombre are protestant pastors here. Thriving manufactures of cloth, linens, flannels, soap, leather, &c.; and a trade in these articles, paper, liqueurs, confectionery. *Hotels* — Du Grand Soleil (Sun); du Nord; Sabatier.

Albi is 39 kil. north of Castres (*see* Route 52).

Puy-Laurens, 20 kil. west of Castres, on the Toulouse road, belonged to the counts of Toulouse, and was made a duchy in favour of Richelieu's niece. It stands on the top of a rock, and was fortified by the protestants, whose academy of sciences here was suppressed by Louis XIV.

Toulouse is 50 kil. further (*see* Route 50).

ROUTE 47.

Narbonne to Carcassonne and Toulouse.

Distance, 163 kil., or 101 miles.

Narbonne, as in Route 43.

Villedaigue (13 kil.)

Moux (15 kil.), to the north of which is the old abbey of Grasse, with some of Spagnoletto's pictures.

Barbeira (13 kil.)

At 15 kil. further, is

Carcassonne. *Hotels*—Bonnet; Nôtre Dame; de l'Ange (Angel); St. Pierre; St. Jean Baptiste. Population, 19,000, many of whom are employed in the manufacture of fine woollens. A very old place, chief town of department Aude, and seat of a diocess, college, tribunal, &c., in a fertile spot, near the canal du Midi, on the Aude, which divides the Cité, or old town, from the Basse Ville, or new town, and is crossed by a bridge. It was a station in *Gallia Ulterior*, in Cæsar's time, and came to the Visigoths, the Saracens, and the counts of Toulouse. A figure of Dame Carcas, who they say founded the town, is shewn by the people.

The modern part is well built, and watered by streams and fountains; one, of Neptune and his horses, is in Grande Place. The promenades are various (on the quay, &c.), and sheltered from the keen winds which blow here. Among the buildings worth notice are the Hôtel de Ville; the préfecture and its large gardens, with a roman inscription to Numerian; library of 6,000 vols. and museum; the bridge, whence you see the Pyrenees; the barracks, theatre, hospitals, &c. St. Vincent's church contains much stained glass.

In the old Cité, higher up, are the ruined walls and battlements of the castle, partly as old as the eleventh century, which the Black Prince tried to take, 1356. St. Nazaire's (Nazarius) *Cathedral*, near it, is a small but good building of the eleventh century, partly in the norman style, with well-stained windows, and the broken tomb of Simon de Montfort (Earl of Leicester), who besieged the town when held by the Albigenses, 400 of whom he burnt alive. A small branch canal, carried over the river Fresquel, on an aqueduct, joins the canal du Midi, which unites the Bay of Biscay and the Mediterranean, and to the planner of which (Riquet) there is a pillar of the coloured marble quarried in this part. Manufactures of cloth for the Levant, &c., eaux-de-vie, leather, paper, &c.; and a trade in these, and wine, grain, fruit, &c.

Conveyances to Toulouse and Béziers (by canal); to Narbonne, Nismes, Perpignan, Montpellier, &c.

ALZONNE (16 k.), on the Aude and canal du Midi.

[Fanjeaux (15 kil. south-west), has an old fort, which encloses remains of a temple to Jupiter.]

VILLEPINTE (8 kil.)

CASTELNAUDARY (12 kil.), a sous-préfecture, in department Aude (population, 9,800), on a gentle slant from the canal du Midi, which has a basin here, 600 toises round, with walks about it whence the Pyrenees are seen. It had a château which Raymond VI. burnt, 1211; and here the Duc de Montmorenci was taken prisoner at the battle of 1632. St. Michel's spire church has a picture by Rivals; there are also a large hospice, founded 1774, by Bishop de Langle; and a cemetery, with the tomb of General Andréossy, a native; as was General Dejean. Pottery, flour, spirits, &c., are made. *Hotels*—De la Flèche (Arrow); Nôtre Dame; de France. Coaches to Toulouse, Carcassonne, &c.

[At 19 kil. north-north-east, is *Revel*, a thriving town of 5,600 souls, in a fertile plain; not far from which (5 kil. east) is

Sorèze, once a fortified town, and having, on the site of abbey de la Paix, founded in the ninth century, by Pepin, a celebrated school or pensionnat for 400, which includes an observatory, botanic garden and cabinet of natural history, swimming school, laboratory, riding and military grounds, and a theatre for declamation; sixty professors are attached, and each student pays 1,000 fr. (£40). To the south of it, in the Montagne Noir, or Black Mountain, is the grotto of Lou Traouc d'el Calel; and the great reservoir of St. Ferreol, which feeds the canal du Midi, by a cut to Naurouze (as below), and is made by shutting up the valley of the Laudot; its circuit is about 6,400 yards.—Puy-Laurens (11 kil. north of Revel), is described in Route 46.]

NAUROUZE (14 kil.), is at the summit level of the canal du Midi (620 feet above the Mediterranean; see Agde, Route 43), marked by a pillar to Riquet, its engineer.

VILLEFRANCHE-DE-LAURAGUAIS (22 kil.) in department Haute-Garonne, a sous-préfecture of 2,770 souls, in the middle of a wide, fertile plain, on the Lers and canal du Midi. Sails for wind-mills, woollens, pottery, &c., are made, and vers à soie (silk worms) reared.

BAZIEGE (11 k.), on the Lers and the canal; as is Castanet (12 kil.); both in a fertile country.

At 12 kil. further is Toulouse (*see* Route 50).

ROUTE 48.

Carcassonne, up the Aude, to Foix, Tarascon, Mont Louis, in the Pyrenees, and Puycerda, in Spain.

Distance (to Mont Louis) 114 kil., or 71 miles.

CARCASSONNE, (Route 47); thence up the Aude to

LIMOUX (25 kil.), a sous-préfecture, in department Aude, as old as the ninth century, in a pretty spot on that river, with 7,000 souls, who carry on the cloth manufactures, &c.

From this, a road turns off to Chalabre (24 kil.), Lavalanet (20 kil.), whence it is 24 kil. to Foix, and 28 kil. to Tarascon (*see* Route 50).

ALET (10 kil.), under the Pyrenees, on the Aude, has good mineral springs.

[*Rennes-des-Bains* (21 kil. from Limoux), on the left, in a fine gorge, on the Sals, has also good springs, which are much frequented.]

QUILLAN (21 kil.), a place of 1,500 souls, engaged in the cloth manufactures and the iron works. The road from Perpignan to Foix crosses here.

The road ascends the Pyrenees, up the course of the Aude, past Axat (12 kil.), Roquefort (12 kil.), and Querigut (8 kil.), whence a road leads about 20 kil. west to Ax (*see* Route 50); then Fourmiquièrs (10 kil.), and the head of the Aude (in a lake), to where Route 43*a* (from Perpignan), falls in at

MONT LOUIS (16 kil.), a small port on a rock over the Tet, fortified by Vauban, to command the pass of Col de la Perche, about 5,200 ft. above the sea. In the Place is the tomb of Gen. Dagobert.

Further on, you cross the Sègre (which rises to the left, under Mont Puymal, about 8600 feet), at Saillagouse (10 kil.), and come to Bourg-Madame (10 kil.), on the very frontier, here marked by the Sègre, which is crossed by a short rustic bridge, and brings you to Puycerda, &c., in SPAIN.

SECTION V.

ROADS TO THE MIDDLE AND SOUTH OF FRANCE;

IN CONNEXION WITH THE PARIS AND ORLEANS RAILWAY (LIGNES D'ORLEANS ET DU CENTRE), SUPPLYING CORBEIL, ORLEANS (THENCE TO BORDEAUX, IN ROUTE 65), NEVERS, MOULIN (THENCE TO LYONS), CLERMONT-FERRAND, LE PUY, GUERET, LIMOGES, TULLE, AURILLAC, CAHORS, ALBI, TOULOUSE, &C.—ROUTES FIFTY TO SIXTY-THREE.

ROUTE 50.

Paris to Orleans.

Station, or embarcadère, Boulevart de l'Hôpital, No. 77, near the Jardin des Plantes; opened May, 1843, (to Corbeil, September, 1840); 122 kil.. or 76 miles, to Orléans. Six trains a-day; three to four hours; 12½, 9¼, and 7 fr. Buffets for refreshments at Etampes and Orléans. Baggage allowed, 30 kil., or 66 lbs. Omnibuses meet all the trains from the branch offices, at Rue Drouot, No. 4; Cours des Domaines, Rue du Bouloi, 21; Rue St. Martin, 295; Rue du Bac, 121; Rue de l'Ancienne Comédie, 14; fare, 30 cent. (3d.), exclusive of baggage.

The stations along this line are

	kil.		kil.		kil.
Choisy	10	Marolles	6	Angerville	5
Juvisy	9	Bouray	4	Toury*	13
Savigny	3	Lardy	2	Artenay	14
Epinay	2	Etrechy	7	Chevilly	6
St. Michel	4	Etampes	7	Cercottes	4
Bretigny	2	Monnerville	14	Orléans	10

The line runs out by Barrière de la Gare and Pont de Bercy, on the Seine, past the bastions at the bac or ferry, Ivry (population, 6,000) and its fort, with Grand Gentilly to the left.

[Gentilly (5 kil. from Paris), on the Bièvre, is near Villeroy château and the

Bicêtre, once a château of Jean, Duke of Berri, and a military hospital, now a vast asylum, in connexion with the Salpêtrière, for 3,000 old people and for lunatics, in a building about 1,000 feet square. In the court is a great well (puits de Bicêtre), 7 feet diameter, and 187 feet deep in the rock; the water is conveyed thence to a reservoir, 57 feet square. Workshops, gardens, a farm, &c., are attached. The Duke of Berri's château replaced a carthusian house, built by Bishop John of Winchester, whence the present name, Winchestre, Bicestre, Bicêtre.]

VITRY-SUR-SEINE (Villejuif to the left), has a seat which belonged to Count Dubois, and is near a spot on the river called Porte à l'Anglais, where the English who held Paris in the time of Charles VI. had a camp to cut off the Dauphin's communication by the river. Population, 2,500. An eight-arch viaduct brings you to

CHOISY-LE-ROI (6¼ miles), in department Seine-et-Oise, at the five-arch bridge on the Seine, built 1802, and so called from a château of Louis XV. which was here. Population, 3,300. There are large glass-works, where painting on glass is carried on; also factories for morocco leather, soap, porcelain, &c.—Thiais is to the south-west, and the Lyons railway on the opposite side of the river.—A little further, at the bridge on the Seine, is Villeneuve-le-Roi, which belonged to Philippe Auguste, and has a good church and several country houses.

ABLON, in a pretty spot, had a protestant church, which Sully used to attend.

ATHIS-MONS on the Orge, near the Seine, a place of the eleventh century, where Louis X. and his son Phillippe had a seat. Fromanteau is near.

JUVISY (5½ miles), where the branch railway turns off to *Corbeil* (*see* Route 50*a*), is on the Orgue, and has the château of Marquis de Montessuy, which belonged to the Brancas and Sevennes families. Population 400.

SAVIGNY-SUR-ORGE (2 miles), a village as old as 925, with the castle built by the chamberlain of Charles VIII., 1480, now belonging to the Princess of Eckmühl. Viaduct to

EPINAY-SUR-ORGE (1¼ miles), a little way from Ville Moisson, on the Orge, where the Yvette joins. A château here, and a church with a good 'John Baptist' in it. St. Geneviève forest is a little further. At Longpont is one of the best churches out of Paris; it belonged to a rich abbey here. Coaches to Longjumeau and Balesy.

St. Michel-sur-Orgue (2½ miles). Coaches to Montlhéry, Linas, Marcoussis.

[*Montlhéry* or Mont-le-héry (2 kil. west), on a hill-side, is noted for the ancient tower, which rises over it, and belonged to the strong feudal castle built 999, by Thibauld-File-Etoupe (*i.e.* tow thread, from his light hair). It had jurisdiction over 133 fiefs and 300 parishes, so that it was troublesome even to the sovereign at Paris. Six gates in the ruined walls lead up to the tower, which looks like the Eddystone lighthouse, and is 101 feet high, and 9 to 4 thick. It has been restored and commands a good range of view. Porte Baudry, built 1015, was rebuilt 1589, and restored by Bonaparte in 'l'An VIII. de la Republique.' A battle was fought here 1465, between Louis XI. and his brother.]

Bretigny (1½ miles), in a pretty valley, where John of France made a treaty with Edward III., then master of the best part of France. Population 750.

Marvolles-en-Hurepoix (3¾ miles), near the railway, has a merino-sheep farm at Chanteloup, which was a country-seat of Phillippe-le-Bel. Coaches to Arpajon, Boissy, and St. Chéron.

[*Arpajon* (2 kil. west), where the Remede joins the Orge, was called Châtres till 1770, when its seigneur, Louis de Saverne, was made marquis of Arpajon. They relate that after the happy marquis received his title, he used to plant himself in the road, with a stick, and inquire of the passers-by, 'What is the name of this seat?' If they said Arpajon,' they were rewarded with praises and something substantial; but woe to the unlucky stranger who called it by its old name of Ghâtres. A large church and timbered halle here.—At St. Chéron (11 kil. south-west), is the fine natural fountain of La Rachée.—At St. Vrain, is a domed pavilion built by Madame Du Barri.

Lonjumeau (3 kil. west), in the pleasant valley of the Yvette, is older than the ninth century. The square church of St. Martin has a good gothic portico.]

Bouray (2½ miles), on the Juine, a little past Mesnil Voisin, seat of the Duke of Choiseul-Praslin. Coaches to La Ferté-Aleps, Vaire, and Malesherbes, all on the Esonne, to which the other river runs. Malesherbes belonged to the bold defender of Louis XVI. at his trial; formerly to one of the mistresses of Henry IV., Henriette d'Entraigues.

Lardy (1½ miles), on the Juine, where they make laces, edgings, &c.

Etrechy (3¾ miles), on the same river, near which, in a wooded spot, are remains of the old feudal castle of Roussay. Gypsum quarries here.

Etampes (5 miles), on the high road to Orléans, and two little branches of the Juine, is a sous-préfecture of 8,200 persons, called *Stampae* in old times, near which Thierry defeated his uncle Clotaire, 604. It is chiefly a long street, with good promenades round it. At the palais de justice, on a rising point, are remains of a castle built by le roi Robert for his wife Constance; the wife of Philippe Auguste retired here; and it was razed by Henry IV. in 1590, except La Quinette tower, the sides of which are rounded on the plan.

Notre Dame church is a large gothic pile of the thirteenth century, with a fine norman tower; St. Martin and St. Basil are also worth notice, as well as the Hôtel de Ville, and the house of Anne de Puisseleu, one of the misresses of Francis I. In the fifteenth century, fireworks were invented here by a townsman, who was nick-named Jean Boutefeu. Petrified fossils are found in the gypsum quarries; and the tour de Brunehaut is near. Geoffrey St. Hilaire, the naturalist, was born here. Trade in grain, flour, soap, &c. *Hotels*—Grands Couriers; Bois de Vincennes. Coaches to Anneau, Dourdan, Pithiviers, Inville, and Sermaise.

[*Dourdan* (15 kil. north-west), an old place in a forest, on the Orgue, with a ruined keep (212 feet high), and eight other towers of its ancient castle, (built they say by Gourtrand, king of Orléans, in the sixth century); a double spire church, and a good timbered hall, built 1223, by Louis VIII. At 28 kil. south-south-east of Etampes, is

Pithiviers, a sous-préfecture, in department Loiret (population 4,000), over a ravine on the Oeuf, was called Piviers and Pluviers, and was a strong plaee, which the Prince of Condé took twice in the League wars, and which Henry IV. dismantled. You see here many gothic houses, the tower of an abbey, a venerable church, the spire of which, 270 feet high, was burnt in 1853, and fragments of the walls, &c. In the neighbourhood are the grotto of St. Gregory, Segrais mineral well, and remains of a castle, which Henry I. of England burnt. At Yèvre-le-Châtel are the extensive ruins of another.

Trade in grain, wine, honey, saffron, gateaux d'amandes (almond cakes), and pâtés d'alouettes (lark pies), for which it is noted. *Hotels*—De l'Ecu (Crown Piece); de la Ville d'Orléans. Coaches to Orléans, Fontainebleau, &c]

MONNERVILLE (8¾ miles), on the railway, from which there is a coach to Méréville, (5 kil. south-east), on the Juine, the seat of Comte de St. Romain, in a fine park, in which are a temple, swiss cottage, statues, and a pillar to two of Lapeyrouse's companions. — Near Champuisteux (16 kil. east of this), is Vignay, where the chancellor Hôpital died.

ANGERVILLE (3 miles), the last place in department Seine-et-Oise. Coach to Chartres, 40 kil. west-north-west, (*see* Route 90).

TOURY (8½ miles), in department Eure-et-Loir, close to the border of Loiret, has a population of 1,400, with sugar works and an old château. Coaches to Janville, Châteaudun, Courtalain (seat of the Montmorencies), Droué (*see* Route 65), Montdoubleau (and its feudal ruin), St. Calais (Route 67), and Chartres.

ARTENAY (8¾ miles). Near this are ruins of a famous château, the lords of which were so powerful in the feudal age, that it resisted all the forces of Louis le Gros in three several attacks. There is also a church of the tenth century.

[At *Patay* (15 kil. west), the great Talbot was for the first time defeated (1428), and taken prisoner by the French, who were led on by Joan of Arc.]

CHEVILLY (3¾ miles), where the sandy plain of the Orléanais begins, and the forest of Orléans, which covers 94,000 acres.

CERCOTTES (2½ miles), in the forest.

At 6½ miles further is the Orléans terminus, near Porte Bannier, in that faubourg.

Orleans. *Hotels*—Du Loiret and Grand Hotel d'Orléans, in Rue Bannier; de Londres and Café de Paris; du Commerce; de France, in Place de Martroy; des Trois Empereurs; de la Boule d'Or (Golden Ball), in Rue d'Illiers near the Poste-aux-Lettres. Rev. MM. Rosselloty, Nougarède, and Duchemin are protestant pastors here.

Conveyances: by railway to Etampes, Epernay, and Paris; to Blois, Tours, Angers, Nantes Bordeaux; to Vierzon, Châteauroux, Bourges and Nevers. Coaches to Boiscommun, Bellegarde, Vitry, Donnery, Fay, Montargis, (*see* Route 25), Lorris, Châteauneuf, Cosne, Gien Sancerre, Sully, Jargeau, (Route 50*b*), Briare, Dampierre, and Châteaudun. Omnibuses to Ormes, Olivet, St. Mesmin, St. Denis, Bionne, Checy, St. Ay, &c. By steamer, daily, up the Loire, to Gien (6 hours), Cosne (18 hours), Nevers (24 hours), and Moulins (30 hours).

Population 42,000. Chief town of department Loiret (once part of *Orléanais*), seat of a bishop, &c., on the north bank of the Loire, in a wide plain, near the forest of Orléans. It was the *Genabum* of the Carnutes when Cæsar burnt it, and being re-built by Aurelian, A.D. 272, took his name, *Aurelianum*, of which the modern name is a corruption. It is noted not only as the head of a duchy, first created by Philippe de Valois for his second son (died 1375), and revived by Louis XIII. for his brother Gaston, whose descendant is the young Count de Paris (grandson of Louis Philippe); but also for the various sieges it has withstood. In 451 it was saved from Attila by Aetius, the Roman commander; about 570, Childeric rescued it from Odoacer; and again it was saved, in 1429, when the English, who held nearly three-fourths of France, and had nearly taken the city, were driven back by the famous Jeanne d'Arc, the Pucelle or 'Maid of Orleans,' a simple shepherdess, of Domremy (*see* Route 19). Believing herself to be inspired, she became the means of turning the tide of conquest against the English, who thenceforth lost ground in France; but revenged themselves on poor Joan by burning her for a witch at Rouen, two years after. It was held by the Huguenots or Protestants in the civil wars of the sixteenth century, when it escaped another siege, by the sudden death of the Duke of Guise.

The river here is free from islands and lined with quays, (one built 1810) at each end of the modern stone bridge, which was built in 1751, on nine arches, and is 1063 feet long (the centre arch 105 feet wide), but has not much water under it in the summer. From this, the best street, Rue Royale, leads up to Place du Martroy, where a tasteless bronze of the Pucelle (put there 1804, instead of that on the old bridge erected by the women of the city, in the fifteenth century), is, or is to be, replaced by Foyatier's statue of her on horseback, representing her in armour, with her banner and sword, returning thanks to God at the crisis of her triumph here.

Much of the old town consists of dirty irregular streets and places, with many curiously carved timber houses. The faubourgs are better built; the largest being that on the Paris road; another, called St. Marceau is across the bridge. Pleasant country houses lie beyond. One of the best promenades is on the boulevard or site of the old walls, of which a piece 26 feet high is left, supposed to be Roman; two old towers also remain at one of the gates, near the Croix de la Pucelle, where the English were driven back. A new street, Rue Jeanne d'Arc, leads to

St. Croix *Cathedral*, one of the best looking in France, rising above everything else in the town. It was rebuilt about 1000 by Bishop Arnoul, but having been ruined by the Huguenots, in 1567, it has been again gradually rebuilt (since Henry IV. began it, 1601), on a regular cross-shaped plan, in the gothic style, with an east apse. Over the three portals and rose windows of the front are two cruciform towers, in four decreasing stories, elegantly carved, and 263 feet high; the central clock-tower is nearly as high; the roof of the nave is very lofty, and the high altar and Virgin chapel are richly decorated.

St. Pierre-le-Puellier, the oldest of all the churches, in the worst part of the town, is part romanesque, small, and ill lit, with a curious inscription to a young girl called Rose of Paris. St. Aignan's, is a good gothic structure, with a romanesque crypt, and was attached to a convent. The chapel of St. Jacques now a salt store, has a good front, and was built about 1155, by Louis le Jeune, it is said. Another St. Euverte's, also a magazine (as well as a third, St. Paul's) has a tower built 1566.

Among other buildings worth notice is the old gothic brick *Hôtel de Ville*, begun by Charles VIII., and finished 1498: it offers a decorated façade, lately restored; and, in the court there stands an ancient square tower or belfry. Opposite it is a copy of the Princess Marie's well-known beautiful *Statue of the Maid* in armour embracing her sword. The public musée is placed here, founded 1825, containing between 500 and 600 paintings and designs of the French school, and a gallery of mediæval antiquities, with a portrait of the Maid. The Palais de Justice, was built 1821, with a portico of four pillars and sphinxes. There are also a bourse, large theatre, halle-aux-grains (corn-market), a public abattoir (built 1825), a bibliothèque of 37,000 volumes, (besides MSS. and coins), a college, protestant orphan house, jardin botanique, &c.

Several of the old gothic houses deserve examination, such as the maison d'Agnes Sorel, No. 15, Rue de Taubоury, with a highly carved front; the maison de Francis I., No. 28, Rue de Recouvrance, so called because of his arms on it; and the hôtel de Crênaux, of the time of Louis XIII. Pothier the lawyer, and Dolet the learned printer, who was burnt as an atheist, 1546, were natives; and Francis II. died here.

Trade in refined sugar, wine, brandy, corn, pottery, &c.

ROUTE 50—*continued.*

By *Ligne du Centre railway from Orléans to Châteauroux.* 90 miles, or 144 kil., in 4 to 5½ hours; thrice a-day. The stations are:—

	kil.		kil.		kil.
La Ferté	23	Vierzon	10	Issoudun	8
Lamotte	16	Chéry	15	Neuvy-Pailloux	11
Nouan	7	Reuilly	4	Châteauroux	16
Salbris	12	Ste.-Lizaigne	9		
Theillay	13				

After crossing the Loire you come to St. Marceau, then

St. Olivet (3 miles), on a hill, (in which crystals are found), at the bridge on the Loiret, where the Duke of Guise, called Le Balafré (from a scar on his face), was assassinated by Poltrot, 1563. Clovis founded a monastery here. A little to the east are St. Denis-en-Val, where the best Orléans wine is produced,—and the Château de la Source, where

Bolingbroke lived, 1719, in his exile, when he married Madame de Maintenon's niece. He improved this seat, which takes its name from the source of the Loiret, bubbling up here out of the limestone in a basin 47 feet across, called the Bouillon; the Abîme is another head. It runs clear, and full of fish, 6 miles north-west to the Loire. The water of the latter river, by filtering through the soil, is supposed to be the secret source of the Loiret, which though small, gives name to the department

LA FERTE-ST. AUBIN (11½ miles) on the Cosson, near a roman camp, in the barren district of La Sologne, has the château of Prince d'Essling (Marshal Massena's son), one part being gothic of the thirteenth century, the other from Mansard's designs.

LA MOTTE BEUVRON (10 miles) on the Beuvron, a branch of the Loire, in department Loir-et-Cher.

[10 kil. west on a rock, is the fine old château of Chaumont, with machiolated towers, &c.]

NOUAN-LE-FUSELIER (4 miles) on a branch of the Beuvron.

[About 40 kil. east-south-east is Aubigny, on the Nere, given by Charles VII. in 1425 to John Stuart, constable of Scotland, and defended by his descendents against the League.]

SALBRIS (7½ miles), a spot on the Sauldre, where many roman antiquities have been found. Population 1,700. Coaches to Romorantin and Aubigny.

[At 24 kil. west-south-west, down the Sauldre is

Romorantin, a sous-préfecture of 7,400 people (who made cloth, &c.), where the Morantin joins in the sandy Sologne district. It grew out of a château of the seigneurs of Lautheny, which came to Francis I., whose wife Claude was born here. Just before Poitiers 1356, the Black Prince besieged it and (as Froissart relates) made use of artillery for the first time. It is further noted for the Edict de Romorantin issued by the wise Chancellor Hôpital, which saved France from the Inquisition. Pajon, a protestant divine, was also a native. *Hotels*—D'Angleterre; de l' Etoile (Star).]

THEILLAY or Theillay-le-Pailleux (7½ miles).

VIERZON or Vierzon-Ville (6¾ miles), where the branch rail to Bourges and Nevers turns off (with a stoppage of ten to twenty minutes; *see* Route 51), is in department Cher, and stands among fertile prairies (meadows) on the Canal de Berri, and the Cher, where the Yèvre joins it. It is mentioned in the old romance of the Knights of the Round Table; and in 1195 when held by the counts de Blois, was destroyed by Richard Cœur de Lion for refusing to acknowledge him as suzerain. The Black Prince held it for a few years; at length it came to the dukes of Berri and the crown. Its old castle stood here till lately; the church is a good one. Population 6,700. Trade in cloth, wine, iron (made at Les Forges), and pottery. *Hotels*—Des Messageries Nationales; de la Croix Blanche (White Cross).

CHERY (9½ miles), on the Auron. About 5 miles west is Massay, where was a benedictine abbey.

REUILLY (2¾ miles), a fine seat on the Auron.

[At 20 kil. to the west is Vatan, in a plain, (population 2,754) where Guy de Chatillon built a collegiate church to the memory of St. Laman, archbishop of Seville, who fled to this part, and was martyred. Parts of the old walls are left.—*Valençay* (22 kil. north-west), a pretty place (population 3,095), on the Nahon, having a fine castle originally built by Philibert de Lorme for the d'Etampes family, and since increased by various holders, till it looks like a palace.]

ST. LIZAIGNE (5½ miles) up the same stream.

ISSOUDUN (5 miles) a sous-préfecture (in department Indre) of 12,000 souls, on a hill-side, by the rapid Théols, among windmills, was made a roman station by Cæsar, and one held by the English. The part called Bas Château is the oldest, but Haut-Château is well built. Among the buildings are the Hôtel-de-Ville near the old Tour-Blanche, which deserves notice; another old tower at the prison; the chapel of the hospital with some curious carvings about it; and a caserne or barrack, which was an ursuline convent. There are also a college, new salle de spectacle, three bridges, &c., and traces of a castle burnt 1135, along with an abbey. Another fire happened 1651, when it was besieged by the Fronde.

Though warmly protestant, it drove off the

party of the League 1589. A treaty was made here 1177 between Louis VII. and Henry II. of England, who were successively husbands of Eleanor of Guienne. Trade in wool, grain, cattle, wine, parchment, &c.; a large sheep fair in September and October. Important iron forges at Boisry, Bellabre, and Alloux, in the neighbourhood near the road called Levée de César (Cæsar's causeway). Roman traces of walls, &c., are noticed also at Levroux the ancient *Gabatum* (30 kil. west-north-west) besides druid stones. Pretty spots at de la Prée old abbey, and Gouers. *Hotels*—Du Lion d' Or (Golden Lion); du Lion d'Argent (Silver Lion). Coaches to La Châtre, (42 kil.); Gueret, (102 kil.); Aubusson, (158 kil.); Lignieres, (26 kil.); St. Amand, (50 kil.); Montluçon, (176 kil.); Vatan, (26 kil.); *see* Routes 53, and 54

[Lignières (26 kil. south-south-east) on the Auron, near a group of lakes, has a castle which was the residence of Jeanne de Valois, the divorced wife of Louis XII.]

NEUVY-PAILLOUX (7 miles). A little north of Châteauroux (10 miles further) is *Déols* or Bourg-Dieu, which has interesting remains of an abbey founded in the tenth century by the 'Princes of Déols' close to their château, originally built they say by a roman proconsul, Léocade, whose son Eude is buried in the church, under a black stone held in great reverence by the people. The abbey became very rich after Raoul-le-Laye founded Châteauroux; so that in the seventeenth century, a prince of Condé made a journey to Rome to beg it of Gregory XV.

CHATEAUROUX. *Hotels*—La Promenade; du Dauphin; la Poste. Population 13,100. The chief town of department Indre (with a tribunal, college, &c.), in the old province of Berri, and centre of the woollen manufactures, on a hill-slope by the Indre, in the middle of a fertile plain. It was founded by Raoul le Déols (whence the name Château-Raoul), who about 940 built an abbey at Déols (1½ miles off, as above), and here built a castle (close to the préfecture, on a hill to the west), in which Condé had his wife (who was Richelieu's niece) imprisoned. She lies in the old ruined church of St. Martin. That of the Cordeliers is a prison. The old narrow streets are some improved. An ancient gate remains in the middle of the town. At the Hôtel de Ville, built 1823 near the castle, are the palais de justice (law court) and library. There is a theatre, a jardin publique, &c. A good prospect from the towers of the old castle. General Bertrand who went with Napoleon to St. Helena, and died a short while ago, was born here.

Trade in woollens, cotton thread, iron (from the forges around), &c. Conveyances by rail to Orléans, Paris, Nantes, &c.; by coach to Périgueux (236 kil.), Limoges (128 kil.), La Souterraine (69 kil.), Argentin (31 kil.), Leblanc (60 kil), Valençay (40 kil.), La Châtre (37 kil.)

The abbey of Fontgombauld, Gargillesse priory, and the château of Valençay, may be visited hence.

From Chateauroux, on the road to Limoges, you pass

LOTHIER (15 kil.), on a heath.

ARGENTIN (14 kil.), on the Creuse, has a bridge dividing the upper town (on a steep rock) from the lower, and remains of a castle, built they say by Pepin. Population, 4,600.

VILLE-AU-BRUN (34 kil.).

[To the right is the prettily seated village of *Benoit-de-Saut*, near the fall of Montgerno. To the left you see the ruined tower of Crosant, on a granite rock, 213 feet above the Creuse.]

MORTEROL (17 kil.), to the left of which is the old château of St. German-Beaupré, which Henry IV once inhabited, and to which Madlle. de Montpensier was exiled. It has portraits of Henry, Madame de Maintenon, &c., with large gardens, an orangery, and hunting forest.

CHAUTELOUBE (12 kil.). And at 29 kil. further is

Limoges. *Hotels* — De l'Aigle d'Argent (Silver Eagle); de la Boule d'Or (Golden Ball) du Perigord; de la Pyramide. *Cafés*—De l'Europe; de la Comédie. Population, 34,300. An old town, capital of department Haute-Vienne (formerly of province of *Limousin*), seat of a diocess, &c., in a healthy spot, on the slant of a gentle hill by the Vienne, which is crossed by two old bridges, and another of stone, built 1830. In Cæsar's time it was the head of the *Lemovices*, and became an important roman town; but afterwards suffered by the ravages of the Visigoths, Normans, &c., and in the religious wars. The Black Prince took it by storm 1370, after a long siege.

Many old timbered houses are seen in the lower parts or Cité, where the roman town stood; the castle was placed in the upper part or ville. The streets are narrow and crooked, for the most part; but adorned with fountains, which are supplied from the country. One, the Fontaine d'Aigoulène, is filled by a roman aqueduct, one of the few pieces of antiquity which time has spared; another is in Place St. Martial. Among the public promenades are the Champ de Juillet, the largest, and Place d'Orsay, which marks the site (called Les Arènes, the Arena) of the roman amphitheatre.

The *Cathedral*, dedicated to St. Etienne (Stephen), of the thirteenth and fourteenth centuries, replaces one destroyed by the English; it is of granite, and looks venerable, though incomplete (a choir only) and mixed in the style; it has a finely carved wood loft, 36 feet wide, put up 1533 by Bishop Langeac, whose beautiful tomb is here; the belfry stands away by itself.

St. Michel-de-Lions is a good church of the fourteenth century, having a door with carved lions on each side, a tower 226 feet high, surmounted by a ball, and a lofty vault. The modern church of St. Pierre du Queyroix is marked by a good tower.

An old convent is turned into the Hôtel de Ville; in front stands a belfry which belonged to the church of St. Martial. In old times a festival or Fête de Branden, was kept up, in the manner of the Boy Bishop. A mock litany was sung, the response to which, in Limousin patois, was 'St. Marceau prega per nous, et nous epingaren per vous' (*i. e.*, St. Martial pray for us, and we will dance for you); and the day ended with merriment and drunkenness.

The bishop's palace (évêché) is a solid structure of granite, and there is a cross in the public ways, of the same material. The library contains 12,000 vols. A few roman stones have been collected by amateurs; one or two are seen in the gardens of the préfecture. There is the usual variety of public buildings, but none of any note.

D'Aguesseau, the chancellor; Vergniaud, the Girondist; Marshal Jourdain; Dupuytren, the physician; Michel Chevalier, were all natives.

Excellent porcelain, cotton and woollens, paper, &c., are made here. Horse fairs are held, the breed being noted.

Conveyances to Bordeaux, Angoulême, Poitiers, Moulin, Chateauroux (on the rail), Toulouse (25 hours by mail), Pau (28 hours), Lyons, Clermont, &c.

From Limoges, on the road to Tulle and Cahors, you pass

CHALUSSET (8 kil.) and its fine old ruined castle.

[To the right, at Solignac, are remains of St. Eloi's abbey, founded in King Dagobert's time, with various eccentric and obscene ornaments about them.]

PIERRE BUFFIERE (12 kil.), at the bridge on the Briance.

[Eymoutiers (30 kil. east), in a pretty spot on the Vienne, having a good gothic church, with some painted windows in it.]

UZERCHE (18 kil.), a town of 3,500 people, on a peak over the Vezère, very prettily seated, and having many good houses, so that a proverb says, 'whoever has a house at Uzerche, has a castle in Limousin' (the name of the province). It has an old parish church; and St. Eulalie's chapel, of an early date.

Here the road to TULLE (30 kil.; *see* Route 56) turns off.

[About 30 kil. to the north-east, up the Vezère, is the village and old castle of Treignac. To the east (about 12 kil.) is the château de *Pompadour*, which Louis XV gave, with the name, to his mistress, whose real name was Poisson. It stands on a long terrace, and has several gothic towers, &c.]

DONZENAC (25 kil.), among vines and poplars.

BRIVES (9 kil.), a sous-préfecture (department Corrèze), of 8,400 souls in a fine wooded valley, among vineyards, &c., has a well built college, near the church, and an old carved house, built by the English. It is sometimes called Brives-la-Gaillarde, *i. e.* the lively, but more for its neighbourhood than for what it is in itself. Cardinal Dubois and Marshal Brune were natives. Trade in wine, truffles, cattle, &c. *Hotels*—De Bordeaux; de Toulouse. The castles of Noailles and Turenne are a little to the south-east, off the road.

SOUILLAC (36 kil.), at the seven-arched bridge on the Dordogne, has manufactures of muskets, linen, &c. Population 3,100. About 3 kil. to the east is Carennac, and remains of a Cluniac abbey, one part of which is visited as the spot where *Fenelon* wrote some of his excellent work. Its bare walls are covered with names.

PEYRAC (10 kil.) on a lake, near which Charles Martel defeated the Saracens, according to some.

[About 20 kil. east is Gramat, in a rocky part of the Alzou, with good mineral springs and a tumulus.—At 15 kil. north-east of it, is St. Ceré on the Bave, among high limestone hills, on one of which are the two towers of St. Laurent, 130 and 90 feet high. Good black hats are made here. There is a fall of the Bave, at Autoire, near this, 106 feet down, close to an old tower.]

PONT-DE-RODEZ (18 kil.) on the Bléon.

[About 8 kil. east-south-east is La Bastide Fortunière, where Napoleon's brother-in-law, *Murat* king of Naples, was born, the son of an innkeeper. A village near it is called after him.]

PELACY (17 kil.)

At 18 kil. further is

CAHORS. *Hotels*—Des Ambassadeurs; des Trois Rois (Three Kings); de l'Europe; du Palais Royal. Population 12,200. Capital of department Lot, seat of a diocess, and a very old city on a rocky height over a bend of the Lot. Ptolemy calls it *Doucona* after the latin Divona (from a sacred spring here), and it was the head of the *Cadurci*, whence the name. The English held it for a time; and Henry of Navarre pillaged it after a hard fight 1580.

The streets are steep and narrow; the oldest part is in upper town, where the houses command a fine prospect (even as far as the Pyrenees) from their terraces.

The *Cathedral* has two cupolas (one 105 feet high) on six pillars, and a nave 184 feet by 49. It is said to be on the site of a temple, or a part of one, with modern additions. There are three other churches. The préfecture was the bishop's palace. Opposite the college is a statue of Fenelon (put up 1820) who was educated here. The Hôtel de Ville is new; and the large priests' seminary is turned into a barrack. Of the three bridges on the river (where the promenades are), one called Pont de Valendré has three gate towers on it; another named after Louis Philippe, replaces the Notre Dame bridge; and Pont Neuf leads to the faubourg St. George. A public library has 12,000 volumes; there are a salle de spectacle, a tobacco factory, &c.

Some pieces of roman wall remain near the Fontaine de Divone (and the site of the Chartreuse and a preceptory of the Knights Templars), which springs up in a fine hollow under the mountains, and runs by several mills, to the Lot. An aqueduct went hence to St. Martén de Vern (25 kil.) past La Roque where some of the arches are seen. Pope John XXII. was born at a house outside the north gate; C. Marot who turned the psalms into fashionable verse, was also a native (time of Francis I).

Trade in wine, truffles, eaux-de-vie, leather, &c. Conveyances daily, to Paris, Toulouse, Rodo (90 kil.; *see* Route 52.) Aurillac, Villeneuve d'Agen, &c., (62 kil.; *see* Route 60). At Capendac, Cæsar's gate marks the ancient *Uxallodunum*.

From Cahors, on the road to Montauban, you pass

CAUSSADE (38 kil.) in a fertile spot on the Léra, with 4,500 people, and a good trade in cattle, wool, bark, black truffles, capons, &c.

Further on you leave to the right, Nègrepelisse, which was visited with terrible slaughter in 1622, by Louis XIII., for the execution of some royal troops in the civil disturbances here.

Montauban is 23 kil. beyond Caussade.

MONTAUBAN. *Hotels*—De France; de l'Europe; du Grand Soleil (Sun); du Tapis Vert (Green Carpet). Population, 23,000. Chief town of department Tarn-et-Garonne (formed by Napoleon, in 1808), seat of a bishopric, of a theological college for protestants, &c., on the Tarn and Tescore, was founded in the twelfth century by the counts of Toulouse, who had a castle here, among the willows (*alba* in the gascon tongue). It was one of the head quarters of the Huguenot or Reformed faith; and successfully resisted Louis XIII. in three sieges, 1621, but opened its gates to him and Richelieu, when Rochelle fell, eight years after. Louis XIV. sent his dragoons here, and razed the walls, which was so far beneficial that it had thenceforth room to extend itself.

Most of the old town is of brick, on a plateau, 50 or 60 feet above the river, with a deep ravine on one side. A brick bridge, of seven pointed arches, has the Hôtel de Ville, St. Jacques' brick church, and the quay, at one end; and at the other, a sort of brick triumphal arch, leading to Faubourg Bourbon, which was founded, 1562, by protestants from Toulouse.

The *Cathedral*, built 1739, by Larroque, is in

the italian style, and shape of a greek cross, 285 feet by 125, with two clock-towers over the pilastered front; the vault, on doric pillars, is 82 feet high; it has the Vow of Louis XIII., a copy, by a lady, of the original done by Ingres a native artist.

Other buildings are, the préfecture and its turrets, the bishop's palace, two priests' seminaries, the French protestant chapel, college, library of 10,500 vols., theatre, &c. Place Royale is the most regular of the squares, having a gate at each corner. In Grande Place the patriots were massacred, 1791.

There is a theological college of the *Reformed Church* here, with seven professors. They have also an orphan house for forty children. Rev. MM. Mollin, Magnan, Cruvellié, &c., are resident pastors.

A turning by Café de l'Etoile, in Faubourg Dumoustiers, leads to Les Terrasses, whence there is a vast prospect of the fertile country beyond, taking in even the Pyrenees, which may be seen in fine weather (50 leagues). Above and below are the pretty falls of the Tarn, which in November, 1766, rose 34 feet above its usual level. Cazalès, an orator of the Constituent Assembly, was a native.

Manufactures of cadis de Montauban, or woollen serges, stuffs, silk stockings, cotton, soap, pottery, eaux-de-vie, &c; with a trade in these, and grain, leather, oil, wool, drugs, spices, &c.

Conveyances to Bordeaux, Toulouse, Rodez, Villefranche, Limoges, Cahors, Agen, &c.

BRESSOLS (6 kil.) up the Tarn.

GRISOLLES, in Route 84, is 16 further, on the Garonne; and 29 kil. beyond is

Toulouse. *Hotels*—Du France, Place St. Etienne; de l'Europe, and Casset, both in Place Lafayette; Bachières, and Grand Soleil, in Rue des Arts; du Midi (the South); Rue des Balances. *Cafés* and *Restaurants* in Place de Capitole, &c. The pâtés de foies canards (duck-liver pies), truffles, ortolans, and fruits, are noted. Population, 84,000.

This ancient town, the capital of department Haute-Garonne (part of High Languedoc, in the province of Guienne, or Aquitaine) and of south France, seat of a military division, an archbishop, cour imperiale, university, academie des jeux-floraux (or floral games, first founded, 1323, by the troubadours), and of many literary and scientific institutions; is on a fertile plain between the Garonne and the canal du Midi(*i.e.* of the South), 404 kil. from Chateauroux, 256 from Bordeaux, 290 from Bayonne, 150 from Pau, 445 from Marseilles, 470 from Lyons. It was the head of the Tectosages, when the Romans took it, and made it a free colony, 106 B.C.; afterwards it was called *Tolosa*, &c., whence comes the present name.

The Visigoths made it their capital till conquered by Clovis, 507; at a later date it was governed, under its counts, by a body of capitulaires, or 'capitouls,' chosen by the people, till Louis XIV. took the privilege away. Among its counts were Raymond IV., one of Tasso's heroes, who died a crusader in Syria. Raymond V. was besieged here by Henry II. of England, for refusing homage to him as lord of Guienne; from the next Raymond, who protected the Albigenses, it was captured, 1215-7, by the fanatic hordes led by De Montfort, who was killed under the walls, 1218; and in 1221, St. Dominic established the inquisition here, till the people drove it across the Pyrenees again. When Charles V. threatened it, 1539, it mustered as many as 35,000 men-at-arms. In the late war, Wellington defeated Soult close at hand.

Though many improvements have been made, Toulouse is still full of irregular narrow streets, paved with pebbles; the houses and buildings are mostly brick, some of the oldest being covered with stucco and wood-work. Here, says Trollope, "on the second or third floor of a house, the colour of the gateway of St. James's palace, may be found living on, say sixty pounds a year, some high-heeled and high-born dame, with her equally ancient *suivante*, or some Monsieur et Madame de ——, too poor, and far too proud, to seek society among the less pure-blooded of the present day."

Its old battlemented walls, with their nine gates, are nearly all replaced by boulevards, beyond which lie six or seven faubourgs, exclusive of St. Cyprien, across the river, built since 1785 (when the quays were made). This suburb is joined to the city by Pont-Neuf, a good seven-arch level brick bridge, 853 feet long (the centre arch is 106 feet span), having a tête-du-pont, in the shape of a triumphal arch, by Mansard, at the south or St. Cyprien end, leading to Cours Dillon, a pleasant promenade.

Other walks are on the quays, esplanade, the allées along the canal, the large jardin des plantes, &c. Near the bridge are the château d'eau, and Ile de Tounis, on which stood the castle of the counts; some old houses are in the Rue des Coutellers, among which the hôtels de Malte, de Levy, de Mac-Carthy, &c., are worth notice. One of its best fountains is in Place de la Trinité; another, 56 feet high, in Place St. Georges. The new Place Lafayette is large. The market for fruit, flowers, &c., in Place du Capitole is worth seeing.

St. Etienne *Cathedral* is an irregular building, the oldest part being the nave, built by Raymond VI., whose arms are in the vault; a portal and large rose window were added by Archbishop Dumoulin; the semi-circular choir, which is *much* out of line with the nave, was re-built, 1609-12 (after a fire), in a handsome gothic style. It has an altar of Languedoc marble, and a great bell of 50,000 lbs. weight in the tower.

A much older church is *St. Sernin*, or Saturnien, built 1090, on the site, they say, of a roman temple, in the romanesque and early gothic styles, having a south porch, with a double arch, a tower of six decreasing stories, with a spire over all, and great pillars inside, where are tombs of the counts, a copy of the splendid shrine of the saint, besides side chapels, and a crypt. Nôtre Dame-de-la-Daurade was re-built lately, on the site of one which belonged to a convent, now used for the government tobacco factory. St. Paul has a large dome, with a statue on it.

Several other churches are left out of the 80 (?) they say were here; some still in use; others turned into magazines, &c. The church of the Cordeliers (which contains mummies in its cellars) with its convent is now a military depôt; that of the Jacobins is an artillery barrack; another makes stables for the cavalry; St. Clair's is a cannon foundry.—The gothic Augustine church is the *Museum*, and contains a few good pictures, with an excellent collection of roman and middle-age relics, such as busts, statuary, and marbles, found at Martres, Nerac, &c, or gathered from the churches and religious houses. The large old palace of the archbishops is turned into the préfecture; the palais de justice, since restored, was the seat of the parliament which condemned Jean Calas to be broken on the wheel, 1762, on a false accusation. It was done in Place St. Géorges, a square of dingy red brick houses.

The *Hôtel de Ville*, in Place du Capitole, is a great pile, 380 feet by 128, fronted by eight red ionic pillars, built 1769: it includes the theatre; an old court where Henry de Montmorenci was executed, 1632; a gallery, or salles des Illustres, in which are 160 busts of natives and others; and the salle de Clémence, so called from a statue (brought from the Daurade church) of the famous Clémence Isaure, a lady of the fourteenth century, and a professor of the gai savoir (gay science), in whose honour prizes of gold and silver flowers are given at the May meeting of the Jeux Floraux Society.

The clerical library comprises 33,000 vols., and Charlemagne's Heures, or prayer book, which he gave to St. Sernin's, 778; that of the Lycée numbers 33,000 vols. There are, besides, two seminaries, the college, an hôtel de monnaies, or mint, the large Hôtel Dieu and another hospital called St. Joseph de la Drave, a good observatory, artillery and veterinary schools, powder factory, the great Basacle and Château flour-mills, each containing 34 grindstones; also a synagogue, and a protestant church, in which are monuments of the English officers who fell in the battle of 10th April, 1814. A short canal (de Brienne), cut by the Archbishop of that name, joins the river to the canal du Midi, at the double bridge of Ponts-Jumeaux (twins), near which, and on the Sypière, Rave, and Calvinet hills, the battle was fought; a brick pillar, dedicated to the French soldiers who fell, marks the site, and commands a view of the distant Pyrenees.

Soult's army occupied a strong position on these heights, with the canal on one side and the Lers, a small branch of the Garonne, on the other, or North, side. The English ascended this river, which had been widened and deepened, and artificially inundated, and then charging up the slope, drove the French from the heights with great loss. At that time Soult was not aware of Napoleon's abdication. That he was beaten is well known, yet the visitor may sometimes come across an account of the 'Victoire du Maréchal Soult sur le Duc de Wellington!'

Rev. MM. Chabrand, Sabatier, and Cazalis, are Protestant pastors here. Don Enrique de

Bourbon, uncle to the queen of Spain, is a resident. When Charles Albert abdicated the crown of Sardinia, after his defeat at Novara, 1848, he stopped here on his way to Portugal. "He arrived in an ordinary carriage, with a valet and courier only, and nobody guessed who he was. He was put into the first bed-room (No. 4, at the Hotel de l'Europe) that happened to be vacant, and might have quitted Toulouse in as strict incognito as he entered it, had not the fille de chambre received from the hands of the valet a silver warming pan (!) for the purpose of warming the royal sheets. On the lid of this magnificent, but tell-tale pan, were emblazoned the royal arms of Sardinia. The maid shewed the pan to her master, and the cat was out of the bag."—(Trollope).

Toulouse is a gay bustling place, a sort of petit Paris, much frequented by persons of moderate income, the remnants of the old noblesse, who, without fortune or privilege, maintain a superiority by the ease and grace of their manners. Cafés, circles, and places of amusement abound; and it is equally distinguished for its pursuit of literature and the arts. House rent and living are cheap, but the weather, though mild, is at times damp and changeable.

The women in this part wear coloured handkerchiefs over the shoulders, and a cap with an immense stiffened front, spreading like a fan, cut at the edges, and trimmed with lace; they are soft and attractive in their manners, and fond of music. The men dress something like muleteers; their patois is the Provençal, which was distinguished from the language of the north of France by the pronunciation of the little shibboleth *oui* (or yes) as *oc*, and hence called the *Langue d'oc* (the language of oc).

Among the natives, besides Clémence Isaure, are Fermat, the mathematician; General Dupuy; the statesmen Bertrand de Molville, de Villèle, and Montbel (the last was a minister of Charles X.); Paul Riquet, the engineer, &c.

The *Manufactures* include hardware goods, steel, oil, brandy, beer, dyes, leather, rope, cotton and woollen yarn, &c., flour, wax candles or bougies, paper, hats, pottery, vermicelli; and a general trade is carried on in the produce of south France, of which Toulouse is an entrepôt, as wine, refined sugar, fruits, essences.

Coaches start from 21, Rue Lafayette, daily, to Nismes, Perpignan, Carcassonne (*see* Route 47), Bordeaux (by Agen or Auch; Routes 84, 62), Moissac, Bayonne (by St. Gaudens, Pau, and Tarbes; Route 63), Aurillac (Route 57), Montauban, Foix, Ax, and Tarascon, Albi, (Route 52); and every two days, to St. Girons and Isle-en Dodon. During the season coaches go to the watering places of Rennes, Dax, d'Ussat, Bagnères-de-Luchon, Vernet, Moligt, Bagnères-de-Bigorre, Cauterets, St. Sauveur, Barèges, Eaux-Bonnes, Eaux-Chaudes. Malle-postes to Paris by way of Limoges (54 hours), Bayonne (22 hours), Marseilles (33 hours), Perpignan. Diligences of the Messageries, to Paris.

Diligences from other offices to Albi, St. Etienne, Villefranche, Muret, Mondonville, St. Lys, Ile-en-Jourdain, Grenade, &c. Cabs, &c. may be hired for the town and neighbourhood, at 1½ fr. an hour. Barques-de-poste or barges, run on the Canal du Midi to Carcassonne, Beziers, Cette, &c., starting daily, early in the morning. A steamer to Bordeaux sometimes runs on the Garonne, in 15 hours; return in 32 hours; but usually it comes no higher than Agen, to which a coach runs.

Routes 40, 46, 47, 52, 57, 62, 63, *and* 84 *meet Route* 50 *here, leading to the places above mentioned.*

From Toulouse, up the Garonne, you come to PORTET (10 kil.), where the Ariége joins. Passing up the latter, by the junctions of the Lèze and Stize, you come to

VIVIERS (16 kil.), on the Ariége.

SAVERDUN (22 kil.), in department Ariége, once a fortified town, and a roman station, where greek and roman coins have been found. Jacques Fournier or Pope Benedict XII. was born here. Population 4,100. At Mazères (14 kil. east-north-east), near the Lers, Gaston de Foix (killed at Ravenna, 1512) was born, and it is noted for its wine.

PAMIERS (15 kil.) on the Ariége, is a sous-préfecture (6,800 population), and seat of a bishop, in a fertile part, and was founded by Count Roger II., a crusader, who built a castle which he called *Apamea* after a town in Syria. It came to the house of Foix, and was sacked by the Kings of Condé 1628. The castle site, is the Castellet walk on a high rock, which commands a fine prospect over the town and river, and the plain and the Pyrenees beyond. The town contains a cathedral, rebuilt by Mansard, except the gothic tower, six other churches, a Carmelite convent, large hospital, and factories of nails and steel. Woollen serges, cheeses, &c. are made. *Hotels*—Catala; Douays.

[At 23 kil. east is *Mirepoix*, an industrious place (3,640 population), at the bridge on the Lers, once a strong post of the Albigenses, from whom it was taken in the thirteenth century, and given to Gui de Levi, one of their leaders, the Marshal of the Faith, as he was called. It has a curious unfinished church, a large hospice, and covered arcades in the public Place. Lalande the astronomer, and Marshal Clauzel were born here.—Maz d'Azil (25 kil. west of Pamiers), on the St. Girons road, in a fertile hollow of the Arize, was a fortified stronghold of the Protestants, who made a successful defence against Marshal de Themines 1625, after three assaults and a month's siege. Near this is Carlat, where *Bayle*, author of the Dictionnaire Critique was born.]

VARILHES (8 kil.), on the Ariége, has a curious grotto near it.

At 11 kil. further is

FOIX. *Hotels*—Du Rocher (Rock); de la Poste; des Voyagers (Travellers). Population 5,180. This small capital of department Ariége, on a river of the same name, where the Arget joins it, is hid away in a gap among the lower Pyrenees. It was the head of a county which grew out of St. Volusien's abbey, founded by the lords of Carcassonne, and of a castle built to protect it by the counts of Foix. Part of the abbey serves as the préfecture, the rest having been burnt down about 1800. Three gothic towers of the castle (used for the prison) stand on a high rock to the west; two are square, and the tallest, or keep, is 136 feet high. It was built 1362 by the famous Gaston de Foix, who lived here, but mostly at Orthes. He was so fond of hunting that he kept 1,600 dogs, and wrote a curious old book on the chase. The earlier counts fought for the Albigenses against Simon de Montfort and his crusaders. Through his wife, a daughter of Philip III. of Navarre, Gaston succeeded to that kingdom, which with the county came to the French crown through Henry IV.

The streets are narrow, and the houses irregular and ancient. An old stone bridge crosses the river. St. Volusien's church was built by Count Roger II. The palais de justice under the castle rocks, is of the fifteenth century. There are barracks, a theatre, college or school, and library of 8,000 vols. The Rev. T. Prat is protestant pastor here.

Small manufactures of woollens, hosiery, &c., with a trade in coal and iron (which are worked in the valleys around), and in cattle, cork, resin, wine, &c.

Conveyances to Toulouse, Bayonne, Carcassonne, Perpignan. There are about a dozen passages through the Pyrenees, but none fit for carriages in this quarter.

From Foix, up the Ariége, you pass

TARASCON (16 kil.), where the valley of Vicdessos from the south-west falls in (noted for La Rancié iron mines), is the *Tascodunitari* of Pliny, and has the round tower of its old castle on a rock, with the church of Notre Dame, near some caves. There are caves or grottos at Bédeillac (to the right) worth notice. Several forges are dispersed about this entrepôt.

The road leads on past the baths of Ussat, and Mont St. Barthelemy, to Cabannes (10 kil.), near Château-Verdun, and a chapel to the Virgin. At Orlu forge (to the left) there is a fine fall of the Ariége. Then you come to

AX (26 kil. from Tarascon), at the point where the three heads of the Ariége join, in a pretty, healthy spot, noted for its hot sulphur springs (aquæ). They rise up on all sides, and are powerful in obstinate cases of rheumatism, skin diseases, scrofula, &c.; the season is from June to October. *Hotels*—De France; d'Espagne, where and at La Tech, about thirty of the springs are in use, either as water or vapour baths, and for drinking. Board 4 fr., bed and bath ½ fr. each. Population, 2,000.

HOSPITALET (18 kil.), near the Col de Puymaurins, or pass over the ridge of the Pyrenees, 6,300 feet above sea. To the right is the little republic of Andorre (population, 15,000); and 20 kil. further on you come to Puycerda across the *Spanish* frontier, where the roads from Carcassonne and Perpignan fall in. (*See* Routes 43*a*, and 48). The more interesting passes of the Pyrenees to the west are described in Routes 60, 86, 87.

ROUTE 50a

Paris to Corbeil.

A short branch railway out of the Orléans line, running four trains a-day, in about an hour

JUVISY (20 kil. from Paris), as in Route 50.

CHATILLON on the Seine, here covered with villas, is noted for a fête champêtre, in May, and is opposite Draveil and Champrosay.

RIZ or RIS-ORANGIS (4 kil.), at the suspension bridge on the Seine, built by Aguado the banker, whose seat was here. The château was inhabited by Henry IV. That of Fromont belongs to M. Soulange Bodin, and has a well-arranged horticultural garden. A little further up the river are Doujons, Soisy, Etioles, and Petit Bourg, so called after the château of the Duc d'Antin, where Louis XIV. used to visit Madame Montespan. It was pulled down after being the seat of Aguado the banker. A hospital, founded by the Duchess of Bourbon, is also here.

CORBEIL (3 kil.), at the bridge on the Seine, in a pleasant spot, where the Esonne joins, and turns forty flour mills, is a sous-préfecture (Seine-et-Oise) of 4,500 souls, having a large trade in grain, a halle-au-blé (corn market), St. Spire's old church, a library of 4,000 vols., and an immense granary of six stories, large enough to feed all Paris for a fortnight. The second wife of Philippe Auguste died here, 1236, and the Prince of Condé attacked it without success, 1562.

Hotels—De la Belle-Image; Mouton-Blanc (White Sheep). A steamer runs hence to Melun and Montereau. Coaches to Melun, Fontainebleau, (*see* Route 24), Milly, Malesherbes, Puiseaux, Beaumont, Mennecy, Ponthierry.

A continuation of this rail is projected *viâ* Pithiviers, Montargis, Gien, to Nevers.

[Essonne (2 kil. south-west) on that river, was the old *Axona* or *Exona*, and a country-seat which Clothaire gave to St. Denis' abbey. Peat is cut here. Population 2,700.]

ROUTE 50b.

Orleans, up the Loire, to Briare and Nevers.

Distance (to Briare) 64 kil. or 40 miles.

ORLEANS, as in Route 50.

COMBLEAUX (8 kil.), where the canal d'Orléans goes off to the Loing, below Montargis.

JARGEAU (10 kil.) on the south side (opposite St. Denis), at the bridge, has a population of 2,450, and was held by the English, under Suffolk 1421, when taken by the Duc d'Alençon and Joan of Arc. A few years before, Charles, Duc of Orleans, and his brother formed a league here to revenge the death of their father by the Duke of Burgundy; whose death they accomplished at Montereau.

CHATEAUNEUF (8 kil.), opposite the pretty village of Siglon (on south side), is so called from an old castle. The church has a fine tomb of M. de la Vrillière. Excellent matelotes (a mixed dish of fish) at the Ville d'Orléans *hotel*.

[*Lorris* (22 kil. east), on the canal d'Orléans, though a marshy spot, was the seat of the kings of France, where St. Louis signed a treaty which regulated the succession of the county of Toulouse. It gives name to the Coutumes or Customs of Lorris, by which certain disputes were settled by duel; gentlemen using swords, and the bourgeois poignards.]

ST. BENOIT (10 kil.) or Fleury-sur-Loire, on the north side of the Loire, takes name from one of the earliest benedictine abbeys in France, of which the cruciform church (of the ninth century) remains, including St. Michel's tower over the entrance, with curious carvings about it. The interior is part romanesque.

SULLY (7 kil.) on the south side (at the suspension bridge to St. Pere), near the old moated castle of the Trémouilles, which Henry IV. gave with the title of duke to his great minister *Rosny* who printed his Memoirs in the Bethune tower. They shew Henri Quatre's chamber, and say that Voltaire began the Henriade when staying here with his literary patron the third duke.

LION (10 kil.) on the south side, opposite Ouzouer and Dampierre.

GIEN (12 kil.) on the north side, at the old twelve-arched stone bridge, in a pleasant spot, is on a gentle slant, at the top of which are the old spire church of St. Louis (where King Jean-sans-Peur was married 1410), and the château (now Hôtel de Ville), built or begun in Charlemagne's time. There are pretty gardens and baths on the river. Steamers from Orléans, Nevers, &c. touch at the quay. Flannel goods and pottery are made.

At 1 kil. north-east is VIEUX (or Old) GIEN, where roman stones, medals, &c. have been found, whence some think this was the ancient

Genabum. About 18 kil. south-west is the old castle of Argent.

BRIARE (9 kil.) on the high-road to Nevers and Lyons (*see* Route 51.)

ROUTE 51.

Orleans to Bourges, Nevers, Moulins, Roanne, and Lyons.

By railway (to Nevers), 113 miles, or 182 kil.; 5 to 6 hours, four trains a day. From Nevers to Lyons, about 288 kil., or 179 miles.

ORLEANS to VIERZON, as in Route 50.

FOECY (6¼ miles).

MEHUN (3½ miles), on the Yèvre, has parts of a chapel, staircase, and tower, of the favourite seat of Charles VII, where he lived with Agnes Sorel, his mistress, and where he afterwards died, starved to death through fear of being poisoned by his wicked son Louis XI. It belonged to the Courtenays, one of whom married St. Louis's nephew, Robert d'Artois, and another was allied to the emperors of Constantinople. The family is now represented by the Earl of Devon, of Powderham Castle.

MARMAGNE (4½ miles), on the Yèvre.

At 5¾ miles further is

Bourges. *Hotels*—De la Poste; du Bœuf Couronné (Crowned Bull); de la Boule d'Or, (Gold Ball); du Cheval Blanc (White Horse); de France. Population, 22,000. Chief place of department Cher, in the old province of Berri, seat of a cour impériale (high court of law), college, archbishopric, military division, &c., and a very ancient town on the Evre where the Auron meets it.

It was the head of the eastern *Bituriges* (whence the name), and is called *Avaricum* by Cæsar, who sacked it without mercy after a siege. Before the revolution it was the chief town of Berri, and noted for its good society from having an university established 1463, by Louis XI (a native), besides 20 churches, an abbey, and many religious houses. The streets are mostly narrow and crooked, with many low gable-ended houses, especially in the old town, which surrounds the hill where the Cathedral stands. The open Places and Sérancourt promenade are well planted.

St. Stephen's *Cathedral*, which commands a fine view of the town and neighbourhood, is one of the best in France; length, 348 feet. The front, 180 feet wide, has five great doors, ascended by steps, and two towers (one 200 feet high), and is richly ornamented with sculptures of scripture subjects, niched statues, &c. The interior is 141 feet wide, and has five naves (the middle one 121 feet high), stained windows (some as old as the thirteenth century), a rose window, 18 chapels, carved stalls, a fine altar, and an old crypt, in which are monuments of Jean, first duke of Berri, and Marshal Montigny. A clock in the tower is as old as 1423.

The archbishop's palace is in the italian style, and has grounds laid out by Le Nôtre, with an obelisk to the Duc de Bethune-Charost. The churches of Notre Dame and St. Bonnet were both burnt 1487, and rebuilt 1510-20. At the préfecture is the norman door of St. Ursin's church, which stood close to the palace of the ducs de Berri.

The *Town Hall* (Hôtel de Ville) was built 1443, by Jacques Cœur, silversmith to Charles VII, in a rich gothic style, and was given to the town by Colbert. Notice the oriel doorway, the curious chimney, the sugar-loaf towers, the chapel, the carvings of hearts (cœurs), &c., the motto 'A vaillans cœurs rien impossible' (nothing is impossible to bold hearts) near the gate, the stained windows, and portraits of the founder and of Bourdaloue.

The caserne d'artillerie (artillery barrack) is a large pile, built 1682, by Archbishop Phelippeaux, for a priests' seminary. In Rue des Arènes stands another barrack, a sort of brick tudor house, which belonged to Cujas, the scholar. Another old building, now a convent of Sœurs Bleues (Blue Sisters), was built by the Lallemand family, 1612, in the renaissance style (a sort of ornamented italian), and has a chapel, where they say Louis XI was baptised.

Other buildings are the museum, which has some portraits, &c., worth notice; the public library of 25,000 volumes; the college, and seminary; salle de spectacle. There are large caves under the old palace of the dukes. Two mineral waters are near. Bourdaloue, the famous preacher, was a native.

Trade in corn, wine, cattle, sheep, fruit. A few coarse woollens, and a little cutlery, are made.

Conveyances, by rail to Orleans and Paris, to

Tours, &c., and to Nevers; by coach to Montluçon, Neris-les-Bains, Clermont, &c.

[At 43 kil. north-east is *Sancerre*, a sous-préfecture (in department Cher) of 3,700 souls, on a hill covered with vineyards. It is ill built, but enjoys fine prospects of the Loire (10 kil. off), &c., especially from the Port de César. It was founded by Charlemagne for a colony of Saxons, and belonged to the princes of Condé, one of whom razed the walls, 1621. As a Protestant stronghold, it was besieged 1573, by Charles IX, with great distress on the town's part; and it is further noted for the royalist insurrection of 1796, headed by Phelippeaux, who afterwards contributed to Bonaparte's defeat at Acre. Most of the houses are gothic looking; an old tower overlooks the town.

Outside it was St. Satur's rich abbey, where stands a famous chesnut 33 feet round, and nearly 1,000 years old. The constable, Louis de Sancerre, and Marshal Macdonald, were born here. Trade in wine (of the district, called Sancerrois), fruit, grain, cattle, marble, &c. The wine is shipped at St. Thibault, on the Loire. *Hotels*—Le Bœuf Couronné (Crowned Ox); le Lion d'Or (Golden Lion).

Pouilly, in a pretty part of the Louvre, is noted for good white wine.]

From Bourges, along the rail to Nevers, you pass

Moulins (6¾ miles), Savigny (3¼ miles), Avor (2½ miles), Bengy (5¾ miles), Neron‹des (3½ miles), La Guerche (8 miles), Le Guetin (6½ miles), none of any consequence; thence after 6½ miles, and crossing the Allier and Loire, you come to

Nevers. *Hotels*—De France; du Lion d'Or (Golden Lion); de l'Image (*i. e.* of St. Louis); de l'Europe (in Rue du Commerce); de Nièvre. Population, 16,000. This capital of department Nièvre (formerly of a province called Nivernais), seat of an archbishop, &c., and the roman *Noviodunum*, is on a gentle slant of the Loire, where the Nièvre joins it (the Allier joins a little lower).

It looks well, but is a dull place, with crooked streets, and many old buildings. Parts of its ancient walls are left; one gate, the Porte des Croux, as rebuilt in the fourteenth century, is machiolated and carved, and has two small turrets, and a high roof; a modern one, on the Paris road, like a triumphal arch, was built 1746, after the battle of Fontenoy; a third leads over the twenty-arched stone bridge towards Moulins. On the hill is the gothic château of its dukes, now turned into a Hôtel de Ville, and its Parc, used as a promenade.

Near it stands St. Cyr *Cathedral*, a long large structure, with a square tower (1509-28), on which are statues; the oldest part of the body is romanesque, of the twelfth century, as well as the crypt; some of the pillars in the nave are of the same date, but the nave itself is of the thirteenth century; the choir and its carved work and stained windows belong to the fourteenth century; a north door was built 1290, the south door as late as 1528. Some old tapestry in it was worked by Marie d'Albret and her ladies.

Other churches are worth notice. St. Etienne is of the twelfth century; St. Pére, which belonged to the Jesuit's college, is small but elegant. Near the Loire is the norman crypt of St. Sauveur's ruined church; there are remains also (besides the refectory and byzantine cloisters) of a benedictine abbey church, called the Oratory. Not far from this, in rue Parcheminerie, they shew the house (with a niched figure in the walls) where Maitre Adam or Master Adam Billaut, the joiner-poet was born. The college was founded 1525; the library contains 8,500 vols. Besides these are priests' seminaries, large barrack, and an arsenal for founding government cannon, a theatre and baths, iron works, &c. The Sisters of Charity and Christian Instruction, numbering about two hundred and forty houses in France, have their head-quarters here.

Tiles, earthenware, and porcelain, are made, as well as enamel and glue; and there is a trade also in wine, eaux-de-vie, salt, wood, coal (from the neighbourhood). There are government foundries for chain cables, bridges, &c., at Imphy and Fourchambault up the Loire, and Guerigny, on the Nièvre.

Conveyances: by coach to Paris (malle-poste), Clermont, Lyons, Clamecy (72 kil.), Château - Chinon, Autun, &c.; by rail to Orléans, Paris, Nantes, &c. (four times a day); by steamer daily to Decize and Digoin (up the Loire), Orléans (down the Loire), Moulins (up the Allier). It is about 150 kil., by Château-

Chinon and Autun (in Route 28), to Chalons-sur-Saône (Route 24).

The Canal Lateral de la Loire, a side cut by the river, passes here on to Decize, where the Nivernais canal joins, and which has a good trade. It stands on a rocky island, joined to the main by two bridges (one suspended), and has an old castle of the Nevers dukes.

From Nevers, by road, to

MAGNY (12 kil.), an old place, with an old church.

ST. PIERRE-LE-MOUTIER (11 kil), near a lake, well stocked with fish. The coiffure or head dress of the women in this part is curious.

At 30 kil. further is

Moulins. *Hotels*—De l'Europe, in Rue de Garceaux; du Dauphin, in Place d'Allier; de la Poste; de l' Ecu. Population 16,000. Capital of department Allier (in the old province of Bourbonnais), and seat of a diocess, is on the flat banks of the Allier; and is pretty well built of brick (ziz-zaged in the façades), having good streets and promenades, with a well-planted Cours, and a thirteen-arched bridge, made solid to resist the river when it floods, against which also high levées or embankments are raised. The bridge was built 1753-63 by Regemortes, after others had been washed away, and is 1,084 feet long, and 45 wide.

Moulins, so called from the mills here, began in a castle of the tenth century, which became a seat of the ducs de Bourbon; a great square tower is the most striking part of it, which survived the fire of 1753. Here Antoine de Bourbon, King of Navarre, married Jeanne d'Albret; and Catherine de Medicis and Charles, in 1566, met the Cardinal of Lorraine, Coligny, &c., before the League was formed.

Notre Dame *Cathedral*, built 1386-1468, has only a large choir finished, with a carved figure of a dead man (near one of the doors), stained windows, paintings of the virgin and child. Below are the ashes of Charles VII.'s daughter, Jeanne. At the church of the visitation, founded by the wife of the gallant Montmorency, god-son to Henry IV., and beheaded 1632, is a good monument of him, including his effigy, with figures of Valour, Liberality, Piety, and Justice.

A clock-tower in one of the Places has a sort of minaret steeple, and figures (called the Jacquemard family, by the people) to strike the hours, &c. There are also a public library of 20,000 volumes, a museum, a district nursery or pepinière, large barracks (over the bridge), a college, seminary for priests, salle de spectacle, hospitals, &c.

At 2 kil. to the east is the romanesque church of Izeure, with its curious carvings, begun in the ninth century; and, near it, the little country house of Beauvoir, where the constable Bourbon spent his honeymoon.

Marshals Berwick and Villars were natives—the former born in Rue de la Cigogne. Cutlery, hats, and furniture prints are made; and there is a trade also in wine, grain, timber, oil and cattle.

Conveyances to Nevers, Paris, &c., and Roanne, Montluçon, Bourbon l'Archambault, Clermont-Ferrand, &c.; by steamer to Orléans in 30 hours.

From Moulins, on the road to Roanne (95 kil.) you pass

BESSAY-SUR-ALLIER (12 k.) VARENNES (15 k.)

ST. GERAND-LE-PUY, (11 kil.) with a ruined château.

[At 18 kil. to the south-south-west is *Cusset*, in a pretty valley made by the Sichon and Jolan; an ancient place with narrow streets, decayed walls, and part of a royal château rebuilt by Louis XI., who, when prince, was pardoned here by his father after the rebellion of the Praguerie. An abbey was founded here in 882, by a bishop of Nevers. Population 5,400.

Vichy, 2 kil. further, on the Allier, at the new suspension bridge, is noted for mineral springs, which are in the new town, or *Vichy-les-Bains*, where is a Thermal establishment, begun 1784 and improved 1820, including baths, ball and news-rooms, &c. At this building are three of the springs, called the Grande Grille (from a railing round it), Chomel or Petit Puits, and Grand Puits (*puit*, a well); near the soldiers' hospital is that called Lucas and Acacias (from the trees round it, and a physician here); H pital, is in Place Rosalie (near the hospital for the poor), and Celestins, on the river (under the site of an old convent).

These waters range between a temperature of 68° and 113°, are clear and bubbling like soda-water, and, as they also contain iron, are excellent in all cases of debility of the stomach and bowels, bad circulation, &c. From 5,000 to7,000 visit here in the season, which lasts from 15th May to 15th September. Lodging-houses are to be had in abundance.

The Avenue des Mesdames, towards Cusset was begun 1785, when the two royal ladies, Mesdames Adelaide and Victoire, took the waters.

Conveyances: by omnibus, to Cusset, Randan, Effiat, &c.; by coach to Paris, Lyons, Clermont, Roanne, Moulins, Gannat, Thiers, &c.]

LA PALISSE (10 kil.), a sous-préfecture of 2,700 population, in the fertile valley of the Bébre, under an old castle which belonged to Marshal de la Palisse (of the house of Chabannes), who is celebrated in a popular song. Boots and shoes or exportation are made.

ST. MARTIN D'ESTREAUX (15 kil.)

LA PACAUDIERE (8 kil.)

[Briennon (18 kil. east), on the Loire, was noted for the Clairvaux Abbey of Bénissons-Dieu, founded 1138, by St. Bernard. Its large and well-preserved gothic church remains, having a chapel cased with marble, and a portal between two elegant spires.]

ST. GERMAIN L'EPINASSE (12 kil.)

[About 7 kil. west is Ambierle and its fine abbey church (founded 938), containing the tombs of the Seigneurs of Pierrefitte.

St. Haond-le-Châtel (7 kil. south-west) takes name from the old Château de Boisy, near it, which was one of the strongest places in Forez; the walls are still so thick that *three* carriages may ride abreast on them. In the time of Charles VII. it belonged to the famous Jacques Cœur, his jeweller, and bore this inscription over the gate :—

"Jacques Cœur fait ce qu'il veut,
Et le Roi ce qu'il peut."

Here Admiral Bonnivet, killed at Pavia, was born.]

At 12 kil. further you come to Roanne, on the Loire and the St. Etienne railway (*see* Route 33), whence it is 140 kil. to Lyons.

ROUTE 51*a*.

Moulins to Macon.

Distance, 124 kil. or 77 miles

MOULINS, as in Route 51.

CHEVAGRES (16 kil.) on the Acotin. Thence across the Loire, to

BOURBON LANCY (20 kil.), in department Saône-et-Loire, on a hill-side on the Loire, under an old castle, begun by Henry III., was the *Aquae Nisinei* of the Romans, on account of its mineral springs, which are much like those of Vichy. Of eight springs only one is cold; the others have a temperature of 68° to 140°, the hottest being that called Lymbe; they are all in Faubourg St. Leger. Roman coins, &c. have been found. The country round is rather fine.

Conveyances, daily, to Moulins, Autun, Nevers, Macon.

DIGOIN (20 kil.) on the Loire, where the Canal du Centre from Chalons-sur-Saône falls in, close to the Arroux's mouth.

CHAROLLES (22 kil.), a sous-préfecture in department Saône-et-Loire, of 3,000 souls, was the capital of *Charolais*, a county in Burgundy, and stands between two hills, on one of which is an old castle, One of its counts, of the royal blood, in the time of Louis XV., amused himself by firing on the passers by, and, having killed a man, asked for letters of pardon; the king granted them, 'But,' said he, 'I have also signed a pardon for the man who may kill you by way of reprisal.'

CURTIL (20 kil.)

ST. SORLIN 18 kil.

At 8 kil. further is Macon (*see* Route 24); from which there is a road to Geneva (Route 32).

ROUTE 52.

Moulins to Clermont, St. Flour, Rodez, Albi, and Toulouse.

Distance, about 430 kil. or 267 miles; a hilly but most interesting road.

MOULINS, as in Route 51.

[From Moulins, on the road to Gueret, you pass *Souvigny* (10 kil.), on the Queune, which has the large benedictine abbey church of the ducs de Bourbon, with their fine monumental effigies. The abbey was founded. 913, by Aymard of Bourbon; the church is mostly of the fifteenth century. Parts of the town walls are left. Population, 3,000. At 8 kil. to the north-west is Menoux, on the Ours; and 8 kil. beyond it, the watering place of

Bourbon l'Archambault, in a pretty valley on the Barge, so called after Charles the Simple's favourite, Aymard d'Archambault, who built a château which had 24 towers, three of which remain, with other parts. At the church is a piece of the 'true cross,' given by St. Louis to his son Robert. The Romans called this place *Aquae Borbonis*. An Hôpital des Eaux stands near the saline springs, on Place des Capucins; they are three, viz., the Fontaine Bourbon, a hot spring (temp. 122°); and the cold springs of Jonas and St. Pardoux; and are useful in paralysis, apoplexy, rheumatism, scrofula, diseases of the skin and bones, &c. There are bath-houses and assembly-rooms, and the season is from June to August. This estate has lately been purchased by the Vicomte des Roys.

Montet-aux-Moines (20 kil.) Then Mont Marault (13 kil.), in a fertile spot; and 16 kil. further is Mont-Luçon (*see* Route 53.)]

CHATEL-DE-NEUVE (18 kil.), on the Allier.

ST. POURÇAIN (12 kil), in a fertile wine country on the Sioule, where the Limon joins, is called *St. Portianus*, after a Christian slave, to whom a monastery was built in the sixth century. Its gothic church contains a very well executed 'Ecce Homo' in marble, as old as the fifteenth century. Population, 5,000.

GANNAT (24 kil.), a sous-préfecture of 5,400 souls, in a pretty spot on the Audelot, grew out of a benedictine cell founded by the Bourbons, and has remains of a château (now the prison), a chapel called St. Procule, which devotees frequent, and a mineral spring. Cardinal Duprat and Abbe Chatel were natives. The baths of Vichy (*see* Route 51) are 19 kil. to the east.

AIGUEPERSE (9 kil.), the roman *Aquae sparsae*, in Auvergne, on the Luzon, has a mineral water, and (at the Hôtel de Ville) a statue of the Chancellor l'Hôpital, born at La Roche chateau, 1505. Abbé Delille, the translator of Virgil, is also a native. Good stone and plaster, &c., are quarried in the hills of Montpensier and Chaptuzat; St. Mion mineral spring, and the old château of Effiat are in the neighbourhood.

[At 4 kil. to the east, is the fine château of *Randan*, with its curious heap of spires and chimneys, and its beautiful grounds,—a good specimen of the old feudal châteaux of France. It has a view of the Limagne, the mountains of Forez, Mont Dore Puy de Dôme, &c.; and, after being held by the Polignacs, came to Louis Philippe's sister, Madame Adelaide; but has been sold with other property of the Orléans family.]

RIOM (16 kil.), where the road from Bourges falls in (*see* Route 53), is a sous-préfecture, on a hill above the Ambone, and the second town in Auvergne, over which it has a good view from the church. The houses are constructed of dark Volvic lava stone. St. Amable church was built as far back as 1077. The palais de justice was part of the seat of the Comtes d'Auvergne. In one of the Places is a statue of Desaix. There are a general hospital, &c., and several fountains. Population, 11,000. *Hotels* — De la Couronne (Crown); de l'Ecu de France (French Crown-piece); du Palais, &c.

[*Volvic* (5 kil. south-west) is remarkable for its quarries of lava, of great extent (with a granite mass in the midst), and for the fine ruins of Tournoel castle, the donjon of which has a noble prospect of the rich basin of Limagne, or valley of the Allier.]

At 16 kil. further is

Clermont, or Clermont-Ferrand. *Hotels*—De l'Ecu de France (French Crown-piece); de la Poste (in Place de Jaude); de l'Europe; de la Paix; des Messageries, &c. *Cafés*—De Paris; Lyonnais; de Clermont. Population, 32,500.

Capital of department Puy-de-Dôme, a bishopric, &c., and a very ancient city (the *Augustonemetum* of Ptolemy, and head of the Arverni), where Pope Urban II. and Peter the Hermit preached the First Crusade, 1095. It was ravaged by the Northmen in the ninth century.

It stands in a fine spot between two small streams, the Tiretaine and Artier, on a low hill (*Mons Clarus*, where the castle stood), surrounded by higher hills, falling one way to the rich plain of Limagne (on the Allier), and rising the other way towards Puy-de-Dôme peak (8 kil. off), which gives name to the department.

Auvergne, the old province which the latter was taken out of, is an extraordinary region of conical peaks (called Puys) of extinct volcanoes, and has a lava soil, very fertile in some parts, with many old castles on the highest points. It has been investigated by Scrope, Elie de Beaumont, and other geologists.

The streets of Clermont are narrow and irregular, and the houses built of dark Volvic lava, mostly whitewashed over. It is well supplied with water from Royat, &c. Promenades on the boulevards, which are well planted: and on the Squares or Places. Among these are, Place du Taureau, which has a fountain in honour of General Desaix, with a prospect of the Limagne, the plateau of Gergovia, and the castle on Mont Rognon; Places de la Pôterne and d'Espagne, commanding good views also; Place des Jacobins, or Delille, which has a mixed gothic fountain of three stories, built 1515, topped by a statue of Delille the poet; and Place d'Armes or de Jaude, 860 feet long, so called after a mineral intermitting spring near it.

The *Cathedral*, built of dark lava stone, between 1248 and 1265, is a rather imposing gothic structure, but unfinished; length, 321 feet; breadth, 139; height, 106, to the open lofty roof, which hangs on 56 light and well carved pillars. It has a good north porch, rose and other stained windows, carved work in the choir, &c.; and there is a fine view from the tower. There were five towers before the revolution.

Notre Dame-du-Port Church, part of which dates from 853, is the oldest building here, and has some curious decorations, with an ancient crypt and an image of the Virgin, held in great esteem by the faithful superstitious. At the church of St. Genès are modern painted windows.

Other objects of note are the préfecture, Hôtel de Ville, lyceum or college, halle au blé (corn market), linen market, theatre, hôtel Dieu and general hospital; also the library of 19,000 vols. (besides MSS.), begun by Massillon when bishop here; the cabinet of mineralogy (very good); the academy of sciences (having some roman marbles and a statue of Pascal, a native); all contained in the large botanic garden. The cattle market and priests' seminary are at Montferrand, to which a fine avenue of a mile runs.

Schools of art and science exist here, where lectures on various subjects are given. In Faubourg St. Alyre, near the benedictine abbey of that name, is a curious mineral water (acid and tonic), and *petrifying spring* in a garden kept by M. Clémentel, which in course of time has made, by gradual deposits of carbonate of lime, a sort of dyke or wall, about 250 feet long and 13 broad, with a natural stalactite bridge at the end hanging over the Tiretaine brook. Flowers, fruit, &c., covered with this sediment are sold.—At St. Mart (1 kil. off), to the west, is a third mineral water of good quality (near the baths of Cæsar), brought into use since 1843.

Rev. M. Collins is protestant pastor here.

Manufactures of stockings, paper, hats, leather, confitures (apricot and other sweetmeats); and a trade in cattle, wool, cheese, hemp, fruit, and wine.

Conveyances to Paris, Moulins, Lyons, St. Etienne, Montpellier, Le Puy, Bordeaux, Toulouse, Rodez, Aurillac, Limoges, &c.

Clermont is one of the places in the Central of France railway scheme, which proposes to unite this with Rodez, Montauban, Perigueux, Limoges, &c., and ultimately with Lyons and Bordeaux.

In the neighbourhood are the plain of Gergovia, Mont Rognon (a peak of basalt), and its old castle, St. Vincent mineral water, Roche Blanche and its caves, Chateaugay and its prospects, the caverns of Gravenoire, Royat and its grottoes, mills, falls, &c.; Puy de Pariou (north-west); Puy de Dôme (west), and other volcanic peaks. Royat is to the west, in a pretty valley, with the waters of Fontanat, and the Puy-Châteix near it, and under Puy de Dôme and Gravenoire (2,722 feet above the sea).

[From Clermont to Puy de Dôme, to the west, you pass over a lava soil to Barraque, where the road turns off to Puy de Pariou, which is 4,000 feet above the sea, having a very regular crater, 300 feet deep and 3,000 feet round the edge. After an ascent of 10 kil. altogether, you come to

Puy de Dôme, which gives name to the department, and overlooks all the other puys, of which about sixty may be seen from the top, stretching in a line 18 miles long (north and south), besides the peaks of Mont Dore (further south), the fertile plain of the Allier, &c. It is 4,839 feet above the sea, or 656 feet higher than the Petit Puy de Dôme near it; and is composed of porous, crumbling stone, here called Domite, after the mountain, which takes its own name from its dome shape. Pascal experimented on the weight of the air from this peak.

Puys Chopine, Sarcoui, and de Côme, to the north, are respectively, 3,908, 3,436, and 1,273 feet high. The forests about here are great places for making Sabots, or wooden shoes;

the men working at the business in the open air. Many millions are made in this quarter, and in the forests round Valenciennes and Fougères.]

From Clermont, on the road to Rodez, you pass (up the fine valley of the Allier) under Gravenoire peak, Mont Rognon, with its old castle of the Dauphins on the top, to

GERGOVIA (9 kil.), a hill, where Cæsar was beaten by the Gauls under Vercingetorix, with traces of a camp on it.

VAYRE (8 kil.), in a beautiful spot near Puy de Marman.

COUDES (24 kil. from Clermont), on the Allier close to Mont Peyroux. Mont D'Or or Dore, and its range of peaks are on the left.

ISSOIRE (11 kil.), a sous-préfecture of 5,600 people (who make copper kettles, &c.), in a hollow, on the Creuze, having an old church of the tenth century. It was the birthplace of Chancellor Duprat. *Mont Dore-les-Bains*, is 35 kil. to the left (*see* Route 57), up the valley of the Creuze; passing the volcanic peaks and basalt cliffs, near Villetour spa and lake Pavin, which was once a crater, 850 feet deep. Not far from this is another lake, called Chambron (abounding with fish), above which rises the old feudal castle of Murol.

LEMPDE (20 k.), where the road to Le Puy turns off.

[It passes *Brioude* (15 kil.), an ancient town and sous-préfecture (department Haute-Loire), on the Allier. Population, 4,800. The norman style church, St. Julien's, one of the oldest in Auvergne, was rebuilt in the tenth century by William of Aquitaine, with five chapels round it. A fine view from the hill where the college stands.—At 23 kil. to the east, on the St. Etienne road is *la Chaise Dieu*, with the abbey church of Casa Dei, 302 feet long, built in a fine gothic style, begun by Clement VI (a native) in 1343, having a well-carved portal, 156 stalls, some old tapestry, the founder's tomb, &c., and a few remains of the abbey adjoining.

La Vieille-Brioude (3 kil.) has a large single-arched lava bridge, on the Allier, 181 feet span.

St. George d'Aurat (18 kil.), near Chavagnac château, where *Lafayette* was born.

Limandre (18), in a lava region beyond which (at 13 kil.) is the ruined château de Polignac, and its old church.

At 6 kil. further is *Le Puy*, on a volcanic peak (*see* Route 40).]

MASSIAC (18 kil.), in a hollow on the Alagnon.

[Here the road turns off to Aurillac, on a series of terraces, passing (at 22 kil.) *Murat*, on the Alagnon, among the basalt hills round Mount Cantal, and a sous-préfecture in department Cantal.

One hill, Roche Bonnavie, with a basalt cliff, in which are prismatic pillars (some 50 feet long) has the old castle of Jacques d'Armagnac on top. To avoid the steep road beyond this, the *Tunnel of Lioran*, about 5,000 feet long, was cut 1839-47, through the volcanic heights which divide the Alagnon and Cère: it comes out near the old road, between Puy de Griou and *Plomb de Cantal*, which is 6,095 feet above the sea, and the centre of a range of extinct volcanos, as Puy Mary, Puy Chavaroche, &c., in continuation of those in Puy de Dôme. It is a smooth cone, round which twenty or thirty streams (the head waters of the Dordogne, Lot, Allier, &c.) take their rise, almost as regularly as the spokes of a wheel. After passing Thièzac (26 kil.) and Vic-sur-Cère, in the beautiful valley of the Cère, you come (27 kil. further) to Aurillac (as in Route 57).]

ST. FLOUR (30 kil.), a sous-préfecture (department Cantal), and seat of a bishopric, on a basalt precipice 330 feet above the high road, was built about the year 1000, and has a gothic cathedral of the fifteenth century, the convent of the jacobins, a priests' seminary, and a view from the bishop's palace, as well as other points of Plomb de Cantal, &c. Population, 5,800. *Hotels*—De France, Amangat. The road to Mende (83 miles) and Nismes, by St. Cheley, turns off here (*see* Route 44).

CHAUDES-AIGUES (33 kil.), *i. e.* Hot Springs, lies in a deep gorge of the mountains between Auvergne and Gévaudan. Five springs varying in temperature from 135° to 177° (the Par is as hot as this), are used not only for the bath and drinking, but for cooking, for hatching chickens, washing fleeces, &c.

LA GUIOLE (32 kil.), in department Aveyron, is a healthy place, of 2,100 people, on a basalt peak nearly 3,300 feet above the sea. They make good cheese here.

Espalion (24 kil.), a small industrious sous-préfecture, in the middle of a large basin, on the Lot, covered with vines, &c. Population, 4,400. A tower on the site of Benneval abbey, and Roquelaure Castle, may be visited.

[*St. Geniès de Riva d'Olt* (21 kil. east-south-east), on the Lot, an industrious place, of 4,000 population, who make flannels, woollens, &c. It stands among vineyards and falls, in a charming valley of the Lot, here crossed by a bridge, and once called Oltis, whence the name, signifying on the 'bank of the Lot.']

At 32 kil. further is

Rodez or Rhodez. *Hotels*—Des Voyageurs (Travellers); des Princes; de la Ville de Paris. Population, 10,000. The chief town of department Aveyron (formerly of the province of Rouergue), seat of a bishop, tribunal, &c., finely seated in a healthy spot, on the crest of a hill, 150 feet above the Aveyron, which winds round the bottom, and 2,170 feet above the sea. It was the ancient *Legodunum*, a capital of the *Rateni* (from whom comes the modern name), so called from their goddess Ruth or Venus. Rhodanois money was coined here by its early counts, in the Rue de Saounario (*i. e.* sous factory), where the mint stood till 1824. Their château is gone, except the Martelière tower, built 1264, now a prison; it was taken by the English in the fourteenth century. The town is badly built, with small dirty steep streets of wooden houses, but the neighbourhood is pleasant.

The *Cathedral*, of reddish sandstone, is the best building, and stands on the site of one founded in the fifth century, which fell 1275, when the new one was commenced, but not finished till the 16th century. It is cross-shaped, 320 feet long by 118 feet wide, and 109 to the vault. Contrary to custom, it has no west entrance, the doors being at the sides. Over one of these stands an excellent carved tower, built 1501, 265 feet high (and seen 18 leagues off), square at the bottom, but eight-sided towards the top, which is crowned by pinnacles (with the four evangelists on them), a dome, and a statue of the Virgin. It contains a good screen and other carved work, and some old-fashioned stained windows. When threatened at the revolution, some friends of art thought of dedicating it to Marat! which device was the means of saving it.

Another church is marked by a tall tower. The Cordeliers house is of the fourteenth century; a government stud is established at the Chartreuse convent. At the college, first built by the Jesuits, is a library of 16,000 vols., and a cabinet of natural history, &c. Other buildings are the préfecture, new Hôtel de Ville, the priests' seminary, bishop's palace, a deaf and dumb school, the pepinière or departmental nursery, &c. In 1784, Abbé Carnus, a man of science, ascended here in a balloon, 55 feet diameter, $1\frac{3}{4}$ miles high, staying up 35 minutes, to the great astonishment of the people in that age.

There is a trade in woollens, linens, silk thread, Roquefort cheese, wax candles, cattle, mules, &c. Coaches to Montpellier, Toulon, Montauban, Albi, Aurillac, Clermont, &c.

The caves of Sollac are 4 kil. off; some pretty falls at Salles-Comtaux (about 12 kil. north), in the rocky and well-wooded valley of Marcillac. This is one of many charming valleys about Rodez, little known or visited. A druid stone or dolmen at Perignagols (8 kil.).

[Rignac is 24 kil. west-north-west, and 24 kil. beyond is Villefranche (*see* Route 57).]

La Mothe (24 kil.). Then comes Les Faguelles (28 kil.). Albi is 20 kil. beyond; you pass near the Saut de Sabo, a fall of the Tarn, close to a large paper-mill.

Albi, or Alby. *Hotels*—Des Ambassadeurs; de l'Europe; du Commerce; de France; du Nord; the last having an eating room full of fine paintings. Population 11,665.

The chief town of department Tarn, seat of an archdiocess, having a tribunal, communal college, &c. It was the roman *Civitas Albiensium*, but is more memorable for giving name to the *Albigeses* or *Albegeois*, exterminated by the papacy in the thirteenth century. It stands over the river Tarn, in the middle of a fine plain; and like all old towns is made up chiefly of narrow irregular streets. The best promenades are in the Vigan quarter, near the public gardens; each quarter is ornamented with fountains, the best being that of Verdusse, where four springs unite, and flow thence into the river. In the Faubourg du Pont, across the latter, are remains of Castelviel fort.

The *Cathedral* of St. Cécile, begun 1282, was

not finished till 1512. Length 345 feet, breadth 89¼, height of the vault 98½, of the west steeple 308½. Three beautifully decorated doors lead into the porch, which divides the choir and nave, and which is covered with sculptures of extraordinary delicacy. The roof of the nave is ornamented with a multitude of subjects from the Bible, including angels, patriarchs, prophets, saints, martyrs, &c., painted in fresco, on a blue ground, set off by arabesques in white and gold. They were begun 1502, and are in the best style of the italian school. Some elegant carvings, and seventy-two statues adorn the choir. A council met here 1176, to condemn the Albigenses.

The tower of St. Salvi's Church is in the moorish style, and it has a large nave. Other buildings are the Hotel de la Préfecture, an immense edifice, which belonged to the Counts of Toulouse and afterwards to the archbishops; a large hospice or convent, with an avenue leading to it the college; a public library of 12,000 vols.; museum, cabinet of natural history, theatre, &c.

Manufactures of linens, agricultural tools, &c., and a trade in grain, saffron, dry fruits, wood.

Conveyances—Daily, to Toulouse (65 kil.) Castres, Rodez and Lower Languedoc, Milhau, Gaillac, Montauban (48 kil.), &c.

GAILLAC (22 kil.) on the road to Toulouse where that to Montauban turns off (*see* Route 50), is a sous-préfecture, on the Tarn, with 7,725 population, in a good wine country. Portal, the physician, was born here. *Hotels*—Austruc; Raffis.

ST. SULPICE (23 kil.) has a camp raised in the wars against the Albigenses, in the time of Louis VIII.

At 31 kil. beyond is TOULOUSE, as in Route 50.

ROUTE 53.

Bourges to Neris-les-Bains and Clermont.

Distance, 185 kil. or 115 miles; nearly following the canal to Montluçon.

BOURGES, as in Route 51.

LEVET (18 kil.)

ST. AMAND (26 kil.), a pretty sous-préfecture on the Marmande, near its joining to the Cher. Population 7,800. It has traces of *Montrond* castle, which belonged to Gaston de Foix (born here), the Duc de Sully, and the great Condé, who was brought up here. *Hotels*—Du Bœuf (Bull); Croix de Fer (Iron Cross).

DREVENT (3 kil.), near remains of a roman theatre, on the Cher, where statues, pavements, &c. have been found.

MONTLUÇON (49 kil. from St. Amand), an old town and sous-préfecture of 4,990 people, in the wine country by the Cher, on a hill, which has remains of a castle of the dukes of Bourbon on the top. Here the canal, from Vierzon *viâ* Bourges, ends. Iron and looking glasses are made here. *Hotels*—De France; du Dauphin.

NERIS-LES-BAINS (8 kil.), a small spa in a healthy spot, was known (as *Aquæ Neri*) to the Romans for its warm mineral baths, which were again brought into notice since 1821, and are used between May and November, in cases of paralysis, rheumatism, tumours, and nervous complaints. The springs are Puits de la Croix, Puits de César, Puits Carré, and La Source Nouvelle; they are also supplied to the houses for cooking, &c. A large bath-room was begun 1831; and there is a hospital with 100 beds for the poor, gratis. The Jardin des Bains is on the site of a roman amphitheatre, which can be plainly traced; columns, statues, coins, &c. have been found here. The old norman church is of the eleventh century. *Hotels*—Grand Hôtel; Léopold.

MONTAIGUT (17 kil.), in the hilly department of Puy de Dôme, has a castle on a pointed (aigu) rock. *Hotel*—De l'Ecu.

MENAT (15 kil.) is the next place, with its tripoli quarries on the Sioule.

ST. PARDOUX (12 kil.), Riom (23 kil.), and Clermont (15 kil.), are described in Route 52.

ROUTE 54.

Chateauroux to Gueret, Aubusson, and Clermont.

Distance, 212 kil. or 132 miles.

CHATEAUROUX, as in Route 50.

LA CHATRE (37 kil.), a town of 4,700 souls, and a sous-préfecture, in a pretty spot on the Indre, with remains of a castle, of which a tower serves as the prison. There are some good points of view around.

[*Chateaumeillant*, about 15 kil. to the left, is a curious mixture of various styles, and stands in a moat.]

GENOUILLAC (27 kil.)

[*Boussac* (12 kil. east-north-east), in department Creuse, is a small sous-préfecture, finely seated on a rock, over the little Creuse (where the Veron joins it), among precipitous hills. Above the village are the large remains of its ancient castle. Population 879.]

At 27 kil. further is

Gueret. *Hotels* — La Poste-aux-Chevaux (Post Horses), in Place d' Armes; du Lion d' Or (Golden Lion); Saint François; Croix d' Or (Golden Cross). Population 4,800. The chief town of department Creuse, and a very dull place, under a hill, between the rivers Creuse and Gartempe, but not near enough for either to be of service to it. It was called *Garactum* or *Varactum*, and grew out of an abbey, founded 720, by Clothaire; it was also the residence of the counts of Marche, at whose old château (a little east), now in ruins, Charles VII. staid when in pursuit of his rebellious son (Louis XI.) The streets are narrow and the buildings of little note. Parts of its old walls remain. It has a library of 4,500 vols., with a lunatic asylum and a pepinière (nursery) for the department. A group of stones in the neighbourhood is called La Peyras. Trade in wool, cattle, butter, &c.

Aldebert, the first count (about 993) of this province of Marche, of which Gueret was the capital, having given himself the title, and captured Tours in spite of the threats of the king Hugh Capet, was asked by him 'Who made you a count?' to which the bold vassal answered, 'Who made you king?'—a difficult question for the usurper, whom Dante has placed in his purgatory. His descendant, Aldebert, sold it to Henry II. of England, who sold it again to Hugh of Lusignan. After some further changes, it was united to the French crown by Francis I. The vine is not cultivated, but other fruits are plentiful; chesnuts are a common article of food. The people of the department speak a kind of Limousin patois. It is the custom for many of them to emigrate in March every year, in search of employment, returning home in December.

Conveyances to Chateauroux (on the rail), Limoges, &c.

[From Gueret, on the road to Limoges, you pass *Bourganeuf* (29 kil.), a sous-préfecture of 3,200 people, on the Thorion or Taurion, where they say, Zizim, a Turkish prince, flying from his brother, Bajazet II., and placed here under the protection of the grand master, D'Aubusson, built a curious tower of great solidity, which still remains. Paper and porcelain are made. *Hotels*—Du Soleil d' Or (Golden Sun, *i.e.* Louis XIV.); de la Poste.

St. Leonard (28 kil.), an old place on the Vienne (which a bridge crosses), with manufactures of paper, &c. Population 6,100.

At 22 kil. further is Limoges.]

From Gueret, on the road to Clermont Ferrand, you pass

Le Montier (20 kil.)

Aubusson (16 kil.), a sous-préfecture of 5,300 people, with manufactures of tapestry, coarse cloth, &c. It stands in a rocky gap on the Creuse, in a poor country, and has the ruins of a château belonging to the grand master D'Aubusson, who received Prince Zizim at Rhodes, and sheltered him at Bourganeuf (as above); it was dilapidated in 1646. *Hotels*—La Boule d'Or (Golden Ball); du Lion d'Or.

[At 8 kil. to the south is *Felletin*, where paper and carpets are made. It stands over the Creuse, on the slant of a hill, above which was a castle in feudal times. An old building here, called Beaumont, which served as the parish church and an Austrian prison, but now pulled down, was said to be part of a pagan temple.

About 16 kil. to the east is Crocq, a little village on a rock, which, in the troubled reign of Henry IV., gave name to a gang of brigands called *Croquans*.]

La Villeneuve (23 kil.); Pont-au-Mur (22 kil.) on a branch of the Sioule; then

Pont Gibaud (18 kil.) on the Sioule, in the lava soil of Auvergne, whose dauphins built a château here, with walls of great thickness, and corner towers. In the neighbourhood are the seat of Comte de Pont Gibaud (or Gibault), the mineral water of Javelle, mines of lead, copper, antimony, &c., and many volcanic peaks.

At 22 kil. further is Clermont (*see* Route 52).

ROUTE 55.

Clermont to Thiers, Montbrison, St. Etienne and Lyons,

Distance, 203 kil. or 126 miles.

Clermont, as in Route 52.

Puy-de-Poix, a basalt peak, with a spring of mineral pitch or bitumen. Puy-de-Crouelle and Gandaillat are near it with similar springs.

Pont-du-Chateau (15 kil.), at the three-arched bridge on the Allier, near the old château of the bishops of Clermont, in a fine part of the Limagne.

[To the right is the ancient town of Billom, among hills, remarkable for the stormy weather and excessive rain to which it is subject. It has an old church.]

Thiers (26 kil.), on a rocky peak above the Durole, is a sous-préfecture (in Puy-de-Dôme) of 13,200 souls, and commands a fine view of the Limagne, Clermont, Monts Dôme, &c., from the terrace near the old castle. Two churches, Du Montier and St. Genès, are of the eighth and twelfth centuries On the river stand many paper mills and forges for cutlery; good powder is also made. A pretty waterfall is seen at Trou d'Enfer. *Hotel*—De l'Europe.

[At 56 kil. to the south-south-east is *Ambert* (62 kil. direct from Clermont), a sous-préfecture, on the Dore, among hills, in the Livradois, with a population of 8,000, who make linen, and excellent paper for printing, engraving, &c. In the neighbourhood there are fine prospects from Pierre-sur-Haute (the Alps seen), and Mont Fournol (the Cantal, Puy-de-Dôme, &c., seen), and the mineral springs of Talaru. Thence to Montbrison is about 30 kil.]

La Bergere (14 kil.) is reached by a precipitous road, commanding views of the distant mountains.

[Thence to Roanne is 43 kil.]

Noiretable (13 kil.) under Montagne de l'Hermitage.

Boen (27 kil.) on the Lignon, from which, *vià* Feurs, it is 87 kil. direct to Lyons.

At 17 kil. further is Montbrison (*see* Route 33), 12 kil. from Montrond, on the rail, which leads one way to Roanne, and the other way (*vià* St. Etienne), to Lyons.

ROUTE 56.

Limoges to Tulle and Aurillac.

Distance. 115 kil. or 71 miles.

Limoges and Uzerche, as in Route 50.

At 30 kil. further is

Tulle. *Hotels*—Des Voyageurs (Travellers); de l'Aigle d'Argent (Silver Eagle); de Lyon; de Perigord. Population 11,000. Chief town of department Corrèze (formerly the province of Bas-Limousin), seat of a bishop, a government factory for fire arms, &c., is in a narrow valley on the Corrèze (where the Solane meets it), the rocky sides of which are lined with houses in the gothic and renaissance styles, surrounded by picturesque hills. Sarrasin or maize is grown. There are pretty walks on the quays and bridges. An old square tower, said to be roman, stands above the town, near the cemetery. The half-gothic cathedral, marked by a fine slender spire, — feet high, in the Grand Place, where also is the Maison Sage, a turreted house of the fourteenth century, ornamented with arabesque and other carvings. The library contains 2,500 volumes; a district prison, a college, good hospittal, &c., are also seen. The small-arms factory is at Souillac (2 kil.) on the Solane, a river bordered by fine granite rocks. Many remains of the roman *Tintiniacum*, destroyed by the Vandals, exist on a plain 6 kil. north, near which you get a view of the Cantal chain; in a valley below is the Gordino fall. Baluze, the historian, was born here; and here races (courses deschevaux) are sometimes held. Bougies, or wax candles, oil, nails, paper, and playing cards are made. Coaches to Paris, Clermont, Cahors Toulouse, &c.

[At 8 kil. north-east, near *Gimel* (which has a finely carved gothic cross and a feudal château), on the Montane, is one of the grandest *falls* in France. The river tumbles over the broken limestone rocks in a succession of five or six leaps, though not visible all together, one of which is 138 feet down and 15 wide; another is 85 feet down.]

Argentat (31 kil.) is on the Dordogne, at the new wire suspension bridge, built 1828, by Vilat, 328 feet long, and 49 feet above the stream. It belonged to Turenne's family, and had an abbey of the twelfth century.

Monvert (26 kil.) in department Cantal.

Aurillac is 28 kil. further (*see* Route 57).

ROUTE 57.

Clermont to Mont Dore-les-Bains, Tulle, Mauriac, Aurillac, Cahors, Montauban.

Distance about 332 kil. or 206 miles.

CLERMONT, as in Route 52. Passing thence under Puy de Dôme and Mont Serre, you come to Chamalière and its old church, near the valley of Royat.

ROCHEFORT (29 kil. from Clermont), in a deep valley on the Sioule, under a puy or peak, with an old castle on the top, which belonged to the Counts of Auvergne. To the south of it is Murat-le-Quaire, near the Bourboule spa, in a pretty spot on the Dordogne.

LAQUILLE (about 10 kil.)

[Bourg-Lastic (24 kil. west) has a good mineral water.]

ST. SAUVES (14 kil.) on the Dordogne.

[At about 22 kil. east-south-east is *Mont d'Or* (or Dore) *les Bains*, a watering place, about 3,400 feet above sea, near the Pic du Sansey (6,224 feet above sea, the highest of the Mont Dore range), at the head of the Dordogne, among volcanic peaks, woods, valleys, and waterfalls. There are two cold and five warm springs, useful in rheumatism, consumption, and inflammatory complaints; the season is from June to September. It has good bath rooms, and some traces of roman occupation. In the neighbourhood are several attractions, as the falls called Grand Cascade, Quereilh, and de Vernière, Lake Pavin, the Vallée d'Enfer (Hell Cut), Capucin Peak (like a monk's head), the castle of Murol, in a forest under Puy de Tartaret, &c.]

TAUVES (about 8 kil.)

[About 24 kil. west is *Ussel* (28 kil), an old town and sous-préfecture, in department Corrèze, among bare hills, between the Diège and the Sarsonne. Further on is Egletons (29 kil.), beyond which, at 32 kil., is Tulle (*see* Route 56).]

BORT (about 30 kil.), in a fine valley of the Dordogne, is under Orgues de Bort, a rugged basaltic peak, with a pyramid at top, left in the trigonometrical survey, whence there is a noble view of great extent; but the place is most remarkable as the birthplace of *Marmontel*, who describes the course of his early life here in his entertaining memoirs.

MAURIAC (about 30 kil.), a sous-préfecture, (department Cantal) under a volcanic peak, near the Dordogne. Population, 3,600. Notre Dame des Miracles is a curious church, of the eleventh and twelfth centuries, with ancient carvings about it, and an image which draws a crowd on the 9th May. The old ruined chapel of St. Mary commands a fine prospect. A fountain to the memory of Montijon has an inscription by Marmontel, who went to school here. Several falls, ruined castles, and points of view are about. One fall is that of the *Auze*, 108 feet down, a little out of the Aurillac road; it is worth seeing, and is not far from the fine château of Mazerolles.

DRUJEAC (8 kil.), in a fine valley, has an old château and a church, sheltered by immense poplars.

At 27 kil. further is

AURILLAC. *Hotels*—des Voyageurs (Travellers); des Trois Frères.—Population, 10,500. A small town, the capital of department Cantal, in Auvergne, in a pretty valley by the Jordanne, on lava deposits which in past times have run from the extinct volcanoes of the Cantal range, which are in sight. Houses built of slate; the streets are broad, and refreshed by running brooks from a reservoir in the upper part of the town. A promenade, called Le Gravier, lies along the river from the Cours Montyon, so called after a benefactor whose column is here; and the country outside is beautiful. In faubourg St. Etienne is a tower of St. Stephen's castle which belonged to the Comtes d'Auvergne. Some remains of a Benedictine abbey or convent and two nunneries are left in the faubourg de Buis (or des Frères, *i.e.* Brothers). The churches of St. Gerard and Notre Dame have pictures, and the latter a good vault. There are also a college, hôtel de la préfecture, Hôtel de Ville, with a public library of 7,000 vols. and a cabinet of minerals, corn-hall, bridge, theatre, stables for hunters, of arab, English, norman, and other breeds, and the hippodrome (1 kil. off), or race-course, where races, attended by great numbers from all quarters, take place the first fortnight in June. Pope Sylvester II., Marshal Noailles, and General Destaing were natives. Manufactures of lace, jewellery, copper and brass goods, paper, leather; and a good trade in horses, mules, cattle, cheese, &c.

Conveyances: Daily to Paris, Toulouse, Clermont, Limoges, Tulle, Rodez, Montauban, St. Flour, &c.

Within a few miles are the old castles of Carlat, Valduces, Misilliac, Espinassol, and Sedaignes-Vouté; the pretty valleys of Raulhac, Marnagnac, the grottoes of Laroqueveille, and the mineral waters of Cropiéres and Tessiéres les Boulies. Near Tournemire (13 kil.), on the Doire, is the feudal château of *Anjony*, with its old towers, furniture, tapestry, paintings, &c., all in good condition.

[From Aurillac, on the road to Rodez, you pass Arpagon (5 kil.), in a beautiful valley, where the Cère falls into the Jordanne.

Montsalvy (25 kil.), a small place under the Puy de l'Arbre mountains on a plain, where Mechin and Dalembert traced an arc of the meridian to serve as a base for the new system of French measures. It has the old castle of Mandulphe, Notre Dame church, founded 1073, an old Hôtel de Ville, a deaf and dumb hospital, founded by Abbé Sicard; and a little outside, the Mur du Diable (Devil's Wall), built of enormous stone blocks.

Entraygues (about 10 kil.), the next place (in department Aveyron), is so called because placed between the two rivers Lot and Truyere, where they join.

Rodez is about 40 kil. further (*see* Route 52).]

From Aurillac, on the road to Montauban, you pass

St. Mamet (18 kil).

Maurs (27 kil.), near the Célé.

Figeac (21 kil.), a sous-préfecture in department Lot, on the Célé, in a most picturesque hollow, grew out of an abbey founded 755, and has, with remains of ramparts and ditches, several quaint old houses in narrow crooked streets, among which are Baleine castle (now the Hôtel de Ville), with a large hall 32 feet high; the old half-romanesque or round-arched abbey church, 198 feet long, with a dome and towers; and the church of Notre Dame de Puy, with a good carved screen. There are also two aiguilles, or pillar stones, at the west and south ends of the village, which served as landmarks. A pyramid has been raised to Champollion Jeune, the reader of hieroglyphic writing, and a native. Population, 6,390. *Hotels*—Born; Pontié.

[Cardaillac (10 kil. on the west) has some towers, &c. of a large castle, and was dismantled by Louis XIV. for its attachment to protestantism.—Assior (16 kil. west-north-west of Figeac), has the fine remains of another castle, built by Gaillot de Genculhac, whose monument is in the old church, with the motto 'Après la mort, bonne renommée demeure;' or, A good name lives after death.—Brengues (18 kil. north-east), on the Célé, has two or three old castles, in a very hilly, romantic spot.

Marsillac (23 kil. west-south-west of Figeac), down the Célé, has an old abbey church, and not far off, in a pretty valley, a famous grotto (in commune of Blars) or cavern, full of stalactites, galleries, and chambers, under various fanciful names.—Cajare (21 kil.), on the Lot, is a village of 2,000 souls, in a beautiful spot among vineyards and hills, with an old gothic church of the thirteenth century, and castle.—Ginouillac, a little west of this, is on the road to Cahors, which is about 35 kil. further, *viâ* Lentillac, Gironde, &c.]

After Figeac, as above, you come, leaving the castle of Cénievières on the left (a vast structure of different dates, with a noble prospect from its terrace), and Aubin, with a very ancient fort, on the right, to

Villefranche (35 kil.), a sous-préfecture of 9,540 souls, in department Aveyron, in a fine valley, where the Aveyron and Alzon meet, founded by Alphonse (brother of Louis IX.), Count of Toulouse, near the site of Carentomagus. Round the market-place are several large old houses, with arcades in front. The collegiate church, which rises above everything else, has a good porch in the plain west front, with a high tower over it. Its cloisters now serve for a hospital. There are a college, a library of 7,000 vols., museum, &c.; and manufactures of linen, copper, iron, leather, paper, with a trade in grain, wine, truffles, hams, cattle, &c. *Hotels*—du Grand Soleil; des Quatre Saisons (Four Seasons).

Caylux (29 kil.).

Caussade (21 kil.), in Route 50.

Montauban is 22 kil. beyond.

ROUTE 58.

Chateauroux to Le Blanc and Poitiers.

Distance, 118 kil. or 73 miles.

Chateauroux, as in Route 50.

LOTHIER (15 kil.), in the same Route.

ST. GAULTHIER (15 kil.). Many marshy lakes are to the right.

LE BLANC (29 kil.), a sous-préfecture of 6,100 people (department Indre), in a well wooded country, on the Creuse, with some remains of its old fortifications.

ST. SAVIN (18 kil.), has an old norman-style church, with ancient wall paintings of the tenth century.

CHAUVIGNY (18 kil.), on the Vienne, offers remains of castles and an old church, of the same age as the above.

At 23 kil. further is Poitiers, on the Bordeaux rail (*see* Route 65).

ROUTE 59.

Limoges to Angouleme.

Distance, 107 kil. or 66 miles.

LIMOGES, as in Route 50

PETIT BUISSON (16 kil.).

ST. JUNIEN (18 kil.), on the Vienne, with 5,900 people, in a pretty spot, where a bridge crosses close to a chapel of the Virgin, restored 1465, by Louis XI., who had a great regard for it. The ancient parish church of the eleventh and twelfth centuries, contains an altar with a fine bas-relief of the disciples at Emmaus, and the relics of St. Junien. Gloves, cloth, pottery, porcelain, paper, &c. are made here.

[At 15 kil. to the left is *Rochechouart*, a small sous-préfecture, on a rock over the Grenne, having the ruined towers of the old castle of the Mortemart family, now used as a prison. Iron is forged. Population 4,400.]

CHABANNAIS (16 kil.), in a pleasant spot on the Vienne, with an old bridge (commanding a good view), and part of a château, which belonged to the statesman Colbert. The road to Confolens turns off near this.

FONTAFIE (15 kil.), near the old castle of Vauguyon, on the edge of a forest.

ROCHEFOUCAULD (19 kil.), a place of 3,000 souls, on the Tardoire, having an old château in the renaissance style, with peaked towers at the corners, where the Duc de la *Rochefoucauld*, another of 'Les Maximes,' was born 1613. Several caves are found along the banks of the river.

At 23 kil. further is Angoulême, on the Bordeaux railway (*see* Route 65.).

ROUTE 60.

Limoges to Perigueux, Agen, Auch, Tarbes, Pau, Bagneres, &c., and the Pyrenees.

Distance (to Bagnères), 409 kil. or 254 miles.

LIMOGES, as in Route 50.

AIXE (12 kil.), on the Vienne, with an old castle which belonged to Jeanne d'Albret, and to Henry II. of England. Some roman traces and the name of the place (*aquæ*, baths) shew that the Romans used it as a watering place.

CHALUS (24 kil.), on the Tardoire, is remarkable for the ruined castle, before which Richard Cœur de Lion was mortally wounded, 1199. Not far off, above Montbrun, are the large remains of another castle.

[About 24 kil. to the south-east is *St. Yrieix* a sous-préfecture, on the Loue, with a church of the twelfth century, and manufactures of porcelain, &c. Much kaolin, of which porcelain is made, is got here, besides antimony and serpentine. Population 7,500.

About 30 kil. to the south-west is a small sous-préfecture (department Dordogne), called *Nontron*, on a fine part of the Bandiat, in the neighbourhood of several grottoes and druid stones. Cutlery is made, and iron and manganese are worked.]

THIVIERS (28 kil.), is not far from the fine castle of Hautefort, which includes an hospice, founded 1669, by that family.

[About 20 kil. to the south-west is Brantôme, a pretty place on the Dronne, having some remains of a rich Benedictine abbey out of which it grew, and a good trade in the best Périgord truffles. *Brantôme*, the historian, was titular abbot of this foundation. Population 2,720.]

At 32 kil. further is

Perigueux. *Hotels*—De France; de Périgord; du Chêne Vert (Green Oak); du Dragon Volant (Flying Dragon). The pâtés de Périgord (made of truffles and partridges), and the hams, are noted, as well as the game and poultry. Population 11,600. Chief town of department Dordogne, seat of a military division, a bishop, tribunal, &c., on a pleasant slant of a hill over the Isle, here crossed by a good bridge. It was the old capital of Périgord, which took its name from the *Petrocorii*; but the Romans called it Vesuna, and have left the half-ruined round *Tour de Vesonne* as a memorial of their occupation,—about 64 feet high, 5 to 6 thick, and 207 round, made of square stones cemented together, with two cornices near the top, but no signs of doors or windows.

There are also parts of the front of a temple of Mars, besides traces of an amphitheatre (290 feet by 230), of five roman ways (to Bordeaux, Agen, Saintes, &c.), and two aqueducts, of a camp on a hill across the river, fragments of baths, &c. In the oldest quarter of the town, called the Cité, the streets are narrow and lined with high solid stone houses, many carved and gothic-looking; but the other half, Puy St. Front, is more modern. Wide boulevards replace the old walls; the Cours de Tourny is a well planted walk on the highest part of the city, overlooking the river, &c.

St. Front *Cathedral* is said to be one of the oldest christian churches in existence, built, some say, as far back as the fifth and sixth centuries; it makes a greek cross (*i.e.* four equal arms), with a later built tower of three stories, 197 feet high; and looks well as a whole, though the details are heavy. It contains a highly carved 'Annunciation' on wood. St. Etienne church is partly of the tenth century, and that of the hospital is nearly as old.

The other buildings are, Hôtel de Ville (once the bishop's palace), newly built préfecture, the palais de justice (opposite the bronze statue of Montaigne), a college and priests' seminary; a library of 13,000 volumes, museum of minerals and antiquities, collected by M. Taillefer, salle de spectacle, the casernes or barracks, and a botanic garden and district nursery. On the amphitheatre site is the museum Chambon, so called after a citizen who gave it to the town, and was buried here under a pillar. A monument to Fénelon was set up 1840.

This place had the privilege of coining from the French kings; for a time it was held by the English as part of Aquitaine, and was one of the eight cities of refuge allowed to the protestants at the peace of 1576. When the states of Périgord used to meet here, the four barons, of Bourdeuil (21 kil. north-west of this), Biron, Breynat, and Mareuil, preceded the other peers as 'premiers barons;' and to save disputes the four were always summoned together, and subscribed their names in a circle.

In the neighbourhood is a deep spring called Source de l'Abîme, which turns several mills; and at Marzac, is an intermitting spring, which changes about 6 p.m.

Trade in coarse woollens, liqueurs, hogs, cattle, chesnuts, wood, &c. Coaches to Bordeaux, Angoulême, Paris, Breves, Sarlac, Riberac, Bergerac, Agen, Toulouse, &c.

ROUTE 60—*continued.*

The next place to Périgueux is

ROSSIGNOL (12 kil.)

ST. MAMEST (17 kil.), on a branch of the Isle.

At 15 kil. east is the old castle of St Alvére on the Luire.

BERGERAC (20 kil.), on the rich plain of the Dordogne (where the Suire joins), in a white wine country, is a sous-préfecture (10,000 population) and a tolerably well-built town, which belonged to the Counts of Périgord, was held by the English for a time, and dismantled of its fortifications by Louis XIII. A five-arch bridge crosses the river; and it has a college, a bibliothèque (with a portrait of La Belle Gabrielle, mistress of Henry IV.), salle de spectacle, &c. Trade in wine, paper, liqueurs.

Rev. MM. Hugues, Vidal, and Bastie, are protestant pastors here. *Hotels*—Des Princes; de la Boule d'Or (Golden Ball); du Voyageur (Traveller). Coaches to Bordeaux, Pau, Périgueux, &c.

[At 21 kil. east-south-east is Beaumont, built by Lucas de Terny, in the thirteenth century, and walled round by the English when they had Guienne, with towers, &c. The church is as old as 1272.]

CASTILLONNES (24 kil.), is on the Dropt, in department Lot-et-Garonne.

[About 22 kil. east, in department Dordogne, is Mont Pazier, another fortified post of the English, built 1284. At 5 kil. south-south-west of it is

Biron, the seat of one of the four premier barons of Guienne, and held for ages by the family of Gontant-Biron. One of them, the marshal and a great soldier, was made a duke by Henry IV., and lost his head 1602; his effigies on a tomb carved with bas-reliefs round the sides, are in the chapel of the château, which stands high, and has a view of the distant Pyrenees.

Lauzan (9 kil. west-south-west of Castillonnés) a small walled place on a hill, with a ruined castle, which belonged to the Biron family and the dukes of Lauzun, in the chapel of which is a votive marble of Roman times brought from Bordeaux.]

CANCON (14 kil.)

[At 13 kil. east is Montflanquin, a picturesque old village of the thirteenth century, on a peak over the Lède.]

VILLENEUVE D'AGEN or Villeneuve-sur-Lot (19 kil.) is a sous-préfecture of 10,000 souls, on both sides of the Lot, joined by an ancient one-arch bridge, 114 feet wide, 58 high, and only 4½ thick. The north part is the largest and best built; arcades go round the public Place. There are remains of the old walls; also a college, protestant church, theatre, a military stud, several mills, hospice of St. Cyr, large convent of St. Croix, baths, and a house once inhabited by Margaret de Valois. At 6 kil. north is a large house of correction, in the old abbey of Eysses (the roman *Excissum*), to which St. Louis's brother gave the new town (Ville Neuve) after restoring it, 1253, on the site of one called Gazac.

In the wars of the League it was besieged by Margaret de Valois, who took the father of Cieutat (its defender) prisoner, and brought him under the walls threatening to kill him if the place was not given up. The father only told the son to do his duty. The young soldier pretending a parley, descended with a few brave followers, dispersed the guard and retook his father; and afterwards defended the town so courageously that Margaret was obliged to raise the siege. Linens, oil, leather, paper, are made; and there is a good trade in grain, prunes, wine, cattle, iron, &c. *Hotels*—De France; Lamoureux. Coaches to Agen, Bordeaux, Cahors, &c.

[At 7 kil. north-west is *Casseneuil*, on the Lot, where the Lède joins, which had a palace or Villa Regia of Charlemagne's, where his wife, Hildégarde, gave birth to twins, one of whom was the feeble Louis-le-Debonnaire. Fumel (26 kil. east-north-east), up the Lot, has the family seat of the ancient seigneurs of Fumel, whose coutumes or laws, written in old gascon of the twelfth century, are cited by writers on old French jurisprudence.]

CROIX-BLANCHE (14 kil.)

At 19 kil. further is Agen, where the road from Bordeaux to Toulouse crosses (*see* Route 84.).

AGEN. *Hotels*—De France; du Petit St. Jean. Population 15,000.

A large and very old town, the chief place of department Lot-et-Garonne, seated on the right side of the Garonne, in a wide and fertile plain, under a hill 420 feet high; and having a communal college, a royal court, normal school, bishop's see, &c. It was the roman *Aginnum*, of which there are still some traces. It is ill built, the best quarters being in the Faubourg (outskirt) on the Bourdeaux road, near the bridge, and the Gravier promenade, which is said to be one of the most beautiful in the middle of France.

Among the buildings are St. Caprais' *Cathedral*, which is a curious monastic pile; the church of the Jacobins; the prefect's hotel, once the episcopal palace, standing in a park, with a triumphal arch in front; the old Hôtel de Ville; the large priests' seminary; a public library of 15,000 vols.; a fine hall on the site of St. Etienne's (Stephen's) old church, which was destroyed in 1793, except the front. Near the eleven-arch'd bridge, is an ancient structure called Le Las, now used for a house of industry. There is a theatre also, and public baths, one being a part of the old bridge. The hermitage on Mont Pompéian, commands a vast and magnificent view of the country around, the course of the Garonne, and the Pyrenees in the distance. It is the native town of the two learned Scaligers, Lacépède the naturalist, Bory de St. Vincent, and other eminent men. Rev. M. Carénou is protestant pastor here.

There are manufactures of sailcloth, serges, moleskins; and an eaux-de-vie distillery; the trade is in grain, wine, prunes, linen, cotton thread, &c.

Conveyances: Daily, to Bordeaux, Toulouse Auch, Périgueux, Aiguillon, Condom, Lectoure, Nerac. Steamer to Bordeaux.

The churches of Moirax and Layrac (4 kil. off) are worth notice.

[*Nerac* (23 kil.) south-west, a sous-préfecture in department Lot-et Garonne, is partly old and partly modern, joined by two bridges over the Baise. It has remains of a castle of the dukes d'Albret, where Henry IV. once lived; and the fountain of St. Jean is shaded by two immense elms, one planted by the king, the other by Marguerite de Valois A bronze of Henry stands on the Gavenne promenade, by the river. There is a good modern church and a large hall. Many roman coins were found here 1831-3, which the Academie des Inscriptions pronounced to be forgeries. Population 7,200. *Hotel*—Du Tertre (the Hill).]

ROUTE 60 continued.

Astaffort (19 kil).

Lectoure (35 kil.) in department Gers, is a sous préfecture and ancient town on the Gers, once occupied by the Romans, under whom it was the capital of the *Lactorates*. Population 6,300. It stands on an immense rock, faced on all sides by deep precipices; but though strongly fortified and almost impregnable, it has frequently suffered from war. Near the old Gothic church is a statue of Marshal Lannes who was a native, and who, they say, in his early days was hired to plant the beautiful promenades at six sous a day. They command very fine prospects; and here the Marshal, when he came to be Duke of Montebello, used to meet his friends and relate the history of his life. He was one of Napoleon's favourite generals; he commanded at the siege of Saragoza, was engaged in about 350 actions, and fell at Essling. Trade in corn, wine, spirits, cattle, leather, &c. *Hotel*—Calomez.

[Castera Verdouza, or Château Vivent (18 kil. south-west), in a charming valley, is noted for its mineral waters, and has a large grecian bath-house, with twenty baignoires. The springs are both iron and sulphuretted, and are very useful.

At 30 kil. west, is *Condom*, a sous-préfecture in department Gers, with 7,144 population, and manufactures of pens, corks, and porcelain. It dates from beyond the ninth century, and is pleasantly situated on a rock above the Baise. A fine large gothic church ornaments the Grand Place; and it has well planted boulevards, and many country seats about. *Hotels*—Du Lion d'Or (Golden Lion); du Grand Soleil (Sun); du Cheval Blanc (White Horse).]

Montastruc (18 kil).

At 18 kil. further is

Auch. *Hotels*—De France; de la Paix (Peace.) Alexandre. A very old town of 11,700 inhabitants, chief place of department Gers, seat of an archbishop (who was called the primate of Aquitaine), tribunal, college, society of agriculture, &c. Before Crassus took it in Cæsar's wars, it was named *Climberis*, and was the capital of the *Auscii*. Augustus planted a colony here on his return from Spain. It makes a picturesque amphitheatre on a hill side, divided into High and Low Town by the Gers, joined by a street of stairs of 200 steps, called the 'pousterlo,' or postern. The streets are narrow and crooked. Haute Ville (or upper town) has the best houses and a fine square, which commands a view of the Pyrenees. The statue here is a memorial of Etigny. Near it is

St. Mary's *Cathedral*, begun 1489, and finished in the time of Louis XIV.; a mixture of the gothic and grecian styles,—the latter appearing in the front, over which are two regular towers. They say it was first founded by Clovis. It has a fine vaulted roof, several good monuments in the side chapels, stained windows, wood carvings, a fine rood-loft (jubé), black marble font, marble figures, and five crypt chapels. The prelate's palace is close by. There are also the hôtel de la préfecture, Hôtel de Ville, college or seminaire with 15,000 vols., public library of 7,000 vols., a theatre, barracks, cavalry barracks, large hospital, &c.

Cardinal Ossat, D. Serres the marine painter, Villaret-Joyeuse the sailor, were natives. Manufactures of hats, serges, cotton, stuffs, leather, and a trade in wines, eaux-de-vie d'Armagnac, furs, wool, timber, 'bon-chretien' pears, &c. Large turquoises are found at Simorre, in the neighbourhood.

Conveyances, to Toulouse, Agen, Montauban Mont-de-Marsan, Pau, Bayonne, Tarbes, Bagnères de Bigorre, and Bagnères de Luchon, in the Pyrenees.

From Auch, on the road to Tarbes, you pass Vicnau (15 kil).

Mirande (10 kil.) a sous-préfecture in department Gers, and very old place on the Baise, founded 1289 by the Counts of Astarac. Parts of the walls remain. Population 2,532. *Hotel*—Dupuy.

[At 18 kil. south-east is Masseube, noted for its mule fairs, on the Gers.]

MIELAN (13 kil.) between the Osse and Bouès, was a place of importance in the fifteenth century, and formerly noted for its mutton.

RABASTENS (16 kil.), in sight of the Pyrenees, is another ancient stronghold in the plain of Bigorre, and figured in the frontier wars here.

At 9 kil. further is

TARBES. *Hotels*—De France, where the coaches stop; de l'Europe; du Grand Soleil (Sun); de la Paix (Peace). Population, 11,200. Chief town of department Hautes-Pyrenées, seat of a bishopric, &c., was formerly called *Turba*, and was the capital of Bigerrones, who gave name to the surrounding district of *Bigorre*, which, as part of Guienne, was held by the English till the time of Charles VII. It stands on the Adour, in the midst of a rich and wide plain (1,000 feet above sea), which is watered by the numerous branches of that river and the Garonne, and crowded with villages and fragments of rock washed from the Pyrenees, with the Pic du Midi de Bigorre in view on the south.

The road to the watering places and passes of the mountains strike out here as from a centre; and a convenient market is held every other week, attended by the country people, when corn, potatoes, cheese, salt provisions, tools, cattle, sheep, goats, horses, mules, linens, and other necessaries are sold. Here you see the Béarnais, with his white blouse, blue berret or cap, and curly hair, the women with their red capulets, the spanish muleteer, and other picturesque costumes.

The town is regular and well built; streams of water run through the streets, which are lined with houses built of brick and pebbles, or of native marble, roofed with slate, and each with its garden. It includes five suburbs or faubourgs, and a good six-arch stone bridge crosses the river, near Place Mercadieu, where the markets are held; Place Maubourguet is at the centre, and there is a well-planted walk on the Prado.

The *Cathedral*, called La Sède, is not remarkable, except for a fine altar under columns of Italian breccia; it stands on the site of the ancient *Castrum Bigorra*. St. Thérèse church has a tall spire. The old palace of the bishops is used as the préfecture, and the château of its counts, in Place de la Portèle, is used for a prison.

There is a cavalry barrack and riding-school; also another barrack in what was the Ursuline convent; a new theatre, a good hospital, priests' seminary, college, school of design, library of 7,000 volumes, baths, &c. Marshal de Castelnau (ambassador to England in the sixteenth century); and General Dembarrère, as well as the infamous Barère, of the convention, were natives.

Paper, copper goods, cutlery, nails, carts, &c., are made; trade in white wines, spirits, leather, marble, oil, grain, hams, horses, cattle, &c.

Coaches to Pau and Bayonne (malle-poste); *see* Routes 86, 87. To Auch, Bordeaux, Agen, Toulouse (Route 63), St. Gaudens, Bagnères-de-Bigorre, and Bagnères-de-Luchon, St. Sauveur, Cauterets.

Excursions may be made to Lourdes, Argelès, Val d'Azur, Arrens and Poucy-la-Huc chapel St. Savin church and its fine view over the Vallée de Devantaygue, Luz, St. Sauveur, Gavarnie fall, Héas chapel, Baréges, the Pic du Midi, &c.

MOMÈRES (7 kil.) up the Adour.

MONT-GALLIARD (6 kil.) where the road to Lourdes and Argelès turns off.

Bagneres-de-Bigorre (8 kil.). *Hotels*—De Paris; de Frascati (a large house in that Rue); de France, near the college; du Commerce and du Grand Soleil, in Place la Fayette; de l'Europe, Rue de la Comédie; du Bon Pasteur (Good Shepherd), Rue des Caoutères; de la Couronne, Rue aux Herbes. Board, 6 to 8 fr. a-day at the hotels, if you intend to stay.

A sous-préfecture of 7,586 population; the second town in the department, and the Bath of France, being the best and most fashionable watering place in the country. It stands on the Adour (crossed by two bridges), at the entrance of the Val de Campan, in a flat cultivated spot, 1,820 feet above sea, between the gave (*i.e.* burn or rivulet) and hill of Olivet, and is irregularly built, with no remarkable structure, though lodgings, hotels, cafés, and other accommodations for strangers are abundant and cheap. The season lasts from May to October, when the population is doubled by invalids and pleasure-seekers. Lodgings cost 1½ to 2 fr. a-day, sometimes much more.

Orchards, vineyards, bright green meadows (a rare thing in France), fields of buckwheat, &c., are seen in the neighbourhood, with woods of oak and beech on the hills, and something like the parks and gardens of England. The air is pure and delightful; the people are tall and well made; their houses are built of limestone, while cool streams run all day long from the river, through the streets, which are paved with pebble mosaic.

Le Coustou. or the Parc, a shady place in the centre of the town, is the chief rendezvous, where are the cafés, theatre (over the chapel of St. Jean, belonging to the Knights of Malta), and the large parish church of St. Vincent, which has a steeple, and some carvings on wood. Other walks are the Allées Bourbon, and Elysées Cottin and Azaïs, named after those authors.

One avenue leads out from the Hôtel des Thermes bathing house (built of marble, in 1823, and 207 feet long) to the Bains de Salut, in a limestone ravine in Monné hill, behind which is Mont Bédat and its grotto; the baths of Lapeyriè, Grand-pré, Carrère-Lannes, Versailles, are on this road. Those of Cazaux, Théas, &c., are under Olivet hill; Petit-Prieur supplies the civil hospital for the poor; the remainder are called Bellevue (from the prospect near it), Morat, Lasserre, Pinac, la Gautière, de Salie (the last for wounds).

About thirty springs are counted, from 90° to 135° temperature, supplying 85 marble baignoires; they are usually taken in the morning, contain iron, with salts of soda and magnesia, and are tasteless, clear, aperient, and tonic. The fontaines d'Angoulême and des Demoiselles Carrère are chiefly iron. A sulphur spring, called Labasserre, is 8 kil. off, on the Loussonet. The price for a bath is 1 fr. To the Romans these waters were known, as the *Vicus Aquensis*, and have kept their reputation to the present day.

The town was given up to the Black Prince by John of France. An old gothic tower of the Jacobins convent remains. There are also Geruzet's marble works (the veined Marbre de Campan), Lasserre's paper factory, Jalons' musée des Pyrenées and reading-room, Dossun's library, the Frascati athenæum and music hall. Horses, at 5 fr. a-day, mules, donkey-chaises, chaises à porteur (20 fr.) for ladies and invalids, and other conveyances abound; guides 5 fr. a-day. Paper, warm woollen and knitted crépes de Barèges are made. The 'Archives Evangeliques,' a protestant journal, edited by Rev. E. Frossard, is published here.

Coaches to Tarbes, Barèges, St. Sauveur, Cauterets, Bagnères-de-Luchon, Pau, Toulouse, Auch, St. Gaudens, Bordeaux, Condom, Marmande, Grip, Oloron, Agen, Périgueux (for Paris).

Excursions.—Near the town are, Rieunol, the heights of Chipolou (above the fontaine d'Angoulême), the farms of Mentilo and Métaon, the promenade of Monto-Pouzac (where the races are held), and its roman camp. Other points of interest are Val de Campan and its grotto (3 kil.), Grip (12 kil.), Vals de Tribons and de l'Esponne, Médous convent, Ordinsède, Barèges, Pic du Midi (16 kil.), Penn de l'Héris, &c.

Ascending the Adour, you pass Aste and Baudéan (where Larrey the surgeon was born), beyond which the fine Val de l'Esponne joins, leading up to lac Bleu in Pic de Montaigu, past Lesponne and Traonessaron. Further up the Adour is

Campan (6 kil. from Bagnères) which gives name to this beautiful valley, one of the richest in the department for its verdure and scenery. Population, 4,171. It stands under the precipices of the Penn de l'Heris, or Lleyris (about 6,300 feet above sea).

Further on is St. Marie (5 kil.), where the south-east head of the Adour runs up past the marble quarries of Peyrehite and Espinadet (8 kil.) to Col d'Aspin, whence it is about 10 kil. to Arreau, in Val d'Aure (*see* Route 63*b*), and from which there is a path over the mountains to Bagnères-de-Luchon.

From St. Marie, up the south-west or main head of the Adour, you come to the pretty falls of Grip and Artigues (8 kil.), thence the path leads (15 kil.) over the *Tourmalet Pass* to Barèges (in Route 60*a* below), leaving the Pic d'Espade, Néouvielle, &c. on the left, and the Pic du Midi de Bigorre on the right. The latter is 9,438 feet above sea to its sharp top, which commands a noble prospect; the pass itself is 2,300 feet lower.

ROUTE 60*a*.

Tarbes to Lourdes, Cauterets, Bareges and St. Sauveur, in the Pyrenees.

Distance about 75 kil. or 46 miles.

TARBES, as in Route 60.

JUILLAN (4 kil.) on the Cher, a branch of the Adour.

[*Ossun* (6 kil. south-west) gives name to a distinguished family, who built an old château here, near which, on another point, is a large roman camp, fortified, they say, by Crassus. On a plain called Lanne Maurine, a bloody battle was fought with the Saracens in the eighth century. Population 3,243.]

LOURDES (15 kil.) on the Gave (*i e.* torrent) de Pau, where four roads or valleys meet, 1,340 feet above the sea, was the old capital of Lavedan-en-Bigorre, and once called *Miraubel* or Fine-view, on account of its picturesque appearance. The old castle on a high rock, which the Black Prince held when the Duc d'Anjou tried to get it 1373, has been for ages a state prison; it consists of a great square tower, a chapel, and small barrack. Population 3,818; who weave coloured kerchiefs and work the slates here. Grottoes are seen in the rocks, and a lake near is 4 kil. round. Roman coins have been found.

[At *St. Pé* (8 kil. west), on the Pau road, they make boxwood combs and nails.]

VIDALOGS (7 kil.) has a castle commanding the road up the river.

ARGELES, or Argelez (5 kil.), where the Gave d'Azien joins, is 1,530 feet above the sea, and is made up of groups of houses (population 1,351) spread over a beautiful and richly-cultivated mountain valley, which extends to Pierrefitte. Mont Balandrau commands a good view over it.

[*Arrens* (12 kil. south-west), up the Auzun, near the junction of the Gave de Bun, is one of the highest villages (population 1,200) in the Pyrenees, and stands under the Col or pass of Azun, which leads over to Eaux-bonnes and Laruns, and is flanked by the Pic d'Arrens (6,360 feet above sea) and Pic de Gabisos (9,300 feet). An old disused chapel with two towers, above Arrens, called Pouey-la-Houe (*i e.* the mountain of the gate), is used as a look-out by the douaniers against the smugglers.]

After passing the gothic chapel of St. Savin's abbey, you come to

PIERFITTE (7 kil.), where the Gave de Pau is divided from that of Cauterets by the Pic de Viscos, 6,030 feet high.

[*Cauterets*, or Cauterez (10 kil. south-south-east), up a deep, narrow defile, 600 feet deep, between mountains 8,000 or 9,000 feet high, is important on account of its sulphur springs, but is a desolate place in the long winter, as it stands 3,190 feet above sea. The season for invalids is from June to September; lodgings, board, and the bath may cost 10 to 12 fr. a-day. It has fourteen springs, dispersed in different directions above the town, by the names of Bruzaud, Pauze, Espanols (the hottest, 117°), César, Raillère (the largest, 23 baths) under a granite rock, Petit St. Sauveur (only 86°), du Pré, Maouhourat (near that fall), and du Bois. They are useful in most chronic complaints, the early stage of consumption, rheumatism, asthma, indigestion, diseases of the skin and nerves, &c. *Hotels*—De France; du Lion d'Or; des Princes; des Ambassadeurs. Population 1,300.

Higher up the pass is *Pont d'Espagne* (7 kil.), a wooden bridge, where the Gaves de Gaube and Marcadaou join at a fall over the granite rock; thence up the latter torrent by the Val de Jaoret, brings you to the frontier pass (about 10 kil.), where there is a descent to Panticosa in Spain. Following the Gaube from the Pont d'Espagne, you come to the Lac de Gaube, one of the highest in the Pyrenees (5,870 feet), and upwards of 4 kil. round, in which an unfortunate English couple were drowned. Above it, the pass ends in the Cirque de Vignemale, under that great frontier mountain, 10,900 feet high.]

From Pierfitte up the narrow defile of the Gave de Pau, past Viscos, Cheze, and Sazos, and over four or five bridges (one called Pont de l'Enfer), you come to

LUZ (12 kil.), an old fortified post of the Templars (population 2,357), in a sort of triangular basin at the junction of the Gave de Bastan, with that of Pau, 2,400 feet above sea. It has a battlemented church, with remains of St. Michel's hermitage, and of the castle of Ste. Marie (a round and square tower joined together), which the count of Clermont took from the English 1404. The Pics de Viscos and d'Ardideu rise over it. Silk and woollen fabrics, to which Barèges gives its name, are made here.

[From Luz up the difficult and rocky pass of Bastan, you go by Viella to

Barèges (7 kil.), a desolate spot in the heart of the Pyrenees, but noted for its valuable sulphur springs, brought into notice by Madame de Maintenon, 1676, and made accessible by the road from Pierfitte, 1744. It stands nearly 4,200 feet above the sea, and consists of a street of about eighty houses, which are mostly deserted in the long and rigorous winter, when it is hid under 15 or 20 feet of snow.

The waters are taken between May and September; there are eight springs, called Grand-Douche (the hottest, 131°), l'Entrée, le Fond, Polard Dassien, Buvette (129°), Petite-Douche, Bains-Neuf, and la Chapelle (the mildest, 102°), which feed twenty-one baignoires. They are aperient, diuretic, and essentially stimulant, and though greasy and disgusting to the sight, they work surprising cures in cases of rheumatism, stiffened tendons, old ulcers, gun-shot wounds.

A government hospital for 500 invalids is established here. Lodging costs 1 to 3 fr. a day; the bath, 1 fr.; board, 3 fr.; altogether, living, &c., may be 9 to 10 fr. In the season as many as 1,200 strangers collect here. The few objects of notice around are the Pics d'Ayré and de Lisse (above 9,000 feet), Liens mountain, the lac d'Escoublons, the Pic du Midi de Bigorre, which is reached by the Tourmalet pass over to Grip (about 15 kil.), as in Route 60.]

From Luz, passing a petrifying spring and Pont de Villelongue, you come to

St. Sauveur (2 kil.), another, but picturesque watering-place, in a Swiss-like spot, near woods and falls, and 2,500 feet above the sea. The houses stand on a ledge of the ravine, 300 feet from the river, and include hotels, a grand *cercle* or assembly rooms, a round church, and a pillar to the Duchesse d'Angoulême. There are thirteen baths in five groups at the bathing house, as la Chapelle (only 86°), Terrasse, Bézégua, Chateguercy, and Milieu (the two last are the hottest, 95°); snakes sometimes get into them, but they are harmless. As these waters are milder than those of Barèges, and the situation infinitely more agreeable, they are much used by ladies for spasmodic, nervous, and other complaints. From the Pic de Bergons above it 6,120 feet high, there is a noble prospect, from the Val de Lavedan to Mont Perdu, above Gavarnie, to which an excursion may be made from St. Sauveur on horseback, or by chaises-à-porteur, or on foot.

The path leads along the face of a precipice in this romantic defile (with the river at the bottom) to Pragnières and Gèdre (10 kil.), which stands in a basin, 3,460 feet above the sea, where you see a pretty fall, a grotto, and a plain church, with a single door and window in it.

[To the south-east is the narrow and rugged pass to *Héas chapel* (5 kil.) to which a pilgrimage is made between 15th August and 18th September, (Jour de la Notre Dame). It is 4,690 feet above the sea. About 8 kil. above, it ends at Mont Troumouse, in the circus or *Oule de Héas* (oule or olla, a deep plate), 2,300 feet high up its sides, and 6 to 7 kil. round, an amphitheatre in which ten millions of spectators might find places as spectators of another three millions at the bottom.]

The path leads on by the Chaos landslips to a point where the snowy peaks of Marboré (9,930 feet above the sea), Pré Blanc, Brèche de Roland, Vignemale, &c., are seen; then you come to the Gave d'Ossonne, and to Gavarnie church (4,860 feet above the sea), which belonged to the knights of St. John, where they show the skulls of Templars, who were beheaded when their order was prescribed. About 5 kil. higher is the famous *Cirque de Gavarnie*, as remarkable a work of nature as the Oule de Héas, but more regular. From the side where the river breaks out you enter a vast area, 3½ kil., or 2 miles in circumference, strewed with broken rocks and bounded by enormous walls of darkish limestone, 1,600 feet high in some parts, and perfectly bare, except of the snow which collects on the ledges, and which, with the glaciers on the peaks above, feeds about a dozen cascades, supplying the stream below. One of them,

The *Fall of Gavarnie* or Marboré, tumbles down in two leaps from a height of 1,300 feet, (though it seems to be not more than 300 feet) and is lost in spray. It exceeds by 300 feet the fall of Lauterbrunnen in Switzerland, and by 500 feet that of Hungry Hill in Ireland. On the side opposite, a steep and difficult path, for which a guide must be taken, leads up to the top, and thence over a glacier with a slant of 45° to the *Brèche de Roland*, a gash or breach, 300 feet wide and high, and 50 thick, cut in the granite ridge, (9,770 feet above the sea) which divides France and Spain, by the famous sword of Roland (Orlando Furioso), when mounted on horseback in pursuit of the Infidels! From this breach or col, used only by contrabandistes, an ascent may be made to Mont Perdu, the second peak in the Pyrenees (1,270 feet), and a descent to Torla in SPAIN.

ROUTE 61.

Perigueux to Cahors.

Distance, 143 kil., or 89 miles.

PERIGUEUX, as in Route 60.

ST. CREPIN (17 kil.).

[At 12 kil. south-east is *Miremont*, with some of the largest caves in France, altogether 4,600 yards long, and including 8,000 rooms and galleries, one of which is like the Thames Tunnel Near this is the so-called volcano of Meyssandrie, which they say burst out 1783. A little to the south-east, at Bugue, is the pit called Trou de Pomaissac, whence flames, or at least, sulphur vapours have issued; and into which robbers used to throw their victims in old times.]

THENON (16 kil.).

[Terrasson, an ancient town on the Vézère, here crossed by a large new bridge, was called *Terracina*, and is 25 kil. east; Brives is 22 kil. further east, and Tulle 30 kil. beyond (*see* Routes, 50, 56).]

MONTIGNAC (14 kil.), on the Vézère, above which is the ruined castle of the Comtes de Pé-rigord. Population, 3,850.

SARLAT (25 kil.), a sous-préfecture of 6,200 souls, in a narrow pass of the hills, and once a fortified town, as old as St. Benoit's abbey, founded by Charlemagne. Good paper is made. Coaches to Périgueux, Cahors.

[Meyral, to the west, is near La Roque, seat of the Comte de Beaumont.]

GOURDON (25 kil.), another sous-préfecture, but in department Lot (population, 5,150), was a strong place, on a hill over the Bléon, whence there is a wide prospect, and is surmounted by a good gothic church, built 1505-14, with two towers of 112 feet in the front, and a rose window 45 feet across; the nave is 67 feet by 85 and 73 high. Another old church belonged to the Cordeliers. On a second hill behind stood the castle (demolished 1619 by the Leaguers) of Bertrand de Gourdon, who was the cause of Cœur de Lion's death at Chalus. Linen, hats, and oil, are made.

PONT-DE-RODEZ (13 kil.) is on Route 50. And at 33 kil. further is Cahors, on the same Route.

ROUTE 62.

Toulouse to Auch.

Distance, 76 kil., or 47 miles.

TOULOUSE, as in Route 50.

LEGUEVIN (18 kil.).

L'ILE-EN-JOURDAIN (15 kil.), in department Gers, a pretty place, on the Save, with a good church, and vast halle or market house. It had a castle of the Jourdains.

[At 20 kil. south-west is *Lombez*, a small sous-préfecture (population, 1,541 only) in a fertile but low spot, up the Save, which frequently breaks its banks here. Formerly it was remarkable for an Augustine abbey, which Pope John XII made the seat of a bishop 1317.]

GIMONT (18 kil.), on the Gimone, one of the many streams which water this department, is made up of a long street, in which is a gothic brick church. Near it is a mine of turquoises. There was a rich Bernardine abbey here before the revolution.

AUBIET (8 kil.), on the Rals.

AUCH is 17 kil. further (*see* Route 60).

ROUTE 63.

Toulouse to Bagneres-de-Luchon, Bagneres-de-Bigorre, Tarbes

(THENCE TO PAU).

Distance, 202 kil., or 125 miles.

TOULOUSE, as in Route 50.

PORTET (10 kil), up the Garonne, which the English army descended 1814.

MURET (10 kil.), higher up, where the Louge joins, at the suspension bridge, is a sous-préfec-fecture, with a population of 4,300. It was besieged 1213 by Pedro of Aragon, who was defeated here by de Montfort. The houses are brick-built. Linens, pottery, &c., are made. *Hotel*—de France

NOE (13 kil.)

MARTRES (27 kil) is the roman *Calagorris Covenarum*, where many busts, coins, and other antiquities have been found, and placed in the Toulouse museum.

ST. MARTORY (10 kil.), a pretty little village on the rocky banks of the Garonne, here crossed by a stone bridge, with an old tower at one end, and an abbey at the other. Remains of feudal castles are near.

[At 26 kil. south-east is St. Ligier, on the rocky side of the Salat, above which is a palace built 1655-80, by Bishop de Marmiesse, now a general hospital.—At 2 kil. further is

St. Girons, up the Salat, where the Lèze and Baup join, another pretty place, in the mountains, and a sous-préfecture (population, 4,380), with a spire church, and two bridges of blue marble, viz., the Pont Neuf and another. The palais de justice occupies the old château. It carries on a good trade with Spain, &c., in wool, mules, horses, sheep, cattle, paper, grain, skins, &c. The road goes on to Foix and Tarascon; and a mule path follows the Salat over the Pyrenees (?)—Montjoie (2 kil. from this), near the Audinac waters, is so called after a temple which stood on Mons Jovis, where a clock-tower now stands.—At Montesquieu is an old château, with Lagnère grotto.]

ST. GAUDENS (28 kil.), is a sous-préfecture of 5,000 souls, on a rocky hill-side of the Garonne, and is a key to this part of the Pyrenees. It was the capital ot Nébouzan, a part of Commengis, in Gascony. The romanesque church is the oldest in this part; and the walks by the river offer many points of view. A good trade in mules, cattle, hogs, &c. *Hotel*—de France. Coaches to Bagnères-de-Luchon, Toulouse, Bagnères-de-Bigorre, Tarbes, Pau, &c. The road to Bagnères-de-Luchon turns off here, as in Route 63*a*, below.

MONTREJEAU (14 kil.), in a fine spot on the Garonne, where the Neste joins it. Population, 3,000, who knit a great deal. A good six-arch bridge crosses the river. To the south of this, near St. Bertrand, are the famous grottoes of *Gargas*, the largest in the south of France, in which a feudal seigneur kept his prisoners, and which a ferocious monster of the last century, called Blaise Ferrage, used as a den. After capturing more than thirty women and girls, and having eaten some of them (for by all accounts he was a cannibal), he was taken and executed at Toulouse, 1782.

LANNEMEZAN (16 kil.), in department Hautes-Pyrenées, where a road turns off south, up the Val de Nestes (*i. e.*, torrents), or Val d' Aure, as in Route 63*b*, below.

From this, by the direct road, it is 14 kil. to l'Escaldieu, and its old abbey; and 12 kil. further to Bagnères-de-Bigorre (*see* Route 60).

TORNAY (16 kil.) on the Arros.

At 18 kil. further is Tarbes (*see* Route 60).

PAU is 40 kil. beyond.

ROUTE 63*a*.

St. Gaudens to Bagneres-de-Luchon, and the Maladetta, in the Pyrenees.

Distance, about 70 kil., or 43 miles.

ST. BERTRAND-DE-COMMENGIS (18 kil.) is clustered round a rock in the Val de Barouse, at the top of which is its old cathedral church. It was the roman *Lugdunum Convenarum*, where many remains have been found, and was a bishopric till the revolution.

ESTENOS (9 kil.).

CIERP (5 kil.), where the Pique turns from the Garonne, in a fine spot.

[At 6 kil. east, up the latter, is *St. Beat*, in a most picturesque part of the Val d'Arran, at the bottom of a narrow defile, 1,750 feet above the sea. It consists of two streets of marble houses, one on each side of the river, joined by a curious stone bridge. On the east side is the Hôtel de Ville and market hall in one; and parts of the decayed fortifications and castle (on a rock) are seen, which defended this gate of the mountains. About 8 kil. above it is Pont du Roi, the last French station on the frontier, in the middle of the Val d'Arran, one of the most beautiful in the Pyrenees, and so fertile that it numbers about 35 villages and hamlets. It is part of Catalonia.

You ascend it to visit the sources of the Garonne. Passing Les Springs and Bososte

(16 kil.), and Castelleon, you come to a bridge, where the gorge of Artiques-Telline turns off from the main stream. This gorge leads up through a forest, in which is the village of Artiques, then a hermit and hospice, and at length, on the Plan de Goueon, two principal sources of the river (14 kil.)—From Bososte it is 18 kil. up the main stream to Viella (2,860 feet above the sea), whence it is 10 kil. to the pass, or Port de Viella (8,145 feet), over the ridge of the Pyrenees; or it is 20 kil. to the eastern source.—The path then descends under the Maladetta (see below) to Tor; or a path may be taken round the west side of the mountain towards Venasque.]

Going up the Val de la Pique, from Cierp, you pass Baren, Sales, Antigna, and come to

Bagneres-de-Luchon (16 kil.), a watering place among the mountains, in the defile of Arbouste, in a beautiful basin, about 2,000 feet above the sea; green, populous, and well sheltered. Its hot sulphur baths were known to the Romans by the name of *Aquæ Balneariæ Lixonienses*, and altars and inscriptions have been found. The principal springs are at the Hôtel des Thermes; they are useful in rheumatism gout, diseases of the skin and glands, paralysis, &c.; some are as high as 150° temperature. The season is from May to October; baths cost ½ to 1½ fr. each. Accommodations of all kinds are plentiful; a room may be had for 2 to 6 fr. a-day, table d' hôte 3 fr. (breakfast and dinner), but dinner is usually got from the traiteur's.

Hotels—du Parc; de France; de Londres; du Commerce; d'Espagne; de l'Europe; du Lion d'Or (Golden Lion). There are also *Cafés* and a literary cabinet, where the journals are taken in. Coaches to Toulouse, Auch, Bagnères-de-Bigorre; a horse-path across the hills to the east, offers very fine scenery. Population, 2,790. Pleasant shaded walks run from the baths to different parts of the town; and guides, horses, mules, and chaises-à-porteur (chairs for ladies), can be hired for distant *excursions*.

Among the most striking objects of notice are,—1st, the falls of Juzé and Montauban; 2nd, the village of Cazeril half way up a mountain of that name; 3rd, the Lac d'Oo, or Seculéjo, 18 kil., up the Val de l' Arbouste (to the west), past Oo, and its old castle, then the beautiful lake (2,000 yards above the sea), in a deep basin, out of which the water slides down 800 feet: then above it, in a wilder spot, the lakes of Epingo, Souansat, and another, covered with ice, beyond which is the dangerous pass over the Pyrenees of the Col d'Oo (9,750 feet above the sea), leading down to Venasque; 4th, the Val de Lys, past the ruin of Castel Vieil (old castle) and several falls, to the snowy peak of Cabrioules (10,450 feet high); and 5th, the Porte de Venasque and the Maladetta. You reach this (about 20 kil.) up a very rough and difficult path, at the end of which you come at a sudden turn to the Col, or Porte de Venasque (7,840 feet high), a mere granite doorway, cut in the ridge of the mountains, and from which the *Maladetta* (*i. e.* the Accursed), the monarch of the Pyrenees opens on the view, to the left. It is covered with snow and glaciers, and was first ascended by an adventurous Russian in 1842. The highest summit, called Pic de Néthou or d'Anethou, is 11,318 feet above the sea; an inaccessible ridge to the west is 1,000 lower. From the Col, which is much used, though impassable in winter, the path descends to Venasque, in Spain.

ROUTE 63b.

Lannemezan (up the Aure), to Arreau, and Mont Glarbide, &c. (in the Pyrenees.)

Distance, about 65 kil. or 40 miles.

Lannemezan, as above.

La Barthe (6 kil.)

Leches (7 kil.), on the Neste.

Sarrancolin (7 kil.) higher up the Neste, between the hills, was once the fortified capital of Aure, and is noted for a bubbling spring, called the Vivier, and its quarries of marble, some deep red, and veined; another sort (the Beyrède), veined also, but of a bright red, and known as Antin marble. Population, 1,114.

Arreau (9 kil.), a most picturesque place (population, 1,550), from any point of view, at the junction of the Aure and Louron, and an entrepôt for the Val d' Aure, which ranks next to Argelès, for life, verdure, and fine scenery. Maize, buckwheat, and rye are grown, but little fruit or wheat. At Arreau is the old church of St. Exupère, and many marble-built houses.

A coach road turns off west to Bagnères-de-Bigorre; and there is a path east over the mountains to Oo (and Seculéjo lakes) and Bagnères-de-Luchon; also a path, up the Neste de Louron, past Bordères Castle, Frechet, Loudervielle, to the Port de la Pez, near the Pic de Génos (30 kil.) From Arreau, up the Aure, you pass Cadéac (4 kil.), which has a feudal ruin, and sulphur waters, and stands under the granite Pic d' Arbizon, 2,723 feet high, to its round top, on which is a needle-shaped rock (9250 feet above the sea); then Vieille (7 kil.), and Tramesaigues (5 kil.), so called from its springs (aquæ), and having an old church of the knights templars. Hence the path mounts up to Port de Plan, near Mont Glarhide (20 kil.); another, to the west, goes by Arragnouet (4330 feet above the sea, near which is the fall of Couplan, 900 feet down) to Port de Bielsa (24 kil.), over the Pyrenees into SPAIN.

SECTION VI.

ROADS TO THE SOUTH-WEST AND WEST;

IN CONNEXION WITH THE RAILWAY FROM PARIS TO BORDEAUX; SUPPLYING ORLEANS, BLOIS, TOURS (THENCE TO ANGERS, NANTES, AND BREST, AS IN ROUTE 71), POITIERS, NAPOLEON-VENDEE, LIMOGES, NIORT, ROCHELLE, ANGOULEME, COGNAC, PERIGUEUX, BORDEAUX, — AND THENCE TO BAYONNE (AND SPAIN), PAU, BAGNERES, TOULOUSE, &c.—ROUTE SIXTY-FIVE TO NINETY FIVE.

The final portion of the railway between Poitiers and Angoulême (about 110 kil. or 68 miles), was opened (officially) June, 1853; making the whole distance from Paris to Bordeaux by railway about 580 kil., or 360 miles, and the time 13 to 16 hours.

ROUTE 65.

Orleans to Tours (DOWN THE LOIRE); thence **to Poitiers, Angouleme, Bordeaux, Bayonne, and Spain.**

This is a continuation of Route 50, from Paris to Orléans. Distance from Orléans to Tours, 115 kil. or 71½ miles, (to Poitiers, 216 kil. or 135 miles). Five trains to Tours, of which two are direct to Poitiers, in 5½ to 7½ hours; fares to Poitiers, 22½, 16¾, and 12 francs. Bouffet for refreshments at Tours.

The stations from Orleans, are

	kil.		kil.		kil.
La Chapelle..	7	Blois	9	Noisay	7
Saint-Ay	7	Chousy	9	Vernou	3
Meung	6	Onzain	6	Vouvray	3
Beaugency ...	7	Limeray	12	Montlouis ...	1
Mer	12	Amboise......	5	Tours	10
Menars	11				

The line keeps the north side of the Loire.

[*Châteaudun* (50 kil. west-north-west of Orléans), is a sous-préfecture (department Eure-et-Loir) of 6,500 souls, who make coverlets, &c., and stands in a picturesque part of the Loir, which here flows between cultivated hills, 426 feet high. Much of the town has been rebuilt since a fire in 1723. Its castle is chiefly of the fifteenth century, but the great keep is as old as Thibault le Tricheur (*i.e.* the Tricker), who founded it 935. The public library contains 5,000 vols. The people are reputed to be quick; so that a proverb says, 'Il est de Châteaudun; il entend à demi-mot.'

Jean Toulain, who invented enamel painting, was born here. *Hotels*—André; Raimond. Conveyances to Chartres, Orléans, Vendôme, &c.]

The first station you pass is

LA CHAPELLE (4¾ miles).

ST. AY (4 miles), in a pretty spot, among vineyards.

[At 5 kil. south is *Cléry-sur-Loire*, on a hill, where stands the fine church of Notre Dame (re-built after the English leader,

Salisbury, had burnt the first one, 1428), by the cruel and superstitious devotee, Louis XI., and containing the Virgin's image, his tomb (not older than 1622), an excellent doorway and choir, with mosaic work, carved stalls, &c. The house of Louis XI. is close to it.]

MEUNG, or MEHUN (3¾ miles), at the suspension bridge on the river, has an old château, built by Louis le Gros, and taken by the English. It contains also an old collegiate church, and was a seat of the Orleans bishops. Population, 4,100, who make hats, leather, paper, &c. Mehun, or Menun, the continuer of the Romance of the Rose, was a native. A viaduct of twenty-nine large arches crosses the Mauves, near

BEAUGENCY (4¼ miles), which stands above the embankment of the Loire (here crossed by a bridge of thirty-nine arches), and has, besides part of its old fortified walls, the keep of a very ancient castle, 122 feet high, and about 70 square. It suffered in almost every contest, from the invasion of the Huns (451) downwards. Roman coins have been found. The Hôtel de Ville is in the renaissance style. Excellent wine, brandy, &c., are produced. Population, 4,700. *Hotels*—De la Forêt; du Grand Cerf (Stag). Near the châtesu d'Avary stands an immense dolmen.—At 5 kil. east is Lailly, where Condillac is buried.

MER (7½ miles), among vineyards and country houses, in department Loir-et-Cher. Population, 3,900.

MENARS (7 miles), or Ménars-le-Château, has a fine château of the seventeenth century (with beautiful terraces on the river), which belonged to Madame de Pompadour and M. de Broglie, now to Prince de Chimay, who, in 1832, established the Prytaneum here, where theoretical and practical education are carried on together.

[At 8 kil. to the south-east, is the château de *Chambord*, on the Casson, in the middle of a great forest, where the deer and wild boar are found. Francis I. began to build it (on the site of a hunting seat of the counts of Blois), after the designs of Primaticcio; and, as completed by his successors, it makes a quadrangle, in the renaissance style, with great high-peaked towers at the corners (60 feet diameter), a central tower and dome, 106 feet high, under which is the double staircase, besides a chapel, picture galleries, &c. The front contains a great many windows, divided by pilasters and small columns, with a picturesque heap of turrets and chimneys above. Some parts are richly carved, and the F. and salamander (for Francis I.*), the H. and D. (for Henry II. and Diana of Poitiers) are noticed. At one time it belonged to Stanislaus of Poland; then to Marshal Saxe, the victor at Fontenoy, who amused himself by playing at soldiers and training horses, and died here; afterwards it came to the Polignacs, and the Prince of Wagram (Marshal Berthier), of whose widow it was bought, 1820, for the Duke of Bordeaux (now Count de Chambord, or Henry V. as he is called), by his friends. At present it is deserted. The "Bourgeois Gentilhomme" was first acted here, 1670, before Louis XIV.]

At 9 kil. further, is

Blois. *Hotels*—D'Angleterre; de l'Europe; la Tête Noire (Black Head). Population, 16,176. A fine old town, the chief place of department Loir-et-Cher, in the old province of Orléanais, on the river Loire, beautifully seated on a hill-slope, and joined to Vienne by a stone bridge of eleven arches, which bends much in the middle, where stands a pyramid 60 feet high. A fine quay of great length fronts the river. It was the head of a county which came to our King Stephen, through his mother, Adela, the Conqueror's daughter, and now belonging to the Orleans family.

The streets are narrow, steep, and winding. At the top of the hill, above the old town, stands the royal castle (now used as a barrack), where Henry III. treacherously killed the Duke of Guise (in the queen's chamber) and his brother, 1588. The north front was built by Francis I.; east front, by Louis XII. (who was born here), 1498; west front, by Gaston, Duke of Orleans, after Mausard's designs. Catherine de Medici's observatory is on the south side, with *uraniæ sacrum* on it. An old gothic tower remains. Another tower is called Château Regnault, because that place (13 miles off) is seen from it. The Salle des Etats, where the country deputies used to meet, is of the thirteenth century.

* In a fit of jealousy he wrote on one of the windows (now gone)—

Souvent femme varie
Mal habile qui s'y fie.

Near the castle stands the cathedral, which was one part of the jesuits' college. Other buildings worth notice are, the préfecture, in the Grand Place; the old préfecture or bishop's palace, built by Gabriel, with fine gardens, commanding a view of great extent along the river, &c.; palais de justice; Hôtel de Ville, with a library of 17,000 vols.; college, or seminary, at Bourg Moyen old abbey; hospital, at St. Lauman's old abbey, the church of which is a curious one of the eleventh and twelfth centuries; botanic gardens; theatre; abattoir, or slaughter-house; lunatic asylum (l'hospice des aliénés); and many public fountains, supplied by a reservoir outside the walls, to which a so-called 'roman' aqueduct (styled Pont de César), half a mile long, brings the water.

The Allées promenade is of great length, leading by a large forest. Each gate has an image of the Virgin, in remembrance of a deliverance from the pestilence, in 1631. Go to the bridge, from which you have a noble view up and down the Loire; the levées, or embankments begin here. Manufactures of good gloves, serge, glass, and hardware; and trade in wine, vinegar, eaux-de-vie, copper, &c.

Conveyances: by railway, to Tours, Nantes, Orléans, Paris, &c.; coaches to Bracieux (18 kil.), Château Regnault (33 kil.), Vendôme, St. Calais, Montaichard (38 kil.), Oucques (27 kil.), Romorantin (40 kil., see Route 50), St. Aignan.

[*St. Aignan* (38 kil. south of Blois), an old town on the Cher (population, 2,770), founded by the abbots of St. Martin de Tours, having an ancient tower, called Tour d'Agar, of a castle, built 1019, by the counts of Blois.—Towards Selles, to the east, is the château of Chenonceaux, in good condition, on a bridge over the Cher.]

From Blois, along the railway to Tours, close by the north bank of the river, which increases in beauty as you descend, you pass

Chousy (5 miles); then Ouzain (4 miles), opposite which is

Chaumont-sur-Loire, in a delightful spot at the foot of a wooded height, crowned by a fine old château, seen a long distance round.

Limeray (6½ miles).

[At 20 kil. north-north-west, is *Château-Regnault*, and the donjon of a castle, built 1100, by one Regnault, its seigneur, and occupied by Henry IV. in the civil wars.]

Amboise (3½ miles), away from the line on the south bank, another fine spot, with a château above it. Population, 4,800. The castle, with its two large towers, stands on the site of a fort, built (so they say) by Julius Cæsar, who gives name to some excavations in the rocks below, called 'Greniers de César' (Cæsar's granaries). It and the chapel were restored by Louis Philippe. Charles VIII. was born here, 1470; and Abd-el-Kader was confined in it, 1848–52, until liberated by Louis Napoleon. The Amasse runs into the Loire, which is crossed by two bridges, resting on an island in the middle. *Hotel*—du Lion d'Or (Golden Lion). The châteaux of Chanteloup (1 kil) and Chenonceaux (4 kil.) are near.

[*Loches* (25 kil. south), an old town and sous-préfecture (5000 population) in department Indre-et-Loire, agreeably placed on the Indre, the arms of which are crossed by a line of bridges to Beaulieu. Above it, on a rock, stand the picturesque remains of the *Castle*, older than the ninth century, now used as a gaol. King John gave it up to France, but Cœur-de Lion retook it 1194, though it was taken back 1205. Louis XI. made it a state prison, and confined Cardinal Balue in one of its oubliettes or iron cages which the Cardinal had invented; Philip de Comines the historian was also a prisoner. The square Donjon tower is 130 feet high, in four stories. That part called Charles the Seventh's château, (now the mairie) was the seat of his mistress, the beautiful and amiable Agnes Sorel; the terrace commands a fine prospect, and in one of the pointed towers is the mausoleum of Agnes, brought here, 1809, from the ancient church of Notre Dame. The latter, founded as far back as 450, rebuilt in the eleventh century, is worth notice for its four towers 164 feet high, and an eight sided vault 85 feet from the ground. Money was struck here as well as at Tours and Chinon. Linens and woollens are made. *Hotels*—De France, de la Promenade. Coaches to Tours, Châteauroux, Amboise, &c. In the neighbourhood are Loches forest, Liget Chartreuse, Chenonceaux château, &c.]

Noizay (3¼ miles), Vernon (2½ miles), Vouvray (2¾ mls.), Mont-Louis (¾ mile) are the next places on the line; and 6½ miles further is

Tours. *Hotels*—Du Faisan, (Pheasant), Boule d'Or, (Golden Ball), de Londres, all in Rue Royale; del'Univers, des Trois Barbeaux, (Three Barbels), de St. Julien. Fish and poultry are good Dinner, 3 fr.; breakfast, 1 fr.; bed, 1½ fr. English chapel, near the préfecture; service at 11½ and 6½. Rev. M. Fuzier is French protestant pastor here.

Population 27,500. An ancient town, the capital of department Indre-et-Loire, seat of a military division, of an archbishop, college, &c , in a flat but pleasant part of the Loire, on a tongue of land between it and the Cher. Several English families live here for cheapness of living, and its agreeable climate. It was the Roman *Caesarodunum*, and the head of the Turones; afterwards of Neustria, &c.; and of the county of Touraine, which was held by the Plantagenets till Philippe Auguste took it from John, 1202. The states-general were summoned here in the fifteenth century when the Leaguers commanded Paris. It had a mint for coining 'livres Tournois' or franc pieces, and still has one, ranking fifth (letter E). Louis XI. established the silk manfacture here, and built his famous château, *Plessis-lès-Tours* (in which he died 1483), close by; parts of it are left (2 kil. off), including his and Cardinal Balue's chambers, and a brick donjon.

Twelve gates surround the town, the old walls of which are replaced by planted boulevards; beyond are the four faubougs of la Priche, St. Eloi, &c. A fifth, St. Symphorien, across the river, is joined to the main part by an excellent level stone bridge of 15 arches, each 80 feet span, built 1762-77; it is 1,752 feet long (174 less than the one at Bordeaux), 48 wide, and 39 above the water. A little above it are remains of the old bridge, built by the Counts of Touraine. Two others of 17 and 8 arches, cross the Cher in the neighbourhood.

From the end of the great bridge, where the Hôtel de Ville and musée stand, the principal street, Rue Royale, runs through for half a mile to the Poitiers road; straight, wide, and bordered with *pavements*, and good three-story houses, of white stone, with slated roofs. Most of the hotels and cafés are here. The old streets out of it are narrow and dirty, but contain some ancient buildings. One of the fountains (de Baune), in the market place, is a gothic obelisk, with many landings on it. Promenades are laid out on the quays; and in the neighbourhood, fruit gardens, vineyards, and cornfields are seen.

St. Gatien gothic *Cathedral*, begun in the twelfth century, was finished 1550; it has a wide west front, with a triple porch, a rose window, and two domed towers, 260 feet high, ornamented with statues and bas-reliefs (some grotesque), and built they say by Henry V. of England; in the interior, which is 262 feet long and 88 high, are some beautiful stained windows, a fine choir, and the tomb of Charles VIIIth's children. The famous abbey church, founded 347 by St. Martin de Tours being burnt 561, was restored by St. Gregory de Tours, and survived till the revolution, when it was pulled down except two towers, one called Tour de Charlemagne, the other used as a belfry. Alcuin was one of its Abbots. Remains of St. Julien's abbey church (now an auberge), and St. Clement's (the corn market) are also left. At the barrack, in Quai Royal, is part of the old château, built by Henry II. of England, from which the Duke of Guise, when a prisoner, escaped 1591.

The archbishop's palace, the préfecture, the palais de justice, are large and handsome structures.

In the préfecture is the bibliothèque of 40,000 vols., besides valuable MSS. and illuminations; open 12 to 4, Tuesday to Friday; and at the museum is a collection of 200 pictures, and natural history specimens. There are also a college, a large general hospital, Hôtel de Ville, botanic garden, bublic baths, and a theatre, near the post office (in Rue de la Scellerie). M. Gouin, formerly minister of commerce, lives in Louis XIth's old gothic chancellurie, in Rue de Commerce, which he has restored. They shew in the town a block of stone (a remnant of some Roman building), said to be the tomb of 'Turnus' its reputed founder. At the Radegonde (3 kil.), are some traces of the Marmoutiers abbey, founded in the fourth century.

It is the native place of Destouches the comic writer, Duchesne the geographer, Heurteloup the mayor, Alfred de Vigny, &c. The famous *battle of Tours* was fought, 732, some think, at Miré (15 kil. south-west), near Artanes, when Charles Martel (*i.e.* Charles the Hammer) defeated Abd-el-rahman and his Saracen hosts, who having conquered Spain had so far overrun France. But for this check, 'the Koran' (says Gibbon) 'might have been taught in the schools of Oxford to a circumcised people.'

Manufactures of silk stuffs (gros de Tours), which flourished till the revocation of the Edict of Nantes, ribbons, lace, carpets, muslins, pottery, powder, wax-candles, soap, saltpetre, &c., and a trade also in grain, wine (of Vouvray, &c.), spirits, dry fruits, and chestnuts. The railway goes on to Angers and Nantes, as in Route 71. Coaches to Château-Lavalliere, La Flèche, La Chatre, Le Mans, and Loches.

ROUTE 65—*continued.*

The stations from Tours to Poitiers are—

	kil.		kil.		kil.
Monts.........	11	Dangé	3	Dissais	4
Villeperdue .	9	Ingrandes...	10	Clan	4
Saint-Maurc	12	Chatellerault	5	Chasseneuil.	3
Port-de-Piles	11	Les Barres..	8	Poitiers	9
Les Ormes...	5	La Tricherie	5		

Monts (8¾ miles), on the Indre. Coaches to Artanes (near the field of Miré, as above), Esvres, Montbazon, Pont-de-Ruan, Vergné.

[Montbazon (5 kil. east) up the Indre, has an old castle built in the eleventh century, by Foulques de Néra, Count of Anjou. Near it are the Ripault powder and sugar works.]

Villeperdue (5½ miles). A little beyond is the old village of Ste. Catherine-de-Fierbras (so called from Guillaume Fier-à-bras, or strong arm, Count of Poitou), near the château of Comonacre where Joan of Arc went, 1429, to fetch the sword of Charles Martel, with which he slew the infidels. The church is in the renaissance style of Francis I.

St. Maurc (7¾ miles) on a branch of the Vienne. Coaches to Chinon (*see* Route 71), Courcoué, Latour-St.-Gelin, Ligueil, L'Isle-Bouchard, Richelieu, St. Epain.

[*Richelieu* (25 kil. south-west) on the Amable, belonged to the father of Armand du Plessis, the famous cardinal, whose seat here, which he enlarged and beautified, was pulled down at the revolution. It was made the head of a dukedom, 1631, and the town rebuilt by him a little after.]

Port-de-Piles (6¾ miles), on the Creuse.

[Haye Descartes (7 miles south-east) higher up the river, so called (since 1802), from the philosopher *Des Cartes;* they show the house he was born in, with his bust, &c. To the east of it is Gralmoont, the old seat of Louis the Eleventh's gossip, Tristan l'Hermite.]

Les Ormes (3 miles) in department Vienne, has a fine château of the Argensons, surmounted by a column eighty feet high, with a staircase in it, whence there is a wide prospect over the Vienne, &c.

Dange (2 miles) on the Vienne.

Ingrandes (5 miles) up the same river.

[Guerche (13 kil. east) on the Creuse, has the château of Agnes Sorel, and a church of the sixteenth century.]

Chatellerault (6 miles) a sous-prefecture in department Vienne (population 11,300), and seat of the cutlery and sword trade, on the Vienne, which a good bridge crosses, with an old four-turreted gate at one end. It stands among pleasant hills and gardens, and has the gothic church of St. Jean, a salle-de-spectacle, &c. The duke of Hamilton claims to be duke of Châtellerault, on account of the title conferred on his ancestor, the Regent Arran. *Hotels*—Du Grand Monarque; de la Tête-Noire (Black Head); de l'Esperance (the Hope).

Steamer, in summer, early in the morning, down the Vienne and Loire to Tours, Saumur, Angers, Nantes. Coaches to Aux-Angles, Plumarten, Le Blanc (*see* Route 58), Laroche, Iscure. Cenon (4 kil.) is another supposed site of the Saracens' defeat by Charles Martel, at what is called the battle of Tours.

[*Laroche* or Roche-Posay (23 kil. east-south east) on the Creuse, where the Gartempe joins, has some cold sulphur waters (discovered 1573), in the limestone, which are taken between July and September, and are useful in scrofula, skin diseases, intermittent fever, &c. To the north-east of it is Boussay (with an old camp), where general Nenon, who succeeded Kléber in Egypt, was born.—Mirebeau (30 kil. west-south-west of Chatellerault) the old capital of Mirebelais, had a castle, built by Foulques Néra, in which Henry of England's widow, Eleanor was beseiged by her grandson, Arthur.

Les-Barres-le-Nintre (3 miles).

La Tricherie (3 miles).

Dissais (2¾ miles), on the Clain, is known for its red wines.

CLAN (2¼ miles).

CHASSENEUIL (1¾ miles).

At 5¼ miles further is

Poictiers, or POITIERS. *Hotels*—De France (noted for its truffle pies); de l' Europe; des Trois Piliers (Three Pillars); d'Evreux; de la Tête Noire (Black Head). Population 24,000.

A very old city, capital of department Vienne, seat of a cour impériale, university, college, bishopric, &c., on a rocky height, above the Clain, where the Boivre joins, and with the other almost surrounds it. As you look at the town it has a most picturesque appearance, with its gardens and meadows, but the streets are crooked, dirty, and steep; and the houses mean, though interesting from their antiquity. Some remains of the gothic walls are left, pierced by six gates, four of which lead out to the Clain. That on the south takes you to the Parc de Blossac walk, on the rise of the opposite hill, whence there is a fine prospect; beyond, at the hermitage, are four arches of a roman aqueduct, which supplied the vast Arènes, or amphitheatre, the ruins of which are in the court-yard of hôtel d' Evreux. Cæsar called this place *Limonum;* it was then the capital of the Pictavi, who gave name to it and the province (Poitou).

The Vandals, Visigoths, Saracens, and Normans, took it in succession, but the most memorable event is the *battle* of 1356 (fought to the south-west) in which Edward III., his son, the Black Prince, and Chandos, with 8,000 men (4,000 of whom were archers), defeated 50,000 French, taking prisoners king John and his son, with an archbishop, and seventy nobles, besides men-at-arms, the English loss being 2,400 killed. By the treaty of Bretigny, four years after, it was given, with the province, to the English, but recovered by France, 1372. The Huguenots held it for a time; and they shew in the Clain's banks, the grotto of Calvin, where he used to meet his disciples.

The *Palais de Justice*, in Rue des Cordeliers, on the hill, includes part of the seat of the counts of Poitou, such as Maubergeon tower, and the Salle des Gardes, a timber-roofed hall, in a half-norman style. At the corner of Rues de St. Paul and du Coy is a house in which Diana de Poitiers lived. The maison de la prévôté is a curious house of the fifteenth century, in that street; another of the same age is in Rue de l'Arceau; and in Rue du Marché stands one in the renaissance style. The ancient juridiction consulaire, in Rue de la Mairie, was built by a native, Girpuard, who is the author of the portal of the Augustine church, in Place d'Armes. Poitiers is remarkable for many old churches.

St. Pierre's *Cathedral*, in a ruined romanesque and gothic style, was begun about 1042, carried on by Henry II. of England, in 1152, and finished in 1379, except part of the front, which is as late as the fifteenth century, and has two towers and a rose window. Length 323 feet by 100 wide, and 97 feet high to the vault of the nave, which stands on sixteen pillars, and is strengthened by buttresses. It contains painted windows, a fine organ by Cliquot, a good choir, and the east walls are immensely thick.

Close to it is the church of *Ste. Radégonde* (Clotaire's wife), a romanesque building of the twelfth century, with a carved portal of the fifteenth century, a good nave, unsupported by pillars, an ancient sacristy, and a crypt, where they shew the tombs of the saint as well of St. Agnes, first abbess of St. Croix. A little further is the very ancient baptistry of St. Jean, built in the fourth or fifth century (some say the third, as a roman temple), now used as a *musée* of antiquities. Another old church is that of Montiernent, built 1076-96, as part of a Benedictine abbey, founded by Guy-Geoffry, Count of Poitiers; it is a mixture, like the rest, of the round and pointed styles, except the choir, which was rebuilt in the fourteenth century, and contains a modern tomb to the founder.

In Place du Marché is the romanesque church of Notre Dame, which some fix in the ninth century, and some in the tenth; it has a rich and highly curious front, carved with statues and sculptures, of Adam and Eve, the Annunciation, Christ in the manger, &c.; and inside, a bas-relief of the Resurrection, a brass reading-desk and a pulpit, are worth notice. St. Porhaire has a tower of the eleventh century, and a carved front, with the tomb of the saint. Near Grande Porte is part of St. Hilaire's, built 1049, on the site of one by Clovis, in honour of Pope Hilary (and burnt 863 by the Normans), and containing a romanesque apse, the saint's shrine (which holds part of his skull and arm bone!), and some statues commemorating the deliverance of the town from the English, 1202.

St. Triaise offers a front of the eleventh century. In the Cordeliers church Madame de Montespan was buried.

There are also the college and museum of natural history, schools of medicine and design, an ancient école de droit, a female deaf and dumb school (école de sourdes-muettes), a public library of 25,000 volumes, besides rare MSS., public baths, a well built theatre, botanic garden, and pepinière or nursery (on the Cours), with a large hospital. Rev. M. Poupot is protestant pastor here.

Paper and a few woollen and cotton caps are made. Trade in wool, paper, iron, grain, wine, spirits, honey, stone, &c., the produce of the neighbourhood.

Coaches to St. Jean d'Angely, Saintes, and Bordeaux, (253 kil.); to Agen (306 kil. by Route 60); to Chateauroux (118 kil., by Route 58); Confolens (81 kil.); Couhé (35 kil.); La Rochelle (129 kil., Route 75); Le Blanc (59 kil., Route 58); Les Sables (85 kil., Route 75); Limoges (121 kil., by Route 77); Niort (63 kil., Route 80); Parthenay (49 kil., Route 76); Rochefort (149 kil., in Route 75).

Some points of interest near this are, the Pierre Levée or druid stone (1 kil. south-east), 33 feet long, noticed by Rabelais; the Cardinerie (6 kil.) near Noaillé abbey ruins, where the battle of Maupertius (as the French historians call the fight of Poitiers), was fought; St. Benoit abbey ruins, near another famous rock, Passeelourdin, celebrated by Rabelais. Béruges (8 kil. west), with its roman vaults, Fleury aqueduct, and Guienne tower. Pin cistercian abbey (12 kil. west), now a thread factory, near the castle of Montreuil-Romien, which belonged to the dukes of Aquitaine, the Lusignans, &c., and was the residence of Cœur-de-Lion, Duguesclin, the Montmorencies, &c.

[At *Vouillé*, or Vougé, or Voulon, on the Auzance, below Latille, 16 kil. to the west of Poitiers, Clovis, in 507, defeated Alaric II. (who was killed), and his Visigoths, and finally drove them out of Gaul.]

ROUTE 65 *continued.*

This part of the line was opened officially (but not fully to the public) June, 1853, with only one line of rail. Distance, about 110 kil. or 68 miles; time, 3½ hours. The stations, as at present arranged, are:—

Ligugné	Civray	Luxé
Vivonne	Ruffec	Vars
Couhé-Vérac	Moussac	Angoulême

N.B.—The distances given below are not official.

Liguené (about 6 kil.), on the Clain, was once the seat of St. Martin de Tours.

Vivonne (12 kil.) up the Clain, where the Vône joins. A good trade in woollens, grain, &c. Population 2,850.

Couhe-Verac (about 16 kil.), on the Dive.

[At 28 kil. south-west is *Melle*, a sous-préfecture of old houses, in department Deux-Sèvres, (population 2,600) on a hill in a fertile spot over the Béronne, which dries in summer. It has a college, a pepinière, remains of old walls, a tower called Mallezeard, and the sulphur spring of Fontadau, which is found useful in cutaneous diseases. Woollens are manufactured, and it has a trade in grain, wool, trefoil seed, cattle, and and especially in asses and mules, the breed of which are of noted excellence. Three old châteaux, Lezay, Marais, and Boissec, are within a short distance.]

Civray (about 16 kil.), a sous-prèfecture (2,400 population), in department Vienne, in a rich hollow on the Charente, includes an old château in the faubourg across the river, and has an ancient and curiously carved church. Trade in woollens, truffles, corn, chesnuts, marrows, cattle, &c. *Hotel*—Des Trois Piliers (Three Pillars).

[Charvoux, 10 kil. east, (past the camp des Anglais, 3 kil.), has some fine ruins of a church, belonging to a monastery founded by Charlemagne, in 785.—At Availles, 20 kil. east-south-east of this, on the Vienne, is a good cold sulphur spring; and it carries on a trade in wine and mill-stones.]

Ruffec (about 16 kil.), on the little rivulet Lien (which produces good trout), is a sous-prèfecture in department Charente, (population 3,100), in a grass and corn country, noted for its truffles, chesnuts, and cream cheeses. The church is of the eleventh century. Near it are the Gondac windmills and several forges, and the old château of Broglie. Ruffec stands about half-way between Tours and Bordeaux. A tunnel made here for the railway is 500 mètres or 1,640 feet long. That of Bachées, on another part of the line is 1,394 feet. *Hotel*—De la Poste.

[About 36 kil. east is the sous-préfecture of *Confolens*, (population 2,070), at the old bridge on the Vienne, where the Goire joins, having the square tower of its ancient castle, and a library of 13,000 volumes. Trade in cattle, which are grazed here, timber for shipping, &c. *Hotel*—Courteau Lagrange.

Half-way to Germains, 2 kil. down the river, is the island of St. Madeleine, having a pagan temple excavated in the rock, about 39 feet by 10, and near it, a cromlech of nine tons, resting on four pillars, of grison stone, a sort of granite found here. It has an altar and benetière, for the use of the priest on the saint's fête day.]

MOUSSAC (— kil.), is near Les Nègres, on the Lien, opposite Verteuil château, a seat of the dukes of Rochefoucauld, lately restored. The next station

LUXE (— kil.), is not far from Mansle, which stands on the Lien, where it joins the Charente, which runs through green meadows, and a high stone bridge; and has a trade in grain, wine, and spirits. Population 1,000. The seat of the famous Rochefoucauld is 24 kil. south-east, as in Route 59.

VARS (— kil.), on the Charente, is about 13 kil. from Angoulême.

ANGOULEME. *Hotels*—Poste; Grand Cerf (Great Stag); Table Royale; Croix d'Or (Golden Cross). Population 16,622.

An ancient town or city, on the Charente, capital of that department, (formerly of the province of Angoumois) seat of a bishopric &c., called *Iculisma* by the Romans. It stands at a good height on the rocks above the river, in a pure but sharp air, looking, at a distance, something like Chester, and commanding, from the old ramparts, a wide prospect over the rich and beautiful wine country round the basins of the Charente and Anguienne, &c. The old town is, as usual, a nest of ill-built narrow streets. In the Place d'Artois, is a fine sloping promenade running from the Hotel de Ville, with a pillar 60 feet high, raised to the memory of her husband by the late Duchesse d'Angoulême.

The *Cathedral*, mostly rebuilt 1816, has a good porch of the twelfth century and a steeple. At the Castle, the sister of Francis I., Marguerite des Marguerites (Pearl of Pearls) was born. A public library of 15,000 vols. is at the palais de justice. Other buildings are, the old college de la marine (naval school) near the Quay, in faubourg de l' Houmeau; the Bridge on the river; the museum; theatre, &c. Our John Lackland's wife, Isabelle de Taillefer, was a native, as were Ravaillac who assassinated Henry IV., and Poltrot the assassin of Duke of Guise. It suffered in the wars of the Huguenots; and first gave title to the Duc d'Angoulême, who commanded at the final siege of Rochelle.

Trade, in excellent paper (made in the various mills around), wine, spirits, grain, truffles, chesnuts, cork, hemp, needles, iron, copper, &c. A government foundry at Ruelle (7 miles) and powder factory at Thouérat.

Conveyances: Daily, to Poitiers, Bordeaux, Rochefort, Limoges, Cognac, Périgueux.

From Angoulême to Bordeaux, by railway, 133 kil. or 83 miles; three trains a day; 3½ to 4½ hours.

The stations of this line which leaves the high road through Barbezieux, &c., much to the left, are

	kil.		kil.		kil.
La Couronne	8	Laroche-Chalais	14	Saint-Sulpice	6
Monthiers ...	7	Coutras........	17	Saint-Loubès	3
Charmant ...	5	Saint-Denis ..	9	La Grave d'Ambèares	10
Montmoreau.	13	Libourne......	7	Lormont	0
Chalais	16	Vayres.........	9	Bordeaux	4

LA COURONNE (5 miles).

MONTHIERS (4½ miles), near the bridge dividing the basins of the Charente and Dronne.

[To the west is *Beaulieu*, a fine spot at the source of the Touvre which springs up among rocks (under the ruins of Ravaillac Castle) and is thought to be like Vaucluse.

CHARMANT (4¼ miles).

MONTMOREAU (8 miles).

[At 28 kil. west-north-west, on the old road, is *Barbezieux*, a sous-préfecture of 3,500 population, (department Charente) and a pretty place on the Dronne, in the cognac brandy country. There are remains of a castle, and it has a good mineral water. *Hotels*—De la Poste, de l'Ecu de France.

Jonsac, about 24 kil. west of this, is another sous-préfecture, (department Charente Inférieure) with a fine old castle over the Seigne. A good trade in wine, brandy, cheese and poultry. Population 2,000.]

Chalais (10 miles).

[*Aubeterre* (12 kil. east) on the Dronne, a pretty little place under a hill, in which the church is scooped out just below the top, where the ruined castle stands. Méré château is near. Riberac, an unimportant sous-préfecture, is 18 kil. further.]

Laroche-Chalais (8¾ miles), in department Dordogne. Montlieu, on the high road, is 28 kil. west-north-west.

[At 27 kil. east-south-east, is Mussidan, on a fertile part of the Isle, once a fortified town, which the protestants took 1569, and which was retaken six years after, by capitulation, when the protestants were put to the sword. This breach of faith is the subject of a chapter in Montaigne's *Essais*, 'L'Heure des parlemens dangereuse.' It has forges round it. —Montpont (18 kil. south-east), lower down the same stream, is near a roman camp, where coins of the emperor Probus have been found, and remains of the chartreux abbey of Vauclaire.]

Coutras (10¾ miles) in department Gironde, between the L'Isle and Dronne, where they join, is the spot where Henry of Navarre defeated the Leaguers, October 1587, under the duke of Joyeuse, who was killed.

[To the east 10 kil., is St. Medard.]

After crossing the L'Isle, you come to

St. Denis (5½ miles).

Libourne, (4½ miles) a fine well-built town and sous-préfecture (in department Gironde) of 10,500 population, on the Dordogne, where the Isle joins it under a handsome suspension bridge. Another of nine arches crosses the main stream, which has a port large enough for 300-tons ships. The walks are beautiful. It has a public library of 3,000 vols., a botanic garden, large cavalry barrack, glass factory, &c.; and a good trade in eaux-de-vie, oil, timber, iron, salt. *Hotels*—De France; de l'Europe.

Cubzac is 20 kil. north-west, and Blaye 30 kil. (*see* Route 75). Bergerac is 60 kil. east, (*see* Route 60).

At 7 miles east, up the Dordogne, in a gorge among vineyards is the old fortified town of *St. Emilion*, having many antiquities to shew: as a parish church of the twelfth century; the façade of Cardinal de Canterac's palace; the hermitage of the saint, near the Place, cut in the rock, close to a fountain, where they shew his stone bed and chair; a 'monolithic' temple or church in the rock, 85 feet by 53, with a vault resting on eight great pillars, and various carvings; and what is called the rotonde or round church, in a light gothic style. There are also remains of the castle. Guadet, the Girondist, was born here.

Castillon, 20 kil. higher up the river, (population 2,900,) is celebrated for the battle of 1453, in which the English under the great Talbot (who with his son was killed) were defeated by the French, and finally driven out of France.—About 5 kil. to the north-east (in department Dordogne) is *St. Michel-Montaigne*, the old feudal château of Montaigne, who wrote his 'Essais' here; they shew his room, in which are sentences from the Bible and the classics, a portrait of his daughter Eléonore, also his writing table, books, and bed, and the clock which he refers to.—To the north is Villefranche de Longchapt, a very old place on a rock, walled round by the English, and taken by assault 1577 by the Huguenots, Sully being among them.]

Vayres (5½ miles).

St. Sulpice (3¾ miles).

St. Loubes (2 miles).

La Grave d'Amberes (6¼ miles).

Lormont (1¾ miles).

At 2¼ miles further is the new Bordeaux station, a building 984 feet long, close to the quay.

Bordeaux. *Hotels*—De France, and de Marin, in Rue Esprit-des-Lois; de la Paix, in Fossés-du-Chapeau Rouge; des Princes; de Paris, Allées d'Orleans; de Richelieu, Fossés-de-l'Intendence; du Midi, Place de la Comédie; des Américaines, Rue de Condé; de la Marine, Rue Dieu; des Sept Frères, opposite the post office; also de Rouen, where English, German, and Spanish are spoken. *Cafés*—de la Comédie, near the theatre; de la Préfecture, Fossés-du-Chapeau Rouge; Helvetius, &c. *Restaurants*—de Richelieu; de la Préfecture, &c. Breakfasts and déjeûners a la fourchette, 75c. to 1 franc at the cafés, or 1½ to 2 francs at the hotels; a good dinner for 3 francs at the hotels.

English consul, T. G. Scott, No. 7, Place du Champ-de-Mars; chaplains, Revs. T. and J. Quin, and C. Campbell. Revs. MM. Villaret, P. Durand, and Pellissier, are French protestant pastors here. Bankers: Barter and Gestur, Quai des Chartrons, 35; Johnston and Sons, Rue Fry, 21. Library and reading room at M. Chaumas-Gayet, opposite the préfecture. Post-office, 5, Rue-Porte-Dijeaux. Omnibuses run to all parts of the town.

Conveyances, by railway to Angoulême, Poitiers, and Paris, twice a day, in about 14 hours. Malle-poste, daily, to Bayonne (15 hours), Nantes (23 hours), Toulouse (16 hours), Lyons (38 hours); diligences to these and other places, as Agen, Montauban, Dax, Pau, Bagnères-de-Bigorre, Auch, Tarbes, Rochefort, La Rochelle, Bourbon-Vendée, Périgueux, Cahors. Steamboats to Mortagne, Blaye, and Pauillac, daily; to Royan, twice a week; to Nantes, twice a week. Sailing packets to Havre every five days; a steamer also runs.

Bordeaux is the third commercial port in France, the centre of the vin de Bordeaux (or claret) trade, chief town of the department Gironde (formerly of the province of Guienne), head of a military division, seat of an archbishop, &c. It stands on the west bank of the Garonne, *à bord-des-eaux*, 70 miles from the sea, where the river is 500 to 800 yards broad (the Thames at London Bridge is 350 yards); and it is from the water that you see to advantage its noble range of quays and buildings, stretching like a crescent three miles long from the ship-yards at the south end to the fine streets and houses at the north extremity, towards the Chartrons and Chapeau Rouge quarters, where the merchants live. A fine stone *Bridge* of 17 arches, 531 yards long, 50 feet broad, was built 1811-21, by Deschamps, from the Porte de Bourgogne to the village of La Bastide opposite. The river below it forms the port, where as many as 1,000 sail may lie; the larger vessels anchor at Pauillac, which is the real port. High water at full and change, 3 o'clock.

The houses are large and well-built; the higher classes are wealthy and luxurious in their habits, and particularly well disposed towards the English, to whom Bordeaux and the province belonged for three centuries down to 1451. Its climate however is damp. The buildings worthy of notice are as follows:—

The *Bourse* (exchange) in Place Royale, near the bridge, is 98 feet by 65, and 78 feet high to the middle of the glazed dome. The douane or custom house is near it. In the Rue Chapeau Rouge (a fine street like Portland-street), is the principal *Theatre*, a large and noble structure, built by Louis XIV, and opened 1780; it has a corinthian portico of twelve columns, with a great vestibule and staircase, and will hold 4,000 persons. It is usually reckoned the best out of Paris. Another theatre called les *Variétés* is in Rue Fossés de l'Intendance.

Hôtel de Ville (or town hall), near the cathedral, was the palace of the archbishops, and was called château royal; it is a large square pile, with a court in the midst, and a picture gallery. Here they shew Napoleon's Cross of the Legion of Honour, a History of his Battles, with notes, and other curiosities, presented by General Bertrand. An older gothic town hall is in the street leading to the bridge. The *Palais de Justice* (law courts), near the Hôtel de Ville, is rather an elegant building, with a statue of Montesquieu (who lived at Château de Brède, 10 miles off); behind it are the prisons; and opposite, the *Hôtel Dieu* or public hospital, with 600 beds. In Rue St. Dominique is the *Bibliothèque* or public library, of 110,000 volumes and 300 MSS., including Montaigne's copy of his *Essais*; also the museums of antiquity and natural history, and the observatory. The hospice des enfans trouvés where 700 foundlings are kept, is on the Quai de la Paludate.

St. André's *Cathedral*, built by the English in the thirteenth century, is large but irregular, with buttresses, &c.; it is 413 feet long, and has two spires 150 feet high, in the north transept, a good rose window, a fine altar, and an arched roof 56 feet broad. Near it is St. Pey Berlaud's gothic tower, 200 *steps* high, built 1440 by Archbishop Pierre Berlaud, and now used for a sho tower.

St. Michael's gothic church, also built by the English, has a north front of later date, and a clock-tower 180 feet high; St. Croix, of the eleventh century, has a good norman west front, with curious figures on it; St. Seurin or Severin to which mothers take their children 16th May, has a bishop's throne, and was that to which the body of Roland was brought after his death at Roncevaux; Notre Dame, a modern church, re-built 1701; and the Feuillant's church has the mailed effigy of Montaigne, who was a judge of the Bordeaux parliament, was twice mayor, and died 1592, in Rue des Minimes. There are, besides these, six other catholic churches, three protestant churches, and a handsome synagogue. Some remains of the Chartreuse abbey church are left in the public cemetery, outside the town.

The amphitheatre or *Palais Gallien*, now hardly to be seen for the houses in it, is a roman remain, near the jardin des plantes (botanic garden. It was 241 feet by 177, and 64 high. Tour de l'horloge or clock-tower, is an old gate built by Henry III. of England, the porte de caillon, another gate, was built by Charles VIII.; in Place d'Aquitaine is the evêché or bishop's house.

The entrepôt réel, for colonial produce, is a large pile on the Quai des Chartrons; on Quai de Bacalan, are the victualling office and Viellard's (formerly Johnston's) large porcelain factory, which communicates by canals with the river; hôtel des monnaies (mint), in Rue de Palais Gallien. Joubert's spinning factory is on a large scale. Kruse's *chais*, or cellars, containing 30,000 barrels of wine, are worth visiting. Excellent public *Bains* (baths) near the bourse, and in Place Lainé; also two swimming schools, mineral baths, &c.

The best *Promenades* are in the Cours d'Albret de Tourny (so called after M. de Tourny, whose statue is near), and du Jardin publique,—but especially in the large Place Louis Philippe or Place Quinconce, on the site of the Château Trompette. All are laid out with fine avenues of trees. Fairs are held the first ten days in July at the hippodrome at Gradignan (10 kil. away).

There are a college or university (as old as 1441), schools of architecture and medicine, royal academy, deaf and dumb institution, and many benevolent societies; an abbatoir (slaughter house), large barracks, &c.

Among the persons born here are Ausonius the latin poet of the fourth century; Richard II. of England; Clement V.; Ducos, and other 'Girondists,' who figured in the revolution. Another native was Girard, the rich merchant of New York, who sailed hence, 1762, as a cabin boy, and died worth two and a half millions sterling.

Bordeaux was called *Burdigala* by Strabo, and was the chief town of the Bituriges. Ausonius praises it for its soft climate, its long spring, and short winter. He describes it as four-sided; with high towers, and broad well-planned streets, and watered by the stream called Devitia (now La Devise); 'and when father ocean flows up, the whole surface is covered with fleets.'

The roman city stood between Place Royale on the Quay, and the Cathedral. It had fourteen gates, of which the last (Porte Basse) was pulled down 1805. The Visigoths burnt it 412, and the Saracens about 732. It was for a time the capital of Gascony; and through Eleanor, wife of Henry II. (of England), it came to the English crown as head of the duchy of Guienne. Henry III., who built the old Hôtel de Ville, made Simon de Montfort governor; Edward I., when prince, lived here; and from hence the Black Prince marched to the battle of Poitiers, and brought back John of France prisoner. Charles VII. took it from the English 1451, and built Château Trompette to defend it, besides Castle Ha (now a prison). L'Ombrière, the old palace of its dukes, remains near the custom house.

Trade.—The produce brought up by the Canal du Midi, and shipped to the French colonies, &c., consists of hides, flour, seeds, brandy, almonds, prunes, chesnuts, cork, resin, verdigris, honey, hams, &c. The manufactures are perfumery, liqueurs, ornamental fruit-boxes, stockings, carpets, cotton, earthenware, bottles, casks, hats, paper, vinegar, tobacco, refined sugar, rope, &c., and gloves from André's factory. Imports of all kinds from abroad. About 100,000 tons of shipping are employed; and it possesses one-fourth of the French colonial trade. The famous claret wine is grown below the city, on the west side of the river, in the district of the Mêdoc; about 50,000 tuns of the 'first growths' (called Château Morgaux, Lafitte, Latour and Haut Brion), are made yearly, and about one-twentieth is sent to England.

From Bordeaux to Lyons is 574 kil., passing through Limoges, Aubusson, and Clermont. To Marseilles, 714 kil., passing Agen, Montauban,

Albi, St. Affrique, Lodeve, Montpellier, Nismes and Arles; or 701 kil. by way of Montauban, Toulouse (256 kil.), and Montpellier. To Nantes, 347 kil., by way of Saintes, La Rochelle, and Bourbon-Vendée.

The roads to Rochelle and Nantes, to the Mêdoc wine country, to the sea at Tête de Buch, and to Toulouse, are described in Routes 75, 82, 83 and 84.

The *Central of France* railway scheme proposes to unite Montauban, Rodez, Périgueux, Limoges, Agen, and Lyons, with each other, and with Bordeaux and Toulouse, on the Bordeaux and Cette line.

ROUTE 65—*continued.*

From Bordeaux, on the road to Mont de Marsan, Bayonne (228 k.), and Pau (190 k.), you pass

CASTRES (24 kil.), up the Gironde (leaving, on the right, the old chateau of *Brède*, where they shew Montesquieu's library, and several portraits, &c.) Leaving this, you see (on the left) the old castles of Benauge (at Arbis), Langoiran, and *Cadillac* (43 kil. from Bordeaux), the last, on the Garonne, being a vast structure built by the ducs d'Epernon. Then you come to

LANGON (23 kil.), a delightful spot on the Garonne (here crossed by a suspension bridge), with 3,570 souls, who trade in excellent white wine, eaux-de-vie, &c. A steamer runs to Bordeaux.

[At 12 kil. from Langon, on the right, is the fine castle of Castres, as old as Edward II. of England, with a noble view of the Garonne.]

BAZAS (15 kil.), a sous-préfecture and bishop's see, of 4,225 people, (department Gironde), and a very old place, on a rock above the Beuve, with a cathedral of the thirteenth century, remarkable for the number of its pillars and its sculptured portals. The father of the roman poet Ausonius was a native. Here you enter the Landes country.

ROQUEFORT (47 kil.), where the road to *Pau* turns off, is on the junction of the Douze and Estampon, and has an old castle.

At 22 kil. further is Mont-de-Marsan.

MONT-DE-MARSAN. *Hotels*—Des Ambassadeurs; de la Couronne; de France. Population, 4,500. Chief town of department Landes (in the old province of Gascony), in a sandy hollow on the Douze, where the Midon joins it (making the Medouze), was built by the Counts de Marsan, 1140, taken by the Protestant leader, Montgomery, 1560, and united to the crown with Henry IV's other possesions. The rivers form a little port at Place de Commerce, and are crossed by five or six bridges. It is regularly built, and has many fountains and public baths. The chief edifices are the préfecture, palais de justice, house of detention, a nursery of plants, &c., for the department, and the barracks. The women are small, but pretty, and simply drest. Trade in cloth, wine, eaux-de-vie. Conveyances to Bordeaux, Bayonne, Pau, &c.

In this district of the *Landes* "nothing is seen for miles but extensive marshy wastes, without any sign of habitation, beyond here and there a turf hovel to afford shelter to the peasantry, who are employed to superintend the flocks of sheep, and whose aspect is sufficiently indicative of the malarious influence of the locality. In the winter, and when the ground is covered in many parts with water, they use for progression high *stilts*, which enable them to see for a considerable distance, and with which they can run and leap the wide chasms, by which the ground is frequently intersected with surprising dexterity. A man, woman, and child frequently go together, walking on these stilts, the woman being usually employed in knitting; and, seen from afar, the group presents rather a grotesque appearance" (Lee, *Companion to the Continent*).

From Mont de Marsan, on the road to Bayonne, you pass

CAMPAGNE, (13 kil.)

TARTAS (14 kil.), on a hillside over the Medouze, is an old place, once fortified, and in 1441 saved from the English by Charles VII. The château was demolished, because of its attachment to the reformed faith. It has a good trade in vinegar, saffron, wine, fruit, Bayonne horses, and resin (from the pine forests around). Population, 3,[illegible]00.

[At 26 kil. to the west, on the old road to Bayonne, is Castets, on the Palue, with a church, supposed to have been built by the English, and an intermitting iron spring.]

PONTOUX (11 kil.), on the Adour. A little further on, to the left, is Ranquines, near Puoy-de-Monsonet, where the excellent *Vincent de Paul* was born. Close to an old ruined chapel is an oak named after him; and from a hill, the highest in the department, you may see Bordeaux. Further off, are the mineral springs of Prechacq and Gamardes.

St. Paul-les-Dax (12 kil.), a place of forges and furnaces, has a gothic church, built 1441, with marble carvings, inside and out, of scripture subjects.

[At 2 kil. to the south-east is *Dax*, a sous-préfecture, on the Adour, founded by the Romans, with the name of *Aquæ Tarbellicæ*, on account of its hot mineral waters, of which the chief spring, called Fontaine de Neale, in the middle of the town, falls into a large basin in front of a kind of triumphal arch, among clouds of steam, the temperature being 160°. The supply is most abundant, especially at spring time; it is very clear, and contains sulphate and carbonate of magnesia, &c.; and is not only used by the sick for rheumatism, paralysis, &c., but by the people to wash, and make their bread with.

Another spring at Baignots, close by, has large bath rooms over it, and a temperature of 90° to 145°. A bridge leads over to Sablar Faubourg, where the old church of St. Paul stands, which was a cathedral till the revolution. The bishop's palace is now the mairie. The town walls are partly roman; and a roman way went to Toulouse. Ducos, the conventionalist, General Ducos, and Borda, the mathematician, were born here. *Hotels*—De St. Etienne; de France; de la Croix d'Or (Gold Cross).

To the south-east of it, up the Arrigan, is the town of Pouillon (population, 3,200), which is noted for a warm mineral spa, and contains the old feudal château of Lamothe.]

St. Geours (13 kil.), in the midst of forests of cork.

[About 18 kil. north-west is the decayed port of Vieux Bocault, among sandhills (some 200 feet high), on the Bay of Biscay, which was of some consequence between 1360, when the course of the Adour was turned into it, and 1560, when it was made to take its old course. A lake is called étang de Moison after an old skipper, who was so unwilling to believe that the river was turned that he kept his vessel at anchor in the stream till there was no water left to carry him out to sea.]

Cantons (13 kil.)

[About 4 kil. west-north-west is Cap Breton, once a good port, when the Adour ran by it into the Bay of Biscay, from which sandhills now hide it. Some say it was founded by Brutus as *Caput Bruti*. Part of a knigh templar's house is seen among the ruins.]

At 19 kil. further is Bayonne, with the Pyrenees in view. It is entered by a wooden bridge over the Adour, from the suburb of *St Esprit* (population, 6,000), which belongs to department Landes, and contains Vauban's citadel upon the heights over the town. Until 1831 the Jews of Bayonne were obliged to retire to this quarter at sunset. The circus has been rebuilt and enlarged for bull-fights, which were first celebrated here September, 1852, and are to be repeated annually after the Spanish ceremonial.

Bayonne. *Hotels*—St. Etienne; du Commerce; de St. Martin; du Grand d'Espagne. Population, 14,773. High water at full and change 3h. 30m., the tide rising 14 feet. English consul, F. Graham, of whom passports for Spain may be had.

A sous-préfecture in department Basses-Pyrénées (part of Gascony), seat of a bishopric, fortress of the first class, on the Spanish frontier, and a thriving port on the Adour, where the Nive joins it, about 3 miles from the Bay of Biscay. It has a good harbour (as the name signifies in the Basque language, *Baia* and *ona*), but the mouth is obstructed by a dangerous bar, near which the Duke of Wellington crossed the Adour, February, 1814, on a bridge of boats.

The town was founded in the tenth or eleventh century; is defended by high and strong ramparts, and divided by the rivers into three parts, viz., Grand and Petit Bayonne, and the suburb of St. Esprit, which stands on the right bank of the Adour, in another department (Landes), and contains Vauban's citadel, which commands the town and country around, and was invested 1814. There is a noble prospect hence over the town, the wide estuary of the Adour, and the forests at its mouth, with the snowy peaks of the Pyrenees to the south. A bridge of boats crosses this part of the Adour, and two bridges cross the Nive.

The main street is good, but the rest are narrow; with houses of stone, and three or four stories high Place Grammont is the best and livelicst spot, and there is a beautiful walk along the Allées Maritimes, a sort of jetty, one mile long, near the quays, with good prospects. The Bayonnaise women are considered pretty. Among the buildings, notice the small cathedral of the twelfth century and its large cloisters, built by the English; the arsenal and military hospital; old château, barrack, near the sous-préfecture; the mint, and naval dock, &c. There are a chamber of commerce and navigation school. (See Pau, for Navarre, &c.)

A large proportion of the population is Jewish, that body being very wealthy, in consequence of the flourishing condition of the extensive smuggling business which is carried on with Spain. General Harispe and Lafitte, the banker, were natives. The *bayonette*, they say, was invented here; and here (at Château de Marrac, Napoleon seized Charles IV. of Spain, with his queen and son, 1808. Rev. M. Nogaret is Protestant pastor.

Manufactures: eaux-de-vie d'Andaye, glass bottles (sand being plentiful), hams (cured at Orthez, &c.), chocolate, sugar, &c.; and a trade with Spain in timber, wool, wines, drugs, resin, &c.

Conveyances to Toulouse, Bordeaux, Pau, Orthez; also to Tolosa, and St. Sebastian (in Spain), on the way to Madrid. A railway is projected in this direction, past Irun, St. Sebastian, Tolosa, Bilboa, Vittoria, Burgos, Valladolid, &c., to Madrid; 685 kil., or 427 miles long. There is a steamer on the Adour.

From Bayonne, on the road to Spain, you pass

Biarritz (4 kil.), a bathing place on the Bay of Biscay, here lined with limestone cliffs, 50 to 60 feet high, hollowed into caves, as the Chamber of Love, &c. It is reached by omnibuses, but the country people ride *en cacolet*, that is, in a pannier on one side of a horse, the other being filled by the driver.

Bidart (11 kil. from Bayonne), where the Basque race begins to appear.

St. Jean de Luz (9 kil. from Bidart), a fortified town of 2,860 souls, at the Nivelle's mouth.

Urrugne (5 kil.), near Montagne d'Arrhune, in the Lower Pyrenees mountains, and the Bidassoa, which divides France and Spain. The heights were defended by Soult against Wellington, who passed this way, October, 1813, into France. A bridge crosses the river at Behobia (the last French post town and custom-house), to Irun, and at its mouth are Andaye (French) and Fuentarabia (truly Spanish).

(*a*) Up the Nive you pass Ureury (20 kil.), near Cambo Spa, which Napoleon visited, 1808, then Irissari (20 kil.), then St. Jean Pied-de-Port (12 kil.), the old capital of Navarre, beyond which is Roncevaux, or *Roncesvalles* (in Spain), where Roland and his brave peers were killed, 778.

ROUTE 67.

Blois to Vendome and Le Mans.

Distance, 132 kil., or 82 miles.

Blois, as in Route 65.

Le Breuil (16 kil).

Vendôme (32 kil.), an old sous-préfecture on the Loir, in department Loir-et-Cher (population 8,000), having the ruined walls and six towers of the castle of the ducs de Vendôme; also the cathedral church of Ste. Croix, a college, a barrack (in the old benedictine convent), marble fountain, &c.

But it is most remarkable for the *boy-crusades* which originated here, 1262, with a shepherd youth, Stephen. About ten thousand children followed him to Marseilles, to embark for the Holy Land; after suffering great hardships, the survivors were trapped on board ships for Alexandria, and sold there as slaves.

Trade in cloth, paper, fruit, &c.

[At 16 kil. north-east, up the river, is *Freteval* where the English suddenly attacked Philippe Auguste, 1194, and captured the royal seal and public acts, which it was the custom till then to carry about with the sovereign. —Morée, a little further, has remains of its old walls.

Montoire (13 kil. west-south-west of Vendôme) down the stream, was the old capital of Bas Vendômois. For a while it was called Kerhoent, after a Breton seigneur who obtained possession; another owner was Marshal Tallard, who laid out the Grande Place. The picturesque remains of St. Oudville château stand above the town. Population, 3,072.

About 30 kil. west is Coutures, near Poissonnière château, where *Ronsard*, the poet, was born, 1524. In Gatine's forest, hard by, is the fountain of Miracon, and Ribauchère Castle, on the Loir; all connected with the poet, who was buried in Coutures Church (pulled down at the revolution).]

Epuise (17 kil.).

[Mont Doubleau (10 kil. north) on the Graisne, has large ruins of a feudal castle as old as the ninth century.]

St. Calais (15 kil.), is a sous-préfecture in department Sarthe, on the Auille; and has two gothic churches and a new palais de justice. Population, 3,900. Woollens &c., are made.

Bouiloire (17 kil.).

Le Mans is 35 kil. further. (*see* Route 90.)

ROUTE 69.

Tours to La Fleche, Le Mans, and Laval.

Distance (to Laval), 135 kil. or 84 miles. A branch railway is projected to Le Mans.

Tours, as in Route 65.

La Roue (20 kil.)

[At 21 kil. north-north-west, on the Le Mans road, is

Chateau-de-Loir (department Sarthe), a well-built, industrious place, in a charming part of the Loir, among vineyards of white wine. Its old castle, perched high on the rocks, sustained a siege of seven years, in the eleventh century, against Geoffrey of Anjou, and was taken by Henry IV., in 1589. St. Guingalais' gothic church has an ancient crypt of the tenth century, and some marble carvings. Several grottoes are in the cliffs. Coaimon bridge commands a fine view of the Loir. Population, 3,100. Good linens, cotton thread, &c., are made, and it is noted for its chesnuts. A large trade in cattle, hemp, flax, poultry, &c. Le Mans is 41 kil. further.]

Chateau-Lavilliere (17 kil.), on the Fare; above which rises an elegant seat built by Louis XIV. for the Duchess de la Vallière.

Le Lude (15 kil.), a pretty place of 3,400 people on the Loir (in department Sarthe), having several old carved houses, and a fine château, half gothic, with enormous towers, commanding the river. They show the room which Henry IV. slept in, and Mongendre's statue of Hercules in the park. *Hotel*—Du Bœuf.

La Fleche (15 kil.), a sous-préfecture in department Sarthe, of 6,400 souls, in the pretty valley of the Loir, and a healthy, well-built town, among woods and vineyards, called by its present name because of a spire (flèche) put on St. Thomas' romanesque church, in the twelfth century, by Count Helie, whose old castle stands in the river. It has a public library of 22,000 volumes, a good Hôtel de Ville, hospital, &c., but is most noted for the Jesuits' college founded 1503, by Henry IV., and a military school; Descartes was educated in it. The spire of St. Thomas, which was 85 feet long, was blown down by a hurricane, 1726, crushing a house in its fall. The Vendeans took the town 1793. Opposite it is the fine château given by Henry IV. to his favourite, La Varonne. *Hotels*—Des Voyageurs (Travellers); de l'Etoile (Star); des Quatre Vents (Four Winds). Coaches to Le Mans, Angers, Saumur, &c. Muslins, linens, gloves, &c., are made and the poultry is noted.

Sable (26 kil.), an old town on the Sarthe, which is crossed by a marble bridge, joining the two parts of it. Above it stands a fine château, built by Mansard for the brother of Colbert the statesman. It commands a noble prospect. The town belonged to Geoffrey of Anjou, and was taken by Henry IV., in person. Gloves, linens &c. are made, and marble is worked. *Hotel*—De Notre Dame. Population 4,900.

[At 4 kil. up the river, near the quarries, is the old abbey of *Solesmes*, founded 993–1095, and mostly rebuilt in the time of Louis XV. The church contains a remarkable collection of fifty bas-reliefs, statues, &c., by Geoffrey Pilon, in the fifteenth century, some the size of life, called the Saints de Solesmes; among these are the sepulchre of the Virgin (a group of fourteen figures), Christ in the grave (by Pilon's father), Christ with the doctors, &c.]

Meslay (21 kil.), a healthy little village on the Vaige.

At 21 kil. further is Laval (*see* Route 90).

ROUTE 71.

Tours to Angers, Nantes, &c.,

DOWN THE LOIRE.

By Railway.—Distance 196 kil. or 122 miles; four trains a-day, in $3\frac{3}{4}$ to $6\frac{1}{2}$ hours; for $20\frac{1}{4}$, $15\frac{1}{4}$, $11\frac{1}{4}$ francs.

The stations on this line are—

	kil.		kil.		kil.
Savonnières	14	La Ménitré	6	Champtocé	8
Cinq-Mars	7	St. Mathurin	3	Ingrandes	5
Langeais	5	La Bohalle	7	Verades	9
St. Patrice	9	Trélaze	6	Ancenis	12
La Chap.-sur-Loire	7	Angers	7	Oudon	9
Port-Boulet	5	Bouchemaine	6	Clermont	4
Varennes	8	La Pointe	2	Mauves	5
Saumur	10	Les Forges	3	Thouaré	5
Saint-Martin	7	La Poissonnière	3	Sainte-Luce	3
Les Rosiers	8	Chalonnes	6	Nantes	7

TOURS, as in Route 65. Passing Plessis-les-Tours, opposite St. Cyr and Vallières, you come to

SAVONNIERES (8¾ miles), on the south bank, near the Cher, and Villandry dropping caves, and opposite to *Luynes*, which was called Maillé as far back as 475, and was made the head of a duchy by Louis XIII. for his favourite Charles-Albert de Luynes, 1619. It stands in a pretty spot under the rocks (and was sometimes styled Rochoir-sur-Loir) which are hollowed out for people to live in; above is the old château. Paul Courvier, assassinated here 1824, was a native. Near it are about fifty pillars of an ancient aqueduct.

CINQ-MARS (4½ miles), at the nineteen-arch viaduct over the Loire, stands on the cliffs, near an old castle, and a famous antiquaries' puzzle, called the *Pile de Cinq Mars*, a solid tower of large bricks, 13 feet square, 92 high to the corner turrets which rise 10½ above. A fifth turret over the middle was blown down 1751. It has neither door nor window, and the builder is unknown, but it is supposed to be a mausoleum. Cinq-Mars, one of the favourites of Louis XIII., is the subject of De Vigny's novel. Coaches to Chateau-la-Vallière, Cléré, Savigné, Rille, Channay Mazières.

LANGEAIS (3¾ miles), on the north bank, has an old gothic château of the tenth century (now a prison), built by Foulques Nera, Count of Anjou, and enlarged by St. Louis' barber, Pierre de Labrosse. In the hall, the marriage of Charles VII. with Anne of Brittany was celebrated, 1491.

[Coach to *Azay-le-Rideau*, (8 miles south-east), which has on an island in the Indre, a beautiful turreted château, in the renaissance style, with a richly carved portico and staircase. The devices of Diana de Poitiers and Francis I. (the salamander), are seen, and the motto '*Ung seul desir*' in one part. It contains a gallery of portraits. Population 2,200.]

ST. PATRICE (5 miles), near the Bois de Bismond. A little further is Trois-Violets, opposite the château d'Ussé, seat of Duc de Duras, formerly of Vauban, who partly built it.

LA CHOUZE-SUR-LOIRE (4½ miles). A little north-east is Bourgeuil, in a charming red-wine country on the Doigt, and having remains of a benedictine abbey of the tenth century, founded by Edme, duchess of Guienne.

PORT-BOULET (2½ miles), at the suspension bridge to Candes, which stands at the Vienne's mouth, near the picturesque ruins of Montsoreâu castle. Candes has the church in which St. Martin de Tours died. Coaches to Chinon, Loudun, Fontevrault. Windmills abound here.

[*Chinon* (13 kil. east-south-east), up the Vienne, in department Indre-et-Loire, is a sous-préfecture (7,000 population), in a pretty part, above which are the large ruins of the castle, built 953, by Thibault-le-Tricheur, where Henry II. of England died, 1189, and which Charles VII. held (the only fortified place remaining to him) when Joan of Arc came to declare her mission. He built the Tour d'Argenton. Richelieu had possession of it 1631. *Rabelais* was born at a farm-house, near at hand, 1483. Trade in prunes, soap, cattle, wine, spirits, &c. The steamer from Châtellerault passes by. *Hotels*—De France; de St. Martin; de la Boule d'Or (Golden Ball); all on the Place.

Fontevrault (5 kil. south of Candes), in department Maine-et-Loire, a village at the bottom of a wooded valley, once noted for its famous abbey, founded for men and women by Robert d'Arbrissel, 1099, and now turned into a prison for eleven departments. It was the burial place of the kings of England when counts of Anjou, and in the fine cathedral church of the twelfth century (one of five attached to the abbey) are monuments of Henry II. and his wife Eleanor, his son Richard Cœur de Lion, and John's wife Isabella. The Tour d'Evrault in the court, is the eight-sided gothic kitchen of the abbey, with a chimney rising over the middle.

Loudun, 20 kil. further, is a sous-préfecture in

department Vienne (population 5,500), and an old town on a hill among woods and vine-yards. It is noted for its delicate wines. The protestants held it till Richelieu razed the castle, and the revocation of the Edict of Nantes which followed. The excellent but unfortunate Urban Grandier, a monk, here, was burnt on pretence of sorcery, 1634. Coarse woollens, jewellery, &c., are made, and there is a trade in corn, wine, oil, walnuts, &c. *Hotels*—De France; du Lion d'Or (Golden Lion).

Moncontour (16 kil. south-south-west of this), on the Dive, is celebrated for the defeat of the Huguenots under Coligny, 1569. "Oh, weep for Moncontour! oh, weep for the hour!"

VARENNES (5½ miles), opposite several river islands, and Dampierre, where Margaret of Anjou died.

SAUMUR (5½ miles), in a fine situation across the Loire, on a hill side, is a sous-préfecture of 11,100 souls, in department Maine-et-Loire, with a college, military riding school, chamber of commerce, &c, and was the capital of Saumurais, taken from the counts of Blois by Foulques Nêra, in the ninth century. Under Du Plessis Mornay it became a flourishing protestant town in the time of Henry IV., having a good trade, a famous academy, and a population of 25,000, but was ruined by the revocation of the Edict of Nantes. The Vendeans seized it 1793.

From La Croix Verte, on the railway side, a stone bridge resting on Ile des Ponts (where King René, Margaret's father, had a seat) runs over to the quay, the half, nearest which, is on twelve arches, and 900 feet long. Another bridge leads out of the town, by Porte Fouchard, over the Thouet, which joins the Loire a little below. The houses in the new quarters are well built of white stone; they are irregular and steep in High town, above which stands the donjon of the old château, built about the thirteenth century (on the site of one of Pepin's, called château du Tronc), once a state prison and an arsenal.

Most of the churches deserve attention. St. Pierre is early gothic, and cross-shaped, with a bold, square tower and spire. That of Nantilly is imperfect, and as old as the sixth century in some parts, with stout romanesque pillars and arches, six windows on the north side, and a good west door. Notre Dame des Ardilliers, under the cliff, on the river side, was begun 1553, and added to by Richelieu and others; the Marquis de Sable gave the painting by Philippe de Champagne, of Simeon at the Temple gate; and A. Servier built the dome 64 feet diameter. It contains the tomb of the Duchesse de Meilleraye, and makes part of the convent and hospice of Providence.

The caserne or *cavalry barrack* one of the largest in France, is H-shaped, of four stories, and comprises riding schools, stables, &c., and an esplanade.

At the gothic Hôtel de Ville, with its high pitched roof and pinnacles, is a musée of antiquities; there is also a public library of 12,000 vols., a theatre on arches over the market-place, two hospitals besides la Providence, good baths, and many wind-mills. Madame Dacier, the greek scholar, was a native. Rev. N. Duvivier is protestant pastor.

Glass and other beads, articles in enamel, copper goods, linens, saltpetre, leather, &c. are made; trade also in white wine, eaux-de-vie, fruit, &c. *Hotels*—Du Belvédère; de Londres; de France; des Trois Pigeons. Coaches to Niort (*see* Route 80), Rochefort, La Rochelles, Napoleon-Vendée (Route 75), Bellay, La Flèche (Route 70), Le Mans (Route 90), Le Lude, Vernantes, Poitiers (Route 65). Steamer to Nantes, Tours, &c. in summer.

[At *Vernantes* (14 kil. north-north-east) are parts of the fortress-looking church (the clock-tower, painted choir window, &c.) of Lourroux cistercian abbey, founded 1121 by Foulques or Fulhe V., count of Anjou.—Brain (14 kil. north-east), contains fragments of Coutancière château which belonged to Bussy d' Amboise, the tyranical governor of Anjou.

At Bagneux (3 kil. south of Saumur), up the Thouet, is the large Poutigné cromlech of fourteen stones, one twenty-four feet long.—Montreuil Bellay and its old castle are 11 kil. further, and beyond it are Thouars, Bressuire, and Parthenay, as in Route 76—Doué (16 kil. south-west), an old place, having remains of a palace of Dagobert, also several caves, and an amphitheatre dug out of the rocks. Its fountain is handsome and abundant.—Vihiers, 17 kil. beyond it, near lake, has remains of one of the most ancient castles in Anjou, near which is a cairn or mort-hill, 300 metres round, 18 high.]

St. Martin (5½ miles), opposite Treves castle, in the Forest de Milly and the village of Chenehutte, which is cut off from Tufeaux and its gypsum quarries by a ravine; above the cliffs are remains of a large roman camp, where coins, pottery, tombs, &c. have been found.

Les Rosieres (3¾ miles) is opposite Gennes, where another roman camp is traced, besides a ruined aqueduct. At Cunault is the curious old church of Nôtre Dame, founded by Dagobert; it consists of three naves, rounded off at the east end, and is 236 feet long by 65 to 75 broad.

La Menitre (3¾ miles). Coaches to Beaufort and Beaugé.

[*Beaugé* or Baugé (20 kil. north-north-east), a sous-préfecture of 3,600 souls, on the Couesnon (here crossed by a bridge), where the English, under the Duke of Clarence, were defeated 1421, by la Fayette. It has an old castle of Foulques Nera, built in the eleventh century, and an excellent hospital. Paper, coarse linens, and woollens are made.]

St. Mathurin (1¾ miles) at the long suspension bridge to St. Maur, so called after St. Benedict's disciple, and one of the seats of the learned Congregation of St. Maur, among whom were Mabillon and Montfaucon.

La Bohalle (5 miles), where the great levées or embankments of the Loire end.

Trelaze (2¾ miles).

La Paperie (3 miles).

At 2½ miles further is

Angers. *Hotels*—de la Boule d'Or (Golden Ball); Trois Trompettes (Three Trumpets). Population, 41,000.—The capital of department Maine-et-Loire, and once of the province of Angers, which belonged to our Henry II., as Duke of Anjou, is the seat of a cour impériale, tribunal, university, college, bishopric, &c., and was, in roman times, the chief town of the *Andecavi*, whence the name is derived, like many others in France. It stands in a fine amphitheatre made by a bend of the Mayenne or Maine, below where the Sarthe joins, and near its own junction with the Loire. The oldest part is a collection of dark, narrow, steep streets (some too steep for carriages) of wooden or slate houses, with carved stone balconies. The new town is regularly built; the boulevards are well planted; and there is a suspension and another bridge. Old walls of brown stone, defended by turrets, go round the town. One of the promenades called Bout du Monde (World's End) overlooks it and the country.

At the top of a hill stands St. Maurice's *Cathedral*, seen for many leagues round. It is a cross, 298 feet long, with one of the largest naves in France. The front has three towers, one being domed, and is ornamented with statues. In the interior are some excellent carvings; stained, rose, and other windows; old tapestry; the high altar, of different coloured marbles; a famous organ, by Danville (from which you may take the round of the walls by a gallery near the roof;) and a benitier (holy water basin), given by le bon roi René, whose tomb, in which his daughter Margaret (wife of our Henry VI.) was buried, was destroyed at the revolution.

His moated castle, on a steep rock over the river, now used as a prison, was begun as early as the time of Philippe Auguste; the walls are high and thick, and strengthened by eighteen towers of slaty stone; the terrace has a good view of the river.

St. Serge's curious old gothic church, is in part of the eleventh century, with a nave of the fifteenth. The great hall of the hôtel dieu, or St. John's hospital, was built by our Henry II.; in faubourg St. Jacques, is the large front of the abbey of St. Nicholas; at the corner of Rue (street) du Figuier, is a fine gothic house called Hôtel d'Anjou. Notice, also, the riding academy; the public library, of 26,000 vols., and many rare MSS.; the picture gallery, a good collection of old and new French masters; the botanic gardens, with many exotics; the cabinet of natural history, deaf and dumb school, baths, theatre, racecourse; and the slate quarries, employing 3,000 men. King René, Bernier the traveller, Ménage, David the sculptor, were natives. The Duke of Wellington spent two years of his early life here.

Manufactures of sailcloth, camlets, handkerchiefs, thread stockings, refined sugar, &c.; and a good trade in these and oil, hemp, grain, wine, dried fruits, (fruits cuits) honey, vinegar, slate, marbles.

Conveyances: Daily, by rail, to Nantes, Tours, Orleans, Paris, &c. Coaches to Brest, Morlaix, St. Brieuc, Rennes (all in Route 90), La Guerche, Craon, Segré (Route 72), Laval (Route 90), Château Gontier (Route 72), Chollet, Beaupréau, Chemille, Caen, Alençon, Sable, Le Mans (Route 90), La Flèche (Route 69). Also, to Ponts de Cé (4 kil.), so called after the wood and stone bridge which skips, by about 100 arches, across the islands of the Loire,—and from a Cæsar's camp here. One of these islands, Béhuard, has a pilgrim's chapel, with a portrait of Louis XI. Across the Loire (12 kil. from Angers), is the ruined château of the Ducs de Brissac.

[About 12 kil. north-east of Angers is the fine old castle of Plessis-Macé, with its towers, moat, square donjon, machicolations, &c.]

From Angers, along the Nantes railway, you pass, going down the right side of the Loire,

BOUCHEMAINE (3¾ miles), La Pointe (1¼ miles), Les Forges (2 miles), Les Poissonnières (1¾ miles), near which, on the river side, are the fine park and château of Savrant, with its orangery and chapel.

CHALONNES (3¾ miles), near the beautiful island of Lombardière, Champtocé (5 miles) or Champtoceau, with its ruined castle, Ingrandes (3¼ miles), are next passed, then

VARADES (5¼ miles). Coaches to Condé and St. Florent (— kil.), where the royalist leader Bonchamps, killed in the Vendéan war, is buried.

ANCENIS (7¾ miles), a sous-préfecture, in department Loire Inférieure, in a charming spot, with a gothic château above it, which belonged to the Bethunes. Population, 3,800. Coaches to Châteaubriant (Route 72), St. Mars-la-Juille, La Chapelle-Glain, St. Julljen. The druid stone, Couvreclair, is near.

OUDON (5¾ miles), with an eight-sided tower, built about 840, Clermont (2¼ miles), Mauves (3 miles), Thouaré (3¼ miles), St. Luce (1¾ miles). Nantes is 4¼ miles further.

Nantes. *Hotels*—De France, in Place Graslin; du Commerce; des Voyageurs (Travellers), near the theatre; des Etrangers; des Colonies; de l'Europe; de Bordeaux; du Cheval Blanc (White Horse); de la Belle Etoile (Star). *Cafés*—in Place Graslin, &c. Living at the hotels, 5 to 6 francs a day.

English consul, H. Newman; Post office, in Rue Boileau.

Protestant church, Rue des Carmelites, in the old chapel of the convent. Rev. MM. Vaurigaud and Sohier, are french protestant pastors here. Omnibuses run through the town.

Population, 89,030. Capital of department Loire-Inférieure, head quarters of a military division, seat of a diocess, and fourth port in France, on the north side of the Loire (where the Erdre joins), 35 miles from the Bay of Biscay. Many English live here, in great comfort and even luxury, on £100 a year. It was the roman *Namnetes*; was ravaged by the Normans in the ninth and tenth centuries; was a principal seat of the dukes of Brittany, till Anne of Brittany married Charles VIII.; is celebrated for the 'Edict of Nantes,' issued here by Henry IV., in favour of the protestants, which Louis XIV. revoked 1685; was attacked by the Vendéans 1793; about which time the atrocious Carrier and his terrorist agents held it, and 25,000 persons, young and old, suspected of loyalty, were drowned in barges (the *noyades*) or shot, or left to die in prison.

The old town is on the corner made by the river ; in Faubourg Le Marchys is the new town, begun by Graslin the financier, 1784; other suburbs lie on the islands in the Loire, such as Feydeau, Gloriette, Biesse, &c.; and a chain of six bridges, from island to island, carries a road of 3 kil. length, across the river to Bere, on the south bank, where the Sevre falls in. There are nine or ten other bridges. La Fosse quay is lined with trees and well-built houses; it is part of a succession of quays extending from the castle for half a league or more. The Erdre is also bordered with quays, and they are carried round Ile Feydeau. The tide flows up to the town, rising only a fathom; enough to bring up small vessels under 200 tons. The entrance to the Loire is rather foggy and dangerous. Larger ships stop at Paimbœuf, 25 miles lower.

From 2,000 to 3,000 vessels visit Nantes in a year, with fish from Newfoundland, sugar and other produce from the French colonies; sardines or pilchards are caught in the season. Small corvettes and brigs are built here. Coarse woollens and cottons are made; besides steam-engines, bottles, pottery, rope, canvas, vinegar, refined sugar, provisions for the navy, &c.

The streets are pretty good; the houses of stone and slate, the latter material being used to face those in the old town (as in La Poissonnerie, Rue de la Juiverie, &c.), where the streets are narrow and dirty, and made up of old-fashioned houses, with projecting gables. Besides the promenades on the quays are those of St. André and St. Pierre (between the Loire and Erdre), on the site of part of the ramparts, and having between them Place Louis XVI., with a statue of that king; at the end are statues of Anne of Brittany and Arthur III. (near the castle), and Oliver de Clisson and Du Guesclin, two famous soldiers. There are about twenty open places, of which, Place Royale and Place Graslin are the best; a theatre, rebuilt 1810, with a corinthian portico, stands in Place Graslin.

St. Peter's *Cathedral* was built 1434-1500, on the site of one founded 555, by Felix. It has a massive norman choir (the oldest existing part, except the crypt) and a lofty flamboyant nave 121 feet high. The west front, with its three well-sculptured portals, carries two low unfinished towers, with a watch-turret at the top of one. Its finest monument is the tomb, in black, white, and red marble, of Francis II. (last Duke of Bretagne) and his wife Margaret. The *château* of the duke, on the river, is a large irregular pile of the fourteenth century (first founded 938), flanked with round towers, &c. Here Anne of Brittany was born; and the late Duchesse de Berri (Madame, as she was called), was confined after her capture in the town by General Dermoncourt, in 1832. Her adventures are related by the general in his entertaining 'La Vendée et Madame.' A many-sided tower of the Château de Bouffay, as old as the tenth century, serves for a belfry.

The préfet's hôtel, one of the best buildings in the town, was the old Chambre des Compts, and has two of its fronts in the ionic style. A colonnade in the same style before the bourse or exchange (built 1812) on the quays, is ornamented with emblematical statues by Bertrand and Debay; another façade (towards the Port-au-Vin) of the doric order, has busts of french seamen, Duquesne, Cassart, Jean Bart, Duguay-Trouin.

Over the marché-aux-grains or corn market, is the public library of 30,000 vols., besides MSS.; the museum of paintings has a collection of 700 or 800 works, among which are two Murillos. A natural history museum in Rue du Port Communeau, contains many good mineral specimens, &c.

Other buildings are, the churches of St. Similien and St. Francis de Sales, and six or seven churches besides a college and priests' seminaries; five hospitals, including the hôtel dieu, built 1655; the general hospital of St. Jean, &c.; the law courts, once the hôtel des monnaies; a halle aux toiles, or linen hall; a large abattoir or public slaughter house; there is also a well stocked botanic garden.

Near the hôtel de commerce is a handsome covered way, built 1843, called Passage Pommeraye, and ornamented with Debay's statues. In the old town are some ancient houses, as, the hôtels Briord, Rosmadec, d'Aux, Deurbroucq, Bourvardière, &c., and the bishop's palace.

Besides Anne of Brittany, Cassart a famous sailor, Fouché the police minister, Caillaud the traveller, Laennec the physician, General Cambrone, &c., were born here. Marshal Gilles de Retz, the French Bluebeard, was burnt here 1440, for his cruelties. Palais or Pallet, in this neighbourhood, was the native place (1079) of Abelard.

Conveyances, by steamer,—to Bordeaux, twice a week, in 24 hours, 15 and 18 francs; to Angers (up the Loire), daily, in — hours; and to Tours (36 hours from Nantes); they run slow, especially in summer, when the water is low, but the views are pleasant. To Nort (up the Erdre) daily; above it in a pretty part where the river is like a lake, is Gâcherie château, where Marguerite de Navarre lived when she wrote the 'Heptameron,' a collection of licentious tales. To Paimbœuf (down the river), twice a day, touching at St. Nazaire, &c. To Brest (touching at Belle Isle and Lorient) weekly, in 20 hours, 18 and 25 francs. — By railway to Angers, Tours, Bordeaux, Paris, &c. (see *Bradshaw's Continental Railway Guide*). — Coaches to Clisson, les Sables, Belle-Ile, Napoleon-Vendée, Nint, St. Hermione, La Rochelle, Rochefort (in Routes 75, 76), Bordeaux (Route 65); Rennes, Morlaix, St. Brieuc, Brest, in Route 90; Vannes, Pontivy, Lorient, Quimper, Redon, La Roche-Bernard, in Route 74; also to Croisic, St. Nazaire, Paimbœuf, and Pornic.

[At Basse-Indre, 7 miles down the Loire, small frigates and steamers are built, the engines being made on the island of Indret opposite it.

Paimbœuf, near the river's mouth (in front of Donzes and its salt marshes), is a sous-préfecture and port of 4,500 souls, with a strong mole 217 feet long, where large ships lie. It is not older than the last century. Coaches go from this to *Pornic*, 12 miles south-west, a healthy watering place, with an old château, in the Bay of Biscay, on Bourgneuf bay, opposite Noirmoutiers island, which had a benedictine or black (noir) abbey.

Fort Mindin below Paimbœuf, commands the mouth of the Loire (here 4 miles broad), and is opposite the little rocky port of St. Nazaire (population, 3,800). Two dolmens or druid stones are near it; and at 12 miles to the north-west, are Batz, Guérande, &c., and their salt works. West of this, on the coast, is the port of Croisic and its large stone spire church; 18 kil. off which is Le Four rock and its lighthouse (?) 98 feet high).]

ROUTE 72.

Angers to Segre, Chateau-Gontier, Laval, Chateaubriant, and Rennes.

Distance, 127 kil., or 79 miles.

ANGERS, as in Route 71.

LE LION D' ANGERS (22 kil.), a pretty place on the Oudon, where it joins the Mayenne.

[To the north-east where the Sarthe falls in, is *Brissarthe*, which has a very old norman church, at the door of which Robert the Strong was killed, 866, by the Normans, who were inside, and who thence gained a footing in France.

Château Gontier (23 kil. north of Lion d'Angers), a sous-préfecture, on the Mayenne, having a charming view of the basin of that river from the promenade. Church, an early gothic. Part of a castle, built by Fulque of Anjou, in the eleventh century, remains. The Vendéans took it, 1793. There is a mineral water; linens, woollens, &c., are made. Population, 6,143, in a good trade. *Hotels*—De la Boule d'Or (Golden Ball); Trois Trompettes (Three Trumpets).

At 30 kil. further is Lavel (*see* Route 90).]

SEGRE (14 kil.), a sous-préfecture (department Maine-et-Loire), on the Oudon, in a fine grain and pasture country, with some druid stones near it, at Chatelais. Population, 2,300.

[About 12 kil. north, in department Mayenne, is the gothic château of St. Ouen, built by Anne, of Brittany, with various excellent carvings about it.]

POUANCE (22 kil.)

[At 21 kil. north-east is *Craon*, in a pleasant part of the Oudon, and as old as the eighth century, but the ancient castle, which the Prince of Conti took 1592, is replaced by a modern seat. It gives name to an illustrious family in French history. Population, 4,100.]

CHATEAUBRIANT (16 kil.), in Loire-Intérieure, a sous-préfecture, with 3,900 inhabitants, and so called after a castle built 1015, by Briant, Count of Penthièvre, of which the donjon keep and two high towers are left, besides the chapel and other old buildings, and the Château Neuf, in which Francis de Foix was bled to death by his wife. It is noted for a sweetmeat called conserve d'angelique. Sabots or wooden shoes are made. *Hotels*—Des Voyageurs (Travellers); du Lion d'Or (Golden Lion).

[About 16 kil. south, on the Nantes road, is the Trappist convent of Le Meilleraye].

THOURIE (18 kil.), in department Ille-et-Vilaine.

[At 12 kil. north-north-east is Essé or Rouvray, on the Seiche, having a druid monument called the *Roche-aux-Fées* composed of 42 stones (schistus) about 12 feet high, of which 34 of various sizes stand in the ground and support eight larger ones, as at Stonehenge. They make a long square of 63 feet by 12, lying north-west and south-east, and cut in two by a line across it.]

CORPS-NUDS (17 kil.), *i.e.* Naked Bodies, has a very old church, and 2,400 population.

At 18 kil. further is Rennes (*see* Route 90).

ROUTE 74.

Nantes to Vannes, Lorient, Quimper and Brest.

Distance, 304 kil., or 189½ miles.

NANTES, as in Route 71.

LA TEMPLE (23 kil.)

LA MOERE (11 kil.), close to Saveny, which is a sous-préfecture in department Loire-Inférieure, of 2,000 people, where the Vendéans were finally routed, December, 1793. Here the road turns off to Guerande and Croisic, (*see* Route 71.)

PONT CHATEAU (15 kil.), on a small stream,

navigable to St. Nazaire, on the Loire. Population, 3,600.

La Roche-Bernard (19 kil.), in department Morbihan, a small port on the Vilaine (16 kil. from the sea), which is crossed by a suspension bridge, 582 feet long, 106 above water.

[About 12 kil. to the south-west, on the road to Croisic, is Herbignac, near the ruined château of Beuronet, with its round towers, &c. Further on near Croisic, is Piriac, a small granite-built bathing place, opposite Belle Ile.—At 24 kil. to the north-east of Roche-Bernard, up the Vilaine, where the Oust joins, is

Redon, a sous-préfecture (in department Ille-et-Vilaine) of 4,500 souls, and a small port, having a good trade in slate, grain, salt, beer, honey, coarse woollens, &c. Its walls were pulled down, 1588. Since a fire, only the tower is left of St. Sauveur's gothic church, which belonged to the abbey here. The clock-tower (horloge) is worth notice, as well as Beaumont château, which includes some ancient towers. *Hotel*—Du Lion d'Or (Golden Lion.]

Muzillac (15 kil.) At 24 kil. further is

Vannes. *Hotels*—Du Commerce; de France; du Dauphin; de la Croix Verte (Green Cross). Population, 11,500. Chief town of department Morbihan, seat of a bishop, and port of the fourth class, on the Marle, 4 kil. from the lagoon or Gulf of Morbihan, to which only small craft come. It was the old capital of the *Venetes*, and after being the scene of various events in the history of Brittany, was joined with it to France, 1532.

Though the neighbourhood is pleasant, it is a dull and ancient-looking place, with narrow streets; five of its six gates are left; le Port and la Gerenue are the chief promenades; a few small vessels are built here. St. Pierre *Cathedral*, rebuilt in the fifteenth century, has a new spire (since 1824), a high vault, two good figures of saints in wood, and the tombs of St. Vincent Ferrier and Bishop Bertin. The small chapel of the college deserves notice.

Carmes convent is now the bishop's palace; the former one, used as the prefect's hôtel, was rebuilt on the site of the château of La Motte. The salle de spectacle was the hall where the states of Brittany met for about seventy years. An ancient tower, called tour du Connétable, was part of Hermine castle, where Jean IV. caught Oliver de Clisson, the constable, and made him pay a heavy sum for his release. The dukes had another seat called the castle of Plaisance in this neighbourhood.

Two heads of 'Vannes et sa femme' (Vannes and his wife), are shewn by the town people, and are as celebrated as Gog and Magog. There is a library of 8,000 vols., besides hospices and old convents. Trade in grain, honey, beer, cider, eaux-de-vie, wine, cottons, lace, &c. Conveyances to Rennes, Brest, Lorient, Nantes.

[At 15 kil. to the north-east is *Elven*, noted for its curious machicolated tower, where the Duke of Brittany kept the Earl of Richmond a prisoner, when wrecked here after the battle of Tewkesbury. It was built, 1256, by a crusader, Eudon de Malestroit, and is eight-sided, each side being 30 to 38 feet long, and 4 to 15 feet thick; the height, in five stages, is 128 feet. Another machicolated tower, but round, stands near it, and is still older. Many druid stones are about.—At 25 kil. further towards Rennes is the sous-préfecture of

Ploermel, on the Duc (near the canal from Nantes to Brest), which makes a fine lake and cascade close by. It grew out of a château of the Bretagne dukes, and is considered so healthy that invalids are sent here for recovery. At the old church of the twelfth century are stained windows, and effigies, in armour, of John II. and III. of Brittany. Another church is at the Ursulines convent. Population, 4,700. *Hotels*—De France; du Commerce.

After passing the Obelisque des Trente, at Mi-Voye, where, according to a silly tradition, 30 Bretons beat 30 English in 1351, you come (12 kil. west of Ploermel) to Josseline castle, the fine gothic seat of the dukes of Rohan, above the Oust, including the room in which Oliver de Clisson (who rebuilt it after it had been razed by Henry II.) died 1407. The device of the present owners (who sprung from Rohan, to the north of this), '*à plus, à moins*,' is carved in the tracery of the balustrades.—At 13 kil. south-east of Vannes, towards the sea, is Sarzeau where *Le Sage*, the author of

'Gil Blas,' was born, and having many druid stones, besides the tumulus of Grand-Mont, 321 feet round, and 107 high. Beyond it on the sands are remains of Rhuys, or St. Gildas' abbey, which Abélard was prior of.]

AURAY (18 kil.), a town of 3,700 souls, noted for the battle of 1364, where Charles de Blois was killed, and his dukedom came to his opponent, John de Montfort. The old castle is gone; it stood near the promenade. St. Esprit romanesque church is large, and of the thirteenth century. At the Chartreuse chapel are the names of the royalists who fell in the Quiberon expedition, 1795. A few small craft are made here, and conveyances may be got to the druid mouuments at Carnac, &c., around the gulf of Morbihan.

[At 12 kil. south-west is *Carnac* or *Karnac*, the most remarkable druidical station in France, consisting of about 4,000 blocks of granite, arranged with tolerable regularity in eleven rows, running east and west, on a space 1½ miles long, and 300 feet wide; some looking like the small kistvaens in England, or balanced like the logan stones, and most of them from 4 to 19 feet high. Their origin is unknown; but, like those in England (where there are usually but two rows) they are supposed to refer to serpent worship. Many remains of this class are about here; as at Locmariaker (12 kil. east-south-east), at the Gulf of Morbihan's mouth, which some say was the roman *Dorioricum*. A circus and roman way may be traced, and it has a great dolmen (or kistvaen), called the Table de César, and a colossal menhir (logan stone) on the ground, as much as 67 feet long. Others at Sarzeau (as above), and Ploermel and Erdeven (north-west of Carnac).—About 10 kil. to the south-west of Carnac is

Quiberon, on the long, sandy presqu'ile, or peninsula, of that name, off which Hawke defeated the French fleet, 1759, but which is more notorious for the unfortunate descent of 1795, made by a body of emigrés under British protection, who were defeated and shot by the republican leaders. —At 13 kil. south-west is *Belle-Ile*, or *Belleisle*, one of the largest of French islands, having, at St. Palais, an old château of its marquises. It belonged to Quimperlé abbey in the tenth century; and was held by the English, 1761-3. The lighthouse is 276 feet high. The Nantes steamer stops here. Houat and Hœdic are near it.]

LANDEVAN (15 kil.), at the head of a creek from the sea, and 19 kil. from Port Louis, has some grottoes near it.

HENNEBON (13 kil.), where five or six roads meet, is a small port near the Blavet's mouth, up which the English fleet sailed to the support of the Countess of Montfort, when she was besieged in her castle (of which a few remains are left) by Charles de Blois, 1342. It has a gothic church of the fourteenth century, a suspension (instead of its ancient) bridge, and parts of old walls and an abbey. A few small vessels trade from it. There are mineral springs near. The direct road to Quimperlé is 16 kil. nearer than by Lorient.

[About 20 kil. to the north-east is *Baud* (population, 5,000), with a lead mine and very old chapel near a fountain. Near it, at Quinpilly château, is a granite figure of a woman, in the egyptian style, brought from a temple which stood on Castannec hill, near Bieuzy (a little north).—Further on (22 kil.), towards the head of the Blavet, is

Pontivy, a sous-préfecture and old place, including a New Town, begun by Bonaparte, who called it Napoleon-ville. Population, 6,500. Parts of the old walls, and the chateau of the dukes of Rohan are left. The Nantes and Brest canal passes here; linen is made. *Hotels*—Des Voyageurs (Travellers); de la Grande Maison.]

LORIENT (10 kil.), a sous-préfecture, seat of a maritime prefect, fortress of the third class, and naval port, near the mouth of the Blavet, & Scorf (5 kil. from the Bay of Biscay), having a dockyard and population of 20,000. It was a little fishing village when given, 1666, to the French East India Company, from whom it received its name, L'Orient, or the East. Upon their dissolution, the crown took it, 1764. The English had attempted it without success, 1746, when they landed at Pouldu, but were driven off by the Count of Tinteniac.

It is well built, the best houses being on the Quai, and in Place Royale; in the market place is a granite pillar to Bisson, a famous sailor. A signal tower, on a hill to the south (121 feet high), where the observatory stands, commands the best view of the town and dock-yards, including the prefect's hôtel, mast house, building slips for frigates and steamers, foundries, block-factory (poulierie), lazaretto on Ile St. Michel, and the military and seamen's barracks, the latter being the old buildings of the Company, where Law, the projector of the Mississippi scheme, lived. There is a small theatre, and a parish church, begun on so large a plan that part was pulled down to finish the rest. The Hôtel de Ville is good. Trade in wax, honey, beer, sardines (pilchards), &c. *Hotels*—De France; des Etrangers; de la Croix Verte (Green Cross).

Conveyances: by coach, daily, to Brest, Bordeaux, Morlaix; by steamer to Bordeaux weekly.

[At 4 kil. south, on the other side of the Scorf, near the mouth, is the bathing place of Port Louis, built and fortified by Louis XIII., and called Port Liberté in the revolution. About 10 kil. south-west of this is Ile de Groix, which has several caves and druid stones, and produces froment d'Espagne (Spanish wheat). It was saved from the English fleet in the last century by the curé, who, while the men were away fishing, dressed up the women, and moved them about like bodies of troops, and so deceived the enemy. Large conger eel, &c. are caught. The light-house on the north-west corner is 1*4 feet high.]

QUIMPERLE (20 kil.), a sous-préfecture, in department Finisterre, of 5,700 souls, in a pretty hollow on the Elle, where the Isole joins it, and makes a little port at the quay. The dukes of Brittany had a seat here, called Carnaet. St. Michel's gothic church stands on a hill above, with two convents, &c., forming a very picturesque group. The old benedictine convent is now the mairie, and has the ancient romanesque church of Ste. Croix behind it.

Conveyances, daily, to Nantes, Lorient, Morlaix.

ROSPORDEN (25 kil.) on the Aren.

[At 10 kil. to the south-west is Concarneau, a thriving little port on the bay of La Forest, on a fortified point or island. It was taken by Duguesclin, 1373, and by the Leaguers in 1579; the harbour is rocky.]

At 21. kil further is.

QUIMPER, or Quimper Corentin. *Hotels*—de l'Epée (Sword); de Provence; de France. Population, 9,700. Chief town of department Finisterre, seat of a bishopric, &c., on a pleasant hill-side, where the Odet and Fleyr meet at the head of a pretty creek, 15 kil. from the sea. It was the capital of part of Cornouailles or Bas-Breton, and ravaged by Charles le Blois, 1345. Ships of 300 tons may come up to the quay, lined with gothic-looking houses; the old town is enclosed by ancient walls and towers; the best point of view is at the platform, on the hill behind the préfecture, some hundred feet high, where a promenade is laid out.

The *Cathedral*, one of the best in Brittany, was begun, 1239, but not finished till 200 years after; length, 302 feet; width, 65 feet. It has a fine portal (once decorated by statues, &c.), between large battlemented towers, with two spires, and long narrow windows in them; the entrance in Rue Ste. Catherine is well proportioned, and has escutcheons of Breton families upon it. Other buildings are the Churches of Locmaria and St. Mathieu, the large jesuits' college, palais de justice, the public baths, barracks, and military hospital, bibliothèque, salle de spectacle, &c. There are also a school of navigation, a pepinière or district nursery; and the neighbourhood offers several good points of view. Pottery and small vessels are made. Trade in grain, wine, spirits, wax, honey, butter, coarse linen, &c.

Conveyances, to Nantes, Brest, Rennes, &c.

[At 16 kil. to the south-west, in the small port of Pont l'Abbey; 11 kil. beyond which, is Penmarck or Penmarch near the coast of the Bay of Audierne, as wild and stormy as the Land's End, having a light-house 135 feet high, and lined with granite rocks, one of which, the Torche, is cut off by a narrow channel called the Saut de Moine (the Monk's Leap), where the sea is most furious. —At 9 kil. west-north-west of Quimper, is Douarnenez, a fishing village on the bay of that name, with a good trade in pilchards. Beyond it (30 kil.), is Plogoff, on the Bec (beak or point) du Raz, which has a light 259 feet high, on the cliffs, which are continually undermined by the sea. One terrible gulf is called the Baie des Trépassés

(Deadmen's bay). The desolate Ile de Sein, on which a few hardy fishermen live, is 10 kil. off; its light is 148 feet high. It was on this dismal coast that Pellew, in the 'Indefatigable,' 1799, drove the 'Droits de l'Homme' ashore, with 1,500 men on board. She was one of Hoche's fleet which invaded Ireland.]

Chateaulin (24 kil), a sous-préfecture of 2,800 souls, on the pretty valley of the Aulne (which runs down to Brest roads), has an old château, and some well wooded points of view around. Small craft come up to the town, but the Brest steamer stops at Port de Launay, 4 kil. below. At Eleuan chapel, near the town, is an intermitting spring, which rises and falls with the tide in the sea. *Hotel*—de la Poste.

[At 24 kil. east of it. up the Aulne, is Châteauneuf-le-Faou, a pretty little village among windmills, where the canal from Nantes to Brest falls in.—Above it is Carhaix, a very old village, with a church of the sixth century. Corret, the republican soldier, called La Tour d'Auvergne, was born here.—About 20 kil. north-east, at Logueffret, is the beautiful fall of St. Darbot, pouring over a granite rock, more than 200 feet down. Between 10 and 20 kil. further are the valuable lead works of Huelgoët and Poullaouen, the former (650 feet deep), opened for three centuries, the latter (where the ore is smelted) since 1741. They yield 500,000 kilogrammes of metal and 700 of silver; and employ about 500 men.]

Le Faou (19 kil.), a little place at the bottom of a creek in the Brest roads, with curious old carved timber houses. The green Kersanton stone is worked near this.

At 19 kil. further is Landerneau; and 20 kil. beyond it is Brest (described in Route 90).

ROUTE 75.

Nantes to Napoleon-Vendee, Rochelle, Niort, Rochefort, Saintes, Cognac, Angouleme and Bordeaux.

By malle-poste to Bordeaux 349 kil., or 216½ miles, in 22 hours.

Aigrefeuille (21 kil.) About 14 kil. east is Clisson (as in Route 76.)

[To the west, about — kil., is Les Lucs, a small village among rocks and druid stones called menhirs and dolmens.]

Montaigu (13 kil.), in department La Vendée, on the Main, has an old château, and was built in the Vendéan war. At 37 kil. further is Napoleon-Vendée.

Napoleon-Vendee. *Hotels*—de l'Europe, des Etrangers, des Trois Pigeons. Population 5,700, —This small capital, of department Vendée, was formerly called Roche-sur-Yon, from an ancient castle on the precipitous rock over the Yon, which Oliver Clisson took from the English, 1373, and which came to the Trêmouilles and Bourbons, and was razed by Louis XIII. On the site is a large caserne or barrack, near the statue of Napoléon, put up 1844. Between it and the modern town is the old bourg and its steep streets. Bonaparte made the town the head of the department, 1805, altering the name to Napoleon-Ville; this was changed to Bourbon-Vendée, 1815, in return for the attachement shewn by the Vendéans to that family; it is for the present called Napoléon-Vendée.

The préfecture is an immense pile, round three sides of a square, including a library of 5,000 volumes, &c. In Place Royale are some public buildings and hotels, with a bronze, by Maindron, of General Travot, a native and the 'pacificateur de la Vendée, 1838,' when the Vendéans again rose in behalf of the Bourbons. The church is in the greek style, with a doric portico, two domes, &c. Behind is the theatre, and a public halle. It has a good hospital and government stud.

Coaches to Nantes, Bordeaux, Les Sables, &c.

[From Napoléon-Vendée, to the west, you pass Fontenettes or Venansault (6 kil.), which has ruins of an abbey, with a good mineral spring in the midst. La Mothe Achard (12 kil.), is the next place. Then comes

Sables d' Olonne (15 kil.) a sous-préfecture in department Vendée (population 5,900), bathing place and port on the sands (sables) of the bay of Biscay. Batteries defend the harbour, which admits vessels of 200 tons. *Hotels*—de France, de Cheval Blanc (White Horse) —Ile Dieu is about 12 leagues north-west.]

From Napoléon-Vendée, on the road to La Rochelle, you pass

Luçon (32 kil.), a bishopric since the fourteenth century, and small town (population 4,300), in a marshy spot, having a gothic cathedral, with a tower spire of 212 feet. Trade in grain, wine, &c. A canal runs down to the sea at Baie d'Aiguillon.

[*Fontenay-le-Comte* (27 kil. east), a sous-préfecture in department Vendée, and prettily placed on a hill over the river Vendée in a plain where four great roads meet. Population 7,963. The college or high school is well built; the fountain which gives name to the town, is rather elegant. Notre Dame church is a fine gothic structure, with a well-proportioned spire of 269 feet, a good portal, a copy of Raphael's Transfiguration, and one of Lefèvre's best productions over the altar. Trade in grain, timber, and wine.

Hotel—Du Chapeau Rouge.

At 31 kil. further is Niort (*see* Route 80.)].

MARANS (27 kil.), a port in a marshy spot, connected with the sea by canals and river Sèvre, with 1,404 souls, trading in corn, wine, and a farinaceous food called minot. It stands in department Charente-Inférieure.

At 26 kil. further is

La Rochelle. *Hotels*—De la Poste; de France; de la Croix d'Or (Golden Cross); du Commerce, &c. Population 14,200. Capital of department Charente Inférieure, (part of Poitou), seat of a bishop, and military division, &c., and port of the third class, on a small inlet of the Bay of Biscay, opposite Iles de Ré and d'Oléron, enclosing the Roads, which are entered by the strait called Pertuis d'Antioche. It belonged to Henry II. of England, through his wife Eleanor; was taken from the English by Duguesclin 1372; and became the head quarters of the Huguenots from 1557 till 1629, when Richelieu (Louis XIII. being present) took it after a memorable *siege* of thirteen months, (which brought down the population from 27,000 to 5,000), by running a great dyke across the harbour, which kept out the English fleet under Buckingham. It is still seen at low water, between Point Coreille and Fort Louis, nearly a mile long, with a passage in the middle for shipping.

Vessels of 500 tons may get into the harbour, which consists of two docks surrounded by quays and houses, whence the Maubec canal crossed by three bridges runs up the town. The fortifications were planned by Vauban; of the five old gates, one called Porte de l'Horloge, is a clock-tower of the sixteenth century; the streets are well built, and most of the houses have covered porticoes. Place du Château, where the old castle of Vauclair stood, has a fine prospect of the sea; and so has the Mail outside the walls.

At the Hôtel de Ville, a building in the renaissance style, they show Henry IVth's chamber, and the chair and portrait of the mayor Guiton, who led the people in the siege.

Besides the cathedral (which is of no mark), and three or four churches (St. Sauveur's gothic tower, 216 feet high, is used for a shot factory), the bishop's palace, priests' seminary, &c., there are a bourse or exchange, St. Louis' hospital, a public library of 20,000 volumes, botanic garden and museum, the arsenal and salle d'armes (armoury), new abattoirs or slaughter houses, good bathing rooms (built 1827), and a protestant chapel.

Rochelle salt (a purgative) was discovered here by Seignette, the chemist. Reaumur the philosopher (whose division of the thermometer is in general use in France), Billaud-Varennes the conventionist, President Dupatz, and Admiral Duperre, were natives. Trade in wine, spirits, wood, salt, iron, cheese, oil, fish, &c. Pottery, glass, refined sugar, &c., are made and a little ship building carried on.

Rev. MM. Fau and Delmas are protestant pastors here.

Conveyances to Rochefort, Nantes, Bordeaux, Poitiers; steamers daily, to Ile de Ré, 2½ and 1½ fr.

[Ile de Ré, 4 kil. from the nearest land, from which it is divided on the north by the Pertuis Breton, is 27 kil. long, and in the middle only 2 broad, being sandy throughout, and yielding good wine and salt. It is strengthened by forts and a citadel at St. Martin, which Buckingham tried to take, 1628. At an old abbey here, was found, 1730, the tomb of Eudes, Duke of Aquitaine, and his wife, he having a copper crown on. The people (17,000) are fishers.]

From La Rochelle, on the road to Bordeaux, you pass

TROIS-CANONS (14 kil.), to the west of which is Ile d'Aix, a strongly fortified rock in the Basque Roads, where Lord Cochrane with his frigates and fireships, in April 1809, attacked the French fleet of nine sail of the line, burning three of them, &c.

Rochefort (17 kil.) a sous-préfecture of 19,000 souls, seat of a maritime prefect, and a naval dock-yard, in a flat part of the Charente, 16 kil. from the sea (at Rade des Basques or *Basque Roads*, inside Ile d' Oleron), was founded 1666, by Louis XIV., and attempted 1757 by the English (who held all this country till the time of Charles VII.), and again in 1809 by Lord Cochrane, when he burnt part of the French fleet. It is fortified and protected by forts on the river, up which large ships may come to the quays; the streets are regular, and the houses not more than two stories high. A large fountain stands in Place d'Armes.

Rochefort has a church rebuilt 1839; an exchange, college, navigation and other schools, public library of 10,000 volumes, foundling hospital, cemetery, and the civil hospital, built by the intendent Bigon, who improved the town generally 1688-1710; but its most important feature is the *Arsenal* at the Port Militaire. This includes the large chantiers de construction (building slips) and floating basin; ateliers des fonderies, for cannon and steam engines; masthouses, workshops, saw mills; corderie or rope house, 1,300 feet long; salle d'armes or armoury, and gun wharf; magasin de vivre or victualling office, an old building, in which are 40 ovens and machinery for making buiscuits; store houses 1300 feet long; the commandant's hotel, close to the public gardens; three casernes or barracks for the sailors and marines; the Bagne or convict depôt, the inmates of which were sent off to Cayenne, 1852; and outside the town, the hôpital de la Marine, a large building by Touffaire, with 1300 beds in it, a museum of natural history, a library of 5,000 volumes, besides the public library. An avenue called the Cours d' Ablois leads up to it.

There are some iron and copper works, with an horlogerie or clock factory; trade in wine cognac brandy, grain, wood, fish, salt, &c. It was here that Napoleon, 15th July, 1815, gave himself up to Captain Maitland in the Bellerophon, stationed off the coast to prevent his escape to America. Captain Doré, now a senator, formed a plan for smuggling the fugitive away, but he could not pass the British squadron. Rev. M. Puaux is protestant pastor here.

Hotels—Du Grand Bacha (Pasha), in Rue Royale; des Etrangers; de la Poste; de la Coquill d'Or (Golden Shell). Excellent vegetables and fish are to be had.

Conveyances by coach, to Tonnay-Charente, Rochelle, Marennes, Royan, Bordeaux, Saintes, Nantes, &c.; by steamer, daily, up the Charente to Saintes.

[At 20 kil. to the south-west, is
Marennes, a sous-préfecture of 4,600 souls, in a marshy spot, and noted for its oysters, beans, and peas. It has a trade in salt, wine, brandy, &c., and is near the mouth of the Seudre, opposite the long flat *Ile d' Oléron*, the roman *Uliaris*, which supplies good vegetables, brandy, and salt, (population 16,000). Under the English rule it had a bishop, and the people were so enterprising, that it gave name to the Ley d'Oléron or laws of Oléron, a code of maritime laws, at one time adopted by all Europe, and ascribed without authority to Richard I. At 10 kil. south-east of Marennes, is the feudal Tour de Brou, as old as the sixth or seventh century. About 23 kil. south of Marennes, is *Royan*, a bathing place at the Gironde's mouth, with the light tower of Cordouan outside, 207 feet high. As a stronghold of the Huguenots, it was taken by Louis XIII. A steamer runs hence to Bordeaux in the season.]

TONNAY-CHARENTE (8 kil.) on the north bank of the Charente (here crossed by a fine suspension bridge from rock to rock, under which large merchantmen may easily pass), has an old château, and a great trade in wine and cognac *brandy*, which is exported hence to England. Population 3,400.

English Consul, J. F. Close. *Hotels*—Du Faisand; du Point du Jour (Break of Day).

ST. HIPPOLYTE (3 kil.) on the opposite side of the Charente.

[About 50 kil. to the east, is *St. Jean d' Angély*, a sous-préfecture of 6,200 souls, in a pleasant part of the Boutenne, having an old benedictine abbey (now a school), and a large trade in cognac.]

ST. PORCHAIRE (13 kil.), on the little river Epine, has a good gothic church.

[A little east of this, on the Charente, are the quarries of St. Savienien (which furnished stone for the new bridge at Bordeaux), and the old castle of Taillebourg.]

SAINTES (14 kil.), a sous-préfecture of 10,500

souls, and a very old town, once the capital of the *Santones*, who gave their name to it, and to the province of *Saintonge*, which, as part of Guienne, came to Henry II. of England, through his wife Eleanor. The Northmen took it, 850, and for a few years it was chief town of the department.

Though pleasantly seated under a hill on the Charente, it consists mostly of small dirty streets and poor houses, with a good walk on Quai Blair. Among its roman remains are, a plain triumphal *Arch* (lately restored, and removed to a more convenient site), on the roman way to Poitiers, built of large uncemented stones, and dedicated to Germanicus, Tiberius, &c, by C. J. Rufus, a priest; parts of a small *Amphitheatre*, once about 70 feet long, in a valley outside the town; with traces of a circus near it. Fragments of baths have been found on the river, which is crossed by a suspension bridge, at the Cours Royal built 1841-2, in place of the old stone one.

The cathedral church, with its fine pinnacled steeple, was rebuilt 1568 (on the site of Charlemagne's), except a good portal of the fourteenth century, which has several niched figures, &c., in its roof. St. Eutrope's church, near the amphitheatre, has an excellent spire, built by Louis XI., and an early norman crypt. To an old abbey here, Eleanor retired, after her separation from Louis le Jeune.

The Hôtel de Ville was the bishop's palace; there are also a college, with a museum and library of 25,000 vols. attached; a district pepinière, or nursery; salle de spectacle (theatre), &c.

Bernard de Palissy, who, after many trials and failures, made his discovery of enamelled pottery, was born here, about 1563. Trade in Cognac brandy, wine, grain, cattle, stone, &c. *Hotels*—Des Messageries; du Bateau à Vapeur (Steamboat).

Rev. J. Dolon is protestant pastor here.

Coveyances to Angoulême (by Cognac, up the Charente), Bordeaux, Niort, &c.

[At 10 kil. north-east, is *St. Vénérand*, which has a spring rising in a rocky gap, and running through a narrow valley. Not far from it, at Doubet, are a château and a small part of a roman fountain and aqueduct which carried the water here to the arena at Saintes.

At 20 kil. to the west, near Sablonceaux, are some other *roman* works; a stone tower, called the Pile de Pirelongue, 103 feet high, and 19 feet square at the base; and another tower, or turret, called Turris Longini, 13 feet high, in the middle of the Camp de César.—At Prieuré des Arènes, 6 kil. south, near the Bordeaux road, are remains of a roman villa, baths, &c. — A temple has been opened at St. Saloine.]

Le Jard (12 kil.), from which a road turns off to Royan and Mortagne, on the Gironde.

Pons (9 kil.), in a pretty valley on the Seugne, has the tower of its old château left, 83 feet high, which the Huguenots held against Louis XIII. It possessed three churches, &c., before the revolution; and has three or four small bridges (ponts), which may have given it its name.

St. Genis (11 kil.), whence roads turn off to Port Maubert (on the Gironde) and Jonzac.

Mirambeau (12 kil.), has a church, built by the English, and a ruined château, which belonged to Mirabeau's family, whence there is a fine prospect.

Etauliers (17 kil.), on a little river which runs down to the Gironde, opposite Pauillac.

Blaye (13 kil.), a sous-préfecture of 4,300 souls, in department Gironde, and a pilot station on the east bank of the Garonne. It was the ancient *Blavia*, and had a strong castle, taken by the Huguenots, 1568, and then by the Leaguers. This now makes part of the citadel, on a rock in Upper Town, commanding the river (about 4 kil. broad), in conjunction with the fort of le Pâté (or the Pie), on an island in the midst, and Fort Médoc on the opposite side. In the old gothic tower of the castle the Duchesse de Berri was confined, 1833.

A good mairie, hospital, theatre, &c., are in the Lower Town, where the merchants and pilots live. At the Austin abbey here, King Caribert of Aquitaine was buried, 631. Ships are built; and there is a good trade in corn, wine, brandy, oil, fruit, and timber. *Hotels*—De l'Union; de France. Coaches to Bordeaux, Rochelle, &c.; steamers to Bordeaux, Pauillac, and Royan.

Cubzac (29 il.), on the Dordogne, here crossed by a splendid wire *suspension bridge*, in five bends, about 2,950 feet long, 59 feet wide, and 98 feet above the water. It was built 1835-9, by Fortuné-de-Vergey, for £120,000. The Bordeaux merchants have large warehouses at this spot, where the high road from Paris falls in.

BORDEAUX is 21 kil. further (*see* Route 65).

ROUTE 76.

Poitiers to Nantes, through La Vendee.

Distance, 177 kil. or 110 miles.

AYRON (25 kil.)

PARTHENAY (24 kil.), on a slope of the Thouet, a sous-préfecture, of 4,700 population, in department Deux-Sèvres (part of Vendée), in a country of hills, valleys, lakes, and forests. It was strongly fortified, and suffered in the English and religious, as well as in the Vendéan wars of the first and later revolution (chiefly in 1793 and 1832). Parts of an old castle of the twelfth century, flanked with five or six towers, are seen; also St. John's church, of the ninth century, and the clock-tower, 74 feet high, once part of the prison. Coarse woollens are made. *Hotel*—Du Cheval Blanc (White Horse).

[At *Airvault* (18 kil. north-north-east), are an old castle, and the gothic church (with a spire on four pillars) of a convent, destroyed in the religious wars.—Secondigny (14 kil. west-south-west) up the Thouet, has remains of its old walls and castle.]

BRESSUIRE (31 kil.), on a hill over the Argenton, is a small sous-préfecture of 1,900 persons, and had good manufactures of cloth till the Vendéan war at the revolution, which left but one house and the old granite church, with its tower of 360 feet. It is again reviving, and makes handkerchiefs and woollens.

[*Argenton-le-Château* (18 kil. north), was also destroyed in the Vendéan war. Trade in white and red wines, and woollens.—At 20 kil. east of it is

Thouars, in a fine part of the Thouet, above which rise the old turreted walls, begun by Pepin and finished by the English, from whom Duguesclin took it, 1312. The Vendéans captured it, 1793. On a granite rock, 108 feet high, stands the old high-walled château, built, 1635, by Marie de la Tremouille, forming a centre and wings, 393 feet long, which, with its garden and terraces, is now the mairie.

Close to it is St. Medard's ancient church, made up in fact, by three or four chapels, one over the other. St. Laon has a fine square tower. One turret on the walls, called Tour du Prince de Galles (Wales), is a prison. Population, 2,300. There are also a college and two hospices.]

CHATILLON-SUR-SEVRE (22 kil.) was once fortified, but ruined by the religious and Vendéan wars.

MORTAGNE (18 kil.), in department Vendée, where the Vendéans were defeated in the civil war of 1793. There are an old convent and part of a castle which Oliver Clisson took from the English, 1373. It was the roman *Segora*, and is prettily placed on the river Sèvre-Nantaise.

[*Les Herbiers* (12 kil. south-west), on the Napoleon-Vendée road, has a ruined church, and remains of the fortifications built when the English held it. From some roman remains found near it, some think it was the ancient *Herbadilla*. Population, 2,826.—At *Chollet* (8 kil. north-east of Mortagne), on the road to Angers, is a castle destroyed in the Vendéan wars.]

TORFOU (15 kil.) has a column (shaped like a factory chimney) commemorating a victory gained by the Vendéans in the same wars.

[About 7 kil. east, are the picturesque ruins of *Tiffauges Castle*, with its machicolated walls and towers, spreading over a rocky height above the Sévre, where the Creonne joins. It was built by the counts of Thouars, 1119, came to the famous Barbe-Blue (Marshal Gilles de Retz, or 'Blue Beard'), and was dismantled by Richelieu. It commands a fine prospect. A colony of Theiphalian Goths settled here, 475, and gave name to the town.]

CLISSON (14 kil.) stands above the picturesque valley of the Sèvre, where the Maine joins it, with the old battered ruins of Clisson castle, which belonged to the Constable de Clisson, a soldier of the fourteenth century. Parts of the walls, ditches, keep, great hall, &c., remain; the well, into which 400 Vendéans were thrown by the republican general, Kleber, 1793, is filled up. At the country seat of La Garenne, they shew the grotto of Heloise, the bath of Diana, temple of Vesta, &c.

TOURNEBRIDE (15 kil.)

At 13 kil. further is Nantes (*see* Route 71.)

ROUTE 77.

Poitiers to Limoges.

Distance 123 kil. or 76 miles.

POITIERS, as in Route 65.

CHAUVIGNY (23 kil.), on a rock above the Vienne, has an old castle, and ancient church, curiously carved; with a trade in wine and druggets.

LUSSAC-LE-CHATEAU (28 kil.), up the Vienne, so called from its old castle.

[At 12 kil. east is *Montmorillon*, a sous-préfecture (population, 3,700), on the Gartempe, in a pretty part, but ill built, having a seminary, hospital, &c., and noted for its biscuits and macaroons. Paper and linen are also made. It is further remarkable for a chapel or temple, partly romanesque, eight-sided and vaulted, over a vault or crypt lit with narrow slits. Four quaint groups, of thirteen figures, are carved above the chapel door, composed of women holding snakes and toads to their breasts, young and bearded men, a man and woman kissing, &c., and supposed to represent the Vices, and other emblems. *Hotel*—Du Grand Monarque.]

BUSSIERE-POITEVINE (22 kil.)

BELLAC (10 kil.), on the slant over the Vincon, is a sous-préfecture in department Haut-Vienne (population, 3,800), and is known by the old castle at the top of the hill, now used as a palais de justice and prison. It was attacked by Pepin's son Robert, and by the Leaguers in the sixteenth century, when they tried to throw a bridge across to the castle. Near are several druid stones, as at Borderiè, Blond, Berneuil, Pierre-Belle, &c.

[Le Dorat (12 kil. north), in a charming part of the Sèvre, commands extensive prospects, and has an ancient, fortified church of the tenth century (the walls being lined with towers and battlements), below which is a crypt called Basse-Eglize. Barometers, weights, cottons, woollens, are made. Population, 2,240. Glass is made at Danac.]

CONORE (20 kil.)

At 20 kil. further is Limoges (*see* Route 50).

ROUTE 80.

Poitiers to Niort and La Rochelle.

Distance 139 kil. or 76 miles.

POITIERS, as in Route 65.

CROUTELLE (7 kil.) is noted for the cunning of its people, so that 'finesse de Croutelle' is a proverb.

LUSIGNAN (17 kil.), on the Vanne, in a pleasant spot in department Vienne, has a good view from the site of the great castle, which was taken and razed by the Duke of Montpensier, 1574, and which gave name to Guy of Lusignan, the crusader, who became King of Jerusalem and Cyprus. The family tombs are at the capital of Cyprus, and his descendant, the King of Sardinia, still claims those dominions through him. Good macaroons are made, and there is a trade in grain, seed, &c. Population, 2,500.

VILLEDIEU-DU-PERRON (14 kil.)

ST. MAIXENT (15 kil.)

[At 14 kil. north is Champdeniers, which has manufactures of hats and tiles, and cattle fairs, which the Spanish dealers attend to buy mules, &c.]

LA CRECHE (10 kil.)

At 13 kil. further is

NIORT, 79 kil., or 49 miles from Poitiers. *Hotels*—De France; des Postes; du Raisin-de-Bourgogne (Burgundy Grape); de l'Aigle d'Or (Golden Eagle); du Grand Cerf (Stag). *Cafés*—Français (in Rue Royale); des Colonnes, &c. Population, 17,300. Capital of the department Deux-Sèvres (formerly of the Niortaise district, a part of Poitou), on a hill-side over the Sèvre-Niortaise, has good promenades, and is on the whole well laid out. Notre Dame, one of its two churches, was built in the gothic style by the English, and has a tower 2v6 feet high. The Hôtel-de-Ville was the palace of Eleanor d'Aquitaine, and has an old horloge, or clock.

But the greatest curiosity is the *Château*, of which the donjon is now the maison d'arret, or prison; Madame de Maintenon's father was confined here when she was born. Other objects of notice are,—the college; musée and school of design; a bibliothèque of 20,000 vols., (many rare,) besides valuable MSS.; the theatre; public baths; large barracks; hospital for 400; the Fontaine de Vivier, an artesian well, 108 feet deep, which supplies the town; and the Passage du Commerce, a covered way, in Rue Royale. A pretty spot in the neighbourhood is the Cambon brook; some druid stones are also to be seen.

Manufactures of chamois leather for gloves and breeches, flannel, &c., and angélique (a sweetmeat); and a trade in grain, wine, vegetables (which are plentiful). Its fairs for cattle, horses, and goods in general, were so famous. and so convenient for match-making, that the ages of marriageable girls were reckoned by the number they had attended—'*Elle a tant de foires, plus seize ans*' (She is so many fairs more than sixteen years old). Two large fairs are now held at Champdeniers above mentioned.

Conveyances to Poitiers, Napoleon-Vendée, La Rochelle, Nantes, Bordeaux, &c.

From Niort, on the road to La Rochelle, you pass

Frontenay (10 kil.)

Mauze (13 kil.), a little village, noted for its breed of asses, and with a good trade in spirits, wine, and linseed oil. The road to Rochefort turns off here.

Ferrieres (15 kil.). Then Groland (16 kil.) And La Rochelle is 9 kil. further (*see* Route 75).

ROUTE 81.

Angouleme to Cognac and Saintes.

Distance, 141 kil. or 88 miles.

Angouleme, as in Route 65.

Hiersac (14 kil.) is noted for its red wines.

Jarnac (15 kil.), with a population of 2,400, and a good brandy trade, is at the suspension bridge on the Charente, in the middle of vast meadows, and is famous for the battle of 1569, when the Duke of Anjou defeated the Huguenots, under Coligny and the Prince of Condé, who was killed.

Cognac (65 kil.) a sous-préfecture, and smal town of 3,409 population, on the south side of the Charente, commanded by an old castle, and standing at the west end of the beautiful country furnishing the *brandies* so well known in Europe. The tract belonging to the growers of La Societié Vignicole Champenoise, who profess to sell the genuine article, is within a circle, 20 to 25 miles in diameter, near the Charente having Segoniac for the centre, and taking in Cognac on the west, Jarnac on the north, Chateauneuf on the east, and nearly to Barbazieux, on the south. Francis I. was born here, under an elm, in the castle grounds. *Hotels*—De France; du Faisan (Pheasant); Trois Marchands (Three Merchants).

Saintes (27 kil.), Rochefort (39 kil.), Rochelle (31 kil.); for which *see* Route 75.

ROUTE 82.

Bordeaux to Tour de Cordovan.

From Bordeaux (as in Route 65), down the west side of the Garonne, in the wine country of *Médoc*, you pass

Blanquefort, which belonged to the Black Prince; then La Barde; *Château Margaux* (noted for its 'first growth' claret) opposite Blaye; Beycheville, and Château Léoville (second growths); *Château Latour* (first growth); *Château Lafitte* (another first growth), near which is Pauillac, a port on the river, 44 kil. from Bordeaux, where large ships stop.

The best clarets (premier crus, or first growths) are grown on the east side of *Médoc*, near the Garonne, on a most unpicturesque gravel strip, about two miles broad, and 50 to 80 feet above the river. The vines are trained about 2 feet high in open fields; vintage takes place in September. The grape-plague appeared here 1852.

Lesparre (68 kil. from Bordeaux), a small sous-préfecture in department Gironde (population, 1,232), among vineyards and meadows. Passing through good pasture land, you come to Soulac (25 kil.), at the mouth of the Garonne, opposite Royan bathing place, and near the *Tour de Cordouan*, a round solid light-house of three stories, 234½ feet high, built 1611, by Louis de Foix, having large refractors on Fresnel's system.

ROUTE 83.

Bordeaux to Tete de Buch.

By rail 53 kil., or 33 miles; twice a day, or in about an hour.

The Stations are—

	kil.		kil.		kil.
Pessac	6	Marcheprime	4	Teich	3
Saint-Médard	2	Biard	2	Cantaranne..	2
Gazinet	3	Argentières..	3	Mestras	2
Toctouco ...	4	Canauleye ...	2	Gujan	1
Pierroton ...	3	Cameleyre ...	3	La Hume ...	3
Verdery	2	Facture	1	La Teste......	2
Chemin de M.	3	Lamothe	3		

Bordeaux, as in Route 65.

Toctouco (15 kil.), or Touche tout doucement,—*i.e.*, touch softly, so called in patois, because the marsh is dangerously soft. Before you get to

Argentieres (16 kil.), you are in the country (but not the department) of Les *Landes*,—all sand, marsh, and pine trees, where the people walk about on tall stilts, or *xcanques*, with which they will sometimes go three leagues an hour. Les Grandes Landes stretch all the way to the Bayonne. The shepherds dress in sheepskins; each carries a gun at his back, for defence against the wolf, with a poële, or *frying-pan*, to serve for cooking. (*See* Mont-de-Marsan, in Route 65).

TETE, or TESTE DE BUCH (22 kil.), a port and bathing place, on a lagoon, called Bassin d' Arcachon, in a flat, dull spot, on the Bay of Biscay. Population, 3,500. *Hotels*—D' Arcachon; de la Providence.

ROUTE 84.

Bordeaux to Agen, Montauban, and Toulouse.

Distance, 253 kil., or 157 miles.

BORDEAUX, as in Route 65.

LANGON (46 kil.), in the same route, where the road to Toulouse turns off, up the Garonne, past the suspension bridge.

CAUDROT (9 kil.)

LA REOLE (9 kil.), a sous-préfecture in department Gironde, on the rocks above the Garonne (crossed by a suspension bridge), having remains of a pagan temple, called La Grand Ecole, and of a castle built by the Visigoths. It has also an intermittent spring, and another of a petrifying quality. Population 4,100. *Hotel*—Lafond. A steamer runs to Langon and Bordeaux. Ascending the river you come next to

MARMANDE (20 kil.), a sous-préfecture in department Lot-et-Garonne, and a bustling-place, (population 8,200,) with a bridge of one wide arch, a palais de justice, college, &c., and several fountains of excellent water. The trade is in grain, wine, fruits, eaux-de-vie, tobacco. *Hotel*—De la Providence. The steamer touches here.

TONNEINS (17 kil.), one of the most beautiful places in the department Lot-et-Garonne, in two parts, above the Garonne, here crossed by a suspension-bridge. Place de l'Esplanade, where an old castle once stood, commands a delightful view, which takes in even the Pyrenees. The houses are well built, but irregularly placed, which gives effect to the prospect of the town. Population 6,490. It has a government tobacco factory. *Hotels*—D'Angleterre; de France. The Bordeaux steamer comes up to this place.

AIGUILLON (11 kil.), on the Garonne, where the Lot joins it, (passing under a semi-arched bridge, built 1825), still shows the thick walls, towers, and turrets of the old castle of the ducs d'Aguillon, whose more modern seat is also here. Near it on the right, is part of a roman tower, called Tour de St. Côme. At 31 kil. further is Agen (*see* Route 60).

From Agen, on the road to Montauban and Toulouse, you pass

CROQUEHARDIT (10 kil.), and La Magistère (10 kil.), both on the Garonne, the latter being in department Tarn-et-Garonne.

MALAUSE (12 kil.), in the same department, is an old place, where many roman remains have been found, and has a ruined château. Population 1,500.

MOISSAC (14 kil.), in a cultivated hollow on the Tarn, at the new bridge, not far from the Garonne, is a sous-préfecture of 10,000 persons, and an ancient town, which suffered in the wars with the English, and the religious wars. It has remains of a rich abbey, founded by Clovis, which came to be attached to Cluni abbey, and governed by an abbey-knight,, a mixture of layman and churchman. The old *church* of this foundation, dedicated to St. Peter and St. Paul, has a porch covered with figures of the Annunciation, Adoration of the Wise Men, Flight into Egypt, the Apostles, &c.; while the capitals of the ruined cloisters are adorned with other bas-reliefs, some grotesque and indecent, of the Virtues and Vices. Trade in wine, saffron, grain, salt, &c. *Hotel*—Du Grand Soleil (Sun).

CASTEL-SARRASIN (7 kil.), another sous-préfecture, with 7,200 population, on the Garonne, where the Azin falls in (whence the name, Sur-Azin), is in a fertile spot, and well built, having remains of its old ramparts, two ancient gates, and a gothic church. The Abbé de Prades was a native. Woollen serges, &c., are made. *Hotel*—Le Grand St. Pierre. At about 20 kil. to the east, is MONTAUBAN.

LA VITARELLE (13 kil.)

[At 20 kil. to the south-west, is Beaumont, a well built little town, in the rich valley of the Gimone, with a good trade. Population 4,200.]

GRISOLLES (16 kil.), just past where the road

from Montauban falls in, has a church of the sixteenth century.

ST. JORY (12 kil.), on the Garonne. At 17 kil. further is Toulouse (*see* Route 50).

ROUTE 86.

Bordeaux to Auch, Tarbes, and Pau,

(THENCE TO OLORON, EAUX BONNES, ETC.)

Distance to Pau, 197 kil., or 122 miles.

ROQUEFORT (as in Route 65), 109 kil. from Bordeaux. It stands on the Douze, where the Estampon joins, among rocks, on which are the old castle and a modern château.

VILLENEUVE-DE-MARSAN (16 kil.), on the Midou, in a sandy plain, now partly cultivated.

CAZERES (15 kil.), where the road from Mont-de-Marsan falls in.

[*Grenade* (11 kil. west-north-west), a little place on this road, down the Adour, where Marshal Perrignon was born. About 6 kil. down the river is

St. Sever, a sous-préfecture of 5,000 people, in a pleasant hollow, having an old church which was part of a Benedictine abbey, founded 993; also remains of the château of the Gascony dukes. It was taken from the English 1426. There is a column to General Lamargue, a native. At Peulvan (near the town), and Peyrelongue (8 kil. off), druid stones are seen. *Hotel*—Des Voyageurs.—About 14 kil. south of St. Sever, on the Loute, at Hagetman, is an old castle of the kings of Navarre.]

AIRE (7 kil.), near the head of the Adour, where the roads to Tarbes (67 kil.) and Agen turn off, is an old decayed place of 4,300 population, and seat of a bishopric, having on Mas d'Aire hill, remains of the seat of the Visigoth king, Alaric II., who promulgated the Theodosian code here. It suffered from the ravages of the Normans and English, and the religious wars which followed. The cathedral is rather old than beautiful; an ancient convent is now the priests' seminary.

GARLIN (17 kil.), in department Basses-Pyrenées. Auriac (12 kil.), is the next place.

At 21 kil. further is Pau, where the road between Bayonne and Tarbes crosses.

Pau. *Hotels*—De France; de l'Europe; de la Poste; de la Dorade; des Ambassadeurs. Bankers: MM. Davantes Brothers, M. Merillon, senior. English clergyman, Rev. E. Hughes, at the English church in Rue de Cordelles; service in French by Rev. M. Buscarlet

English physicians, Dr. Taylor, Dr. Smythe, and Dr. Hill.

Vice-Consul, G. Hodgson, who also banks for the English.

Post office, near the préfecture.

Population 14,500. Chief town of department Basses-Pyrenées, seat of a cour impériale, university, &c., and a favourite resort of English and others on account of its soft and beautiful climate, and its delightful situation within view of the Pyrenees, which are about 50 kil. or 30 miles off.

It stands in a rich plain, above the Gave, *i. e.* torrent, de Pau, (which rises at the celebrated fall of Gavarnie), on a height crowned by its old castle, memorable for the birth of Henry IV. or *Henri Quatre*, the darling hero of the French people. The town began in a château of the tenth century, built its vicomtes, who marked the bounds by stakes or *paous* (in Béarnais), whence the name derived. About 1364 Gaston de Foix made it the capital of Béarn, and rebuilt the castle; and a parliament and university were afterwards granted.

The little brooks of Heas, Ousse, &c., traverse the town, which is cut in two by a ravine, crossed by a bridge from the Place de la Comédie, the largest square, where the theatre, &c. stand. From Basse Ville or low town, a seven-arch bridge spans the river, towards the hills of Jurançon, which are noted for white wine. The main street, about one-mile long, is crossed by several short ones; the houses are of pebbles and cement.

Place Grammont is surrounded with porticoes; Place Nationale, near the castle and St. Louis' church, is planted with trees, and has Raggi's marble statue of Henry IV., which replaces one of Louis XIV., overturned at the revolution. When the people, during that king's time, asked leave to erect a monument to their favourite, all they could get was permission to build one to the reigning sovereign. As a consolation they cut this inscription upon it in the Béarnais tongue, '*A ciou qu'ey l'arrahil de nouste grand Enric*' (To him who is the grandson of our great Henri).

The préfecture is well built, and contains the

archives, with letters of Henry IV., many of which have been published by M. Berger de Xivrey. At the college, founded as a convent by Henry, is a collection of minerals from the Pyrenees, &c. There is a public library of 15,000 vols., a normal school, and school of design, and circulating library; a public fountain stands near the musée and market halle; also a theatre, government stud, baths, and the house (Rue de Trau) in which *Bernadotte*, king of Sweden was born 1764, the son of a lawyer. The hôtel de Gaisson commemorates another soldier, Marshal Gaisson, who fought under Gustavus Adolphus and at Rocroi. He never despaired: 'I have that in my head, and at my side,' said he, 'which makes me sure of victory.' One more native, the Vicomte d'Orthe, deserves to be remembered. When governor of Bayonne, in the days of the St. Bartholemew massacre, he wrote to Charles IX.: 'I have communicated your majesty's letter to the garrison and townspeople. They are brave soldiers and loyal subjects, but I cannot find a single executioner.'

A drawbridge leads to the gothic château, piled on the rock, and to the Basse-Plante walk in its gardens, on to a beautiful shady terrace high over the river, called the *Parc*, where stood Castel-Beziat town, and whence there is a noble prospect of the fine Val d'Ossau, the Pic du Midi, Mont Perdu, Mont d'Aspey, &c., in the snowy range of the Pyrenees. "This Parc has been compared to the Engi at Berne. I think it decidedly superior. It is true that there are no mountain masses equal to those of the Oberland. But the extent of the chain open to your view is far wider; the principal objects are nearer the eye; and, above all, the foreground and middle distance are far superior at Pau. It is the most splendid and enjoyable *town walk* that I know; and others, of a yet wider experience than mine, have pronounced it unequalled in Europe."—(Trollope's *Impressions*).

The old *château* includes four towers, with low pyramid tops, and a square brick donjon, 115 feet high, in which Abd-el-Kader was a prisoner (1848), till removed to Amboise; a broad staircase carved with arabesques; an elegant chapel, restored by Louis Philippe (who beautified the whole structure with chefs d'œuvre of tapestry and carvings); the presence chamber; the apartments of Marguerite of Navarre, or Marguerite the Pearl, sister of Francis I., and Henri's grandmother; and those of Henri's mother, Jeanne d' Albret (who was born here), with his own bed chamber, and the room in which he was born, 1553, containing his tortoise-shell *cradle* and the carved bedstead of La Belle Gabrielle. The last fine room was occupied by the Emir's harem, who used to roast their mutton in the middle of its oak floor.

When his mother's time drew near, Henri's grandfather told her to *sing*,* that she might not give birth to a puling and crabbed infant. As soon as he was born, the old king shewed him to the people, crying out '*Ma brebis a enfanté un lion!*'—then rubbed his mouth with garlic, and made him drink a few drops of Jurançon wine, to ensure a hardy and robust constitution. That Henri possessed an excellent one is well known; but the wonder is that he survived such vigorous treatment. He was afterwards nursed by a peasant at Bilhère (to the north-west).

Calmness according to Sir J. Clarke and other authorities, is a striking character of the climate. Westerly winds are most prevalent; northerly are feeble and infrequent. "A sense of fulness is the first effect produced upon healthy strangers; and to congestive patients, therefore, the climate is injurious" (Dr. Taylor); but it is beneficial in cases of chronic indigestion, weak throats, and asthma.

The west part of this *department* includes the Pays Basque, and Bas, or Low, Navarre, a small part of a kingdom, which included Navarra, Bizcaya, &c., in north Spain, the country of the Vascones, or Gascons, who gave their name to

* She sung, they say, an anthem to the Virgin, in the Béarnais, beginning

Nouste Dame deü cap deü poün,
Adyudat-me à d'aquest' hore;
Pregats au Dioü deü ceü
Qu'emboulle bié délioura leü
D'u maynat qu'em hassie lou doun.

Which in modern French runs

Nôtre Dame du Bout-du-Pont, secourez-moi à cette heure; priez le Dieu du ciel quil veuille bien me delivrez promptement; qu'il me fasse le don d'un garçon; (Ask God to deliver me soon and give me a boy).

Gascony. What was left in France, after the seizure of the Spanish portion, by Ferdinand the Catholic, came to Henri, who was King of Navarre, before he succeeded, as Henri IV., to the crown of France. Both the Béarnais and Basque people wear the beret, or round Scotch cap, but the latter dress in gayer colours, and are further distinguished by a language of their own, one of the most ancient in Europe. It is full of long expressive compounds, and its purity is a proof of the independence which they have maintained for 3,000 years, in spite of the changes around them. They are a proud and boastful race, fond of their own customs, but hospitable, and so lively and active that '*léger comme un Basque*' is a proverb. General Harispe was a Biscayan.

Coloured handkerchiefs, Béarn linens, carpets, woollens, &c., are made; and there is a trade in wine, Bayonne hams, salted goose legs, poultry, chesnuts. Coaches daily to Bordeaux (22 hours), Tarbes, Toulouse, Bayonne (10 hours) and Spain, Oloron, St. Sauveur, Barèges, Bagnères-de-Bigorre (*see* Route 60), Eaux-Bonnes, &c.

[At Morlaas (10 kil. north-east) on the Luy-de-France, was a château and mint of the Viscomtes of Béarn, called Forquie, on a hill of that name.—At 8 kil. south-east of Pau, up the Gave, is Meillon; and 8 kil. beyond, is Nay, in a fertile spot, covered with vineyards, &c., an industrious place of 3,300 persons, who manufacture woollens, established since 1542.—Coarraze, 3 kil. higher, has the tower of an old château, where Henri IV. was brought up when a youngster. Then comes the chapel of Notre Dame de Béthoram (4 kil.), in a fine valley at the bridge on the Gave, to which pilgrimages are made, 15th August to 8th September; a priests' seminary stands near it, and the nine stations on the hills above, command fine prospects.—Lestelle and its grotto are a little further; and then St. Pé, as in Route 60*a*.]

ROUTE 86—*continued.*

Gau (8 kil.) like Jurançon and Gelos, which the road passes, is noted for its wine, and is in the beautiful valley of the Néez river, which falls over several little cascades.

Rebenac (8 kil.) at the head of the little Néez above which is a château.

[At 16 kil. west-north-west is the sous-préfecture of

Oloron, on a hill by the Gave d'Oloron, which is made by the union of the Gaves, d'Aspe and d'Ossau. It was known to the Romans as *Iluro*, which being ruined by the Saracens (732) and Normans, was rebuilt by the Vicounts of Béarn. Population, 6,458, inclusive of 4,400 in St. Marie, at the other end of the high bridge, over the Gave. There are two mineral springs near. Manufactures of woollens, caps, stockings, paper; and a trade in wool, Bayonne hams, salt provisions, horses, &c; and timber for the navy. *Hotels*—De France; des Voyageurs (Travellers); de la Providence.

Up the Val d'Aspe, by a bold road, first cut by the Romans, you pass by Asasp (10 kil); Escot, under the Pène d'Escot, and Sarrance, to Bédous (13 kil.) in a pleasant part of the Gave; then to Accous (population 1606); the roman *Aspaluca*, near the lukewarm mineral spring of Superlaché, and Mont Argarry (to the west). To the east is a road over the mountains to Eaux-Bonnes. A little beyond Accous, near Cette, is a pass (to the west) over to Castillo d'Anso in *Spain*.

Following the defile up the Gave, you come to Ardos (17 kil.) under Montagnes Rouges, whence a mule path leads by Paillette (11 kil.) under Mont d'Aspe, over the frontier, by a pass 6,713 feet above the sea, to Campfranc (28 kil.), in *Spain*.]

Arudi (7 kil.) Bielle, Bellestein, are next passed, in a fine part of the Val d'Ossau. Then Louvie, and

Laruns (11 kil.) in the middle of a deep valley, a depôt for navy timber, from the forests of the Gabas mountains.

[At 4 kil. south-east is

Eaux-Bonnes, or Aigues-Bonnes, a small but noted watering place, at the end of the Gave-de-Valentin, and of a deep pass, under the Pic-de-Gers, in a healthy spot, with forests, pretty cascades and good walks, on the marble cliffs, round it. About four hundred persons (many of them soldiers) between May and October, use the sulphur springs, which are called La Vieille, or Buvette (93° temperature), La Neuve, Ortech, and la Froide (59°), and are beneficial in cases of old wounds, chronic affections, intermittent fevers, skin diseases, early consumption, &c. Drs. Darralde and Crouseilhes are the medical inspectors.]

EAUX-CHAUDES (4 kil.) or Aigues-Chaudes, up the wild gorge of Val d'Ossau, watered by the Gave-de-Gabas, is another sulphur spa, less fashionable than the other, with a large bath-house, fed by the Esquirette, Fontaine du Roi, Clot, Arresec, and other hot springs, up to 97° temperature. That of Mainville is cold, and taken in draughts. Season, June to September. The government inspectors are Drs. Laffore and Laffaille. Chronic rheumatism and diarrhœa, colic, vertigo, paralysis and derangements of the viscera, are successfully met by a course of these waters.

Proceeding up the pass, which is broken and well wooded, you come to the Pont de l'Enfer (Hell Bridge), and Fairies' grotto; then to Gabas custom house (10 kil.), whence a mule path over the frontier leads to the famous Panticosa spa, in *Spain* (which is most beneficial in consumption); and from which also the double headed *Pic du Midi d'Ossau* may be ascended. It is 9,696 feet above sea, in the midst of a circle of other peaks, some of whose sides are darkened with forests of pines &c., and commands a view of the valleys of Aspe and Ossau, the Pic du Midi de Bigorre, Monts Vignemale, Perdu, and the Maladetta.

ROUTE 87.

Tarbes to Pau, Orthez, Bayonne.

DOWN THE GAVE DE PAU.

Distance 134 kil., or 73 miles.

TARBES as in Route 60.

GER (10 kil.), in department Basses-Pyrenées.

BORDES D'EXPOEY (12 kil.).

PAU (17 kil.), described in Route 86.

LESCAR (6 kil.), the ancient *Beneharnum*, and seat of a bishopric, was destroyed by the Normans, 856, rebuilt by Guillaume Duc de Gascogne, and ravaged by the Calvinists in 1569. In the old romanesque church, the grandfather of Henry IV. was buried. Population 2,093.

ARTIX (20 kil.), on the Gave de Pau.

MASLACQ (11 kil.), has a large paper factory.

ORTHES or Orthez (9 kil.), a well built sous-préfecture of 7,100 souls in department Basses-Pyrenées, pleasantly seated where six roads join, on a hill side by the Gave de Pau, at the old gothic bridge which has a ruined tower on it. It was taken from the Counts of Dax by Gaston III., one of the Princes of Béarn, whose seat was at the decayed château de Moncade, where Blanche of Castile was poisoned by her sister, the wife of Gaston IV., and where Gaston, surnamed Phœbus, killed his own son, and died. The castle tower commands a view over the fertile district of Béarn.

In the town is a new Hôtel de Ville, a market hall, and fountains. It was a flourishing place, and the seat of a protestant university founded by Henri Quatre's mother, till the revocation of the Edict of Nantes.

On the hills above, the Duke of Wellington beat the French, 27th February, 1814, after crossing the Pyrenees.

Woollen stuffs, linseed oil, leather, &c., are made, and Bayonne hams cured; there are large saw-works, and a trade in goose feathers. *Hotels*—Bergerot; Sené. Coaches to Bayonne, Pau, Mont de Marsan, Toulouse.

About 5 kil. out of Orthez, a road turns off as in Route 87a below, to St. Jean de Port.

[Amou (13 kil. north), a town of 2,000 population, on the Luy de Béarn has a good church, with one of the best gothic spires in the department (Landes), and a château by Mansard.]

PUYOO (7 kil.) a pretty place, as is

PEYREHORADE (16 kil.), in department Les Landes, where the Gave d'Orloron joins that of Pau, and which has an old castle, flanked by great towers, and stone quarries. Population 2,700. About 8 kil. further you cross the Adour.

BIANDOS (9 kil.), has but the posting-house.

At 17 kil. further is Bayonne (*see* Route 62.)

ROUTE 87a.

Orthez to St. Jean Pied de Port.

ORTHEZ, as in Route 87. A turning 5 kil. west of it leads to

SALIES (9 kil.) or Sailles, so called from a brine spring used to cure the Bayonne hams.

[About 8 kil. south-west is La Bastide-Villefranche, which has an old tower called Tour de Béarn.]

Sauveterrae (9 kil.), on the Gave d'Oloron, is remarkable for a decayed tower and other antique ruins.

St. Palais (14 kil.), on the Bidouze, was an important place in French Navarro, where Henri d'Albret established his chancery after the loss of Pampeluna.

Larceveau (15 kil.), up the Bidouze.

[About 21 kil. east, by a winding road among the hills is the small sous-préfecture of *Mauléon* (population 1,145) on the Saison, or Gave de Mauléon, and divided into Low and High town,—the latter including the ancient château.

Higher up the Gave and Val de Soule you come to Gottein, and Tardets (10 kil.), from which a road turns off east to Oloron, and another west, to the paths over Monts Solumongagna and St. Sauveur, to St. Jean. Further on is Licq in the Val de Soule, whence the Gave turns up east towards Engrace, and Monts Leche and Argarry; to the west it brings you to Larrau, where there is a pass over Mont Bethaudy on the frontier, to Ocagavia on the Salozax, under Mont Abaudy.

St. Jean-Pied-de-Port (13 kil.) as in Route 65*a*.

ROUTE 89.

Paris to Sceaux.

By railway (Ligne de Paris à Sceaux). Embarcadère or station, Barrière d'Enfer, behind the Luxembourg, opened 1846; 6½ miles. Trains, nearly every hour, in 25 minutes; omnibuses to all, from Rue du Bouloi, Place St. Sulpice, &c.

This line having many small curves in it, they use the patent jointed carriages and trains of M. Arnoux, which are about to be employed also on the Calais railway. The gauge is 6 feet; little wheels on the rims of the greater ones keep the carriages on the rail; the carriages turn freely on their wheels, and require no buffer. Curves of even 82 feet radius are safely passed.

The stations are—

Arcueil-Cachan,	Fontenay-aux-Roses,
Bourg-la-Reine,	Sceaux.

Passing Petit Montrouge and the fortification; then Montrouge quarries and its new fort, all on the left; you come to

Arcueil (7 kil.) from Paris), so called from the aqueduct made by the Romans over the Biévres, two arches of which are seen in the modern aqueduct, built 1613-24 by Desbrosses, for Mary de Medicis' palace at Luxembourg; it stands on 25 arches, 72 feet high, 1,200 long. Country seats are about. Cachan is across the valley.

Bour-la-Reine (9 kil. from Paris), on the high road to Etampes and Orleans, a pretty place, with a country seat of Gabrielle d'Estrées, 'la Belle Gabrielle,' mistress of Henry IV., whose decorated chamber is still shewn. It was in the prison here that Condorcet, the philosopher and Girondist, poisoned himself, 1794. The cattle market or Marché de Sceaux, is held near this, every Monday.

To the north-west are Chatillon on a hill, and Bagneux on another,—the latter a healthy village with an old church of the twelfth or thirteenth century. L'Hay and Chevilly lie to the south-west, and Berni château to the south beyond the viaduct.

Fontenay-aux-Roses (9 kil. from Paris), a charming village, so called from the rose trees cultivated here, and spreading over the walls and houses. The vine, strawberry, &c. are also grown.

Sceaux (11 kil. from Paris), a sous-préfecture in department Seine (population 1,800), had a château, built 1670 by Colbert the statesman, which came to Madame de Montespan and the Duc de Penthièvre. It was pulled down at the Revolution, except the orangerie, now a public garden for Sunday balls.

Near the gothic church of St. Jean is a pillar to Florian the novelist. The Hôtel de Ville is a good building. Plessis and the forest of Meudon are to the west.

Coaches to Antony, Lonjumeau, Lenas, Arpajon, Massy, Palaiseau, Orsay (to which the railway is to be carried), Limours, Bonnelle, Epilly, Verrières, Chatenay, and Amblainvilliers.

[Chatenay (2 kil. south) was the birthplace of *Voltaire* 1694.—Palaiseau (9 kil. south-south-west) on the Yvette, so called from its palatium or château, has a church of the eleventh and twelfth centuries.—At Orsay, 5 kil. above it, up the Yvette, is a fine moated château.]

SECTION VII.

ROADS TO THE WEST.

IN CONNEXION WITH THE RAILWAY FROM PARIS TO VERSAILLES (RIVE GAUCHE), RAMBOUILLET, CHARTRES AND LA LOUPE (CHEMIN DE FER DE L'OUEST), SUPPLYING DREUX, LE MANS, ALENÇON, LAVAL, RENNES, ST. MALO, BREST, ETC.—ROUTES NINETY TO NINETY-FIVE.

ROUTE 90.

Paris to Versailles and La Loupe.

Opened to La Loupe 1852; 124 kil. or 77 miles. Embarcadères, as the traveller may prefer; either 24, Boulevard Mont Parnasse, for the rive gauche (or left bank of the Seine); or 24, Rue St. Lazaire, for the rive droite (or right bank); the first reaches Versailles by Bellevue, the second by St. Cloud. Omnibuses to all the trains; four trains a day, in 3½ to 6 hours: fares, 12fr. 80c., 9fr. 65c., and 7fr. 10c. Trains to Versailles every hour, in twenty to thirty-five minutes; 1¼ and 1½ fr. Versailles park and the Trianons are open daily; the museum every day, except Thursday and Friday.

The stations of this line to Versailles (17 kil.) are:

	kil.		kil.		kil.
Clamart	5	Sèvres.........		Viroflay	1
Meudon	2	Chaville	4	Versailles ...	4
Bellevue	1				

Beyond Versailles:

	kil.		kil.		kil.
Saint-Cyr ...	5	Rambouillet.	8	Chartres	10
Trappes	6	Epernon......	13	Courville......	18
Laverrière ...	5	Maintenon...	8	Pontgouin ...	8
Lartoire	7	Jouy	9	La Loupe ...	10

Leaving the station at Mont Parnasse, near Barrière du Maine, you have the cemetery on the left, and the large suburb of Vaugirard on the right, towards the river Seine. Beyond the lines are Vanvres and Issy, and their detached forts.

[Across the Seine are the following:—

Auteuil (4 kil. west of Paris), near Bois de Boulogne, St. Cloud, &c., was the favourite residence of Boileau, Molière, Rasine, Lafontaine, Franklin, Condorcet, Helvetius, Count Rumford, Cabanis. Boileau's house is still shewn in the sixth street, to the left from the church on the St. Cloud road. The spire church of the twelfth century has the tomb of Nicolai; and there is a pillar to Chancellor d'Aguessau in the Place.

Passy, near this, on a hill-side by the Seine, is equally celebrated for its residents. Franklin lived here (1788), and gives name to a street; also Abbé Raynal (died here 1796); the Comte d'Estaing, who fought with Rodney: Picini and Bellini, the composers. It has a Ranelagh Garden, near the site of La Muette Château, and a good iron spa, which is useful in indigestion, &c.

Near is the *Longchamp* promenade. Before the revolution there was an abbey close to Suresnes, founded by St. Louis' sister Isabella, which the ladies of Louis XIV.th's court used to attend in Passion Week; and hence arose the custom of appearing here in gay equipages at this time of the year.]

CLAMART-SOUS-MEUDON (5 kil.), near Meudon forest. A little further is Pont-du-Val viaduct, on a double row of arches, 108 feet high, with Fleury to the left, and Les Moulineceaux on the Seine to the right.

MEUDON (2 kil.), in department Seine-et-Oise, is a pretty place, near Meudon forest, under the château built by Louis XIV th's son, and restored by Napoleon for Marie Louise. An avenue leads up to the fine terrace in front of it (where stood the Cardinal of Lorraine's older château, made an ammunition factory at the revolution, and pulled down 1804), 450 yards long by 80 broad, and commanding a vast prospect over Paris, the Seine, &c.

The *château* has some pictures and tapestry

and was the residence latterly of the Dukes of Bordeaux and Orleans; a small park laid out by Lenôtre, of 500 arpents (250 hectares, or 618 acres), is taken out of the wood. Near the railway is Notre Dames des Flammes chapel, triangular, with spires at the corners, commemorating the death of nearly 150 persons, 8th May, 1842, burnt to death by the carriages taking fire. One of the sufferers was Admiral D'Urville. Rabelais was titular curé of Meudon. Glass and pottery are made.

Bellevue (1 kil.), with a good prospect, is near Sèvres (*see* Route 3), and the rive droite line beyond.

Chaville (4 kil.)

Viroflay (1 kil.), where the branch of 4 kil. to Versailles turns off, past Petit Montreuil, to Avenue de la Mairie, opposite the palace.

Versailles, 17 kil. or 10½ miles, from Paris. *Hotels*—Des Reservoirs; de France; de la Chasse Royale; de l'Europe. Population, 35,000. The capital of department Seine-et-Oise (formerly Ile de France, Hugh Capet's patrimony), seat of a bishop, tribunals, &c., and of a magnificent palace of the later Bourbon kings, which has been turned into a national museum since 1837. It was a mere hunting lodge of Henry IV. and others, till Louis XIII., in 1624, built a brick château here, to which Louis XIV., 'le Grand Monarque,' as he is styled, added the palace (1661-72), gardens and parks (twenty miles in circuit), at a vast expense; some say ten millions, some forty millions sterling.

At Place d'Armes, opposite the palace, the avenues de St. Cloud and de Sceaux meet each other and a third or centre avenue, de Paris, which is 288 feet wide, and well-planted, and divides the town into two parishes.

That of Notre Dame to the north includes J. Mansard's doric church, built 1684, the palais de justice behind the great stables, the english church near Place Hoche (which has that general's statue), barracks, a large market, the Venerie, or grand huntsman's house, a fine hospital near the Austin college, founded by Louis XV th's queen (with an elegant chapel), the rive droite railway station, &c.

In the south or St. Louis parish are the Hôtel de Ville and rive gauche station, close to another pile of stables (now a barrack), the grecian *Cathedral*, built 1743, the préfecture in the old gard meuble, and a small building called Jeu de Paume, where the States-General or National Assembly met 1789, before they moved to Paris, with the marché St. Louis, the Menus Plaisirs, and barracks. There are also baths, a public library of 48,000 vols., priests' seminary, &c. All the streets are regular and well built. Blucher pillaged it 1815.

The Place d'Armes, 800 feet broad, brings you to the Cour d'Honneur and the marble court, 380 feet broad, in front of Louis XIII.th's château, with Louis XIV.th's and sixteen other statues; to the right and left are ranges of buildings, as Louis XV.th's opera house, the bibliothèque, the Grand Commun (now a military hospital), and Louis XIV.th's beautiful chapel, with its high-pitched roof, where Marie Antoinette was married. Behind the old château, facing the gardens, is the main or west front of the *Palace*, a noble ionic range, 1,400 feet long, something in the style of Somerset House (from the river), but with the wings thrown back from the domed centre; it was the work of Mansard, and has 102 columns, in groups of four to eight each, and 375 windows and doors, with a profusion of vases, busts, &c. Inside are splendid rooms and galleries, restored by Louis Philippe, as the Gallerie des Glaces, 242 feet long, the cabinet of Louis XIV. (who privately married Madame de Maintenon here), Louis XVI th's chamber, where he showed himself with the cap of liberty to the people below (a young officer, Bonaparte, and his friend Bourienne, being spectators), also the chamber where the ferocious mob broke in on Marie Antoinette, and other rooms, now filled with marbles, china, tapestry, busts and statues of eminent french soldiers, a marine gallery, and above 1,100 paintings dedicated to the glory of France, including portraits of admirals, marshals, generals, &c., works of the time of Louis XIV., views of royal palaces, paintings of battles from Clovis, down to H. Vernet's battle of Isly, in Algerie. (See Galignani's *Paris Guide*).

The *Gardens* or Little Park were laid out by Lenótre or his disciples, and comprise a beautiful Orangery (one tree as old as 1421), and a great number of terraces, allées, parterres, bosquets, pieces of water, &c., ornamented with vases and statuary (that, by Lebrun, at the Bassin d'Apollon, for example). The centre walk, called

Tapis vert, or green carpet, leads to the Grand canal (a cross-shaped piece of water), and the fountains, supplied by forcing pumps at Marly (though Louis XIV.th's intention was to bring water from the Eure, by the aqueduct he began at Maintenon). The petites eaux play first Sunday of every month, but the *grandes eaux* only on especial fête days. The potager or kitchen garden is near the jardin Anglais made by Louis XVIII. when Count of Provence, and the lake called Pieces des Suisses.

Towards the north-west are, *Grand Trianon* (on the site of the village of *Triarnum*), a centre and wings in the italian style, built by Mansard of Campan marble, for Madame de Maintenon, and lately occupied by Madame Adelaide; and *Petit Trianon* to the right, a pavilion, 72 feet square, built by Louis XV. (who died in it) for Madame du Barry. Marie Antoinette, and the Duchess of Orleans, lived in it.

Philip V. of Spain (Louis XIV.th's grandson), Louis XVI., and his brothers Louis XVIII. and Charles X., were born in the palace. Marshal Berthier, Generals Hoche and Gourgaud, and the excellent Abbé de l'Epée, were also natives; Marchaud's statue of the last was put up 1843; many fossil shells are found round this place. The agricultural college at Grignon, near Thiverbal, was discontinued 1852. Rev. N. Vers is protestant pastor here.

Fire-arms, clocks, and watches, and jewellery are made. Coaches to St. Nom, Villepreux, Dreux, Jouy, St. Cyr, Chevreuse, Houdan, Montfort, Septeuil.

[*Buc*, 2 kil. south of Versailles, is a charming little place in the woods above the Bièvre, here crossed by an aqueduct on nineteen arches, 70 feet high, built 1688 to supply Versailles with water. Among other seats is that called La Guerinière.—Jouy-en-Josas, 2 kil. east of it, down the Bièvre, was *Gaugiacum* in the ninth century, when it belonged to St. Germain's abbey. The river turns many mills; and M. Oberkampf's painted paper factory is here, as well as a fine château. Population, 1,244.]

ROUTE 90—*Continued.*

VIROFLAY, as above.

ST. CYR (3½ miles), in the great park of Versailles, is known for its military school for 300 infantry cadets, established here 1806 by Napoleon, in place of the school for young ladies of rank, founded 1686 by Madame de Maintenon, who received a visit from Peter the Great, and died here 1719. As built by J. Mansard it forms five large courts. Racine's Esther was performed here for the first time.

TRAPPES (3¾ miles). Coaches to Le Château, Neauphle, Thoiry, Pontel, Septeuil, &c.

[About 5 kil. south-east near Vaumurier, in a deep valley, are a few fragments of *Port Royal des Champs*, originally a bernardine monastery, founded 1204 by Matthew de Marli, and called Portus regius, Porréal, &c., after Philippe Auguste found shelter when hunting; but having become, about 1640-60, the head quarters of the Jansenist leaders, Arnauld d'Andilly, Lancelot, Le Maistre (who translated the Bible), Pierre Nicole (who shared in Pascal's 'Provincial Letters') and other learned and pious recluses, it was suppressed 1708. Arnauld's house was at Les Granges, a farm still standing on the hill above.]

LAVERRIERE (3½ miles). Coaches to Le Tremblay, Dampierre,—Chevreuse (8 kil. east-south-east), and the old castle of its seigneurs and dukes, on the Yvette,—Montfort, and La Queue, on the Dreux road.

LARTOIRE (4½ miles). Coach to Menuts, and to Montfort-la-Maury, which is 11 miles north, under the remains of a castle built by one Amalric or Amaury. It has also a fine old church, with stained windows.

RAMBOUILLET (5¾ miles), a sous-préfecture of 3,100 souls, in a valley, having a royal château in the midst of a park of 3,000 acres (laid out by Lenôtre), and a hunting forest of 30,000 acres. The *château*, a large plain brick pile, flanked by turrets and a great tower, includes a grand saloon with a marble floor, the room in which Francis I. died, in 1547, stables for 500 horses, &c. Here Marie Louise and her son met the Allied sovereigns, and Charles X. abdicated here 1830, in favour of the Duc de Bordeaux, and set off for Cherbourg and Poole. Some of the earliest merinos in France were bred here. Hats and lace are made. *Hotels*—Du Lion d'Or (Golden Lion); St. Pierre. Coaches to Ablis, Auneau, St. Arnoult, Dourdan (*see* Route 50), St. Léger, Houdan, &c.

[Houdan (28 kil. north-west), on the Vesgre, where the Opton joins, has a fine gothic church, built by Robert le Pieux, and an old tower, with some remains of its ancient fortifications.—Auneau (22 kil. south of Rambouillet), in department Eure-et-Loir, has a tower left of the old castle of its seigneurs, one of whom was Henry de Joyeuse, marshal of France in the sixteenth century.]

EPERNON (8 miles), in a pretty well-watered spot, on the Guesle, in department Eure-et-Loir, has remains of the old château of its dukes, the first of whom was the favourite of Henry III., Nogarêt de la Valette, whose pride was so ridiculous that he was styled king of Epernon. Formerly it was called Sparnonum, and strongly fortified. Population,1,700. Coaches to Gas and Gallardon.

MAINTENON (5 miles), in the fertile valley of the Eure (here crossed by a fine viaduct on 32 arches), where the Voise joins, gave title of marchioness to the widow of Scarron, whom Louis XIV. privately married at Versailles. A square and several round high-peaked towers are seen in the moated château, now belonging to the Duc de Broglie, but in part as old as Philippe Auguste's time; they shew Madame's portrait (by Mignard), and her bed-room. The chapel has stained glass of the fifteenth century.

At the end of the park are druid stones, called the Berceau (cradle), the Pierres de Gargantua, &c. The remains of an *aqueduct*, begun from Pont-Gouin, about 60 kil. west-south-west, up the Eure, 1684-8, by Louis XIV., to supply Versailles with water, are also seen; supported by 47 or 48 arches or piles, above 80 feet high, and to make which 60,000 troops were sometimes employed. Colin d'Harleville, the comic writer, was born here. Population, 2,100. Coaches to Nogent- le-Roi and Dreux (*see* Route 91).

JOUY (5½ miles), up the Eure.

At 4½ miles beyond is

Chartres. *Hotels*—De France; du Grand Monarque (*i.e.* Louis XIV.); du Duc de Chartres; de l'Ecritoire (Writing table). Population, 16,000. The chief town of department Eure-et-Loir, seat of a tribunal, bishopric, &c., in the fertile corn plain of the Beauce, on a hill, (crowned by its noble cathedral) by the Eure, which runs round the old ramparts, now turned into public walks. The other promenades are near St. Pierre's church and Places des Epares, or des Barricades, &c, Basse Ville, or Lower Town, is full of narrow streets and gothic-looking houses of wood, with their gables to the front, and is joined by very steep ascents to Upper Town, where the best buildings are. Among these are the vast and imposing

Cathedral, built 1140-1260, in the shape of a cross, 422 feet long, 208 broad through the transept, and 113 to the roof. The front, 160 feet broad, consists of a noble portal between two towers of equal breadth with it; one tower has a spire 364 feet high; the other 402 feet high, is later built (1514) and in a more florid style. Three entrances, covered with carvings of prophets and apostles, are in the portal, which is 40 feet by 30 and recessed 18 feet, having statues in the jambs, with a fine rose window above. Two other ornamented porches and rose windows are in the north and south sides. The nave is 239 feet long, but the interior is dark on account of the painted windows, of which there are 130. A beautifully carved screen of the fifteenth or sixteenth century, leads to the choir, which has 45 niches in it, and a multitude of sculpture, besides bas-reliefs of the Descent from the Cross and the Presentation, by Bridan; another over the altar by the same artist, of the Assumption of the Virgin, was saved at the revolution by putting a cap of liberty on her head. The crypt and chapels of the older foundations are below.

St. André's large old church, in Basse Ville, of the twelfth century, is a store house; St. Pierre's, now a barrack, belonged to the benedictines, and has some stained windows.

The préfecture stands in a good garden. At the Hôtel de Ville, which was the ursuline convent, the museum is kept, where they shew several objects of natural history, Charlemagne's glass, Philippe le Bel's armour, and the sword of General Marceau (a native), of whom a pillar in Place Marceau, or the herb market, states that he was 'Soldat à 16 ans, Géneral à 23. Il mourut à 27,' when he fell at Altenkirchen.

The public library contains 30,000 volumes and 1 000 MSS. There is a theatre, also a college, normal school, school of design, public baths, a bridge, by Vauban.

Porte Guillaume, with its old towers remains; and there are some traces of aqueducts made by the Romans, who called this place *Autricum*, when it was the capital of the Carnutes. The Northmen attacked it under Hastings, and again under Rollo, the founder of Normandy. It gave title of duke to the Orleans family.

Nicolle, one of the Port Royal writers, and the advocate Pétion were born here. A very large market for corn and flour every Saturday, lasting an hour, when six millions of quintals are sold. Leather, woollens, excellent pâtés (at Lemoine's, &c.) are made.

Conveyances: by rail, to Paris; coaches to Orleans (80 kil.), Châteauneuf-en-Themerais (24 kil. north-west), Illiers (25 kil. south-west), Brou (13 kil. further), Bonneval, Châteaudun, and Courtalain.

[At Morancez (5 kil.) is a very old church, having no side chapel, but a lombard porch and buttresses in front. It is supposed to be at least of the tenth century.

Bonneval (31 kil. south-south-west), a pretty place of 2,800 population, on the Loir, having a church with a good spire, and a mill which was once a benedictine college. Coudreaux, which belonged to Ney, is near, and there are several druid stones (menhirs, dolmen, &c.) in the neighbourhood. One dolmen near Baudouin mill on the river, towards St. Germain, is 12 feet long; another of 10 feet is on the Houssay road, besides peulvans, or ring stones.

Châteaudun (14 kil. further), the ancient *Castellodunum*, and a sous-préfecture of 6,500 population, in the valley of the Loir, was rebuilt after the fire of 1723 on a regular plan. It has a square where you command a view of the whole; also remains of a convent (now the sous-préfect's house), and the old tower of the castle of Thibaut-le-Tricheur (the cheater or tricker), Count of Dunois, built in the tenth century. It is 96 feet high and 188 round. J. Toulain, the inventor of painting on enamel, was born here.

From this, *viâ* Tournoisin, it is 48 kil. to Orleans.—Vendôme is 40 kil. further; and 56 kil. beyond that is Tours (*see* Route 65).—Blois is 32 kil. from Vendôme.]

Courville (11½ miles), on a hill, in a fertile part of the Eure valley.

[*Villebon* (4 kil. south), has the fine old feudal brick castle, with towers, moats, battlements, &c., in which Sully, the great minister of Henry IV. died. It preserves its old decorations and furniture.]

Courville is near Louis XIVth's aqueduct, which begins at the next station,

Pontgouin (5 miles), on the Eure, and was completed as far as Maintenon, following a zig-zag course of upwards of 30 miles.

La Loupe (6½ miles) is the present terminus of the rail, which will pass on to Le Mans, Laval, Rennes, and Brest. Coaches to Nogent-le-Rotrou, La Ferté, Bernard, Regni Malard, and its old chateaux; Bellesme and its springs, Mamers (*see* Route 91); Alençon (Route 91); Longuy, Toutouvre, Mortagne (Route 91); Séez (Route 92); Carouges, La Ferté-Mené, Laigle, and Verneuil (Route 91).

ROUTE 90.—*continued*,

Distance (to Brest) 477 kil. or 296 miles.

From La Loupe

St. Victor (7 kil., to the east of which (3 kil.) is Montlandon and its old castle.

Nogent-le-Rotrou (15 kil.) a sous-préfecture, in department Eure-et-Loir, of 7,000 population, on the Huisne (which has a fall at the entrance of the town), under a hill, crowned by remains of the castle of the famous Duc de Sully, whose tomb, with that of his wife, is at the Hôtel Dieu, founded by Count Rotrou, 1598. Excellent trout and cray fish are caught.

[Bellesme (about 20 kil. west-north-west), in a forest, has the Herse mineral waters (2 kil.) near it, discovered 1607, rising out of a fountain marked by a roman inscription (?)]

La Ferte-Bernard (22 kil.), on the Huisne, and so called from the fertility of the soil, was one of the keys of France when the English held Normandy, &c. It is a miniature town, having a moat round its ancient battlemented walls, a castle-like gate, with two solid towers, now used for prisons, an Hôtel de Ville, and a fine gothic church of the sixteenth century, looking like a cathedral. It is 190 feet by 70, and 80 high to the vault, or about 160 to the low spire over the west front, which is supported by buttresses. The English, under Salisbury, took the to n 1424, and it was given up to the Prince of Conti, 1590. Population, 2,600.

[About 14 kil. west-south-west, is Bonnetable, a town of 6,000 population, in a fertile spot, having the old castle of its seigneurs, surmounted by six towers, and ornamented inside with wood carvings and portraits.]

CONNERE (19 kil.), is near *Dollon*, so called after a dolmen or cromlech of one stone, 20 feet long, resting on eight others.

[Before you reach this, you leave on the right, at Croix-de-Fer, another dolmen called the Pierre-de-Vouvray.]

At 25 kil. further is

LE MANS. *Hotels*—Le Dolphin; La Boule d'Or (Golden Ball); de la France. Population, 24,290. The chief town of department Sarthe, seat of a bishopric, &c., on a hill side by the Sarthe, near to the junction of the Huisne, or Huine, was the roman *Suindunum*, or capital of the *Cennomanni* (whence the modern name), afterwards of the province of Maine, which was held by Geoffrey Plantagenet, whose son, Henry II., was born here 1133. It was many times besieged in old French history, and in 1793, was occupied by 60,000 Vendéans, who were driven out with great slaughter by Marceau. The Chouans also took it in their rising, 1799.

Three bridges cross the Sarthe. Pont Ysoir joins Gourdane quarter to that of the Pré; Pont Perrin leads to St. Jean, and Pont Napoléon is opposite Place des Halles, the largest square in the city. Another square called Place des Jacobins, and planted with poplars, was the site of a convent, and of a roman amphitheatre; Place du Greffier is a walk by the Sarthe, near the quais, with prospects of the fertile country beyond. The best part of the town is up the hill, that on the river, being a collection of narrow, steep, and dirty streets. The houses are of stone and slate; many old ones are in Grande Rue, Place du Château, Rue des Chanoines, &c. An ancient seat of the knights templars yet remains, and there are four or five modern fountains.

St. Julien's *Cathedral*, 446 feet long, is on the site of a roman temple, of which traces are said to be visible in the oldest part, the norman nave, which is of the tenth and eleventh centuries, and has a good south door; the fine lofty choir and the transepts are of the thirteenth to fifteenth centuries, the former being 106 feet high; a square tower, ornamented with niches, &c., stands over one transept, 217 feet from the ground, or 331 from the river. The rose and other windows are beautifully stained; in the thirteen side chapels are monuments of Richard the First's queen Berengaria, of Charles IV. of Anjou, L. Dubellay, &c. At No. 1, in Rue St. Michel, close by, lived Scarron, the comic writer, who held a canonry here, till he married his wife, who afterwards, as Madame de Maintenon, became mistress or wife to Louis XIV.

La Couture church is partly norman and partly gothic, of the eleventh and thirteenth centuries; it has a good west portal (with carvings of the Judgment), and an ancient crypt. The abbey buildings near it are used for a préfecture, which contains a library of 42,000 vols., with 7,000 MSS., also a gallery of paintings (including a portrait on copper of Geoffrey Plantagenet), and a museum of natural history, armour, roman stones, &c., besides an Egyptian mummy.

Notre Dame du Pré church of the eleventh century, is cruciform, and has a carved doorway. At St. Benoit's is a good painting of a Dead Christ. St. Vincent's abbey church, with an excellent front, is used for the priests' seminary. St. Pierre's old church is altered into a school; the residence of the monks of the Oratory is used for the college, and that of the Visitation for the palais de justice, prison, &c. An old seat of the counts of Maine is now the Hôtel de Ville, and they still shew remains of an earlier building, which it replaced. Parts of the ancient town walls yet remain; the circular hall on the Grande Place, was rebuilt 1822, on the site of a wooden one as old as 1568. There are a good theatre and public baths.

Ledru Rollin, one of the republican leaders in the Revolution of 1848, and author of the Décadence de l' Angleterre, was born here.

Manufactures of cotton, woollen, wax candles, black soap, leather, paper, and beer; and a trade in these, and in cattle, fruit, fat poultry, grain clover-seed, wine, eaux-de-vie, and honey. Conveyances: to Tours, Blois, and Angers, on the Nantes rail; and to Alençon, Chartres, Caen, Rouen, Laval, Rennes, &c.

[*Beaumont-sur-Sarthe*, or Le Vicomte, (27 kil. north-north-west) in an amphitheatre over the Sarthe, which is crossed by two bridges, is a small bustling place of 2,400 people, who trade in cattle, &c., and make linen and carding machines. The old castle serves for a prison, and a well-preserved tumulus near has been planted and made accessible by a spiral road. At 23 kil. beyond is Alençon (*see* Route 91).

From Le Mans, on the way to Laval, you pass ST. DENIS-D'ORQUES (40 kil.), which has remains of a Chartreuse convent, and some rocks in the neighbourhood.

ST. JEAN-SUR-ERVE (10 kil.) is on the Erve (in department Mayenne), so called after the ancient *Arvii*, whose capital was about 8 kil. south, further down the river, near the grottoes of Saulge, or Caves de Margot, which are in the limestone cliffs on its banks; one is about 64 feet in diameter.

[St. Suzanne, about 10 kil. up the Erve, from St. Jean, stands on a rock, commanding a wide prospect, near a lake; it has an old château, and the ramparts are rather remarkable as being vitrified, like some of the Pictish forts in Scotland. Six or seven menhirs, or druid stones, are near this.]

At 27 kil. further is

LAVAL. *Hotels*—La Tête Noire (Black Head); du Louvre; le Cœur Royal (Royal Heart). Population 18,000. A manufacturing town, and capital of department Mayenne (formerly the province of Lower Maine), on a cultivated slope in the valley of the Mayenne. Much linen and cotton cloth, and thread is made. The plain around was formerly called the Forest of Concise; the town grew out of a castle built by Guyon, son of the counts of Maine, in 840. It was taken and retaken in the wars between the English and French, 1466.

An old tower (near the bridge), with its peaked top, is all that remains of the castle, which came to the Dukes of Laval and the Trêmouilles, and is used as a prison.

It is a picturesque old place, having many curious gothic timbered houses, and narrow streets, some rather steep. The Champ de Foire and especially a house called Bel Air, command the best prospects. Two bridges cross the river, the view up which takes in the pretty spire of Avnières church. Parts of the ancient walls are left. Among the buildings to be noticed are the churches of la Trinité and St. Vénérand—the former being the old cathedral, in the gothic style of the twelfth century; the prêfecture and palais de justice (law court); the college; a large linen hall (halle aux toiles); a public library of 25,000 volumes; two hospices; part of the cordeliers old convent, &c.; but none are of much note.

Ambrose Paré, of whom there is a bronze statue, was a native. The Chouans, fighting on behalf of the royalists, gained a victory over the republicans here, 1793. Trade in grain, wine, eaux-de-vie, linens, wood, iron, marble, &c. Conveyances to Rennes, Angers, Mayenne, Le Mans, &c.

From Laval, on the road to Rennes, you pass LA GRAVILLE (20 kil.), then

VITRE (16 kil.) a sous-préfecture (in department Ille-et Vilaine), on the Vilaine, having regular gothic ramparts, strengthened by machicolated towers, between two of which is a house once inhabited by Madame de Sévigné. The houses are ancient-looking. At the mairie, once a benedictine convent, there is a good prospect of the country. The old castle of the ducs de Trêmouille, at the west end of the town, is used for a prison. A stone pulpit is seen outside the gothic church of Notre Dame.

Goat skin dresses are made here for the country people to wear in winter time; besides a few linens, &c. Cantharides flies are also prepared. Savary, the antiquary, was a native. Population 8,650. *Hotel*—La Poste.

A road to Fougères, St. Malo, Avranches, &c. turns off here (*see* Routes 94, 95).

[About 2 kil. south is château des *Rochers*, the old seat of Madame de Sévigné, with a court, tower, the cabinet of Madame, eight-sided chapel in the grounds, &c.]

CHATEAUBOURG (15 kil.), on the Vilaine.

At 21 kil. further is

Rennes. *Hotels*—De France, in Rue de la Monnaie; de la Corne de Cerf (Stag-horn) Rue Louis Philippe; du Commerce, Rue de Bordeaux; du Bout du Monde (World's End). Population 39,300. The chief town of department Ille-et-Vilaine, seat of a military division, of a bishop, cour impèriale, university, &c., on a slight hill, in a wide plain, on the Ille, where the Vilaine joins it, and eleven or twelve roads meet. The Romans called it *Condate-Rhedonum*, from its situation at the junction (condate) of the rivers, in the country of the Rhedones, a Celtic people of Armorica (*i. e.* the sea-side), as this peninsula, from St. Malo round to Nantes, was called. Afterwards it took the name of Bretagne, or Brittany, when the natives of Britain, who fled from the Romans in the third and fourth centuries, settled here; and came to the French crown by the marriage of Duchess Anne to Louis XII.

Rennes, in Haute Bretagne, was the capital of the whole province; the Normans beseiged it 873-4, and John-of-Gaunt, 1336, in behalf of de Montfort. A great fire, 1720, burnt twenty-seven streets, and eight hundred and fifty houses in the heart of the town. These have been rebuilt of darkish granite and sand-stone; and the suburbs beyond the old walls are regularly laid out; but there are many small, low, curiously carved timber houses, especially near the river, in Basse Ville.

One old gate, the Porte Mordelaise, by which the dukes entered on their accession, has some traces of a roman inscription to the Emperor Gordian. Two out of eleven Places are tolerably large; the Place d'Armes, planted with trees, and Place du Palais, where a bronze of Louis XIV. stood. It takes name from the large *Palais de Justice*, on the north side, built 1670, with a tuscan portico, and façade 152 feet long: the provincial states used to meet in it; it has some gallery paintings by Jouvenet. There are pleasant walks along the quay, nearly a mile long; and on the Thabor, la Motte, le Maille, and other promenades. That of le Thabor, where stands a statue of Duguesclin, is the garden of the old benedictine house of St. Mélaine, and commands a fine prospect of the river &c.; la Motte faces the préfecture.

The *Hôtel de Ville*, built since the fire of 1720, by Gabriel, near Place de la Comédie, is a grecian pile, about 213 feet by 82, including a clock-tower, rooms for the tribunals, schools of design, gallery of paintings, and a public library of 30,000 volumes, among which are many ancient books and MSS.

St. Pierre *Cathedral*, opposite Porte Mordelaise replaces the old gothic one, with a tower of the seventeenth century, and is a very modern structure, in the grecian style, having a portal 127 feet high, decorated with rows of columns, above which rise two tall towers. Its shape is a greek cross; the timber roof rests on pillars, which terminate in thirty-three ionic columns, at the rotonde at the east end. St. Sauveur is the best of the other churches.

The ancient Benedictine abbey of St. George's, which was once a pagan temple, is now a barrack; another barrack is placed in the Hôtel Kergus, formerly a high school. Hôtel Blossac, is a building worth notice; so is the theatre. There are also a college, priests' seminary, jardin des plantes, public baths. A gold roman vase, with a bas-relief of the Triumph of Bacchus, now at Paris, was found here, 1774.

Guinguiné, author of the 'Literary History of Italy,' A. Duval, the dramatist, Lanjuinais, of the convention, are among the natives. Rennes, like Toulouse, is a sort of provincial capital, where some of the decayed noblesse may be found, living in quiet obscurity.

Many of the country people dress in sheepskins in winter, and wear their hair long; the women put on high or wide square caps, over their locks, which they sell to the dealers, who come round periodically to clip them. The men make good sailors, and are noted for probity, so that '*La parole d'un Brêton vaut or*' (The word of a Breton is worth gold), is a proverb.

Sail cloth, linens, &c., are made; and there is a trade in grain, cider, butter (beurre de la Prévalaye), fowls (poulardes de Jauzé), cattle, &c. Rennes lies beyond the region in which the vine flourishes in France.

Conveyances to Paris, Nantes, Lorient, Vannes, Brest, Dinan, St. Malo, St. Brieuc, Morlaix, Avranches, Caen, Havre, Rouen, St. Lô, Cherbourg, &c. The canal d'Ille-et-Rance is a series of cuttings to improve the course of the upper part of the Ille, and join it to the Rance at Dinan.

From Rennes, on the road to Brest, you pass

PACE (10 kil.).

BEDEE (13 kil.).

[At 5 kil. south-south-west is *Montfort*, a small sous-préfecture (population, 1,715), on a hill over the Meu (where the Chailloux joins), having remains of a moat, ramparts, and old towers. Among its counts were Jean de Montfort, who became Jean IV., duke of Brittany, by the help of his heroic wife Jeanne of Flandres, and of Edward III. of England; and the famous Simon de Montfort, Earl of Leicester, who fell at Evesham in the previous reign. It was taken from the English by Duguesclin.

Some good mineral springs are here. At the

Thermes or roman baths are two basins 76 ft. by 63 each, descended by step. In the neighbourhood is an ancient oak, six or seven centuries old; also the tomb of the enchanter Merlin, on a hill in Brescilien forest, near the ruins of the famous fountain of Jouvence. Good beer is made.]

LA BARETTE (14 kil.),

BROONS (16 kil.), in department Côtes-du-Nord, and Basse-Bretagne, is a place of 2,000 population, a little beyond which is the site of Lamotte Broons, the seat of the famous soldier *Duguesclin*, who died here 1311, and to whom a pillar is set up. The country people here begin to speak the Bas-Bréton or Brezounecq language, a dialect of the Celtic.

LARGOUEDRE (12 kil.), on the Arguenon.

LAMBALLE (15 kil.), on the Gouessan, was the old seat of the counts and dukes of Penthièvre (a title now in the Orleans family), whose old castle, built near a monastery founded 1084 by Geoffrey I., was pulled down by Richelieu 1626, except Notre Dame chapel, and its minaret-like tower. The site is a pretty walk, with good views. Population, 4,300; trade in woollens, honey, wax, corn, leather, cattle, horses. *Hotel*—du Croissant.

[About 30 kil. north-east is Cape Frehel and its revolving light, standing 246 feet high, and shining for 2¾ minutes to a distance of 16 or 18 miles.—At 15 kil. south-west is Moncontour, then Plougenast (14 kil.), then

Loudéac (11 kil.), a sous-préfecture of 6,740 population, in a forest, of no consequence except for its toiles de Bretagne or linens. The church has a tall spire, and there is a linen hall, college, chamber of commerce, &c. *Hotel*—de la Croix Blanche (White Cross.—Pontivy is 22 kil. further (*see* Route 74).]

At 20 kil. further is St. Brieuc.

ST. BRIEUC or St. Brieux. *Hotels*—de la Croix Rouge (Red Cross); de la Croix Blanche (White Cross); du Chapeau Rouge (Red Hat). Population, 13,300. A port on a bay in the Channel, chief town of department Côtes-du-Nord (in Lower Brittany), and seat of a diocess, is among hills (which shut out the sea-view), on the Gouet, the mouth of which makes the harbour at Legué, for vessels of 400 tons. Two bridges cross it, one being of granite. A promenade made 1788 is carried round the site of the old walls, and has a fine prospect at the terrace. In Place Duguesclin, is a statue of that warrior.

The *Cathedral*, with its low plain towers, is of the thirteenth century, on the site of a druid temple, which St. Brieuc, an Irishman, turned into a monastery in the fifth century. It has an altar by Corlay, and two pieces of Gobelins tapestry. St. Michel is an ugly structure, with nothing noticeable about it.

Hôtel de Ville is an old building. The public library is large, containing 24,000 volumes. There are a museum, college, navigation school, theatre, several fountains, and an hospital, besides a race-course or hippodrome, near the old tower of Cesson (which has a double ditch round it), and the large public gardens which belonged to the Cordeliers convent. Trade in grain, cider, butter, honey, cattle, paper, thread, fish.

From St. Brieuc on the road to Brest, you pass CHATELAUDREN (17 kil.), which commands a fine view from the ruins of its old castle.

GUINGAMP (14 kil.), on the plain of the Trieux, is a sous-préfecture (7,000 population) in department Côtes-du-Nord, and in the old duchy of Penthièvre, with some remains of its old walls, a college, and a good market halle near the fountain in the Place. Its church is large, and ornamented with a tall spire at one end, and a sort of domed tower at the other. *Hotels*—des Voyageurs (Travellers); de Bretagne.

[Pontrieux (16 kil. north), down the river, here crossed by a bridge to which the tide comes. Pierre de Rohan sacked the old castle of Châteaulin, which stands near, in the fifteenth century. The church is one of the ugliest in the department.

Paimpol (13 kil. north-west of this) is a bustling little port in the Channel, with a ship-yard, &c. Population, 2,108. To the south and south-east of it are the old round church of Lanleff and Beauport abbey.

Tréguier (12 kil. north-north-west of Pontrieux), a pleasant place, where the Gwindy and Jaudy join not far from the sea, grew out of a monastery founded by St. Tugdual in the sixth century, and made the seat of a bishop. The Spaniards took it in their descent 1592. Some of the streets are good; there is a large octagon halle and a priests' seminary The old cathedral church is a curious structure, with an open tower, and many quaint carvings on it. Formerly it held the tombs of a duke of Brittany, and St. Yves (or St. Ives) the patron saint, who was born near this. Population, 3,178.]

BELLEISLE-EN-TERRE (20 kil.), on the Guer.

[About 24 kil. north down the river is *Lannion*, an old-fashioned sous-préfecture (with 5,400 population), in department Côtes-du-Nord, and a smuggling port, with a quay, about 7 kil. from the sea. The spire church is of the twelfth century; and there are a college and two hospitals,—one on the quay, near a mineral water, which is useful in cases of stone. Traces of the site of the roman *Lexovium* have been found on the river; and on the Plæmeur road is a menhir stone 26 feet by 10. *Hotel*—des Marchands.]

MORLAIX (33 kil.), a port and sous-préfecture in department Finisterre, where the Jarleau and Kevleut fall into the Channel, under some picturesque hills, and lined by quays which offer good prospects. Population 11,600. Some curious old houses are seen at Lances and on the Trigieux side of the creek, which runs up to the principal place. Others are seen in Rues des Nobles and du Pavé. Of the four churches, St. Mathieu's is in the pointed style, St. Martin's stands on a hill. The mairie and markets are in the Place, on the site of a large hôtel de ville, pulled down 1836. It has a salle de spectacle, and large tobacco factory, navigation school, &c. and walks near the fontaine des Anglais. General Moreau was a native. The English held it in the fourteenth century.

Conveyances, daily, to Paris, Brest, St. Malo, Rennes, St. Pol, Lannion, &c.; and by steam to Havre, on Wednesdays, in 20 hours. Druid stones are to be seen at Breumlis and Meneguen, and other spots in the neighbourhood; and at Touquedoc (to the east), are fine remains of a castle of the thirteenth century.

[*St. Pol-de-Leon*, (20 kil. north-west) to the right of the road to Brest, on the coast, is a decayed cathedral town, with several old gothic houses; and takes its name from the roman *legion* stationed in this part. Population 6,500. The beautiful granite spire of Kreisker church, 394 feet high, was built, in the fourteenth century, by an English architect: and the cathedral, with its two good towers, rose window, carved porch, stalls, &c., and tombs of Conan Méridec, Bishop Visdelon, and the patron saint, deserves notice.]

LANDIVISIAU (20 kil.), has a good church.

LANDERNEAU (16 kil.), on the Elorn, which fall into the east end of Brest harbour, is a place of 5,000 population, to which vessels of 300 tons come, having large barracks for sailors, long quays, a church of the sixteenth century, and the Plaudiry fountain in the shape of an obelisk.

[On the road to Lesneven (to the west) in a wild heath, are the beautiful ruins of Notre Dame du Folgoat, a church built 1423 by the dukes of Brittany; it abounds with delicate carving and tracery.]

At 20 kil. further is

Brest. *Hotels*—De Provence, Grand Monarque (*i. e.* Louis XIV.), de Nantes, de la Tête d'Argent (Silver Head). *Cafés*—Parisien; Prosper; Laplanche. Population 29,860.

A naval dock yard and arsenal, chief place of a maritime préfecture, first class military station, &c., on the fine harbour or Road of Brest; had a castle of the dukes of Brittany, which Robert Knolles held for Richard II. of England against Duguesclin in 1373, and which was given up to the French, 1395. Louis XIV. made it a naval station, 1631, by the advice of Richelieu, and built the arsenal after Vauban's plan round the old tower of the castle, which is 100 feet high, standing at the mouth of a creek of the Penfeld (on the north side of the harbour), along which the town and dock yard lie.

The town is divided into upper and lower, so steep as to be joined by steps in several places; some of the newest houses are in the suburb of Recouvrance on the west. The Cours d'Ajot has a good view of the harbour; and there are promenades at Champ de Bataille, Place de la Liberté, &c.

A narrow passage, called Le Goulet (the gullet), about one mile wide, leads in from the Bay of Biscay on the west, to the noble land-locked *Harbour*, which is about nine leagues in circuit, would hold about 500 ships of the line, and towards the east divides off into two channels to Landerneau and Châteaulin. It is strongly defended by batteries on every point, numbering about 1000 pieces of cannon; a telegraph communicates with Paris; and outside the Goulet, about 10 miles off, is Ouessant or *Ushant* light, at the mouth of the channel, where Keppel had an action with the French, 1778.

The *Dock Yard* includes 10 building slips, large dry docks, rope works (corderies), of great length, shears (machine à mâter), sail lofts (voilerie), cannon-foundry, and general magazine, forges, &c., the Cayenne, or sailors' barracks for 4,000, victualling office (parc aux vivres), museum of models (salle des modèles), the Clermont-Tonnerre hospital (a large building with 1,340 beds in it), marine library of 15,000 volumes, and observatory, &c.

At the *Bagne*, an immense building about 850 feet long, on a hill, about 3,000 forçats or convicts are kept. In the town are a naval school, called the college Joinville, Hôtel de Ville, St. Louis' church, salle de spectacle (theatre) with a good front, bibliothèque of 8000 volumes, museum, botanic garden, medical school with a library of 8,000 volumes, &c. *Howe* fought the battle of the 1st June, 1794, off Brest. One of the boats of the unfortunate Amazon escaped in here, 1852. High water at moon's fall and change 3h. 40m. The climate is moist and cloudy.

English Consul, Sir A. Perrier.

Rev. M. Lefoardrey, is protestant pastor here.

Trade in wine, eaux-de-vie, sail-cloth, rope, &c.

Conveyances, by coach, to Paris, Nantes, Rennes, St. Malo, Lorient, &c.; by steam to Châteaulin, up the Aulne. Across the harbour and thence to Camaret, brings you to a druid circle of about 60 stones called Foull-Inguet, 44 feet apart, and some 18 feet high; two rows of 12 each lead to the circle. Near it is a view of the Bec de la Chèvre and Bec du Raz, at the mouth of Douarnenes Bay, (*see* Route 74.)

(*a*) From Brest, along the coast towards the west, you pass Conquet (20 kil.), at the mouth of the Roads, near St. Mathieu's old abbey, and the light on St. Matthew's Point, and overlooking the Bay where the French were so carefully watched by the English fleet in the war; also the Passage du Four which lies inside the Ushant, and the other wild rocky islands in the Atlantic. Further on (to the north) you come to the Menhir of Pleuarsel, a druid rock 30 feet high (called Maen hir in Cornwall, *i. e.* long stone), near St. Renan. Then come the Porçal rocks, Abervrach haven, Lannion, and other churches, on the road to Morlaix.

ROUTE 91.

Maintenon to Dreux, Mortagne, Alençon, Mayenne, and Laval.

Distance, 220 kil. or 137 miles.

MAINTENON, as in Route 90.

NOGENT-LE-ROI (9 kil.), down the Eure, was so called after Philip de Valois, who died here, 1350, and suffered much in the civil and religious wars. The English, under Salisbury, carried it sword-in-hand in the time of Henry V.

[Near Le Péage (8 kil. west-south-west), is a cromlech of one stone on two others.]

DREUX (18 kil.), in a fertile part of the Blaise, near the Eure, is a well-built sous-préfecture of 6,800 population, who make cloth, hats, linens, &c., and stands under a hill covered by the remains of its old castle. It was the capital of the *Durocasses* in Cæsar's time; Louis le Gros gave it to his son Robert; it was burnt by the English (being on the border of Normandy) 1188, and taken by Henry IV. 1593, after repeated assaults.

The church is early and later gothic; the square Hôtel de Ville, a mixture of gothic and renaissance, has a curious chimney and a carved clock-tower; there are also a college, good hospital, theatre, and several timbered houses.

Of the old château, which Catherine de Medicis gave to her son the Duc d'Alençon, 1559, you see an enormous brick donjon (now used as a telegraph), a ruined chapel with sculptures as old as 1142, and a highly finished modern chapel in the greek style, built by Louis Philippe, in which his family are buried, including his mother (who began the chapel), his aunt the Duchesse de Condé-Bourbon (the poor Duc d'Enghien's mother), his sister, Madame Adelaïde (died 1847), his son the Duc d'Orleans (killed 1842), his daughter Marie of Wurtemburg, &c. A high tower close to it leads by a subterranean way to the chapel.

On the plain close by, in 1562, the Calvinists under the Prince of Condé and Coligny were defeated by the royalists under Montmorency, after a severe action, Condé being taken prisoner.

Rotrou, a dramatic writer; Philidor, the chess-player; and General Sénarmont were born here.

Hotels—Du Paradis; du Lion d'Or (Golden Lion); du Saumon (Salmon). Coaches to Chartres, Le Mans, Falaise, &c.

[About 15 or 20 kil. north-east, down the Eure, are Anet and Ivry (*see* Route 1.).—Up the Blaise (10 kil. south-west), are remains of Crécy château, built by Louis XIV. for Madame de Pompadour.]

NONANCOURT (14 kil.), on the Avre, in department Eure, contains the house where Henry IV. slept before the battle of Ivry.

TILLIERES (11 kil.), higher up the stream, is near Mesnil-sur-l'Estrées, the paper factory of Firmin Didot frères, the first printers in France, employing about 400 hands, who make about five leagues or twelve miles of paper daily, in strips four feet broad. A willow in the garden was produced from that which overhung Napoleon's grave at St. Helena.

VERNEUIL (10 kil.), in the fertile part of the Avre, was fortified by Henry I., of England, and repeatedly taken and retaken till given up to the French, 1449. The Duke of Bedford defeated Charles VII. here, 1424. Among remains of antiquity are the cathedral church and its spire (seen ten miles off), with quaint carvings on it; the beautiful tower of the Madeleine church; the Tour Grise on the old walls, large and round, about 66 feet diameter; and many gothic houses of timber or brick. The public library has 3,000 vols., and the walks are pleasant. Population 4,100. Leather for bookbinders is prepared here. *Hotels*—De la Poste; du Cygne (Swan); Grand St. Martin. Coaches to Falaise, Evreux.

[L'Aigle or Laigle (22 kil. west) already noticed in Route 6, must be again mentioned on account of a remarkable fall of about 2,000 aerolites, which occurred in 1795. The cause of it was investigated by Vaquelin and Bicot, the astronomers.]

ST. MAURICE (16 kil.), in department Orne.

MORTAGNE (12 kil.), a sous-préfecture of 4,900 souls, once a strong place and the capital of the Perche, is on a hill over the Chippe, and was founded by Yves de Bellême 968, and strengthened with a double moat, forts, &c. In the wars of the League it was pillaged twenty-two times. The streets are steep. It has the old gothic church of St. Jean, with richly carved culs-de-lampe (pendants) in the vaulting of the nave. The hospice was founded 1523, by Margaret de Lorraine. There are large market halls, a prison, public fountains, &c.

Manufactures of hemp, strong linens, sheep skins, &c.; the old church of the Capucins is now a linen factory. Its langues fourrées or stuffed tongues are noted. *Hotels*—Des Trois Lions; de la Bouteille. About 6 kil. from it, near the road to Soligny, is the old romanesque church of Champs, with stained windows.

[*Soligny-la-Trappe* (12 kil. north), in a sandy spot, has remains of the cistercian abbey of La Trappe, founded in the twelfth century by Rotrou II. Count of Perche, reformed by the severe discipline of Abbé de Rancé, 1666, and suppressed at the revolution. After taking shelter in Switzerland, the Trappists settled in England, and returned here 1815, but in 1824, on a dispute with the bishop, moved to Meilleraye.]

MESLE-SUR-SARTHE (16 kil.), on the Sarthe. Séez, 30 kil. north-west of it, on the Orne, is described in Route 92.

LE MENIL BROUST (10 kil.), lower down the Sarthe.

At 13 kil. further is

Alençon. *Hotels*—D'Angleterre; de la Poste; du Maure (the Moor); du Grand Cerf (Stag); du Petit Dauphin. Population 14,400.

This old seat of the ducs d'Alençon is a pleasant, well-built town, the capital of department Orne, in a wide fertile plain, covered with forests, where the Sarthe and Briante join. It belonged to the county of Perche, which was once part of Normandy.

The Hôtel de Ville (town hall), on the site of the old Castle (of which two or three round towers are left at the prison opposite it), has a fine promenade something like the grand avenue at the Luxembourg at Paris.

Notre Dame *Cathedral* was built between 1353 and 1617. It is a small latin cross, 107 feet by 32. The porch and nave have some good carvings; and the altar is decorated with the Assumption in black marble, and a copper canopy; a spire, 156 feet high, was struck down by lightning 1744. Montsort church is of the eighth century.

There are also a palais de justice, public library of 7,000 vols. in the Jesuits' old church, two hospitals, markets for corn, fish, linens, public abattoir or slaughter-house, theatre, &c. Hébert, an infamous revolutionary hero, who edited the Père Duchesne paper, General Bonnet, Desgenettes the physician, were natives.

A trade in grain, cider coarse linens (toiles d'Alençon), thread, goose feathers, &c., and horses of a good breed.

Conveyances, daily, to Paris, Rennes, Mans; the old castle and church of St. Cénery le Gérey (12 kil.), stormed by the Earl of Arundel 1484, the Dugos glass-works in Ecouve forest (8 kil.), and remains of a monastery in Persaigne forest, may be visited hence.

[*Mamers* (25 kil. south-east), a sous-préfecture of 6,000 population, in department Orne, on the Dive, having a church founded 1145 and restored 1831, and an old convent, now the mairie, &c. Some ditches called after Robert le Diable are traced; and at 6 kil. off is a roman camp. To the north are the ruined walls and arches of Persaignes abbey, founded 1145 by the counts of Alençon, who were buried here till 1377. Abbé Rancé, who reformed the Trappists, was a monk here.

Fresnay-le-Vicomte (15 kil. south of Alençon), on the Sarthe, in a pretty spot, containing several linen factories (population, about 3,000), and a norman-style church, besides two round towers of an old château.]

St. Denis (11 kil.)

Prez-en-Pail (13 kil.), in department Mayenne, where good cider may be had.

Mayenne (37 kil.), a sous-préfecture in the same department, among the hills on the river Mayenne, very irregularly built, and remarkable for little besides the old château of its seigneurs, now a linen factory. Linen goods, of various kinds, are made and bleached, and iron is forged near it. Population, 9,797. *Hotels*—De la Belle Etoile (Beautiful Star); de l'Europe; du Petit Pavilion.

Conveyances to Laval, Rennes, &c.

[*Ambrières* (10 kil. north), an ancient place on the Mayenne, fortified by William the Conqueror, to defend the Normandy frontier. It has an old bridge, a pretty spire church, and a halle on the castle site. Population, 2,490.]

Martigné (13 kil.) has some mineral springs.

Laval is 17 kil. further (*see* Route 90).

ROUTE 92.

Alençon to Falaise and Caen.

Distance, 101 kil., or 63 miles.

Alençon, as in Route 91.

Seez (21 kil.) on the Orne, the old *Civitas Sagiorum*, and a bishop's see, with a gothic cathedral of the twelfth century, having a good porch, &c. At the episcopal palace are portraits of all the prelates. Population, 5,049, linen weavers, &c.

[To the east (5 kil.) is the old moated château d'O or Mortrée, built, they say, by Isabelle de Bavière, but now restored.]

Argentan (23 kil.), a sous-préfecture of 6,147 inhabitants, on a hill by the Orne, in a fertile plain, near the forest of Gouffern. The ditch of the old castle of the Comtes d'Argentan makes a beautiful promenade; and the portico of St. Germain's church is worth notice.

Manufactures of gloves and linens; and a trade in grain, leather, fruit, cattle, poultry, and good cheese. *Hotels*—Dévary; de Trois Maures (Three Moors); du Pont de Paris. A roman camp and some druid stones are near. Population, 5,700.

Falaise (22 kil.), a sous-préfecture in department Calvados, in Normandy, is a curious old town, founded by the Normans, and noted as the birthplace of *William the Conqueror*, whose statue on horseback was set up October, 1851, in the presence of Guizot and others.

Perched on the highest rocks is the once impregnable norman *castle* where the Conqueror drew breath, including the walls sixteen to forty-two feet high, the keep and the tower (100 feet) built by the great Talbot, who took the castle in the time of Henry V. It was re-taken by Henri Quatre, 1589; and is now partly used as the communal college.

The old town adjoining is hemmed in by remains of fortifications. East of it is the faubourg of Guibray where a celebrated *fair*, of very ancient date, for horses, &c., is held 15th to 25th August; and at the bottom stand the picturesque quarters of Val d'Ante and St. Laurent, watered by the small river Ante. The public library contains 4,000 vols. Pop. 9,500.

Manufactures of cotton caps, bone-lace; and a trade in cotton thread, wool, merinoes. *Hotels*—De France; du Grand Cerf (Stag).

Caen is 35 kil. further (*see* Route 4)

ROUTE 93.

Alençon to Bagnoles, Mortain, Vire, and St. Lo.

Distance, 146 kil., or 91 miles.

ALENÇON, as in Route 91.

PREZ-EN-PAIL (24 kil.), in the same route, where the road turns off to

COUTERNE (18 kil.), to the right of which (5 kil.) is the

Spa of Bagnoles, in a pretty, quiet valley, surrounded by good promenades. The establishment is well managed, lodgings are good, and the season for taking the waters is between May and September. They are tonic and purgative; and are useful in cutaneous complaints, chronic rheumatism, gout, ulcers, and diseases of the joints. Temperature, 22° Reaumur, or 81° Fahrenheit. Several objects of notice are near, as the châteaux of Bermondière and Couterne, St. Orler chapel, Bonvouloir watch tower, in Andienne forest, the iron works of Varennes and Cossé.

DOMFRONT (19 kil. from Couterne), on a rock over the Varennes, is a small sous-préfecture, in department Orne (population, 2,700), but was once an important walled town, defended by a strong castle, built by Guillaume de Bellesme, now a picturesque ruin. It is near Mont Halouze, one of the highest points in this quarter of France.

William the Conqueror and his sons, Henry I. and II., made it their residence; Eleanor of Guienne, wife of the latter, gave birth to a daughter here; Charles VIII. stopped here on his way to Mont St. Michel; and Charles IX. also, about the time that Montgomery, the protestant leader, was imprisoned in it, 1694. It stood several sieges, the last of which was when Henry IV. took it, 1589.

Notre Dame church, one of the oldest about here, is a ruin. There is a prison, built, they say, by the English. The houses are old fashioned, and the streets crooked and steep; the water is bad, but the air is pure though sharp.

'*Domfront, ville de malheur; arrivé à midi, pendu à une heure; pas seulement le temps de diner?*' (A bad place for me! Come at twelve, hung at one! Not even time for dinner!) This curious speech, which has become current here, is attributed to an unlucky Calvinist officer in the religious wars, who, having fallen into the enemy's hands, was forthwith led to execution by his inhospitable captors. Iron, glass, and paper works are near.

MORTAIN (23 kil.), a small town and sous-préfecture (population, 2,500), in department Manche, on the Cance. The fine remains of its castle, are close to a pyramid-shaped rock, near a *waterfall* of 115 feet among some picturesque cliffs covered with shrubs and lichens. The old and curious half norman church was founded 1082. A road to Avranches here.

[At 20 kil. north-east is *Tinchebray* (department Calvados), on the Noireau, which had a castle where Robert Courthose, Duke of Normandy, was finally defeated and taken prisoner by his brother, Henry I. of England, 1106.

Condé-sur-Noireau (18 kil. further), down the river, where the Druane falls in, was held by the Huguenots, who met in synod here, 1674. Population, 6,500, who manufacture linens, nails, cotton thread, &c. St. Martin, one of its two old churches, is decorated with stained windows, and has a statue of Admiral D'Urville, burnt to death, 1842, on the Versailles railway. There are remains of a château which St. Louis inhabited 1256, and the English took, 1418.]

SOURDEVAL (10 kil.), on the little river Sée, which works many paper factories in the neighbourhood, at Beaufigel, Bronhains, &c. Population, 4,300.

VIRE (13 kil.), an old place and sous-préfecture, in department Calvados, with 8,043 inhabitants, is noted for its good-looking, sprightly women. It is well placed on a rock, where the Vire and the Vaux join; and the environs, being hilly, are very pleasing. Among the best buildings are the foundling hospital, a general hospital founded by the norman dukes, Notre Dame gothic church, public library of 7,000 vols., many fountains. Cards, linens of the best quality, and paper (by machinery) are made here. *Hotel*—Du Cheval Blanc (White Horse).

Several grottoes and druid stones are near; and at Brimbal Hill, the highest in this quarter, the Vire, the Vey, the Seez, the Noireau, and the Grenne, all take their rise.

THORIGNY (25 kil.), has, at the Hôtel de Ville, part of a noble château (which was mostly destroyed, 1789), with some pictures, and a piece of Gobelins tapestry. It is further known for the marbre de Thorigny, a roman gallic relic of the third century, now in the town-house of Caen.

St. Lô is 14 kil. further (*see* Route 7).

ROUTE 94.

Laval to Fougeres, Pontorson (St. Malo), Mont St. Michel, and Avranches.

Distance, 110 kil., or 68 miles.

Laval, as in Route 90.

La Bacconnière (17 kil.)

Ernee (14 kil.), a pretty, industrious place, on the Ernée, which the Vendéan army crossed, 1793. Linens are made. *Hotel*—La Poste. Population, 5,500.

Fougeres (21 kil.), a handsome, well-built sous-préfecture, in department Ille-et-Vilaine, in a healthy spot, where several roads join, and formerly one of the most important keys of Brittany, before its union with the crown. A point behind the church commands a view of the charming valley of the Nonçon, and the old gothic towers of Raoul de Fougères' ruined château. In the forest near this, are the Monument and Pierre de Trésor druid stones; also a subterranean passage, called the Celliers de Landeau. Vast numbers of sabots, or wooden shoes, are made.

Manufactures of linen and hemp cloths; and a trade in grain, oatmeal of well-known quality, beer, honey, &c. *Hotels*—St. Jacques (James); des Voyageurs (Travellers). Population, 10,000.

[About 20 kil. south-west, on the Rennes road, is *St. Aubin-du-Cormier*, in a forest, with its tall, picturesque tower of the castle, built, 1222, by Pierre, Duc de Bretagne. It is celebrated for the great defeat sustained by Duke Francis II. (father of Anne of Brittany) and the Duke of Orleans (afterwards Louis XII.), from the forces of Charles VIII., commanded by Vicomte de la Trêmouille then a young man of 18, in the year 1488.]

St. Brice (15 kil.), on the Oisance.

Antrain (11 kil.), lower down the stream, where it joins the Couesnon.—Dol (*see* Route 95) is 24 kil. north-west.

Pontorson (12 kil.), at the mouth of the Couesnon, in department Manche, an old place, fortified by Robert Duke of Normandy, and nearly all burnt, 1736. The castle of the Montmorencies was pulled down by Louis XIII. Trade in linen and eggs. Population, 1,900.

A road, made 1842, leads to the famous Mont St. Michel (9 kil. north), which, as well as Avranches, 20 kil. from Pontorson (by way of Pont-aux-Beaux, on the Celune), is described in Route 7.

ROUTE 95.

Rennes to Dinan, Dol and St. Malo.

Distance (to St. Malo), 69 kil. or 43 miles.

Rennes, as in Route 90.

Hede (23 kil.), a village, with remains of a castle, approached by a causeway which overlooks a lake on one side, and a brook and several mills on the other. Each house has its pretty garden. The direct road to St. Malo, by St. Pierre de Plerguen (20 kil.) and Châteauneuf (13 kil.), and that to Dol unite here; but we leave them to follow that to the south-west, about 20 kil. by Bécherel, to

Dinan, a sous-préfecture, in department Côtes-du-Nord, and a fine old town, most picturesquely seated on a steep granite rock, 200 feet above the Rance, up which river small craft from St. Malo (30 kil.) come, taking advantage of the tide, which rises 30 to 40 feet with great suddenness. It was a roman station in the county of the Curiosolites. Duguesclin took it from the English, 1373, and de Clisson again a few years later. The Leaguers of this part made it their head quarters, but gave it up to Marshal Brissac, 1598.

Its old walls remain, so thick that you might drive a carriage on them; the moat outside is planted. In one part, near Porte St. Louis, is the tall machicolated donjon, built 1300, by Duchess Anne, now serving for a prison. Like all old towns, it has many narrow dark streets, of old-fashioned wooden houses; but the more modern ones are built of granite. Place Duguesclin is the site of a combat in 1359, between that warrior and a 'Thomas of Canterbury;' his statue ornaments one end, and his house stands in Rue de la Croix.

St. Malo's gothic church, with its spire, has various carvings of sacred and profane subjects. That of St. Sauveur is marked by another tall spire, and contains bas-reliefs of the Loves of Pysche, and a monument over Duguesclin's heart, brought here in 1810, from the dominican church.

The granite horloge or clock-tower ends in a spire, near the Hôtel de Ville; the latter was formerly a hospice, and holds the public library of 3,000 volumes, besides portraits of Duclos the historian, the excellent La Garaye, and the soldiers Duguesclin and Beaumanoir. Two pillars, of a single block of granite each, front the tribunal. There are also a hospital, college, salle-de-concert, and a chapel for the English residents here.

A pretty road leads out to the Coninaic mineral springs (1 kil.), in a deep valley: useful in cases of indigestion, &c.

The neighbourhood is exceedingly pleasant, abounding in many charming walks and points of view. Within a distance of 6 or 8 kil. are the following:—At *Léhon* or Léon, only 1 kil. off, on a round hill, are the massive walls and eight round towers of a *castle*, built, they say, on the site of a roman fort, and rebuilt about 1408. Close by is the gothic chapel of St. Magliore's priory (founded 850, by Nominoé), where the Beaumanoir family were buried. Near St. Esprit and the large lunatic asylum (1 kil. west), under the care of the brothers of St. Jean de Dieu, is a gothic cross of granite, worth notice.

La Garaye château (2 kil. north-west), in the renaissance style, is the ruined seat of its benevolent owner, who in the last century retired here with his wife, and turned it into a dispensary, &c., for the benefit of the poor.—Chesnan, in the forest of Coëtquen, was the seat of Abbé F. Delamennais.

CORSEUL, (4 kil. north-west) was the capital of the *Curiosolites*, a gaulic people, where remains of a temple of Mars (30 feet high), roman epitaphs, altars, pieces of columns, coins, bronzes, &c. have been found. Many of the tiles in its walls (which were 3 inches square) were used to repair those of St. Malo. An inscription is seen on the church; and a roman way may be traced. Montafilan château is a ruin.—At St. Jurat, Quiou, &c. (8 kil. south), fossil shells are abundant.—Ganterie (6 kil.) has remains of Roche-aux-Fées (Fairies' Rock), in granite; another druid stone (quartz rock) is at Lesmonts (4 kil.), near Plouer; and a granite menhir of large size at St. Samson or Tremblaie (4 kil.).

A steamer from the bridge runs up and down the Rance daily, with the tide; the banks are high and rocky, and in some parts well wooded.

Trade in butter, flax, honey, linens, souliers de pacotille (shoes for exportation), pottery, salt, refined sugar, &c. *Hotels*—Du Commerce; de la Poste. Coaches to Rennes, Brest, Morlaix, Loudéac, St. Malo, Dol, &c.

[About 25 kil. north-east is *Dol*, an old fortified place (population 4,200), on a rock above a marshy inlet of the sea (6 kil. off), in a fertile spot, on the norman frontier. It was held by the Vendéans, 1793, against the republicans. Some of the houses are granite built—in Grand Rue, for instance—but most of them are like those at Dinan, the first floor overhanging that on the ground, and supported by pillars, making an arcade in front. The old cathedral church, once the seat of a bishop from the sixth century, is a large gothic pile of granite, with high towers, and a fine lofty nave, resting on four-shafted columns. It has a college, &c. On the sands, at the mouth of the creek, is a granite rock called Mont Dol, with a telegraph on it.

About 2 kil. south of Dol, is the Champ Dolent menhir, or druid stone, an immense granite block, 40 feet high and 30 round at the ground, below which it sinks 30 feet.—Pontorson (*see* Route 94) is 19 kil. west.]

From Dinan to St. Malo, you pass

CHATEAUNEUF (14 kil.), down the Rance, in department Ille-et-Vilaine, a small old place, defended by a fort on Vauban's system, constructed 1777. Above is a seat and park including remains of the old castle.

ST. SERVAN (12 kil.), a port and bathing place, with 10,000 population (many of them English), separated from St. Malo only by a small bay which dries at low water, when you may cross the sands in a cart in ten minutes; but at high water it is 50 feet deep.

A vast stone causeway 87 feet wide, begun to St. Malo, will make a harbour (326 acres) of this bay, which includes two little ports in it, St. Pére and Solidor,—the latter taking name from a fort between them, on a rock, built 1382; it is above 60 feet high, exclusive of the machicolated top, and shaped like a trefoil, having round towers at each of the three corners.

The town is well built, and the neighbourhood

a pleasant one; good bathing and mineral waters may be taken. *Hotels*—Royal; de Constantine; de France; du Pelican; de l'Union.

St. Malo (1 kil.), *Hotels*—De France et des Voyageurs (Travellers); de la Paix; Maison Brecey; all in Rue des Juifs (Jew Street). Dinner 1½ fr., breakfast 1¼ fr., bed 1 fr.

Coaches to Dinan, Brest, St. Brieuc, Rennes, Dol, Caen, &c. Steamer to Jersey, Monday and Thursday, calling at Granville. Passports are required to visit the Channel Islands, which are 40 miles to the north.

A sous-préfecture of 9,000 population, third class fortress, &c., is the best haven in this part of France, lying in the throat of a difficult bay at the Rance's mouth, five miles across from Pointe de la Verde to Pointe du Decollé, and covered with rocks above and below water.

The town stands on the Ile d'Aron, joined by a solid causeway (called le Sillon), 200 yards wide to the main, which often demands repair on account of injuries occasioned by the sea. To the east of the mole (carrying a fixed light) is the port, which is left dry at low water, but is perfectly safe.

The anchorage in the Rade or Roads on the west is protected by seven forts; one of which, on Ile Canchée (3 miles out) was built by Vauban; another is on Cezembre; and a third on Beys rock, near the bar and the Rocher aux Anglais. Beacons are placed here and there to mark the channels between the rocks, some of which are 20 to 30 feet high, and bear such names as Crolante, Durand, Benetin, Grandes et Petites Pointus, Grand Conchée, Pierre aux Normands, Ronfleresse, Buharats, &c. The light on Cape Frehel, 13 miles off, is within view. Near this light is St. Cast château, 'celebrated,' say the French, 'for the victory of that name over the English in 1758'?

St. Malo replaces the ancient *Aletum*, the memory of which is preserved by Guich Alet point near this. It looks well, and has good hotels and streets of tall houses, but is rather a dull place. There are pleasant walks with prospects of the sea, &c., on the large high walls round the edge of the rock and strengthened by old towers and Vauban's bastions.

Two of its four portes or gates, St. Vincent and St. Thomas, are close to the old *château*, built by the Duchess Anne of Brittany, and making part of the fortifications. This is a square pile with corner towers, one of which is called 'Qui qu'en grogne,' from an inscription put upon it by that strong-minded lady—'*Qui qu'en grogne, ainsi sera; c'est mon plaisir,*' (Let them growl as they like; it is my will to have it so)

The old cathedral church, the seat of a bishop before the revolution, is in the gothic style; there are two other churches, with a bourse or exchange, two hospitals (one for foundlings), a high school, school of navigation, theatre, a government tobacco factory, &c. Under Fort de la Cité is a suspension bridge built 1847, and leading to the telegraph. A casino and ball rooms are attached to the baths, which are much frequented in the season.

Opposite the cathedral is the statue of Duguay-Trouin a brave seaman, and a native; Chateaubriand was born in Rue des Juifs, and is buried on an island near Solidor fort. Cartier, who discovered Canada, 1534; Maupertuis, the astronomer; Labourdonnaye, who took Madras and Abbé Lamennais, are also natives.

It is a great place for privateers in war-time, and, as might be expected, was noted for smuggling, but this has fallen off. Some of the best sailors in France are found here. Ships are fitted out for the whale and cod fisheries and the coasting trade (petit cabotage).

Cordage, lines, fish-hooks, sails, soap, &c. are made; and there is a brisk trade in grain, fruit, wine, spirits, salt provisions, toiles de Bretagne (linens), cider, honey, butter, wax, oysters, fish, &c., the produce of the department or of the colonies.

From St. Malo along the Dol road you come to Paramé, where you leave it for St. Columb and

Cancale or Cancalle (15 kil. to the east), a town on the cliffs, overlooking a sandy bay, which stretches round by Mont Dol and Mont St. Michel to Granville. With the little port of La Houle, it contains a population of 5,100, fishermen and oyster catchers. The oysters are sent to Paris, or to replenish the beds of natives in the Thames. A church on the height commands a fine view of the bay, the Herpin rocks at the Grouin de Cancale, and other objects.

BRADSHAW AND BLACKLOCK, PRINTERS, 47, BROWN STREET, MANCHESTER.

PARIS—Continued.

GRAND HOTEL DE LYON, No. 12, Rue des Filles St. Thomas, with a large frontage in the Rue Richelieu, and near the Bourse. No hotel is better situated for travellers who visit Paris for pleasure or business. Board and lodging at 5fr., 6fr., or 6½fr.; admission to dinner 'de famille,' at 2frs., wine included; single room, at 1½, 2, or 3 francs. Also small and large apartments for families. Restaurant à la Carte, or board and lodging by the week, month, or year. Newspapers and periodicals are provided for the use of travellers. Mr. MERIMEE, the landlord, being in communication with the principal Hotels throughout France and Europe, recommends those best suited to travellers. Omnibuses for all parts of Paris; also to and from every train. English, German, and Spanish spoken

HOTEL VICTORIA, Rue Chauveau la Garde, No. 3, near the Madeleine, the best quarter of Paris.—Established in 1837, and patronised by the ex-Royal Family.—The accommodation is superior, and the charges moderate; for the daily expense of apartment, breakfast, dinner with wine, tea or supper in the evening, and servants, does not exceed seven shillings per day.

HOTEL DE NORMANDIE, 240, Rue St. Honoré.—The above Hotel possesses advantages for Travellers rarely to be met with. It is in the vicinity of the principal Public Establishments, in the most favourable situation for pleasure as well as business, and it is the constant aim of the Proprietor to merit patronage by affording every comfort at the most moderate charges. Each Visitor may be furnished with a Bed-room, Breakfast, Dinner at Table d'Hôte, with a bottle of good Burgundy Wine at 5s. and 5s. 6d. per day, including light and servants.

N.B.—ENGLISH SPOKEN BY THE LANDLORD AND SERVANTS.

HOTEL FOLKSTONE, 9, Rue Castellane.—This Establishment is situated in the fine quarter of the *Madeleine Church*, near the Boulevards, Tuilleries, and the Champs Elysées, it is particularly noted for its elegant furniture, comfort, and cleanliness, nothing being spared by the Proprietor to render this Hotel one of the most comfortable in Paris. Bed-rooms at 2 and 3 francs per day. Apartments for Families. Arrangements made by Week or Month. Breakfasts at 1 franc 50 cents. Table d'Hôte at 3 francs. English attendants.

L. OLIVIER, PROPRIETOR.

HOTEL DES ETRANGERS AND WALTER SCOTT, No. 11, Rue Joquelet, near the *Exchange*, *Palais Royal*, Boulevards, and principal Theatres, an excellent Hotel for accommodation, and a well-supplied Kitchen, superintended by the Proprietor himself.

BRITISH TAVERN, 104, Rue Richelieu, near the Boulevard. — English Restaurant, suited to the accommodation of the superior orders. This Establishment, situate in the centre of Paris, is distinguished by the noble elegance of its *locale*, combining the advantage of free respiration, both in its lofty salons, and its GARDEN, in which latter can be taken one's repast in the fine weather of summer; and is remarkable for the true character and quality of its Wines, which are served without the absurdly exorbitant prices exacted in almost all the public establishments, and that for wines neither true nor in good order.

JEWELLERY.—GOLDSMITHS and JEWELLERS.—DUPONCHEL & CO., 47, Rue Neuve St. Augustin, Orfevre, Bijoutier, Joallier. The assortment of Works of Art, the stock of Set and Un-set Jewellery, Gold and Silver Ornaments, at this Establishment is unrivalled. Travellers visiting this extensive and old-established house will find a great variety of exquisite and highly-finished Jewellery, of the newest designs and patterns, and of the best materials, at reasonable prices.

LACE.—FRENCH AND BELGIAN MANUFACTORY,
57, RUE NEUVE VIVIENNE, 15, BOULEVARD, MONTMARTRE,

corner of the Rue Vivienne and of the Boulevard.

White and Black Lace, Brussels Application Lace, English Point Lace, Alençon Point Lace Shawls, Scarfs, Robes, Veils, Pelerines, &c., Mantles or Mantillas for Ladies.
Gold or Silver Lace. Marriage Corbeilles.

ENGLISH SPOKEN.

PARIS—Continued.

NOUVEAUTES—AUX TROIS QUARTIERS.—GALLOIS, GIGNOUX, & CO. MAGASIN DE NOUVEAUTES, 21 and 23, Boulevard de la Madeleine.—This well-known Establishment, by its immense sale, and the constant supply of the newest articles from the first manufactories of France, is enabled to offer an unrivalled choice of Silks and Velvets of special patterns; Mantles, Merinos, French Cashmeres, Woollen Stuffs, Lace, &c., &c., at comparatively low prices. The business is conducted on the strictest principles of honour.

ENGLISH ASSISTANTS IN ATTENDANCE.

DENTIST.—WM. ROGERS, formerly of London, now of 270 Rue St. Honoré,

FACING THE PASSAGE DELORME,

Author of "The Dictionary of the Dental Sciences;" "The Dental Encyclopedia;" "The Manual of Dental Hygiène;" and of the "Buccomancie; or, The Art of Knowing the Past, Present, and Future;" Works received by the Faculty of Medicine.

ENGLISH PHARMACY.

T. DALPIAZ, 381, Rue St. Honoré, near the Madeleine. Messrs. SAVORY AND MOORE, of London, think it proper to inform the English Traveller that Mr. DALPIAZ (formerly their principal Dispensary Assistant) is their sole Agent in Paris.

DANCING ACADEMY, No. 320, Rue St. Honoré, exactly opposite the Hotel de Lille and d'Albion. At this admirably conducted Establishment, now under the direction of MADEMOISELLE VICTORINE and MONSIEUR COULON, of the Grand Opera, the elite of Parisian society dance the Valse à 2 et à 3 Temps, Polka, Redowa, Schottische, Sicilienne, &c. For terms and hours of public repetitions, private lessons, &c., see the Prospectus, in English and French, to be had gratis at the above address. N.B.—Pupils attended at their own residences.

LESSONS OF GRACE AND DEPORTMENT.

MR. SCOTT, SURGEON DENTIST,

No. 0, RUE ROYALE, ST. HONORE, PARIS,

may be consulted on every branch of his profession from TEN to FOUR.

Mr. S. has had twelve years practical experience in London and Paris, and can be relied on with all confidence, either in the surgical or mechanical parts of his profession.

TEACHERS OF MODERN LANGUAGES IN PARIS.—The following list is furnished by our Paris Correspondent, to whom the gentlemen, whose morality and ability he guarantees, are personally known—SPANISH, Mr. Florez;—ITALIAN, Dr. Monti;—GERMAN, Mr. Eichendorff;—PORTUGUESE, Mr. S. De Vasco;—RUSSIAN, Mr. Kêdnoff;—TURKISH and ARABIC, Mr. Benna;—MODERN GREEK, Mr. Pogri. Cards may be had at Messrs. GALIGNANIS' Library, and of Mr. HOGG, Chemist to the British Embassy.

WATCH AND CLOCK MAKER.—RABY, Watch Maker to the ex-Royal Family, 17, Boulevards des Italiens, first floor, opposite Tortoni's. MANUFACTORY AT VERSAILLES. Great assortment of Gold and Silver Watches, warranted three years. Agents in London, New York, Philadelphia, and St. Petersburgh.

MR. SEYMOUR, SURGEON DENTIST,

No. 10, RUE CASTIGLIONE,

may be consulted daily from NINE to FIVE, on all branches of his Profession. First-rate attendance, and workmanship to the highest perfection.

RAILWAY FROM ANTWERP TO ROTTERDAM.

ARRIVAL & DEPARTURE OF TRAINS ON & AFTER JULY 3RD, 1854.

ANTWERP TO ROOSENDAEL.

Trains leave		1 Morn.	2 Morn.	3 Aft.
Antwerp		6 0	9 45	4 30
Eeckeren		6 15	10 0	4 45
Cappellen		6 20	10 5	4 50
Calmpthout		6 35	10 20	5 5
Esschen	arr.	6 45	10 30	5 15
	dep.	6 55	10 40	5 25
Roosendael	arr.	7 5	10 50	5 35

ROOSENDAEL TO ANTWERP.

Trains leave		4 Morn	5 Aft.	6 Aft.
Roosendael		8 25	1 20	7 25
Esschen	arr.	8 35	1 30	7 35
	dep.	8 50	1 45	7 50
Calmpthout		9 0	1 55	8 0
Cappellen		9 15	2 10	8 15
Eeckeren		9 20	2 15	8 20
Antwerp	arr.	9 30	2 25	8 35

Train No. 1 corresponds at Breda with the Railway from Gueldres, Germany, Utrecht and Rotterdam. Train No. 2 corresponds at Breda at 2 p.m. with Dordrecht, Rotterdam, Delft, The Hague, Leyden, Haarlem and Amsterdam. This train leaves Antwerp after the arrival of the train which leaves Brussels at 8 30 a.m. Train No. 3, leaving Antwerp after the arrival of the train which leaves Brussels at 3 20 p.m., corresponds with Paris, Valenciennes, Lille, Ostend, Ghent, Cologne and Liége.

N.B.—All the trains correspond by Omnibus between Bergen-op-Zoom and Roosendael.

Train No. 4 corresponds with the train leaving Antwerp at 9 45 a.m. for Brussels, Liége, Cologne, Ghent, Ostend, Lille and Paris. Train No. 5 takes on passengers arriving at Breda at 9 a.m. from Amsterdam, Tilburg and Bois-le-Duc, and corresponds with the train leaving Antwerp at 2 45 p.m. for Brussels, Liége, Cologne, Ghent, Ostend, Lille and Paris. Train No. 6 takes on passengers arriving at Breda at 2 30 p.m. from Bois-le-Duc and Tilburg, also at 3 30 p.m. from Amsterdam and Utrecht, and at 3 45 p.m. by Railway from Haarlem and Rotterdam. Corresponds with Brussels, Liége, and Cologne, by train leaving Antwerp at 9 p.m.

POUR ROOSENDAEL.

	1 Matin.	2 Matin.	3 Soir.
Départ **d'Anvers**	6	9,45	4,30
„ d'Eeckeren	6,15	10	4,45
„ de Cappellen	6,20	10,05	4,50
„ de Calmpthout	6,35	10,20	5,05
Arrivée à Esschen	6,45	10,30	5,15
Départ d'Esschen	6,55	10,40	5,25
Arrivée à **Roosendael**	7,05	10,50	5,35

POUR ANVERS.

	4 Matin.	5 Soir.	6 Soir.
Départ de **Roosendael**	8,25	1,20	7,25
Arrivee à Esschen	8,35	1,30	7,35
Départ d'Esschen	8,50	1,45	7,50
„ de Calmpthout	9	1,55	8
„ de Cappellen	9,15	2,10	8,15
„ d'Eeckeren	9,20	2,15	8,20
Arrivée à **Anvers**	9,30	2,25	8,35

Par le convoi (1) correspondance à Breda avec le chemin de fer de Gueldre, l'Allemagne, Utrecht et Rotterdam. Par le convoi (2) correspondance à Breda à 2 h. avec Dordrecht, Rotterdam, Delft, La Haye, Leyden, Haarlem et Amsterdam. Départ d'Anvers après l'arrivée du convoi partant de Bruxelles à 8 h. 30. Par le convoi (3) départ d'Anvers après l'arrivée du convoi partant de Bruxelles à 3 h. 20, en correspondance avec Paris, Valenciennes, Lille, Ostende, Gand, Cologne et Liége.

Par le convoi (4) correspondance avec le convoi partant d'Anvers à 9 h. 45 pour Bruxelles, les lignes de Liége, Cologne, Gand, Ostende, Lille et Paris. Par le convoi (5) départ des voyageurs arrivés à Breda à 9 h. du matin d'Amsterdam, de Tilburg et Bois-le-Duc. Correspondance avec le convoi partant d'Anvers à 2 h. 45 pour Bruxelles, Liége, Cologne, Gand, Ostende, Lille et Paris. Par le convoi (6) départ des voyageurs arrivés à Breda à 2 h. 30 de Bois-le-Duc et Tilburg, *id.* à 3. 30 d'Amsterdam et Utrecht, *id.* à 3,45 arrivés par le chemin de fer d'Haarlem et Rotterdam. Correspondance pour Bruxelles, Liége et Cologne, par le convoi partant d'Anvers à 9 heures du soir.

N.B.—A tous les convois correspondance par omnibus, entre Berg-op-Zoom et Roosendael.

NAAR ROOSENDAEL.

	1 s'morgens.	2 s'morgens.	3 naar midd.
Vertrek van **Antwerpen**	6	9,45	4,30
„ van Eeckeren	6,15	10	4,45
„ van Cappellen	6,20	10,05	4,50
„ van Calmpthout	6,35	10,20	5,05
Aankomst te Esschen	6,45	10,30	5,15
Vertrek van Esschen	6,55	10,40	5,25
Aankomst te **Roosendael**	7,05	10,50	5,35

NAAR ANTWERPEN.

	4 s'morgens.	5 naar midd.	6 narr midd.
Vertrek van **Roosendael**	8,25	1,20	7,25
Aankomst te Esschen	8,35	1,30	7,35
Vertrek van Esschen	8,50	1,45	7,50
„ van Calmpthout	9	1,55	8
„ van Cappellen	9,15	2,10	8,15
„ van Eeckeren	9,20	2,15	8,20
Aankomst te **Antwerpen**	9,30	2,25	8,35

Met den trein (1) correspondentie te Breda met den spoor weg van Gelderland en Duitschland, Utrecht en Rotterdam. Met den trein (2) correspondentie te Breda, ten 2 ure, met Dordrecht, Rotterdam, Delft, 's Gravenhage, Leijden, Haarlem en Amsterdam. Vertrek van Antwerpen na de aankomst van den trein ten 8 ure 30 van Brussel vertrekkende. Met den trein (3) vertrek van Antwerpen na de aankomst van den trein van Brussel vertrekkende ten 3 ure 20 in correspondentie met Parijs, Valencijn, Rijssel, Oostende, Gent, Keulen en Luik.

Met den trein (4) correspondentie met den trein vertrekkende ten 9 ure 45 naar Brussel, met de lijnen van Luik, Keulen, Gent, Oostende, Brussel en Parijs. Met den trein (5) vertrek der reizigers ten 9 ure te Breda aangekomen van Amsterdam, Tilburg en, s' Hertogenbosch, correspondentie met den trein ten 2 ure 45 van Antwerpen vertrekkende naar Brussel, Luik, Keulen, Gent, Oostende, Rijssel en Parijs. Met den trein (6) vertrek der reizigers ten 2 ure 30 te Breda aangekomen van 's Hertogenbosch en Tilburgh ; *id.* ten 3 ure 30 van Amsterdam en Utrecht ; *id.* ten 3,45 voor degene aangekomen langs den spoor weg van Haarlem en Rotterdam. Correspondentie met Brussel, Luik en Keulen met den trein van Antwerpen vertrekkende ten 9 ure 's avonds.

N.B.—Met al de treinen correspondentie, per omnibus, tusschen Berg-op-Zoom en Roosendael.

PASSPORTS AND VISES.

OFFICE FOR BRADSHAW'S BRITISH AND CONTINENTAL GUIDES.

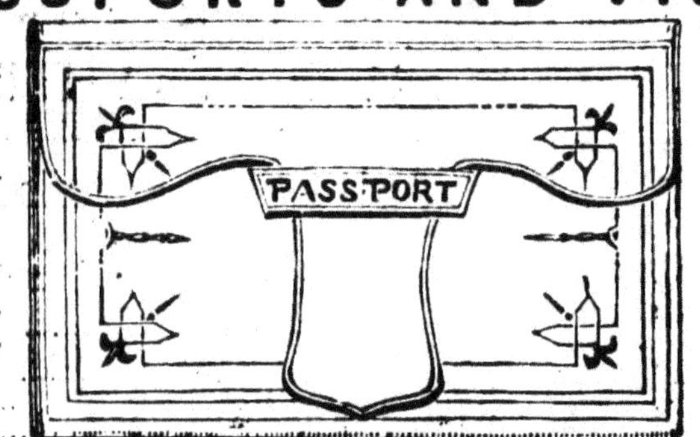

LONDON, 59, FLEET STREET.

Every information relative to Passports may be obtained on application at the above office, to Mr W. J. Adams, Publisher of "Bradshaw's British and Continental Guides and Handbooks," &c.

Parties residing in the Country, or London, *who desire to avoid delay and trouble*, can have their Passports obtained and duly *viséd*, with the utmost expedition and dispatch, upon application by letter, or otherwise, to W. J. Adams, as above. Parties in the Country, by this arrangement, are saved the trouble of coming to London about their Passport, as it can be forwarded to them by post *(en régle)*. It is necessary, in sending instructions, to name the Countries about to be visited, so that the proper counter-signatures or *visés* of the Ambassadors or Authorities in London may be attached.

In order to obtain the privilege of a Foreign Office Passport, a Banker's Letter of recommendation is necessary, which must give the name of the applicants, and their addresses, in full, and state that they are British subjects. For further information respecting Passports, see "Bradshaw's Continental Guide," page 19.

Fee for obtaining Passports, 2s. 6d.; Ditto for each Visé, 1s., in addition to the charges made by the several Authorities

PASSPORTS CAREFULLY MOUNTED, AND NAMES LETTERED THEREON, IN GOLD, IF REQUIRED.

Passport Cases from **1s.** to **6s.**, Traveller's Portfolios, Courier's Bags, Foreign Post Papers, and every description of Stationery useful to Continental Travellers.

N.B.—Bankers' Letters of recommendation should be at the Office, 59, Fleet Street, before Two o'clock p m., to insure the Passport being obtained on the following day.

CORDING'S WATERPROOFS

HAVING been tested for several years, their general use by the Nobility and Gentry of the United Kingdom and the Officers of the Army and Navy in all parts of the world, is a guarantee for their service and durability. They are made of various fabrics, suitable for Ladies and Gentlemen's wear, and are acknowledged by those who have used them, to be the best and only ones to be relied on in all climates.

CORDING'S GOSSAMER WATERPROOF COAT FOR THE POCKET

Weight only Nine ounces.

CORDING'S FISHING BOOTS

Are superior to anything hitherto made for the comfort of Anglers and Snipe shooters; they are light, pliable, and never crack; impervious to water for any length of time, and require no dressing to keep them in condition.

AIR BEDS FOR SEA AND LAND; TRAVELLING CUSHIONS FOR RAILWAYS AND INVALIDS.

COMPRESSIBLE SPONGING BATHS,

PORTABLE INDIA-RUBBER BOATS, FOR ONE, TWO, OR SIX PERSONS.

LIFE BELTS, 10s. EACH.

A LARGE STOCK OF WATERPROOFS ON HAND, AND ANY ARTICLE MADE TO ORDER.

CAUTION.—All Genuine Goods are stamped with the Name

J. C. CORDING,

231, STRAND, LONDON,

Five Doors West of Temple Bar.

www.ingramcontent.com/pod-product-compliance
Lightning Source LLC
Chambersburg PA
CBHW062034090426
42740CB00016B/2902

* 9 7 8 1 5 3 5 8 0 1 6 1 4 *